The Chemistry of the Terpenes

THE CHEMISTRY OF THE TERPENES

HEUSLER–POND.

THE CHEMISTRY

OF

THE TERPENES

BY

F. HEUSLER, PH.D.,
PRIVATDOCENT OF CHEMISTRY IN THE UNIVERSITY AT BONN.

AUTHORIZED TRANSLATION

BY

FRANCIS J. POND, M.A., PH.D.,
ASSISTANT PROFESSOR IN THE PENNSYLVANIA STATE COLLEGE.

CAREFULLY REVISED, ENLARGED AND CORRECTED.

PHILADELPHIA:
P. BLAKISTON'S SON & CO.
1012 WALNUT STREET.
1902

TO

GEHEIMRATH PROFESSOR OTTO WALLACH

THIS VOLUME IS

GRATEFULLY DEDICATED

BY THE AUTHOR AND TRANSLATOR.

PREFACE TO THE AMERICAN EDITION.

THE favorable reception of the German edition of Dr. Heusler's work renders it unnecessary to offer an excuse for presenting this translation and revision of "The Terpenes." The chemistry of the terpenes covers a portion of organic chemistry which has experienced a very remarkable development in the past few years, and, since the chapter on the terpenes in most works on organic chemistry is necessarily very limited, it seemed desirable to have at least one book in English which should be devoted exclusively to this subject. It is desired that this translation shall serve this purpose.

That the German edition has already proved of great value to chemists especially active in this field is evidenced by the remark of Doctors Gildemeister and Hoffmann in their book, "The Volatile Oils": "The monograph by Heusler on the terpenes has proved itself well-nigh indispensable for the scientific investigations of terpenes and their derivatives."

Before presenting this translation, it has been necessary to carefully review the very numerous contributions on the terpenes which have been published since the German edition was issued, and to introduce the results of these investigations in this edition; in doing this, it will be obvious that, although a vast amount of literature has been condensed into as small a space as possible and many important compounds are merely mentioned with references to original papers, the book has been enlarged to a degree very unusual in a translation. The task has proved a severe one, but I have endeavored to keep the plan of Dr. Heusler's work intact, and have introduced the large amount of new material in those places which appeared to me the most desirable. I have not distinguished in any way the separation of the old and new material, as such a plan did not seem advisable.

In the translation I have studied to keep as close to the original as possible, and yet give a clear version. The chapter of introduction is without change from the original edition. The table of constituents of the ethereal oils, which was added to the German work, has been omitted because such a list is no longer of so great importance since the translation of "The Volatile Oils" by Professor Kremers. Following Dr. Heusler's plan, the many researches on the derivatives of Japan camphor, such as the investigations on camphoric acid, etc., have not been introduced. An index has also been added.

The writer desires to express his obligation to Mr. Jesse B. Churchill, Instructor of Chemistry at The Pennsylvania State College, for valuable assistance in the reviewing of literature, preparation of index and proof-reading.

F. J. Pond.

State College, Pa.,
May, 1902.

PREFACE TO THE GERMAN EDITION.

THE following monograph was originally compiled for the "Handwörterbuch der Chemie." The article which was written for this collective work on chemistry was printed some months after the completion of the manuscript; at this time a review of the work which had appeared during these months was added, the effort being made to render this review as complete as possible. The fact that at the present time the chemistry of the terpenes occupies a very prominent position in scientific interest led the author and publishers to publish the article separately in book form.

The outward form of the "Handwörterbuch" was of course retained in the publication of this book. Most of the literature of the intervening months has been reviewed, and certain inaccuracies which appeared in the original article have been corrected. The publication of this book may be justified by the fact that the recent advances of the chemistry of the terpenes are, perhaps, not generally recognized.

I may refer to the chapter of introduction for the principal points of view from which the compilation of the monograph has proceeded; I still regard these principles as correct.

I wish to express my thanks for the valued assistance which Mr. E. Gildemeister of Leipzig and Mr. J. Bredt of Bonn have repeatedly extended to me in the course of my work. I am indebted to my friend, Dr. Gildemeister, not only for the table of constituents of the ethereal oils, but he has repeatedly placed his experience at my disposal in reviewing certain parts of the work, and finally in reviewing the entire book. My honored colleague, Dr. J. Bredt, has frequently given me valuable suggestions, and has kindly read one proof.

F. HEUSLER.

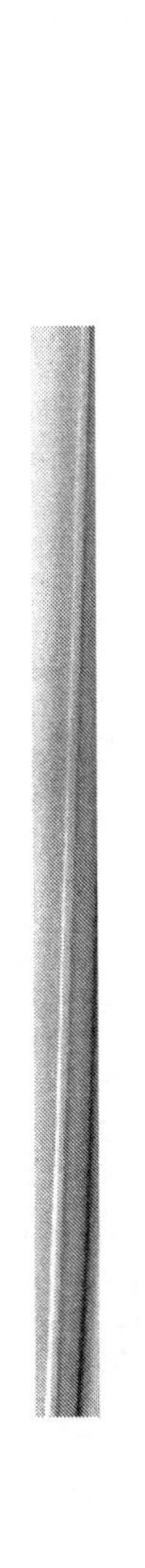

TABLE OF CONTENTS.

THE TERPENES.

THOSE hydrocarbons which have the empirical constitution, C_5H_8, are termed terpenes. Four main classes are recognized:

Hemiterpenes, C_5H_8,
Terpenes proper, $C_{10}H_{16}$,
Sesquiterpenes, $C_{15}H_{24}$,
Polyterpenes, $(C_5H_8)_x$.

The terpenes proper and the sesquiterpenes form the most important constituents of the ethereal oils. In the latter, several terpenes often occur together, and further, the ethereal oils frequently contain oxidized compounds which in many cases are not separable from the terpenes by fractional distillation, or only imperfectly so.

The result of these conditions was, that during the period before it was known how to sharply characterize the separate terpenes by chemical reactions, and to determine them as individuals, mixtures of this character were often regarded as chemical individuals, and were accordingly given independent names.

To Professor O. Wallach belongs the distinction of having elevated the methods of the terpene chemistry, by a series of superior experimental investigations, to such a plane, that the recognition and separation of the several terpene hydrocarbons have become relatively simple matters for the chemist.

These methods gave the first possibility of an actual working system to these substances, and moreover permitted the accurate establishment for the first time of the numerous transformations, which, under the influence of the greatest variety of reagents, take place so easily in this group of hydrocarbons.

It has already been mentioned that many oxidation products are present with the terpenes in the ethereal oils. It is evident that these compounds, occurring together in the plants, are very closely related to each other. What these relations are is rendered entirely clear by the study of the terpenes. Not only have many terpenes been artificially prepared from such natural oxidized compounds, but also a complete series of oxidation products have been successfully secured from natural terpenes, and these substances are isomeric with, or closely related to, the natural oxygen-containing members of the terpene group.

The so-called camphors, a name long used to designate these oxidized compounds, have been brought into so close a relation to the terpenes that a separate consideration of these two classes of compounds is no longer justifiable. In fact, it is impossible to develop the chemistry of the terpenes unless these oxygen-containing compounds are considered as members of the terpene series.

With this point in view the following monograph has been compiled, and only the one reason of outward conformity has prevented the carrying out of this fundamental idea to the end.

Japan camphor, while very closely allied to the terpenes, has, however, such an extremely large number of derivatives that an exhaustive description of them would demand as large a space as the derivatives of all the remaining members of the terpene group taken together. Hence the only derivatives of this compound to be mentioned will be those which stand in an especially close relation to other members of the terpene group.

While the discussion of camphor and its derivatives will be limited, an equally exhaustive treatment for the remaining oxygen- and nitrogen-containing compounds of the terpene group will be sought, as for the terpenes themselves.

The terpenes proper may be divided into two groups. The hydrocarbons of the first group contain one; those of the other group contain two ethylene linkages. As a class, the terpenes of the latter group may apparently be regarded as true dihydrocymenes. The known tetrahydrocymenes and hexahydrocymene, which are closely related to these terpenes, are discussed in the following treatise.

Corresponding to hexahydrocymene, which does not occur naturally, are oxygen-containing compounds which are widely distributed in nature, namely, menthone, $C_{10}H_{18}O$, and the alcohol corresponding to this ketone, menthol, $C_{10}H_{19}OH$. Two compounds, carvomenthone, $C_{10}H_{18}O$, and carvomenthol (tetrahydrocarveol), $C_{10}H_{19}OH$, structural isomerides of the above-mentioned substances, are to be considered as the completely hydrated parent-substances of an extremely large number of unsaturated, oxygenated members of the terpene group. Nevertheless, they do not themselves occur in nature.

If one molecule of water be eliminated from menthol or carvomenthol, hydrocarbons, $C_{10}H_{18}$, are formed, which can be considered as structural isomerides of tetrahydrocymene. The following formulas illustrate the constitution of these compounds. (For the nomenclature, see page 23.)

CH$_3$
CH
H$_2$C CH$_2$
H$_2$C CH$_2$
CH
CH
H$_3$C CH$_3$

Hexahydrocymene
(Terpane, Menthane).

CH$_3$
CH
H$_2$C CH$_2$
H$_2$C CO
CH
CH
H$_3$C CH$_3$

Menthone
(β-Ketohexahydrocymene,
Terpan-3-one, Menthan-3-one).

CH$_3$
CH
H$_2$C CO
H$_2$C CH$_2$
CH
CH
H$_3$C CH$_3$

Carvomenthone
(α-Ketohexahydrocymene,
Terpan-2-one, Menthan-2-one).

CH$_3$
CH
H$_2$C CH$_2$
H$_2$C CHOH
CH
CH
H$_3$C CH$_3$

Menthol
(β-Oxyhexahydrocymene,
Terpan-3-ol, Menthan-3-ol).

CH$_3$
CH
H$_2$C CHOH
H$_2$C CH$_2$
CH
CH
H$_3$C CH$_3$

Carvomenthol
(α-Oxyhexahydrocymene,
Terpan-2-ol, Menthan-2-ol).

CH$_3$
CH
H$_2$C CH$_2$
H$_2$C CH
C
CH
H$_3$C CH$_3$

Menthene
(Δ^3-Tetrahydrocymene,
Δ^3-Terpene, Δ^3-Menthene).

CH$_3$
C
H$_2$C CH
H$_2$C CH$_2$
CH
CH
H$_3$C CH$_3$

Carvomenthene
(Δ^1-Tetrahydrocymene,
Δ^1-Terpene, Δ^1-Menthene).

Other compounds, isomeric with menthol and carvomenthol, are known, which possess the character of tertiary alcohols, and, according to Baeyer, have the following constitution :

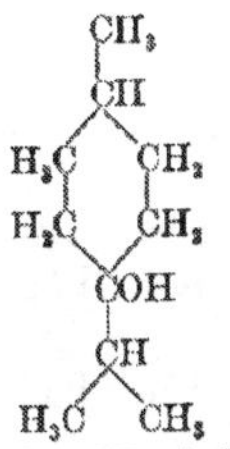

CH_3
CH
H_2C CH_2
H_2C CH_2
COH
CH
H_3C CH_3

Tertiary Menthol.

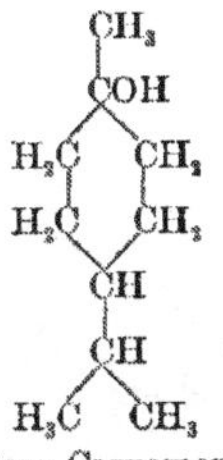

CH_3
COH
H_2C CH_2
H_2C CH_2
CH
CH
H_3C CH_3

Tertiary Carvomenthol.

Theory also clearly allows other isomeric tetrahydrocymenes to be predicted, although they are still unknown.

By consideration of the above-mentioned derivatives of hexahydrocymene, it had to be accepted as a fact, according to the views prevailing at that time, that a third ketohexahydrocymene, isomeric with menthone and carvomenthone, could not exist.

The fact more recently established by Wallach that such an isomeric ketone, thujamenthone, and its corresponding alcohol do exist, deserves therefore to be emphasized at this point as a matter of especially great theoretical importance.

If we suppose one methylene group in the hydrocarbons, $C_{10}H_{18}$, to be replaced by a carbonyl group, we arrive at the ketones, $C_{10}H_{16}O$, which contain one double linkage, and are to be regarded as derivatives of tetrahydrocymene. By reduction of these ketones, $C_{10}H_{16}O$, secondary alcohols, $C_{10}H_{17}OH$, are formed which may be transformed into terpenes, $C_{10}H_{16}$, by the elimination of one molecule of water. The reverse process, by which the alcohols may to some extent be prepared from the terpenes, $C_{10}H_{16}$, by the addition of the elements of water, is also possible.

Ketones, $C_{10}H_{16}O$, of this character, which may be considered as ketotetrahydrocymenes, and their corresponding secondary alcohols (oxytetrahydrocymenes), have recently been discovered in exceedingly large numbers. The constitution of these compounds has not yet been determined with such a degree of accuracy that an extended discussion of the various views held in regard to the constitution of the separate members of this class would be of value here. Nevertheless, we recognize certain of these substances which must be regarded as derivatives of menthone, and certain others which are to be considered as derivatives of carvomenthone. The following compounds are derived from menthone: pulegone, and also in all probability the ketone, menthenone, which is formed by heating nitrosomenthene with hydrochloric acid.

From carvomenthone are derived: dihydrocarvone and dihydrocarveol; carvenone; dihydroeucarvone and dihydroeucarveol; thujone (tanacetone) and thujyl alcohol; and carvotanacetone.

According to Wallach, isothujone appears to correspond to neither menthone nor carvomenthone. By reduction it yields the above-mentioned thujamenthone.

Aside from the secondary alcohols, $C_{10}H_{17}OH$, just referred to, tertiary alcohols, $C_{10}H_{17}OH$, are known, which are also to be considered as oxytetrahydrocymenes. The constitution of one of these tertiary alcohols, terpineol (melting point 35°), was determined by Wallach and Baeyer independently of each other, but with perfect agreement in result, and until quite recently terpineol was represented by their formula:

```
        CH3
        |
        C
      /   \\
  H2C       CH
   |         |
  H2C       CH2
      \   /
       COH
        |
        CH
      /   \
  H3C       CH3
```

Later experiments by Wallach, on the one hand, and Tiemann, Semmler, and Schmidt on the other, however, entitle the formula

```
        CH3
        |
        C
      /   \\
  H2C       CH
   |         |
  H2C       CH2
      \   /
        CH
        |
       COH
      /   \
  H3C       CH3
```

to an equal consideration, and, indeed, it appears in all probability to be the correct representation of the constitution of terpineol.

A large number of bases, $C_{10}H_{17}NH_2$, which have been prepared by various methods from the ketones, $C_{10}H_{16}O$, or the alcohols, $C_{10}H_{17}OH$, are to be considered with the latter.

If a molecule of water is withdrawn from the alcohols, $C_{10}H_{17}OH$, or ammonia from the bases, $C_{10}H_{17}NH_2$, a class of terpenes, $C_{10}H_{16}$, is derived, which contain two ethylene linkages, and are to be regarded as dihydrocymenes. To this group of terpenes belong:

Limonene (Dipentene),	Carvestrene,
Sylvestrene,	Terpinolene.

In regard to another terpene, thujene, which belongs here, only a few statements have hitherto been submitted.

Regarding the constitution of these hydrocarbons, it is worthy of note that Baeyer believes the constitution of terpinolene, which results by the elimination of water from the above-mentioned terpineol (melting point 35°), to be proved with a degree of accuracy equal to that of any other organic compound.

```
        CH3
        |
        C
      /   \\
  H2C       CH
   |         |
  H2C       CH2
      \   /
        C
        ||
        C
      /   \
   H3C     CH3
```

Terpinolene.

It will be judicious, however, to use this formula cautiously for the present, since Baeyer's proofs rest to some extent on conclusions drawn from analogy, and their strength must at all events be supported by the presentation of an extended series of observations.

Various views have been held from time to time with respect to the position of the double linkage in the other terpenes of the limonene group; but it would be of little interest at this time to discuss the proposed formulas, since the investigations regarding these have not yet reached definite conclusions.

If it be imagined that one of the methylene groups in the terpenes of the limonene series is oxidized to a carbonyl group, ketones, $C_{10}H_{14}O$, are derived, which contain two ethylene linkages, and are to be considered as ketodihydrocymenes. Again theory allows two classes of these ketones to be predicted, of which one corresponds to menthone, the other to carvomenthone. Both classes may be transformed into these two saturated ketones by hydration. With the ketones, $C_{10}H_{14}O$, which are derived from menthone, we are as yet unacquainted. The known ketones, $C_{10}H_{14}O$,

Carvone,
Eucarvone,
Pinocarvone,

are all derivatives of carvomenthone, and this substance owes its name to precisely this relation which it bears to carvone. An alcohol, $C_{10}H_{15}OH$, corresponding to carvone, is known only in its methyl ether, but, on the other hand, an alcohol, $C_{10}H_{15}OH$, pinocarveol, exists corresponding to pinocarvone.

These theoretical considerations render it apparent that all the hydro-derivatives of cymene can be transformed into each other by the greatest variety of methods.

The nomenclature of the above-mentioned group of hydrocymene derivatives is rendered difficult, if it be desired to rationally express the structure of a compound in its relation to hexahydrocymene as the parent-substance. Baeyer[1] has therefore advanced the proposition to designate hexahydrocymene as *terpane;* the tetrahydrocymenes, according to the Geneva commission, as *terpenes;* and the hydrocarbons, $C_{10}H_{16}$, hitherto known as terpenes, as *terpadiënes.*

The position of the double linkage is indicated by the same method as that introduced by Baeyer in the case of the hydrophthalic acids; thus, as an example, the above-mentioned structural formula of terpinolene would be designated as follows:

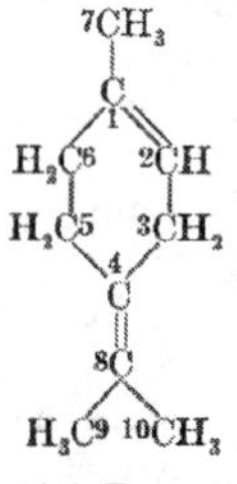

7CH$_3$
C
1
H$_2$C6 2CH
H$_2$C5 3CH$_2$
4
C
8C
H$_3$C9 10CH$_3$

Δ-1, 4(8)-Terpadiëne.

According to Baeyer, the ketones, $C_{10}H_{18}O$, are termed *terpanones,* the alcohols, $C_{10}H_{19}OH$, *terpanols,* with an index figure to designate the carbon atom to which the oxygen is attached. The ketones, $C_{10}H_{16}O$, and the alcohols, $C_{10}H_{17}OH$, Baeyer designates as *terpenones* and *terpenols.*

[1] Baeyer, Ber., 27, 436.

This system of nomenclature, introduced by Baeyer, has the one disadvantage of giving the old familiar name terpene to the hydrocarbons, $C_{10}H_{18}$. In order to avoid this difficulty, but, at the same time, to preserve the unquestionable advantage of Baeyer's system of nomenclature, Wagner[1] has suggested that hexahydrocymene be called *menthane*. The hydrocarbons, $C_{10}H_{18}$, retain the name *menthene*, which has already been employed for one member of this group, while the dihydrocymenes, $C_{10}H_{16}$, may be called *menthadiënes*, or *terpenes* as hitherto.

In the meantime no agreement has been reached as to whether Baeyer's or Wagner's nomenclature shall be introduced.

For the sake of completeness it might be noticed at this point, that in accordance with a proposition by Wallach,[2] menthone is often designated as β-, carvomenthone as α-keto-hexahydrocymene, and, correspondingly, all unsaturated ketones which yield menthone by hydration are termed β-, but all ketones which form carvomenthone by hydration, α-keto-derivatives.

It has already been mentioned that in addition to the terpenes of the limonene series, other terpenes are known which contain only one ethylene linkage, and can not be regarded as simple hydration products of cymene. Especially is this the case in a family of closely related terpenes consisting of:

Pinene,
Camphene,
Fenchene.

To these terpenes correspond also saturated hydrocarbons, $C_{10}H_{18}$. If it be imagined, in a manner similar to that above, that one methylene group in these hydrocarbons, $C_{10}H_{18}$, be replaced by a carbonyl group, the ketones, $C_{10}H_{16}O$, are derived, which are *saturated* compounds. These ketones, camphor and fenchone, sustain the same relation to the three terpenes of this class, as the above-mentioned ketotetrahydrocymenes to the terpenes of the limonene series.

The saturated nature of camphor has caused this compound to be regarded as a ketotetrahydrocymene containing a so-called para-linkage (Kannonikow,[3] Bredt[4]) :—

[1] Wagner, Ber., 27, 1636.
[2] Wallach, Ann. Chem., 277, 105.
[3] Kannonikow, Journ. Russ. Phys. Chem. Soc., *1*, 434.
[4] Bredt, Ann. Chem., 226, 261.

```
          CH3
          |
          C
        /   \
    H2C   |   CH2
    H2C   |   CO
        \   /
          C
          |
          CH
        /    \
    H3C       CH3
```

According to this, Wallach[1] has gradually brought the following constitutional formula of pinene into consideration :—

```
          CH3
          |
          C
        /   \\
     HC   \   CH
    H2C     \ CH
        \   /
          CH
          |
          CH
        /    \
    H3C       CH3
```

During the course of further investigations, however, these formulas have proved untenable, and Bredt[2] has proposed the following formulas for camphor, pinene and camphene :—

```
CH2———CH———CH2              CH2———CH———CH2
|  H3C—C—CH3  |             |  H3C—C—CH3  |
CH2————C——————CO            CH2————C——————CHOH
       |                           |
       CH3                         CH3
    Camphor.                    Borneol.

CH2———CH———CH               CH2————C═══CH
|  H3C—C—CH3  ||            |  H3C—C—CH3  |
CH2————C——————CH            CH2————C——————CH2
       |                           |
       CH3                         CH3
    Camphene.                   Pinene.
```

Bredt's camphor formula interprets the conduct of this compound especially well in the formation of trimethylsuccinic acid

[1]Wallach, Ber., *24*, 1545.
[2]Bredt, Ber., *26*, 3047.

from camphoronic acid resulting from the oxidation of camphor. The behavior of pinene can be explained with the help of the above formula, if we assume with Bredt that, by the action of certain reagents, especially aqueous acids, the formation of an atomic group $C(CH_3)_2$ may result, by which an isopropyl group is formed, accompanied by a break in the pentamethylene ring. Thus the formation of a hexahydrocymene derivative is made possible. For example, Bredt explains the formation of terpine in the following manner:

```
                                                   CH3  CH3
 CH2———C=====CH                                       \/
 |  H3C—C—CH3 |                                        CH
 |      |  :  |            +2H2O =  H2C—C(OH)—CH2
 CH2———C———————CH2                   |      |
        |                           H2C—C(OH)—CH2
        CH3                                 |
                                            CH3
    Pinene.                              Terpine.
```

Whether this formula proposed by Bredt will be proved correct in all points, time alone will tell. Some investigators have already proposed modifications of Bredt's formulas, which seem to better suit certain facts.[1] As a rule, in the present state of our knowledge, criticisms arise against all such formulas. It would, therefore, be too early at this time to pass a critical judgment concerning the value of the extremely large number of formulas proposed for pinene.

Fenchone, which very closely resembles camphor, stands in its relation to the latter, as a meta- to a para-compound (Wallach). Fenchene undoubtedly possesses a similar relation to camphene.

Aside from the terpenes, $C_{10}H_{16}$, already mentioned, two others are known, terpinene and phellandrene, both of which appear to possess but one ethylene linkage. They do not, however, admit of classification in the same group with pinene, camphene and fenchene. Both are without doubt closely allied to cymene.

The relations of the terpenes, $C_{10}H_{16}$, to the numerous ketones occurring in nature or artificially prepared, and to the monobasic alcohols have now been presented. There remains for conclusion the consideration of a series of polyvalent alcohols known in the terpene series. Several of these alcohols lose water with great readiness, forming anhydrides which possess the character of oxides. To these anhydrides belong the saturated *cineole*, $C_{10}H_{18}O$, *pinole hydrate*, $C_{10}H_{17}O \cdot OH$, and *fenchenole*, $C_{10}H_{18}O$.

[1] Wagner, Ber., 27, 2270; Tiemann and Semmler, Ber., 28, 1345.

After it was recognized that certain terpenes were to be considered as dihydrocymenes, the next step was to synthesize the latter hydrocarbons, and to identify them with known terpenes. The long familiar reaction by which a terpene, $C_{10}H_{16}$, results from heating isoprene to a high temperature, and which Wallach[1] has characterized as dipentene, can be looked upon as the first synthesis of a terpene; the course of the reaction was not, however, clear, and the constitution of isoprene, which had not been prepared by synthetical methods, was not known.

After Wallach[2] in the year 1890 had demonstrated that certain unsaturated aliphatic ketones (methyl hexylene ketone, $C_8H_{14}O$, and methyl heptylene ketone, $C_9H_{16}O$), could easily be converted, by the elimination of water, into lower homologues of the terpenes (dihydro-meta-xylene, C_8H_{12}, and dihydro-pseudocumene, C_9H_{14}), Bertram and Walbaum[3] in 1892 succeeded in accomplishing the partial synthesis of two terpenes, dipentene and terpinene, by the elimination of water from an unsaturated alcohol of the fatty series, linalool, $C_{10}H_{17}OH$, which is found in nature.

The complete synthesis of a dihydrocymene, $C_{10}H_{16}$, was accomplished in the year 1893 by Baeyer,[4] who distilled the dibromide of methylisopropyl-succino-succinic ester with quinoline. The resultant dihydrocymene, boiling at 174°, has not yet, however, been identified with any known terpene.

In this connection it might further be recalled that a ketotetrahydrocymene, $C_{10}H_{16}O$, has been synthetically prepared by Knoevenagel.[5] This compound, to which Knoevenagel ascribes the formula

```
        CH
      /    \\
    OC      C—CH3
     |      |
   H2C      CH2
      \    /
        CH
        |
        CH
      /    \
   H3C      CH3
```

is derived from isobutylidene diaceto-acetic ester,

[1]Wallach, Ann. Chem., *227*, 295 and 302.
[2]Wallach, Ann. Chem., *258*, 338; *272*, 120; Ber., *24*, 1573.
[3]Bertram and Walbaum, Journ. pr. Chem., N. F., *45*, 601.
[4]Baeyer, Ber., *26*, 233.
[5]Knoevenagel, Ber., *26*, 1085; Ann. Chem., *281*, 44.

$$(CH_3)_2CH—CH\begin{cases}CH<\begin{matrix}COOC_2H_5\\COCH_3\end{matrix}\\CH<\begin{matrix}COCH_3\\COOC_2H_5\end{matrix}\end{cases}$$

Although all the above-mentioned terpenes, $C_{10}H_{16}$, as well as their related oxidized compounds, possess a ring formation of the carbon atoms, nevertheless, another series of hydrocarbons, $C_{10}H_{16}$, and several oxygen-containing compounds, $C_{10}H_{16}O$, $C_{10}H_{18}O$, and $C_{10}H_{20}O$, are known, which belong to the aliphatic series. These compounds also form important constituents of very many ethereal oils; and, since they possess a close connection to the terpenes and camphors with a ring formation of carbon atoms, these hydrocarbons, $C_{10}H_{16}$, are designated as *olefinic terpenes*, according to a proposition of Semmler,[1] while the oxidized compounds are classed under the group name, *olefinic camphors.*

Our knowledge in regard to the olefinic terpenes is still very meager, but it should be mentioned that such terpenes result, not only by the elimination of water from olefinic terpene alcohols, $C_{10}H_{17}OH$, but exist as well already formed in nature. It should further be mentioned that hydrocarbons, $C_{10}H_{18}$, are known, which belong to the aliphatic series, and correspond to menthene.

The olefinic camphors are better known. They are widely distributed, and, in consequence of their agreeable odor form, to some extent, very valuable constituents of numerous ethereal oils. Two primary alcohols, $C_{10}H_{17}OH$, are known, the optically active *linalool,* and the optically inactive *geraniol,* the latter standing perhaps in the same relation to linalool, as dipentene to the active limonene. Both alcohols yield, by oxidation, the same aldehyde, *geranial* (*citral*), $C_{10}H_{16}O$, which also occurs in nature. According to Tiemann and Semmler, geranial is probably a dimethyl-2-6 octdiën-2-6-al-8 :

$$\underset{}{CH_3}—\underset{\substack{|\\CH_3}}{C}=CH—CH_2—CH_2—\underset{\substack{|\\CH_3}}{C}=CH—CHO$$

Citronellal, $C_{10}H_{18}O$, is a second aldehyde, which belongs to this class and which likewise occurs in many ethereal oils.

The close relations of these substances to the ordinary terpenes are first suggested by the circumstance that geranial, by the elimination of water, is quantitatively converted into cymene (Semmler[2]). According to Tiemann and Semmler, this reaction is preceded by a transposition of the double linkage :

[1]Semmler, Ber., *24*, 682.
[2]Semmler, Ber., *23*, 2965 ; *24*, 201.

```
        CH3                        CH3
        |                          |
        C                          C
      /   \\                     //   \
   HC      CH                HC      CH
   ||                        |        ||
   HC      CHO    -H2O =     HC      CH
     \                         \\   /
      CH2                         C
      |                           |
      CH                          CH
     /  \                        /  \
  H3C    CH3                  H3C    CH3
   Geranial.                   Cymene.
```

More important, however, is the fact that, according to Bertram and Walbaum,[1] two well known terpenes, dipentene and terpinene, may be obtained by the removal of water from linalool or geraniol, $C_{10}H_{17}OH$. In a similar manner, Tiemann and Semmler[2] have succeeded in the transformation of an extended series of linalool and geraniol derivatives into isomeric cyclic compounds by treatment with sulphuric acid.

While the naturally occurring olefinic terpenes and camphors can thus be easily converted into ring compounds which are in part identical with those occurring in nature, the investigations of Wallach[3] have shown that, conversely, cyclic compounds may be transformed into substances which occur in nature, and which must be designated as olefinic camphors. Thus, according to Wallach, menthonoxime, $C_{10}H_{18}NOH$, yields menthonitrile, $C_9H_{17}CN$, by the elimination of water. Although menthonoxime is a saturated cyclic compound, menthonitrile possesses the character of an unsaturated aliphatic substance. By reduction, menthonitrile is easily converted into menthonylamine, $C_{10}H_{19}NH_2$. This base, which is isomeric with the cyclic compound menthylamine, yields, by the action of nitrous acid, *menthonyl alcohol* (*menthocitronellol*), $C_{10}H_{19}OH$, which is a primary olefinic alcohol and is converted by oxidation into an *aldehyde* (*menthocitronellal*), $C_{10}H_{18}O$. The intimate relation of these two compounds with the olefinic camphors occurring in nature is revealed by their similar odors. It is, therefore, a matter of practical importance to artificially prepare the olefinic camphors from the more accessible cyclic compounds, since the former are to an extent very valuable perfumes. For this reason a rapid extension of our knowledge in regard to the olefinic terpenes and camphors is to be expected, and it follows from this that more light will be thrown upon the constitution of the closed-chain terpenes and camphors.

[1] Bertram and Walbaum, Journ. pr. Chem., N. F., *45*, 590.
[2] Tiemann and Semmler, Ber., *26*, 2708.
[3] Wallach, Ann. Chem., *278*, 315.

It has been the aim of the foregoing to somewhat facilitate the study of the ten-carbon terpenes and their derivatives by a short survey of this extensive field. It should, however, be especially mentioned that to those who intend to study the chemistry of the terpenes, a very valuable aid will be found by a careful examination of an address given by Wallach[1] in the year 1891.

Although the investigations of Wallach have made possible a systematic classification of the terpenes proper, $C_{10}H_{16}$, and the work of this chemist, as well as of numerous others, has already determined with a certain degree of accuracy the constitution of some members of this group, nevertheless, nothing comparable with this has yet been accomplished for the terpenes having five, fifteen, and more carbon atoms. It should be noted, however, at this point that Wallach[2] has made efforts to compile at least a classification for the sesquiterpenes, $C_{15}H_{24}$. Still, this work has not been in any degree as successful as in the analogous case of the terpenes, $C_{10}H_{16}$. Several alcohols, $C_{15}H_{25}OH$, related to the sesquiterpenes, are associated with the latter to some extent in their natural occurrence. For the remaining polyterpenes, reference is made to the special part.

In the compilation of this monograph, it has been assumed that only such material is to be accepted from the numerous publications as possesses permanent value for science. The experience of past years has proved that structural formulas, which have been suggested in extremely large numbers for many members of the terpene series, are often in a very short time rendered valueless by facts. The time has not yet arrived when it is possible to give an objective and hence scientifically valuable criticism of the views expressed in these constitutional formulas. For this reason it has been the design to present all the constitutional formulas which have been proposed for a few members of the terpene series. In general, however, the structural formulas are only presented in the consideration of those substances whose constitution has been determined with certainty, or with a high degree of probability ; or in certain cases where the presentation of a formula, which, although not determined with scientific accuracy, can nevertheless be used to more clearly illustrate the relation of several compounds to one another.

In regard to the actual observations which have been published, the author has exerted himself to the utmost to present them in a complete form.

[1]Wallach, Ber., *24*, 1525.
[2]Wallach, Ann. Chem., *271*, 285 and 297.

SPECIAL PART.

Hemiterpenes, C_5H_8.

For the numerous isomeric hydrocarbons, C_5H_8, Beilstein's "Handbuch der organischen Chemie" (third edition, Vol. I., page 131), may be consulted. Isoprene, however, stands in an especially close relation to the terpenes, and should be more closely considered here.

Isoprene, C_5H_8.

If the oil obtained by the dry distillation of caoutchouc or guttapercha be submitted to a fractional distillation, a distillate is obtained which consists of isoprene. Williams,[1] Bouchardat,[2] Tilden,[3] Wallach,[4] Euler[5] and Mokiewsky[6] have published investigations concerning this hydrocarbon.

Euler[5] prepared isoprene by the following method. 3-Methylpyrrolidine, $C_5H_{10}NH$, on treating with methyl iodide, yields a compound, which, when distilled with potash, yields 2, 3, 5-trimethylpyrrolidine, $C_7H_{14}NH$. This again unites with methyl iodide, giving a substance which, on distilling with potash, yields trimethylamine and isoprene. The latter is given the constitution,

$$CH_2 = C(CH_3) - CH = CH_2.$$

Pure isoprene[6] is regenerated from its dibromide by treatment with zinc dust; it is very unstable, boils at 33.5° (impure isoprene boils at 33° to 39°), has a specific gravity of 0.6989 at 0° and 0.6794 at 19°. It is polymerized on heating to 250° or 270° into dipentene. When acted upon by concentrated hydrochloric acid, a polymerization product resembling caoutchouc results, together with oily chlorides. Isoprene does not form compounds with ammoniacal solutions of silver and cuprous salts; oxidation with a chromic acid solution or with nitric acid converts it into carbonic acid, acetic acid, formic acid and oxalic acid.

[1] Williams, Journ., *1860*, 495.
[2] Bouchardat, Compt. rend., *80*, 1446; *89*, 1217; Bull. Soc. Chim., *1879*, 577.
[3] Tilden, Journ. Chem. Soc., *1884* (45), 410; Journ., *1882*, 410.
[4] Wallach, Ann. Chem., *227*, 295.
[5] Euler, Ber., *30*, 1989.
[6] Mokiewsky, Journ. Russ. Phys. Chem. Soc., *30* (1898), 885; *32* (1900), 207.

According to Bouchardat, it combines with dry halogen acids, adding one and two molecules of the halogen hydride.

Isoprene hydrochloride, $C_5H_8 \cdot HCl$, boils at 85° to 91°, and has a specific gravity 0.885 at 0°; when treated with silver oxide, it yields an *alcohol* which possesses an agreeable odor, boils at 120° to 130°, and is somewhat soluble in water. The hydrochloride gives an oily *dibromide* when treated with bromine.

Isoprene dihydrochloride, $C_5H_8 \cdot 2HCl$, boils at 143° to 145°, and has the specific gravity 1.079 at 0°.

Isoprene hydrobromide, $C_5H_8 \cdot HBr$, boils at 104° to 108°, and at 0° has the specific gravity 1.192.

According to Mokiewsky,[1] the action of an acetic acid solution of hydrogen bromide on isoprene gives a hydrobromide, C_5H_9Br, which boils at 66° to 67°, and has the specific gravity 1.3075 at 0° and 1.2819 at 20°. On treating this bromide with alcoholic potash, an *alcohol*, $C_5H_{10}O$, is formed; it boils at 97° to 99°, and has the specific gravity 0.8417 at 0° and 0.8242 at 20°.

Isoprene dihydrobromide, $C_5H_8 \cdot 2HBr$, has the specific gravity 1.623, and boils at 175° to 180°.

Isoprene dibromide, $C_5H_8Br_2$, is formed, together with an amylene bromine derivative, by adding one molecular proportion of bromine to a cold, ethereal solution of isoprene. It is a very unstable liquid, has a penetrating odor, boils at 90° to 94° at 12 mm. pressure, and easily chars. When treated with zinc dust it yields 70 per cent. of pure isoprene. It combines with one molecule of bromine with difficulty, forming the *tetrabromide*. On oxidizing the dibromide with a one per cent. solution of potassium permanganate, the corresponding *glycol*, $C_5H_8Br_2(OH)_2$, is formed; it crystallizes from ether in long, colorless prisms, melts at 126.5°, sublimes when heated above its melting point, and is converted into isoprene by the action of zinc dust.

Isoprene tetrabromide, $C_5H_8Br_4$, was first prepared by Tilden. It is an oil which decomposes by distillation, but, according to Wallach,[2] it may be purified by distillation with steam. If the bromide be covered with ammonia, and allowed to remain for a short time at a low temperature, a white amorphous mass results, which is insoluble in all solvents (Wallach).

Isoprene dichlorhydrin, $C_5H_8Cl_2(OH)_2$, is formed, together with the chlorhydrin of trimethylene glycol, $C_5H_{11}ClO$, by the action of a cold, dilute solution of hypochlorous acid on isoprene; the product is a yellowish-brown, viscous liquid, from which the two compounds are isolated. The dichlorhydrin crystallizes from al-

[1]Mokiewsky, Journ. Russ. Phys. Chem. Soc., *32* (1900), 207.
[2]Wallach, Ann. Chem., *238*, 88.

cohol, ether or benzene, melts at 82.5°, and, when heated with water at 120°, forms a *compound*, $C_5H_9Cl \cdot OH$, which melts at 72.5° to 73°. The compound, $C_5H_{11}ClO$, boils at 141°, and has a specific gravity 1.0562 at 0°.

Isoprene dibromhydrin, $C_5H_8Br_2(OH)_2$, is formed by treating isoprene with hypobromous acid; it crystallizes in hexagonal plates, and melts at 86°. It is more readily prepared than the corresponding chlorine derivative.

TERPENES PROPER, $C_{10}H_{16}$.

I. PINENE.

In its two physical isomeric modifications, the levorotatory and the dextrorotatory, pinene forms a widely distributed constituent of numerous ethereal oils. Before Wallach had recognized the identity of the pinene derived from different sources, it was believed that an extremely large number of terpenes existed, and were designated as terebentene (levo-pinene), australene (dextro-pinene), eucalyptene, laurene, olibene, massoyene and others. Wallach's [1] investigations then determined that all these substances contain pinene as their chief constituent, whose physical and chemical properties are modified by the presence of larger or smaller amounts of isomeric hydrocarbons, or oxygen-containing compounds of the terpene series.

The ethereal oils, prepared from the different varieties of pines and from various other coniferous plants, are especially rich in pinene, hence the name. Thus, pinene is the chief ingredient of turpentine oil; the American, Russian, Swedish and German turpentine oils contain dextro-pinene; the French oil consists almost wholly of levo-pinene.

The latter modification has also been found by Bertram and Walbaum [2] in the pine needle oils from *Abies alba, Picea excelsa, Pinus montana,* and *Pinus silvestris* L.,[3] oil from cones of *Abies alba,* and hemlock needle oil. Among the numerous oils in which pinene occurs the following may be mentioned: pine needle oil from *Pinus silvestris,*[4] oil of Siberian pine needles,[5] oil of pine-resin,[6] oil of juniper berries,[7] oil of eucalyptus (*E. globulus*),[9] oil of mace,[7] oil of sage,[10] oil of lemon,[7] oil of basil,[8] oil of laurel berries and laurel leaves,[10] oil of olibanum,[10] valerian

[1] Wallach, Ann. Chem., *227*, 282; *230*, 245; *252*, 94; *258*, 340.
[2] Bertram and Walbaum, Arch. Pharm., *231*, 290.
[3] Schimmel & Co., Chem. Centr., 1898, 258.
[4] Bertram and Walbaum, Arch. Pharm., *231*, 290.
[5] Flawitzky, Journ. pr. Chem., N. F., *45*, 115.
[6] Kurilow, Journ. pr. Chem., N. F., *45*, 123.
[7] Wallach, Ann. Chem., *227*, 282.
[8] Bertram and Walbaum, Arch. Pharm., *235*, 176.
[9] Wallach and Gildemeister, Ann. Chem., *246*, 283.
[10] Wallach, Ann. Chem., *252*, 94.

oil, bay oil,[1] camphor oil, coriander oil, fennel oil, oil of massoy bark,[2] oil of myrtle,[3] parsley oil, oil of rosemary, oil of spike, oil of star anise, oil of thyme, oil of water fennel, oil from sassafras bark and sassafras leaves,[4] and oil of valerian (Japanese).[5] The presence of pinene is also reported in the oils of galbanum, niaouli, canella, cheken leaves, French basilicum, tansy, cajeput, kesso-root, spearmint, elderberry, thuja, nutmeg, peppermint and lavender. Pinene is likewise found in the products resulting from the dry distillation of vegetable resins. Thus, Wallach and Rheindorf[6] recognized this hydrocarbon in the distillation products of copal resin, olibanum and colophonium. Commercial resin oil also contains pinene as shown by Renard,[7] who isolated from this product a levorotatory hydrocarbon having the properties of pinene. Pinene also occurs in the distillation products of resinous woods; an example may be cited in the investigations of Aschan and Hjelt,[8] who recognized it in the products of distillation of pine roots and trunks of the Scotch fir.

Preparation.—In order to prepare the optically active modifications of pinene, we must resort to the fractional distillation of the ethereal oils containing it. For the preparation of dextro-pinene, it is most convenient to employ American oil of turpentine, while for the preparation of levo-pinene, the French oil is best adapted. Should the oil at command be old, it must first be distilled with steam, dried with potassium hydroxide and fractionated, using some form of fractionating apparatus; the fraction boiling up to 160° is to be further purified by repeated fractionations. The product thus obtained is, of course, not strictly pure. Chemically pure pinene is optically inactive, and may be prepared by an excellent method suggested by Wallach;[9] this method is based on the fact that when pinene nitrosochloride is heated with an excess of aniline, nitrosyl chloride is eliminated with the formation of amido-azo-benzene and inactive pinene:

$$C_{10}H_{16}NOCl + 2C_6H_5NH_2 = H_2O + HCl + C_6H_5N{:}NC_6H_4NH_2 + C_{10}H_{16}.$$

Since it is not advisable to operate with too large quantities at a time, ten grams of pinene nitrosochloride are heated for a

[1] Mittmann, Arch. Pharm., *227*, 529.

[2] Wallach, Ann. Chem., *258*, 340; Arch. Pharm., *229*, 1.

[3] Jahns, Arch. Pharm., *227*, 174.

[4] Power and Kleber, Pharm. Review, 1896.

[5] Bertram and Gildemeister, Arch. Pharm., *228*, 483.

[6] Wallach and Rheindorf, Ann. Chem., *271*, 308.

[7] Renard, Ann. Chim. Phys. [6], *1*, 223.

[8] Aschan and Hjelt, Chem. Ztg., *18*, 1566; compare Renard, Comp. rend., *119*, 165.

[9] Wallach, Ann. Chem., *252*, 132; *258*, 343.

short time with a mixture of thirty cc. of aniline and eighty cc. of alcohol in a flask provided with a vertical condenser. After the violent reaction has taken place, the product is distilled with steam. The aqueous distillate is then treated with an excess of acetic acid to remove the unchanged aniline, the hydrocarbon is separated and again washed with acetic acid, and rectified.

PROPERTIES.—According to Wallach, chemically pure pinene, obtained by the method just suggested, is an optically inactive liquid, boiling at 155° to 156°. At 20° its specific gravity is 0.858; at 25° it is 0.854; its coefficient of refraction at 21° is $n_D = 1.46553$.

According to their sources, the optically active modifications have a specific gravity of 0.8587 to 0.8600, and a rotatory power, $[\alpha]_D = +32°$ to $[\alpha]_D = -43.4°$.[1]

The spectrometric behavior of levo-pinene has been closely examined by Brühl.[2]

Before we consider more carefully the characteristics of pinene, it would seem expedient to present a series of transformations of pinene, which had been performed before Wallach's investigations; it is doubtful, however, whether all the reaction-products obtained by these transformations result directly from pinene.

If the vapor of oil of turpentine be passed through a tube heated to redness, hydrogen, isoprene, C_5H_8, benzene, toluene, metaxylene, cymene, naphthalene, anthracene, methylanthracene, phenanthrene, and terpilene (terpinene) are formed (G. Schultz[3]). Pinene absorbs oxygen from the air forming acetic acid, hydrogen peroxide,[4] and a compound resembling an aldehyde, and is eventually converted into a resinous mass. By the electrolysis of a mixture of dilute sulphuric acid, oil of turpentine and alcohol, terpine hydrate, terpine, cymene, and two acids are formed. Renard[5] has examined some of the salts of these acids.

Nitric acid readily oxidizes turpentine oil, while fuming nitric acid or a mixture of nitric and sulphuric acids ignites it. A series of products have been obtained by the action of dilute nitric acid on oil of turpentine; among these may be mentioned acetic acid, propionic acid, butyric acid, an acid of the formula, $C_5H_6O_2$, dimethyl fumaric acid, $C_6H_8O_4$, oxalic acid, para-toluic acid, $C_8H_8O_2$, terephthalic acid, $C_8H_6O_4$, terebic acid, $C_7H_{10}O_4$, terechrysinic

[1]Kannonikow, Ber., *1881*, 1697.
[2]Brühl, Ber., *25*, 153.
[3]G. Schultz, Ber., *1877*, 114; compare Tilden, Journ. Chem. Soc., *45*, 411.
[4]Kingzett, Jahresb. Chem., *1876*, 402.
[5]Renard, Jahresb. Chem., *1880*, 448.

acid, $C_6H_8O_5$, and nitro-benzene.[1] Chromic acid solution oxidizes turpentine oil into acetic acid, terebic acid, terpenylic acid, $C_8H_{12}O_4$, and a little terephthalic acid.[1]

Reducing agents, such as phosphonium iodide at 300°,[2] hydriodic acid and red phosphorus at 275°,[3] and a hydriodic acid solution of specific gravity 2.02 at 280°,[4] convert turpentine oil into the hydrocarbons, $C_{10}H_{20}$ or $C_{10}H_{18}$ (b. p. 165°), $C_{10}H_{20}$ (b. p. 170° to 175°), $C_{10}H_{22}$ (b. p. 155° to 162°), and C_5H_{12} (b. p. 40°). When heated with iodine at 230° to 250°, meta-xylene, a little para-xylene and cymene, pseudocumene, mesitylene, a hydrocarbon, $C_{11}H_{16}$ (b. p. 189° to 193°), durene and polyterpenes, $(C_{10}H_{16})_n$, are formed.

To return to the consideration of pure pinene, we find that it is distinguished by the readiness with which it can be converted into isomeric terpenes. The transformation into the closely related camphene can be accomplished either by the action of concentrated sulphuric acid, or by passing dry hydrogen chloride into dry pinene, and heating the pinene hydrochloride thus formed with sodium acetate, or aniline. On the other hand, the action of moist hydrochloric acid forms dipentene dihydrochloride, which, by elimination of the hydrogen chloride, yields dipentene. A direct transformation of pinene into dipentene can, however, be effected by heating pinene to 250° to 270°.[5]

Dilute nitric[6] or sulphuric acid converts pinene into dipentene and terpine hydrate.

According to Wallach, the terpenes, terpinolene and terpinene,[7] resulting by the action of alcoholic sulphuric acid on pinene, are not to be considered as the primary products of the reaction, but rather as resulting from a transformation of dipentene, which is first formed.

According to Genvresse,[8] when a mixture of pinene, alcohol and nitrous acid (purified from nitric acid) is left at the ordinary temperature, reaction takes place slowly, and at the end of two months about two-thirds of the pinene is changed. By fractional distillation of the product, a liquid is obtained which is identical

[1]Roser, Ber., *1882*, 293; Fittig and Kraft, Ann. Chem., *208*, 74; compare publications of Schryver, Journ. Chem. Soc., *1893* (1), 1327; Ber., *27*, 133 Ref.

[2]Baeyer, Ann. Chem., *155*, 276.

[3]Orlow, Journ. Russ. Phys. Chem. Soc., *15*, 44; Ber., *16*, 799.

[4]Berthelot, Journ., *1869*, 332.

[5]Wallach, Ann. Chem., *227*, 282.

[6]Hempel, Ann. Chem., *180*, 73.

[7]Wallach, Ann. Chem., *227*, 282; *230*, 262.

[8]P. Genvresse, Compt. rend. (1901), *132*, 637.

with terpineol; the yield is about seventy-five per cent. of the pinene transformed. The melting point of its nitrosochloride is 83°.

Pinene picrate, $C_{10}H_{16} \cdot C_6H_2(NO_2)_3OH$, is prepared, according to Lextreit,[1] by heating pinene with picric acid at 150°; it forms crystals, which, by boiling with potassium hydroxide, yield inactive borneol. Camphene is obtained by heating the compound with pyridine, or by dry distillation of its potassium salt (Tilden and Forster[2]).

Pinene hydrochloride,[3] $C_{10}H_{16} \cdot HCl$ (so-called "artificial camphor"), is obtained by saturating well cooled, dry pinene with dry hydrochloric acid gas. If rise of temperature during the operation is prevented, the oil solidifies almost completely after saturation with the gas to a camphor-like mass. It is necessary to avoid the presence of moisture and to prevent the rising of the temperature, as otherwise some dipentene dihydrochloride is formed, and prevents the complete solidification of the reaction-product; for, as Tilden[4] first observed, pinene hydrochloride and dipentene dihydrochloride form a mixture, which has a low melting point.

Pinene hydrochloride is very volatile at ordinary temperature, and smells like camphor. It crystallizes from alcohol in feathery crystals, which press together, forming a sticky mass. It melts at about 125°, and boils at 207° to 208°, suffering almost no decomposition (Wallach).

The hydrochloride of dextro-pinene is optically inactive according to the observations of Pesci,[5] which have been confirmed by Wallach and Conrady; that prepared from levo-pinene is levorotatory, $[\alpha]_D = -30.687°$ and $-26.3°$.

According to more recent investigations by J. H. Long,[6] pinene hydrochloride melts at 131° and not at 125°, and the different values (from 0° to + 30°), which have been given by different investigators for the specific rotatory power of the hydrochloride, are due to the fact that the hydrocarbon employed contained varying amounts of dextro- and levo-pinene. Long finds that the hydrochloride of levo-pinene has a higher rotatory power than l-pinene, and that the hydrochloride from dextro-pinene has a slightly lower rotatory power than d-pinene.

[1] Lextreit, Compt. rend., *102*, 555; Ber., *19*, 237, Ref.

[2] Tilden and Forster, Journ. Chem. Soc., *1893* (1), 1388; Ber., *27*, 136, Ref.

[3] Wallach, Ann. Chem., *239*, 4; compare J. Kondakow, Chem. Zeit., *25* (1901), 609.

[4] Tilden, Ber., *12*, 1131.

[5] Pesci, Gazz. Chim., *1888*, 223; Wallach and Conrady, Ann. Chem., *252*, 156.

[6] John H. Long, Journ. Amer. Chem. Soc., *21*, 637.

Camphene[1] is formed when pinene hydrochloride is heated to 200° with sodium acetate and acetic acid; according to earlier experiments of Ribau and Berthelot, the same result can be obtained by heating with alcoholic potash, or other reagents capable of eliminating the elements of hydrogen chloride. The latter reactions require, however, a relatively high temperature.

Armstrong[2] regards the hydrochloride as more closely related to camphene than to pinene, and, since it may be converted into dihydrocamphene,[3] $C_{10}H_{18}$ (which he calls *camphydrene*), by the action of sodium and alcohol, he introduces the term *chlorocamphydrene* for this hydrochloride.

By oxidizing one part of the hydrochloride with five parts of concentrated nitric acid at a temperature of about 20°, Armstrong[4] obtained *ketopinic acid*, $C_{10}H_{14}O_3$, which crystallizes from water in colorless plates, melting at 234°, and is optically inactive; its *hydrazone* melts at 146°, and its *oxime* fuses at 216°.

When the hydrochloride is oxidized on the water-bath with nitric acid diluted with half its volume of water, it is converted into acetic acid, camphoric acid, $C_{10}H_{16}O_4$, camphopyric or camphoic acid, and other acids.[5]

According to Wagner,[6] pinene hydrochloride is the true chloride of borneol; this view is also supported by Semmler.[3] Attempts to convert the hydrochloride into bornyl acetate by heating with silver acetate and acetic acid gave camphene and isobornyl acetate, but no bornyl acetate.

Tetrahydropinene, $C_{10}H_{20}$, was obtained by Wallach and Berkenheim[7] as a reduction product of pinene by heating pinene hydrochloride to 200° with hydriodic acid and red phosphorus. It boils at 162°, has the specific gravity 0.795, and the refractive index 1.437 at 20°.

Pinene hydrobromide, $C_{10}H_{16}\cdot HBr$, was first obtained by Deville.[8] It is prepared by the action of dry hydrobromic acid on pinene, and melts at about 90°; it boils with decomposition. It resembles the hydrochloride in its optical behavior, and, like this,

[1] Wallach, Ann. Chem., *252*, 6.

[2] Armstrong, Journ. Chem. Soc., *69* (1896), 1398.

[3] Semmler, Ber., *33*, 774.

[4] Armstrong, Journ. Chem. Soc., *69* (1896), 1401.

[5] Gardner and Cockburn, Journ. Chem. Soc., *73* (1898), 278.

[6] Wagner and Brickner, Ber., *32*, 2302.

[7] Wallach and Berkenheim, Ann. Chem., *268*, 225.

[8] Deville, Ann. Chim. Phys., *75*, 45 and 54; compare Papasogli, Gazz. Chim., *1876*, 542.

is converted into camphene by the elimination of hydrogen bromide (Wallach[1]).

Pinene hydriodide,[2] $C_{10}H_{16}\cdot HI$, is best prepared by the action of dry hydrogen iodide on French turpentine oil. It is a stable, heavy, colorless oil, boils at 118° to 119° under a pressure of 15 mm., solidifies in a freezing mixture, melts at − 3° and has the specific gravity 1.4826 at 0° and 1.4635 at 20° (Wagner[3]).

When prepared from a turpentine oil having a specific rotatory power, $[\alpha]_D = -37° 50'$, and washed with aqueous caustic potash, it had the rotatory power, $[\alpha]_D = -33° 34'$, in a one decimeter tube; on heating with alcoholic potash, this value decreased until after forty hours of this treatment the value was $[\alpha]_D = -31° 25'$.

It is converted into camphene by heating with alcoholic potash at 160° to 170° for a short time. It is only slowly attacked by a hot solution of potassium permanganate, but is readily oxidized by fuming nitric acid in the cold with elimination of iodine. When treated with silver acetate and acetic acid, it is converted into a mixture of dipentene, terpinyl acetate, camphene, bornyl acetate, and isobornyl acetate; Wagner[3] regards the two first-mentioned compounds as the normal products of the action, while camphene and isobornyl acetate are produced in larger quantities at higher temperatures, and are regarded as secondary products.

Wagner regards pinene hydriodide as identical with *bornyl iodide* in all respects except its rotatory power.

The Action of Hypochlorous Acid on Pinene.[4]

When French turpentine oil, boiling at 155° to 156° and having the specific rotation, $[\alpha]_D = -37° 30'$, is treated with hypochlorous acid, and the resulting product is acted upon by potash, a mixture is obtained from which Wagner[5] has isolated the following compounds: *cis-pinole oxide* (Wallach's *anhydride of pinole glycol*), $C_{10}H_{16}O_2$, *cis-sobrerytrite* (*menthane*-1, 2, 6, 8-*tetrol*), $C_{10}H_{20}O_4$, *cis-pinole glycol-2-chlorhydrin*, $C_{10}H_{16}O\cdot Cl(OH)$, *cis-menthane-1, 2-dichlor-6, 8-diol*, $C_{10}H_{18}O_2Cl_2$, a *chlorhydrin* of

[1] Wallach, Ann. Chem., *239*, 7.

[2] Deville, Ann. Chem., *37*, 176; Baeyer, Ber., *26*, 826.

[3] Wagner and Brickner, Ber., *32*, 2302.

[4] Wagner and Slawinski, Ber., *32*, 2064; Wagner and Ginzberg, Ber., *29*, 886; Ginzberg and E. Wagner, Journ. Russ. Chem. Soc., *30*, 675.

[5] Wagner and Ginzberg, Ber., *29*, 886.

unknown composition, *nopinole glycol*, $C_{10}H_{18}O_3$, and unsaturated compounds.

Only nopinole glycol will be considered here; the remaining compounds, being derivatives of pinole, will be mentioned more in detail under pinole.

Nopinole glycol, $C_{10}H_{18}O_3$, is regarded by Wagner as a derivative of an isomeride of pinene; it crystallizes from ether in splendid prisms, and melts at 126° to 127°. It differs from the pinole glycols in that its *diacetate* is a liquid, and it gives a red coloration with concentrated sulphuric acid, while the pinole glycols at first give a light yellow color which passes into a bright red. When oxidized with permanganate, it yields formic acid and a non-volatile, syrupy acid, but no acetic acid; under similar conditions the pinole glycols give acetic and terpenylic acids.

When an emulsion of pinene in water is treated with hypochlorous acid and the product is treated with potassium carbonate, a compound,[1] $C_{10}H_{16}Cl_2$, which Wagner calls *tricyclene dichloride*, is produced; it melts at 165° to 168°.

Additive Compound of Formaldehyde and Pinene.[2]—A compound, $C_{11}H_{18}O$, is obtained by heating twenty grams of pinene, 4.4 grams of paraformaldehyde and ten grams of alcohol in a sealed tube at 170° to 175° for twelve hours; the contents of the tube are poured into water, extracted with ether, and distilled. Considerable unchanged terpene is recovered, together with an oil boiling at 225° to 240°. After purification by steam distillation, it boils at 232° to 236°, and has the composition $C_{11}H_{18}O$. It is a clear, strongly dextrorotatory liquid, and is readily soluble in most solvents, but insoluble in water; it has a specific gravity of 0.961 at 20°, and a turpentine-like odor. It forms a *dihydrochloride* melting at 74°, a *dihydrobromide* melting at 77°, and liquid *acetyl-* and *benzoyl*-derivatives.

The action of nitrous acid upon pinene, see *pinenol*, $C_{10}H_{15}OH$.

Pinene nitrosochloride, $C_{10}H_{16} \cdot NOCl$, was discovered by Tilden,[3] who obtained it by passing nitrosyl chloride into a mixture of pinene and chloroform, the liquid being cooled by a freezing mixture. Later, Goldschmidt[4] investigated this compound, and prepared from it nitrosopinene (see below). The importance of pinene nitrosochloride and similar products prepared from other terpenes for the characterization of the terpenes was recognized by

[1]Ginzberg and E. Wagner, Journ. Russ. Chem. Soc., *30* (1898), 675.

[2]O. Kriewitz, Ber., *32*, 57.

[3]Tilden, Jahresb. Chem., *1874*, 214; *1875*, 390; *1877*, 427; *1878*, 979; *1879*, 396.

[4]Goldschmidt, Ber., *18*, 2223.

Wallach, who studied especially the pinene nitrolamines resulting from pinene nitrosochloride. Although Wallach gives the above suggested simple formula for this substance, Baeyer[1] considers it as a bisnitrosyl-derivative:—

$$C_{10}H_{16}Cl - N_2O_2 - C_{10}H_{16}Cl.$$

Wallach[2] recommends the following method for the preparation of this compound.

To a mixture of fifty grams each of oil of turpentine, acetic acid, and ethyl nitrite, well cooled by a freezing mixture of salt and ice, add gradually fifteen cc. of crude, thirty-three per cent. hydrochloric acid. Pinene nitrosochloride separates at once as a crystalline precipitate, which is filtered with the pump and purified by washing with alcohol. After standing in a cool place, and especially on the addition of alcohol, more pinene nitrosochloride separates from the filtrate. The filtrate from pinene nitrosochloride, when distilled with steam, yields *pinole.*

If carefully washed with alcohol, pinene nitrosochloride can be immediately used for the preparation of pure pinene, or of the following derivatives. A more perfect purification may, however, be accomplished by solution in chloroform and subsequent precipitation with methyl alcohol. Thus purified, the product may then be recrystallized from benzene. Pure pinene nitrosochloride melts at 103° (according to Schimmel & Co.,[3] it melts at 108°). This compound and its derivatives are optically inactive. Baeyer[4] found that carvoxime hydrochloride is formed by allowing a solution of pinene nitrosochloride in ethereal hydrochloric acid to stand for a long time.

Pinene nitrosobromide, $C_{10}H_{16}.NOBr$, is obtained by a similar process. It melts at 91° to 92° with decomposition (Wallach[5]).

Pinene Nitrolamines.

Pinene nitrolpropylamine[6] melts at 96°.

Pinene nitrolamylamine[6] melts at 105° to 106°.

Pinene nitrolallylamine[6] melts at 94°.

Pinene nitrolpiperidide[7] is formed when pinene nitrosochloride is dissolved in excess of an aqueous or alcoholic solution of piperi-

[1] Baeyer, Ber., *28*, 648.
[2] Wallach, Ann. Chem., *253*, 251; *245*, 251.
[3] Schimmel & Co., Semi-Annual Report, April, 1901, 11.
[4] Baeyer, Ber., *29*, 3.
[5] Wallach, Ann. Chem., *253*, 251.
[6] Wallach and Früstück, Ann. Chem., *268*, 216.
[7] Wallach, Ann. Chem., *245*, 251.

dine, and gently warmed. When the energetic reaction is complete, the resulting nitrolamine is precipitated by the addition of water. It melts at 118° to 119°.

Pinene nitrolbenzylamine[1] is obtained by the action of an alcoholic solution of benzylamine (two molecules) on pinene nitrosochloride. It separates from a mixture of ether and alcohol in beautiful, hemihedral, rhombic crystals, melting at 122° to 123°.

Dextro- and levo-pinene yield the same optically inactive nitrolamines. When heated to a rather high temperature, the pinene nitrolamines decompose into a polymeric modification of nitrosopinene and the corresponding primary base; for example, pinene nitrolbenzylamine, when heated to 160° to 180° in a paraffin bath, decomposes, yielding benzylamine.

Although Wallach ascribes to the pinene nitrolamines the formula,

$$C_{10}H_{16}\begin{cases} NO \\ NHR \end{cases}$$

Baeyer considers them as constituted similar to pinene nitrosochloride:

$$C_{10}H_{16}\begin{cases} NHR \quad RHN \\ N_2O_2 \end{cases}C_{10}H_{16}$$

It should be mentioned that secondary amines, for example diethylamine, convert pinene nitrosochloride into nitrosopinene. On the other hand, as has already been mentioned, aniline and other aromatic bases convert it into inactive pinene, with a simultaneous formation of amidoazo-compounds.

Nitrosopinene, $C_{10}H_{15}NO$, was obtained by Tilden[2] by the action of alcoholic potash on pinene nitrosochloride:

$$C_{10}H_{16}NOCl + KOH = C_{10}H_{15}NO + KCl + H_2O.$$

Wallach and Lorentz[3] give the following method for the preparation of nitrosopinene.

To a solution of twelve grams of sodium in thirty cc. of ninety per cent. alcohol, add one hundred grams of pinene nitrosochloride. Boil the mixture on the water-bath, using a reflux condenser, until all nitrosochloride has entered into the reaction. Then add sufficient water to the liquid to dissolve the sodium chloride, which is thrown out; filter off any impurities which may appear, and pour the clear liquid into a large excess of

[1] Wallach, Ann. Chem., *252*, 130.
[2] Tilden, Jahresb. Chem., *1875*, 390.
[3] Wallach and Lorentz, Ann. Chem., *268*, 198.

water acidified with acetic acid. Nitrosopinene is at first thrown out as an oil, but after standing for several days it solidifies to a very hard, yellowish mass. This is broken up, thoroughly washed with water and dried on a porous plate. The most convenient method of purification is to rub up the crude product with petroleum ether, in which nitrosopinene is sparingly soluble; an absolutely pure product is obtained by recrystallization from ethyl acetate in the form of monoclinic crystals,[1] melting at 132°.

Nitrosopinene is optically inactive. Alcoholic hydrochloric acid converts it into carvoxime hydrochloride.[2]

As a result of their observations that nitrosopinene forms a sodium salt and a methyl ester, Goldschmidt and Zuerrer[3] classify this substance as an *isonitroso-compound*, $C_{10}H_{14}=NOH$, whilst Wallach[4] is inclined to regard it as having the constitution of a true nitroso-compound, $C_{10}H_{15}NO$.

The statements on which Wallach bases his views, and in accordance with which nitrosopinene should be very stable towards acids, are faulty, according to Baeyer,[5] and the latter investigator agrees with Goldschmidt in ascribing the isonitroso-structure to nitrosopinene.

Meanwhile, however, Urban and Kremers[6] mentioned in a preliminary publication, that when nitrosopinene is boiled with hydrochloric acid, the product consists of hydroxylamine and an oil. According to Baeyer,[5] carvacrol and hydroxylamine are formed by long-continued boiling of nitrosopinene with hydrochloric acid. Mead and Kremers[7] have also obtained the same result.

When nitrosopinene is reduced with zinc dust and acetic acid, it yields a mixture of pinocamphone, $C_{10}H_{16}O$, and pinylamine, $C_{10}H_{15}NH_2$.[8] Cymene is readily formed by the distillation of pinylamine hydrochloride. The same hydrocarbon is likewise obtained by the elimination of hydrogen bromide from pinene dibromide. Nitrosopinene unites with bromine forming nitrosopinene dibromides.

Behavior of Pinene toward Bromines.

Although the action of bromine on pinene has been the subject of much study, very divergent results have been obtained. Wal-

[1] Maskelyne, Jahresb. Chem., *1879*, 396; Hintze, Ann. Chem., *252*, 133.
[2] Baeyer, Ber., *29*, 3.
[3] Goldschmidt and Zuerrer, Ber., *18*, 2223.
[4] Wallach, Ber., *24*, 1547.
[5] Baeyer, Ber., *28*, 646.
[6] Urban and Kremers, Amer. Chem. Journ., *16*, 404; Ber., *27*, 793, Ref.
[7] Mead and Kremers, Amer. Chem. Journ., *17*, 607.
[8] Wallach, Ann. Chem., *258*, 346; *268*, 197; *300*, 287; *313*, 345.

lach's investigations[1] have shown that the various reactions are extremely complicated, a condition which the varying results of the investigations of Oppenheim,[2] Tilden[3] and others have sufficiently explained.

If dry bromine be added drop by drop to well cooled, absolutely dry pinene, diluted with pure carbon tetrachloride, two atoms of bromine are united to one molecule of pinene, accompanied by an immediate removal of the color of the bromine. If more bromine be added, the color of the bromine will disappear quickly or slowly, according to the conditions under which the experiment is performed, especially the temperature. However, the facts that the decolorization is not immediate, and that it is accompanied by an evolution of hydrogen bromide, prove that a simple addition no longer takes place. The absorption of four atoms of bromine can be accomplished in this manner.[4]

The course of the reaction is, however, further complicated since the elimination of hydrogen bromide can be observed even in the first phase of the interaction. The hydrogen bromide so formed also reacts on some unchanged pinene, forming the monohydrobromide.

In accordance with the above-described method, if two atoms of bromine be added to one molecule of pinene, and, after removal of the carbon tetrachloride, the reaction-product be boiled with alcoholic potash, two reaction-products are obtained: an oil boiling in vacuum at 80° to 140°, and a solid pinene dibromide.

The oil boiling at 80° to 140° contains bromine, and on boiling with aniline yields a large quantity of camphene. This hydrocarbon probably results from the pinene hydrobromide, which is formed during the bromination of pinene, and which is stable towards alcoholic potash at low temperatures. When this liquid pinene dibromide is reduced with alcohol and sodium, dihydrocamphene, $C_{10}H_{18}$, is obtained.[5]

Crystallized pinene dibromide, $C_{10}H_{16}Br_2$, is obtained by the bromination of pinene according to the above method, the yield amounting to about seven per cent. of the pinene used. It is recovered from the residues, which remain after distilling off the lower boiling products, by recrystallization from alcohol.

[1] Wallach, Ann. Chem., *264*, 1.

[2] Oppenheim, Ber., *5*, 94 and 627.

[3] Tilden, Journ. Chem. Soc., *1888*, 882; Ber., *22*, 135; Journ. Chem. Soc., *69* (1896), 1009.

[4] Stschukareff, Journ. pr. Chem., N. F., *47*, 191; see also Tilden, Journ. Chem. Soc., *69* (1896), 1009.

[5] Semmler, Ber., *33*, 3420.

This substance crystallizes from alcohol or from acetic ether and chloroform, in which it is more easily soluble, in characteristic, hexagonal crystals, whose faces are almost never sharply defined, but grow pyramid-shaped and are often hollow. Pinene dibromide melts at 169° to 170°, and is optically inactive.

When heated with aniline in a sealed tube at 180° it readily yields cymene.

According to Wagner,[1] this pinene dibromide, melting at 169° to 170°, may be more readily obtained and in a larger quantity by the action of hypobromous acid on pinene.

Wagner[2] also states that when pinene dibromide, melting at 169° to 170°, is treated with zinc dust and acetic acid, it is converted into a new terpene, melting at 65° to 66° and boiling at 153°; he terms this hydrocarbon, *tricyclene.*

Pinene dichloride (?), $C_{10}H_{16}Cl_2$.—A compound, $C_{10}H_{16}Cl_2$, which is called *tricyclene dichloride*,[3] is formed by adding hypochlorous acid to an emulsion of pinene in water, treating the product with potassium carbonate, extracting with ether, and distilling with steam. It crystallizes in monoclinic crystals, and melts at 165° to 168°.

Oxidation of Pinene.

Two neutral reaction-products have been found by G. Wagner[4] to result from the action of a *one per cent. solution of potassium permanganate on pinene at 0°*. These substances are separated by repeated fractionation in vacuum.

1. **Pinene glycol,** $C_{10}H_{16}(OH)_2$.—The higher boiling of these two substances is regarded by Wagner as pinene glycol. It boils at 145° to 147° under 14 mm. pressure, and at 150° to 152° under 21 mm. It is a "fairly solid, crystalline, extremely hygroscopic mass," which apparently has not been obtained quite free from the adhering mother-liquors. A homogeneous compound does not appear to have been isolated, although it should be added that Wagner separated a compound, melting at 76° to 78°, which he regards as the pure glycol; it does not react with hydroxylamine or ammoniacal silver solution.

The transformation which this substance undergoes when heated with very dilute hydrochloric acid should be mentioned. One of the products is an oil which is volatile with steam, and boils at 180° to 220°; the chief portion boils at 180° to 190°

[1] G. Wagner and Ginzberg, Ber., *29*, 886.
[2] G. Wagner and Godlewski, Journ. Russ. Chem. Soc., *29* (1896), 121.
[3] Ginzberg and E. Wagner, Journ. Russ. Chem. Soc., *30* (1898), 675.
[4] G. Wagner, Ber., 27, 2270.

and is composed chiefly of *pinole* (when treated with bromine it yields pinole bromide, melting at 92° to 93°), while the smaller quantity of the higher boiling fractions contains a ketone of unknown composition, which yields a crystalline oxime. The other product is non-volatile with steam, forms quadratic tablets, melting at 191° to 191.5°, has the composition, $C_{10}H_{18}O_2$, and is probably an a-glycolene.

2. **Keto-alcohol,** $C_{10}H_{16}O_2$.—The substance, formed together with pinene glycol, boils at 122° to 124° under 14 mm. pressure, and at 130° to 132° under 21 mm.; after remaining some time, it deposits crystals, which melt at 97° and have the empirical composition, $C_{10}H_{16}O_2$. Wagner regards it as a keto-alcohol, although it does not react with carbanile; it gives a crystalline oxime, $C_{10}H_{16}(NOH)_2$, which melts at 130°.

When this compound is allowed to remain in contact with silver oxide, it is converted into *pinononic acid*,[1] $C_9H_{14}O_3$.

A third neutral product of the oxidation of French turpentine oil is described by Wagner[1] as an aldehyde, which is oxidized by the air to an acid resembling camphenilic acid, $C_{10}H_{16}O_3$, melting at 171.5° to 172.5°, which is obtained from camphene.

Wagner[1] has also described two acids resulting from the oxidation of French turpentine with a one per cent. solution of permanganate at 0°.

1. **Pinononic acid,** $C_9H_{14}O_3$.—It crystallizes from chloroform in transparent prisms, melts at 128° to 129°, is sparingly soluble in cold water, and insoluble in petroleum. It yields an *oxime*, which separates from water in plates and melts at 178° to 180°. Alkaline hypobromite converts pinononic acid into an *acid*, $C_8H_{12}O_4$, melting at 173° to 174°, bromoform, and carbon tetrabromide (see norpic acid).

2. An *acid* separating from water in fine crystals, and melting at 103° to 104°; it is not a ketonic acid.

As a result of his investigations on pinene, Wagner[2] proposed the following formula for this terpene,

```
CH2————CH————CH2
|   H3C—C—CH3   |
|               |
CH=====C———————CH
       |
       CH3
```

In the critical consideration of the constitutional formulas of

[1] G. Wagner and Ertschikowsky, Ber., *29*, 881.

[2] G. Wagner, Ber., *27*, 1636.

pinene, and other members of the terpene series, which have been advanced by G. Wagner during the course of his investigations above referred to, the incompleteness of the experimental foundations for these formulas, as is sufficiently observed from what has been mentioned, must not be neglected.

Tiemann and Semmler[1] have published accounts of their researches in regard to the action of potassium permanganate on pinene. They isolated the following compounds:

d-Pinonic acid, $C_{10}H_{16}O_3$.—This is prepared by gradually adding a solution of seven hundred grams of potassium permanganate in six liters of water to an emulsion of three hundred grams of pinene in two liters of water. The filtered liquid is evaporated to about two liters, saturated with carbon dioxide, and the neutral compounds are removed either by distillation with steam or by extraction with ether. The crude pinonic acid is separated from its potassium salt by sulphuric acid, and is extracted with ether. According to the conditions of temperature which prevail during the oxidation, the products are different, but they may be entirely controlled; thus, when the temperature is maintained at about 6°, a liquid pinonic acid results, while at 25° to 40°, Baeyer's *α-pinonic acid*, melting at 103° to 105°, is the chief product.[2]

The liquid pinonic acid, which is to be regarded as a mixture of isomerides,[3] boils at 193° to 195° under 22 mm. pressure, while at ordinary pressure it distills with slight decomposition at 310° to 315°. When a crystal of α-pinonic acid is introduced into the liquid pinonic acid, one-half of the weight of the latter is converted into the solid α-pinonic acid.

Liquid pinonic acid, when freshly distilled, has the specific rotatory power, $[\alpha]_D = + 6°$, in a one decimeter tube, but this is increased to $[\alpha]_D = + 13°$, when all of the α-pinonic acid is removed; the latter acid has the specific rotatory power, $[\alpha]_D = + 2°$, in a one decimeter tube, which is probably due to imperfect separation of all of the liquid d-pinonic acid.

According to Tiemann and Semmler,[1] this liquid pinonic acid is a saturated ketonic acid, and forms two isomeric *oximes;* one of these melts at 125° with loss of water, the other melting at 160° without elimination of water. Its *semicarbazone*[2] melts at 207°.

It yields the keto-lactone, $C_{10}H_{16}O_3$ (methoethylheptanonolide), melting at 63° to 65°, when treated with acids, or when slowly distilled at atmospheric pressure.[2]

[1]Tiemann and Semmler, Ber., *28*, 1344 and 1778.
[2]Tiemann and Semmler, Ber., *29*, 529.
[3]F. Tiemann, Ber., *29*, 119.

It is slowly acted upon by an alkaline hypobromite solution with the formation of bromoform.

l-Pinonic acid,[1] $C_{10}H_{16}O_3$, is a ketonic acid formed together with α-dioxydihydrocampholenic acid, by the oxidation of α-campholenic acid, $C_{10}H_{16}O_2$ (oxycamphor), boiling at 256°. It is also produced by the dry distillation of α-dioxydihydrocampholenic acid, $C_{10}H_{18}O_4$, water being split off.

l-Pinonic acid crystallizes from water, and melts at 98° to 99°, forming a colorless oil, which boils at 178° to 180° under 12 mm. pressure. It has the specific rotatory power, $[\alpha]_D = -21.4°$. It yields an *oxime*, melting at 147°, and a *semicarbazone*, melting at 232°. It is acted upon by alkaline hypobromite with formation of bromoform or carbon tetrabromide. It is converted by concentrated sulphuric acid into the *keto-lactone*, $C_{10}H_{16}O_3$ (methoethylheptanonolide), which in this case appears to be optically active.

i-Pinonic acid,[2] $C_{10}H_{16}O_3$, is formed, together with some liquid d-pinonic acid, by the oxidation of French turpentine oil with a dilute solution of potassium permanganate, at a temperature not exceeding 30°. The solid, optically inactive acid is separated by filtration from the active liquid acid, and is purified by recrystallization from water; it melts at 105°, and is to be regarded as identical with Baeyer's α-pinonic acid. Its *semicarbazone* melts at 206° to 207°.

i-Pinolic acid,[2] $C_{10}H_{18}O_3$, is an alcoholic acid formed by the reduction of the solid i-pinonic acid or α-pinonic acid (m. p. 105°). It is prepared by heating either of these solid pinonic acids with alcoholic potash for six or seven hours at 185° to 200°; it crystallizes in needles, melting at 99° to 100°. It boils at 195° to 205° (20 mm.), is sparingly soluble in hot or cold water, dissolves readily in alcohol, ethyl acetate or ether, and yields the crystalline i-pinonic acid on oxidation with potassium permanganate; the semicarbazone of the pinonic acid thus formed melts at 206° to 207°.

l-Pinolic acid,[2] $C_{10}H_{18}O_3$, is prepared from the liquid d-pinonic acid in the same manner as i-pinolic acid from the crystalline α- or i-pinonic acid. It crystallizes in well formed needles, melting at 114° to 115°. In a thirty-three per cent. alcoholic solution it has a rotation $-7°$ in a 100 mm. tube. On oxidation with permanganate it is reconverted into the liquid d-pinonic acid, which yields a semicarbazone, melting at 206° to 207°.

[1] F. Tiemann, Ber., *29*, 3006.

[2] F. Tiemann, Ber., *30*, 409; *33*, 2662.

i-Pinocampholenic acid,[1] $C_{10}H_{16}O_2$, is formed when crude i-pinolic acid, which has not been subjected to treatment with a current of steam, is distilled under reduced pressure; the distillate also contains pinodihydrocampholenolactone (see below). It is an oily liquid having a faint odor, boils at 140° to 141° (13 mm.), has a sp. gr. 0.9925 at 17°, and a refractive index, $n_D = 1.46702$. It yields inactive pinodihydrocampholenolactone when treated with hydriodic acid, and yields the same products on oxidation with permanganate as *α*-campholenic acid, namely, l-pinonic acid, whose semicarbazone melts at 232°.

l-Pinocampholenic acid, $C_{10}H_{16}O_2$, is prepared from the liquid d-pinonic acid or the l-pinolic acid in the same manner as the preceding compound is obtained from i-pinonic or i-pinolic acid. It boils at 136° to 138° (10 mm.), and at 248° to 252° under atmospheric pressure. Sp. gr. is 0.9897 at 20°, $n_D = 1.47096$. In other properties it is identical with the inactive acid; thus reduction converts it into the inactive lactone, and oxidation with permanganate gives rise to l-pinonic acid (semicarbazone melting at 231° to 232°), which, in turn, is oxidized by chromic and sulphuric acids yielding isocamphoronic acid (m. p. 166°) (Tiemann).

i-Pinodihydrocampholenolactone, $C_{10}H_{16}O_2$, is obtained by the reduction of both pinolic acids and pinocampholenic acids with hydriodic acid; it is a colorless oil, boils at 128° to 130° (12 mm.), and at 254° to 257° under atmospheric pressure. Sp. gr. is 1.014 at 18°, $n_D = 1.4640$. When hydrolyzed, it yields an oxy-acid which does not crystallize, but on distillation yields crystalline i-pinolic acid (m. p. 99° to 100°) (Tiemann).

According to Tiemann, pinolic acid, pinocampholenic acid and pinodihydrocampholenolactone, which result from pinonic acid, have the same chemical structure as oxydihydrocampholenic acid, *α*-campholenic acid and dihydrocampholenolactone which may be converted into pinonic acid. The differences in the behavior of the oxy-acids, as well as in the melting points of the members of both series and of their various derivatives, are to be explained by the assumption of a condition of *cis*- and *cis-trans*-isomerism. Thus the close relations existing between the constitution of pinene and that of camphor are emphasized, for it is not only possible, starting from *α*-campholenic acid, $C_{10}H_{16}O_2$, to arrive at the optically active l-pinonic acid, but also to convert members of the pinene series into derivatives of the camphor series.

For the crystallographic relations of the pinonic acids, see Fock, Zeit. Kryst. Min., **31** (1899), 479.

[1] F. Tiemann, Ber., *33*, 2665.

Terebic acid, $C_7H_{10}O_4$, melting at 174°, and oxalic acid are formed by the oxidation of the above-mentioned liquid d-pinonic acid with nitric acid of specific gravity 1.18. If, on the other hand, liquid d-pinonic acid be oxidized by means of a chromic acid mixture, the following acids [1] result.

1. **Isoketocamphoric acid,** $C_{10}H_{16}O_5$, melts at 128° to 129°. It is a dibasic ketonic acid, identical with the acid prepared by Thiel [2] in the oxidation of α-campholenic acid and described under the name of isoxycamphoric acid, $C_{10}H_{16}O_5$. It forms an *oxime*, melting at 185° to 186°, and a *semicarbazone*, melting at 187°. It is decomposed by an alkaline hypobromite solution into isocamphoronic acid and carbon tetrabromide.

It is also prepared by the oxidation of α-dioxydihydrocampholenic acid or of l-pinonic acid with chromic acid.[3]

2. **Isocamphoronic acid,**[4] $C_9H_{14}O_6$, melts at 166° to 167°. It is a tribasic acid, and has been described by Thiel [2] as an oxidation product of α-campholenic acid. It is identical with oxycamphoronic acid, obtained, together with other products, by Kachler [5] in the oxidation of camphor with nitric acid. Concentrated sulphuric acid converts it into terpenylic acid [6] and carbon monoxide; and acetyl chloride changes it into an anhydromonocarboxylic acid, which, in turn, yields terpenylic acid by the action of concentrated sulphuric acid, carbon monoxide being eliminated.

This acid [3] may also be obtained from α-dioxydihydrocampholenic acid or l-pinonic acid by the more vigorous oxidation with chromic acid than is allowed when isoketocamphoric acid is required.

3. **Terebic acid,** $C_7H_{10}O_4$, melts at 174°.

According to Tiemann and Semmler,[1] if liquid d-pinonic acid be dissolved in soda, and heated with an excess of a four per cent. solution of potassium permanganate on the water-bath, the following acids are formed.

1. **Dimethyltricarballylic acid,** $C_8H_{12}O_6$, melts at 147°. This acid is obtained by extracting the oxidation products with chloroform, from which solvent the crystals of this acid are deposited.

When heated above its melting point, it loses water, and yields

[1] Tiemann and Semmler, Ber., *28*, 1344.
[2] W. Thiel, Ber., *26*, 922.
[3] F. Tiemann, Ber., *29*, 3006.
[4] W. H. Perkin, jun., and Thorpe, Journ. Chem. Soc., *75* (1899), 1897.
[5] Kachler, Ann. Chem., *191*, 143.
[6] F. Tiemann, Ber., *29*, 2612.

anhydrodimethyltricarballylic acid, which melts at 142.5°, and boils at 225° under 16 mm. pressure.

2. **Oxytrimethylsuccinic acid**, $C_7H_{12}O_5$, melts at 141°. This acid is obtained from the filtrate from the dimethyltricarballylic acid. It has also been found by Kachler in the oxidation products of camphor. When treated with hydriodic acid, it is converted into trimethylsuccinic acid, melting at 145°.

3. An *acid,* which accompanies the above-mentioned acid, and which was not isolated in a condition of purity; when distilled in a vacuum, this acid loses water, and, apparently, carbon dioxide, forming *isocamphoranic acid,* $C_9H_{12}O_6$. The latter is a lactonic acid, and melts at 143.5°.

Oxyisocamphoronic acid, $C_9H_{14}O_7$, is a tribasic acid, and is produced by heating isocamphoranic acid with potassium hydroxide; it had previously been prepared in an impure condition by Kachler[1] from camphor.

Isocamphoranic acid is perhaps isomeric with isocamphorenic acid, melting at 226°, which Kachler obtained from isocamphoronic acid.

By the careful investigation of the above oxidation products obtained from pinene, Tiemann and Semmler[2] claim to have established the following constitutional formula for this terpene,

```
CH3
   >C————CH————CH2
CH3 |     |      |
    |    CH2     |
CH3 |     |      |
   >C————C=====CH
 H
```

If crude pinene be oxidized with potassium permanganate, the *keto-lactone,* $C_{10}H_{16}O_3$, melting at 63° to 64°, is formed from an impurity contained in commercial pinene. Tiemann and Semmler[3] have designated this compound as methyl-3¹-ethyl-3-heptanon-6-olide-1-3¹. Wallach first described it as a product of the oxidation of terpineol.

As a result of his researches on the oxidation products of pinene, Baeyer[4] came to quite different conclusions regarding the

[1] Kachler, Ann. Chem., *191,* 152.
[2] Tiemann and Semmler, Ber., *29,* 3027.
[3] Tiemann and Semmler, Ber., *28,* 1778.
[4] A. von Baeyer, Ber., *29,* 3, 326, 1907, 1923 and 2775.

constitution of pinene than Tiemann and Semmler; his results seem to support Wagner's formula of pinene. Some of the products which Baeyer prepared during these investigations are as follows.

1. **α-Pinonic acid,** $C_{10}H_{16}O_3$. This acid is readily obtained by the oxidation of pinene at 30° with potassium permanganate, according to the method of Tiemann and Semmler. It melts at 103° to 105°, and boils at 180° to 187° under 14 mm. pressure. It constitutes the chief product of the oxidation, and may be readily separated from the liquid products, owing to the fact that it is insoluble in ethyl nitrite. It is difficultly soluble in cold water and ether, readily soluble in hot water and chloroform. On heating with sulphuric acid it is converted into the keto-lactone, $C_{10}H_{16}O_3$ (m. p. 63° to 65°). This solid α-pinonic acid is a ketonic acid, and yields an *α-oxime*, which crystallizes in large plates or prisms, and melts at 150°. The acid is optically inactive, and is to be regarded as identical with Tiemann and Semmler's i-pinonic acid.

When the syrupy mother-liquor, from which α-pinonic acid is separated, is treated with hydroxylamine, it yields two oximes, isomeric with the α-oxime, which Baeyer designates as *β-oxime* and *γ-oxime*. The *β-oxime* melts at 128° and is identical with the oxime melting at 125°, which Tiemann and Semmler obtained from their liquid d-pinonic acid; it is dextrorotatory, $[\alpha]_D = +2° 18'$ (8.2 per cent. solution in ether in a one decimeter tube). The *γ-oxime* is less readily soluble than the β-oxime, and separates from glacial acetic acid as a powder; it melts at 190° to 191°, and is levorotatory.

The *phenylhydrazone* of α-pinonic acid melts with decomposition below 100°.

α-Pinonic acid is oxidized by alkaline hypobromite, yielding *pinic acid*, $C_9H_{14}O_4$, and bromoform, while dilute nitric acid oxidizes it to pinic, oxalic and terebic acids.

2. **Nopic acid,** $C_{10}H_{16}O_3$. This is a product of the oxidation of commercial pinene or French turpentine oil with permanganate. It is isomeric with α-pinonic acid, but it is not a ketonic acid. It is sparingly soluble in water, but crystallizes from it in long needles, melting at 126° to 128°. It forms crystalline salts with the metals. It is an oxy-monobasic acid.

Bromotetrahydrocumic acid, $C_{10}H_{15}BrO_2$, is formed by the action of a glacial acetic acid solution of hydrogen bromide on nopic acid. It is readily soluble in chloroform, sparingly in ether, and insoluble in petroleum; it crystallizes in leaflets, melting and decomposing at 175°. It decolorizes a solution of permanganate, and is an unsaturated compound.

Dihydrocumic acid, $C_{10}H_{14}O_2$, is formed by the action of hot, twenty-five per cent. sulphuric acid or alcoholic potash on the preceding compound. It is sparingly soluble in water, crystallizes from alcohol, melts at 130° to 133°, sublimes at about 100°, and boils at 176° under 14 mm. pressure. It reduces a cold alkaline solution of permanganate, and is oxidized by potassium ferricyanide to cumic acid, $C_{10}H_{12}O_2$.

Nopinone, $C_9H_{14}O$, is a ketone which is produced by passing steam through water in which lead peroxide and nopic acid are suspended. It is a volatile oil, having a pleasant odor. Its *oxime* is an oil, and its *semicarbazone* separates from methyl alcohol in needles, which melt at 188.5°. With benzaldehyde it forms a condensation-product, *benzylidene nopinone*.[1]

According to Wallach,[2] nopinone is also formed, together with α-pinonic acid, during the oxidation of turpentine oil with potassium permanganate. It originates probably from nopic acid, $C_{10}H_{16}O_3$, which, in addition to pinonic acid, is produced by the oxidation of crude pinene, and which by continued oxidation is decomposed into nopinone and carbon dioxide according to the equation,

$$C_{10}H_{16}O_3 + O = C_9H_{14}O + CO_2 + H_2O.$$

Homoterpenylic acid is formed by the oxidation of nopinone with fuming nitric acid.

3. **Pinoylformic acid**, $C_{10}H_{14}O_5$, is a dibasic ketonic acid, which is formed, together with α-pinonic acid, by the oxidation of pinene under certain conditions. It is separated from the α-pinonic acid by adding potassium carbonate in quantity insufficient to neutralize the latter acid, which is then removed by ether; the solution of potassium pinoylformate is acidified, the free acid is taken up in ether and, after evaporation of the ether, the resulting oil is treated with potassium acid sulphite; the resulting compound is then decomposed by a concentrated solution of barium hydroxide, and free pinoylformic acid is obtained. It is readily soluble in cold water and melts at 78° to 80°. Its *silver salt* crystallizes in leaflets. The *potassium-* and *sodium-hydrogen sulphite compounds* are crystalline; the *phenylhydrazone* crystallizes in prisms, and melts with decomposition at 192.5°. Oxidation converts pinoylformic acid into pinic acid, while fuming nitric acid changes it into oxalic and terpenylic acids.

Homoterpenoylformic acid, $C_{10}H_{14}O_5$, is a lactonic acid, which is formed by treating pinoylformic acid with hot, dilute sulphuric

[1] Wallach, Nachr. k. Ges. Wiss., Goettingen, *1899*, No. 2.
[2] Wallach and Schäfer, Ann. Chem., *313*, 363.

acid. It is difficultly soluble in cold water and ether, crystallizes in prisms, and melts at 126° to 129°. Its formation from pinoylformic acid is analogous to the conversion of *α*-pinonic acid into methyl-ethyl-heptanonolide (m. p. 63° to 65°). It yields an *oxime*, which crystallizes in needles, and melts at about 170°.

Homoterpenylic acid, $C_9H_{14}O_4$, is produced by the action of lead peroxide or fuming nitric acid on homoterpenoylformic acid. It is sparingly soluble in water, but crystallizes from it in large prisms, melting at 98° to 101°; it separates from ether in crystals, melting at 100° to 102.5°. It is a lactonic acid, and stands in the same relation to adipic acid that terebic acid does to succinic acid.

Oxyhomopinic acid, $C_{10}H_{16}O_5$, is an oxydibasic acid, which is formed by the reduction of an alkaline solution of pinoylformic acid with sodium amalgam. It crystallizes from water, and melts at 130° to 133°.

α-Ketoisocamphoronic acid (dimethyltricarballoylformic acid), $C_9H_{12}O_7$, is a keto-tribasic acid, which is obtained by the action of sodium hypochlorite or hypobromite on pinoylformic acid. It crystallizes from water in plates and leaflets, and melts with evolution of gas at 186° to 187°. On heating its aqueous solution with lead peroxide, it yields *dimethyltricarballylic acid;* the *anhydro-acid* melts at 145° to 146°, and on boiling with water gives dimethyltricarballylic acid, melting at 149° to 151°, while by heating with water at 230° it gives the same acid, melting at 156° to 157°.

The *lactone of α-oxyisocamphoronic acid,* $C_9H_{12}O_6$, is formed by reducing *α*-ketoisocamphoronic acid with sodium amalgam. It crystallizes from water in prisms containing one molecule of water, sinters at 160°, again solidifies, and finally melts at 185° to 186°. When it is heated with hydriodic acid at 170° for four hours, it yields *isocamphoronic acid,* $C_9H_{14}O_6$.

The *lactone of α-oxydimethyltricarballylic acid,* $C_8H_{10}O_6$, is prepared by the action of phosphorus tribromide and bromine on dimethyltricarballylic acid and the treatment of the product with boiling water. It is deposited in large crystals from ethyl acetate, it melts at 196° on slow heating, and at 207° by rapid heating. It forms crystalline salts with certain metals. Fusion with potash converts it into oxalic acid and *as*-dimethylsuccinic acids.

4. **Pinarin,** $C_{10}H_{14}O_3$, is deposited in crystals from the fraction of the neutral oxidation product of pinene, boiling at 150° to 180° at 15 mm. pressure. It separates from petroleum in needles, melts at 66° to 68°, and exhibits certain properties of a lactone.

5. **Pinic acid**, $C_9H_{14}O_4$, is produced, together with bromoform, by the action of alkaline hypobromite solution on *a*-pinonic acid; the yield is quantitative. It is a dibasic acid. It crystallizes in splendid prisms, melting at 101° to 102.5°, does not form an anhydride when treated with acetyl chloride, and is stable towards a cold solution of permanganate and towards hydrobromic acid; at 100° its solution is slowly oxidized by potassium permanganate.

Bromopinic acid, $C_9H_{13}BrO_4$, is prepared by the action of phosphorus tribromide and bromine on pinic acid; the product is then treated with boiling water and extracted with ether, yielding an oil from which crystals are slowly deposited.

Oxypinic acid, $C_9H_{14}O_5$, is obtained from the preceding compound, either by the action of barium hydroxide, or by treating bromopinic acid with silver acetate and hydrolyzing the resultant acetyl compound. This separates from water in prisms, melting at 193° to 194°.

Norpic acid aldehyde, $C_8H_{12}O_3$, is formed by the oxidation of oxypinic acid in a hot, dilute acetic acid solution with lead peroxide. It is an oil, and is soluble in water. Its *semicarbazone* melts at 188° to 189°.

Norpic acid, $C_8H_{12}O_4$, is obtained by the oxidation of norpic acid aldehyde. It crystallizes from ether in large crystals, melts at 173° to 175°, and sublimes at about 100° in needles. It does not yield an anhydride by the action of boiling acetyl chloride, and is very stable towards oxidizing agents. It is a dibasic acid, and forms a crystalline *silver salt*. Norpic acid is probably identical with the acid, $C_8H_{12}O_4$, which Wagner[1] obtained by the action of alkaline hypobromite on pinononic acid, $C_9H_{14}O_3$.

Baeyer regards pinic acid and norpic acid as derivatives of a dimethyltetramethylene ring,

```
          /CH3
         C—CH3
  —HC<       >CH—
         CH2
```

which he calls the "*picean-ring*."[2]

2. CAMPHENE.

Since camphene is the only well known solid hydrocarbon of the terpene series, its recognition in ethereal oils might be expected to be especially easy; there is, however, only one ethereal

[1] G. Wagner and Ertschikowsky, Ber., 29, 881.
[2] Baeyer, Ber., 29, 2775.

oil known from which a solid hydrocarbon, $C_{10}H_{16}$, melting at about 30° and boiling at 162°, can be separated. This oil is obtained from *Pinus sibirica,* and from it Goluboff[1] isolated a solid hydrocarbon, which, according to Bertram and Walbaum,[2] may be considered an impure camphene. It was therefore believed until about the year 1894 that camphene did not occur free in nature. The transformation of camphene into isoborneol, which was accomplished by Bertram and Walbaum by the action of glacial acetic acid and sulphuric acid on this hydrocarbon, constitutes a method by means of which the presence of camphene in mixtures can be determined. The presence of camphene has thus been detected by these chemists in citronella oil, camphor oil, lemon oil, ginger oil, and oil of valerian (Japanese). According to Bouchardat,[3] camphene occurs in small quantity in oil of spike. Rosemary oil[4] contains inactive camphene. Schimmel & Co.[5] have also reported camphene present in Dalmatian and Italian oils of rosemary, hemlock oil, and American turpentine oil. In all probability camphene occurs together with pinene in many other oils.

Camphene is artificially prepared by the action of concentrated sulphuric acid upon pinene (Armstrong and Tilden[6]); by heating pinene hydrobromide or hydrochloride with sodium acetate and glacial acetic acid at 200°, or by heating with other reagents capable of withdrawing the elements of the halogen acids (Wallach[7]); by heating pinene hydriodide with potassium phenolate at 160° to 170°, a very pure camphene is obtained (Wagner[8]), and it may also be made in the same manner from pinene hydrochloride (Reychler[9]). It is also formed from borneol by heating with acid potassium sulphate at 200° (Wallach[10]), or by heating borneol with dilute sulphuric acid (two parts of water and one part concentrated acid) at 60° to 100° for six to eight hours; by the latter method the yield is said to be 90 per cent. of the theoretical (Konowaloff[11]). It results also by heating isoborneol (300 grams) with benzene (150 grams) and zinc chloride (200 grams), or by boiling isoborneol with dilute sulphuric acid in a flask provided

[1]Goluboff, Chem. Centr., *1888*, 1622.
[2]Bertram and Walbaum, Journ. pr. Chem., N. F., *49*, 15.
[3]G. Bouchardat, Compt. rend., *117*, 1094.
[4]Gildemeister and Stephan, Arch. Pharm., *235* (1897), 582.
[5]Semi-annual report of Schimmel & Co., for October, 1897.
[6]Armstrong and Tilden, Ber., *12*, 1753.
[7]Wallach, Ann. Chem., *239*, 6.
[8]Wagner and Brykner, Ber., *33*, 2121.
[9]A. Reychler, Ber., *29*, 695.
[10]Wallach, Ann. Chem., *230*, 239.
[11]M. I. Konowaloff, Journ. Russ. Phys. Chem. Soc., *32* (1900), 76.

with a reflux condenser (Bertram and Walbaum[1]). Camphene is also formed, together with "terpilene" (terpinene), isoborneol ("levo-camphenol"), and "isocamphol" (fenchyl alcohol), by heating French turpentine oil with benzoic acid at 150° (Bouchardat and Lafont[2]).

According to Wallach and Griepenkerl,[3] bornylamine, the base corresponding to borneol, can also be converted into camphene, if the free amine or its formyl derivative is heated with acetic anhydride at 200° to 210°:

$$C_{10}H_{17}NH_2 = C_{10}H_{16} + NH_3.$$

In order to prepare camphene, it is most convenient to start with borneol, from which bornyl chloride is first obtained. This compound yields camphene by heating with an excess of water to which potassium hydroxide or magnesia has been added (Kachler[4]).

According to Wallach,[5] dry bornyl chloride is gently warmed with an equal weight of aniline. At first the chloride dissolves to a clear solution. The mixture is then heated to the boiling point of aniline, when the reaction, accompanied by an ebullition of the liquid and separation of aniline hydrochloride, occurs suddenly, and is complete after a short time. The reaction-product is then neutralized with hydrochloric acid and distilled with steam; camphene quickly passes over as a colorless liquid, which at once solidifies to a crystalline mass, resembling paraffin. The camphene which passes over toward the end of the distillation is collected separately, since it contains impurities due to some undecomposed chloride. The resulting camphene is pressed on a porous plate, and after drying the melted hydrocarbon with potassium hydroxide, it is rectified.

PROPERTIES.—Camphene is a solid hydrocarbon, melting at 48° to 49° and boiling at 160° to 161° (Wallach[6]).

According to Brühl, camphene prepared from pinene melts at 51° to 52°, solidifies at 50°, and boils at 158.5° to 159.5°; the same investigator finds camphene, obtained from bornyl chloride, to melt at 53.4° to 54°, and to solidify at 53° to 52.5°.

It crystallizes from alcohol, in which it is comparatively difficultly soluble. It exists in an optically inactive, a levo- and a

[1] Bertram and Walbaum, Journ. pr. Chem., N. F., *49*, 8.
[2] Bouchardat and Lafont, Compt. rend., *113*, 551.
[3] Wallach and Griepenkerl, Ann. Chem., *269*, 349.
[4] Kachler, Ann. Chem., *197*, 96.
[5] Wallach, Ann. Chem., *230*, 233; Ber., *25*, 916.
[6] Wallach, Ann. Chem., *230*, 234.

dextrorotatory modification. These three varieties of this hydrocarbon, which are analogous to those of pinene, agree completely in all other physical and chemical properties. The specific gravity of melted camphene is:

According to Wallach,[1] 0.850 at 48°.
According to Brühl,[2] 0.84224 at 54°.
According to Brühl,[2] 0.83449 at 63.7°.
The coefficients of refraction are:

$n_c = 1.4555$ at 48° (Wallach and Pulfrich [1]).
$n_{Na} = 1.4514$ at 54° (Brühl [2]).
$n_{Na} = 1.45085$ at 63.7° (Brühl [2]).

From this, a value for the molecular refraction is found which agrees with the calculated value, if we consider camphene to possess one double linkage.

The molecular heat of combustion of camphene derived from pinene has been determined by Stohmann [3] to be 1466.7 calorimetric units, while that of camphene obtained from borneol is 1470.3 calories.

Levo-camphene, prepared from pinene hydrochloride by the action of an alcoholic solution of potassium acetate, has the specific rotatory power, $[\alpha]_D = -80° 37'$ (Bouchardat and Lafont [4]).

Camphene is not stable at a high temperature. By continued heating at 250° to 270°, it is converted into a liquid consisting of unchanged camphene and products of higher and lower boiling points. Dehydrating agents also decompose camphene; thus phosphoric anhydride converts it into an oil apparently containing cymene, and partially into resin; a similar reaction takes place when camphene is heated with zinc chloride at 200°. Concentrated sulphuric acid acts very energetically on camphene,[5] while in contrast to pinene, dilute sulphuric acid acts slowly upon it.[6]

According to Marsh and Gardner,[7] phosphorus pentachloride converts camphene into a reaction-product, which, when treated with water, is resolved into two crystalline acids, α-camphene-phosphorous acid, $(C_{10}H_{15}PO_3H_2)_2+H_2O$, and β-camphene-phosphorous acid, $C_{10}H_{15}PO_3H_2$; the salts of the latter decompose readily on heating into meta-phosphoric acid and camphene.

[1] Wallach, Ann. Chem., *245*, 210; *252*, 136.
[2] Brühl, Ber., *25*, 160.
[3] Compare Brühl, Ber., *25*, 170.
[4] Bouchardat and Lafont, Compt. rend., *104*, 693.
[5] Wallach, Ann. Chem., *230*, 234.
[6] Wallach, Ann. Chem., *239*, 9.
[7] Marsh and Gardner, Journ. Chem. Soc., *1894*, 35.

When camphene is heated with glacial acetic and sulphuric acids, the acetyl derivative of *isoborneol* is formed (Bertram and Walbaum[1]). This reaction also demonstrates that the camphene molecule is more stable than that of pinene, since the latter hydrocarbon is converted by an analogous reaction, first into dipentene and then into terpineol.

The action of trichloracetic acid on camphene[2] converts the latter into an ester of isoborneol, which, on saponification, yields isoborneol.

A compound of camphene with nitrosyl chloride has not been obtained.[3]

The action of nitrous acid on camphene has been investigated by Jagelki;[4] he obtained the following compounds.

1. **Camphene nitronitrosite,** $C_{10}H_{16}\cdot N_3O_5$.—This compound separates as a white, crystalline powder, when a well cooled mixture of a solution of camphene in ligroine and a concentrated solution of sodium nitrite is treated very slowly with acetic acid. Its color changes to a blue when it is heated, and it decomposes at about 149°, with elimination of water and oxides of nitrogen. It is insoluble in the ordinary solvents, but dissolves in hot nitrobenzene, forming a blue colored solution.

2. **Camphene nitrosite,** $C_{10}H_{16}\cdot N_2O_3$.—The ligroine solution, freed from the preceding compound by filtration, is agitated with a concentrated solution of potassium hydroxide, which removes the nitrosite in the form of its potassium salt; when the latter is decomposed with acids it yields the free nitrosite. It is a greenish oil, having a pleasant odor, which decomposes readily at 50° when heated under reduced pressure, yielding nitrous oxide, water, and camphenilic nitrite. Its *potassium salt* separates in red crystals from alcohol, which detonate on heating; the *benzoyl* derivative is an oil, which decomposes on distillation.

3. **Camphenilic nitrite,** $C_{10}H_{15}NO_2$.—This substance is obtained from the ligroine solution, which has been freed from the nitronitrosite and nitrosite as above described, by the evaporation of the ligroine. It crystallizes from petroleum in needles, melts at 66°, boils at 147° under a pressure of 12 mm., and detonates on heating strongly. It gives a cherry-red coloration on warming with concentrated sulphuric acid. It is converted into *camphenilan aldehyde*, $C_{10}H_{16}O$, by the reduction with tin and hydrochloric acid or with zinc dust and acetic acid; this aldehyde is

[1] Bertram and Walbaum, Journ. pr. Chem., N. F., *49*, 1.
[2] A. Reychler, Ber., *29*, 695.
[3] Wallach, Ann. Chem., *245*, 255.
[4] W. Jagelki, Per., *32*, 1498.

also obtained by Bredt and Jagelki[1] in the oxidation of camphene with chromyl chloride. Oxidation with potassium permanganate or treatment with alcoholic potash converts camphenilic nitrite into *camphenilone*[2] (camphenylone), $C_9H_{14}O$. Camphenilic nitrite is also one of the products which are formed during the oxidation of camphene with nitric acid, although in this case its production depends on the initial formation of camphene nitrosite, formed by the addition of the elements of nitrous acid to camphene, which then loses water and nitrous oxide, and yields camphenilic nitrite.

Camphene hydrochloride, $C_{10}H_{16}\cdot HCl$.—According to Reychler,[3] this addition-product is formed when hydrogen chloride is led into an alcoholic solution of camphene, and isobornyl chloride is produced by a similar treatment of isoborneol. Reychler[4] gives the melting point of camphene hydrochloride, crystallized from alcohol containing hydrogen chloride, at 149° to 151°, and that of isobornyl chloride at 150° to 152°; he regards these two compounds as identical, and stereoisomeric with bornyl chloride.

According to Jünger and Klages,[5] camphene hydrochloride melts at 165°, but after standing for four hours it melts at 158°; after crystallization from alcohol containing hydrogen chloride, it melts at 152°. When treated with glacial acetic acid, it yields isobornyl acetate from which isoborneol is obtained by hydrolysis. When reduced with sodium and alcohol, the hydrochloride loses hydrogen chloride and yields a mixture of camphene and dihydrocamphene identical with that from pinene hydrochloride.[6]

Camphene hydrobromide,[6] $C_{10}H_{16}\cdot HBr$, separates from alcohol in well formed crystals and melts at 133°. It is reconverted into camphene by alcoholic alkalis and also by reduction with sodium and alcohol.

Camphene hydriodide,[7] $C_{10}H_{16}\cdot HI$, forms colorless crystals, melting at 48° to 55°; when it is treated with alcoholic potash, it gives camphene, melting at 49°, together with some unaltered iodide. It reacts with silver oxide, yielding camphene and borneol (?).

By the action of phosphorus trichloride and bromine on camphor, Marsh and Gardner[8] obtained *α- and β-tribromocamphene*

[1]Bredt and Jagelki, Ann. Chem., *310*, 112.
[2]Balaise and Blanc, Compt. rend., *129* (1899), 886.
[3]A. Reychler, Ber., *29*, 697.
[4]A. Reychler, Bull. Soc. Chim., 1896 (III.), *15*, 366.
[5]Jünger and Klages, Ber., *29*, 544.
[6]Semmler, Ber., *33*, 3420.
[7]Kondakoff and Lutschinin, Chem. Zeit., *25*, 131.
[8]Marsh and Gardner, Journ. Chem. Soc., *71*, 285.

hydrobromide, $C_{10}H_{14}Br_4$, melting at 168°, and 143° to 144°, respectively; both compounds yield *tribromocamphene*, $C_{10}H_{13}Br_3$, melting at 75° to 76°, when treated with sodium methylate. The action of phosphorus pentachloride on camphor yields *α-chlorocamphene hydrochloride*, $C_{10}H_{16}Cl_2$, melting at 165°, and the latter is converted into *α-chlorocamphene*, $C_{10}H_{15}Cl$, by the action of zinc dust and glacial acetic acid. By the action of sulphuric acid containing five per cent. of water, α-chlorocamphene is converted into a compound, $C_{10}H_{16}O$, which was at first called "*oxycamphene*" or "*camphenol*"[1]; this oxygen-containing compound was subsequently investigated by Marsh and Hartridge, who changed its name to *carvenol*, $C_{10}H_{16}O$; it is quite probable that this compound is identical with the ketone, $C_{10}H_{16}O$, previously described by Wallach[2] under the name of *carvenone*.

α-**Dichlorocamphene**, $C_{10}H_{14}Cl_2$, is a derivative of camphor, which was prepared by Lapworth and Kipping[3] by heating *α-chlorocamphenesulphonic chloride;* it crystallizes from methyl alcohol in prisms or needles, melts at 72° to 73°, sublimes readily, and is volatile with steam.

Monobromocamphene, $C_{10}H_{15}Br$.—According to Wallach,[4] a solution of camphene in four parts of alcohol and four parts of ether removes the color of two atoms of bromine, the reaction proceeding with less vigor than in the bromination of pinene; when the reaction-product is distilled with steam, an oily liquid is obtained, which contains only one atom of bromine. On reduction with sodium and alcohol, it yields camphene.[5]

A bromocamphene, prepared by treating camphene hydrochloride (m. p. 165°) with bromine and distilling the reaction-product with quinoline, is described by Jünger and Klages[6] as an oil, boiling at 226° to 227°; it has the specific gravity 1.265 at 15°, the index of refraction, $n_D = 1.52605$ at 15°, and the molecular refraction, M = 52.36.

Camphene dibromide, $C_{10}H_{16}Br_2$.—According to Reychler,[7] when camphene is brominated according to Wallach's method and the monobromocamphene, $C_{10}H_{15}Br$, is removed by distillation with steam, a compound, non-volatile with steam, remains in the distilling flask; it crystallizes from alcohol in colorless prisms,

[1]Marsh and Hartridge, Journ. Chem. Soc., *73*, 852.
[2]Wallach, Ann. Chem., *277*, 122.
[3]Lapworth and Kipping, Journ. Chem. Soc., *69*, 1559; see also, *69*, 1546; *63*, 548.
[4]Wallach, Ann. Chem., *230*, 235.
[5]Semmler, Ber., *33*, 3420.
[6]Jünger and Klages, Ber., *29*, 544.
[7]A. Reychler, Ber., *29*, 900.

melts at 90°, and has the composition, $C_{10}H_{16}Br_2$. It is likewise formed by slowly adding bromine to a solution of camphene in light petroleum, cooled to − 10°.

According to Semmler,[1] camphene dibromide is probably formed by the addition of hydrogen bromide to the bromocamphene which is the primary product of the action; it may be reconverted into bromocamphene by distilling with quinoline. It is not readily acted on by alcoholic potash, but is reduced by sodium and alcohol to a dihydrocamphene identical with that from pinene hydrochloride.

Oxidation of Camphene.

A chromic acid mixture converts camphene into camphor, oxycamphor, $C_{10}H_{16}O_2$, carbonic acid, acetic acid and camphoric acid (Kachler and Spitzer[2]). (According to more recent investigations by Semmler,[1] it is stated that camphene is never oxidized to camphoric acid.)

According to Wagner,[3] the oxidation of camphene with a dilute solution of potassium permanganate in the cold yields *camphene glycol*, $C_{10}H_{16}(OH)_2$, melting at 192°, and *camphenilic acid*, $C_{10}H_{16}O_3$, melting at 170° to 172°.

By the oxidation of camphene with dilute nitric acid, Marsh and Gardner[4] obtained the following acids.

1. **Camphoic acid (camphoylic or carboxyl-apocamphoric acid)**, $C_{10}H_{14}O_6$.—This tribasic acid is prepared by heating camphene with nitric acid of specific gravity 1.3 on the water-bath; the crud eacid is purified by recrystallization from hot nitric acid, sp. gr. 1.42. When crystallized from nitric acid or water, it melts with decomposition at 196°; crystallized from ether, it melts at 197° to 198°; but when a pure specimen is prepared from anhydrocamphoic acid, it melts and decomposes at 199° to 200°.

It is also produced by the oxidation of chlorocamphene phosphoric acid, $C_{10}H_{14}Cl{\cdot}PO_3H_2$ (prepared by the action of phosphorus pentachloride on camphene and subsequent treatment of the product with water), by means of nitric acid. On distillation it loses water and carbon dioxide, and yields *camphopyric anhydride*, $C_9H_{12}O_3$, and *isocamphopyric acid*, $C_9H_{14}O_4$ (m. p. 209°).

Anhydrocamphoic acid, $C_{10}H_{12}O_5$, is formed by the action of acetyl chloride on camphoic acid; it crystallizes from ether in large, transparent plates, melting at 205°.

[1] Semmler, Ber., *33*, 3420.
[2] Kachler and Spitzer, Ann. Chem., *200*, 341.
[3] G. Wagner, Ber., *23*, 2311.
[4] Marsh and Gardner, Journ. Chem. Soc., *1891* (1), 648; *1896* (1), 74.

Other derivatives of camphoic acid are *cis-, meso- and trans-camphopyric acids*,[1] $C_9H_{14}O_4$, melting at 203° to 204°, 160° to 170°, and 190° to 191°, respectively; and *cis-camphopyric anhydride*, $C_9H_{12}O_3$, melting at 178°.

2. **Terephthalic acid, camphoric acid,** $C_{10}H_{16}O_4$, **and succinic acid.**

In addition to camphoic acid, Jagelki[2] obtained the following compounds by the oxidation of camphene with dilute nitric acid.

1. **Anhydrocamphenilic acid,** $C_{10}H_{14}O_2$, crystallizes in plates and melts at 147.5° to 148°. Since it is indifferent towards potassium permanganate, Wagner[3] regards it as a derivative of a class of compounds which he terms *tricyclenes*.

2. **Camphenilone,** $C_9H_{14}O$, is a ketone, melting at 36° to 38° and boiling at 195° under 738 mm. pressure.[4] It is also formed by the oxidation of camphenilic acid, $C_{10}H_{16}O_3$, with lead peroxide. Its *oxime* melts at 105° to 106°, and the *semicarbazone* melts and decomposes at 220° to 222°. Camphenilone is readily reduced to an *alcohol*, $C_9H_{15}OH$, which, in turn, may be converted into a *chloride*, $C_9H_{15}Cl$; when the latter is heated with aniline, it yields an unsaturated hydrocarbon, *camphenilene*, C_9H_{14}, boiling at 142°.

When camphenilone oxime is heated with dilute sulphuric acid, it loses water and is converted into the *nitrile* of an unsaturated acid, $C_9H_{13}N$; by hydrolysis, this yields the unsaturated *camphoceenic acid*, $C_9H_{14}O_2$, melting at 54°. If this acid be oxidized with a cold, dilute solution of potassium permanganate, it gives rise to *dioxycamphoceanic acid*, $C_9H_{16}O_4$, melting at 163°; on distillation in vacuum this dioxy-acid is converted into a mixture of a ketonic acid, *camphoceonic acid*, $C_9H_{14}O_3$, melting at 173°, and the *lactone* of *oxycamphoceonic acid*, $C_9H_{14}O_3$, melting at 58°. When dioxycamphoceanic acid is oxidized with dilute nitric acid, it yields *dimethyltricarballylic acid*, $C_8H_{12}O_6$, melting at 157° to 158°, which, on fusion with potash, gives rise to oxalic acid and *as*-dimethylsuccinic acid, $C_6H_{10}O_4$.

3. **Camphenilic nitrite,** $C_{10}H_{15}NO_2$ (see above).

By the action of nitric anhydride on a solution of camphene in chloroform, an *acid*,[5] $C_{10}H_{15}O_5N$, is formed, which crystallizes from dilute alcohol in prisms, melting at 140° to 141° and decomposing at 165° to 170°. It forms a soluble potassium salt,

[1] For complete synthesis of camphopyric (apocamphoric) acid, compare Komppa, Ber., *34*, 2472.

[2] W. Jagelki, Ber., *32*, 1498; compare Bredt and Jagelki, Chem. Zeit., *20* (1896), 842.

[3] Majewski and G. Wagner, Journ. Russ. Chem. Soc., *29* (1896), 124; Chem. Centr., *1897* (I.), 1056.

[4] Blaise and Blanc, Compt. rend., *129* (1899), 886.

[5] Demjanoff, Journ. Russ. Phys. Chem. Soc., *33*, 283.

and a sparingly soluble silver salt. On reduction with tin and hydrochloric acid, or on heating with concentrated potash, the acid is converted into anhydrocamphenilic acid, $C_{10}H_{14}O_2$ (m. p. 148°).

The *compound*,[1] $C_{10}H_{16}\cdot 2CrO_2Cl_2$, is formed when a solution of camphene in carbon bisulphide is treated with chromyl dichloride. It is a pale brown powder, very hygroscopic, and is somewhat soluble in ether.

Camphenilan aldehyde, $C_{10}H_{16}O$, is obtained by the treatment of the preceding double compound with water. It melts at about 70°, and boils at 96° under 14 mm. pressure. It is identical with *camphene aldehyde*, $C_{10}H_{14}O$, previously prepared by Étard, and also by Wagner from camphene glycol and hydrochloric acid.

Camphenilanic acid, $C_{10}H_{16}O_2$, results by the oxidation of camphenilan aldehyde with a current of air; it melts at 65°. When the aldehyde is oxidized by the usual oxidizing agents it yields *isocamphenilanic acid*, $C_{10}H_{16}O_2$, melting at 118°; this acid is also formed by heating camphenilanic acid with nitric or chromic acid. When camphenilanic acid is treated with bromine and the resultant monobromo-derivative is boiled with alcoholic potash, it is converted into *oxycamphenilanic acid*, $C_{10}H_{16}O_3$; this acid melts at 170° to 172°, and is identical with *camphenilic acid*, $C_{10}H_{16}O_3$, which Wagner obtained in the oxidation of camphene with potassium permanganate.

Two isomeric *nitrates*, $C_{10}H_{16}\cdot HNO_3$, have been obtained by Bouveault[2] by gradually adding a solution of camphene in chloroform to cold fuming nitric acid. One of these nitrates decomposes when distilled under diminished pressure, and the other boils at 110° under 10 mm. pressure, has a specific gravity 1.0988 at 0°, and is reverted into camphene by alcoholic potash.

Ethylcamphene, $C_{10}H_{15}\cdot C_2H_5$, and *isobutylcamphene*, $C_{10}H_{15}\cdot C_4H_9$, were prepared by Spitzer,[3] and *hydrazocamphene*, $C_{10}H_{17}NO_2$, was obtained by Tanret.[4]

Camphene alcoholate,[5] $C_{10}H_{17}\cdot OC_2H_5$, is prepared by boiling a mixture of camphene, alcohol, and sulphuric acid; it is an oil, boils at about 200°, has a sp. gr. 0.895 and a refractive index, $n_D = 1.4589$; it is identical with isoborneol ethyl ether.

In addition to the above-mentioned derivatives of camphene, a series of very interesting and important compounds has been ob-

[1] Bredt and Jagelki, Ann. Chem., *310*, 112.
[2] L. Bouveault, Bull. Soc. Chim., *23* (1900, III.), 535.
[3] Spitzer, Ann. Chem., *197*, 133.
[4] Tanret, Compt. rend., *102*, 791; *104*, 917; *106*, 660 and 749; Ber., *20*, 253 and 285, Ref.; *21*, 237 and 352, Ref.
[5] Semmler, Ber., *33*, 3420.

tained by Forster; for a description of the method of preparation, properties, etc., of these substances (bromonitrocamphane, $C_{10}H_{16}BrNO_2$, nitrocamphene, $C_{10}H_{15}NO_2$, amidocamphene, $C_{10}H_{15}NH_2$, hydroxycamphene, $C_{10}H_{15}OH$, etc.), reference must be made to the original publications under the title, "Studies in the Camphane Series."[1]

3. FENCHENE.

Although fenchene has not yet been found in nature, nevertheless it may form a constituent of many turpentine oils (compare with fenchyl alcohol).

The methods for the artificial preparation of this terpene are limited to the reduction of fenchone, $C_{10}H_{16}O$, and elimination of the elements of water from the resulting fenchyl alcohol, $C_{10}H_{17}OH$. Fenchene is formed when fenchyl alcohol is heated with acid potassium sulphate.

In order to prepare fenchene, it is most convenient to convert fenchyl alcohol into fenchyl chloride. Equal weights of fenchyl chloride and aniline are warmed in a flask connected with reflux condenser, and the mixture is heated to the completion of the somewhat violent reaction. The mass is then allowed to cool, treated with an equal volume of glacial acetic acid, and the fenchene is distilled off with steam; phenyl fenchylamine remains in the residue in the distilling flask. The hydrocarbon is purified by fractional distillation (Wallach[2]).

Properties.—According to Wallach,[2] fenchene is a liquid hydrocarbon, which boils at 155° to 156°, has a specific gravity of 0.867 and a refractive index equal to 1.4690 at 20° and 1.47047 at 18°; its odor resembles that of camphene. According to Gardner and Cockburn,[3] fenchene, prepared by Wallach's method and purified by careful fractionation, distills chiefly at 150° to 152°, with small fractions from 152° to 160°; the fraction boiling at 150° to 154° has a specific gravity 0.8667 at 18°, and a specific rotatory power, $[\alpha]_D = -6.46°$ (not in solution).

In a more recent investigation, Wallach[4] finds that when levorotatory fenchyl alcohol, prepared by the reduction of dextrorotatory fenchone, is treated with phosphorus pentachloride, it gives rise to two fenchyl chlorides, and these, in turn, yield two fenchenes, the one dextrorotatory, and the other levorotatory;

[1] M. O. Forster, Journ. Chem. Soc., 77, 251; 79, 644, 653, 987 and 1003.

[2] Wallach, Ann. Chem., *263*, 149; *302*, 376.

[3] Gardner and Cockburn, Journ. Chem. Soc., 73 (1898), 276; compare with Bertram and Helle, Journ. pr. Chem., *61*, 1900 (II.), 293.

[4] Wallach, Ann. Chem., *302*, 371; *315*, 273.

since both fenchenes are derived from dextro-fenchone, Wallach designates them as *D-d-fenchene* and *D-l-fenchene*, respectively.[1] The optical rotation of fenchyl chloride, obtained from D-l-fenchyl alcohol, varies between the limits, $[\alpha]_D = -13°$ and $+5.1°$, in a one decimeter tube; the direct product, prepared at a relatively low temperature, is always levorotatory, but the subsequent treatment which it receives, especially repeated distillations, modifies its rotatory power. When prepared by heating on the water-bath a dextro-fenchyl chloride results. By the elimination of the elements of hydrogen chloride by means of aniline or quinoline from *strongly levorotatory* fenchyl chloride, *levo-fenchene* is always formed; but feebly levorotatory, or nearly inactive, fenchyl chloride yields a mixture of l- and d-fenchene, which is optically inactive or dextrorotatory. The limits of rotation for l- and d-fenchene are, $[\alpha]_D = \pm 21°$, in a one decimeter tube. Dextro-fenchene is best prepared from fenchyl chloride which has not been distilled. Levo-fenchene may be obtained by heating d-fenchene with alcoholic sulphuric acid for several hours; the reverse transformation does not appear to take place. l-Fenchene may be isolated from a mixture of the two modifications by fractional oxidation with a three per cent. solution of potassium permanganate; by this treatment, D-d-fenchene is oxidized in a few minutes, while D-l-fenchene is only slowly attacked, and may be removed from the reaction-product by distillation with steam.

An optically inactive fenchene was obtained by Wallach[2] in his first investigation of fenchene.

Levo-fenchyl chloride[3] is formed by saturating a solution of either d- or l-fenchene in glacial acetic acid with hydrogen chloride, pouring the product into water, and distilling with steam. When the resultant l-fenchyl chloride is heated with aniline, l-fenchene is obtained; by this method, therefore, d-fenchene may be converted into l-fenchene.

L-d-Fenchyl alcohol, obtained from l-fenchone, acts in a similar manner to D-l-fenchyl alcohol, when it is converted into its chloride; the fenchene obtained from it yields L-d-oxyfenchenic acid (m. p. 152° to 153°), when it is treated with alcoholic sulphuric acid and is subsequently oxidized with a permanganate solution (see below).

[1]The capital letters designate the optical rotation of the original compound, and the small letters that of the final product; thus, D-l-fenchene is the levorotatory terpene obtained from dextrorotatory fenchone, and D-l-fenchyl alcohol is the levorotatory alcohol derived from dextro-fenchone.

[2]Wallach, Ann. Chem., *263*, 150.

[3]Wallach, Ann. Chem., *302*, 382.

According to Kondakoff,[1] the action of alcoholic potash on fenchyl bromide, and to a less extent on the chloride, gives a product which consists of two isomeric fenchenes; one of these has been isolated in a pure form. It boils at 140° to 141°, has a sp. gr. 0.8385 at 20°, the rotatory power is $[\alpha]_D = -55°$; it shows the properties of a reduced aromatic compound with a double linking in the ring.

Fenchene hydrochloride,[2] $C_{10}H_{16}.HCl$, closely resembles fenchyl chloride, $C_{10}H_{17}Cl$, and is probably almost all tertiary; moist silver oxide converts it into isofenchyl alcohol.

Fenchene hydrobromide,[2] $C_{10}H_{16}.HBr$, resembles fenchyl bromide; $[\alpha]_D = -27° 16'$.

Fenchene hydriodide,[3] $C_{10}H_{16}.HI$, boils at 120° to 120.5° (23 mm.), has a sp. gr. 1.427 at 21°/4° and $[\alpha]_D = +42°57'$ at 40°; when treated with alcoholic potash, it yields a mixture of fenchene (b. p. 143° to 150°, sp. gr. 0.8482 at 19°/4°), and unaltered hydriodide; the latter reacts with moist silver oxide, yielding solid fenchyl alcohol.

Fenchene unites with two atoms of bromine forming an oily dibromide, which, however, has not been obtained in a condition of purity.

When fenchene is treated with a mixture of glacial acetic and sulphuric acids, it is converted into isofenchyl alcohol,[4] $C_{10}H_{17}OH$, melting at 61.5° to 62°. This transformation is similar to that of camphene into isoborneol.

Fenchene alcoholate,[5] $C_{10}H_{17}OC_2H_5$, is produced by heating D-d-fenchene with alcoholic sulphuric acid; it boils at 200° to 201°, and on treatment with sodium it yields the sodium derivative of the alcohol, $C_{10}H_{17}OH$. This alcohol melts at 61°, and is identical with isofenchyl alcohol.

Oxidation Products of Fenchene.

As is mentioned above, D-d- and D-l-fenchene react quite differently toward potassium permanganate. Twenty grams of D-l-fenchene require about twelve hours to be oxidized in the cold with a three per cent. solution of permanganate, while under the same

[1] Kondakoff and Lutschinin, Journ. pr. Chem., 1900 (II.), *62*, 1; Chem. Zeit., 25, 131.

[2] Kondakoff, Journ. pr. Chem., 1900 (II.), *62*, 1.

[3] Kondakoff, Chem. Zeit., *25*, 131.

[4] Bertram and Helle, Journ. pr. Chem., *61*, 1900 (II.), 293.

[5] Wallach, Ann. Chem., *315*, 273.

conditions D-d-fenchene is completely oxidized in a few minutes. The product is in each case an oxyfenchenic acid,[1] $C_{10}H_{16}O_3$.

1. **D-l-Oxyfenchenic acid,**[2] $C_{10}H_{16}O_3$, is the oxidation product of pure D-l-fenchene. It crystallizes from dilute acetone in leaflets, and melts at 152° to 153°; like the hydrocarbon from which it is derived, it is levorotatory, $[\alpha]_D = -56.8°$. The same acid may also be obtained by the oxidation of D-l-fenchyl chloride with permanganate. Its *acetyl* derivative melts at 109° to 110°.

D-d-Fenchocamphorone,[3] $C_9H_{14}O$, is formed by the oxidation of D-l-oxyfenchenic acid in an acid solution. It melts at 109° to 110°, boils at 202°, and is dextrorotatory, $[\alpha]_D = +14.64°$. It is a ketone isomeric with phorone, has the odor of camphor, and is very similar to it. Its *oxime*, $C_9H_{14}NOH$, melts at 69° to 71°, is levorotatory, $[\alpha]_D = -50.30°$, and yields fenchocamphonitrile,[3] $C_9H_{13}N$, on treating with dilute sulphuric acid. On reducing this nitrile with alcohol and sodium, a *base*, $C_9H_{15}\cdot NH_2$, is obtained, and is identified by means of its platinochloride and carbamide. An isomeric *fenchocamphylamine*, $C_9H_{15}\cdot NH_2$, produced by the direct reduction of fenchocamphoronoxime with amyl alcohol and sodium, boils at 196° to 199°, and solidifies at low temperatures; its *hydrochloride*, $C_9H_{15}\cdot NH_2\cdot HCl$, is very stable, and crystallizes from a mixture of ether and alcohol.

Fenchocamphorone semicarbazone melts at 210° to 212°, and is levorotatory, $[\alpha]_D = -131.3°$.

Fenchocamphorone[4] is oxidized by nitric acid, sp. gr. 1.25, yielding two acids, which melt at 124° and 202°, respectively; the acid melting at 202° has the formula, $C_9H_{14}O_4$, and yields the *anhydride*, $C_9H_{12}O_3$ (m. p. 176° to 177°), and a *monanilide* (m. p. 211°). These compounds agree in their properties with the corresponding derivatives of *cis-camphopyric acid*,[5] and hence the two acids are identical (see page 64).

When fenchocamphorone is reduced by sodium and aqueous ether, *fenchocamphorol*,[6] $C_9H_{15}OH$, is obtained; it crystallizes from dilute methyl alcohol in needles, melting at 128° to 130°. A *pinacone*, $C_{18}H_{30}O_2$, melting at 192° to 193°, is also formed during the reduction.

[1] Wallach, Ann. Chem., *284*, 333; *300*, 313; *315*, 273.

[2] Wallach, Ann. Chem., *302*, 377.

[3] Wallach, Ann. Chem. *300*, 313; *302*, 383; *315*, 273; Chem. Centr., *1899* (II.), 1052.

[4] Wallach, Ann. Chem., *300*, 313; *315*, 273.

[5] Marsh and Gardner, Journ. Chem. Soc., *69*, 77.

[6] Wallach, Ann. Chem., *300*, 313.

2. **D-d-Oxyfenchenic acid,**[1] $C_{10}H_{16}O_3$, is the oxidation product of pure D-d-fenchene. It crystallizes from dilute acetone in well formed, transparent prisms, melting at 138° to 139°; it is dextrorotatory, $[\alpha]_D = +7.696°$. Other acids are simultaneously formed with this compound, but they have not yet been obtained pure. Its *acetyl* derivative crystallizes in prisms, and melts at 122° to 124°.

D-l-Fenchocamphorone,[1] $C_9H_{14}O$, is produced by the oxidation of D-d-oxyfenchenic acid; it melts at 62° to 63°, boils at 201° to 202°, is very volatile with steam, and slightly soluble in water. It is levorotatory, $[\alpha]_D = -16.69°$. Its *oxime* is very soluble in all solvents, melts at 54° to 56°, and is dextrorotatory, $[\alpha]_D = +49.03°$; a nitrile is formed at once by heating the oxime with mineral acids.

Its *semicarbazone* crystallizes from hot alcohol in prisms, melting at 204° to 206°, and is dextrorotatory, $[\alpha]_D = +58.11°$.

D-l-Fenchocamphorone differs from its D-d-isomeride in not yielding a camphopyric acid with dilute nitric acid. The principal product of this action is an acid whose mono- and di-anilides agree in properties with those of *as*-dimethylsuccinic acid; but there is a discrepancy in the melting points of their anhydrides, that from the acid derived from D-l-fenchocamphorone melts at 125° to 130°, whilst *as*-dimethylsuccinic anhydride melts at 29° (Wallach[2]).

3. **L-d-Oxyfenchenic acid,**[3] $C_{10}H_{16}O_3$.—This compound is prepared as follows. l-Fenchone is reduced to L-d-fenchyl alcohol ($[\alpha]_D = +10.36°$), and the latter is converted into fenchyl chloride, and this, in turn, into fenchene; the hydrocarbon is heated for several hours with alcoholic sulphuric acid, and then the strongly dextrorotatory terpene is oxidized with permanganate. The resulting L-d-oxyfenchenic acid melts at 152° to 153°, and is dextrorotatory, $[\alpha]_D = +57.29°$.

The *racemic oxyfenchenic acid,*[3] $C_{10}H_{16}O_3$, is prepared by crystallizing from ether a mixture of equal quantities of D-l-oxyfenchenic acid and L-d-oxyfenchenic acid; it melts at 142° to 143°, lower than either of its components.

The L-l-oxyfenchenic acid and the corresponding inactive, racemic modification have not yet been prepared.

In general it may be stated that different specimens of crude fenchene vary greatly in their behavior towards permanganate, and usually yield a mixture of D-l- and D-d-oxyfenchenic acids,

[1] Wallach, Ann. Chem., *302*, 378 and 384.
[2] Wallach, Ann. Chem., *315*, 273.
[3] Wallach, Ann. Chem., *302*, 378 and 379.

the levo-isomeride predominating. Some samples of fenchene contain readily oxidizable compounds, and in such cases the product of oxidation is a complex mixture consisting of the two oxyfenchenic acids, together with acids of the acetic series and a *ketonic acid*,[1] $C_8H_{12}O_3$; the latter gives a *semicarbazone*, melting at 210°, and a *silver salt*. This ketonic acid may possibly be formed from a third isomeric fenchene, which is contained in crude fenchene.

Fenchene differs from other terpenes in being relatively stable towards strong nitric acid in the cold, but it is vigorously attacked by the hot acid. According to Gardner and Cockburn,[2] when twenty grams of fenchene are heated on the water-bath with 100 cc. of water and 100 cc. of concentrated nitric acid, and the product is distilled with steam, the following oxidation products are obtained.

1. **Acetic acid.**
2. **Cis-camphopyric acid,** $C_9H_{14}O_4$, is obtained from the non-volatile oil remaining in the distilling flask; it melts at 207°.
3. **Cis-camphopyric anhydride,** $C_9H_{12}O_3$, melts at 178°.
4. An *acid* whose constitution is not yet determined.

4a. LIMONENE.

Limonene is the optically active modification of dipentene. While pinene and camphene exist in the active and inactive modifications, agreeing in all properties except in their action on polarized light, limonene bears the same relation to dipentene as the optically active tartaric acids to racemic acid. For this reason, the name dipentene has been retained for inactive limonene, and both modifications will be separately considered.

Limonene (designated in the early literature as hesperidene, citrene, and carvene), is, next to pinene, the most widely distributed terpene occurring in nature. Dextrorotatory limonene[3] is found in the following ethereal oils: oil of orange[4] and orange peel,[4] lemon,[4] bergamot,[4] caraway,[4] dill,[4] erigeron,[5] kuromoji,[6] massoy bark,[7] and celery. Levo-limonene occurs in the oil from

[1] Wallach, Ann. Chem., *315*, 273.

[2] Gardner and Cockburn, Journ. Chem. Soc., *73*, 277.

[3] Gildemeister and Stephan, Arch. Pharm., *235* (1897), 582; see also J. Flatan and Labbé, Bull. Soc. Chim., *19*, 1898 (III.), 361 and 364.

[4] Wallach, Ann. Chem., *227*, 287.

[5] Beilstein and Wiegand, Ber., *15*, 2854.

[6] Kwasnick, Ber., *24*, 81.

[7] Wallach, Ann. Chem., *258*, 340.

cones [1] and needles [2] of *Abies alba,* Russian peppermint oil,[3] and Russian and American spearmint oil.

PREPARATION.—The most convenient source of this terpene is oil of orange peel or caraway oil, and oil of *Abies alba.* These oils are dried and fractionally distilled. The fraction boiling at 175° to 180° is collected separately, and on redistillation yields limonene, boiling at 175° to 177°, which is not a chemically pure product.

PROPERTIES.—The odor of limonene somewhat resembles that of lemons. It is optically active and boils at 175° to 176°. The specific rotatory power has been determined by Wallach and Conrady,[4] as follows:—

Levo-limonene, $[\alpha]_D = -105.0°$.

Dextro-limonene, $[\alpha]_D = +106.8°$.

Kremers [5] found the specific rotatory power of freshly distilled limonene to be higher, viz.:—

$$[\alpha]_D = 121.3°.$$

He also investigated the rotatory power of limonene in different solvents.

The specific gravity of levo-limonene at 20° is 0.846, the refractive index, $n_D = 1.47459$, corresponding to a molecular refraction of 45.23 (Wallach).

According to Godlewsky,[6] when limonene tetrabromide (prepared from *carvene,* and melting at 104°), is reduced in alcoholic solution with zinc dust, a limonene is obtained, which, after drying and distilling over sodium, has the following properties: it boils at 177.5° under 759 mm. pressure, has a specific gravity 0.8441 at 20°, and a specific rotatory power, $[\alpha]_D = +125° 36'$, at 20°; bromine converts it into the original tetrabromide.

When treated with perfectly dry hydrogen chloride, limonene yields an optically active monohydrochloride; with nitrosyl chloride an optically active additive product is formed, and with bromine an active tetrabromide results. If, on the other hand, limonene be treated with hydrogen chloride in the presence of water, it is rendered inactive, and yields dipentene dihydrochloride; moist hydrogen bromide and iodide act in an analogous man-

[1] Wallach, Ann. Chem., *246,* 221.

[2] Bertram and Walbaum, Arch. Pharm., *231,* 290.

[3] Andres and Andrejew, Ber., *1892,* 609.

[4] Wallach and Conrady, Ann. Chem., *252,* 144.

[5] Kremers, Amer. Chem. Journ., *17,* 692.

[6] J. Godlewsky and Roshanowitsch, Chem. Centr., *1899,* I., 1241; J. Russ. Chem. Soc., *31,* 209.

ner. Limonene is also rendered inactive by heating to high temperatures (Wallach[1]).

Limonene tetrabromide,[2] $C_{10}H_{16}Br_4$, is prepared from the fraction boiling at 174° to 176° of the oil of sweet orange peel, or oil from cones of *Abies alba*.

Dissolve the terpene in four times its volume of glacial acetic acid, cool with ice water, and gradually add bromine from a dropping funnel until the liquid no longer absorbs it. Crystals separate at once, and are filtered off with the aid of the pump; they are pressed on a porous plate, and recrystallized from an equal weight of acetic ether. The yield is about the same as the weight of limonene employed.

In regard to the preparation of limonene tetrabromide, compare Baeyer and Villiger,[3] and Power and Kleber.[4]

Limonene tetrabromide is optically active, and separates in hemihedral rhombic crystals,[5] which melt at 104° to 105°.

If hydrobromic acid is eliminated from limonene tetrabromide by heating with alcoholic potassium hydroxide, two molecules of hydrogen bromide are split off, while one bromine atom suffers replacement by one alcohol radical.[6] Thus, if a solution of potassium hydroxide in *methyl* alcohol be employed, the reactions take place in accordance with the following equations:—

$$\text{I. } C_{10}H_{16}Br_4 - 2HBr = C_{10}H_{14}Br_2,$$
$$\text{II. } C_{10}H_{14}Br_2 + KOCH_3 = C_{10}H_{14}BrOCH_3 + KBr.$$

The resulting compound, $C_{10}H_{14}BrOCH_3$, is an oil, which boils at 137° to 140° under 14 mm. pressure, and has a specific gravity of 1.251 and coefficient of refraction, $n_D = 1.51963$, at 18°. When treated with a solution of hydrogen bromide in glacial acetic acid, this oil gives a quantitative yield of dipentene tetrabromide. If sodium is added to an alcoholic solution of this oil, the atom of bromine in this compound, $C_{10}H_{14}BrOCH_3$, is replaced by hydrogen, and *carveol methyl ether*, $C_{10}H_{15}OCH_3$, is formed. The latter compound is an optically active oil, boiling at 208° to 212°, and has a specific gravity of 0.9065 and coefficient of refraction, $n_D = 1.47586$, at 18°. This carveol methyl

[1] Wallach, Ann. Chem., *227*, 301.

[2] Wallach, Ann. Chem., *225*, 318; *239*, 3; *264*, 12; Scheidt, Inaug. Diss., Bonn, 1890.

[3] Baeyer and Villiger, Ber., *27*, 448; compare Godlewsky, Chem. Zeit., *22*, 827.

[4] Power and Kleber, Arch. Pharm., *232*, 646.

[5] Hintze, Zeitschrift für Krystallographie, 10 [2].

[6] Wallach, Ann. Chem., *281*, 127; *264*, 12.

ether is converted into *inactive carvone* by oxidation with a solution of chromic acid in acetic acid.

On the other hand, a conversion of carvone into limonene is said to be accomplished by the following method.[1] Dextro-carvone is reduced to dihydrocarveol, which is readily converted into *methyl dihydrocarvyl xanthate*, $C_{10}H_{17}.O.CS_2.CH_3$; this substance is a thick oil, and, on distillation, yields two hydrocarbons, boiling at 172° to 173.5° and 174° to 176°, respectively. The higher boiling hydrocarbon may be converted into limonene tetrabromide, which, by the action of zinc dust on its alcoholic solution, yields pure dextro-limonene.

A liquid limonene tetrabromide is also known, and is readily formed when bromine is added to the hydrocarbon dissolved in a perfectly dry solvent.[2]

Limonene nitrosochlorides, $C_{10}H_{16}.NOCl$, are known in four modifications; by the action of nitrosyl chloride, dextro- and levo-limonene each yields two optically active isomerides, distinguished as α- and β-limonene nitrosochlorides. There are, therefore, four isomeric, optically active limonene nitrosochlorides, and corresponding to them, are two inactive modifications, the α- and β-dipentene nitrosochlorides.

PREPARATION OF THE NITROSOCHLORIDES FROM DEXTRO- AND LEVO-LIMONENE.[3]

To a mixture of five cc. of limonene, seven cc. of amyl nitrite (or eleven cc. of ethyl nitrite), and twelve cc. of glacial acetic acid, well cooled by a mixture of ice and salt, add slowly and in small portions at a time a mixture of six cc. of crude hydrochloric acid and six cc. of glacial acetic acid. Finally add five cc. of alcohol and allow to stand for some time in the freezing mixture. A mass of crystals consisting of the crude nitrosochloride separates, is filtered with the pump and washed with alcohol. One hundred grams of nitrosochloride are obtained from 120 grams of limonene.

SEPARATION OF THE α- AND β-LIMONENE NITROSOCHLORIDES.

One hundred grams of the white and perfectly dry, crude product are digested with 300 grams of chloroform for a few

[1] L. Tschügaeff, Ber., *33*, 735.
[2] Wallach, Ann. Chem., *281*, 137.
[3] Wallach, Ann. Chem., *252*, 106; *270*, 174.

moments in the cold. It is then filtered, and the crude β-compound remaining on the filter is washed with a little chloroform.

An excess of methyl alcohol is added to the filtrate, thus precipitating the α-compound as a crystalline powder. The crude α-nitrosochloride is filtered, dried, and digested in a flask with two to three times its quantity of dry ether for one-quarter of an hour, care being taken to keep the mixture cold. It is then filtered, and the ether allowed to evaporate, when the α-compound generally separates in large crystals; they are rubbed up with methyl alcohol, again dissolved in twice their weight of ether, filtered, and some methyl alcohol is added to the filtrate. By the slow evaporation of the solution, pure α-limonene nitrosochloride is obtained in large, brilliant crystals, which melt at 103° to 104°.

α-Limonene nitrosochloride separates in monoclinic crystals; together with holohedral forms, hemimorphic crystals are always found, which in the case of the dextro-limonene derivative have the clinodome on the left, while those of the levo-compound have the clinodome on the right.

α-Limonene nitrosochloride is soluble at ordinary temperature in one part of chloroform, and in two parts of ether. It quickly decomposes on standing.

The crude β-limonene nitrosochloride is dried and dissolved in ten times its weight of chloroform. The solution is filtered and precipitated with methyl alcohol in such a manner that a further addition of this reagent causes a slight additional precipitate. Thus, the most difficultly soluble portion of the nitrosochloride is obtained; it is filtered, washed with ether and dried. The dry substance is again digested with three times its weight of ether, and, on evaporation of this solvent, pure β-limonene nitrosochloride is obtained; after drying, this compound forms soft needles, which melt at about 100°. The β-nitrosochlorides may be kept for a long time without decomposing. The crude limonene nitrosochlorides contain only about twenty per cent. of the β-nitrosochlorides.

(For the influence of the concentration of the hydrochloric acid on the yield of β-nitrosochlorides, compare experiments of Wallach.[1])

According to Wallach,[2] the α- and β-nitrosochlorides are physical, and not chemical isomerides. While Wallach gives them the formula,

$$C_{10}H_{15}\begin{cases}Cl\\NOH\end{cases}$$

[1]Wallach, Ber., *28*, 1308 and 1474.

[2]Wallach, Ann. Chem., *252*, 113; *270*, 185.

Baeyer[1] is inclined to consider these compounds as possessing double that molecular weight, and to regard them as bisnitrosyl-derivatives. Wallach[2] has, however, published the results of experiments, which indicate that the α- and β-nitrosochlorides actually possess twice the molecular weight of the above formula, but in all other relations they both behave as mono-molecular compounds.

When heated with alcoholic potash, α- and β-limonene nitrosochlorides form the same carvoxime, melting at 72°.

Benzoyl limonene nitrosochloride,[3]

$$C_{10}H_{15}\langle{}^{Cl}_{NOCOC_6H_5}$$

is formed by adding one molecule of benzoyl chloride to a solution of one part of α-limonene nitrosochloride in two parts by weight of dry ether and allowing the mixture to stand for one or two weeks.

It may also be readily obtained by warming β-limonene nitrosochloride with one molecule of benzoyl chloride and eighty times its weight of dry ether for several days on a water-bath. Benzoyl limonene nitrosochloride melts at 109° to 110°, is difficultly soluble in ether, easily soluble in acetic ether, and is optically active. It yields carvoxime[4] by boiling with sodium alcoholate.

Limonene nitrosobromide,[5] $C_{10}H_{16}\cdot NOBr$, is obtained by a method analogous to that used in the preparation of the nitrosochloride. It melts at 90.5°.

Limonene nitrosate,[5]

$$C_{10}H_{15}\langle{}^{ONO_2}_{NOH}$$

is an oil, which solidifies only at a very low temperature; it also yields carvoxime by treatment with alcoholic potassium hydroxide.

LIMONENE NITROLAMINES.[6]

If dextro-α-limonene nitrosochloride be treated with an organic base, two isomeric nitrolamines are formed, one of which is

[1] Baeyer, Ber., *28*, 648.
[2] Wallach, Ber., *28*, 1308 and 1474.
[3] Wallach, Ann. Chem., *270*, 175.
[4] Wallach, Ber., *28*, 1311.
[5] Wallach, Ann. Chem., *245*, 258.
[6] Wallach, Ann. Chem., *252*, 113; *270*, 180.

optically dextrorotatory and is called α-nitrolamine, the other is levorotatory, and termed β-nitrolamine. If dextro-β-limonene nitrosochloride be treated with the same base, exactly the same reaction-products are obtained, namely, a dextrorotatory α-limonene nitrolamine, together with a levorotatory β-limonene nitrolamine. If, on the other hand, levo-α- or levo-β-limonene nitrosochloride be treated with an amine, a mixture of a levorotatory α- and a dextrorotatory β-limonene nitrolamine is formed. These α- and β-nitrolamines have simple molecules (Wallach[1]).

If equal proportions of the two oppositely active α-, or β-limonene nitrolamines are recrystallized together, the corresponding α- or β-dipentene nitrolamine is obtained. These may also be prepared together by a precisely analogous method from the α-, as well as from the β-, dipentene nitrosochloride. The following table may serve to explain these transformations (page 78).

1. **Limonene nitrolanilides,**

$$C_{10}H_{15}\begin{cases} NOH \\ NHC_6H_5 \end{cases}$$

Twenty grams of pure α-limonene nitrosochloride are pulverized and warmed with twenty cc. of aniline and thirty cc. of alcohol in a flask fitted with a reflux condenser. The mixture is heated with constant shaking until a reaction commences. After the violent reaction has taken place, the mass is allowed to cool, and treated in the cold with an excess of concentrated hydrochloric acid. The resulting mass of crystals is filtered, and washed with alcohol and ether. These crystals consist of the hydrochloric acid salt of α-limonene nitrolanilide. The free α-base is obtained by treating the hydrochloride with ammonia. α-Limonene nitrolanilide crystallizes from alcohol in monoclinic crystals, which melt at 112° to 113°. The yield of the α-base is about eighty per cent. of the theoretical.

In order to obtain the β-anilide, the alcholic-acid filtrate from the hydrochloride of the α-base is poured into a large excess of ammonium hydroxide. The β-anilide gradually solidifies, and is dissolved in three times its weight of benzene in order to remove any aniline which may cling to it. Most of the β-anilide separates from this solution on cooling, while the remainder may be precipitated by the addition of petroleum ether. β-Limonene nitrolanilide crystallizes from alcohol in moss-like needles, which melt at 153°. It is difficultly soluble in ether, readily soluble in chloroform.

[1] Wallach, Ber., 28, 1311.

Isomerism in the Limonene Series.

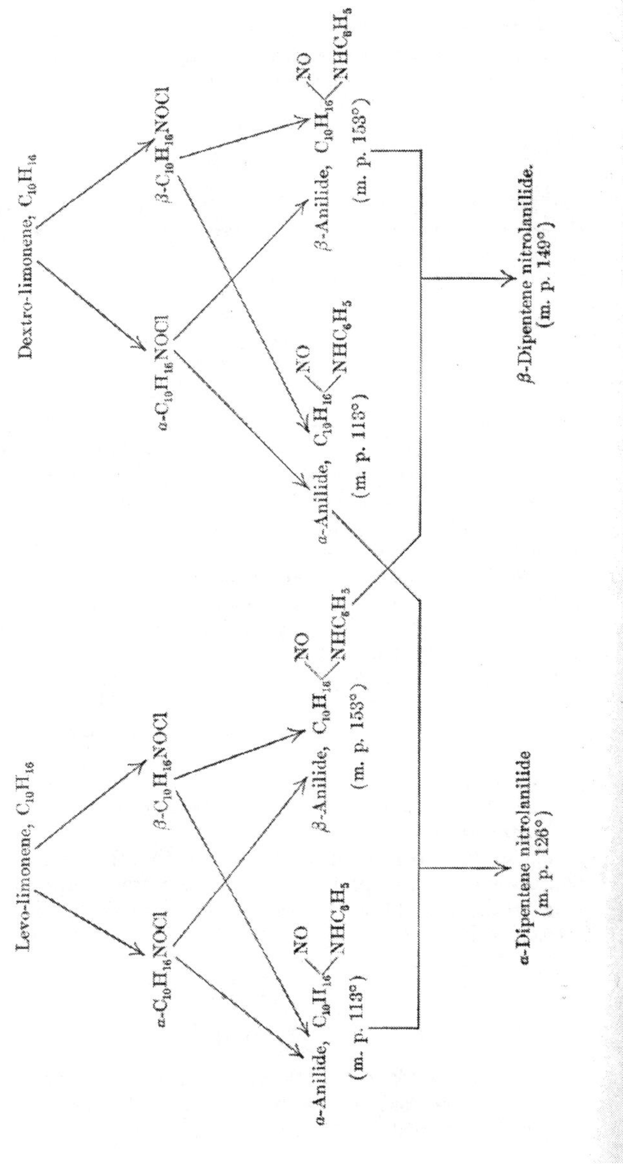

When the glacial acetic acid solution of the α-, or the hydrochloric acid solution of β-, limonene nitrolanilide is treated with a solution of sodium nitrite, *nitroso-compounds*,

$$C_{10}H_{15} \begin{cases} NOH \\ N(NO)C_6H_5 \end{cases}$$

are formed. The α-nitroso-compound melts at 142°, while the β-derivative, characterized by its great power of crystallization, melts at 136°.

2. **Limonene nitrolpiperidides,**

$$C_{10}H_{15} \begin{cases} NOH \\ NC_5H_{10} \end{cases}$$

Twenty grams of pure pulverized α-limonene nitrosochloride are covered with twenty grams of piperidine and sixty grams of alcohol, and gently warmed with frequent shaking. When a clear solution is obtained, the warm liquid is poured into an evaporating dish and a small quantity of water added. On cooling, crystals of the very sparingly soluble, impure β-base separate. These are filtered, and the readily soluble, impure α-base is precipitated from the filtrate by water. The purification of these compounds is based on the circumstance that the β-piperidide is sparingly, the α-base extremely easily, soluble in petroleum ether. The crude α-base is first dissolved in acetic acid, filtered to remove the non-basic impurities, and again thrown out with ammonia. It first appears as an oil which solidifies after a little time. It is dried, digested with a small amount of petroleum ether, decanted from the undissolved β-base, and, after evaporation of the petroleum ether, is recrystallized from alcohol.

α-Limonene nitrolpiperidide separates in orthorhombic crystals, and melts at 93° to 94°.

The crude β-base is dried, digested with cold petroleum ether, and the undissolved portion recrystallized from warm petroleum ether with the addition of some methyl alcohol. β-Limonene nitrolpiperidide melts at 110° to 111°.

3. **Limonene nitrolbenzylamines,**

$$C_{10}H_{15} \begin{cases} NOH \\ NHCH_2C_6H_5 \end{cases}$$

Two bases are formed by the action of limonene nitrosochloride on benzylamine; only the α-amine, however, has been obtained in a condition of purity. It forms hard needles, melting at 93°.

This base yields a nitrate, which forms splendid crystals, and is very sparingly soluble in water.

Emil Fischer[1] and other investigators have suggested that the isomerism of the α- and β-limonene nitrolamines is to be explained as stereo-chemical isomerism. According to Wallach,[2] however, the known facts do not determine whether the α- and β-limonene nitrolamines, in contrast to the nitrosochlorides, have the same or different chemical structure. The following observations argue against the stereo-chemical theory.[2]

1. No transformations of the α- into the β-limonene nitrolamines, or the β- into the α-derivatives, have yet succeeded.

2. α-Limonene nitrolanilide is a weaker base than β-limonene nitrolanilide.

3. On heating, the α-anilide yields aniline and a product containing carvoxime; the β-anilide, under the same circumstances, gives aniline and an isonitrile.

4. α-Limonene nitrolanilide in a methyl alcohol solution is capable of adding the elements of hydrochloric acid, forming a compound which melts at 115°. The latter substance is apparently identical with hydrochlorolimonene nitrolanilide,

$$C_{10}H_{17}Cl\left\langle\begin{matrix} NO \\ NH.C_6H_5 \end{matrix}\right.$$

obtained from hydrochlorolimonene nitrosochloride. Under the same conditions, β-limonene nitrolanilide forms a compound, $C_{16}H_{23}ClN_2O$, which melts at 78°; a substance similar to this compound has not yet been prepared from hydrochlorolimonene nitrosochloride.

It should be noted that α- and β-limonene nitrolanilides possess the same molecular weight (determined by the boiling point method, dry ether being the solvent).

Limonene hydrochloride, $C_{10}H_{16}\cdot HCl$.

Limonene, well dried over metallic sodium, is diluted with an equal volume of perfectly dry carbon bisulphide, and saturated with dry hydrochloric acid gas. The liquid must be well cooled with ice, and every precaution used to avoid the presence of any trace of water. One hundred grams of limonene require twenty-four hours for the saturation. When this point is reached, the excess of hydrochloric acid and carbon bisulphide is removed

[1]Emil Fischer, Ber., 23, 3687; 24, 2686.
[2]Wallach, Ann. Chem., 270, 186.

by distillation under diminished pressure, and the resulting limonene monohydrochloride rectified in vacuum (Wallach, Kremers[1]).

Optically active limonene hydrochloride forms a colorless oil, boiling at 97° to 98° under 11 mm. to 12 mm. pressure. A product obtained from dextro-limonene had the specific gravity of 0.973 at 17.8°, while that obtained from levo-limonene had the specific gravity of 0.982 to 16°.[1]

Limonene hydrochloride appears to readily change into an inactive modification on standing. This transformation is accompanied by polymerization of the substance.

Although limonene hydrochloride (like its inactive modification, dipentene hydrochloride) behaves as a saturated compound towards dry hydrochloric acid, it unites with the halogens, nitrosyl chloride, etc., forming additive compounds.

When allowed to remain in contact with water in a sealed glass tube for some months, limonene hydrochloride forms crystals of terpine hydrate. Alcoholic potassium hydroxide eliminates the elements of hydrogen chloride from limonene hydrochloride. In an acetic acid solution it unites with hydrochloric acid, forming dipentene dihydrochloride, while under the same conditions, hydrogen bromide converts it into a compound melting at 47° to 48°.

According to a preliminary notice by Semmler,[2] the chlorine atom in limonene hydrochloride can be replaced by a hydroxyl-group, thus forming an optically active terpineol.

Hydrochlorolimonene nitrosochloride, $C_{10}H_{17}Cl \cdot NOCl$, is obtained by the gradual addition of twenty-five cc. of a five to six per cent. solution of hydrochloric acid in glacial acetic acid to a well cooled mixture of five cc. of limonene hydrochloride, ten cc. of methyl alcohol and seven and one-half cc. of amyl nitrite. Water is then added until the liquid commences to appear cloudy, when the nitrosochloride separates gradually. It is purified by dissolving in chloroform and precipitating with methyl alcohol. It melts at 109° (Wallach[3]).

Hydrochlorolimonene nitrosate,[3] $C_{10}H_{17}Cl \cdot NO(ONO_2)$, is prepared by treating a very cold mixture of one molecule of limonene hydrochloride and one molecule of amyl nitrite with one molecular proportion of sixty per cent. nitric acid. The mixture should be agitated during the addition of the nitric acid. The nitrosate separates as a white, crystalline precipitate. The yield can be increased by the final addition of alcohol. Hydrochlorolimonene

[1] Wallach and Kremers, Ann. Chem., *270*, 188.

[2] Semmler, Ber., 28, 2189.

[3] Wallach, Ann. Chem., *245*, 260.

6

nitrosate was first obtained by Maissen[1]; its constitution was explained by Wallach's investigation. It melts at 108° to 109°.

Hydrochlorolimonene nitrolamines,

$$C_{10}H_{17}Cl\langle{}^{NO}_{NHR}$$

Hydrochlorolimonene nitrosate is best employed for the preparation of these compounds, since it is more difficultly soluble, and more readily obtained than the corresponding nitrosochloride; the following general observation, however, should be noted in preparing these amines. It has been mentioned that limonene hydrochloride is readily converted into the inactive modification. Consequently, some inactive hydrochlorodipentene nitrosate is often obtained during the preparation of hydrochlorolimonene nitrosate.

If the preparation of the active hydrochlorolimonene nitrolamines be desired, the *most soluble portions* of hydrochlorolimonene nitrosate, prepared according to method described, are employed, since hydrochlorodipentene nitrosate is more difficultly soluble than the active modifications, and separates out before the active derivatives (Wallach[2]).

Hydrochlorolimonene nitrolbenzylamine,[2]

$$C_{10}H_{17}Cl\langle{}^{NO}_{NHCH_2C_6H_5}$$

is prepared by warming a mixture of five parts of hydrochlorolimonene nitrosate, ten parts of alcohol and four parts of benzylamine for a short time, until the reaction begins. The inactive dipentene base separates in fine needles on cooling. The active base is precipitated from the filtered solution by the addition of water. It is very readily soluble in alcohol, ether and benzene, only sparingly soluble in cold petroleum ether from which it is recrystallized. It is optically active, melts at 103° to 104°, and yields an optically active hydrochloride, which crystallizes from alcohol in fine needles, melting at 163° to 164.°

Hydrochlorolimonene nitrolanilide,[2]

$$C_{10}H_{17}Cl\langle{}^{NO}_{NHC_6H_5}$$

is conveniently prepared by the following method. Three and one-half cc. of aniline are added to a warm solution of five grams

[1] Maissen, Gazz. Chim., *13*, 99.
[2] Wallach, Ann. Chem., *270*, 191.

of hydrochlorolimonene nitrosate in thirty-five grams of benzene. Aniline nitrate is formed, and after a few minutes is filtered off; small quantities of inactive hydrochlorodipentene nitrolanilide separate with the aniline nitrate.

To obtain the hydrochlorolimonene nitrolanilide, the benzene filtrate is shaken with hydrochloric acid. The hydrochloride of the nitrolanilide separates as a solid, while the excess of aniline is taken up by the hydrochloric acid solution, and other impurities are dissolved in the benzene. The filtered hydrochloride is rubbed up with ammonium hydroxide, and the free nitrolamine crystallized from alcohol.

Hydrochlorolimonene nitrolanilide melts at 117° to 118°. A compound,

$$C_{10}H_{17}Cl\begin{cases}NO\\NHC_6H_5\end{cases}$$

obtained by the addition of hydrogen chloride to limonene nitrolanilide, melts at 115°; it has not been determined with certainty whether this compound is identical with hydrochlorolimonene nitrolanilide.[1]

When hydrochlorolimonene nitrolanilide is treated with alcoholic potash, tarry products are obtained from which no bases free of chlorine have yet been separated in a crystalline condition. (Compare with dipentene derivative, page 97.)

The *condensation-product*,[2] $C_{10}H_{18}O$, is produced by heating limonene and paraformaldehyde in alcoholic solution in a closed tube, at 190° to 195°, for several hours; it is a colorless liquid, boils at 246° to 250°, has the specific gravity 0.9568 at 20°, and its optical rotation corresponds to that of the limonene employed. Its *acetyl* derivative boils at 259° to 263°.

The action of nitrous fumes on dextro-limonene cooled by ice and salt gives rise to an alcohol, *limonenol*,[3] $C_{10}H_{15}OH$.

OXIDATION PRODUCTS OF LIMONENE.

The earlier publications[4] regarding the oxidation of limonene state that a chromic acid mixture converts limonene into carbonic anhydride, acetic acid, and a liquid camphor, $C_{10}H_{16}O$, but that nitric acid oxidizes it to oxalic acid and hesperic acid, $C_{20}H_{26}O_{17} + 2H_2O$. Tilden and Williamson[5] showed that when

[1] Wallach, Ann. Chem., *270*, 187 and 194.

[2] O. Kriewitz, Ber., *32*, 57.

[3] P. Genvresse, Compt. rend., *132*, 414.

[4] Wright, Jahresb. Chem., *1873*, 369; Sauer and Grünling, Ann. Chem., *208*, 75.

[5] Tilden and Williamson, Journ. Chem. Soc., *63* (1893), 293; *53* (1888), 880.

this terpene is oxidized with nitric acid, neither toluic acid nor terephthalic acid is formed.

G. Wagner[1] obtained a tetrahydric alcohol, *limonetrol*, $C_{10}H_{16}\cdot(OH)_4$, by the oxidation of limonene with potassium permanganate.

According to Godlewski,[2] *oxyterpenylic acid*, $C_8H_{12}O_5$, is produced, when limonene, free from carvone, is oxidized with potassium permanganate; it melts at 174.5°, and is identical with the acid obtained by Best[3] in the oxidation of carvone with permanganate. The *dilactone* of the acid, $C_8H_{10}O_4$, melts at 129° to 130°, and is reconverted into oxyterpenylic acid by the action of potassium hydroxide.

Semmler[4] has suggested that those terpene derivatives which contain a double linkage between the nucleus and the side chain shall be termed *pseudo*-derivatives, and the isomeric compounds containing the double bond in the nucleus, *ortho*-derivatives. In accordance with this suggestion, limonene, which is regarded as having the formula,

```
      CH3
       |
       C
     // \
   HC    CH2
    |     |
  H2C    CH2
     \  /
      CH
       |
       C
     /  \\
  H3C    CH2
```

should be called *ortho-limonene*. The isomeric, *pseudo-limonene*, would have the formula,

```
      CH2
       ||
       C
     /   \
  H2C    CH2
    |     |
  H2C    CH2
     \  /
      CH
       |
       C
     /  \\
  H3C    CH2
```

[1] G. Wagner, Ber., *1890*, 2315.
[2] J. Godlewsky, Chem. Centr., *1899* (I.), 1241; Journ. Russ. Chem. Soc., *31* (1899), 211.
[3] O. Best, Ber., *27*, 1218.
[4] F. Semmler, Ber., *33*, 1455.

Semmler thinks that it is not improbable that dipentene has the latter formula, and that it is not an inactive modification of limonene, as is generally assumed. He further states that both compounds would yield the same derivatives by the action of halogen acids. (In a subsequent investigation Semmler[1] concludes that terpinene is to be regarded as *pseudo-limonene.*)

It should also be mentioned that Baeyer[2] has succeeded in converting certain monocyclic terpenes into corresponding derivatives of benzene. Thus, limonene is converted into dipentene dihydrobromide by treatment with a glacial acetic acid solution of hydrogen bromide; the dry dihydrobromide is added to bromine, some iodine being introduced, and the mixture allowed to stand until no further evolution of hydrogen bromide is noticed. On treating the product with an alcoholic solution of hydrochloric acid and zinc dust, and then with sodium and alcohol, *para-cymene* is obtained.

The values for the rotatory powers of the limonene derivatives are given in the following table. These values were obtained in the extended investigations of Wallach, Conrady and Kremers.

The dextro- and levo-limonene derivatives agree completely in their power of rotation, provided they are obtained in a pure condition. A reversal in the direction of rotation takes place when salts are prepared from basic compounds, when limonene nitrosochloride is converted into carvoxime, and when β-nitrolamines are formed from the nitrosochlorides; the α-nitrolamines, which are formed together with the β-nitrolamines, rotate the plane of polarized light in the same direction as the original nitrosochlorides.

4b. DIPENTENE.

Dipentene is the optically inactive modification of limonene and bears the same relation to the latter as racemic acid to the optically active tartaric acids (Wallach).

Dipentene is widely distributed in many ethereal oils, and is also formed by heating different terpenes and polyterpenes to a high temperature. According to its source, it has been described under various names, such as di-isoprene, terpilene, caoutchin, cinene, cajeputene, isoterebentene, etc. Wallach[3] showed, however, that all these substances contain dipentene as their principal constituent, and are, therefore, to be regarded as identical.

[1]Semmler, Ber., *34*, 708.

[2]Baeyer and Villiger, Ber., *31*, 1401.

[3]Wallach and Brass, Ann. Chem., *225*, 309; Wallach, Ann. Chem., *225*, 314; *227*, 293.

Compounds of the Limonene Series.	Prepared from		Observer.
	Levo-limonene (—) $[\alpha]_D$	Dextro-limonene. (+) $[\alpha]_D$	
Limonene	— 105°	+ 106.80°	Wallach and Conrady, Ann. Chem., *252*, 141.
Limonene tetrabromide	— 73.45°	+ 73.27°	
α-Limonene nitrosochloride	— 314.80°	+ 313.40°	
β-Limonene nitrosochloride	— 242.20°	+ 240.30°	
Benzoyl limonene nitrosochloride	— 101.84°	+ 101.75°	Wallach and Macheleidt, Ann. Chem., *270*, 176.
α-Limonene nitrolanilide	— 102.62°	+ 101.97°	Wallach and Kremers, Ann, Chem., *270*, 182 and 189 and 192.
β-Limonene nitrolanilide	+ 87.17°	— 88.33°	
Nitroso-derivative of α-limonene nitrolanilide	— 47.82°	+ 46.20°	
α-Limonene nitrolpiperidide	— 67.60°	+ 67.75°	Wallach and Conrady.
β-Limonene nitrolpiperidide	+ 60.18°	— 60.48°	
α-Limonene nitrolbenzylamine	— 163.60°	+ 163.80°	
α-Limonene nitrolbenzylamine hydrochloride	+ 83.06°	— 82.26°	
α-Limonene nitrolbenzylamine nitrate	+ 81.00°	— 81.50°	
" " d-tartrate	+ 69.60°	— 49.90°	
" " l- "	+ 51.00°	— 69.90°	
Carvoxime	+ 39.71°	— 39.34°	
Limonene hydrochloride	+ 39.50°	— 40.00°	Wallach and Kremers.
Hydrochlorolimonene nitrolbenzylamine	— 147.40°	+ 149.60°	

Dipentene is contained in camphor oil,[1] Russian [3] and Swedish turpentine oil,[2] oil of pine needle from *Picea excelsa*,[3] oil of cubebs, oil of limetta leaf, oil of kesso-root, oil of olibanum,[4] oil of mace,[4] oil of wormwood,[1] oil of bergamot, oil of fennel, oil of kuromoji,[5] oil of myrtle, oil of pepper, oil of cardamom, oil of nutmeg, oil of golden rod, oil of massoy bark, oil of thyme (from *Thymus capitatus*), and oil of wormseed.

It is always formed when terpenes are heated to high temperatures, hence it is found in Russian and Swedish turpentine oils,[2] as well as in the products of the distillation of pine roots and fir-wood.[6] Dipentene is also obtained from the distillation products of vegetable resins, as copal resin, soft Elemi resin and colophonium.[7] Essence of resin also contains dipentene as shown by Renard's [8] experiments, which will be mentioned later.

Dipentene is produced under various conditions from many compounds of the terpene series. It is formed, together with higher boiling polymerides, by heating isoprene,[9] C_5H_8, at 250° to 270°; it is also found with isoprene in the products of the dry distillation of caoutchouc.[10] Pinene is converted into dipentene by heating to 250° to 270°.[12] Dipentene is obtained by mixing equal quantities of dextro- and levo-limonene;[11] limonene also becomes inactive by heating to high temperatures. A transformation of pinene into dipentene may also be effected by the action of dilute, or alcoholic, sulphuric acid.

Dipentene is derived from many oxidized compounds of the terpene series by the elimination of water. According to Wallach and Brass,[13] cineole, $C_{10}H_{18}O$, may be converted into dipentene by heating with hydrochloric acid gas, or by heating with benzoyl chloride, or by an indirect method depending on the formation of dipentene dihydriodide from cineole and hydriodic acid; by elimination of hydrogen iodide from this dihydriodide, dipentene is prepared. Terpine hydrate gives dipentene on warming with

[1] Wallach, Ann. Chem., *227*, 296.

[2] Wallach, Ann. Chem., *230*, 244 and 246.

[3] Bertram and Walbaum, Arch. Pharm., *231*, 290.

[4] Wallach, Ann. Chem., *252*, 100.

[5] Kwasnick, Ber., *24*, 81.

[6] Aschan and Hjelt, Chem. Ztg., *18*, 1566.

[7] Wallach and Rheindorf, Ann. Chem., *271*, 310.

[8] Renard, Ann. Chim. Phys. (6), 1, 223.

[9] Wallach, Ann. Chem., *227*, 295; Bouchardat, Compt. rend., *89*, 1217.

[10] Wallach, Ann. Chem., *227*, 295; Bouchardat, Compt. rend., *80*, 1446; *89*, 1217; Tilden, Journ. Chem. Soc., *1884* (45), 410; Jahresb. Chem., *1882*, 405.

[11] Wallach, Ann. Chem., *246*, 225.

[12] Wallach, Ann. Chem., *227*, 289.

[13] Wallach, Ann. Chem., *230*, 255.

acid potassium sulphate,[1] or by boiling with a twenty per cent. phosphoric acid solution. Terpineol, $C_{10}H_{17}OH$, yields dipentene when heated with acid potassium sulphate.[2]

Of especial interest is the formation of dipentene from linalool; according to Bertram and Walbaum,[3] the action of formic acid, sp. gr. 1.22, converts linalool, an unsaturated, optically active, aliphatic alcohol, into dipentene and terpinene.

All these methods of preparation of this terpene yield an impure product. In order to obtain chemically pure dipentene, the halogen hydride addition products are employed, the dihydrochloride being particularly well adapted. Hydrochloric acid may be eliminated from this substance by boiling with aniline,[4] or better with sodium acetate.

PREPARATION.[5]—One part by weight of dipentene dihydrochloride is boiled with one part of anhydrous sodium acetate and two parts of glacial acetic acid for half an hour in a flask provided with a reflux condenser. The product is distilled with steam, the volatile oil separated and boiled for some time with potassium hydroxide; it is then redistilled with steam, dried and purified by fractional distillation (Wallach).

PROPERTIES.—Since dipentene is inactive limonene, the boiling points of both compounds, when pure, are the same. The bibliographical references, however, give the boiling point of dipentene rather higher than that of limonene. These differences are to be traced to the varying degrees of purity of the hydrocarbons. Wallach found the boiling point of dipentene, prepared from the dihydrochloride by means of aniline, to be 178°; it had the specific gravity of 0.845 at 20° and the refractive index, $n_\epsilon = 1.47308$.[6]

A relatively pure dipentene, prepared by the dry distillation of caoutchouc, boils at 175° to 176°, has the sp. gr. 0.844 and the refractive index, $n_D = 1.47194$, at 20° (Schimmel & Co.).

According to Tilden and Williamson,[7] dipentene, obtained from the dihydrochloride by the action of aniline, contains cymene, terpinene, terpinolene and a saturated hydrocarbon similar to paraffin; when oxidized with nitric acid it gives a considerable quantity of toluic acid.

[1]Wallach, Ann. Chem., *230*, 255.
[2]Wallach, Ann. Chem., *275*, 104; *291*, 342.
[3]Bertram and Walbaum, Journ. pr. Chem., N. F., *45*, 601.
[4]Wallach, Ann. Chem., *227*, 286; *245*, 196.
[5]Wallach, Ann. Chem., *239*, 3.
[6]Wallach, Ann. Chem., *245*, 197.
[7]Tilden and Williamson, Journ. Chem. Soc., *1893* (63), 292.

Dipentene polymerizes at high temperatures without previous conversion into an isomeric terpene. It is, therefore, characterized by its relative stability; but, nevertheless, it may be changed into terpinene.[1]

This transformation into terpinene, accompanied by a considerable polymerization of the terpene, takes place when dipentene is warmed with alcoholic sulphuric acid. Further, if dipentene dihydrochloride be boiled with alcohol for some time, terpinene is produced by the withdrawal of hydrochloric acid. These reactions indicate that terpinene, which is always obtained together with dipentene by boiling terpine hydrate or terpineol with concentrated mineral acids, is a secondary product, resulting from the dipentene primarily formed. On shaking with an equal volume of concentrated sulphuric acid, dipentene is converted into cymeme sulphonic acid and cymeme, with evolution of sulphur dioxide; cymene also results by the action of phosphorus pentasulphide on dipentene.

The following derivatives of dipentene, without exception, may be prepared not only from dipentene, but also by combining equal parts by weight of the corresponding dextro- and levo-limonene derivatives.

Dipentene hydrochloride,[2] $C_{10}H_{16}.HCl$, is obtained by the same method as limonene hydrochloride; it is likewise formed when equal volumes of dextro- and levo-limonene hydrochlorides are mixed (Wallach[3]). This compound, like its active components, is not changed by *dry* hydrogen chloride; with moist hydrochloric acid, it forms dipentene dihydrochloride. It forms additive products with bromine, nitrosyl chloride, etc. It is only distinguished from limonene hydrochloride by its lack of optical activity.

Dipentene dihydrochloride, $C_{10}H_{16}.2HCl$, is formed by the action of moist hydrochloric acid on numerous compounds of the terpene series which are related to dipentene. It is obtained by saturating the alcoholic, ethereal or acetic acid solution of dipentene, and also of pinene and limonene, with hydrochloric acid gas. It further results by the action of hydrochloric acid on terpine hydrate, terpineol and cineole.

In order to prepare dipentene dihydrochloride, dilute limonene with one-half its volume of glacial acetic acid, and pass a current of hydrochloric acid gas *over, not into,* the well cooled liquid, with frequent shaking. Every rise in temperature of the liquid, which would lead to the formation of oily by-products, may thus

[1] Wallach, Ann. Chem., *239*, 15.

[2] Wallach, Ann. Chem., *245*, 247; *270*, 188.

[3] Wallach, Ann. Chem., *270*, 189; *245*, 247; Riban, Jahresb. Chem., *1874*, 397; Bouchardat, Bull. Soc. Chim., *24*, 108.

be prevented. As soon as the mass becomes solid, shake with water, filter, press on a porous plate, and purify the product by dissolving in alcohol and precipitating with water (Wallach [1]).

Dipentene dihydrochloride melts at 50°, and boils at 118° to 120° under a pressure of 10 mm.[2] It is easily soluble in alcohol, ether, chloroform, ligroine, benzene, and glacial acetic acid. Its conversion into dipentene, as well as its transformation into terpinene by boiling with alcohol, has already been mentioned; on standing with alcohol, terpine hydrate is formed. The products of the action of sodium, and sodium ethylate on this compound have been investigated by Montgolfier,[3] and Tilden.[4] By warming with a little ferric chloride solution, dipentene dihydrochloride gives a rose color, which passes into a violet-red and finally into a blue (Riban).

This dipentene dihydrochloride belongs to the *trans*-series. According to Baeyer,[5] a *cis*-dipentene dihydrochloride, melting at about 25°, is obtained if a well cooled glacial acetic acid solution of cineole be treated with hydrochloric acid.

Monochlorodipentene dihydrochloride,[6] $C_{10}H_{17}Cl_3$, is obtained when dry chlorine is conducted into a solution of dipentene dihydrochloride in three times its amount of carbon bisulphide; the chlorination is best performed in the direct sunlight, or after the addition of some aluminium chloride to the solution. The liquid first becomes cloudy, and then exceedingly warm; during the course of the reaction a violent evolution of hydrogen chloride takes place. The chlorinating action is continued until the liquid appears clear, and has a yellow color. If the operation is successful, the carbon bisulphide is allowed to evaporate, and the resulting crystalline product is pressed on a porous plate and recrystallized from alcohol. In other cases, the trichloride is separated from admixed dipentene dihydrochloride and tetrachloride, the latter remaining in the residue, by fractional distillation in vacuum; the trichloride boils at 145° to 150° under 10 mm. pressure. It crystallizes from alcohol in brilliant, white leaflets, which melt at 87°.

The behavior of this trichloride and of the corresponding bromine derivative towards reagents capable of eliminating halogen hydrides is quite different. Thus, when monobromodipentene

[1] Wallach, Ann. Chem., *245*, 267.
[2] Wallach, Ann. Chem., *270*, 198.
[3] Montgolfier, Ann. Chim. Phys. (5), *19*, 155.
[4] Tilden, Jahresb. Chem., *1878*, 639.
[5] Baeyer, Ber., *26*, 2863.
[6] Wallach and Hesse, Ann. Chem., *270*, 196.

dihydrobromide, which melts at 110° and is prepared from dipentene dihydrobromide, is treated with alcoholic potash, a hydrocarbon, $C_{10}H_{14}$, is obtained; the trichloride, however, yields a product consisting principally of an *unsaturated, liquid dipentene dichloride* when it is submitted to the action of sodium alcoholate or sodium acetate (Wallach and Hesse[1]). This liquid dichloride was not obtained pure, but was converted into the original trichloride (m. p. 87°) by the action of hydrochloric acid; with bromine, it gave a compound, $C_{10}H_{16}Cl_2Br_2$, melting at 98°. It formed a *nitrosochloride*, melting at 111°, which was converted into a *nitrolanilide*,

$$C_{10}H_{16}Cl_2\langle^{NO}_{NHC_6H_5}$$

melting at 140° to 141°, and a *nitrolpiperidide*, melting at 147° and crystallizing from alcohol in brilliant tablets.

Dichlorodipentene dihydrochloride, $C_{10}H_{16}Cl_4$, is prepared when dipentene dihydrochloride, or the above-described trichloride, is dissolved in carbon bisulphide and treated with chlorine for a long time; the reaction-products are then distilled in vacuum. The fraction boiling at 160° to 165° contains most of the tetrachloride, and solidifies in the cold. This compound is separated from admixed trichloride by means of petroleum ether, and is recrystallized from ethyl acetate; it melts at 108° (Wallach and Hesse[1]).

Dipentene dihydrobromide, $C_{10}H_{16}\cdot 2HBr$, was first obtained by Oppenheim[2] by treating terpine with phosphorus tribromide. Hell and Ritter[3] prepared the same compound by the action of hydrobromic acid on wormseed oil. According to Wallach,[4] dipentene dihydrobromide is formed by the addition of hydrogen bromide to dipentene and limonene, or by the treatment of terpine with hydrobromic acid. The dipentene dihydrobromide, prepared in a manner similar to that of the trans-dipentene dihydrochloride, melts at 64°, and, according to Baeyer, belongs to the trans-series.

Cis-dipentene dihydrobromide is produced as a by-product by some of the above-mentioned methods of preparation of the trans-compound. It is formed in exceedingly large quantities in the action of a glacial acetic acid solution of hydrobromic acid on a well cooled solution of cineole in glacial acetic acid (Baeyer[5]).

[1] Wallach and Hesse, Ann. Chem., *270*, 196.
[2] Oppenheim, Jahresb. Chem., *1862*, 459.
[3] Hell and Ritter, Ber., *17*, 2610.
[4] Wallach, Ann. Chem., *239*, 12.
[5] Baeyer, Ber., *26*, 2863.

The melting point of this compound is about 39°. If the solution is not well cooled during the preparation of this substance, the trans-compound is formed in large quantities.

When cis-dipentene dihydrobromide is treated with silver acetate in an acetic acid solution, the acetate of the long known terpine hydrate (cis-terpine hydrate, m. p. 117.5°) is formed. Under the same conditions, trans-dipentene dihydrobromide (m. p. 64°) yields the acetate of a new crystalline, anhydrous terpine, melting at 156° to 158°, which is termed trans-terpine (Baeyer).

Dipentene is formed by the elimination of hydrobromic acid from the trans-, as well as from the cis-, dipentene dihydrobromide.

Monobromodipentene dihydrobromide, $C_{10}H_{17}Br_3$ (according to Baeyer, 1, 4, 8-tribromoterpane), is derived from dipentene dihydrobromide. As one or two hydrogen atoms in dipentene dihydrochloride may be replaced by chlorine, so higher brominated derivatives of dipentene may be prepared from dipentene dihydrobromide by substitution. Among these, the tribromide is characterized by its power of crystallization.

In order to prepare this compound, two hundred grams of dipentene dihydrobromide, contained in a flask, are covered with 400 cc. of glacial acetic acid, and thirty-four cc. (not more!) of bromine are added to the slightly cooled mass, with constant agitation. During this process the temperature should not rise too high, but, nevertheless, must increase to such an extent that all dipentene dihydrobromide is dissolved. The liquid is allowed to stand until the color of the bromine has disappeared, and is then poured into a crystallizing dish; three hundred cc. of absolute alcohol are added, and the whole is allowed to remain for one day at the lowest possible temperature. The preparation is most successful in the winter.

The resultant crystals are collected; water is added to the mother-liquor, and the heavy oil which separates is washed with water, and dissolved in an equal volume of methyl alcohol. Additional quantities of the solid tribromide are obtained by placing this solution in a freezing mixture. The yield of the crude tribromide is about one-third of the weight of the dihydrobromide employed. It is purified by dissolving fifty grams of the product in one hundred cc. of warm acetic ether, and subsequently adding twenty-five cc. of methyl alcohol. The tribromide separates in brilliant, white leaflets, which melt at 110° (Wallach[1]).

Baeyer[2] obtained the same tribromide by the addition of hydrobromic acid to terpinolene dibromide.

[1]Wallach, Ann. Chem., *264*, 25.
[2]Baeyer, Ber., 27, 450.

If fifty grams of the tribromide are warmed with a solution of twelve grams of sodium is one hundred and fifty cc. of alcohol, an *unsaturated hydrocarbon*, $C_{10}H_{14}$, isomeric with cymene, results; it boils at 183° to 184°, has the specific gravity of 0.863 at 20°, the refractive index, $n_D = 1.49693$, and the molecular refraction, 45.435 (Wallach[1]).

Tetrabromide,[1] $C_{10}H_{14}Br_4$.—The above-mentioned hydrocarbon, $C_{10}H_{14}$, forms oily addition-products with the halogen hydrides; it yields no crystalline derivatives with the oxides of nitrogen. On the other hand, a characteristic additive compound with bromine is obtained if bromine be added to a cold solution of the hydrocarbon in a mixture of ten volumes of glacial acetic acid and a little alcohol. The resulting, sparingly soluble bromide, $C_{10}H_{14}Br_4$, separates from ethyl acetate in asymmetric crystals, which melt at 154° to 155°.

A readily soluble bromide, $C_{10}H_{14}Br_4$ (or $C_{10}H_{16}Br_4$?), melting at 103° to 104°, is formed as a by-product during the bromination of the hydrocarbon, $C_{10}H_{14}$.

Baeyer[2] found that by reducing the above-described tribromide, $C_{10}H_{17}Br_3$, melting point 110°, with zinc dust and glacial acetic acid, the mixture being well cooled, the liquid acetate of a crystalline alcohol, $C_{10}H_{17}OH$, melting at 69° to 70°, is formed. In accordance with Baeyer's proposed nomenclature, this alcohol is called Δ 4(8)-terpen (1)-ol:

```
        CH3
        |
        C—OH
       / \
   H2C     CH2
    |       |
   H2C     CH2
       \ /
        C
        ||
        C
       / \
    CH3   CH3
```

The tribromide (m. p. 110°) is obtained by the action of hydrobromic acid on the dibromide of this alcohol (terpenol), as well as on the dibromide of its acetate.

If the reduction of tribromoterpane (m. p. 110°) be performed with zinc dust in an alcoholic solution, the bromide, $C_{10}H_{17}Br$ (1-bromo-Δ (8)-terpene), corresponding to the terpenol above mentioned, is formed. It melts at 34° to 35°, and yields a blue nitrosobromide, which melts at 44° (Baeyer and Blau[3]).

[1] Wallach, Ann. Chem., *264*, 25.

[2] Baeyer, Ber., *27*, 444.

[3] Baeyer and Blau, Ber., *28*, 2290.

Dipentene dihydriodide, $C_{10}H_{16}\cdot 2HI$, results if hydriodic acid be passed through well cooled cineole. When the reaction is complete, the crystalline mass is filtered by a pump, washed with a little alcohol, and recrystallized from petroleum ether (Wallach and Brass[1]). Dipentene dihydriodide is also very conveniently prepared from terpine hydrate, if this compound be well agitated in the cold with a concentrated aqueous solution of hydriodic acid (Wallach[2]). It may further be obtained from pinene, limonene, dipentene and terpineol by methods analogous to those for the preparation of the dihydrochloride and dihydrobromide.[3]

When recrystallized from petroleum ether, dipentene dihydriodide exhibits two different crystalline forms; it sometimes crystallizes in rhombic prisms, melting point 77°, often in monoclinic tablets melting at 78° to 79° (Hintze[4]).

After Baeyer discovered that dipentene dihydrochloride and dihydrobromide exist in cis- and trans-modifications, the presumption followed that the difference in the two modifications of dipentene dihydriodide could be explained in a similar manner. Wallach[5] found, however, that this conjecture was not confirmed; moreover, he showed that both crystallographically different modifications of trans-dipentene dihydriodide are formed by the action of phosphorus triiodide on terpine, and that at the same time small quantities of a compound, melting at 50°, are produced; the latter substance is much more readily soluble in petroleum ether than the trans-derivative, and is to be regarded as cis-dipentene dihydriodide.

Dipentene dihydriodide is readily soluble in ether, benzene, chloroform and carbon bisulphide, more sparingly in cold alcohol. It is rather unstable; iodine is readily and completely removed from it by an alcoholic silver nitrate solution. It can not, therefore, be long preserved, but remains for some time undecomposed if kept under water with a small piece of phosphorus.

With aniline, alcoholic potash or sodium acetate, dipentene dihydriodide yields dipentene.[6]

Dipentene tetrabromide,[7] $C_{10}H_{16}Br_4$, is prepared in a perfectly similar manner to limonene tetrabromide. It has a certain historical interest in so far as its discovery marks the beginning of

[1] Wallach and Brass, Ann. Chem., *225*, 300.
[2] Wallach, Ann. Chem., *230*, 249.
[3] Wallach, Ann. Chem., *239*, 13.
[4] Hintze, Ann. Chem., *239*, 14.
[5] Wallach, Ber., *26*, 3072; Ann. Chem., *252*, 128.
[6] Wallach, Ann. Chem., *281*, 243.
[7] Wallach and Brass, Ann. Chem., *225*, 305; *227*, 279; *246*, 226.

Wallach's investigations. It should also be mentioned that, almost simultaneous with Wallach, Renard[1] obtained a solid tetrabromide, melting at 120°, from a terpene boiling at 170° to 173° which occurs in essence of resin; this bromide is without doubt to be regarded as impure dipentene tetrabromide.

Dipentene tetrabromide crystallizes from acetic ether in very characteristic rhombic crystals, which are more sparingly soluble in ether than those of limonene tetrabromide. They melt at 125° to 126°, are brittle, and show reed-like striations on the faces in the vertical zone (Hintze[2]).

According to Baeyer,[3] dipentene tetrabromide is formed indirectly from terpineol. Terpineol (m. p. 35°) is first converted into its liquid dibromide,[4] and this in turn is changed into a liquid 1, 2, 4-tribromoterpane, $C_{10}H_{17}Br_3$, by the action of hydrobromic acid. When the tribromoterpane is dissolved in glacial acetic acid and treated with two atoms of bromine, a bromide, melting at 124°, is obtained whose crystals, according to crystallographic measurement by Villiger, are "undoubtedly" identical with the crystals of dipentene tetrabromide measured by Hintze.[2]

It should, however, be mentioned that Hintze[4] has intimated that this identity does not appear to have been definitely proved by Villiger's results. On the other hand, Wallach[5] confirmed Baeyer's statement that dipentene tetrabromide results by the action of bromine on 1, 2, 4-tribromoterpane.

The products[6] obtained by the action of alcoholic potash on dipentene tetrabromide have not yet been carefully investigated.

Dipentene nitrosochlorides, $C_{10}H_{16} \cdot NOCl$, are known in two modifications, which are much more soluble, hence less characteristic, than the corresponding optically active compounds. *α*-Dipentene nitrosochloride, prepared by mixing the solutions of equal quantities by weight of dextro- and levo-*α*-limonene nitrosochloride, does not crystallize as well as the active modifications; when heated to 78°, it becomes liquid, again solidifies, and, on increasing the heat, melts at 103° to 104°. *β*-Dipentene nitrosochloride has not been isolated in a condition of purity; it is very readily soluble (Wallach[7]).

[1] Renard, Ann. Chim. Phys. (6), *1*, 223.
[2] Hintze, Ann. Chem., *227*, 279.
[3] Baeyer, Ber., *27*, 439.
[4] Hintze, Ann. Chem., *279*, 363.
[5] Wallach, Ann. Chem., *281*, 140.
[6] Wallach, Ann. Chem., *275*, 109.
[7] Wallach, Ann. Chem., *252*, 124; *270*, 175; *245*, 268.

When dipentene nitrosochloride is warmed with alcoholic potash, *inactive carvoxime*,[1] melting point 93°, is formed.

Benzoyl dipentene nitrosochloride,[2]

$$C_{10}H_{15}\begin{cases}Cl\\NOCOC_6H_5\end{cases}$$

is obtained by mixing the solutions of the corresponding active compounds. It melts at 90°, and is much more readily soluble than the active modifications.

Dipentene nitrosate, $C_{10}H_{16}\cdot NO(ONO_2)$, is prepared by adding three and one-half grams of nitric acid, sp. gr. 1.4, to a well cooled mixture of five grams of dipentene, four grams of amyl nitrite, and two cc. of glacial acetic acid; the resultant nitrosate is precipitated by successive additions of alcohol and a little water. It is recrystallized from benzene, and melts at 84°. It also yields inactive carvoxime when treated with alcoholic potash (Wallach [3]).

DIPENTENE NITROLAMINES.

The dipentene nitrolamines, like limonene nitrolamines, exist in two isomeric modifications, and are prepared from dipentene nitrosochloride, or by mixing the solutions of equal weights of the corresponding dextro- and levo-limonene nitrolamines (Wallach [4]).

α-Dipentene nitrolpiperidide,

$$C_{10}H_{16}\begin{cases}NO\\NC_5H_{10}\end{cases}$$

separates almost immediately when the petroleum ether solutions of the corresponding active bases, melting at 93° to 94°, are mixed. It crystallizes from alcohol in monoclinic crystals, which melt at 154°.

β-Dipentene nitrolpiperidide is similarly formed from the limonene bases, melting at 110°; it is more readily soluble than the α-dipentene nitrolpiperidide, and melts at 152°.

α-Dipentene nitrolanilide,

$$C_{10}H_{16}\begin{cases}NO\\NHC_6H_5\end{cases}$$

results by the union of the limonene bases, melting point 112° to 113°. It melts at 125° to 126°.

[1] Wallach, Ann. Chem., *245*, 268.
[2] Wallach, Ann. Chem., *270*, 177.
[3] Wallach, Ann. Chem., *245*, 270.
[4] Wallach, Ann. Chem., *252*, 123; *270*, 180.

β-Dipentene nitrolanilide is prepared from the limonene bases, melting at 159°. It melts at 149°.

Nitroso-dipentene-α-nitrolanilide,

$$C_{10}H_{16}\langle^{NO}_{N(NO)C_6H_5}$$

is more difficultly soluble than the corresponding limonene derivative. It melts at 147° with decomposition.

Nitroso-dipentene-β-nitrolanilide is very easily soluble, and melts at 129°.

α-Dipentene nitrolbenzylamine,

$$C_{10}H_{16}\langle^{NO}_{NHCH_2C_6H_5}$$

is distinguished from its active components, melting at 92° to 93°, by its superior power of crystallization. The base is obtained from dilute alcohol in monoclinic crystals, melting at 109° to 110°.

The compounds, $C_{10}H_{17}ClNO(NHC_6H_5)$, melting at 78° and resulting by the addition of hydrochloric acid to dextro- and levo-β-limonene nitrolanilide in a methyl alcohol solution, combine and yield a substance,[1] which belongs to the dipentene series and melts at 90°.

As has already been mentioned, hydrochlorodipentene nitrosochloride and hydrochlorodipentene nitrosate are contained, together with the corresponding active modifications, in the most insoluble parts of the compounds described as hydrochlorolimonene nitrosochloride and nitrosate. (See page 82.) Accordingly, the hydrochlorodipentene nitrolamines are obtained either from these difficultly soluble portions of hydrochlorodipentene nitrosate and thus result as by-products during the preparation of the corresponding active modifications, or they are prepared by mixing the active components.

Hydrochlorodipentene nitrolanilide,[2]

$$C_{10}H_{17}Cl\langle^{NO}_{NHC_6H_5}$$

is almost insoluble in cold alcohol, and melts at 140° to 141°. By the action of alcoholic potash on this amine, two bases containing no chlorine are obtained; one melts at 123° to 124° and yields a difficultly soluble hydrochloric acid salt, while the other

[1] Wallach, Ann. Chem., *270*, 188.

[2] Wallach, Ann. Chem., *270*, 195; *245*, 262.

melts at 158° and forms an easily soluble salt. According to Wallach, both bases closely resemble the α- and β-dipentene nitrolanilides, but whether they are identical with the latter compounds has not yet been determined.

Hydrochlorodipentene nitrolbenzylamine,[1]

$$C_{10}H_{17}Cl\begin{cases}NO\\NHCH_2C_6H_5\end{cases}$$

is almost insoluble in cold alcohol and is sparingly soluble in all other solvents. It melts at 150°.

Hydrochlorodipentene nitrol-p-toluidide,

$$C_{10}H_{17}Cl\begin{cases}NO\\NHC_6H_4CH_3\end{cases}$$

was represented by Wallach[2] as a limonene compound, but it has been proved by further investigation to belong to the dipentene series. It crystallizes with alcohol of crystallization, and melts at 135°. It is precipitated from its solution in benzene by petroleum ether as a white mass, which melts at 145° to 146°.

Two compounds should be mentioned which Wallach obtained by the action of dimethyl aniline and ethyl or methyl alcohol on a substance called "hydrochlorolimonene nitrosate"; this substance consists to some extent of hydrochlorodipentene nitrosate.[3] According to Wallach, dimethyl aniline acts only in the elimination of hydrochloric acid, while the ONO_2-group appears to be replaced by the ethoxyl- or methoxyl-group.

The *compound*,

$$C_{12}H_{22}NO_2Cl = C_{10}H_{17}Cl\begin{cases}NO\\OC_2H_5\end{cases}$$

forms splendid crystals, which melt at 114° to 115°.

The *compound*,

$$C_{11}H_{20}NO_2Cl = C_{10}H_{17}Cl\begin{cases}NO\\OCH_3\end{cases}$$

crystallizes in prisms, melting at 139°.

A *condensation-product*,[4] $C_{11}H_{18}O$, is formed by heating an alcoholic solution of dipentene and paraformaldehyde in a sealed tube

[1] Wallach, Ann. Chem., *270*, 193.
[2] Wallach, Ann. Chem., *245*, 263.
[3] Wallach, Ann. Chem., *245*, 265.
[4] O. Kriewitz, Ber., *32*, 57.

at 190° to 195°, for several hours; it boils at 242° to 248°, and has the specific gravity 0.9459 at 20°. Its *acetyl* derivative boils at 258° to 261°.

The following table presents a convenient synopsis of the most important derivatives of limonene and dipentene, and of the relations of these substances to oxygenated compounds of the terpene series.

5. SYLVESTRENE.

Sylvestrene was discovered by Atterberg[1] in Swedish turpentine oil; Wallach[2] confirmed this observation, and at the same time found sylvestrene to occur in Russian turpentine oil. Aschan and Hjelt[3] further recognized it in the products of the distillation of pine roots, and Bertram and Walbaum[4] detected it in the pine needle oils from *Pinus montana* and *Pinus silvestris*.

For the preparation of sylvestrene, the fraction boiling at 174° to 178° of Swedish oil of turpentine is employed. This is diluted with an equal volume of ether, saturated with hydrochloric acid gas and, after one to two days standing, the ether is distilled off, and the residue allowed to crystallize in an extremely cold place.

The preparation of this compound is attended with the best results only in winter. The crude sylvestrene dihydrochloride, which is very soluble in the mother-liquor, is filtered by the pump, pressed on a porous plate, and dissolved in an equal weight of alcohol, in order to remove the admixed dipentene dihydrochloride. It crystallizes from the very cold, alcoholic solution, and is recrystallized from ether until it melts at 72°. The mother-liquors contain a mixture of sylvestrene- and dipentene-dihydrochlorides (Wallach[5]).

Pure sylvestrene is obtained by heating the dihydrochloride with an equal weight of aniline[6] and a small quantity of alcohol (Atterberg[1]), or better by boiling with the same weight of fused sodium acetate and twice its weight of glacial acetic acid for half an hour in a flask fitted with an upright condenser.[5] The hydrocarbon is distilled with steam, heated with a potassium hydroxide solution, again distilled with steam, and fractionated.

[1]Atterberg, Ber., *10*, 1202.
[2]Wallach, Ann. Chem., *230*, 240 and 247.
[3]Aschan and Hjelt, Chem. Ztg., *18*, 1566.
[4]Bertram and Walbaum, Arch. Pharm., *231*, 290.
[5]Wallach, Ann. Chem., *239*, 24.
[6]Wallach, Ann. Chem., *247*, 197.

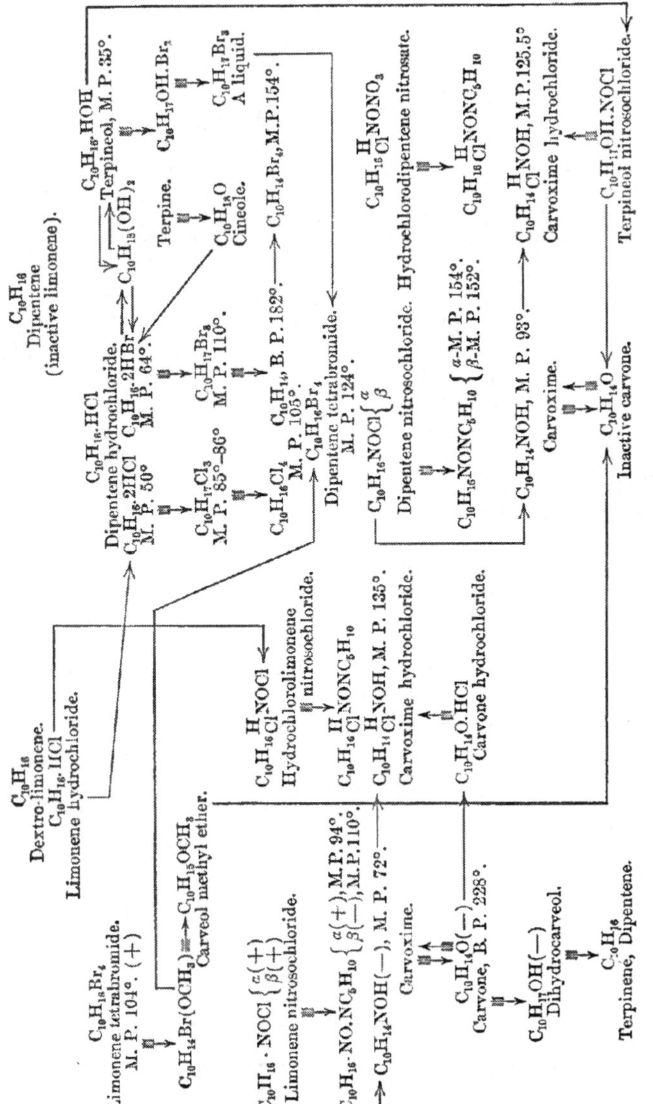
$C_{10}H_{16}$
Dextro-limonene.
$C_{10}H_{16}.HCl$
Limonene hydrochloride.
$C_{10}H_{16}Br_4$
Limonene tetrabromide.
M. P. 104°. (+)
$C_{10}H_{14}Br(OCH_3)$
$C_{10}H_{15}OCH_3$
Carveol methyl ether.
$C_{10}H_{16}\cdot NOCl \left\{ \begin{matrix} \alpha(+) \\ \beta(+) \end{matrix} \right.$
Limonene nitrosochloride.
$C_{10}H_{16}\cdot NO.NC_5H_{10} \left\{ \begin{matrix} \alpha(+), M.P. 94°. \\ \beta(-), M.P. 110°. \end{matrix} \right.$
$C_{10}H_{14}NOH(-)$, M. P. 72°.
Carvoxime.
$C_{10}H_{14}O(-)$
Carvone, B. P. 228°.
$C_{10}H_{17}OH(-)$
Dihydrocarveol.
$C_{10}H_{16}$
Terpinene, Dipentene.
$C_{10}H_{16}{}^{H}_{Cl}NOCl$
Hydrochlorolimonene nitrosochloride.
$C_{10}H_{16}{}^{H}_{Cl}NONC_5H_{10}$
$C_{10}H_{14}{}^{H}_{Cl}NOH$, M. P. 135°.
Carvoxime hydrochloride.
$C_{10}H_{14}O.HCl$
Carvone hydrochloride.
$C_{10}H_{16}$
Dipentene
(inactive limonene).
$C_{10}H_{16}.HCl$
Dipentene hydrochloride.
$C_{10}H_{16}.2HCl$
M. P. 50°
$C_{10}H_{16}.2HBr$
M. P. 64°.
$C_{10}H_{16}.HOH$
Terpineol, M. P. 35°.
$C_{10}H_{18}(OH)_2$
Terpine.
$C_{10}H_{17}OH.Br_2$
$C_{10}H_{17}Cl_3$
M. P. 85°–86°
$C_{10}H_{17}Br_3$
M. P. 110°.
$C_{10}H_{18}O$
Cineole.
$C_{10}H_{17}Br_3$
A liquid.
$C_{10}H_{16}Cl_4$
$C_{10}H_{14}$, B. P. 182°.
M. P. 105°.
$C_{10}H_{14}Br_4$, M.P. 154°.
$C_{10}H_{16}Br_4$
Dipentene tetrabromide.
M. P. 124°.
$C_{10}H_{16}NOCl \left\{ \begin{matrix} \alpha \\ \beta \end{matrix} \right.$
Dipentene nitrosochloride.
$C_{10}H_{16}{}^{H}_{Cl}NONO_3$
Hydrochlorodipentene nitrosate.
$C_{10}H_{16}NONC_5H_{10} \left\{ \begin{matrix} \alpha\text{-M. P. 154°.} \\ \beta\text{-M. P. 152°.} \end{matrix} \right.$
$C_{10}H_{16}{}^{H}_{Cl}NONC_5H_{10}$
$C_{10}H_{14}NOH$, M. P. 93°.
Carvoxime.
$C_{10}H_{14}{}^{H}_{Cl}NOH$, M.P. 125.5°
Carvoxime hydrochloride.
$C_{10}H_{14}O$
Inactive carvone.
$C_{10}H_{17}OH.NOCl$
Terpineol nitrosochloride.

PROPERTIES.—Sylvestrene has a very agreeable odor, which is somewhat similar to that of lemons, but for the most part resembles that of the oil of bergamot. It boils at 176° to 177°, has the sp. gr. of 0.8510 at 16°, and the refractive index, $n_c = 1.47468$.[1] Another specimen boiled at 175° to 176°, and at 20° had the sp. gr. of 0.848 and the refractive index, $n_D = 1.47573$.[2] Sylvestrene is optically dextrorotatory. The specimen above referred to had the specific rotatory power, $[\alpha]_D = +66.32°$.[2]

The addition of a drop of concentrated sulphuric acid (or fuming sulphuric acid) to a solution of one drop of sylvestrene in acetic anhydride produces a deep blue coloration. A similar reaction is shown only by carvestrene; all other terpenes under like conditions give a red to yellowish-red coloration. This sylvestrene reaction, therefore, is produced only by mixtures of terpenes which contain considerable quantities of sylvestrene (Wallach[3]).

Sylvestrene is one of the most stable of the terpenes. On heating to 250° it is partially polymerized, without a previous transformation into other terpenes. In a similar manner alcoholic sulphuric acid appears to merely change it into resinous products, but also without previous conversion into isomerides.

Sylvestrene dihydrochloride, $C_{10}H_{16}\cdot 2HCl$.—The formation of this compound from Swedish turpentine oil has already been suggested. It may further be prepared direct from pure sylvestrene by saturating the cold, *dry* hydrocarbon with *dry* hydrochloric acid gas, or more conveniently and readily by adding a solution of hydrochloric acid in glacial acetic acid to a solution of sylvestrene in glacial acetic acid, and then pouring the liquid into cold water.[3]

Sylvestrene dihydrochloride crystallizes in monosymmetric tablets, which melt at 72° and have a specific rotatory power, $[\alpha]_D = +18.99°$[2].

Sylvestrene dihydrobromide,[4] $C_{10}H_{16}\cdot 2HBr$, is obtained in a similar manner to the dihydrochloride; it crystallizes in monoclinic crystals, melts at 72°, and possesses the specific rotatory power,[2] $[\alpha]_D = +17.89°$.

Sylvestrene dihydriodide,[4] $C_{10}H_{16}\cdot 2HI$, is prepared like the two

[1] Wallach and Pulfrich, Ann. Chem., *245*, 197.
[2] Wallach and Conrady, Ann. Chem., *252*, 149.
[3] Wallach, Ann. Chem., *239*, 27.
[4] Wallach, Ann. Chem., *239*, 28.

preceding compounds, and crystallizes from petroleum ether in small plates, which melt at 66° to 67°.

Sylvestrene tetrabromide,[1] $C_{10}H_{16}Br_4$.—This compound can only be obtained from *pure* sylvestrene, regenerated from the dihydrochloride. Bromine is slowly added to a cold solution of the terpene in glacial acetic acid until a yellow color is produced, and after the addition of a small quantity of water to the reaction-mixture, it is allowed to stand in an open vessel in a cold place; crystals separate, and are purified by recrystallization from ethyl acetate or ether. Sylvestrene tetrabromide is so obtained in the form of monosymmetric crystals, which melt at 135° to 136°, and are optically dextrorotatory. Wallach and Conrady found the specific rotatory power, $[\alpha]_D = + 73.74°$.

Considerable amounts of an oily tetrabromide are always formed, together with the solid compound; this is probably the reason why sylvestrene can not be separated in the form of its tetrabromide from mixtures of sylvestrene and other ethereal oils.

Sylvestrene nitrosochloride, $C_{10}H_{16} \cdot NOCl$, is prepared from pure sylvestrene, obtained from its dihydrochloride, by the following method. To a well cooled mixture of four cc. of the terpene and six cc. of amyl nitrite, four cc. or five cc. of fuming hydrochloric acid are added with constant agitation. When the heavy oil which separates is shaken with a little ethyl alcohol, it solidifies to a crystalline mass. It is purified by dissolving in a small quantity of chloroform and precipitating with petroleum ether; the product is then recrystallized from methyl alcohol. It melts at 106° to 107°, and is dextrorotatory (Wallach[2]).

Sylvestrene nitrolbenzylamine,

$$C_{10}H_{16}\left\langle\begin{matrix}NO\\NHCH_2C_6H_5\end{matrix}\right.$$

is obtained by warming an alcoholic solution of sylvestrene nitrosochloride with benzylamine (Wallach[3]). The base separates from methyl alcohol in well defined crystals, melting at 71° to 72°. It has a specific rotatory power, $[\alpha]_D = + 185.6°$, while that of its hydrochloride is $[\alpha]_D = + 79.2°$.[4]

[1]Wallach, Ann. Chem., *239*, 28.
[2]Wallach, Ann. Chem., *245*, 272.
[3]Wallach, Ann. Chem., *252*, 135.
[4]Wallach and Conrady, Ann. Chem., *252*, 150.

According to Baeyer,[1] sylvestrene may be converted into *meta-cymene* by a method similar to that employed in the conversion of limonene into para-cymene. Dry sylvestrene dihydrobromide is brominated by bromine in the presence of iodine, and the resulting product is reduced with zinc dust and alcoholic hydrochloric acid, and finally with sodium and alcohol; a hydrocarbon is obtained, which, when freed from unsaturated compounds by the action of potassium permanganate, is identical with *meta-cymene.*

6. CARVESTRENE.

This optically inactive terpene was obtained by Baeyer[2] in the distillation of carylamine hydrochloride and vestrylamine hydrochloride. Since it has no rotatory power, and yields the sylvestrene reaction, Baeyer regards it as inactive sylvestrene. Its similarity with sylvestrene and its formation from a carvone derivative suggested the name carvestrene.

Wallach[3] obtained dihydrocarvone, $C_{10}H_{16}O$, by the oxidation of dihydrocarveol; subsequently, Baeyer[4] prepared the same compound by the reduction of carvone. Dihydrocarvone is converted into the isomeric ketone carone, $C_{10}H_{16}O$, by the successive addition and removal of hydrobromic acid (Baeyer[5]). When the oxime of this optically active carone is reduced with sodium and alcohol, it yields an active base carylamine, which in turn may be changed into the hydrochloride of an isomeric, but optically inactive, base, vestrylamine,[2] $C_{10}H_{17}NH_2$, by heating with hydrochloric acid.

When vestrylamine hydrochloride[2] is distilled in an atmosphere of dry hydrochloric acid gas, it decomposes into ammonium chloride and a hydrocarbon, $C_{10}H_{16}$, whilst carylamine hydrochloride, under the same conditions, partially volatilizes without change, but a little of it is converted into vestrylamine hydrochloride, which then yields the same hydrocarbon; the latter consists of crude carvestrene:

$$C_{10}H_{17}NH_2 \cdot HCl = NH_4Cl + C_{10}H_{16}.$$

The impure carvestrene is boiled for half an hour with fused sodium acetate and glacial acetate acid in order to destroy ad-

[1]Baeyer and Villiger, Ber., *31*, 2067.
[2]Baeyer, Ber., *27*, 3485.
[3]Wallach, Ann. Chem., *275*, 115; *279*, 378.
[4]Baeyer, Ber., *26*, 823.
[5]Baeyer, Ber., *27*, 1919.

mixed hydrochlorides. The resultant terpene boils at 180° to 186°, and gives the sylvestrene reaction (the addition of a drop of concentrated sulphuric acid to a solution of one drop of the terpene in one or two cc. of acetic anhydride produces a blue coloration). The product is then dissolved in glacial acetic acid, treated with an acetic acid solution of hydrogen bromide, and allowed to remain at a low temperature for forty-eight hours, since the addition of hydrobromic acid to carvestrene takes place very slowly. The reaction-mixture is poured onto ice; the resulting crystals are filtered, pressed on a plate and purified by recrystallizing from ether, to which a little glacial acetic acid is added. The dihydrobromide is readily soluble in ether, more sparingly in glacial acetic acid.

Pure carvestrene is formed by distilling the dihydrobromide with four parts of quinoline, and shaking the distillate with dilute sulphuric acid; the terpene remains undissolved, and is rectified over sodium.

PROPERTIES.[1]—Carvestrene has an odor somewhat like that of dipentene; it boils at 178° (corr.), and is optically inactive. Baeyer gives no statements relative to its specific gravity. It rapidly becomes resinous on exposure to air, and then smells like turpentine oil. It decolorizes potassium permanganate at once, and, like terpinene, is oxidized by chromic acid in the cold. It has already been suggested that since carvestrene gives the sylvestrene reaction, it is perhaps to be regarded as the optically inactive modification of sylvestrene.

According to Semmler,[2] the crude carvestrene, boiling at 180° to 186°, obtained by the elimination of ammonia from vestrylamine, probably contains some *pseudo-carvestrene;* while the pure terpene, boiling at 178°, prepared by heating the dihydrobromide with quinoline, is to be regarded as the true *ortho-carvestrene.*

Carvestrene dihydrochloride, $C_{10}H_{16} \cdot 2HCl$, is prepared by treating pure carvestrene (regenerated from the dihydrobromide) in a glacial acetic solution with hydrogen chloride, and, after standing for twenty-four hours, pouring the product onto ice. The heavy oil which separates solidifies on the addition of an extremely small crystal of the dihydrobromide. It crystallizes from glacial acetic acid in long prisms, and melts at 52.5°.

Carvestrene dihydrobromide, $C_{10}H_{16} \cdot 2HBr$, obtained by the method given above, crystallizes in well formed, rhombic tablets whose solid angles are truncated. These crystals may be easily

[1] Baeyer, Ber., *27*, 3490.
[2] Semmler, Ber., *34*, 708.

distinguished from those of the isomeric dipentene dihydrobromide. Carvestrene dihydrobromide melts at 48° to 50°, and is more readily soluble than dipentene dihydrobromide.

By the action of silver acetate and glacial acetic acid on the dihydrobromide, a terpine results, which melts at 127° and crystallizes in splendid, flat, rhombic pyramids.

Baeyer[1] has also succeeded in converting carvestrene into *metacymene* by the bromination of carvestrene dihydrobromide, and subsequent reduction with zinc and hydrochloric acid, and finally with sodium and alcohol.

7. TERPINOLENE.

Terpinolene is one of the terpenes which have not yet been found in nature. It was discovered, and characterized as a chemical individual, by Wallach [2] in 1885. He showed that when turpentine oil is heated with alcoholic sulphuric acid, according to Flawitzky's [3] method, a terpene is formed, which had hitherto been overlooked. According to further observations [4] of Wallach, terpinolene is obtained by boiling terpine hydrate, terpineol or cineole with dilute sulphuric acid or phosphoric acid. In all these reactions, terpinene and other products are formed; among the latter, cymene should be especially noted as it results whenever the sulphuric acid method is employed. Wallach and Kerkhoff[5] found that solid terpineol (m. p. 35°) is remarkably well adapted for the preparation of terpinolene, and that the formation of by-products can be prevented by using a solution of oxalic acid for the removal of the elements of water; however, it is well to boil for a short time only, since otherwise a conversion into terpinene results. Terpinolene may also be prepared with great facility by dissolving terpineol in anhydrous formic acid, and gently heating the liquid for a few minutes, when terpinolene separates rapidly.[6]

According to Baeyer,[7] terpinolene is formed from the tribromide, $C_{10}H_{17}Br_3$ (m. p. 110°), which is derived from dipentene dihydrobromide by bromination. This tribromide is converted into the acetate of Δ-4(8)-terpen-1-ol, an alcohol melting at 69°

[1] Baeyer and Villiger, Ber., *31*, 1402.
[2] Wallach, Ann. Chem., *227*, 283; *230*, 262.
[3] Flawitzky, Ber., *12*, 1022.
[4] Wallach, Ann. Chem., *239*, 23.
[5] Wallach and Kerkhoff, Ann. Chem., *275*, 106.
[6] Wallach, Ann. Chem., *291*, 342.
[7] Baeyer, Ber., *27*, 436.

to 70°, by the action of zinc dust and glacial acetic acid, and when this acetate is distilled with quinoline, terpinolene results:

$$C_{10}H_{17}OCOCH_3 - CH_3COOH = C_{10}H_{16}.$$

Baeyer expresses these transformations by the following formulas:

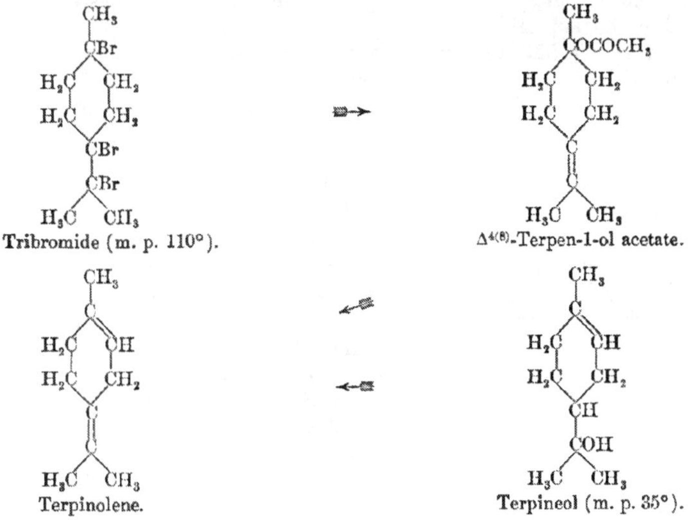

CH_3
CBr
H_2C CH_2
H_2C CH_2
CBr
CBr
H_3C CH_3
Tribromide (m. p. 110°).

→

CH_3
$COCOCH_3$
H_2C CH_2
H_2C CH_2
C
C
H_3C CH_3
$\Delta^{4(8)}$-Terpen-1-ol acetate.

CH_3
C
H_2C CH
H_2C CH_2
C
C
H_3C CH_3
Terpinolene.

←

CH_3
C
H_2C CH
H_2C CH_2
CH
COH
H_3C CH_3
Terpineol (m. p. 35°).

It is worthy of notice that terpinolene tetrabromide may be converted into terpinolene by treatment with zinc dust and glacial acetic acid.

Preparation.[1]—Melted terpineol (m. p. 35°) is added drop by drop to a boiling solution of oxalic acid (one part of acid to two parts of water) through which a current of steam is passing. The addition of the terpineol is so regulated that one gram is introduced every minute, thus accomplishing the decomposition almost completely, while the resulting terpinolene is at once removed from the action of the acid by means of the steam distillation. The oil so obtained is distilled in vacuum, since terpinolene is partially changed by distillation at ordinary pressure.

A purer product is obtained by treating terpinolene tetrabromide with zinc dust and glacial acetic acid at a low temperature.

Properties.—Terpinolene is an optically inactive hydrocarbon whose physical constants have not been determined because its instability prevents the preparation of a chemically pure product.

[1] Wallach and Kerkhoff, Ann. Chem., *275*, 106; Baeyer, Ber., *27*, 448.

According to Wallach,[1] it boils between 185° and 190°. Baeyer states that terpinolene prepared from the tetrabromide boils at 75° under 14 mm. pressure; on distilling under the ordinary pressure it boils at 183° to 185° (corr.), but by continued boiling for ten minutes in a flask connected with reflux condenser, terpinolene is changed into a thick oil which no longer gives the crystalline tetrabromide.

It is very sensitive toward acids, being converted into a product which consists largely of terpinene.

A solution of terpinolene in glacial acetic acid absorbs hydrochloric or hydrobromic acid, producing dipentene dihydrochloride or dihydrobromide.[1]

Terpinolene dibromide, $C_{10}H_{16}Br_2$.—Baeyer [2] obtained this compound from terpinolene (regenerated from the tetrabromide by means of zinc dust) by adding two atoms of bromine to the hydrocarbon dissolved in a mixture of alcohol and ether. On evaporation of the solution, the dibromide separates in beautiful prisms, which melt at 69° to 70°.

When the glacial acetic acid solution of terpinolene dibromide is treated with hydrobromic acid, the same tribromide (1, 4, 8-tribromoterpane, m. p. 110°) results which Wallach obtained by the bromination of dipentene dihydrobromide. This tribromide is further identified by its conversion into the characteristic, blue nitrosochloride of Δ-4-(8)-terpen-1-ol acetate, melting at 82° (Baeyer [2]).

Terpinolene tetrabromide, $C_{10}H_{16}Br_4$, was first prepared by Wallach by brominating terpinolene in a glacial acetic acid solution at a low temperature.[3] According to Baeyer and Villiger,[4] it is better to dilute crude terpinolene in portions of ten grams or less with an equal volume of amyl alcohol and twice its volume of ether, and then to add bromine to the well cooled mixture. After evaporation of the ether, the tetrabromide crystallizes in voluminous leaflets.

Optically inactive terpinolene tetrabromide crystallizes from ether in monoclinic tablets,[5] which melt at 116°. It is not a very stable compound; after keeping for some time it melts at a lower temperature, and changes into a porcelain-like mass, which, on crystallization from ether, yields only partially the pure tetrabromide.

[1] Wallach, Ann. Chem., *239*, 23.
[2] Baeyer, Ber., *27*, 447 and 448.
[3] Wallach, Ann. Chem., *227*, 283; *230*, 263; *239*, 23; *275*, 107.
[4] Baeyer and Villiger, Ber., *27*, 448.
[5] Hintze, Ann. Chem., *230*, 263.

When it is treated with zinc dust and glacial acetic acid, it is reverted into terpinolene (Baeyer); alcoholic potash seems to react less readily (Wallach and Kerkhoff).

8. PHELLANDRENE.

Phellandrene is characterized by its nitrosite, which was discovered by Cahours, and has, therefore, long been recognized as a constituent of many ethereal oils. The name phellandrene was introduced by Pesci,[1] who proved the presence of this terpene in the oil of water fennel (*Phellandrium aquaticum*). It is also a constituent of bitter fennel oil in which Cahours[2] discovered it, and which later served as the material for investigations regarding phellandrene nitrosite. The occurrence of phellandrene in these two oils was confirmed by Wallach,[3] who further showed that phellandrene occurs in the oil of elemi,[4] and that these three oils contain dextro-phellandrene whose nitrosite is levorotatory. Levo-phellandrene was afterwards discovered by Wallach and Gildemeister[5] in eucalyptus oil (*Eucalyptus amygdalina*); its nitrosite rotates the plane of polarization to the right. Bertram and Walbaum[6] found levo-phellandrene in the pine needle oils from *Pinus montana* and *Picea excelsa*, while Power and Kleber[7] proved its presence in bay oil. According to Wallach and Rheindorf,[8] dextro-phellandrene is contained in the distillation-products of the soft and hard elemi resins. The results of experiments performed in the laboratory of Schimmel & Co. indicate that phellandrene is widely distributed, and that it is contained in the following oils:—andropogon oil, angelica oil, bay oil, peppermint oil, camphor oil, curcuma oil, oils from sassafras bark and leaves, ginger oil, star anise oil, pepper oil, dill oil, wormwood oil, golden rod oil, lemon oil, olibanum oil and cinnamon oil.

Phellandrene is found in the fractions boiling at about 170° of the above-mentioned oils; a method for the preparation of pure phellandrene is not at present known. Oils containing this hydro-

[1]Pesci, Gazz. Chim., *16*, 225.

[2]Cahours, Ann. Chem., *41*, 74; compare Bunge, Zeitschr. Chem., *1869*, 579; Chiozza, Gerhardt's Lehrb., German edition, *3*, 394.

[3]Wallach, Ann. Chem., *239*, 40.

[4]Wallach, Ann. Chem., *246*, 233.

[5]Wallach and Gildemeister, Ann. Chem., *246*, 282 and 233.

[6]Bertram and Walbaum, Arch. Pharm., *231*, 290.

[7]Power and Kleber, Pharm. Rundschau, *1895*, No. 13; compare Schimmel's Semi-Annual Report, April, *1895*, 13; see also Pharm. Review, *1896*.

[8]Wallach and Rheindorf, Ann. Chem., *271*, 310.

carbon are fractionated in a vacuum[1] since it is partially decomposed by distillation at ordinary pressure.

PROPERTIES.—Phellandrene occurs in two modifications which are distinguished by opposite rotatory powers, and boils at about 170°. By the distillation of the oil of water fennel, Pesci[2] obtained a fraction which contained about eighty per cent. of phellandrene, boiled at 171° to 172°, had the specific gravity 0.8558 at 10° and the specific rotatory power, $[\alpha]_D = +17.64°$.

Wallach[4] found that phellandrene from an Australian eucalyptus oil boiled at 65° (12 mm.), had the sp. gr. 0.8465 and refractive index, $n_D = 1.488$, at 19°. Gildemeister and Stephan[3] found the optical rotation of phellandrene from schinus oil to be $[\alpha]_D = +60° 21'$.

It is one of the most unstable of the terpenes. If the fractions of the oils of fennel which contain phellanderne are saturated with hydrobromic acid, a violent reaction takes place, and when the reaction-product is poured into water, a heavy oil separates; this oil yields dipentene by heating with sodium acetate and glacial acetic acid. If the same fractions of the fennel oils are warmed with alcoholic sulphuric acid, the phellandrene is converted into terpinene (Wallach[5]). Although the substances which occur together with phellandrene in the fennel oils influence to some extent the character of the products resulting in the above-mentioned reactions, nevertheless it is remarkable that in both cases no trace of phellandrene can be detected in the reaction-products.

Phellandrene dibromide[1] is an oil, and is probably a mixture. It yields considerable cymene by boiling with alcoholic potash.

Phellandrene nitrosite,[6] $C_{10}H_{16} \cdot N_2O_3$, is prepared by adding a solution of five grams of sodium nitrite in eight cc. of water to a solution of five cc. of the fraction of the ethereal oil containing phellandrene in ten cc. of petroleum ether, and then adding slowly, with constant stirring, five cc. of glacial acetic acid. The resulting crystals are filtered, washed with water and methyl alcohol, and finally purified by dissolving in chloroform and precipitating with methyl alcohol. It dissolves easily in ethyl acetate, and melts at 104° to 105°. Only the perfectly pure substance can be recrystallized without decomposition, the crude nitrosite suffering complete decomposition by such treatment.

[1] Wallach and Herbig, Ann. Chem., *287*, 371.
[2] Pesci, Gazz. Chim., *16*, 225; Ber., *19*, 874, Ref.
[3] Gildemeister and Stephan, Arch. Pharm., *235*, 591.
[4] Wallach, Ann. Chem., *287*, 383.
[5] Wallach, Ann. Chem., *239*, 43.
[6] Wallach and Gildemeister, Ann. Chem., *246*, 282.

Bertram and Walbaum[1] recommend the purification of this compound by solution in ethyl acetate and precipitation with sixty per cent. alcohol. For the preparation of large quantities of phellandrene nitrosite, compare Wallach and Herbig.[2]

The nitrosite prepared from dextro-phellandrene is optically levorotatory; Pesci[3] found its specific rotatory power, $[\alpha]_D = -183.50°$. The nitrosite of levo-phellandrene is dextrorotatory. By mixing the solutions of equal quantities of dextro- and levo-phellandrene nitrosite, an optically inactive modification[4] is obtained, which is identical in all other properties with the two active derivatives.

According to a more recent investigation by Schreiner,[5] crude phellandrene nitrosite, prepared from a levorotatory fraction of an eucalyptus oil containing phellandrene, has the rotatory power, $[\alpha]_D = +28.5°$. When the crude nitrosite is rapidly dissolved in boiling ethyl acetate and then cooled with ice-water, a nitrosite separates which melts at 120° to 121°, has the rotation, $[\alpha]_D = +123.5°$, and forms long, well defined needles; on precipitating the ethyl acetate mother-liquor with sixty per cent. alcohol, a second nitrosite is obtained, which melts at 100° to 101°, has the optical rotation, $[\alpha]_D = -36°$, and crystallizes in confused aggregates. When the lower melting compound is recrystallized from methyl alcohol, the melting point is raised to 105° to 106°. The relationship between these two phellandrene nitrosites has not yet been explained. Since the highest melting point given by Wallach and Herbig is 105°, Schreiner concludes that they did not have the pure phellandrene nitrosite.

A solution of phellandrene nitrosite in chloroform does not decolorize bromine so that it is regarded as a saturated compound (Wallach). In other respects it is more unstable than the isomeric terpinene nitrosite, and unlike the latter it is not converted into nitrolamines by the action of organic bases. According to Pesci,[3] phellandrene nitrosite yields *phellandrene diamine*, $C_{10}H_{16}(NH_2)_2$, by reduction with nascent hydrogen, and it is, therefore, to be considered as having the formula,

$$C_{10}H_{16}\begin{matrix} \diagup NO \\ \diagdown NO_2 \end{matrix}$$

[1]Bertram and Walbaum, Arch. Pharm., *231*, 298.

[2]Wallach and Herbig, Ann. Chem., *287*, 371.

[3]Pesci, Gazz. Chim., *16*, 225; Ber., *19*, 874, Ref.

[4]Wallach, Ann. Chem., *246*, 235.

[5]O. Schreiner, Pharm. Arch., *1901*, *4*, 90; compare Gildemeister and Stephan, Arch. Pharm., *235*, 591; Schimmel & Co., Semi-Annual Report, October, *1901*, 62.

By the action of ammonia on the nitrosite Pesci obtained a substance having acid properties, which has the empirical constitution, $C_{10}H_{17}N_3O_4$, and crystallizes in needles. *Nitrophellandrene*, $C_{10}H_{15}NO_2$, is formed, together with the preceding compound, by the action of ammonia on the nitrosite; it is a yellow oil, which is converted into *amidophellandrene*, $C_{10}H_{15}NH_2$, on reduction.

According to Wallach,[1] when pure phellandrene nitrosite is treated with ammonium hydroxide, sp. gr. 0.93, it is slowly dissolved with evolution of nitrous oxide; a white solid results, which gives nitrophellandrene on heating with water, acids or alkalis. This disagreement with the observations of Pesci is explained by the assumption that Pesci's nitrosite was not purified sufficiently.

Nitrophellandrene is also formed by adding the nitrosite to acetyl chloride.

When phellandrene nitrosite is oxidized with nitric acid it yields terephthalic acid, isopropyl succinic acid, and an isomeride of this acid, $C_7H_{12}O_4$, together with a neutral *compound*, $C_7H_{10}O_4N_2$; the latter substance melts at 88° to 89°, and gives the Liebermann reaction for nitroso-compounds. The acid, $C_7H_{12}O_4$, melts at 85° to 88°. Isopropyl succinic acid is also produced when the nitrosite is oxidized with potassium permanganate.

A detailed investigation regarding the constitution of phellandrene and its nitrosite was carried out by Wallach and Herbig.[2] If phellandrene nitrosite be treated with sodium ethylate, pure nitrous oxide is evolved, and an oil is formed, which boils in a vacuum at 134° to 138°; it has the formula, $C_{10}H_{15}NO_2$, is heavier than water, and smells like a quinone. This substance, which Wallach and Herbig regard as chemically identical, and physically isomeric with the "nitrophellandrene" obtained by Pesci, is not a nitro-compound; if it be reduced with sodium and alcohol, or even by the direct reduction of phellandrene nitrosite, the following reaction-products are obtained:

1. Optically active tetrahydrocarveol, $C_{10}H_{19}OH$.
2. Optically active tetrahydrocarvone, $C_{10}H_{18}O$.
3. Optically active tetrahydrocarvylamine, $C_{10}H_{19}NH_2$.

The tetrahydrocarvone thus obtained has a rotatory power opposite to that of the phellandrene from which it is derived.

Since optically inactive tetrahydrocarveol is formed by the reduction of carvone and carvenone, it follows that phellandrene must have the same cyclic structure of the carbon atoms as carvenone, and that it must also have a double linkage on that atom of carbon which in carvone is attached to an oxygen atom.

[1]Wallach, Ann. Chem., *313*, 345.

[2]Wallach and Herbig, Ann. Chem., *287*, 371.

9. TERPINENE.

Terpinene escaped the notice of the earlier investigators because they assumed that it was identical with dipentene. Wallach,[1] however, recognized it as a definite terpene, and Wallach [2] and Weber [3] distinctly characterized it by its transformation into terpinene nitrosite. Weber [3] first obtained the nitrosite during an investigation of cardamom oil. Terpinene occurs in oil of cardamom, and this, together with marjoram oil, are the only ethereal oils in which terpinene has been observed.[4]

The methods of preparation of this terpene are based upon a characteristic property of terpinene, its stability towards dilute mineral acids. It is formed by boiling dipentene [5] and phellandrene [6] with dilute or alcoholic sulphuric acid; it is also obtained by boiling terpine hydrate,[1] cineole,[7] terpineol [8] or dihydrocarveol [9] with dilute or alcoholic sulphuric acid. The transformation of dihydrocarvylamine, $C_{10}H_{17}NH_2$, an amine corresponding to the alcohol, dihydrocarveol, into terpinene is of special interest. By the dry distillation of dihydrocarvylamine hydrochloride, Wallach [10] obtained terpinene, admixed with para-cymene; the latter hydrocarbon is very readily formed by the oxidation of terpinene (see below). Terpinene is further prepared by heating dihydrocarvylamine with acid potassium sulphate. The formation of this terpene by the action of formic acid on linalool [11] has already been referred to. Turpentine oil is well adapted for the preparation of terpinene. A product containing this substance is obtained by agitating oil of turpentine with concentrated sulphuric acid, care being taken to avoid a rapid increase in temperature; hence it forms a constituent of the oil which Armstrong and Tilden [12] formerly designated "*terpilene.*"

[1] Wallach, Ann. Chem., *230*, 254 and 260.
[2] Wallach, Ann. Chem., *239*, 33.
[3] Er. Weber, Ann. Chem., *238*, 107.
[4] W. Biltz (Ber., *32*, 995), finds that the fractions, boiling at 77° to 81° at 30 mm. pressure, of the crude oil of *Origanum majorana* consist largely of terpinene, which was identified by the formation of the nitrosite.
[5] Wallach, Ann. Chem., *239*, 15.
[6] Wallach, Ann. Chem., *239*, 43.
[7] Wallach, Ann. Chem., *239*, 22.
[8] Wallach and Kerkhoff, Ann. Chem., *275*, 106.
[9] Wallach, Ann. Chem., *275*, 113.
[10] Wallach, Ann. Chem., *275*, 125.
[11] Bertram and Walbaum, Journ. pr. Chem. [2], *45*, 601.
[12] Armstrong and Tilden, Ber., *12*, 752.

A product especially rich in terpinene is obtained by the following method.

Seventy cc. of concentrated sulphuric acid are added gradually, in portions of five cc. at a time, to two liters of turpentine oil, contained in a thick-walled vessel. The introduction of the acid is so regulated that the temperature does not rise so high that the vessel cannot be conveniently handled, and after every addition of acid the liquid is well agitated. When all of the sulphuric acid is added, the mixture is shaken at frequent intervals for a day, allowed to stand for one or two days, neutralized with sodium carbonate or hydroxide, and the product distilled with steam. The greater part of the resultant oil boils between 170° and 190°, and may be directly employed for the preparation of terpinene nitrosite (Wallach[1]).

Properties.—Absolutely pure terpinene has not been obtained. The product prepared by the transformation of pinene, or by other methods, is obviously not entirely free of isomeric terpenes, and, moreover, always contains cymene. Terpinene is readily converted into cymene by the oxidizing influence of sulphuric acid. (Wallach and Kerkhoff observed the formation of sulphurous acid during the preparation of terpinene from terpineol and dilute sulphuric acid.) The presence of cymene may have possibly caused the formation of toluic acid, which Tilden and Williamson obtained in the oxidation of terpinene with nitric acid.[2]

Terpinene boils at 179° to 181°. The product obtained by boiling dihydrocarveol with dilute sulphuric acid boils at 178° to 180°, has the specific gravity 0.847 and the refractive index, $n_D = 1.48458$, at 20°. It smells like cymene, is optically inactive, and is one of the most stable of the terpenes. If it be heated with alcoholic sulphuric acid or treated with concentrated sulphuric acid, it is partially converted into resin; the remaining portion, however, forms large quantities of terpinene nitrosite, and contains no other terpene than terpinene (Wallach[3]).

It is very sensitive towards Beckmann's chromic acid mixture (six parts of potassium dichromate or the corresponding quantity of sodium dichromate, five parts of concentrated sulphuric acid and thirty parts of water). This reagent easily and quickly decomposes terpinene, even in the cold, with formation of a brown

[1]Wallach, Ann. Chem., *239*, 35.
[2]Tilden and Williamson, Journ. Chem. Soc., *63* (1893), 295.
[3]Wallach, Ann. Chem., *239*, 38.

precipitate, but it is without action on other terpenes as pinene, limonene, camphene and terpinolene, as well as the oxides cineole and pinole, at ordinary temperature; therefore, terpinene is very readily removed from these substances by repeated treatment with the oxidizing mixture until a brown precipitate is no longer produced (Baeyer[1]).

According to Semmler,[2] terpinene is to be regarded as *pseudo*-limonene. He further states that Beckmann's solution is a characteristic reagent for *pseudo*-terpenes and terpene alcohols.

Hydrochloric, hydrobromic and hydriodic acids unite with terpinene forming liquid addition-products; the hydrochloride, however, solidifies at a very low temperature. Dipentene dihydrochloride is always formed together with the hydrochloride, but it has not been determined whether this is produced from terpinene, or from small quantities of dipentene which may be present in the terpinene employed. Terpinene also combines with bromine, yielding an oily dibromide (Wallach[3]).

Terpinene nitrosite,

$$C_{10}H_{16}\left\langle\begin{matrix}NO\\ ONO\end{matrix}\right.$$

The identification of terpinene in an oil is effected quickly and without any considerable loss of material by diluting two or three grams of the fraction having the boiling point of terpinene with petroleum ether, adding a solution of two or three grams of sodium nitrite, and treating this mixture carefully and with constant agitation with the necessary quantity of acid. The vessel containing the mixture is held in warm water for a moment, and then allowed to remain in a cold place. Terpinene nitrosite, which is insoluble in petroleum ether, separates after standing for a few hours, or certainly in the course of two days (Wallach[3]).

Large quantities of terpinene nitrosite are prepared as follows. To a mixture of 250 grams of terpinene, obtained by the inversion of pinene by the above-described method, 110 grams of glacial acetic acid, and forty-four grams of water, a concentrated aqueous solution of 125 grams of sodium nitrite is added in small portions at a time and with constant shaking. About two hours should be allowed for the addition of the sodium nitrite solution. The separation of crystals commences in a short time and

[1]Baeyer, Ber., 27, 815.
[2]Semmler, Ber., *34*, 708.
[3]Wallach, Ann. Chem., *239*, 38.

is nearly complete in the course of two days. The crystals are filtered, washed with water and then with cold alcohol, and finally pressed on a porous plate. The nitrosite is purified by dissolving in glacial acetic acid, reprecipitating with water, and recrystallizing from hot alcohol (Wallach[1]).

Terpinene nitrosite[1] is very easily soluble in warm alcohol, ether and ethyl acetate, difficultly in petroleum ether, and separates from alcohol in snow-white, monoclinic[2] crystals, which melt at 155°. Its solutions are optically inactive.

According to Wallach,[1] its solutions do not decolorize bromine, so that it behaves as a saturated compound; more recent investigations by Semmler[3] indicate that the nitrosite combines directly with bromine in glacial acetic acid solution forming a number of compounds, one of which is crystalline and melts at 102°.

It dissolves readily without decomposition in strong acids and may be reprecipitated with water; but it is decomposed by continued boiling with concentrated alkalis. It is decomposed by concentrated sulphuric acid only on heating to a high temperature; it does not give the nitroso-reaction when treated with phenol and sulphuric acid. It may be recrystallized without decomposition from boiling, concentrated hydrochloric acid.

When terpinene nitrosite is warmed with alcoholic potash, nitrous fumes are given off, and on immediately pouring the reaction-product into water, *terpinene oxide oxime*,[3] $C_{10}H_{14}O \cdot NOH$, separates as a white mass; it melts at 85°, decomposes on distillation under reduced pressure, and is converted into a liquid *isomeride* when dried in a vacuum; it may be kept unchanged in the air. When the oxime is reduced with sodium and alcohol, it yields a *base*, $C_{10}H_{15}O \cdot NH_2$, boiling at 140° to 150° (20 mm.).

By the reduction of terpinene nitrosite with sodium and alcohol, the following compounds have been obtained.

1. The *base*,[4] $C_{10}H_{17}NH_2$. It boils at 209° to 210°, has a sp. gr. 0.8725, and $n_D = 1.4717$ at 20°; its *carbamide* melts at 171°. It may be converted into an alcohol, which, in turn, yields a ketone, the *oxime* of which melts at 96° to 98°.
2. A crystalline *base*,[3] melting at 88°.
3. **p-Cymene.**[4]
4. A **hydrocarbon,**[3] C_9H_{14}, boiling at 160° to 164°.

When terpinene nitrosite is reduced in an alcoholic solution

[1] Wallach, Ann. Chem., *239*, 35.
[2] Hintze, Ann. Chem., *241*, 315.
[3] Semmler, Ber., *34*, 708.
[4] Wallach, Ann. Chem., *313*, 345.

with stannous chloride, it yields a basic compound whose odor is similar to that of naphthylamine (Wallach).

Two formulas have been suggested for terpinene nitrosite:

$$\text{I. } C_{10}H_{16}\left\langle\begin{matrix} N=O \\ O-N=O \end{matrix}\right. \quad \text{and} \quad \text{II. } C_{10}H_{15}\left\langle\begin{matrix} N-O-H \\ O-N=O \end{matrix}\right.$$

Brühl[1] and Semmler[2] favor the second formula, which represents the nitrosite as an isonitroso-compound. Wallach,[3] however, in consideration of the insolubility of the compound in alkalis, is inclined to regard formula I. as the more probable, although he assumes the existence of the isonitroso-group in the terpinene nitrolamines (terpinene nitrolethylamine is soluble in alkalis). Whatever the constitution of terpinene nitrosite may be, it is converted under certain conditions into compounds which undoubtedly contain the isonitroso-group.

Terpinene benzoyl isonitrosite,[3]

$$C_{10}H_{15}\left\langle\begin{matrix} NO(COC_6H_5) \\ ONO \end{matrix}\right.$$

is formed when terpinene nitrosite (thirty grams) is allowed to stand with dry ether (300 grams) and benzoyl chloride (twenty grams) for some days. The nitrosite is gradually dissolved, and on spontaneous evaporation of the ether the benzoyl compound separates. It is recrystallized from alcohol, and melts at 77° to 78°.

TERPINENE NITROLAMINES.

Terpinene nitrosite, like the nitrosochlorides of other terpenes, is readily converted into nitrolamines. Thus it reacts with ammonia according to the equation:

$$C_{10}H_{16}NO.ONO + NH_3 = C_{10}H_{15}\left\langle\begin{matrix} NOH \\ NH_2 \end{matrix}\right. + HNO_2$$

This transformation is most readily accomplished with aliphatic amines; aromatic bases do not form terpinene nitrolamines, probably because of a secondary formation of diazo-compounds due

[1] Brühl, Ber., *21*, 175.
[2] Semmler, Ber., *34*, 713.
[3] Wallach, Ann. Chem., *245*, 274.

to the action of the free nitrous acid, and the reaction-product is completely decomposed.

Terpinene nitrolamine,[1]

$$C_{10}H_{15}\langle{}^{NOH}_{NH_2}$$

is prepared by the following method. Ten cc. of concentrated ammonia are added in small portions at a time to a hot solution of five grams of terpinene nitrosite in twenty cc. of ninety-five per cent. alcohol. When the reaction is complete, forty or fifty cc. of water are added, and the alcohol and ammonia boiled off. The solution of the amine is now filtered from a red, resinous impurity, and, after the addition of a few drops of ammonia to the filtrate, terpinene nitrolamine crystallizes in a fairly pure condition. The mother-liquor is concentrated in vacuum, and yields further quantities of the nitrolamine. The yield is about ten per cent. It crystallizes from hot water, decomposes very easily, and melts at 118°. Werner[1] obtained the dibenzoyl derivative of this base by the Baumann-Schotten method; it melts at 146°.

For the preparation of substituted terpinene nitrolamines, Wallach[2] employs the following method. Terpinene nitrosite is covered with four times its weight of alcohol, and heated in a flask with upright condenser until all is dissolved; two molecular proportions of the aliphatic amine are then added to the warm liquid, and, after the completion of the reaction which usually takes place immediately, the mixture is boiled. The resulting base is separated by pouring the reaction-product into water; after standing for some time it forms a solid mass, which is washed with water, dissolved in hydrochloric acid, filtered off from resinous substances, and is precipitated by ammonia. The nitrolamine so purified is obtained as a semi-solid mass, which, however, gradually becomes solid and crystalline. It is recrystallized from alcohol.

Terpinene nitrolmethylamine,

$$C_{10}H_{15}\langle{}^{NOH}_{NHCH_3}$$

crystallizes in splendid prisms, which melt at 141°.

Terpinene nitroldimethylamine,

$$C_{10}H_{15}\langle{}^{NOH}_{N(CH_3)_2}$$

[1] Wallach, Ann. Chem., *241*, 320; Werner, Inaug. Diss., Bonn, 1890.
[2] Wallach, Ann. Chem., *241*, 316.

is easily soluble in chloroform, sparingly in alcohol, and melts at 160° to 161°.

Terpinene nitrolethylamine,

$$C_{10}H_{15}\begin{cases}=NOH\\-NHC_2H_5\end{cases}$$

is sparingly soluble in hot water, more readily in warm dilute sodium hydroxide, and very readily in boiling alcohol, ether and chloroform. It melts at 130° to 131°, and is decomposed into hydroxylamine and other products by boiling with hydrochloric acid. Its *nitroso-derivative* crystallizes from alcohol in needles, and melts at 132° to 133°.

Terpinene nitroldiethylamine,

$$C_{10}H_{15}\begin{cases}=NOH\\-N(C_2H_5)_2\end{cases}$$

melts at 117° to 118°.

Terpinene nitrolamylamine,

$$C_{10}H_{15}\begin{cases}=NOH\\-NHC_5H_{11}\end{cases}$$

is characterized by its splendid power of crystallization. It dissolves sparingly in alcohol and ether, and melts at 118° to 119°.

Terpinene nitrolpiperidide,

$$C_{10}H_{15}\begin{cases}=NOH\\-NC_5H_{10}\end{cases}$$

is quite insoluble in sodium hydroxide; it forms splendid crystals, which melt at 153° to 154°.

Terpinene nitrolbenzylamine,[1]

$$C_{10}H_{15}\begin{cases}=NOH\\-NHCH_2C_6H_5\end{cases}$$

is prepared by warming five grams of terpinene nitrosite with five and one-half grams of benzylamine and ten grams of alcohol. The crude product is purified by dissolving in acetic acid and precipitating the filtered solution with ammonia. It crystallizes from alcohol in fragile, brilliant leaflets, and melts at 137°.

10. THUJENE (TANACETENE).

Thujene appears to be different from all the terpenes which have been mentioned in the preceding, but the information regarding this compound is very incomplete. It is formed in the dry distillation of thujylamine hydrochloride and isothujylamine hydrochloride.

[1] Wallach, Ann. Chem., 252, 134.

According to Semmler,[1] tanacetene boils at 60° to 63° under 14 mm. pressure, has the sp. gr. 0.8508 and refractive index, $n_D = 1.476$, at 20°. It contains two ethylene linkages.

According to Wallach,[2] thujene boils at 170° to 172°, has the sp. gr. 0.836 and refractive power, $n_D = 1.47145$, at 22°.

In a more recent publication, Tschugaeff[3] states that thujyl alcohol, $C_{10}H_{17}OH$, may be converted into a methyl xanthate, and that when this compound is dry distilled it yields a new terpene, $C_{10}H_{16}$; the latter boils at 151° to 152.5°, has a sp. gr. 0.8275 at 20°/4°, and the refractive index, $n_D = 1.45042$, at 20°; the molecular refraction is 44.21, while the calculated value for a dicyclic terpene is 43.54. It does not form a crystalline nitroso-chloride, does not form an additive compound with bromine, but instantly decolorizes permanganate solution; in the air it is rapidly oxidized to a resin. It forms a crystalline compound with hot mercuric acetate solution.

Tschugaeff regards this new terpene as belonging to the true thujone series and designates it as "*thujene.*" The terpene above mentioned under the name thujene or tanacetene is considered as a derivative of isothujone and is therefore called "*isothujene*" (Tschugaeff).

By the dry distillation of trimethyl thujylammonium hydroxide, $C_{10}H_{17}N(CH_3)_3 \cdot OH$, Tschugaeff[4] obtained a thujene which boils at 151° to 153°, has a sp. gr. 0.8263 at 20°/4°, refractive index, $n_D = 1.45022$, at 20°, and a rotatory power, $[\alpha]_D = -8.23°$. Since this rotatory power is much greater than that of the thujene obtained from thujyl alcohol as above described, it is perhaps possible that thujone, $C_{10}H_{16}O$, gives rise to two stereoisomeric thujyl alcohols, $C_{10}H_{17}OH$, on reduction, and these yield two stereoisomeric thujenes.

A dextrorotatory thujene[4] ($[\alpha]_D = +21.83°$ in a ten cm. tube) has been obtained from the last fraction formed in the distillation of methyl thujylxanthate.

11. TERPENE FROM THE RESIN OF INDIAN HEMP.

A terpene, which appears to be different from those previously described, is found in the distillate, boiling from 160° to 180°, of the resin of Indian hemp.[5] It has the composition, $C_{10}H_{16}$, boils

[1] Semmler, Ber., *25*, 3345.
[2] Wallach, Ann. Chem., *286*, 97.
[3] Tschugaeff, Ber., *33*, 3118.
[4] Tschugaeff, Ber., *34*, 2276.
[5] Wood, Spivey, and Easterfield, Journ. Chem. Soc., *69*, 541.

at 170° to 175°, and has the specific gravity 0.819 at 17°; it is slightly levorotatory. It has a pleasant odor, and resinifies very rapidly on exposure to the air. It combines with hydrogen chloride, forming an oily monohydrochloride.

12. SYNTHETICAL TERPENE.

A terpene, $C_{10}H_{16}$, which may possibly prove to be the first representative of the class of *ortho*-terpenes, was obtained by Wallach[1] during his investigation of synthetical (*ortho*-?) pulegone, $C_{10}H_{16}O$.

By reducing synthetical pulegone with sodium and alcohol, pulegol, $C_{10}H_{17}OH$, is formed. When pulegol is heated with phosphoric anhydride, and the reaction-product is distilled with steam, the above-mentioned terpene is produced. Its odor resembles that of limonene and of terpinolene; it boils at 173° to 175°, has the specific gravity 0.823 and refractive index, $n_D =$ 1.4601, at 18°. Further investigations may show some changes in these physical constants, since the terpene has not been prepared in an absolutely pure condition.

13. FENCHELENE.

This terpene[2] is produced as a by-product in the formation of fencholenyl alcohol, $C_{10}H_{17}OH$. It boils at 66° to 70° under 20 mm. pressure, and at 175° to 178° under 760 mm. pressure. It has the specific gravity 0.842, and the index of refraction, $n_D =$ 1.47439, at 20°.

14. EUTERPENE.

This terpene[3] is formed when dihydroeucarveol, $C_{10}H_{17}OH$, is treated with phosphorus pentachloride, and the resulting chloride, after removal of the phosphorus oxychloride, is boiled with quinoline for thirty minutes. It boils at 161° to 165°. It yields acetic, oxalic, and *gem*-dimethylsuccinic acids, when it is oxidized with permanganate.

Euterpene forms a dihydrobromide, which, when acted upon by bromine in the presence of iodine and then is reduced with zinc and alcoholic hydrochloric acid and finally with sodium and alcohol, yields *1.2.4-dimethyl-ethyl-benzene*, boiling at 185° to 191°.

[1] Wallach, Ber., *29*, 2957.
[2] Wallach, Ann. Chem., *300*, 294.
[3] Baeyer and Villiger, Ber., *31*, 2067.

15. TRICYCLENE.

This hydrocarbon was obtained by Wagner[1] by treating pinene dibromide, $C_{10}H_{16}Br_2$ (m. p. 169° to 170°), with zinc dust and acetic acid. It has the composition, $C_{10}H_{16}$, melts at 65° to 66°, and boils at 153°; it is indifferent towards potassium permanganate. It forms a solid addition-product with hydrogen chloride.

16. BORNYLENE.

When pinene hydriodide is heated with forty per cent. alcoholic potash in an autoclave at 170° for four hours, a mixture of camphene and another hydrocarbon is produced. This mixture is fractionally distilled, and the fraction boiling at 152° to 160° is heated with acetic acid in a sealed tube at 55° to 60°; the camphene is thus converted into isobornyl acetate, while the other hydrocarbon remains unchanged and is separated by fractionation. This hydrocarbon, $C_{10}H_{16}$, which Wagner[2] calls *bornylene*, melts at 97.5° to 98°, boils at 149° to 150° under 750 mm. pressure, and sublimes readily at the ordinary temperature. It is oxidized at the ordinary temperature by a dilute solution of potassium permanganate yielding camphoric acid. Wagner regards it as the hydrocarbon corresponding to camphor and borneol, and suggests the name bornylene to show this relation; for camphene, which may be readily converted into isoborneol, he proposes the name *isobornylene*.

17. SABINENE.

The fraction of oil of savin which distills below 195° constitutes about thirty per cent. of the crude oil, and consists mainly of terpenes. On redistillation of this fraction, an oil is obtained which boils between 162° and 170°, and consists principally of a terpene, $C_{10}H_{16}$, which Semmler[3] calls sabinene.

It has a specific gravity 0.840, a refractive index, $\mu_D = 1.466$, and a molecular refraction, $M = 44.9$. It forms a liquid *dibromide*, having the specific gravity 1.50, but yields no definite compound with nitrous acid. It is regarded as a *pseudo*-terpene.

Sabinene glycol, $C_{10}H_{16}(OH)_2$, results on the oxidation of sabinene with ice-cold, aqueous potassium permanganate; it boils at 148° to 150° under 15 mm. pressure, crystallizes from water, and

[1] Godlewski and G. Wagner, Chem. Centr., *1897* (I.), 1055; Journ. Russ. Chem. Soc., *29*, 121.

[2] G. Wagner and Brykner, Ber., *33*, 2121.

[3] F. Semmler, Ber., *33*, 1455; *34*, 708.

melts at 54°. It has the specific gravity, 1.021, the refractive index, $\mu_D = 1.402$, and a molecular refraction, $M = 47.41$.

Dihydrocuminyl alcohol, $C_{10}H_{15}OH$, is produced by warming the glycol with acidified water; it boils at 242°, has a sp. gr. 0.9572, $\mu_D = 1.5018$, and $M = 46.80$. Chromic acid oxidizes it to cuminyl alcohol and cumin aldehyde.

Sabinenic acid, $C_{10}H_{16}O_3$, is formed together with sabinene glycol; it is an oxy-acid, crystallizes from water, melts at 57°, and forms a sparingly soluble, crystalline *sodium salt*.

When this acid is distilled in vacuum, it loses water and hydrogen, and yields *cumic acid*, $C_{10}H_{12}O_2$ (m. p. 117° to 118°).

Sabinene, sabinene glycol and sabinenic acid are all dextrorotatory.

Sabinene ketone, $C_9H_{14}O$, is obtained on the oxidation of sabinenic acid with lead peroxide; it boils at 213°, has a specific gravity 0.945, a refractive index, $\mu_D = 1.4629$, and a molecular refraction, $M = 40.26$. Its *semicarbazone* crystallizes from alcohol, and melts at 135° to 137°. The ketone is levorotatory, $[\alpha]_D = -18°$ in a ten cm. tube.

In conclusion, the most important transformations of the several terpenes into each other are briefly presented in the following table:

TRANSFORMATIONS IN THE TERPENE SERIES.

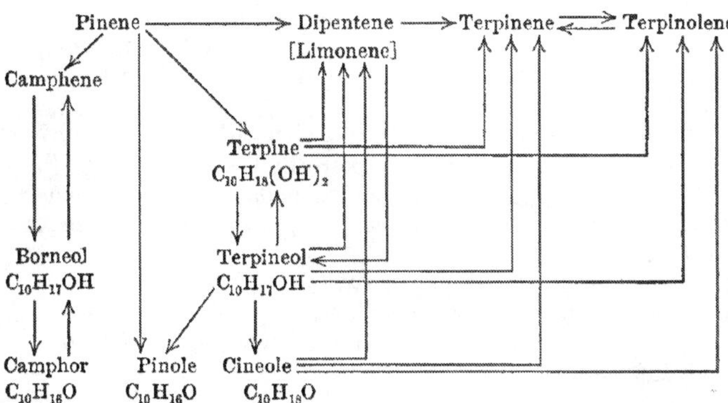

HYDROCARBONS, $C_{10}H_{18}$.

1. DIHYDROCAMPHENE, $C_{10}H_{18}$.

Baeyer[1] seems to have first prepared this hydrocarbon by the action of zinc dust and glacial acetic acid at a low temperature on pinene hydriodide and on bornyl iodide, $C_{10}H_{17}I$.

Bredt and v. Rosenberg[2] obtained dihydrocamphene by the reduction of pinene hydrochloride and of bornyl chloride with sodium and alcohol.

Armstrong[3] speaks of dihydrocamphene under the term *camphydrene*, and he mentions its preparation from pinene hydrochloride by the action of sodium.

Semmler[4] has also recently prepared this hydrocarbon by the reduction of pinene hydrochloride, pinene dibromide, camphene hydrochloride, and camphene dibromide with sodium and alcohol.

Dihydrocamphene[5] is a *saturated* hydrocarbon, and may be freed from impurities by treatment with fuming nitric acid. It melts at 155.3°, and boils at 159.5°. According to Semmler, it separates from alcohol in crystals belonging to the *hexagonal* system, melts at 155°, and boils at 160° to 162° (uncorr.).

Aschan[6] describes a compound, $C_{10}H_{18}$, which is probably dihydrocamphene, under the name *camphane*. He obtains it by the reduction of a nearly inactive pinene hydriodide in an acetic acid solution by means of zinc and hydriodic acid; the product, an inactive camphane (dihydrocamphene), crystallizes in six-sided plates, and melts at 153° to 154°.

This saturated hydrocarbon, $C_{10}H_{18}$, is also called *camphane* by Forster[7] in a paper entitled, "Studies in the Camphane Series"; thus, the compound $C_{10}H_{16}BrNO_2$, which is obtained from camphoroxime, is called *bromonitrocamphane*, and the compound, $C_{10}H_{17}NO_2$, *nitrocamphane*, etc.

It may be mentioned that a hydrocarbon, $C_{20}H_{34}$, termed *dihydrodicamphene*,[8] is formed by the action of metallic sodium upon molten pinene hydrochloride. It is a solid, melting at 75° and boiling at 326° to 327°.

[1]Baeyer, Ber., *26*, 826.
[2]Private communication to Dr. Heusler.
[3]Armstrong, Journ. Chem. Soc., *69* (1896), 1398.
[4]F. Semmler, Ber., *33*, 774 and 3420.
[5]Bredt and v. Rosenberg.
[6]O. Aschan, Ber., *33*, 1006.
[7]M. O. Forster, Journ. Chem. Soc., 77 (1900), 251.
[8]Etard and Meker, Compt. rend., *126*, 526.

2. ISODIHYDROCAMPHENE, $C_{10}H_{18}$.

According to Semmler,[1] when isoborneol is heated with zinc dust for thirty minutes at 220°, it is converted into a mixture of a small quantity of camphene and a much larger amount of a hydrocarbon, $C_{10}H_{18}$; the latter compound is designated as *isodihydrocamphene*. It crystallizes from alcohol in fern-like aggregates, which belong to the *isometric* system. It melts at 85° and boils at 162° (uncorr.).

While the dihydrocamphenes may be termed the parent-substances of the terpenes, pinene and camphene, as well as of camphor, the following hydrocarbons, carvomenthene and menthene, are to be regarded as tetrahydrocymenes.

3. CARVOMENTHENE, $C_{10}H_{18}$.

By the separation of the elements of water from carvomenthol (tetrahydrocarveol), $C_{10}H_{19}OH$, it may be converted into a hydrocarbon, $C_{10}H_{18}$, which differs from menthene, $C_{10}H_{18}$, obtained from menthol in an analogous manner. Therefore, the constitution of carvomenthene and of menthene can not be expressed by formula I., according to which both compounds must be identical, but should rather be regarded as corresponding to formulas II. and III. (Baeyer).

```
      CH3                 CH3                 CH3
      |                   |                   |
      CH                  CH                  CH
     /  \                /  \                /  \
 H2C    CHOH         H2C    CH2          H2C    CH
  |      |            |      |            |     ||     I.
 H2C    CH2          H2C    CHOH         H2C    CH
     \  /                \  /                \  /
      CH                  CH                  CH
      |                   |                   |
      CH                  CH                  CH
     /  \                /  \                /  \
  H3C    CH3          H3C    CH3          H3C    CH3
  Carvomenthol         Menthol.
(tetrahydrocarveol).
```

```
          CH3                      CH3
          |                        |
          C                        CH
         // \                     /  \
   H2C    CH              H2C    CH2
    |      |     II.        |      |      III.
   H2C    CH2             H2C    CH
       \  /                   \  //
        CH                      C
        |                       |
        CH                      CH
       /  \                    /  \
    H3C    CH3              H3C    CH3
   Carvomenthene.            Menthene.
```

[1] F. Semmler, Ber., *33*, 774.

Baeyer[1] prepared carvomenthene by treating tetrahydrocarveol (carvomenthol) with hydrobromic acid, and distilling the resultant bromide with quinoline, while Wallach[2] obtained it by heating tetrahydrocarveol with acid potassium sulphate for one hour at 200°. When purified in the usual manner, it boils at 175° to 176° (corr.).

According to more recent investigations by Kondakoff and Lutschinin,[3] carvomenthene is formed by heating carvomenthyl chloride or bromide with alcoholic potash; on fractional distillation, the resultant hydrocarbon may be separated into two portions, about ninety per cent. of the whole boiling at 172° to 174.5°, and the remainder at 174.5° to 178°.

PROPERTIES.—The fraction of carvomenthene of the lower boiling point has the specific gravity 0.8230 at 16.3°/4°, a refractive index, $n_D = 1.45979$, a molecular refraction, $M = 45.68$, and a specific rotation, $[\alpha]_D = -2° 4'$. The higher boiling fraction has the sp. gr. of 0.8230 at 19°/4°, an index of refraction, $n_D = 1.46108$, a molecular refraction, $M = 45.89$, and a specific rotatory power, $[\alpha]_D = -1° 28'$.

Carvomenthene is a colorless, mobile liquid having an odor of menthene; it is changed on exposure to air, is readily oxidized by permanganate, and unites with two atoms of bromine, forming an oily bromide. According to Baeyer, it combines with hydrogen bromide or iodide in the cold, yielding tertiary carvomenthyl halogen derivatives, which may be converted into a mixture of carvomenthene and tertiary carvomenthol. (See tertiary carvomenthol.)

Carvomenthene hydrochloride, $C_{10}H_{18}{\cdot}HCl$, boils at 90° to 98° under 18 mm. pressure, and at 89° to 95° under 16 mm. It has a specific gravity 0.9390 at 19°/4°, a refractive index $n_D = 1.464941$, a molecular refraction, $M = 50.95$, and a specific rotatory power, $[\alpha]_D = -1° 22'$. Its properties are identical with those of carvomenthyl chloride, with the one exception of its rotatory power (Kondakoff and Lutschinin).

Carvomenthene hydrobromide, $C_{10}H_{18}{\cdot}HBr$, may be obtained by heating carvomenthene with concentrated hydrobromic acid at 160° to 170°; it boils at 92° to 98° under 10 mm. pressure, has a specific gravity 1.1620 at 20.5°/4°, a refractive index, $n_D =$ 1.48822, at 20.5°, a molecular refraction, $M = 54.27$, and it is optically inactive. Its properties are almost identical with those of carvomenthyl bromide, but it seems probable that it consists of

[1] Baeyer, Ber., *26*, 824.
[2] Wallach, Ann. Chem., *277*, 130.
[3] Kondakoff and Lutschinin, Journ. pr. Chem., *60* (II.), 257.

a mixture of secondary and tertiary bromine derivatives, which are derived from two isomeric carvomenthenes present in the parent hydrocarbon.

The carvomenthene regenerated from the hydrobromide boils at 172° to 175°, has the specific gravity 0.8230, at 20°/4°, a refractive index, $n_D = 1.45959$, a molecular refraction, $M = 45.69$, and a specific rotatory power, $[\alpha]_D = -0° 23'$ (Kondakoff and Lutschinin).

4. MENTHENE, $C_{10}H_{18}$.

The structural formula of menthene has already been referred to. This hydrocarbon is prepared from menthol by a method analogous to that used in the preparation of carvomenthene from tetrahydrocarveol. In the year 1838 Walter obtained menthene by treating menthol with vitreous phosphoric acid.

According to Brühl,[1] it is prepared by boiling menthol with fused zinc chloride or anhydrous copper sulphate, while Sicker and Kremers [2] obtain it by heating menthol with twice its weight of acid potassium sulphate at 180° to 200°. For its preparation, Wagner[3] recommends the method that Wallach gives for the preparation of camphene from borneol; thus, menthol is converted into menthyl chloride, $C_{10}H_{19}Cl$, by treatment with phosphorus pentachloride, and this is boiled with aniline for a long time; the yield of menthene is almost theoretical. According to Berkenheim,[4] menthene is formed as a by-product in the preparation of menthyl chloride (b. p. 210°) from menthol and phosphoric chloride; it is also produced by heating menthyl chloride with potassium acetate and glacial acetic acid at a high temperature.

Menthyl chloride, prepared from l-menthol, may be converted into menthene [5] by heating with a solution of potassium phenolate for twelve minutes at 150°. Menthol may be directly converted into menthene[6] by heating with dilute sulphuric acid (one part acid to two parts water) at 60° to 100°, for six to eight hours; the yield is said to be 90 per cent. of the theoretical.

According to Tschugaeff,[7] a menthene of very high rotatory power is obtained by the distillation of the *methyl ester of menthylxanthogenic acid;* the latter compound is produced by treat-

[1]Brühl, Ber., *25*, 142.
[2]Sicker and Kremers, Ammer. Chem. Journ., *14*, 291.
[3]Wagner, Ber., *27*, 1636.
[4]Berkenheim, Ber., *25*, 686.
[5]Masson and Reychler, Ber., *29*, 1843.
[6]Konowaloff, Journ. Russ. Phys. Chem. Soc., *32* (1900), 76.
[7]Tschugaeff, Ber., *32*, 3332.

ing menthol, dissolved in dry toluene, successively with sodium, carbon bisulphide, and methyl iodide. *Menthyldixanthogenate* also yields menthene on distillation; the specific rotatory power of the menthene derived from these two compounds is $[\alpha]_D =$ 111.56° to 116.06°.

Andres and Andreef[1] state that the fraction boiling between 160° and 170° of peppermint oil consists of a mixture of a terpene, $C_{10}H_{16}$, with a hydrocarbon, $C_{10}H_{18}$. The experiments published by these chemists do not determine whether the latter hydrocarbon is identical with menthene, as might be supposed from the occurrence of menthol and menthone in peppermint oil. According to Labbé,[2] menthene occurs in the oil of thyme.

Menthene is an oil having a slight odor unlike that of menthol, and boils at 167° to 168°, considerably lower than carvomenthene; according to Sicker and Kremers, its specific gravity is 0.814 at 20°, while Brühl[3] gives the sp. gr. 0.8064 at 20°. Brühl has also determined other physical constants of menthene. It is optically dextrorotatory, $[\alpha]_D = + 32.77°$ (Urban & Kremers[4]). Masson and Reychler[5] appear to have prepared a levorotatory menthene from menthyl chloride, and they give its specific rotatory power, $[\alpha]_D = - 48.5°$. Of especial interest is Berkenheim's observation that dextrorotatory menthene and levorotatory menthyl chloride are obtained by heating inactive menthyl chloride with potassium acetate and glacial acetic acid; under the influence of potassium acetate the dextrorotatory portion of inactive menthyl chloride is converted into menthene, whilst the levorotatory portion remains unchanged. In this connection, attention should be called to the fact that Berkenheim found the boiling point of this menthene at 170° to 171° (mercury of thermometer in vapor). In general, the results of different investigators do not agree on all points concerning this hydrocarbon.

According to Baeyer, menthene unites with hydrogen iodide, forming tertiary menthyl iodide; menthene may also be converted into tertiary menthol[5] by heating the hydrocarbon with trichloracetic acid for half an hour at 70° to 90°, and agitating the product for several hours with potash (see tertiary menthol).

[1]Andres and Andreef, Ber., *25*, 609.

[2]H. Labbé, Bull. Soc. Chim., *19* (1898, III.), 1009.

[3]Brühl, Ber., *25*, 151.

[4]Urban and Kremers, Ammer. Chem. Journ., *16*, 395; Proc. Ammer. Pharm. Assoc., *1892*, 273; *1893*, 185.

[5]Masson and Reychler, Ber., *29*, 1843.

It combines with bromine producing an oil. Brühl[1] found that cymene is quite readily obtained by heating menthene with anhydrous copper sulphate at 250°.

The compounds resulting from the addition of hydrochloric and hydrobromic acids to menthene appear to be identical with the menthyl chloride and bromide obtained from menthol.[2]

Menthene nitrosochloride, $C_{10}H_{18} \cdot NOCl$, has been investigated by Kremers[3] and his students. It is prepared by slowly adding a solution of eighteen cc. of concentrated hydrochloric acid in eighteen cc. of glacial acetic acid to a well cooled mixture of forty-five cc. of menthene, forty-five cc. of glacial acetic acid, and thirty-three cc. of ethyl nitrite. The resulting nitrosochloride is purified by dissolving in chloroform, and precipitating with alcohol. The products thus obtained from various fractions of dextro-menthene, boiling from 166.5° to 168.5°, have different melting points, from 106° to 122°; the compound having the highest melting point, 121° to 122°, is levorotatory, $[\alpha]_D = -2.4508°$, while the other nitrosochlorides are inactive or dextrorotatory, $[\alpha]_D = +1.015°$ to $+20.64°$, and melt from 106° to 119°. No satisfactory method has yet been found by means of which the different modifications of the nitrosochloride can be separated from the mixture.

It should further be noted that Urban and Kremers[4] obtained an inactive nitrosochloride, melting at 128°, and that Baeyer[5] has mentioned a menthene nitrosochloride, melting at 146°. Tschugaeff[6] has also prepared a nitrosochloride, melting at 127° and having $[\alpha]_D = 242.5°$.

Menthene nitrosate, $C_{10}H_{18} \cdot N_2O_4$, melts at 98°, and is optically inactive (Urban and Kremers).

Menthene nitrolbenzylamine,

$$C_{10}H_{18}\begin{cases} NO \\ NH \cdot CH_2 \cdot C_6H_5 \end{cases}$$

is prepared in the usual manner from the nitrosochloride or nitrosate. It is optically inactive, and melts at 105.5° to 107°. Ac-

[1]Brühl, Ber., *25*, 151.

[2]Wagner, Ber., *27*, 1636; Kondakoff, Ber., *28*, 1618; Journ. pr. Chem., *60* [II.], 257.

[3]Sicker and Kremers, Amer. Chem. Journ., *14*, 292; Urban and Kremers, Amer. Chem. Journ., *16*, 395; Richtmann and Kremers, Amer. Chem. Journ., *18*, 762.

[4]Urban and Kremers, Amer. Chem. Journ., *16*, 395.

[5]Baeyer, Ber., *26*, 2561.

[6]Tschugaeff, Ber., *32*, 3332.

cording to Richtmann and Kremers, the nitrosochlorides having specific rotatory powers differing by 30° all yield optically inactive benzylamine bases, melting at 105.5° to 106.5°.

Nitrosomenthene,[1] $C_{10}H_{16}NOH$, is obtained by boiling menthene nitrosochloride with alcoholic potash. It also results when the nitrosochloride is heated in a tube at about 115°; in this case hydrochloric acid is given off, and the resultant nitrosomenthene sublimes slowly, and condenses in the cooler parts of the tube. It is purified by distilling in a current of steam, and melts at 65° to 67°. Nitrosomenthene prepared from dextrorotatory menthene nitrosochloride is levorotatory, and the inactive modification is formed from the inactive nitrosochloride.

By reduction of nitrosomenthene with zinc dust and acetic acid, Urban and Kremers obtained inactive menthone and a menthylamine; this base forms a crystalline nitrate, which, on treating with nitrous acid, yields an alcohol, $C_{10}H_{17}OH$, boiling at 210° to 215°.

Nitrosomenthene is fairly stable towards sulphuric and acetic acids. When it is warmed with hydrochloric acid, a ketone, *menthenone*, $C_{10}H_{16}O$, is formed; it boils at 206° to 208°, and is reconverted into nitrosomenthene by heating with hydroxylamine.

The oxidation of menthene with potassium permanganate has been studied by Wagner[2] and Tolloczko.[3] According to Wagner, the following products are obtained by oxidizing menthene at about 0° with a one per cent. solution of permanganate.

1. **Menthene glycol,** $C_{10}H_{18}(OH)_2$.—This glycol is an oily, viscid liquid, boiling at 129.5° to 131.5° under 13 mm. pressure; it partially solidifies after a time and crystallizes from ether, melting at 76.5° to 77°; the permanent liquid portions yield a diacetate, a monoacetate, and a terpene, $C_{10}H_{16}$, when treated with acetic anhydride.

2. **Ketone alcohol,** $C_{10}H_{17}O(OH)$.—This compound is a liquid, having the specific gravity 0.9881 at 0°, and boils at 104.5° to 105.5° at 13.5 mm. pressure. It yields a *phenylurethane*, $C_{17}H_{23}O_3N$, melting at 157°, and an *oxime*, $C_{10}H_{19}O_2N$, which crystallizes from ether in microscopic tablets, melting at 132° to 133°.

3. **Acetic acid, methyl adipic acid,** and **γ-isobutyryl-β-methyl valeric acid (oxymenthylic acid).**—These acids are also formed in the oxidation of menthone with potassium permanganate.

[1] Urban and Kremers, and Richtmann and Kremers.
[2] Wagner, Ber., 27, 1636.
[3] Tolloczko, Ber., 28, 926, Ref.

Meta-menthene (1 : 3-methyl-isopropyl-cyclohexene), $C_{10}H_{18}$, is a hydrocarbon, which has been prepared by Knoevenagel[1] by heating *cis*-symmetrical menthol with phosphoric anhydride at 110° to 130°. It is a liquid, having an odor resembling that of turpentine, and is an unsaturated compound; it boils at 169° to 170° under a pressure of 746 mm., has a specific gravity 0.8197 at 16°/4°, the index of refraction, $n_D = 1.45609$, and the molecular refraction, R = 45.67.

According to Kondakoff,[2] a *hydrocarbon*, $C_{10}H_{18}$, is obtained from the *oil of buchu leaves;* it boils at 174° to 176° at 762 mm. pressure, at 65° to 67° under 14 mm., has a specific gravity 0.8648 at 18.5°, and a specific rotatory power, $\alpha_D = +60.20°$. Its odor resembles that of peppermint.

Cyclo-linalolene, $C_{10}H_{18}$, will be described under linalolene.

HYDROCARBONS, $C_{10}H_{20}$.

Many members of the terpene series are converted into hydrocarbons, $C_{10}H_{20}$, by heating with hydriodic acid and red phosphorus at about 200°. A sharp characterization and identification of these compounds have been impossible, since they are chemically very indifferent substances, and their transformations into crystalline derivatives have not yet succeeded. It is probable, therefore, that some of the following hydrocarbons, which are chiefly named after the products from which they are derived, are identical. It is to be noted that, according to Baeyer's nomenclature, hexahydrocymene is called *terpane*, while Wagner suggests the name *menthane*.

Tetrahydropinene, $C_{10}H_{20}$, is described by Wallach and Berkenheim[3] as a hydrocarbon produced by the hydration of pinene hydrochloride; it boils at 162°, has the specific gravity 0.795, and the refractive index, $n_D = 1.43701°$, at 20°. Bromine acts on it, forming substitution products; nitric acid and a mixture of nitric and sulphuric acids do not attack this hydrocarbon in the cold, but warm nitric acid dissolves and oxidizes it. A warm solution of permanganate oxidizes it very slowly, forming valeric acid. The hydrocarbon obtained by Orlow[4] by the direct hydration of oil of turpentine should in all probability be regarded as tetrahydropinene.

[1] Knoevenagel and Wiedermann, Ann. Chem., *297*, 169.
[2] Kondakoff, Journ. pr. Chem., *54*, 433.
[3] Wallach and Berkenheim, Ann. Chem., *268*, 225.
[4] Orlow, Ber., *16*, 799.

Tetrahydrofenchene, $C_{10}H_{20}$, was obtained by Wallach[1] in the reduction of fenchyl alcohol, fenchone and fenchylamine with hydriodic acid and phosphorus. It boils at 160° to 165°, and has the specific gravity 0.7945 and index of refraction, $n_D = 1.4370$, at 22°. In its chemical behavior it resembles tetrahydropinene; bromine acts upon it forming a solid substitution-product, although the yield is extremely small. This bromide crystallizes from ethyl acetate in the form of needles, which melt above 200°, but they have not been analyzed.

Starodubsky obtained a *hydrocarbon*, $C_{10}H_{20}$, in a similar manner from camphor; it boils at 167° to 169°, and has the specific gravity of 0.8114 at 15°.

A *hydrocarbon*, $C_{10}H_{20}$, is obtained by the reduction of terpine hydrate; it boils at 168° to 170°, and has the specific gravity 0.797 at 15° (Schtschukarew[2]).

The *hydrocarbon*, $C_{10}H_{20}$, prepared by Wagner[3] by the action of concentrated sulphuric acid on menthol, is to be regarded as hexahydrocymene, and, according to Wagner, is called *menthane*. The same compound is also formed by the reduction of menthol with hydriodic acid and phosphorus, and is designated by Berkenheim[4] as *menthonaphthene*. According to Wagner, it boils at 168° to 169°, and has the sp. gr. 0.8066 at 0°; according to Berkenheim, it boils at 169° to 170.5°, and has the specific gravity 0.8067 at 0° and 0.796 at 15°.

Jünger and Klages[5] state that this hexahydrocymene is best prepared by reducing menthyl chloride with sodium and alcohol, and shaking the reaction-product with concentrated sulphuric acid.

Meta-menthane[6] (**1 : 3-methyl-isopropylcyclohexane**), $C_{10}H_{20}$, is prepared by the reduction of symmetrical menthyl iodide. It boils at 167° to 168° under a pressure of 756 mm., has a specific gravity 0.8033 at 14°/4°, refractive index, $n_D = 1.44204$, and molecular refraction, $R = 46.02$. It is not acted upon by concentrated sulphuric and nitric acids, bromine, and solutions of potassium permanganate.

A **hexahydrocymene**, $C_{10}H_{20}$, isolated by Renard[7] from the essence of resin by means of sulphuric acid, boils at 171° to 173°, and has the specific gravity 0.8116 at 17°.

[1] Wallach, Ann. Chem., *284*, 326.
[2] Schtschukarew, Ber., *23*, 433c.
[3] Wagner, Ber., *27*, 1638.
[4] Berkenheim, Ber., *25*, 686.
[5] Jünger and Klages, Ber., *29*, 317.
[6] Knoevenagel and Wiedermann, Ann. Chem., *297*, 169.
[7] Renard, Ann. Chim. Phys. [6], *1*, 223.

Berkenheim[1] has published the results of experiments on the relations of the naphthenes, $C_{10}H_{20}$, occurring in Russian petroleum, to the hydrocarbons under consideration, and to the terpenes.

Diethyl hexamethylene, $C_{10}H_{20}$, was synthetically prepared by Zelinsky and Rudewitsch.[2] According to these chemists, *diethyl-keto-hexamethylene*, $C_{10}H_{18}O$, is obtained by the distillation of diethyl pimelic acid over calcium hydroxide; it boils at 205° to 207°. This ketone is converted by reduction into the *alcohol*, $C_{10}H_{19}OH$, which boils at 209° to 211°, and partially solidifies, the crystalline portion melting at 77° to 78°. This alcohol is converted into the *iodide*, $C_{10}H_{19}I$, by treatment with hydriodic acid, and when the iodide is reduced with zinc and hydrochloric acid in alcoholic solution it yields diethyl hexamethylene. The following formulas express these reactions:

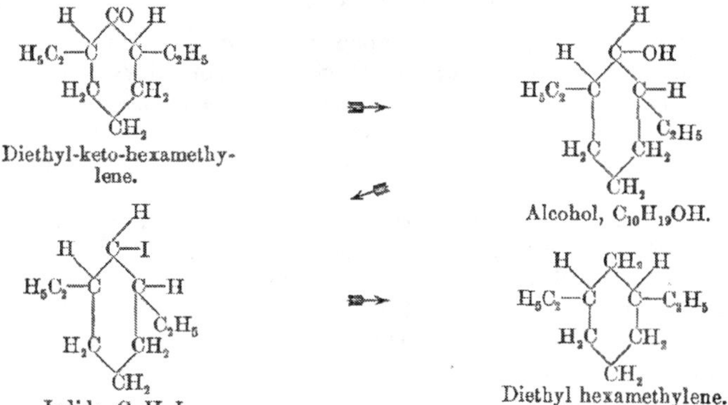

Diethyl-keto-hexamethylene.

Alcohol, $C_{10}H_{19}OH$.

Iodide, $C_{10}H_{19}I$.

Diethyl hexamethylene.

Diethyl hexamethylene is a colorless liquid with a petroleum-like odor. It boils at 169° to 171°, has the specific gravity, d 22°/4° = 0.7957, and the refractive index, $n_D = 1.4388$, at 20°. It is a saturated hydrocarbon, and is immediately colored by bromine vapor.

[1] Berkenheim, Ber., *25*, 686.
[2] Zelinsky and Rudewitsch, Ber., *28*, 1341.

OXIDIZED COMPOUNDS RELATED TO THE TERPENES, $C_{10}H_{16}$.

1. SUBSTANCES WHICH CAN NOT BE REGARDED AS DERIVATIVES OF THE HYDROCYMENES.

(ANALOGUES OF PINENE, CAMPHENE AND FENCHENE.)

1. CAMPHOR, $C_{10}H_{16}O$.

Dextrorotatory camphor (Japan camphor) is found in the camphor tree (*Laurus camphora*), while levorotatory camphor occurs in the oil of *Matricaria parthenium*, and has, therefore, been designated as *Matricaria camphor*. Camphor may be prepared artificially by oxidizing borneol and isoborneol with nitric acid.

Of especial interest is a partial synthesis of camphor which Bredt and v. Rosenberg[1] have accomplished. They obtained camphor by the dry distillation of the calcium salt of homocamphoric acid, prepared from camphonitrile;[2] accepting Bredt's formula of camphor (see page 25), this reaction may be expressed by the equation:

$$\begin{array}{l} CH_2 — CH — CH_2—COO \diagdown \\ \quad H_3C—C—CH_3 \qquad\qquad Ca \\ CH_2 — C — COO \diagup \\ \qquad\;\; CH_3 \end{array} = CaCO_3 + \begin{array}{l} CH_2 — CH — CH_2 \\ \quad H_3C—C—CH_3 \\ CH_2 — C — CO \\ \qquad\;\; CH_3 \end{array}$$

This synthesis of camphor[3] is quite analogous to the syntheses of many keto-pentamethylenes, which have been prepared by J. Wislicenus and his students.

[1]Bredt and v. Rosenberg, Ann. Chem., *289*, 1.

[2]Haller, Thèses présentées à la faculté des sciences de Paris; compare Claisen, Ann. Chem., *281*, 349.

[3]A. Haller, Bull. Soc. Chim., *15*, 1896 (III.), 324.

Camphor forms a colorless, transparent, tough mass, which crystallizes from alcohol; it is very volatile, sublimes easily, melts at 175° and boils at 204°. Its specific rotatory power is $[\alpha]_D = \pm 44.22°$.

Optically inactive camphor is obtained by mixing together the solutions of equal weights of the active modifications, or by oxidizing inactive borneol; it melts at 178.6°.

Camphor is resolved into para-cymene and water when it is treated with phosphorus pentoxide; it is converted into carvacrol by heating with iodine. According to Bredt,[1] both of these changes involve the formation of carvenone, $C_{10}H_{16}O$, as an intermediate product. The transformation of camphor into carvenone also takes place under the influence of concentrated sulphuric acid at 105° to 110°; the carvenone is either the direct product, or, more probably, results from dihydrocarvone, which is readily converted into carvenone by the influence of acids.

"**Camphren**"[2] is formed by heating 200 grams of camphor with 800 grams of concentrated sulphuric acid at 105° to 110°.

A mixture of borneol with about twenty per cent. of isoborneol is formed by reducing camphor in an alcoholic solution with sodium. Nitric acid oxidizes camphor into a product which consists chiefly of camphoric acid (m. p. 187°) and camphoronic acid (m. p. 139°); Bredt formulates this reaction as follows:

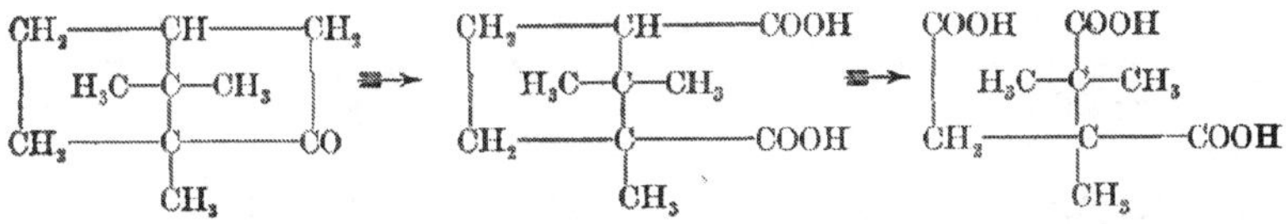

```
CH2————CH————CH2         CH2————CH————COOH        COOH   COOH
|                |       |                         |      |
|   H3C—C—CH3    |  →    |   H3C—C—CH3       →     |  H3C—C—CH3
|       |        |       |       |                 |      |
CH2—————C————————CO      CH2—————C————COOH         CH2————C————COOH
        |                        |                        |
        CH3                      CH3                      CH3

   Camphor.              Camphoric acid.          Camphoronic acid.
```

The discussion of camphor and its derivatives must necessarily be limited owing to the reasons mentioned in the introduction. Only those compounds will be briefly considered which are very nearly related to other members of the terpene group, and which are to be regarded as the parent-substances of certain terpene amido-compounds derived from camphor, or which may be converted by simple reactions into camphene, a terpene closely allied to cam-

[1] Bredt, Rochussen, and Monheim, Ann. Chem., *314*, 369.

[2] Armstrong and Kipping, Journ. Chem. Soc., *63*, 77; compare Bredt, Ann. Chem., *314*, 369.

phor. The most important of these derivatives are camphoroxime, borneol, isoborneol, and substances obtained from them.

Camphoroxime,[1] $C_{10}H_{16}$ NOH, was discovered by Nageli.[2] In order to prepare it, dissolve twenty parts of camphor in two and one-half times its quantity of ninety per cent. alcohol, add twelve parts of hydroxylamine hydrochloride and a little more than the calculated amount of sodium bicarbonate, and warm the mixture for some time. The reaction is complete when the product wholly dissolves in dilute sulphuric acid. It crystallizes from petroleum ether in brilliant, hard, monoclinic[3] prisms, which, like those of the active tartaric acids, are hemimorphic (Beckmann[4]).

Camphoroxime melts at 118° to 119°, boils with slight decomposition at 249° to 250°, and smells like camphor. The presence of an oximid group is proved by the formation of a sodium salt, an ethyl ester, and a compound with phenylcyanate,[5] which melts at 94°.

Leuckart and Bach[6] obtained *bornylamine*, $C_{10}H_{17}NH_2$, by reduction of camphoroxime with sodium and alcohol; they also prepared the same base by the action of ammonium formate on camphor.

The action of nitrous acid on camphoroxime has been investigated by Angeli and Tiemann.[7]

Camphordioxime, see Angelico, Atti. Real. Accad. Lincei, 1900 (V.), *9* (II.), 47.

Camphoroxime anhydride (**α-campholenonitrile**), $C_{10}H_{15}N$, was first prepared by Nägeli[8] by the action of acetyl chloride on camphoroxime; it may also be obtained by the action of other dehydrating agents[9] on camphoroxime, most readily by boiling with dilute sulphuric acid.

[1]Forster, Journ. Chem. Soc., *71*, 191 and 1030; *75*, 1141; *77*, 251.

[2]Nägeli, Ber, *16*, 497, see Konowaloff, Journ. Russ. Phys. Chem. Soc., *33* (1901), 45; Auwers, Ber, *22*, 605

[3]Muthmann, Ann. Chem, *250*, 354.

[4]Beckmann, Ann. Chem, *250*, 354.

[5]Goldschmidt, Ber, *22*, 3104.

[6]Leuckart and Bach, Ber., *20*, 104; see Konowaloff, Journ Russ. Phys. Chem Soc, *33*, 45; Forster, Journ. Chem. Soc, *73*, 386

[7]Angeli and Rimini, Ber., *28*, 1077, Angeli, Ber., *28*, 1127; Tiemann, Ber., *28*, 1079, Angeli and Rimini, Gazz. Chim., *25* [1], 406; Ber., *28*, 618, Ref. Tiemann, Ber., *29*, 2807; Angeli, Gazz. Chim, *26* (II.), 29, 34, 45, 228, 502 and 517; *28* (I.), 11, Mahla and Tiemann, Ber., *33*, 1929.

[8]Nägeli, Ber., *16*, 497.

[9]Goldschmidt and Zurrer, Ber, *17*, 2069 and 2717; Goldschmidt and Koreff, Ber, *18*, 1632, Leuckart, Ber, *20*, 104; Goldschmidt, Ber., *20*, 483.

It boils at 226° to 227°, and at 20° has the specific gravity 0.910 and the coefficient of refraction 1.46648, corresponding to the molecular refraction 45.39 (Wallach[1]). Its specific rotatory power in a one decimeter tube is $[\alpha]_D = +7.5$ (Tiemann[2]).

It is an unsaturated compound and combines directly with halogen acids, forming oily addition-products (Wallach[1]).

By reduction with zinc and sulphuric acid,[3] or better with sodium and alcohol,[4] *a*-campholenonitrile yields *a-camphylamine*, $C_{10}H_{17}NH_2$. When hydrogen chloride is passed into an alcoholic solution of the nitrile,[5] *a-campholenic acid* is produced, together with some *isoamidocamphor*, $C_{10}H_{15}O \cdot NH_2$.

a-**Campholenamidoxime**, $C_{10}H_{15}(NOH) \cdot NH_2$, is produced by heating *a*-campholenonitrile with aqueous hydroxylamine under pressure; it crystallizes in white needles, and melts at 102°.

Isocamphoroxime (*a*-**campholenamide**), $C_9H_{15}CONH_2$, is formed, together with *a*-campholenic acid, by heating camphoroxime anhydride with alcoholic potash; it crystallizes in leaflets, melting at 125° (Nägeli[6]). It has the specific rotatory power, $[\alpha]_D = -4.06°$. Warm, dilute sulphuric acid converts it into the sulphate of isoamidocamphor, and, under certain conditions, into *dihydrocampholenolactone*, $C_{10}H_{16}O_2$. It is quite readily changed into *a*-campholenic acid by boiling with alcoholic potash.

a-**Campholenic acid**, $C_9H_{15} \cdot COOH$ (Goldschmidt and Zürrer,[7] and Tiemann). This acid is identical with the "*oxycamphor*" obtained by Kachler and Spitzer;[8] it boils at 256°, has the specific gravity 0.992 at 19°, and the refractive index, $n_D = 1.47125$, from which the molecular refraction equals 47.36. Its specific rotatory power in a one decimeter tube is $[\alpha]_D = +9° 37'$.

a-**Dioxydihydrocampholenic acid**,[9] $C_9H_{17}O_2 \cdot COOH$, was first prepared by Wallach. It is formed by the oxidation of an ice-cold solution of sodium *a*-campholenate with a two per cent. solution of potassium permanganate.[10] It melts at 144°, and has $[\alpha]_D = +58.03°$.

[1] Wallach, Ann. Chem., *269*, 330.
[2] Tiemann, Ber., *29*, 3006.
[3] Goldschmidt and Koreff, Ber., *18*, 1632.
[4] Goldschmidt, Ber., *18*, 3297; Goldschmidt and Schulhoff, Ber., *19*, 708.
[5] F. Tiemann, Ber., *29*, 3006; *30*, 242, 321 and 404.
[6] Nägeli, Ber., *17*, 805; Tiemann, Ber., *29*, 3006.
[7] Goldschmidt and Zürrer, Ber., *17*, 2069 and 2717.
[8] Kachler and Spitzer, Ber., *17*, 2400; Monatsch. für Chem., *3*, 216; *4*, 643.
[9] Tiemann, Ber., *29*, 3006; Wallach, Ann. Chem., *269*, 327 and 343.
[10] Compare with Bouveault, Bull. Soc. Chim., *19*, 1898 (III.), 565.

In the following is presented a very brief outline of a discussion which was carried on between Leuckart and Goldschmidt regarding the structure of the compounds described above (these compounds were not at that time designated as alpha-derivatives). The formulas of these substances are :

According to Leuckart, Ber., *20*, 104.		According to Goldschmidt, Ber., *20*, 483.
$C_8H_{14}\left\langle\begin{matrix}CH_2\\ \vert\\ CO\end{matrix}\right.$	...........Camphor...........	$C_8H_{14}\left\langle\begin{matrix}CH_2\\ \vert\\ CO\end{matrix}\right.$
	↓	
$C_8H_{14}\left\langle\begin{matrix}CH_2\\ \vert\\ CNOH\end{matrix}\right.$	........Camphoroxime........	$C_8H_{14}\left\langle\begin{matrix}CH_2\\ \vert\\ CNOH\end{matrix}\right.$
↓		↓
$C_8H_{14}\left\langle\begin{matrix}CH_2\\ \vert\\ CH.NH_2\end{matrix}\right.$	............Bornylamine.........	$C_8H_{14}\left\langle\begin{matrix}CH_2\\ \vert\\ CH.NH_2\end{matrix}\right.$
↓		↓
$C_8H_{14}\left\langle\begin{matrix}CH\\ \vert\\ C\end{matrix}\right\rangle N$	.....Camphoroxime anhydride.........	$C_8H_{13}\left\langle\begin{matrix}=CH_2\\ CN\end{matrix}\right.$
↓		↓
$C_8H_{14}\left\langle\begin{matrix}CH.NH_2\\ \vert\\ CH_2\end{matrix}\right.$	......Camphylamine.......	$C_8H_{13}\left\langle\begin{matrix}=CH_2\\ CH_2.NH_2\end{matrix}\right.$
↓		↓
$C_8H_{14}\left\langle\begin{matrix}CH.NH_2\\ \vert\\ CO\end{matrix}\right.$	Isocamphoroxime.	$C_8H_{13}\left\langle\begin{matrix}=CH_2\\ CONH_2\end{matrix}\right.$
	↓	
$C_8H_{14}\left\langle\begin{matrix}CHOH\\ \vert\\ CO\end{matrix}\right.$	......Campholenic acid.......	$C_8H_{13}\left\langle\begin{matrix}=CH_2\\ COOH\end{matrix}\right.$
	↓	
	.........Campholene..............	$C_8H_{14}=CH_2$

The most important fact which Goldschmidt and Zürrer adduce to support their view that camphoroxime anhydride is to be regarded as a nitrile of a monobasic acid, is their observation that a hydrocarbon, C_9H_{16}, campholene (b. p. 130° to 140°), is obtained by the dry distillation of the calcium salt of campholenic acid ; further, an amidine[1] (m. p. 114° to 115°), is formed by

[1] Goldschmidt and Koreff, Ber., *18*, 1633.

heating the anhydride with toluidine hydrochloride according to Bernthsen's method.

It should also be mentioned that Bamberger[1] has accepted Goldschmidt's views, but has advanced the opinion that campholenonitrile is a cyanide having an open chain of carbon atoms, and has the formula:

```
   H  C3H7                          C3H7
    \ /                              |
     C                               C
    / \                             / \\
 H2C   CH2                       H2C   CH2
  |     |          ==>            |     |
 HC    CNOH                      HC    CN
   \\  /                            \\ /
     C                               C
     |                               |
    CH3                             CH3
 Camphoroxime.                Campholenonitrile.
```

Wallach's experiments, however, have proved that Bamberger's assumption is not well founded, hence a brief consideration of these experiments is given in the following.

According to Wallach, [2] campholenic acid is unsaturated; when bromine is added to its alcoholic or acetic acid solution, it forms a product which eventually becomes crystalline, and is insoluble in alkalis. Potassium permanganate, which is decolorized by sodium campholenate even in the cold, converts campholenic acid into *α*-dioxydihydrocampholenic acid, $C_{10}H_{18}O_4$; it separates from hot water in splendid crystals, melts at 144° to 145°, and yields a silver salt, $C_{10}H_{17}O_4Ag$, and is, therefore, a monobasic acid.

A saturated hydrocarbon is produced when campholenic acid is heated with concentrated hydriodic acid and red phosphorus; it boils at 135° to 145°, and probably contains as chief constituent, *dihydrocampholene*, C_9H_{18}.

These experiments show that campholenic acid, and likewise campholenonitrile, contain a cyclic structure of the carbon atoms, and one double linkage.

That campholenic acid is unsaturated and has a cyclic arrangement of its carbon atoms, has also been proved by W. Thiel.[3] In consideration of these facts, and by employing the formula of camphor proposed by himself, Bredt[4] explains the constitution of

[1] Bamberger, Ber., *21*, 1125.

[2] Wallach, Ann. Chem., *269*, 327 and 343.

[3] Thiel, Ber., *26*, 922; compare also under pinene.

[4] Bredt, Ber., *26*, 3054.

campholenonitrile and of campholenic acid by the following formulas, which he regards as the most probable:

CH_2—CH—CH_2 ; H_3C—C—CH_3 ; CH_2—C(CH_3)—CNOH

Camphoroxime.

→

CH_2—CH—CH_2 ; H_3C—C—CH_3 ; CH_2—C(CH_3)—CO—NH

Intermediary product.

→

CH_2—CH—CH_2—CN ; H_3C—C—CH_3 ; CH=C(CH_3)

Campholenonitrile.

→

CH_2—CH—CH_2—COOH ; H_3C—C—CH_3 ; CH=C—CH_3

Campholenic acid.

According to researches of Béhal,[1] and of Tiemann,[2] a second group of isomeric compounds is derived from camphoroxime; Tiemann designates these as beta-compounds.

β-Campholenonitrile,[2] $C_9H_{15}\cdot CN$, is obtained when camphoroxime is boiled for some time with dilute hydriodic acid. It boils at 225° and is optically inactive; when reduced in alcoholic solution with sodium, it gives rise to *β-camphylamine,* $C_{10}H_{17}NH_2$.

β-Campholenamide,[2] $C_9H_{15}CONH_2$, is prepared by the saponification of the β-nitrile. It melts at 86°, and is optically inactive.

β-Campholenic acid,[2] $C_9H_{15}COOH$, is formed by the hydrolysis of β-campholenamide. It melts at 52°, and boils at 245°.

β-Dioxydihydrocampholenic acid,[3] $C_9H_{17}O_2\cdot COOH$, is formed by the oxidation of β-campholenic acid with potassium permanganate. It crystallizes from chloroform or water in needles, and melts at 146°.

Isocamphorone,[3] $C_9H_{14}O$, boiling at 217°, and *campholonic acid,*[3] $C_{10}H_{16}O_3$, a liquid ketonic acid, isomeric with the pinonic acids, are also products of the oxidation of β-campholenic acid.

Isoamidocamphor,[4] $C_{10}H_{15}O\cdot NH_2$, is prepared by treating camphoroxime with twice its weight of hydriodic acid, sp. gr. 1.96. It crystallizes in prisms, melts at 39°, and boils at 254°.

Dihydrocampholenimide,[4] $C_{10}H_{16}O\cdot NH$, is obtained by distilling isoamidocamphor under atmospheric pressure in such a

[1] Béhal, Compt. rend., *119,* 799; *120,* 858 and 1167; *121,* 213.

[2] Tiemann, Ber., *28,* 1082; *30,* 242; see Blaise and Blanc, Compt. rend., *129* (1899), 106; *131* (1900), 803.

[3] Tiemann, Ber., *30,* 242.

[4] Tiemann, Ber., *30,* 321 and 404; see Mahla and Tiemann, Ber., *33,* 1929; Tiemann, Ber., *33,* 2953 and 2960.

manner that the substance becomes slightly superheated. It crystallizes in white needles, melts at 108°, and boils at 266°.

Dihydrocampholenolactone,[1] $C_{10}H_{16}O_2$, is produced when camphoroxime is decomposed with moderately concentrated sulphuric acid, the liquid diluted with water, and then boiled for some time. Tiemann explains this change by assuming that α-campholenonitrile is the first product, and that this compound passes at once into the β-modification, which, in turn, is hydrolyzed to β-campholenamide; this is changed into isoamidocamphor, which loses ammonia forming dihydrocampholenolactone. It melts at 30°, boils at 256°, has the specific gravity 1.0303, the refractive index, $n_D = 1.46801$, and the molecular refraction, $M = 45.79$. It is optically inactive.

Campholene,[2] C_9H_{16}, is formed by boiling α- and β-campholenic acids so that the material becomes slightly superheated. It boils at 133° to 135°, has a specific gravity 0.8034 at 20°, refractive index, $n_D = 1.44406$, at 20°, and molecular refraction, $M = 41.00$.

As a result of his investigations[3] on camphor and the campholene group, as well as from the researches of Tiemann and Mahla[4] on the oxidation products of camphoric acid, Tiemann concludes that the formula of camphor, which he has proposed and made to conform with Bredt's acceptance of a hexamethylene ring formed by the combination of two pentamethylene rings, is proved. Whether this opinion is correct, the future investigations must determine. At the present time, the question regarding the constitution of camphor seems to be an open one, notwithstanding the great amount of work which has been carried on regarding it.

Camphor semicarbazone, $C_{10}H_{16} = N \cdot NH \cdot CO \cdot NH_2$, melts at 236° to 238° (Tiemann[5]).

Oxymethylene camphor,

$$C_8H_{14}\langle\begin{matrix} C = CHOH \\ | \\ CO \end{matrix}$$

is obtained by the action of sodium and amyl formate on a solution of camphor in ether (Claisen). It is a white, crystalline substance, melts at 80° to 81°, and when dissolved in water or

[1] Tiemann, Ber., *30*, 321 and 404; Bouveault, Bull. Soc. Chim., *19*, 1898 (III.), 565.

[2] Tiemann, Ber., *30*, 594.

[3] Tiemann, Ber., *28*, 1079, 2166; *29*, 119, 3006; *30*, 242, 321, 404, 594; *33*, 2935; compare Bredt, Ann. Chem., *289*, 15; Forster, Journ. Chem. Soc., *75*, 1141; *79*, 108; Walker, Journ. Chem. Soc., *63*, 495; *67*, 347; *77*, 394; Blanc, Bull. Soc. Chim., 1900 [III.], *23*, 695.

[4] Mahla and Tiemann, Ber., *28*, 2151; *29*, 2807; *33*, 1929; compare Balbiano, Ber., *30*, 289, 1901; Real. Accad. dei Lincei, *8* (1899), 422; Gazz. Chim., *29* (II.), 490.

[5] Tiemann, Ber., *28*, 2191; see also Rimini, Gazz. Chim., *30* (I.), 600.

aqueous alcohol, it turns blue litmus paper red. Its alcoholic solution is colored reddish-violet by the addition of ferric chloride; a further addition of this reagent produces a blue, and finally a dark green color. It has been carefully investigated by Bishop, Claisen, and Sinclair.[1]

Campholic acid, $C_9H_{17}COOH$, is the parent-substance of campholamine and camphol alcohol; it is prepared by the method given by Errera.[2] To a boiling solution of 500 grams of camphor in 250 grams of benzene, thirty-eight grams of sodium are gradually added; the benzene is then distilled off, and the residual mass is heated at 280° for twenty-four hours. The reaction-product is treated with water, shaken with ether, and the aqueous solution acidified with hydrochloric acid; the resultant campholic acid is distilled with steam. A yield of twenty per cent. may be obtained by careful treatment of the mother-liquor.

Campholamide, $C_9H_{17}CONH_2$, is produced by heating ammonium campholate at 230°, or by treating the acid chloride with ammonia. It crystallizes from water or petroleum ether in needles, and melts at 79° to 80°.

Campholonitrile, $C_9H_{17}CN$, is formed in large quantities as a by-product in the preparation of campholamide, and is separated from the latter by distillation with steam. It melts at 72° to 73°, boils at 217° to 219°, and resembles camphor in odor and appearance. It yields *campholamine* on reduction with sodium and alcohol (Errera[3]).

For condensation-products of camphor with aldehydes, see investigations of Haller.[4]

Camphor pinacone, $C_{20}H_{34}O_2$, is formed, together with borneol, by the reduction of camphor in indifferent solvents; it is odorless, tasteless, very slightly volatile with steam, crystallizes in rhombic pyramids, and melts at 157° to 158°. Dextro-camphor yields a levorotatory pinacone, while levo-camphor gives rise to a dextrorotatory derivative. Various derivatives of this pinacone have been prepared (Beckmann[5]).

2. BORNEOL, $C_{10}H_{17}OH$.

Borneol occurs in nature in an optically dextrorotatory and levorotatory, as well as in an inactive, modification; it is found

[1]Bishop, Claisen and Sinclair, Ann. Chem., *281*, 314.

[2]Errera, Gazz. Chim., *22* [1], 205; Ber., *25*, 466, Ref.

[3]Errera, Gazz. Chim., *22* [2], 109; Ber., *26*, 21, Ref.

[4]A. Haller, Compt. rend., *128*, 1270; *130*, 688; *133*, 79; see also Helbronner, Compt. rend., *133*, 43.

[5]E. Beckmann, Ber., *22*, 92; *27*, 2348; Ann. Chem., *292*, 1; Journ. pr. Chem. [II.], *55*, 31.

free, and also in the form of esters. The most important occurrence of dextro-borneol is in the pith cavities of *Dryobalanops camphora* ("Borneo-camphor"); it is also found in oil of rosemary and oil of spike. The so-called "*Ngai-camphor*" from *Blumea balsamifera* consists of levorotatory borneol. Valerian oil contains levo-borneol ("*Valerian-camphor*"), and some inactive borneol; the latter modification has also been found in oil of sage. In the form of esters of the lower fatty acids, especially acetic acid, levo-borneol is a constituent of many fir and pine oils; thus, Bertram and Walbaum[1] have detected it in pine needle oil from *Abies alba*, Canadian pine oil, hemlock oil, pine needle oils from *Picea excelsa* and *Pinus montana*, while Hirschsohn[2] has found it in the oil of *Abies siberica* L. In the same manner borneol occurs in oil from *Satureja thymbra* L., oil of golden rod, sage oil, and oil of thyme. According to Kremers,[3] the oil of *Picea nigra* is especially rich in levo-bornyl acetate.

Borneol ("levo-camphenol"[4]) is produced by heating French oil of turpentine with benzoic acid at 150° for fifty hours.

For the preparation of borneol from camphor the following method is employed; it is Wallach's[5] modification of the old method proposed by Jackson and Menke,[6] and Immendorf.[7]

Fifty grams of camphor are dissolved in 500 cc. of ninety-six per cent. alcohol in a spacious flask connected with a wide reflux condenser, through which sixty grams of sodium are gradually added. The operation should require about one hour for its completion, and the spontaneous rise of temperature must not be prevented by cooling; it is in fact advisable when the reaction eventually becomes moderate, to accelerate the solution of the last portions of sodium by the careful addition of about fifty cc. of water. When the sodium is dissolved the product is poured into three or four liters of water, the separated borneol is filtered, pressed on a porous plate and crystallized from petroleum ether.

According to Bertram and Walbaum,[8] the borneol so prepared is not pure, but contains about twenty per cent. of isoborneol.

[1] Bertram and Walbaum, Arch. Pharm., *231*, 290.

[2] Hirschsohn, Pharm. Zeitsch. f. Russland, *1892*, No. 38.

[3] Kremers, Pharm. Rundschau, *13*, 135.

[4] Bouchardat and Lafont, Compt. rend., *113*, 551; *125*, 111.

[5] Wallach, Ann. Chem., *230*, 225.

[6] Jackson and Menke, Ber., *15*, 16 and 2730.

[7] Immendorf, Ber., *17*, 1036.

[8] Bertram and Walbaum, Journ. pr. Chem., N. F., *49*, 12; see Beckmann, Journ. pr. Chem., *55*, 1897 (II.), 31.

These chemists obtained chemically pure borneol by saponification of crystalline bornyl acetate.

Beckmann [1] effected the reduction of camphor into borneol by repeated, alternate treatment of a solution of camphor in ether with sodium and water.

PROPERTIES.—Borneol, prepared by Wallach's method, melts at 206° to 207°; pure borneol derived from its acetate, or from "borneo-camphor," or from oil of valerian, melts at 203° to 204°. It boils at 212°, and crystallizes in hexagonal plates (Traube [2]).

Its solution in petroleum ether unites with bromine, forming a yellowish-red, unstable additive compound, which soon decomposes on standing in the air (Wallach [3]).

Two molecules of borneol combine with one molecule of hydrobromic or hydriodic acid, yielding compounds which are easily decomposed.

If borneol be oxidized with nitric acid (sp. gr. 1.4), camphor results. Camphene is formed when borneol is heated with acid potassium sulphate.

Several esters of borneol have been synthetically prepared by Bertram and Walbaum; [4] the properties of these compounds are given in the following table:

	Boiling Point, (10 mm.).	Optical Rotation in 100 mm. Tube.	Sp. Gr. at 15°.	Refraction n_D at 15°.	Percentage of Ester Determined by Titration.
Formate.	90°	+31°	1.013	1.47078	97.89
Acetate.	80°	—38° 20′	0.991	1.46635	100.60
Propionate.	109° to 110°	+24°	0.979	1.46435	97.07
Butyrate.	120° to 121°	+22°	0.966	1.46380	99.20
Valerate.	128° to 130°	+20°	0.956	1.46280	98.56

Bornyl acetate, $C_{10}H_{17}O{\cdot}COCH_3$, is of especial importance, since it is a constituent of the oil of pine needles, and because it is a solid and possesses great power of crystallization. It melts at 29° and forms orthorhombic, hemihedral crystals (Traube).

Methyl bornyl ether, $C_{10}H_{17}OCH_3$, was prepared by Baubigny [5] and by Brühl. [6] It is a liquid, boiling at 194° to 195°.

[1] Beckmann, German patent, No. 42458; Ber., *21*, 321, Ref.; *22*, 912.

[2] Traube, Journ. pr. Chem., N. F., *49*, 3.

[3] Wallach, Ann. Chem., *230*, 226.

[4] Bertram and Walbaum, Arch. Pharm., *231*, 303; see also Minguin, Compt. rend., *123*, 1296.

[5] Baubigny, Ann. Chim. Phys. [4], 19 (1870), 221.

[6] Brühl, Ber., *24*, 3377 and 3713.

Ethyl bornyl ether, $C_{10}H_{17}OC_2H_5$, is obtained by repeated treatment of a solution of borneol in xylene with sodium and ethyl iodide. It is a thick liquid having an unpleasant odor, and boils at 97° at 20 mm. and at 204° to 204.5° under 750 mm. pressure; its specific gravity is 0.9008 at 20°.

A compound[1] called ethyl bornyl ether (?) is formed, together with camphene, by the action of alcoholic potash on pinene hydrochloride; it has a sp. gr. 0.9495 at 0° and a rotatory power, $[\alpha]_D = +26.3°$.

Methylene bornyl ether, $(C_{10}H_{17}O)_2CH_2$, is formed in a similar manner to the ethyl ether. It separates from ligroine in well formed, orthorhombic crystals, and melts at 167° to 168° (Brühl[2]). Brühl has also examined the physical properties of this compound.

Borneol, like other alcohols, combines with chloral and bromal to form compounds, which are analogous to the chloral-alcoholates. The borneol-chloral compound melts at 55° to 56°, and the bromal derivative melts at 98° to 99° (Haller[3] and Minguin[4]).

Bornyl phenylurethane, $C_6H_5NH \cdot CO \cdot OC_{10}H_{17}$, was first prepared by Leuckart[5] by the action of phenyl isocyanate on borneol. It melts at 138° to 139° (Bertram and Walbaum[6]).

The urethane and the above-mentioned compounds of borneol with chloral and bromal yield borneol on treatment with alcoholic potash.

Bornyl xanthic acid, $C_{10}H_{17}O \cdot CS \cdot SH$, was obtained by Bamberger and Lodter[7] by the action of carbon bisulphide on sodium bornylate, and analyzed in the form of its cuprous salt.

Bornyl chloride, $C_{10}H_{17}Cl$, was described by Kachler[8] as borneol chloride. It is most conveniently prepared by the following method.[9]

Sixty grams (one molecule) of phosphorus pentachloride are placed in a flask fitted with a tube containing sulphuric acid to prevent access of moisture, and are covered with eighty cc. of very low boiling petroleum ether; forty-five grams (one molecule) of borneol are added in small portions (about five to eight grams)

[1]Bouchardat and Lafont, Compt. rend., *104*, 639.
[2]Brühl, Ber., *24*, 3377 and 3713.
[3]Haller, Compt. rend., *112*, 143.
[4]Minguin, Compt. rend., *116*, 889.
[5]Leuckart, Ber., *20*, 115.
[6]Bertram and Walbaum, Arch. Pharm., *231*, 303.
[7]Bamberger and Lodter, Ber., *23*, 214.
[8]Kachler, Ann. Chem., *197*, 93.
[9]Wallach, Ann. Chem., *230*, 231.

at a time. After every addition of borneol a vigorous evolution of hydrochloric acid takes place, due to the action of the pentachloride on the borneol, and a new portion of borneol is not added until this evolution of gas is finished. The operation is complete in about half an hour. The clear liquid is now poured off from any excess of phosphoric chloride into a thick-walled separating funnel of about one liter capacity, and the phosphorus compounds are removed by careful and frequent agitation with a large quantity of water. In case there is some doubt whether all of the phosphorus oxychloride is decomposed, the petroleum ether solution of the bornyl chloride is eventually treated with alcohol, which is removed by shaking with water. The solution is poured into a shallow dish, and care is taken that the petroleum ether evaporates as quickly as possible in a cold place. Pure bornyl chloride is so obtained in a yield of about forty-five grams.

It appears and smells like camphor, melts at 157°, and dissolves readily in petroleum ether, less readily in alcohol, from which it may be obtained in thread-like crystals. It yields camphene when heated with aniline.

According to Reychler,[1] and Jünger and Klages,[2] bornyl chloride is stereoisomeric with isobornyl chloride and camphene hydrochloride, the two latter being identical.

According to Wagner,[3] most of the bornyl chloride, prepared as above described, is readily converted into camphene by boiling with alcoholic potash, and therefore consists chiefly of isobornyl chloride (camphene hydrochloride), the borneol being at first changed into camphene which then unites with one molecule of hydrogen chloride; a small proportion of the bornyl chloride, however, is not as easily acted upon by the alcoholic potash, and Wagner regards this as the true bornyl chloride, and that it is identical with pinene hydrochloride.

Recent investigations by Semmler[4] also seem to indicate that pinene hydrochloride is the true chloride corresponding with borneol.

Bornyl Iodide, $C_{10}H_{17}I$.—According to Wagner,[3] a mixture of bornyl iodide and another substance is formed when borneol is moistened with a little water and saturated with hydrogen iodide at the temperature of the water-bath; the two compounds are separated by boiling with alcoholic potash for thirty hours, the bornyl

[1] A. Reychler, Ber., *29*, 697; Bull. Soc. Chim., *15*, 1896 (III.), 366.
[2] Jünger and Klages, Ber., 29, 544.
[3] G. Wagner and Brickner, Ber., *32*, 2302.
[4] F. Semmler, Ber., *33*, 774.

iodide being only slowly attacked, yielding camphene, while the other substance is readily acted upon by the potash, giving an oily hydrocarbon.

Bornyl iodide boils at 118° to 119° at 16 mm. pressure, has the specific gravity 1.4799 at 0° and 1.4617 at 20°, solidifies in a freezing mixture, and melts at −13°; it is almost optically inactive. Silver nitrate and acetic acid convert it into a mixture of camphene, dipentene, and the acetates of borneol, isoborneol and terpineol. Wagner regards it as identical with pinene hydriodide in all respects except its optical rotation.

Methylenic acetal of borneol (diborneolic formal), $CH_2(O \cdot C_{10}H_{17})_2$, is a compound prepared by Brochet[1] by the condensation of borneol with formaldehyde in the presence of mineral acids. It melts at 166°, and boils without decomposition at 344° to 345°.

According to a recent publication by Semmler,[2] borneol is to be regarded as a secondary alcohol, and is not stereoisomeric with isoborneol.

3. ISOBORNEOL, $C_{10}H_{17}OH$.

It has been mentioned that camphene, $C_{10}H_{16}$, may be obtained from borneol by a variety of methods based on the elimination of water; on the other hand, methods are known by means of which hydrocarbons of the terpene group may be converted into alcohols. The most important of these methods is that proposed by Bertram.[3] While studying the effect of this method on camphene, Bertram and Walbaum[4] made the interesting observation that borneol was *not* formed from camphene, but that the isomeric alcohol isoborneol was obtained. Since the latter is also produced, together with borneol, by the reduction of camphor with sodium and alcohol, the isomerism of borneol and isoborneol cannot be explained by a difference in position of the hydroxyl-group (isomerism of position).

Montgolfier[5] had already shown that borneol ("stable camphol") and a compound isomeric with borneol ("instable camphol") are obtained by the action of alcoholic potash or of sodium on camphor. Haller[6] isolated the latter compound in a pure condition, and called it "*isocamphol.*" This substance is identical with Bertram and Walbaum's isoborneol.

[1] A. Brochet, Compt. rend., *128*, 612.
[2] F. Semmler, Ber., *33*, 774.
[3] Bertram, German patent, No. 67255.
[4] Bertram and Walbaum, Journ. pr. Chem., N. F., *49*, 1.
[5] Montgolfier, Compt. rend., *83*, 341.
[6] Haller, Compt. rend., *109*, 187.

Preparation of Isoborneol.[1]

One hundred grams of camphene are heated with a mixture of 250 grams of glacial acetic acid and ten grams of fifty per cent. sulphuric acid at 50° to 60° for a few hours, the mixture being frequently agitated. Since the acid mixture is not sufficient for the perfect solution of the camphene, two layers are at first formed; the volume of the upper one becomes gradually less, and in a short time a perfectly clear, colorless or slightly reddish solution results. The reaction is complete in two or three hours, and the product is diluted with water, the resultant isobornyl acetate separating as an oil. This is washed with water to remove the free acid, and without further purification it is boiled for a short time with a solution of fifty grams of potassium hydroxide in 250 grams of ethyl alcohol in a flask, fitted with a reversed condenser. The greater part of the alcohol is then distilled off, and the residue poured into a large quantity of water; isoborneol is precipitated as a solid mass, which is filtered and recrystallized from petroleum ether.

It crystallizes in thin leaflets, and dissolves readily in alcohol, ether, chloroform and benzene. It smells very like borneol, and is so volatile and sublimes so easily that its melting point, 212°, must be determined in sealed tubes, while its boiling point cannot be determined. It is further distinguished from borneol by its greater solubility in benzene and petroleum ether. According to Traube's measurements, published by Bertram and Walbaum, isoborneol, like borneol, crystallizes in hexagonal plates, but differs from borneol in its positive character of double refraction.

Isoborneol is changed into ordinary camphor by oxidation[2] with nitric acid or with a solution of chromic anhydride in glacial acetic acid; the identity of this product with Japan camphor is especially established by the observation that it yields a mixture of borneol and isoborneol by reduction with sodium and alcohol.

Camphene is formed much more readily by the removal of water from isoborneol than from borneol; this reaction is particularly characteristic. When a solution of isoborneol in benzene is heated with zinc chloride for one hour, a quantitative yield of camphene is obtained; a result almost as favorable as this is produced by boiling isoborneol with dilute sulphuric acid for several hours. Under these conditions pure borneol (m. p. 203° to 204°), prepared from bornyl acetate, is not changed.

Semmler[3] has further shown that when isoborneol is heated

[1] Bertram and Walbaum, Journ. pr. Chem., N. F., *49*, 1.

[2] According to Semmler (Ber., *33*, 3420), isoborneol gives a small yield of camphor on oxidation with dichromate and sulphuric acid.

[3] F. Semmler, Ber., *33*, 774.

with zinc dust for half an hour at 220°, it is converted into a small quantity of camphene, together with a larger amount of isodihydrocamphene, $C_{10}H_{18}$ (m. p. 85°); under similar conditions borneol remains unchanged. From this it appears that isoborneol is a *tertiary* alcohol, and borneol a *secondary* alcohol.

The acetic acid ester of isoborneol may be obtained from camphene by the method given under the preparation of isoborneol. Isobornyl formate can be prepared in a similar manner; it is also formed by adding fifty grams of isoborneol to a mixture of one hundred grams of formic acid (sp. gr. 1.22) and two grams of sulphuric acid, and warming to 30°. The acetyl ester is produced by a like process, but at a somewhat higher temperature. The esters may further be obtained by boiling isoborneol with acid anhydrides.

Isobornyl formate is a liquid, boiling at 100° under a pressure of 14 mm., and has a specific gravity of 1.017 at 15°.

Isobornyl acetate is also a liquid, which boils at 107° at 13 mm. pressure, and has the specific gravity 0.9905 at 15°.

The odors of these esters are like those of the isomeric bornyl esters.

The readiness with which the hydroxyl-group in isoborneol may be replaced by the ethoxyl- or methoxyl-groups is very characteristic. While the corresponding derivatives of borneol are prepared by treating its sodium salt with alkyl haloids, the formation of ethers from isoborneol takes place on mixing and warming an alcohol with isoborneol and sulphuric acid.

Methyl isobornyl ether, $C_{10}H_{17}OCH_3$, is prepared by heating sixty grams of isoborneol with one hundred and twenty grams of methyl alcohol and thirty grams of sulphuric acid. After boiling for twenty to thirty minutes, the mixture becomes cloudy, two layers are formed, and, in the course of one hour, the product is diluted with water. The resulting methyl ether boils at 192° to 193° (at 77° under a pressure of 15 mm.), and has a sp. gr. 0.9265 at 15°.

Ethyl isobornyl ether, $C_{10}H_{17}OC_2H_5$, is formed in an analogous manner; it boils at 203° to 204,° and has the sp. gr. 0.907 at 15°. According to Semmler,[1] this compound is also prepared by boiling a mixture of camphene, alcohol, and sulphuric acid.

Methylene isobornyl ether, $(C_{10}H_{17}O)_2CH_2$, is obtained by the method adopted by Brühl for the preparation of methylene bornyl ether; like the latter, it melts at 167°. It is distinguished from the bornyl derivative by its greatly diminished solubility in

[1]Semmler, Ber., *33*, 3420.

petroleum ether and alcohol, and by its slight power of crystallization; it separates in groups of fine crystals.

The compound of isoborneol with chloral is a liquid. The bromal derivative is a solid, but does not crystallize well; it melts at 71° to 72°.

Isobornyl phenylurethane, $C_6H_5NH \cdot CO \cdot OC_{10}H_{17}$, is difficultly soluble in petroleum ether, more readily in warm alcohol and benzene. It melts at 138° to 139° (bornyl phenylurethane melts at the same temperature), and yields isoborneol when warmed with alcoholic potash.

The differences between isoborneol and derivatives, and borneol and its compounds are rendered more apparent by the following table:

<table>
<tr><th></th><th colspan="2">Isoborneol.</th><th colspan="2">Borneol.</th></tr>
<tr><td>Crystal form,</td><td colspan="2">hexagonal, double refraction +,</td><td colspan="2">hexagonal, double refraction —.</td></tr>
<tr><td>Melting point,</td><td colspan="2">212°,</td><td colspan="2">203° to 204°.</td></tr>
<tr><td>Boiling point,</td><td colspan="2">undetermined,</td><td colspan="2">212°.</td></tr>
<tr><td>Solubility in benzene at 0°,</td><td colspan="2">1 : 2.5 to 3,</td><td colspan="2">1 : 6.5 to 7.</td></tr>
<tr><td>Solubility in benzene at 20°,</td><td colspan="2">1 : 1.5 to 2,</td><td colspan="2">1 : 4 to 4.5.</td></tr>
<tr><td>Solubility in petroleum ether at 0°,</td><td colspan="2">1 : 4 to 4.5,</td><td colspan="2">1 : 10 to 11.</td></tr>
<tr><td>Solubility in petroleum ether at 20°,</td><td colspan="2">1 : 2.5,</td><td colspan="2">1 : 6.</td></tr>
<tr><td>Phenylurethane,</td><td>m. p. 138° to 139°,</td><td rowspan="3">isoborneol is regenerated by treatment with alcoholic potash,</td><td>m. p. 138° to 139°,</td><td rowspan="3">borneol is regenerated by treatment with alcoholic potash.</td></tr>
<tr><td>Chloral compound,</td><td>liquid,</td><td>m. p. 55° to 56°,</td></tr>
<tr><td>Bromal compound,</td><td>m. p. 72°,</td><td>m. p. 98° to 99°,</td></tr>
<tr><td>Formyl ester,</td><td colspan="2">liquid, b. p. 100° (14 mm.),</td><td colspan="2">liquid, b. p. 98° to 99° (15 mm.).</td></tr>
<tr><td>Acetyl ester,</td><td colspan="2">liquid, b. p. 107° (13 mm.),</td><td colspan="2">m. p. 29°; b. p. 106° to 107° (15 mm.).</td></tr>
<tr><td>Behavior towards zinc chloride or dilute sulphuric acid,</td><td colspan="2">forms camphene,</td><td colspan="2">unchanged.</td></tr>
<tr><td>Behavior towards sulphuric acid and methyl or ethyl alcohol.</td><td colspan="2">forms methyl or ethyl isobornyl ether,</td><td colspan="2">does not yield ethers by this treatment.</td></tr>
</table>

Isobornyl chloride,[1] $C_{10}H_{17}Cl$, is obtained when hydrogen chloride is led into an alcoholic solution of isoborneol. It melts at 150° to 152°, and is identical with camphene hydrochloride.

A brief statement regarding the *rotatory powers of the more important derivatives of camphor* is presented in the following.

According to Beckmann,[2] camphor has the specific rotatory power, $[\alpha]_D = \pm 44.22°$. The direction and degree of rotation is not changed by heating camphor to high temperatures (230° to 250°), or by boiling it with alcohol or glacial acetic acid, or by dissolving in concentrated sulphuric acid.

The same investigator finds that camphoroxime prepared from levo-camphor is dextrorotatory, whilst the oxime from dextro-camphor is levorotatory. He gives these values for the rotatory power of camphoroxime:

Dissolved in 5 parts of alcohol, $[\alpha]_D = - 42.4°$ and $+ 42.51°$,
" " 12 " " " $[\alpha]_D = - 41.38°$ and $+ 42.38°$.

Camphoroxime hydrochloride (m. p. 162°) has the specific rotatory power, $[\alpha]_D = - 43.98°$ and $+ 42.52°$.

Borneol has a different rotatory power according to its origin; thus Beckmann[3] found the rotatory power of d-borneol to be $[\alpha]_D = + 37.44°$, and Haller[4] determined the rotatory power of borneol regenerated from the crystalline acetate, $[\alpha]_D = + 37.63°$. Natural l-borneol has $[\alpha]_D = - 37.74°$ (Beckmann[3]), and $- 37.77°$ (Haller[5]); a l-borneol occurring under the name of *Ngai fên* has $[\alpha]_D = - 39° 25'$ (Schimmel & Co.[6]).

According to Bertram and Walbaum,[7] the rotatory power of isoborneol changes under the influence of the sulphuric acid used in its preparation. This substance further shows a change in strength of its optical rotation when dissolved in different solvents. Isoborneol obtained from the camphene of citronella oil has the rotatory power:

Dissolved in alcohol, $[\alpha]_D = + 4.71°$.
Dissolved in benzene, $[\alpha]_D = + 2.88°$.

[1] A. Reychler, Ber., *29*, 697; Bull. Soc. Chim., *15*, 1896 (III.), 366; see also Jünger and Klages, Ber., *29*, 544.
[2] Beckmann, Ann. Chem., *250*, 352.
[3] Beckmann, Ann. Chem., *250*, 353; Journ. pr. Chem. [II.], *55*, 31.
[4] Haller, Compt. rend., *109*, 30; *112*, 143.
[5] Haller, Compt. rend., *108*, 456; *109*, 456.
[6] Schimmel & Co., Semi-Annual Report, April, *1895*, 76.
[7] Bertram and Walbaum, Journ. pr. Chem., *49*, 14.

4. CAMPHENE GLYCOL, $C_{10}H_{16}(OH)_2$.

Camphene glycol is closely allied to borneol; it was obtained by G. Wagner[1] by the oxidation of camphene with potassium permanganate.

Seventy grams of camphene dissolved in twenty-five grams of benzene are added to six liters of a one per cent. solution of potassium permanganate. If the color of the permanganate is entirely removed after four hours of constant agitation, the mixture is allowed to stand for some time, and the clear alkaline solution removed in a current of carbon dioxide by means of Zulkowsky's suction apparatus. The residue consisting of manganese oxides is washed with water, and again shaken with four and one-half liters of a one per cent. solution of permanganate. After decolorization, the liquid is removed as above suggested, and the manganese oxides are treated for a third time with three liters of permanganate. The filtrates thus obtained are saturated with carbonic anhydride, and extracted thirty times with benzene. The benzene is then distilled off, and a small amount of camphene which remains in the residue is driven over with steam; camphene glycol is only slightly volatile with steam, and after the addition of potassium hydroxide to the aqueous residue it is extracted with ether. On evaporation of the latter the solid glycol is obtained, and repeatedly recrystallized from benzene. It separates in prismatic needles, which melt at 192°. It is very readily soluble in ether, alcohol, carbon bisulphide and chloroform, sparingly in benzene; when thrown upon water it rotates in the same manner as camphor. It melts when warmed with water, and is only slightly soluble in hot water; it sublimes very readily when heated above 100°.

ALDEHYDE, $C_{10}H_{16}O$, FROM CAMPHENE GLYCOL.

When camphene glycol is heated with hydrochloric acid, it loses one molecule of water, forming a solid substance which smells like camphor; it has the formula, $C_{10}H_{16}O$, and is characterized as an aldehyde by its behavior towards fuchsinesulphurous acid and towards an ammoniacal silver solution. Hydroxylamine reacts with it, yielding a liquid compound; bromine acts slowly upon its solution in chloroform, giving rise to substitution products. When it is allowed to stand with water in the air, the water at once gives an acid reaction, and the substance becomes liquid (Wagner[1]). (See camphenilanic acid, page 65.)

[1]G. Wagner, Ber., 23, 2311.

This aldehyde is also formed in small quantities in the preparation of camphene glycol.

According to recent investigations of Bredt and Jagelki,[1] it seems probable that this aldehyde is identical with camphenilan aldehyde (m. p. 70°), which is formed by the action of water on the double compound of camphene with chromyl dichloride.

Pinene glycol, $C_{10}H_{16}(OH)_2$, is described by Wagner; it is mentioned under pinene (see page 46).

5. CAMPHOL ALCOHOL, $C_{10}H_{19}OH$.

According to Errera,[2] if a solution of campholamine hydrochloride be warmed with silver nitrite, camphol alcohol, $C_{10}H_{19}OH$, is produced, together with a hydrocarbon, $C_{10}H_{18}$. This alcohol is a liquid having an agreeable odor, and boils at 203°.

Since campholamine contains the group, $-CH_2NH_2$, it would be expected to yield a primary alcohol; Errera,[3] however, determined by the speed of the ester formation that camphol alcohol is a tertiary alcohol.

6. CAMPHENONE, $C_{10}H_{14}O$.

Claisen and Manasse[4] prepared amidocamphor by reduction of isonitroso-camphor,

$$C_8H_{14}\left\langle\begin{matrix} C{=}NOH \\ | \\ C{=}O \end{matrix}\right.$$

with zinc dust and acetic acid; by treating amidocamphor with nitrous acid, Angeli[5] obtained diazo-camphor,

$$C_8H_{14}\left\langle\begin{matrix} CN_2 \\ | \\ C{=}O \end{matrix}\right.$$

which, according to Curtius' nomenclature, may be called monoketazo-camphor-quinone or monoketazocamphadione. When this substance is heated and the resultant product is distilled with steam, camphenone, $C_{10}H_{14}O$, is formed. It has an odor similar to that of camphor, and separates from petroleum ether in splendid, colorless crystals, which melt at 168° to 170° (Angeli[6]).

[1] Bredt and Jagelki, Ann. Chem., *310*, 112.
[2] Errera, Gazz. Chim., *22* [2], 114; Ber., *26*, 21, Ref.
[3] Errera, Gazz. Chim., *23* [2], 497; Ber., *27*, 126, Ref.
[4] Claisen and Manasse, Ann. Chem., *274*, 88.
[5] Angeli, Ber., *26*, 1718; Rimini, Gazz. Chim., *26* [2], 290.
[6] Angeli, Gazz. Chim., *24* [2], 44 and 317; Ber., *27*, 590, 797 and 892, Ref.

Camphenone behaves as an unsaturated compound; it is immediately oxidized by a permanganate solution, and is reduced to camphor by the action of nascent hydrogen.

Camphenone hydrobromide,[1] $C_{10}H_{14}O \cdot HBr$, is produced by treating camphenone with hydrogen bromide in a glacial acetic acid solution; it is isomeric with monobromocamphor. It melts at 113°, is stable towards acids, but is converted into camphenone by alkalis, and yields camphenonoxime on treatment with an alkaline solution of hydroxylamine.

Camphenone dibromide,[1] $C_{10}H_{14}O \cdot Br_2$, is formed by the addition of bromine to a solution of camphenone in carbon bisulphide; it is isomeric with dibromocamphor, but is readily distinguished from the latter by yielding monobromocamphenone on treatment with alcoholic potash. It separates from alcohol or petroleum in large crystals, and melts at 58° to 59°.

Monobromocamphenone, $C_{10}H_{13}BrO$, is obtained by treating camphenone dibromide with alcoholic potash; it forms large, well defined crystals, melting at 70°.

Camphenonoxime,[2] $C_{10}H_{14}NOH$, is formed by the action of hydroxylamine on camphenone; it crystallizes from petroleum ether in tablets, and melts at 132°. It is isomeric with nitrosopinene, and melts at the same temperature as the latter. By the action of mineral acids it is gradually converted into a nitrile.

Pernitrosocamphenone,[2] $C_{10}H_{14}N_2O_2$, is prepared by the action of nitrous acid on camphenonoxime; it melts at 47°, is insoluble in acids and alkalis, and does not give the Liebermann's reaction.

Pernitrosocamphenone dibromide (dibromopernitrosocamphor), $C_{10}H_{14}N_2O_2 \cdot Br_2$, is produced by the addition of bromine to a chloroform solution of pernitrosocamphenone. It crystallizes from petroleum and melts at 133°.

Isocamphenone, $C_{10}H_{14}O$.—When *pernitrosocamphor,* $C_{10}H_{16}N_2O_2$ (obtained by the action of nitrous acid on camphoroxime), is dissolved in a glacial acetic acid solution of dry hydrogen bromide, and is then treated with bromine, *bromopernitrosocamphor,* $C_{10}H_{15}BrN_2O_2$ (m. p. 114°), is formed; this is converted into *isobromopernitrosocamphor,* $C_{10}H_{15}BrN_2O_2$ (m. p. 67°), by the action of dilute alcoholic potash. When the latter compound is treated with cold, concentrated sulphuric acid, isocamphenone is obtained; it separates from petroleum in yellowish crystals, melts at 92°, and soon resinifies in the air. Its *oxime* melts at 170°.

[1] Angeli and Rimini, Atti. d. R. Acc. d. Lincei Rudct., *1895* [1], 390; Gazz. Chim., *26* [2], 34 and 45.

[2] Angeli, Gazz. Chim., *24* [2], 44 and 317; Angeli and Rimini, Gazz. Chim., *26* [2], 34 and 45; Ber., *28*, 1077.

7. PINOCAMPHONE, $C_{10}H_{16}O$.

This ketone, which is isomeric with camphor, is formed as a by-product in the preparation of pinylamine, $C_{10}H_{15}NH_2$, from nitrosopinene, $C_{10}H_{17}NOH$. Wallach[1] observed the formation of this ketone during his first researches on the reduction-products of nitrosopinene, but it was not until the year 1898 that he published a detailed account of its method of preparation and its properties.[2]

Pinocamphone is prepared by the following method. Five grams of nitrosopinene are dissolved in forty cc. of warm glacial acetic acid, and, after diluting with sufficient water to produce a slight cloudiness, the solution is treated with a large excess of zinc dust. After the first violent reaction has ceased, the mixture is heated in a reflux apparatus on the water-bath for three or four hours. The excess of zinc is then removed by filtration, the filtrate is distilled with steam, and the distillate is extracted several times with ether; the ethereal solution is dried with solid potash, the ether is distilled off, and the residue is fractionated in vacuum. The yield of pinocamphone is over twenty per cent. of the nitrosopinene employed.

The odor of pinocamphone is somewhat similar to that of turpentine, but on warming it suggests that of peppermint oil. It boils at 211° to 213°, has the specific gravity 0.959, and the refractive index, $n_D = 1.47273$, at 21°; its molecular refraction is 44.44, while that calculated for the compound, $C_{10}H_{16}O$, is 44.11.

Pinocamphonoxime, $C_{10}H_{16}NOH$, is readily obtained, and is characterized by its splendid power of crystallization. It is volatile with steam, crystallizes in large, transparent plates, and melts at 86° to 87°. On reduction with sodium and alcohol, it yields *pinocamphylamine*,[3] $C_{10}H_{17}NH_2$, which is a liquid; it rapidly absorbs carbon dioxide, forms a *carbamide* (m. p. 204°), and an *acetyl* derivative (m. p. 120°).

Pinocampholenonitrile, $C_{10}H_{15}N$.—Pinocamphonoxime is not attacked by boiling dilute sulphuric acid. When the oxime is boiled for a considerable time with concentrated sulphuric acid (one part acid to one part water), a small proportion is converted into a nitrile, while much of the oxime remains unaltered. The nitrile is obtained by distilling the reaction-product with steam.

[1] Wallach, Ann. Chem., *268*, 210.
[2] Wallach, Ann. Chem., *300*, 287.
[3] Wallach, Ann. Chem., *313*, 345.

The nitrile[1] is an oil, having an odor similar to that of campholenonitrile, and is volatile with steam; it boils at 224° to 226°. It is converted into *pinocampholenic acid*, $C_{10}H_{16}O_2$, by heating with alcoholic potash; this acid yields an *amide* melting at 116°.

Pinocamphone semicarbazone melts at 199° to 200°.

Wallach is inclined to regard pinocamphone, $C_{10}H_{16}O$, as the dihydro-derivative of an unknown ketone, $C_{10}H_{14}O$, which corresponds with nitrosopinene, $C_{10}H_{14}NOH$.

A *ketone*, $C_{10}H_{16}O$, *isomeric* with pinocamphone, is formed when nitrosopinene dibromide is reduced with zinc and acetic acid in exactly the same manner as described above. This compound is an oil, having an odor similar to that of carvone. It yields an *oxime*, which crystallizes from dilute alcohol in needles, and melts at 113° to 114°.

The properties of this isomeric ketone and of its oxime resemble so closely those of *inactive dihydrocarvone*, that Wallach is inclined to consider the ketone as identical with inactive dihydrocarvone.

8. PINOCAMPHEOL, $C_{10}H_{17}OH$.

This alcohol, isomeric with borneol, is prepared by reducing pinocamphone with sodium in aqueous ether according to Beckmann's method of reducing camphor to borneol.

It is a viscous liquid, having the odor of terpineol and turpentine. It boils at 218° to 219°, has the specific gravity 0.9655, and the refractive index, $n_D = 1.48612$, at 20°. When it is heated with zinc chloride, it loses water and yields products among which *cymene* has been identified.

Pinocamphyl phenylurethane,

$$CO\begin{matrix} \diagup NHC_6H_5 \\ \diagdown OC_{10}H_{17} \end{matrix}$$

forms a crystalline mass, and melts at 98°.

9. FENCHONE, $C_{10}H_{16}O$.

Fenchone occurs in nature in a dextrorotatory and a levorotatory modification, and in its total behavior shows the greatest similarity to camphor. Dextro-fenchone is present in fennel oil,[2] while levo-fenchone forms a constituent of thuja oil.[3]

[1]Wallach, Ann. Chem., *313*, 345.
[2]Wallach and Hartmann, Ann. Chem., *259*, 324.
[3]Wallach, Ann. Chem., *272*, 102.

The fractions boiling between 190° and 195° of fennel oil and thuja oil consist almost wholly of fenchone. Its purification is easily accomplished, since fenchone is much more stable towards oxidizing agents than the substances accompanying it. However, the compounds occurring with fenchone in fennel oil differ in character and in quantity from those found in thuja oil, hence the two oils cannot be treated in the same manner.

Preparation of Dextrorotatory Fenchone.[1]—The fraction of fennel oil boiling at 190° to 195° contains considerable quantities of anethol and other impurities, even after repeated distillations. Two hundred grams of this fraction are heated with three times its amount of ordinary concentrated nitric acid in a large flask, connected with a reflux condenser, over a free flame. A vigorous reaction takes place, accompanied by evolution of nitrogen oxides. At this point, it is well to somewhat diminish the heat in order to prevent a too violent action. The mixture is then warmed until the fumes, which are at first reddish brown in color, are light colored. It is then allowed to cool; the contents of the flask are poured into water, and the resulting oil is separated. This oil is washed with a solution of sodium hydroxide, distilled with steam, and the fenchone obtained in the distillate is dried with potash; the product is now quite pure. It is then cooled in a freezing mixture and brought to crystallization by the addition of a small crystal of pure fenchone. Large crystals of pure fenchone separate, and are filtered from the residual oil.

The fraction boiling at 190° to 195° of thuja oil contains a much smaller quantity, about twenty to twenty-five per cent., of fenchone. Thujone isthe chief constituent of this fraction.

Pure levorotatory fenchone is prepared by one of three following methods (Wallach[2]).

1. Oxidation with Nitric Acid.

To eighty cc. of hot concentrated nitric acid contained in a capacious flask provided with a reflux condenser (the tube of the condenser should be sealed onto the flask), twenty cc. of the abovementioned fraction of thuja oil are added drop by drop. After all of the oil has been introduced, the mixture is boiled for an hour, and then distilled with steam; the resulting oil is washed with sodium hydroxide, again distilled with steam, and the pure levo-fenchone is crystallized by the method suggested above.

[1] Wallach, Ann. Chem., *263*, 130.
[2] Wallach, Ann. Chem., *272*, 102.

2. Oxidation with Permanganate.

Levorotatory fenchone and thujaketonic acid may be very conveniently prepared at the same time. For this purpose, one hundred and thirty grams of the fraction of thuja oil boiling at 190° to 200° are shaken with a solution of three hundred and ninety grams of potassium permanganate in five liters of water, until the permanganate solution is decolorized; some form of shaking machine is employed to constantly agitate the mixture. The unchanged oil is distilled with steam, separated and treated with hot nitric acid according to method 1. By this operation larger quantities of levo-fenchone may be obtained in one treatment.

3. Treatment with Dilute Sulphuric Acid.

The thujone in thuja oil may be more readily separated from levorotatory fenchone by heating the fraction of this oil boiling at 190° to 200° with dilute sulphuric acid (one volume of concentrated acid with two volumes of water). Thujone is so converted into isothujone, which boils 30° higher than thujone, while fenchone remains unchanged (Wallach [1]).

Fenchone is further obtained by boiling fenchyl alcohol with three times its amount of nitric acid.[2] The product thus formed has the same optical rotation, respecting direction and power, as the fenchone from which the alcohol is prepared by reduction.

PROPERTIES.[3]—The properties of dextro- and levo-fenchone agree completely with the exception of the opposite rotatory powers. Wallach found the specific rotatory powers as follows:

Dextro-fenchone (chemically pure) = + 71.97°.

Levo-fenchone (not absolutely pure) = − 66.94°.

Inactive fenchone,[4] prepared by mixing equal parts of dextro- and levo-fenchone, has the same properties as its active components, but its derivatives, however, often differ considerably from the corresponding active compounds in melting points, forms of crystals and solubilities. Inactive fenchone bears the same relation to its active constituents as racemic acid does to the dextro- and levo-tartaric acids.

Pure fenchone is an oil, smells like camphor, boils at 192° to 193°, and has the sp. gr. 0.9465 at 19°; its refractive index is $n_D = 1.46306$ at 19°, corresponding to a molecular refraction of

[1]Wallach, Ann. Chem., *286*, 103.
[2]Wallach, Ann. Chem., *263*, 146.
[3]Wallach, Ann. Chem., *263*, 131; *272*, 103.
[4]Wallach, Ann. Chem., *272*, 107.

44.23 while the calculated value for a compound of the composition, $C_{10}H_{16}O$, containing no ethylene linkage, is 44.11. It solidifies at a low temperature, and melts at 5° to 6°.

Fenchone is a saturated compound. It combines with bromine in a cold petroleum ether solution, yielding a red, crystalline, unstable additive product which is reconverted into fenchone on treatment with alkalis. Substitution takes place if bromine acts upon fenchone for a long time, or at a high temperature.

Fenchone is quite readily dissolved by cold concentrated hydrochloric acid or sulphuric acid, and is thrown out of this solution on the addition of water.

When it is warmed with strong sulphuric acid at about 80°, sulphur dioxide is given off and *acetoxylene*, $C_{10}H_{12}O$ [$CH_3 : CH_3 : CH_3CO = 1 : 2 : 4$], is formed; this is an oil, smelling somewhat of cinnamon. It boils at 131° at 20 mm. pressure, yields an *oxime*, melting at 86° to 87°, and is converted into *para-xylic acid*, $C_9H_{10}O_2$, by oxidation (Marsh[1]).

With fuming nitric acid fenchone forms a clear mixture without any apparent reaction, and is precipitated unchanged by water. It may even be boiled with fuming nitric acid without visible change; by long continued boiling it is acted upon by nitric acid, being converted into a mixture of organic acids. Thus, according to Gardner and Cockburn,[2] when fenchone is heated with concentrated nitric acid on the water-bath for six days, it is oxidized to isocamphoronic acid, $C_9H_{14}O_6$ (m. p. 163° to 164°), dimethyltricarballylic acid, $C_8H_{12}O_6$ (m. p. 152°), dimethylmalonic acid, $C_5H_8O_4$ (m. p. 190°), isobutyric acid, and acetic acid; in addition to these acids a *nitrofenchone*, $C_{10}H_{15}O \cdot NO_2$, is formed. The latter is an oil, which boils at 146° to 151° under 14 mm. pressure, and, on reduction with stannous chloride, yields an amine.

Fenchone is more vigorously attacked by heating with three times its amount of fuming nitric acid in a sealed tube at 120°; hydrocyanic acid is one of the products of this reaction.

Potassium permanganate oxidizes fenchone to a mixture of acetic, oxalic and dimethylmalonic acids (Wallach[3]).

When phosphorus pentachloride is allowed to act upon fenchone for six weeks in the cold, and the product is subsequently treated with water, *chlorofenchene-phosphoric acid*, $C_{10}H_{14}ClPO(OH)$, melting at 196°, *α*- and *β-chlorofenchene hydrochlorides*,

[1] J. E. Marsh, Journ. Chem. Soc., *75*, 1058; compare with Claus, Journ. pr. Chem., *41* (II.), 396; Armstrong and Kipping, Journ. Chem. Soc., *63*, 75.

[2] Gardner and Cockburn, Journ. Chem. Soc., *73*, 708.

[3] Wallach, Ann. Chem., *263*, 134.

$C_{10}H_{16}Cl_2$, and *chlorofenchene*, $C_{10}H_{15}Cl$, a solid, boiling at 80° to 83° under 16 mm. pressure, are produced.[1]

Bromofenchone,[2] $C_{10}H_{15}OBr$, is formed by heating fenchone with bromine for twenty hours at 100° in a sealed tube; it is a colorless oil which boils at 131° to 134° under 18 mm. pressure, has a faint camphor-like odor, a sp. gr. 1.348 at 12°, a refractive index 1.51013, and a rotation + 11.6° in a 100 mm. tube. It is not readily volatile with steam, and yields neither an oxime nor a semicarbazone. Fenchone is regenerated by heating the compound with zinc dust and acetic acid.

When bromofenchone is heated with an excess of alcoholic potash, α-fencholenic acid, $C_{10}H_{16}O_2$, is produced, identical with that obtained by Wallach; when cooled with liquid air, it crystallizes. An isomeric *compound*,[3] $C_{10}H_{16}O_2$, is formed by dissolving the acid in concentrated sulphuric acid and pouring the solution on ice; it crystallizes from light petroleum in leaflets, melts at 77°, is not soluble in solutions of sodium carbonate or hydroxide, and does not decolorize solutions of permanganate. (See "Biological Oxidation of Fenchone." Rimini, Atti. Real. Accad. Lincei, 1901 [V.], 10 (I.), 244.)

Tribromofenchone,[3] $C_{10}H_{15}OBr \cdot Br_2$, is obtained by gradually adding bromine to a solution of fenchone in phosphorus trichloride; it is a yellow oil, boils at 181° to 186° under 18 mm. pressure and darkens in the air.

When tribromofenchone is boiled with zinc dust and acetic acid, it yields a crystalline *compound*, $C_{10}H_{15}Br$, melting at 115° to 116°; it has a camphor-like odor, and in general properties resembles the chlorofenchene above mentioned. It sublimes readily and decolorizes permanganate.

Tetrahydrofenchene,[4] $C_{10}H_{20}$, results when fenchone is heated with phosphorus and hydriodic acid; the same hydrocarbon is obtained from fenchyl alcohol under analogous conditions.

That fenchone is a ketone follows from the formation of fenchonoxime and fenchyl alcohol. On heating fenchone with ammonium formate according to Leuckart's method, fenchylamine, $C_{10}H_{17}NH_2$, a base isomeric with bornylamine, is formed.

It differs from camphor in that it does not form an oxymethylene compound.[5]

[1] Gardner and Cockburn, Journ. Chem. Soc., *71*, 1156; *73*, 704.
[2] Czerny, Ber., *33*, 2287; see Balbiano, Gazzetta, *30* [II.], 382.
[3] Czerny, Ber., *33*, 2287.
[4] Wallach, Göttinger Nachrichten, *1891*, 309; Ann. Chem., *284*, 326.
[5] Wallach, Ber., *28*, 34.

The behavior of fenchone towards phosphorus pentoxide is of especial interest in showing the resemblance of the reactions of fenchone and of camphor. According to Wallach,[1] twenty grams of fenchone and thirty grams of phosphorus pentoxide were well mixed in a small, round flask, and, after a further addition of thirty grams of phosphorus pentoxide, the mixture was heated for thirty minutes in a paraffin-bath at 115° to 130°. After cooling, water was carefully added and the resulting oil identified as *meta-cymene*, boiling at 175° to 176°. A comparison was made of this cymene with meta-cymene isolated by Kelbe from the distillation products of colophonium and resin oil, and they were found to be identical.

Since para-cymene is formed by the action of phosphorus pentoxide on camphor, and nearly all of the properties of camphor closely resemble those of fenchone, it is probable that these two substances bear the same relation to each other that a para-compound does to a meta-compound.

It may also be mentioned that by oxidation of dextrorotatory and inactive fenchyl alcohols, obtained by Bouchardat and Lafont[2] by the action of benzoic acid and other acids on French (levorotatory) turpentine, levorotatory and inactive fenchones are obtained; the former is the optical antipode of d-fenchone prepared from oil of fennel. This synthetically prepared l-fenchone forms an oxime (m. p. 161° to 163°), but it is produced less readily than that obtained from the fenchone prepared from oil of fennel.

Fenchone does not react with alkaline bisulphites.

Fenchone semicarbazone,[3] $C_{10}H_{16} \cdot N \cdot NH \cdot CO \cdot NH_2$, cannot be prepared directly from fenchone and a semicarbazide solution. It is formed, however, by gently heating pernitrosofenchone, $C_{10}H_{16}N_2O_2$, with semicarbazide acetate on the water-bath. It separates from alcohol in white crystals, and melts at 186° to 187°.

Fenchonoxime, $C_{10}H_{16}NOH$, is conveniently prepared in *small* quantities by the following method (Wallach[4]). To five grams of fenchone dissolved in eighty cc. of absolute alcohol, a solution of eleven grams of hydroxylamine hydrochloride in eleven grams of hot water and six grams of pulverized potash are added. The sparingly soluble oxime separates in the course of one or two days by the gradual evaporation of the alcohol.

[1] Wallach, Ann. Chem., *275*, 157.
[2] Bouchardat and Lafont, Compt. rend., *126*, 755.
[3] Rimini, Gazz. Chim., *30* (I.), 600.
[4] Wallach, Ann. Chem., *284*, 324; *272*, 104.

For the preparation of *larger* quantities of fenchonoxime, Wallach[1] employs the following method. One hundred grams of fenchone are dissolved in four hundred grams of absolute alcohol and treated with a warm solution of eighty grams of hydroxylamine hydrochloride in eighty grams of water. The solution is then rendered alkaline by the addition of fifty grams of potassium hydroxide dissolved in fifty grams of water; the potassium chloride is filtered off, and the filtrate boiled for a few hours on the water-bath. A large quantity of the oxime separates out on cooling. An additional amount may be obtained by warming the mother-liquor, and precipitating with water.[2]

Fenchonoxime crystallizes from alcohol in fine needles, and from ethyl acetate or ether in well formed, monoclinic[3] crystals, which melt at 161° when heated rapidly.[4] It is volatile with steam, and boils at 240° with slight decomposition (elimination of water). It is insoluble in sodium hydroxide.

The oxime of dextro-fenchone is dextrorotatory,[5] $[\alpha]_D = 52.54°$; that obtained from levo-fenchone is levorotatory.

Inactive fenchonoxime is formed by mixing the ethereal solutions of equal parts of dextro- and levorotatory oximes; it separates in crystals which differ in form from those of the active modifications, and melt slightly lower than these, at 158° to 160°.

Wallach and Hartman obtained *fenchonoxime hydrochloride* by precipitating an ethereal solution of the dextro-oxime with hydrochloric acid; it melts at 118° to 119°.

Fenchylamine, $C_{10}H_{17}NH_2$, analogous to bornylamine, is prepared by reducing fenchonoxime with sodium and alcohol.

Fenchonoxime anhydride,[6] $C_{10}H_{15}N$ (α- and β-**fencholenonitrile,** $C_9H_{15} \cdot CN$), is formed very easily and quickly by the action of dehydrating agents on fenchonoxime. When the oxime is dissolved in warm, dilute sulphuric acid, a clear solution is at first obtained, but if this be heated to a higher temperature, fenchonoxime anhydride separates at once as an oil, which may be readily distilled with steam.

[1] Wallach, Ann. Chem., *263*, 136.

[2] For preparation of fenchonoxime, see also Rimini, Gazz. Chim., *26* (II.), 502.

[3] Zander, Ann. Chem., *259*, 327.

[4] Mahla and Tiemann (Ber., *29*, 2807) give the melting point of the active modifications at 163°; Rimini (Gazz. Chim., *26* (II.), 502) finds them to melt at 165°.

[5] Wallach and Binz, Ann. Chem., *276*, 317; *272*, 104.

[6] Wallach and Hartmann, Ann. Chem., *259*, 328; Wallach, Ann. Chem., *263*, 137.

The anhydride prepared from dextro-fenchonoxime is dextrorotatory, $[\alpha]_D = +43.31°$. It boils at 217° to 218°,[1] has a specific gravity 0.898 and the refractive power, $n_D = 1.46108$, at 20°.

Although fenchone and fenchonoxime are saturated compounds, the anhydride is unsaturated, and forms a liquid bromide when treated with bromine; it also combines with hydrobromic and hydriodic acids, forming the solid, but unstable, addition-products, $C_{10}H_{15}N \cdot HBr$ and $C_{10}H_{15}N \cdot HI$. These two compounds can only be crystallized from alcohol when great care is taken; the hydrobromide melts at 60°, and hydriodide at 54° to 55°.

Hydrochlorofenchonoxime anhydride, $C_{10}H_{15}N \cdot HCl$, is more stable than the hydrobromide and hydriodide, and is prepared by shaking the anhydride with concentrated hydrochloric acid; after a short time the product becomes solid, is pressed on a porous plate, and recrystallized from petroleum ether. The pure hydrochloride melts at 57° to 58°, and decomposes into its constituents on boiling with water or alcohol (Wallach [2]).

Fenchonoxime anhydride is to be regarded as a nitrile, $C_9H_{15}CN$, since it may be converted into α- and β-fencholenic acids, $C_9H_{15}COOH$, and α-fencholenamide; the latter is identical with α-isofenchonoxime.

When it is reduced with sodium and alcohol, an unsaturated base, fencholenamine,[3] $C_{10}H_{17}NH_2$, is formed; this amine is isomeric with camphylamine.

α-Isofenchonoxime, $C_{10}H_{17}NO$ (**α-fencholenamide,** $C_9H_{15}CONH_2$). The transformation of fenchonoxime anhydride into the corresponding acid amide, and more especially into the acid itself, is effected much more slowly than the like transformation of camphoroxime anhydride into α-campholenamide and α-campholenic acid.

α-Isofenchonoxime is prepared by warming thirty grams of fenchonoxime anhydride with a solution of 130 grams of potassium hydroxide in 450 cc. of absolute alcohol and twenty cc. of water for four or five days. A small quantity of ammonia is constantly given off, thus forming fencholenic acid, but the greater part of the anhydride is converted into α-isofenchonoxime. The solution is diluted with water, and the alcohol is removed by distillation; on cooling, yellowish, crystalline leaflets are obtained, which are purified by boiling with animal charcoal and recrystallizing from alcohol. It melts at 113° to 114°, and dissolves in

[1] According to Cockburn (Journ. Chem. Soc., *75*, 503), it boils at 214° to 219°.

[2] Wallach, Ann. Chem., *269*, 330.

[3] Wallach and Jenkel, Ann. Chem., *260*, 369.

alcohol, ether and acids; it may be reprecipitated from an acid solution by alkalis (Wallach[1]).

α-Fencholenic acid, α-isofenchonoxime and α-fencholenonitrile, which is produced by gently warming α-isofenchonoxime with phosphoric anhydride, are unsaturated compounds. The α-isoxime is optically active.

When the solutions of equal quantities of dextro- and levo-α-isofenchonoxime are mixed, an inactive modification is formed, which melts at 98° to 99°.

If the α-isoxime be reduced in an alcoholic solution with sodium, α-fencholenic acid and α-fencholenamine are formed, together with isofencholenyl alcohol (see page 176).

β-Isofenchonoxime,[2] $C_{10}H_{17}NO$, is a saturated compound, and is obtained when α-isofenchonoxime is boiled for several hours with dilute sulphuric acid. By this treatment the α-isoxime is gradually dissolved, and when the cold solution is neutralized with alkali, β-isofenchonoxime is precipitated as a white, crystalline substance, which is more readily soluble in hot water than the isomeric α-compound. It is readily soluble in alcohol, from which it may be recrystallized; it melts at 137°, has pronounced basic properties and is probably a lactam. (See dihydrofencholenic acid lactam.)

By the oxidation of a sulphuric acid solution of the β-isoxime with permanganate, dimethylmalonic acid is formed; therefore, it has in all probability the same atomic structure as fenchone.

β-Isofenchonoxime is optically active; an inactive modification may be obtained, and melts at 160° to 161°.

The *hydrochloric acid salt* is prepared by precipitating an ethereal solution of the β-isoxime with hydrogen chloride; it soon loses hydrochloric acid by standing in the air.

The *sulphate*, obtained by treating the ethereal solution of the β-isoxime with concentrated sulphuric acid, forms brilliant needles.

α-Fencholenic acid,[3] $C_9H_{15}COOH$, is formed, as indicated above, by the saponification of fenchonoxime anhydride or of α-isofenchonoxime with alcoholic potash; it is obtained from the alkaline solution, from which some unchanged α-isofenchonoxime also crystallizes. For the complete separation of the latter, the alkaline solution is shaken with ether, and then evaporated to such a degree of concentration that the liquid separates into two layers; the upper, dark-colored layer, which contains the fencholenic acid salt, is separated from the lower one, consisting for the most part

[1] Wallach, Ann. Chem., *269*, 332; *259*, 330; *315*, 273.
[2] Wallach, Ann. Chem., *269*, 332; *284*, 333.
[3] Wallach, Ann. Chem., *269*, 334; *259*, 330.

of potassium hydroxide, and is acidified with sulphuric acid after proper dilution with water. The liquid α-fencholenic acid is completely removed from the acid solution by means of ether, and is distilled in a current of hydrogen. It boils at 260° to 261°, and has the specific gravity 1.0045 at 16°; its coefficient of refraction is 1.4768 at 16°, corresponding to the molecular refraction 47.24.

By the action of sodium hypobromite on the cold solution of sodium α-fencholenate, a brominated *lactone*[1] is formed, which melts at 76°.

Silver α-fencholenate, $C_{10}H_{15}O_2Ag$, is sparingly soluble in water and alcohol. The salts of the alkali metals and of the alkaline earths are not characteristic. Ammonium α-fencholenate yields α-isofenchonoxime (α-fencholenamide), when heated in a sealed tube at 205° to 210°.

α-Fencholenic acid is unsaturated, and when shaken with hydrogen iodide or chloride it forms solid addition-products.

Hydrochlorofencholenic acid, $C_{10}H_{17}ClO_2$, prepared by shaking α-fencholenic acid with concentrated hydrochloric acid, separates from petroleum ether in small, hard crystals, and melts at 97° to 98°. The *hydrobromide*,[2] $C_{10}H_{17}BrO_2$, melts at 96° to 100°.

α-Fencholenic acid is immediately oxidized by a cold solution of potassium permanganate with the production of an acid, which has a syrup-like consistency.

The electrical conductivity of α-fencholenic acid has been determined by Binz.[3]

When sodium α-fencholenate is distilled with soda-lime, it gives a complicated mixture of hydrocarbons and compounds containing oxygen (Wallach).

A saturated hydrocarbon is formed when α-fencholenic acid is reduced by heating with phosphorus and concentrated hydriodic acid at 180° to 200°; this compound distills almost completely at 138° to 145°, and the analyses and determinations of its vapor density indicate that it consists chiefly of *dihydrofencholene*, C_9H_{18}.

Dihydrofencholene boils at 140° to 141°; its specific gravity is 0.790 and refractive power, $n_D = 1.43146$, at 20°. The same hydrocarbon is also obtained by reducing fenchonoxime anhydride in like manner.

The formation of this hydrocarbon shows that fencholenic acid and fencholenonitrile possess a closed carbon chain.

According to the investigations of Cockburn,[4] a second series

[1] Wallach, Ann. Chem., *315*, 273.

[2] Cockburn, Journ. Chem. Soc., *75*, 506.

[3] Binz, Ann. Chem., *269*, 338.

[4] Cockburn, Journ. Chem. Soc., *75*, 501. Wallach has also confirmed these observations, see Ann. Chem., *315*, 273.

of isomeric substances is derived from fenchonoxime; Cockburn designates these as beta-compounds.

β-Fencholenonitrile, $C_9H_{15}\cdot CN$.—According to Cockburn, the fencholenonitrile, prepared as described under fenchonoxime anhydride by the action of dilute sulphuric acid on fenchonoxime, is a mixture of the α- and β-nitriles, and boils at 214° to 219°; on saponification it yields α- and β-fencholenic acids. The *pure α-nitrile* may be prepared from α-isofenchonoxime (m. p. 113° to 114°); it boils at 211° to 212°, has the sp. gr. 0.9136 at 15.6°, and the specific rotatory power $[\alpha]_D = +28.98°$. On boiling with alcoholic potash, it is *readily* converted into the α-amide (α-isofenchonoxime, m. p. 113° to 114°), but only *with difficulty* into the liquid α-fencholenic acid.

Pure β-fencholenonitrile, prepared from the β-amide by warming with phosphorus pentoxide, is a colorless liquid, boils at 217° to 219°, has the specific gravity 0.9203 at 15.6°, and the specific rotatory power, $[\alpha]_D = +43.66°$. It is *quantitatively* and *very readily* converted into β-fencholenic acid on hydrolysis, but apparently *cannot* be changed into the β-amide by the action of alcoholic potash.

β-Fencholenamide, $C_9H_{15}\cdot CONH_2$.—By the hydrolysis of the mixture of nitriles, formed in the dehydration of fenchonoxime, only the α-amide melting at 113° to 114° can be obtained. The β-amide is produced, however, by heating the ammonium salt of β-fencholenic acid in a sealed tube, at 180°, for five hours; it is readily soluble in ether and alcohol, and crystallizes from a mixture of alcohol and light petroleum in soft, silky needles, melting at 86.5° to 87.5°.

β-Fencholenic acid,[1] $C_9H_{15}\cdot COOH$, is prepared by the hydrolysis of the mixture of α- and β-nitriles by heating with alcoholic potash for two and one-half days; all of the β-nitrile is thus converted into the β-acid while only a small quantity of the α-acid is produced, owing to the difficulty with which the α-amide is saponified. The α-amide which is formed is separated, and can be used for the preparation of the pure α-acid. The yield of the β-acid is about 55 to 60 per cent., and of α-amide 35 per cent. of the theoretical, the remainder being the α-acid.

β-Fencholenic acid is purified by recrystallization from light petroleum; it melts at 72° to 73°, boils without decomposition at 259° to 260°, and has the specific rotatory power, $[\alpha]_D = +19.64°$. It is readily soluble in alcohol, ether, and acetone, less so in benzene and glacial acetic acid. It is an unsaturated acid,

[1] Cockburn, Journ. Chem. Soc., *75*, 503; see Wallach, Chem. Centr., *1899* (II.), 1052; Nachr. k. Ges. Wiss. Göttingen, *1899*, No. 2.

and immediately decolorizes bromine and permanganate solutions. Its salts of the alkali metals are not very characteristic, but the salts of the alkaline earths are well defined, crystalline compounds, thus differing from the corresponding salts of the α-acid.

β-Fencholenic acid yields a brominated *lactone*,[1] melting at 80°, by the action of sodium hypobromite on the cold solution of the sodium salt.

According to Cockburn, *pure* α*-fencholenic acid*, prepared by the hydrolysis of the α-amide, melting at 113° to 114°, boils with slight decomposition at 254° to 256°, has the specific gravity 1.0069 at 16°, and the specific rotatory power, $[\alpha]_D = +30.73°$.

Hydrobromo-β-fencholenic acid, $C_{10}H_{17}BrO_2$, is formed during the action of bromine on a solution of the β-acid in petroleum ether, cooled by a freezing mixture. It crystallizes from light petroleum in long, thin needles, and melts without decomposition at 80° to 81°.

The Action of Nitrous Acid upon Fenchonoxime.[2]

According to Mahla and Tiemann, when an ethereal solution of fenchonoxime is treated with nitrous acid, two compounds are formed; one is insoluble in ether, and is termed *fenchonimine nitrate*, $C_{10}H_{17}N \cdot HNO_3$, melting at 152°, while the other remains in the ethereal liquid after separation of the nitrate, and is called *fenchonitrimine*, $C_{10}H_{16}N_2O_2$, melting at 58°.

According to Angeli and Rimini, when a dilute hydrochloric acid solution of fenchonoxime is treated with sodium nitrite, *pernitrosofenchone*, $C_{10}H_{16}N_2O_2$, is obtained; it crystallizes in transparent scales, melts at 66° to 67°, and is probably identical with Tiemann's fenchonitrimine. It is converted into fenchone by heating with alcoholic potash, but when treated with *cold* alcoholic potash or ammonia, it is changed into *isopernitrosofenchone*, $C_{10}H_{16}N_2O_2$; this compound melts at 88°. Pernitrosofenchone and its isomeride are both converted into *isocamphor*, $C_{10}H_{16}O$, by treatment with concentrated sulphuric acid; isocamphor is an oil, boiling at 216°, and yields an *oxime* (m. p. 106°), and a *semicarbazone* (m. p. 215°). When pernitrosofenchone and semicarbazide acetate are heated on the water-bath, *fenchone semicarbazone* (m. p. 186° to 187°) is obtained.

Fenchimine,[3] $C_{10}H_{16} \cdot NH$, results by the action of twenty-five per cent. aqueous ammonia on fenchonitrimine, $C_{10}H_{16}N_2O_2$. It

[1] Wallach, Ann. Chem., *315*, 273.

[2] Mahla and Tiemann, Ber., *29*, 2807; Angeli and Rimini, Gazz. Chim., **26** [II.], 228; Rimini, Gazz. Chim., *26* [II.], 502; *30* [I.], 600.

[3] F. Mahla, Ber., *34*, 3777.

boils at 83° (15 mm.), has the specific rotatory power, $[\alpha]_D = +$ 76.3°, at 19.5° (10 cm. tube), sp. gr. is 0.9322 at 11.5°, refractive index is $n_D = 1.47809$ at 17°, and the molecular refraction 45.78. It is a strong base and forms crystalline salts; the *picrate* forms splendid crystals and melts at 202°; the *hydrochloride* melts at 278°, and on heating to 180° for eight hours is decomposed with the formation of cymene. *Methylfenchimine iodide* forms well defined crystals.

When a current of dry air is passed through warm, pure fenchimine, it is converted into dihydrofencholenonitrile and oxydihydrofencholenonitrile.

Dihydrofencholenonitrile, $C_9H_{17} \cdot CN$, is formed by leading a current of dry air through fenchimine heated in an oil-bath at 105°; after the action has continued for thirty-six to forty-eight hours, the nitrile is distilled over with steam, and is obtained in a yield of about forty per cent. The oxy-nitrile remains in the distilling flask.

Dihydrofencholenonitrile boils at 98° to 104° (23 mm.), has the sp. gr. 0.8951 at 16.5°, $n_D = 1.44743$ at 17.5°, $M = 45.15$, and $[\alpha]_D = + 25°$ at 19° (10 cm. tube). It is insoluble in water and is saponified only with difficulty. When boiled vigorously for eight hours with thirty per cent. alcoholic potash, it is changed into a small quantity of the corresponding acid and a large proportion of the amide. On distilling off the alcohol, the amide is found in the residue and is purified by recrystallization from dilute alcohol.

Dihydrofencholenamide, $C_9H_{17} \cdot CONH_2$, is formed as above mentioned by hydrolysis of the nitrile. It is crystallized from dilute alcohol and then from ethyl acetate; it melts at 130.5°, and sublimes slowly at 107°.

Dihydrofencholenic acid, $C_9H_{17} \cdot COOH$, is obtained by the hydrolysis of the amide with concentrated hydrochloric acid; it boils at 145° to 146° (13 mm.), sp. gr. = 0.9816 at 15°, $[\alpha]_D = + 4.3°$ at 15.5° (10 cm. tube). It forms silver and ammonium salts, of which the latter may be reconverted into the amide.

Oxydihydrofencholenonitrile, $C_9H_{17}O \cdot CN$, is produced in a yield of about thirty-five per cent. by the action of air on fenchimine. It is non-volatile with steam, boils at 153° to 154° (23 mm.) and is insoluble in water. Sp. gr. is 0.9792 at 15°, $n_D = 1.46464$ at 18°, $M = 47.11$, and $[\alpha]_D = - 8°$ at 18° (10 cm. tube).

Oxydihydrofencholenamide, $C_9H_{17}O \cdot CONH_2$, is obtained by hydrolysis of the oxy-nitrile with thirty per cent. alcoholic potash; it is recrystallized from ethyl acetate and melts at 78°. It is readily soluble in boiling water, ethyl and methyl alcohol and boiling ether, sparingly in cold water.

Dihydrofencholenic acid lactam, $C_{10}H_{17}ON$, is formed, together with an oil which has not yet been investigated, by gently warming a solution of oxydihydrofencholenamide in dilute hydrochloric acid. It separates from the filtered solution on cooling in brilliant crystals, which melt at 136° to 137°; it is soluble in hot alcohol and may be recrystallized from this solvent. It is not attacked by permanganate; when heated above its melting point, it distills without decomposition. It is identical with Wallach's β-isofenchonoxime (m. p. 137°), which is prepared by dissolving α-fencholenamide (m. p. 113° to 114°) in hot, dilute sulphuric acid and precipitating the filtered solution with alkali.

δ-Oxydihydrofencholenic acid, $C_9H_{17}O \cdot COOH$, is obtained, together with the oxy-amide, by the hydrolysis of the oxy-nitrile with alcoholic potash; a small quantity of the lactone of this acid is also formed at the same time. This acid crystallizes from hot water or ethyl acetate in splendid, hard crystals, which melt at 113° to 114°. It is a monobasic acid, is soluble in boiling water, readily soluble in alcohol, ether and ethyl acetate, sparingly soluble in ligroine; it forms silver and copper salts.

δ-Oxydihydrofencholenic acid lactone, $C_{10}H_{16}O_2$, is readily produced by warming the oxy-acid with dilute sulphuric acid; it separates from ethyl acetate in splendid, well formed crystals, which melt at 72° and boil at 130° to 150° (10 mm.). It is very volatile with steam, somewhat soluble in boiling water and insoluble in sodium carbonate. It is dissolved by long continued boiling with caustic alkalis.

Fenchocarboxylic Acids,[1] $C_{10}H_{16}(OH) \cdot COOH$.

When carbon dioxide is passed through a solution of fenchone in ether to which sodium has been added, a mixture of different compounds is obtained; in order to separate them, the crude product is distilled under 15 mm. pressure. The fraction boiling at 150° to 180° solidifies in the receiver, and consists of the two isomeric fenchocarboxylic acids, carbofenchonone, $C_{11}H_{16}O_2$, anhydrofenchocarboxylic acid, $C_{11}H_{16}O_2$, and a pinacone, $C_{20}H_{34}O_2$, or a difenchone, $C_{20}H_{32}O_2$. This mixture is treated with sodium hydroxide or ammonia, shaken with ether, and the aqueous liquor is acidified; α-fenchocarboxylic acid crystallizes from this liquid more rapidly than the β-acid. The β-acid is also more soluble in petroleum ether than the α-acid, and a final separation may be made by means of this solvent.

[1] Wallach, Ann. Chem., *284*, 324; *300*, 294; Chem. Centr., *1899* (II.), 1052; Nach. k. Ges. Wiss., Göttingen, *1899*, No. 2; Ann. Chem., *315*, 273.

α-Fenchocarboxylic acid, $C_{11}H_{18}O_3$, crystallizes from acetic acid, melts at 141° to 142°, and boils without decomposition at 175° at 11 mm. pressure. It is optically active, having a specific rotatory power, $[\alpha]_D = +11.28°$, in a 4.5 per cent. ethereal solution; by mixing equal weights of the active acids prepared from d- and l-fenchone, an inactive acid is obtained, which melts at 91° to 92°. It forms *lead* and *silver* salts.

β-Fenchocarboxylic acid, $C_{11}H_{18}O_3$, melts at 76° to 77°, is dextrorotatory, and is less stable than the α-acid; it forms fenchyl alcohol and anhydrofenchocarboxylic acid by heating at ordinary pressure, and it is partially converted into the α-acid by distillation in vacuum. It is changed into fenchone by the action of sodium hypobromite or by an acid solution of permanganate. It forms *lead* and *silver* salts similar to those of the α-acid. This acid is also formed by warming carbofenchonone with an excess of a dilute solution of sodium hydroxide on the water-bath.

Wallach regards α- and β-fenchocarboxylic acids as *trans*- and *cis*-modifications.

Anhydrofenchocarboxylic acid, $C_{11}H_{16}O_2$, is prepared by boiling α-fenchocarboxylic acid at atmospheric pressure, or by fusing the α-acid with potash. It crystallizes from dilute acetone, melts at 175° and boils at 275° to 277° under ordinary pressure; it is difficultly soluble in water, is volatile with steam, and forms a *lead* salt.

Carbofenchonone,[1] $C_{11}H_{16}O_2$, results by the distillation of lead α-fenchocarboxylate in vacuum; it separates from petroleum ether in yellow crystals, has a slight odor resembling that of camphor, melts at 96°, and boils at 273° to 274° under atmospheric pressure. It dissolves in warm caustic soda, being converted into β-fenchocarboxylic acid. It yields a *monoxime*, $C_{11}H_{16}O \cdot NOH$, which crystallizes from methyl alcohol in needles, melting at 108°; and a *dioxime*, $C_{11}H_{16}(NOH)_2$, which is soluble in water, and melts at 198° to 199°. By the action of ammonia it forms a *compound*, $C_{11}H_{17}NO$, which crystallizes from alcohol and melts at 205°.

Carbofenchonone is an *ortho-diketone.*[1] By the action of zinc dust and acetic acid it is converted into an *alcohol*, $C_{11}H_{18}O_2$, which crystallizes from dilute alcohol and melts at 89°. When the diketone is oxidized, it yields a *dicarboxylic acid*, $C_{11}H_{18}O_4$, which melts at 172° to 173°.

A *lactone*, $C_{10}H_{16}O_2$, is produced by the oxidation of α-fenchocarboxylic acid with potassium permanganate; it crystallizes from dilute methyl alcohol, melts at 64.5°, and boils at 150° under 14 mm. pressure.

[1] Wallach, Ann. Chem., *315*, 273.

A *pinacone*,[1] $C_{20}H_{34}O_2$, or a *difenchone*, $C_{20}H_{32}O_2$, is the neutral crystalline compound formed as a by-product during the preparation of the fenchocarboxylic acids from fenchone; it melts at 122°. It yields no well defined derivatives, and decomposes, when heated under reduced pressure at temperatures below 100°, into fenchone and a non-crystalline product.

As a result of his extended investigations on fenchone and its derivatives, Wallach suggests the following formula as the most probable representation of the constitution of fenchone:

```
CH2——CH——CH—CH3
|      |     |
| H3C—C—CH3  |
|      |     |
CH2——CH——CO
```

Fenchone.

10. FENCHYL ALCOHOL, $C_{10}H_{17}OH$.

Fenchyl alcohol is formed by the reduction of fenchone in an alcoholic solution with sodium (Wallach[2]).

Thirty grams of fenchone are dissolved in 135 to 140 grams of alcohol in a capacious flask, and eighteen grams of sodium are gradually added. When the evolution of hydrogen slackens, the flask is warmed on a water-bath, and the solution of the last particles of sodium may eventually be accelerated by the cautious addition of a small quantity of water. When all of the sodium is consumed, enough water is added to dissolve the sodium alcoholate which tends to separate; two layers are thus formed, the one an aqueous solution of sodium hydroxide, the other a lighter, alcoholic solution which contains fenchyl alcohol. The sodium hydroxide solution is removed, and the fenchyl alcohol separated by shaking the alcoholic solution with water; at first it forms an oil, which solidifies when agitated with ice-water. It is then pressed on a porous plate, fused, dried with potassium hydroxide, and rectified.

Larger quantities of fenchyl alcohol may also be prepared in one operation by this method.

According to Bouchardat and Tardy,[3] the benzoyl esters of fenchyl alcohol and isoborneol are formed by heating the dextrorotatory terpene (pinene[4]), obtained from eucalyptus oil of *Eucalyptus*

[1] Wallach, Ann. Chem., *315*, 273.

[2] Wallach, Ann. Chem., *263*, 143; see also Gardner and Cockburn, Journ. Chem. Soc., *73*, 276.

[3] Bouchardat and Tardy, Compt. rend., *120*, 1417.

[4] Compare with Wallach and Gildemeister, Ann. Chem., *246*, 283.

globulus, with benzoic acid. By the action of certain acids (sulphuric, benzoic) on French (levorotatory) turpentine, Bouchardat and Lafont[1] obtained a mixture of dextrorotatory and inactive fenchyl alcohols, which they at first designated as "*isocamphenol*" and "*synthetical isoborneol*"; on oxidation these two alcohols yield levorotatory and inactive fenchone, respectively.

Fenchyl alcohol forms a colorless, crystalline mass, having a penetrating and extremely disagreeable odor; it is readily volatile with steam, and is freely soluble in alcohol, ether, petroleum ether, and ethyl acetate, but is insoluble in water. It has the specific gravity 0.933 at 50°, boils at 201°, and, as usually prepared, melts at 40° to 42°; *pure* fenchyl alcohol, however, formed as a by-product in the preparation of the fenchocarboxylic acids[2] or obtained by the hydrolysis of fenchyl hydrogen phthalate,[3] melts at 45°.

Fenchyl alcohol prepared from dextrorotatory fenchone is levorotatory;[4] its specific rotatory power is $[\alpha]_D = -10.35°$ (Wallach), and $[\alpha]_D = -13.37°$ (Gardner and Cockburn[5]). By reduction, levo-fenchone yields dextro-fenchyl alcohol,[6] whose specific rotatory power is $[\alpha]_D = +10.36°$. Inactive fenchyl alcohol results by mixing the two active modifications, and melts at 33° to 35° (Wallach).

Wallach[7] designates the levo-fenchyl alcohol obtained from dextro-fenchone as D-l-fenchyl alcohol, and the dextro-alcohol derived from levo-fenchone as L-d-fenchyl alcohol.

By heating the optically active modifications with three times their amount of concentrated nitric acid, a fenchone is obtained, which, respecting the direction and power of rotation, is identical with that from which the fenchyl alcohol was prepared.

Fenchene, $C_{10}H_{16}$, is formed by warming fenchyl alcohol with acid potassium sulphate, while tetrahydrofenchene, $C_{10}H_{20}$, is produced by reducing it with hydriodic acid and phosphorus.

The following derivatives of fenchyl alcohol have been prepared by Bertram and Helle.[3]

Fenchyl formate, $C_{10}H_{17}O{\cdot}COH$, boils at 115° under 40 mm. pressure, and at 84° to 85° under 13 mm. pressure; it has a

[1] Bouchardat and Lafont, Compt. rend., *113*, 905; *125*, 111; *126*, 755.
[2] Wallach, Ann. Chem., *284*, 331.
[3] Bertram and Helle, Journ. pr. Chem., *16*, 1900 (II.), 293.
[4] See Kondakoff and Lutschinin, Journ. pr. Chem., *62* (II.), 1.
[5] Gardner and Cockburn, Journ. Chem. Soc., *73*, 276.
[6] Wallach, Ann. Chem., *272*, 106.
[7] Wallach, Ann. Chem., *302*, 371.

specific gravity 0.988 at 15°, and the optical rotation, $[\alpha]_D = -73° 14'$.

Fenchyl acetate, $C_{10}H_{17}O \cdot COCH_3$, boils at 87° to 88° under 10 mm. pressure, has a specific gravity 0.9748 at 15°, and a specific rotation $[\alpha]_D = -58.08°$. Bouchardat and Lafont[1] obtained an acetic acid ester of their dextro-fenchyl alcohol, prepared by the action of acids on French turpentine oil, which boils at 125° to 127° (5 mm.), is strongly dextrorotatory, and has the specific gravity 0.9817 at 0°.

Fenchyl benzoate,[1] $C_{10}H_{17}O \cdot COC_6H_5$, boils at 183° to 188° under 2 mm. pressure, and has the specific gravity 1.129 at 0°. The alcohol regenerated from it has a lower optical rotation than the original fenchyl alcohol.

Fenchyl phenylurethane,

$$CO\begin{cases} NHC_6H_5 \\ OC_{10}H_{17} \end{cases}$$

crystallizes in needles or tablets, and melts at 82° to 82.5°.

Fenchyl hydrogen phthalate, $C_{18}H_{22}O_4$, crystallizes from alcohol, and melts at 145° to 145.5°. By hydrolysis it is readily converted into pure fenchyl alcohol (m. p. 45°), hence this compound is well adapted for the purification of fenchyl alcohol.

Fenchyl chloride, $C_{10}H_{17}Cl$, may be readily prepared by the following method (Wallach[2]).

Forty-five grams of fenchyl alcohol are dissolved in eighty grams of dry light petroleum or chloroform, and treated slowly with sixty grams of phosphorus pentachloride. An energetic reaction takes place, after which the liquid is poured off from small quantities of unchanged phosphorus pentachloride, and the petroleum ether and phosphorus oxychloride are removed as completely as possible by distillation in vacuum. The residue containing fenchyl chloride is distilled in a current of steam, the volatile oil dried over calcium chloride, and fractionated in vacuum. Most of the substance boils at 84° to 86° under a pressure of 14 mm.

The product thus obtained has a specific gravity of 0.983 at 21°, and contains considerable quantities of non-chlorinated products as impurities. The phosphoric acid ester of fenchyl alcohol is formed during the preparation of the chloride, and remains in the residue from the steam distillation.[3]

[1] Bouchardat and Lafont, Compt. rend., *126*, 755.

[2] Wallach, Ann. Chem., *269*, 148; see also Gardner and Cockburn, Journ. Chem. Soc., *73*, 276; Kondakoff and Lutschinin, Journ. pr. Chem., *62* (II.), 1.

[3] Wallach, Ann. Chem., *284*, 331.

According to more recent investigations by Wallach,[1] fenchyl chloride, prepared as above described, is not an individual substance. The optical rotation of the chloride, obtained from D-l-fenchyl alcohol, varies between the limits $[\alpha]_D = -13°$ and $+5.1°$, in a one decimeter tube; the direct product of the action of phosphorus pentachloride on the alcohol is always levorotatory, but subsequent treatment, as repeated distillations, modifies the rotatory power to a degree which has not yet been accurately determined. It is probable, therefore, that D-l-fenchyl alcohol gives D-l-fenchyl chloride and D-d-fenchyl chloride; for when pure D-l-fenchyl alcohol, phosphorus pentachloride and light petroleum are mixed together at low temperatures, a strongly levorotatory chloride is formed; but when the reagents are mixed without cooling and the reaction is completed on the water-bath, a dextrorotatory fenchyl chloride may be obtained.

According to Kondakoff,[2] the action of phosphorus pentachloride on fenchyl alcohol gives an impure chloride containing fenchene; the crude chloride appears to be a mixture of a solid secondary chloride with a much larger amount of liquid tertiary chloride, which is much more easily decomposed by alcoholic potash than the secondary chloride. Thus, by the action of alcoholic potash on the crude fenchyl chloride at 100°, there is produced, together with fenchene, a *secondary fenchyl chloride*, $C_{10}H_{17}Cl$, which crystallizes from alcohol, melts at 79° to 80°, and has the specific rotatory power $[\alpha]_D = +16° 33'$; it does not react with moist silver oxide, and resembles bornyl chloride in odor and other properties; fenchene is the only product at 150°.

A much purer fenchyl chloride[2] is obtained by heating fenchyl alcohol on the water-bath with concentrated hydrochloric acid; at higher temperatures a *dichloride* is formed.

Fenchyl bromide, $C_{10}H_{17}Br$, is produced by the action of cold hydrobromic acid on D-l-fenchyl alcohol; it boils at 92° to 96° (11 mm.), has the sp. gr. 1.2368 at 19.5°, $n_D = 1.4988$ and $[\alpha]_D = -43°17'$. A small quantity of a *dibromide* is also formed; it crystallizes from alcohol and melts at 49°. Fenchene is produced by the action of alcoholic potash on fenchyl bromide (Kondakoff and Lutschinin).

Fenchyl iodide,[3] $C_{10}H_{17}I$, is prepared by the action of a solution of hydrogen iodide saturated at − 20° on fenchyl alcohol at the ordinary temperature; it boils at 120° to 123° under 23 mm.

[1]Wallach, Ann. Chem., *302*, 371; *315*, 273.

Kondakoff and Lutschinin, Journ. pr. Chem., 1900 [II.], *62*, 1.

[3]Kondakoff and Lutschinin, Chem. Zeit., *25*, 131.

pressure, has a sp. gr. 1.4199 at 21°/4°, and a slight levorotation. On treatment with alcoholic potash, it yields a fenchene boiling at 148° to 158°.

11. ISOFENCHYL ALCOHOL, $C_{10}H_{17}OH$.

As a result of experiments[1] conducted in the laboratories of Schimmel & Co., Leipzig, it has been found that an alcohol, isomeric with fenchyl alcohol, is obtained by treating fenchene, $C_{10}H_{16}$, with a mixture of acetic and sulphuric acids in the same manner as in the preparation of isoborneol[2] from camphene. This alcohol is called isofenchyl alcohol, and while its method of preparation is analogous to that of isoborneol, its chemical behavior is quite different from the latter compound. Thus camphor may be converted into borneol, and the latter, by means of camphene, into isoborneol; when this substance is oxidized, camphor is again obtained. On the other hand, fenchone is reduced to fenchyl alcohol, and this compound may be converted into isofenchyl alcohol by first preparing fenchyl chloride and fenchene; here the similarity ceases, for, when isofenchyl alcohol is oxidized it is *not* converted into fenchone, but yields an isomeric ketone, $C_{10}H_{16}O$. When this ketone is reduced, it gives rise to a new alcohol, $C_{10}H_{17}OH$, which apparently is *not* identical with fenchyl or isofenchyl alcohol.

Isofenchyl alcohol is prepared[3] by heating fenchene with glacial acetic acid and sulphuric acid, according to Bertram and Walbaum's method of preparing isoborneol. It crystallizes in colorless needles, melts at 61.5° to 62°, and boils at 97° to 98° under a pressure of 13 mm.; it has a specific gravity 0.9613 at 15°, a refractive index, $n_D = 1.48005$, at the same temperature, and a specific rotation, $[\alpha]_D = -25.73°$, in an alcoholic solution. It reacts like a saturated secondary alcohol.

When a benzene solution of isofenchyl alcohol is boiled with zinc chloride, it loses water and yields a hydrocarbon, $C_{10}H_{16}$, which is probably identical with fenchene.

Isofenchyl acetate, $C_{10}H_{17}O \cdot COCH_3$, boils at 98° to 99° under 14 mm. pressure, and has a specific gravity 0.974 at 15°. The acetate, formed directly from fenchene by the action of glacial

[1] Schimmel & Co., Semi-Annual Report for Oct., *1898*, 49; April, *1900*, 55 and 60; Bertram and Helle, Journ. pr. Chem., *61*, 1900 (II.), 293.

[2] Bertram and Walbaum, Journ. pr. Chem., *49* (II.), 1.

[3] According to Wallach, Ann. Chem., *315*, 273, it is also formed from fenchene alcoholate, $C_{10}H_{17}OC_2H_5$.

acetic acid, boils at 89° to 90° at 8 mm. pressure, and at 15° it has the specific gravity 0.9724.

Isofenchyl phenylurethane,

$$CO\begin{matrix}\diagup NHC_6H_5 \\ \diagdown OC_{10}H_{17}\end{matrix}$$

crystallizes from alcohol, and melts at 106° to 107°.

Isofenchyl hydrogen phthalate, $C_{18}H_{22}O_4$, is a colorless, crystalline powder, and melts at 149° to 150°. It is converted into pure isofenchyl alcohol on hydrolysis, hence it may be employed for the purification of the alcohol.

The *ketone,* $C_{10}H_{16}O$, is produced by the oxidation of isofenchyl alcohol with chromic acid; it is isomeric, but not identical, with fenchone. It boils at 193° to 194°, has the specific gravity 0.950, and the refractive index, $n_D = 1.46189$, at 15°. Its *oxime* melts at 82°.

The *alcohol,* $C_{10}H_{17}OH$, is formed by the reduction of the preceding ketone with alcohol and sodium. It boils at 83° to 84° under 8 mm. pressure, and forms a *hydrogen phthalate* melting at 110° to 111°.

Some of the characteristic differences between isofenchyl alcohol and its derivatives, and fenchyl alcohol and its compounds are more readily observed from the following table.[1] It will be noted that the compounds derived from isofenchyl alcohol have, in most instances, higher boiling and melting points, than the corresponding fenchyl alcohol derivatives.

	Isofenchyl alcohol.	Fenchyl alcohol.
Melting point,	61.5° to 62°,	45°.
Boiling point,	97° to 98° (13 mm.),	91° to 92° (11 mm.).
Phenylurethane,	m. p. 106° to 107°,	m. p. 82° to 82.5°.
Acetyl ester,	liquid, b. p. 98° to 99° (14 mm.),	liquid, b. p. 88° (10 mm.).
Hydrogen phthalate,	m. p. 149° to 150°,	m. p. 145° to 145.5°.
Hydrocarbon resulting by dehydration of alcohol,	Fenchene (?) b. p. 155° to 156°,	Fenchene b. p. 154° to 156°.
Compound formed by oxidation of alcohol,	Ketone, $C_{10}H_{16}O$, liquid, b. p. 193° to 194°,	Fenchone, $C_{10}H_{16}O$, m. p. + 6°; b. p. 191° to 192°.
Oxime of preceding compound,	m. p. 82°,	m. p. 164° to 165°.

[1] Schimmel & Co., Semi-Annual Report, April, *1900*, 56.

12. FENCHOLENYL ALCOHOL AND ISOFENCHOLENYL ALCOHOL, $C_{10}H_{17}OH$.

Fencholenyl alcohol is the alcohol corresponding to *α*-fencholenamine, a reduction product of *α*-fencholenonitrile, $C_9H_{15}CN$. The following process is well adapted for its preparation (Wallach and Jenkel[1]).

Fifty grams of *α*-fencholenamine nitrate are dissolved in 100 cc. of water, and treated with a solution of sixteen grams of sodium nitrite in thirty cc. of water. A vigorous evolution of gas takes place when this mixture is heated in a flask, fitted with a reflux condenser, and a dark colored oil results. The product is submitted to steam distillation, and the distillate, which contains a mixture of fencholenyl alcohol and unchanged *α*-fencholenamine, is treated with a solution of oxalic acid; this is again distilled in a current of steam. A small quantity of a hydrocarbon is formed, together with the alcohol.

Fencholenyl alcohol boils at 94° to 96° under a pressure of 17 mm., has a specific gravity 0.898 and a refractive power, $n_D = 1.4739$, at 20°; it has an agreeable odor, very similar to that of terpineol. It is not converted into fenchenole, $C_{10}H_{18}O$, by treatment with hot, dilute sulphuric acid. Its acetic acid solution is colored a deep violet on the addition of hydrochloric acid. A detailed investigation of the chemical behavior of this alcohol has not yet been made.

Isofencholenyl alcohol, $C_{10}H_{17}OH$, is apparently *not* identical with the preceding compound (Wallach[2]). When *α*-isofenchonoxime (*α*-fencholenamide) is reduced with sodium and alcohol, *α*-fencholenic acid, *α*-fencholenamine and isofencholenyl alcohol are formed; the reaction-product is then distilled with steam, isofencholenyl alcohol and *α*-fencholenamine being obtained in the distillate. These two compounds are extracted with ether, and the amine is removed from the ethereal solution by precipitation with hydrochloric acid gas. The alcohol is redistilled with steam and rectified (Wallach[3]).

It is an unsaturated compound, boils at 218°, and has the specific gravity 0.927 and the index of refraction, $n_D = 1.476$, at 20°; $M = 47.04$, while the calculated value for its molecular refraction is $M = 47.15$. Its solution in glacial acetic acid is colored deep red on the addition of concentrated sulphuric acid.

[1] Wallach and Jenkel, Ann. Chem., *269*, 375; Wallach, Ann. Chem., *300*, 294.

[2] Wallach, Ann. Chem., *300*, 294.

[3] Wallach, Ann. Chem., *284*, 336.

13. FENCHENOLE, $C_{10}H_{18}O$.

Fenchenole is produced when isofencholenyl alcohol is heated with dilute sulphuric acid (one volume of concentrated acid and seven volumes of water) in a reflux apparatus, for six to eight hours; the sulphuric acid solution at first assumes a beautiful rose color, but soon becomes colorless. The last traces of the unsaturated isofencholenyl alcohol are removed by agitation with permanganate, and pure fenchenole is obtained by distilling the product in a current of steam (Wallach [1]).

Fenchenole is isomeric with cineole, which it closely resembles, and is a saturated compound. It boils at 183° to 184°, has the specific gravity 0.925 and the refractive power, $n_D =$ 1.46108, at 20°. It does not react with hydroxylamine, and is similar to cineole in its odor and behavior. Thus, an additive product is formed by passing a current of dry hydrobromic acid gas into a solution of fenchenole in petroleum ether; it separates in white crystals, which are decomposed by moisture into a dark colored liquid.

The formation of fenchenole from isofencholenyl alcohol resembles the conversion of the alcohols methyl hexylene carbinol and methyl heptylene carbinol into saturated oxides (Wallach [2]).

[1] Wallach, Ann. Chem., *284*, 336.
[2] Wallach, Ann. Chem., *275*, 170 and 172.

II. COMPOUNDS WHICH MAY BE REGARDED AS DERIVATIVES OF THE HYDROCYMENES.

A. SUBSTANCES CONTAINING TWO ETHYLENE LINKAGES. KETONES, $C_{10}H_{14}O$, AND ALCOHOLS, $C_{10}H_{15}OH$.

1. CARVONE, $C_{10}H_{14}O$.

Carvone (formerly called carvol) occurs in nature in two modifications distinguished by their optical behavior. It has long been known that dextrorotatory carvone is the characteristic constituent of the fractions boiling above 200° of the oil of caraway (*Carum carvi*), and of the oil of dill (*Oleum anethi*). On the other hand, levorotatory carvone is found in the oil of spearmint,[1] and in kuromoji oil.[2]

When equal quantities of dextro- and levo-carvone, or their optically active derivatives, are mixed, optically inactive compounds are obtained, which stand in the same relation to their active components as racemic acid does to the optically active tartaric acids, or dipentene to dextro- and levo-limonene. Carvone may be considered as limonene in which two atoms of hydrogen of a methylene group are replaced by an oxygen atom; in fact, transformations of limonene and dipentene into carvone have been observed. The first of these consists in the formation of carvoxime from limonene and dipentene nitrosochlorides, and carvone is obtained by boiling carvoxime with dilute sulphuric acid. A second transformation must be considered more in detail.

According to Wallach,[3] if limonene tetrabromide, $C_{10}H_{16}Br_4$, be treated with methyl alcoholic potash, two molecules of hydrobromic acid are eliminated, and another atom of bromine is replaced by a methoxyl-group; the resultant compound, $C_{10}H_{14}Br\text{-}OCH_3$, may be reduced to carveol methyl ether, and when this optically active substance is dissolved in acetic acid and oxidized with chromic acid, inactive carvone is obtained.

On the other hand, a conversion[4] of carvone into limonene may be accomplished as follows. On reduction with alcohol and

[1] Flückiger, Ber., *9*, 468.
[2] Kwasnick, Ber., *24*, 81.
[3] Wallach, Ann. Chem., *281*, 127; compare Ann. Chem., *264*, 12.
[4] L. Tschugaeff, Ber., *33*, 735.

sodium, d-carvone yields dihydrocarveol, which is then converted into methyl dihydrocarvyl xanthate, $C_{10}H_{17}O{\cdot}CS_2CH_3$; this compound, on distillation, forms two hydrocarbons, one of which yields limonene tetrabromide when it is treated with bromine. By the action of zinc dust on the alcoholic solution of the tetrabromide, pure dextro-limonene is obtained.

Another interesting transformation which should be mentioned here is the conversion of terpineol into carvone.[1] When terpineol nitrosochloride is heated with an alcoholic solution of sodium ethylate, oxydihydrocarvoxime, $C_{10}H_{15}(OH)NOH$, is formed, and dilute sulphuric acid converts this compound into inactive carvone.

Pinole may also be converted into carvone by oxidizing pinole hydrate with a glacial acetic acid solution of chromic acid, when oxydihydrocarvone,[2] $C_{10}H_{15}O(OH)$, is obtained; the latter yields an oxime, which is converted into inactive carvone by warming with dilute sulphuric acid.

Pinole tribromide,[3] $C_{10}H_{17}OBr_3$, and isopinole dibromide,[3] $C_{10}H_{16}O{\cdot}Br_2$, also yield inactive carvone by gently boiling with a ten per cent. aqueous solution of potassium hydroxide.

Dextrorotatory carvone may be obtained in quite a pure condition by repeated fractional distillations of the oil of caraway. In the preparation of levo-carvone, however, it is essential to prepare the hydrogen sulphide derivative, and to decompose it with alcoholic potash, and to distill the resulting carvone with steam.[4]

Properties.—Pure carvone, regenerated from the hydrogen sulphide compound, boils at 223.5°, and has the specific gravity 0.9598 at 0°.[5]

When carvone is treated with certain reagents, as potassium hydroxide or better with glacial phosphoric acid, it is converted into the isomeric compound, *carvacrol;* in this transformation, however, it is most advantageous to first convert carvone into its hydrochloride, and to treat this with anhydrous zinc chloride (Reychler). According to Klages,[6] carvacrol is produced quantitatively by heating carvone with formic acid in a reflux apparatus.

Carvone hydrogen sulphide,

$$C_{10}H_{14}\Big\langle{OH \atop SH}$$

[1] Wallach, Ber., *28*, 1773; Ann. Chem., *291*, 342.

[2] Wallach, Ann. Chem., *291*, 342.

[3] Wallach, Ann. Chem., *306*, 273.

[4] Macheleidt, Inaug. Diss., Göttingen, *1890*; Walla[illegible] 224.

[5] A. Beyer, Ber., *16*, 1387; Schreiner, Pharm. R[illegible]

[6] A. Klages, Ber., *32*, 1516.

is produced by passing hydrogen sulphide into the strongly ammoniacal alcoholic solutions of the fractions of the above-mentioned ethereal oils which contain carvone. The compound is purified by recrystallization from a mixture [1] of chloroform and alcohol, or better from glacial acetic acid; it separates from the latter solvent in long needles,[2] and melts at 187°. The melting point 210° has also been frequently reported for this compound.[3]

Hydrochlorocarvone, $C_{10}H_{14}O \cdot HCl$, was first prepared by Varrentrap. Goldschmidt and Kisser[4] obtained it by saturating carvone with dry hydrochloric acid gas. It is an oily liquid, and decomposes on distillation; it corresponds to hydrochlorolimonene. When treated with hydroxylamine, it yields hydrochlorocarvoxime, which is isomeric with limonene nitrosochloride. The *phenylhydrazone* of hydrochlorocarvone melts at 137°.

It is worthy of note that it is most convenient to employ hydrochlorocarvone to effect the well known transformation of carvone into its isomeride, carvacrol. To this end, hydrochlorocarvone is heated with not more than two per cent. of its weight of anhydrous zinc chloride, and, in order to modify the violent reaction, thirty-three parts of glacial acetic acid are added. At 95° hydrogen chloride is given off, and the reaction is complete at 110° to 120° in twenty minutes. The resulting carvacrol is washed with water, and rectified. The yield amounts to ninety per cent. of the theoretical (Reychler [5]).

Hydrobromocarvone, $C_{10}H_{14}O \cdot HBr$, was obtained by Goldschmidt and Kisser [6] as a thick oily compound by treating carvone with hydrogen bromide. According to Baeyer,[7] it is prepared by gradually adding carvone to a solution of three molecules of hydrogen bromide in glacial acetic acid, in the cold; after standing for fifteen minutes the liquid is poured onto ice, and the oil which separates is washed with water, extracted with ether, and the ethereal solution agitated with sodium carbonate. The solution is then dried with fused sodium sulphate, and allowed to remain in a vac[illegible] desiccator, when hydrobromocarvone is deposited in crystalline masses; these are pressed on a porous plate at a low

[1] A. Beyer, Arch. Pharm., *221*, 283.
[2] [illegible]cheleidt, Inaug. Diss. Göttingen, *1890*.
[3] [illegible]el & Co., Semi-Annual Report, April, *1898*, 47; see also Claus Journ. pr. Chem., *39*, 365.
[4] [illegible] and Kisser, Ber., *20*, 488.
[5] [illegible]oc. Chim., [3], 7, 31; Ber., *25*, 208; Ref. German patent,
[6] [illegible]
[7] [illegible]. Ber., *20*, 2071.

temperature, and washed with methyl alcohol. It is crystallized from ether, and melts at 32°.

Hydrobromocarvoxime is produced by the action of hydroxylamine on hydrobromocarvone, and melts at 136°. When hydrobromocarvone is treated with phenylhydrazine, a *phenylhydrazone*, melting at 123° to 125°, is formed.

According to Baeyer, alcoholic potash withdraws the elements of hydrogen bromide from hydrobromocarvone, and converts it into *eucarvone*, a ketone isomeric with carvone.

According to Harries,[1] when hydrobromocarvone is dissolved in methyl alcohol and is reduced with zinc dust, about one-quarter of the product is carvone, while the remainder consists of a ketone, *Δ^6-menthene-2-one*, $C_{10}H_{16}O$, which is isomeric with dihydrocarvone.

Hydrobromocarvone dibromide, $C_{10}H_{14}O \cdot HBr \cdot Br_2$, is formed when bromine (one molecule) is added to a solution of carvone in glacial acetic acid containing hydrobromic acid. The compound obtained from optically active carvone is an oil, while that derived from inactive carvone is a solid. The latter is prepared by dissolving thirty grams of inactive carvone in sixty cc. of a cold, concentrated solution of hydrobromic acid in glacial acetic acid, and treating the well cooled solution with thirty cc. of a solution of one volume of bromine in two volumes of glacial acetic acid. The tribromide thus formed is precipitated with water, and crystallized from moderately warm ethyl acetate; it separates in splendid, well defined, monoclinic crystals, which melt at 74° to 76° (Wallach[2]).

When an amyl alcoholic solution of the liquid active, or crystalline inactive, tribromide is saturated with dry ammonia, ammonium bromide and a *keto-amine*,[3] $C_{10}H_{13}O \cdot NH_2$, are formed:

$$C_{10}H_{15}OBr \cdot Br_2 + 4NH_3 = 3NH_4Br + C_{10}H_{13}ONH_2$$

This keto-amine is a liquid, but yields a solid *hydrochloric acid salt*.

When the keto-amine is treated with hydroxylamine, it is converted into an *oxy-oxime*, $C_{10}H_{13}(OH)NOH$; it crystallizes from methyl alcohol or hot water in needles; the oxy-oxime resulting from the active tribromide melts at 100°, and that prepared from the inactive modification melts at 105°.

When the hydrochloride of the keto-amine, $C_{10}H_{13}ONH_2 \cdot HCl$, is submitted to dry distillation, hydrogen chloride is eliminated and a solid *amine*, $C_{10}H_{15}ON$, results; this base separates from

[1] Harries, Ber., *34*, 1924.

[2] Wallach, Ann. Chem., *286*, 119.

[3] Wallach, Ann. Chem., *286*, 119, *305*, 245.

methyl alcohol in white crystals, melts at 165° to 167° (when the active carvone tribromide was originally employed), and appears to be isomeric with the liquid keto-amine.

When the keto-amine hydrochloride is treated with an aqueous solution of an alkali, the free base separates as an oil; if the mixture be allowed to stand for a considerable time, or if it be boiled for a short time, the liquid base is converted into a solid *lactone*, $C_{10}H_{14}O_2$ (carvenolide), ammonia being eliminated:

$$C_{10}H_{13}ONH_2 + H_2O = NH_3 + C_{10}H_{14}O_2.$$

Carvenolides, $C_{10}H_{14}O_2$.—**D-l-Carvenolide** is the lactone corresponding with the keto-amine derived from dextro-carvone. Thirty grams of d-carvone are dissolved in sixty cc. of a saturated solution of hydrogen bromide in glacial acetic acid, and the well cooled solution is treated slowly with ten cc. of bromine; the product is poured into ice-water, and the oily carvone tribromide is separated and washed well with water. The oil is then dissolved in 200 cc. to 350 cc. of amyl alcohol, the solution is cooled and saturated with ammonia; after standing for two hours, the product is distilled with steam. A heavy oil is obtained, which is separated, dried and distilled in vacuum; the fraction boiling at 130° to 140° solidifies gradually when placed in a freezing mixture, and after recrystallization from methyl alcohol it melts at 41° to 42°. It is levorotatory, $[\alpha]_D = -138.5°$. It unites with one molecule of bromine, forming a *dibromide*, $C_{10}H_{14}O_2 \cdot Br_2$, which crystallizes from ethyl acetate, melts at 97° to 99°, and is levorotatory, $[\alpha]_D = -67.05°$.

L-d-Carvenolide is prepared as above described from levo-carvone; it melts at 41° to 42°, and is dextrorotatory, $[\alpha]_D = +143.3°$. Its *dibromide* melts at 97° to 99°, and is dextrorotatory.

Inactive carvenolide is prepared by crystallizing a mixture of equal quantities of D-l- and L-d-carvenolide, or it may be obtained directly from the crystalline, inactive carvone tribromide; it melts at 71° to 72°. Its *dibromide* is inactive, melts at 95° to 96°, and is reconverted into i-carvenolide by treating with zinc and glacial acetic acid.

Carvenolic acids, $C_{10}H_{16}O_3$.—These acids are formed by heating the carvenolides with a *large excess* of a solution of sodium methylate, for eight or nine hours, on the water-bath. D-d-Carvenolic acid is produced from D-l-carvenolide, which is obtained from dextro-carvone; it melts at 133°, and has the specific rotatory power, $[\alpha]_D = +178.7°$. L-l-Carvenolic acid melts at 133°, and is obtained from L-d-carvenolide; inactive carvenolic acid melts at 135° to 136°. These acids are unsaturated compounds, like the corresponding carvenolides, and in a glacial acetic acid solution they add bromine.

When D-d-carvenolic acid is fused with potash, it gives rise to some volatile, liquid acids, together with a solid *acid*, $C_7H_{10}O_2$; this is volatile with steam, melts at 130° to 131°, and is levorotatory, $[\alpha]_D = -2.04°$. It is an unsaturated compound, and adds bromine, forming a *dibromide*, $C_7H_{10}O_2Br_2$, which melts at 150°.

Carvenolic acid is oxidized by chromic acid or nitric acid, yielding in each case the same monobasic *acid*, $C_7H_{10}O_4$, which melts at 201° to 202°.

Carvone tetrabromide, $C_{10}H_{14}O{\cdot}Br_4$, is obtained by the careful addition of 6.6 cc. of bromine to a cold solution of ten cc. of dextro- or levo-carvone in ten cc. of glacial acetic acid; towards the end of the operation the liquid becomes cloudy, and very soon solidifies. The crystals are filtered and washed with methyl alcohol; the mother-liquors contain a liquid α-carvone tetrabromide. The crystalline β-tetrabromide is recrystallized from acetone to which a small quantity of methyl alcohol is subsequently added; it separates in beautiful, brilliant, orthorhombic crystals, and melts at 120° to 122°. The crystals are optically active, and have hemihedral, enantiomorphous forms, which in the case of those obtained from levorotatory carvone have the hemihedral faces in the opposite position from those derived from dextrorotatory carvone (Wallach[1]).

Inactive β-carvone tetrabromide is formed by mixing the solutions of equal quantities of the dextro- and levorotatory modifications, or by the bromination of inactive carvone; it separates in monoclinic crystals and melts at 107° to 109°. Racemic α-carvone tetrabromide is an oil.

α- or β-**Carvone pentabromide**, $C_{10}H_{13}Br_5O$, is obtained by treating α- or β-carvone tetrabromide in glacial acetic acid or carbon tetrachloride solution with bromine. The active modifications of the α-pentabromide separate in monoclinic crystals and melt at 142° to 143°, and the inactive melts at 124° to 126°. The active β-pentabromide melts at 86° to 87°, while the racemic derivative melts at 96° to 98°.

Hydrobromocarvone dibromide, carvone tetrabromide and the corresponding pentabromides yield carvone when they are reduced with zinc dust and glacial acetic acid in the cold (Wallach[2]).

Carvone dichloride,[3] $C_{10}H_{14}Cl_2$, is formed by the action of phosphorus pentachloride on carvone; it is an oil, having the specific

[1] Wallach, Ann. Chem., *286*, 119

[2] Wallach, Ann Chem, *279*, 390; *286*, 120.

[3] Klages and Kraith, Ber, *32*, 2550

gravity 1.188 at 18°, and is converted into 2-chlorocymene by heating with quinoline, dilute sulphuric acid, or alcoholic potash. 2-Chlorocymene or 2-bromocymene may be obtained directly from carvone by adding the latter to phosphorus pentachloride or pentabromide covered with a layer of petroleum ether.

When carvone is reduced with alcohol and sodium, one double linkage in the molecule becomes single by the addition of hydrogen, and an alcohol, *dihydrocarveol*,[1] $C_{10}H_{17}OH$, results:

$$C_{10}H_{14}O + 4H = C_{10}H_{17}OH.$$

In a similar manner, *dihydrocarvylamine*,[2] $C_{10}H_{17}NH_2$, corresponding to dihydrocarveol, and *not* the base, $C_{10}H_{15}NH_2$, is formed by treating carvone with ammonium formate (Leuckhart).

Goldschmidt and Kisser[3] obtained a *hydrazone* by the action of phenylhydrazine on carvone; according to Baeyer,[4] it melts at 123° to 124°.

CARVOXIME AND ITS DERIVATIVES.

Carvoxime, $C_{10}H_{14} \cdot NOH$, was first prepared by Goldschmidt[5] by the action of hydroxylamine on dextrorotatory carvone. Tilden[6] had previously obtained a compound, $C_{10}H_{14}NOH$ (*nitrosoterpene*), by treatment of limonene nitrosochloride with alcoholic potash. Goldschmidt recognized the identity of Tilden's product with carvoxime, and thereby demonstrated for the first time the close relation of carvone to limonene. A more complete explanation of this relation was then given by Wallach's researches. The facts discovered by Wallach[7] are briefly presented in the following.

1. Carvoxime (m. p. 72°) obtained from dextro-limonene nitrosochloride is optically levorotatory, as Tilden had already observed, and may also be prepared from levo-carvone and hydroxylamine. On the other hand, levo-limonene nitrosochloride yields a dextrorotatory carvoxime, which has the same melting point (72°), and possesses a rotatory power of equal strength but of op-

[1] Wallach, Ann. Chem., *275*, 110; compare Leuckart, Ber., *20*, 114, and Lampe, Inaug. Diss. Göttingen, *1889*.

[2] Wallach, Ann. Chem., *275*, 119; Leuckart and Bach, Ber., *20*, 105; Lampe, Inaug. Diss. Göttingen, *1889*.

[3] Goldschmidt and Kisser, Ber., *20*, 2071.

[4] Baeyer, Ber., *27*, 811.

[5] Goldschmidt, Ber., *17*, 1577.

[6] Tilden, Jahresb. Chem., *1877*, 429.

[7] Wallach, Ann. Chem., *245*, 256 and 268; *246*, 226; *270*, 171.

posite direction to that of the oxime obtained from dextro-limonene nitrosochloride; it is identical with the dextrorotatory carvoxime obtained from the oil of caraway.

2. The carvoximes obtained from α- and β-limonene nitrosochlorides are identical.

3. Optically inactive carvoxime (m. p. 93°) is obtained by the elimination of hydrochloric acid from α- and β-dipentene nitrosochlorides. It may also be prepared by the combination of equal portions of levo- and dextro-carvoximes.

The above-mentioned modifications of carvoxime combine with the halogen hydrides; the hydrochlorocarvoximes obtained in this manner may also be prepared from the hydrochlorocarvones and hydroxylamine. The carvoximes and hydrochlorocarvoximes also form benzoyl esters, but it should be especially noted that the benzoyl derivatives of hydrochlorocarvoximes are not identical with the benzoyl derivatives of limonene or dipentene nitrosochlorides, and that the hydrochlorocarvoximes are not identical with the limonene or dipentene nitrosochlorides.

If hydrogen chloride be removed from hydrochlorocarvoxime, carvoxime is not regenerated, but *isocarvoxime* is formed. It must be observed that isocarvoxime does not stand in any known relation to eucarvone, which is produced by the splitting off of hydrobromic acid from hydrobromocarvone.

The following tables (pp. 186, 187), may serve to illustrate what has already been mentioned, together with that which follows in the more detailed description of carvoxime and its derivatives.

Optically active carvoxime, $C_{10}H_{14}NOH$, may be prepared by the action of hydroxylamine on carvone (Goldschmidt), or by treating limonene nitrosochloride with alcoholic potash (Tilden, Goldschmidt and Wallach). Dextrorotatory carvoxime is most readily obtained from carvone of oil of caraway, while levorotatory carvoxime is best prepared from dextro-limonene nitrosochloride, since this is more accessible than levo-carvone of the oil of *Mentha crispa.*

Wallach[1] recommends the following method for the preparation of dextro-carvoxime from the carvone obtained from caraway oil.

Fifty grams of carvone are dissolved in 250 cc. of alcohol and treated, with frequent shaking, with a hot solution of fifty grams of hydroxylamine hydrochloride in fifty grams of water; a warm solution of fifty grams of potassium hydroxide in forty cc. of water is then added to the clear liquid. The solution assumes a yellow color, and is then allowed to cool, without further heating;

[1] Wallach, Ann. Chem., 275, 118; 277, 133.

TABLE I. LIMONENE NITROSOCHLORIDE AND COMPOUNDS DERIVED FROM IT.

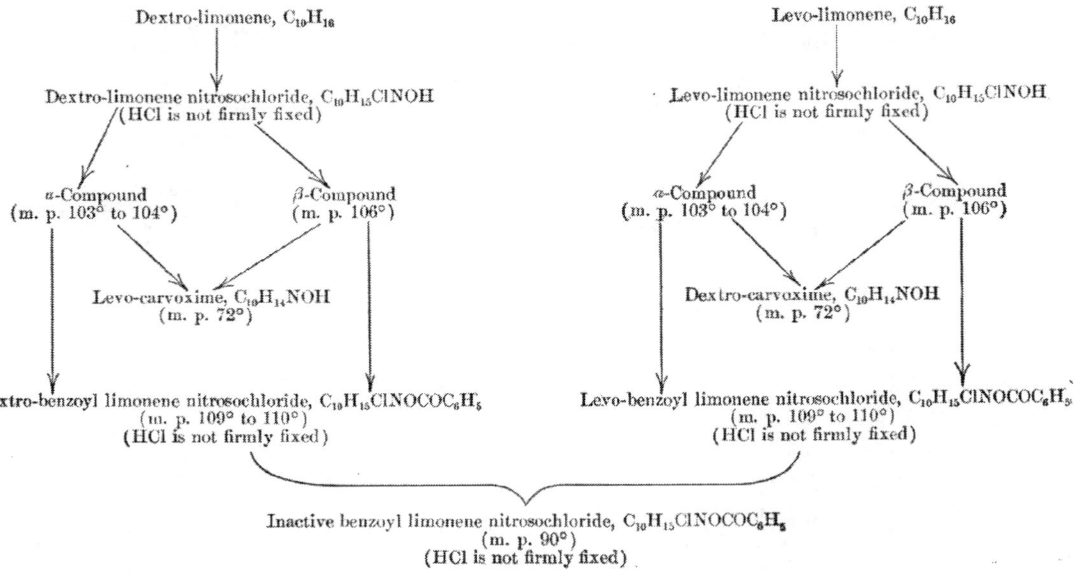

TABLE II. CARVOXIME AND ITS DERIVATIVES.

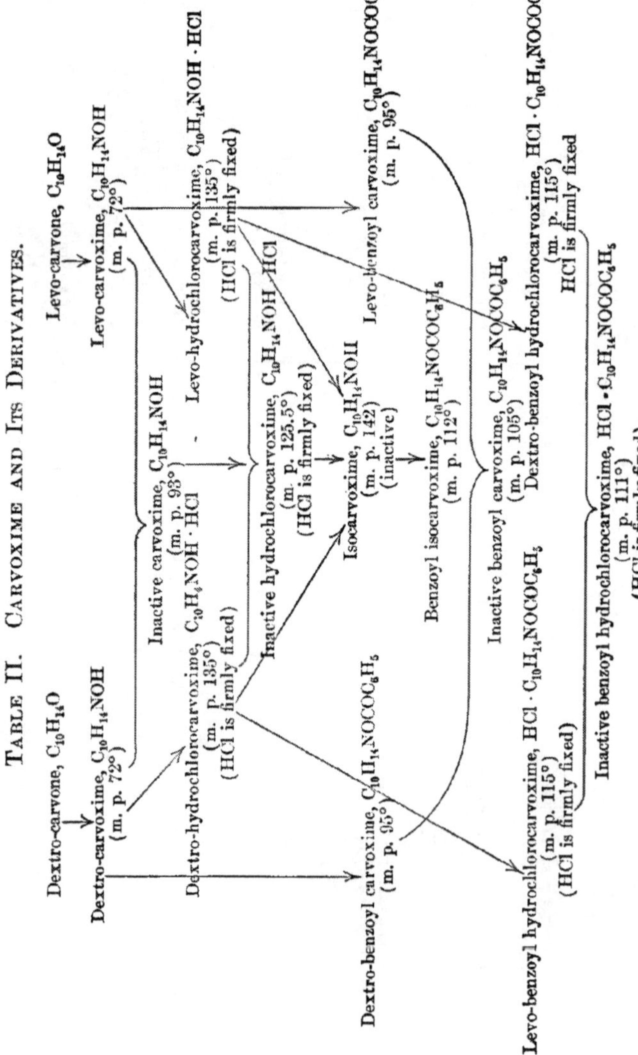

potassium chloride is thrown out, and the liquid is poured into cold water. Most of the carvoxime separates at once in solid flakes, and is collected on a cloth filter and pressed. It is recrystallized by dissolving 100 grams of the dry compound in 200 grams of hot alcohol, to which some ether is added directly before filtering. The yield of carvoxime is large, but not quantitative. Small quantities of a liquid compound are always formed, which, together with some solid carvoxime, remain dissolved in the alcoholic, alkaline solution. (For the method of determining the carvone in ethereal oils as carvoxime, see Kremers, Journ. Soc. Chem Indus., *20*, 16.)

Levorotatory carvoxime is obtained by adding fresh α- or β-dextro-limonene nitrosochloride, in small portions at once, to a solution of sodium in alcohol; the mixture is boiled for a few minutes, and the resultant carvoxime precipitated by pouring the reaction-product into water. It is crystallized from a mixture of alcohol and ether.

Dextro- and levo-carvoximes melt at 72°.

That carvoxime contains the isonitroso-group is proved by numerous observations, which were made for the most part by Goldschmidt.[1] Thus, carvoxime reacts with acetyl and benzoyl chloride; it may also be converted into a methyl ether. Hydrochloric acid precipitates a hydrochloric acid salt from the ethereal solution of the oxime. Carvoxime is soluble in acids and alkalis.

By boiling with dilute sulphuric acid, carvoxime is decomposed into carvone and hydroxylamine.

Carvoxime is an unsaturated compound, and, like carvone, is capable of combining with one molecule of a halogen hydride.

When the oxime is reduced with sodium and alcohol, dihydrocarvylamine, $C_{10}H_{17}NH_2$, is formed; this is the same base that is obtained by the treatment of carvone with ammonium formate by Leuckart's method (Wallach [2]).

Just as carvone may be changed into carvacrol, so carvoxime is convertible into aromatic amines. When ten grams of carvoxime are added gradually to twenty grams of concentrated sulphuric acid, the acid becomes dark colored and warm. Care must be taken that the liquid does not become too hot. When the reaction is complete, the product is diluted with water, and a clear solution of amidothymol is obtained (Wallach [3]). The formation of this amine is probably preceded by a conversion of

[1] Goldschmidt, Ber, *17*, 1577 and 2072, *18*, 1729

[2] Wallach, Ann Chem, *275*, 119

[3] Wallach, Ann Chem, *279*, 369

carvoxime into cymylhydroxylamine, which is analogous to the transformation of carvone into carvacrol :

```
     CH3            CH3              CH3                  CH3
     C              C                C                    C
HC      CO  →  HC      COH      HC      C=NOH    →   HC      C—NH·OH
HC      CH2    HC      CH       HC      CH2          HC      CH
     C              C                C                    C
     C3H7           C3H7             C3H7                 C3H7
  Carvone.      Carvacrol.       Carvoxime.        Cymylhydroxylamine.
```

The investigations of Friedländer [1] and Gattermann [2] have shown that the aromatic hydroxylamines are instantly converted into the isomeric para-amido-phenols. In an analogous manner cymylhydroxylamine must be converted into para-amidothymol :

```
       CH3                              CH3
       C                                C
  HC      C—NH·OH          →       HC      CNH2
  HC      CH                       HOC     CH
       C                                C
       C3H7                             C3H7
Cymylhydroxylamine.              Para-amidothymol.
```

The constitution of para-amidothymol (m. p. 166° to 167°) is proved by its conversion into thymoquinone.

If, according to the recent conception of terpineol as a Δ^1-terpen-8-ol, we ascribe to carvone the formula,

```
        CH3
        C
   HC       CO
   H2C      CH2
        CH
        C
   H3C      CH2
```

then we must consider that the transformations into carvacrol and p-amidothymol are accompanied by transpositions of the double linkage.

[1] Friedländer, Ber., *26*, 177; *27*, 192.

[2] Gattermann, Ber., *26*, 1845 and 2812.

Carvoxime undergoes a molecular change in another manner when a mixture of twelve cc. of sulphuric acid, twenty cc. of water and ten cc. of alcohol is added slowly, drop by drop, to a warm solution of ten grams of carvoxime in thirty cc. of alcohol,[1] or when carvoxime is heated with concentrated aqueous potash at 230° to 240°.[2] In both cases *carvacrylamine*, $C_{10}H_{13}NH_2$, is produced, probably by the reduction of the primarily formed cymylhydroxylamine:

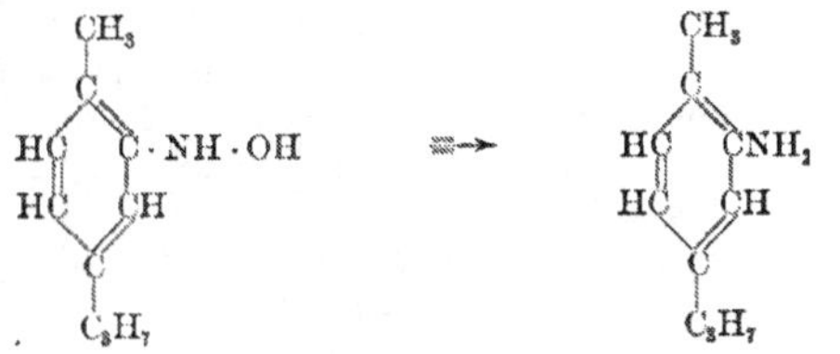

CH$_3$ — C — HC C·NH·OH — HC CH — C — C$_3$H$_7$ → CH$_3$ — C — HC CNH$_2$ — HC CH — C — C$_3$H$_7$

Inactive carvoxime, $C_{10}H_{14}$·NOH, is obtained when dipentene nitrosochloride is boiled with alcoholic potash, hence it was long known by the name "*nitrosodipentene.*" It may also be prepared by mixing the solutions of equal weights of dextro- and levo-carvoximes.[3] It is further formed as a by-product, together with carvacrol and hydroxylamine, when isocarvoxime (m. p. 142°) is boiled with dilute sulphuric acid.[4] It is more sparingly soluble in all solvents than the active carvoximes, and possesses the same molecular weight as these.[3] It melts at 93°. Its chemical behavior is the same as that of active carvoxime.

According to investigations of Roozeboom[5] on the solidifying points of mixtures of d- and l-carvoxime, inactive carvoxime is not a racemic compound, but is a pseudo-racemic mixed crystal.

Isocarvoxime, $C_{10}H_{14}NOH$, was prepared by Goldschmidt[4] by the elimination of hydrobromic acid from hydrobromocarvoxime. This may be effected by an excess of hydroxylamine or by alcoholic potash; small quantities of carvoxime are formed at the same time. It crystallizes from ligroine in needles, which melt at 142° to 143°. It is soluble in acids and alkalis, and has more pronounced basic properties than carvoxime, but, nevertheless,

[1] Wallach, Ann. Chem., *275*, 118.
[2] Wallach, Ann. Chem., *279*, 369.
[3] Wallach, Ann. Chem., *246*, 227.
[4] Goldschmidt, Ber., *20*, 2071.
[5] Roozeboom, Proc. K. Akad. Wetensch. Amsterdam, 1899, *2*, 160.

when treated with sodium alcoholate, it forms a sodium salt which is insoluble in ether. It combines with hydrochloric acid to form hydrochlorocarvoxime (Baeyer[1]). When its ethereal solution is treated with benzoyl chloride, *benzoyl isocarvoxime* results; it crystallizes in leaflets, and melts at 112°. Isocarvoxime and its benzoyl derivative are optically inactive.

Phenylisocyanate unites with isocarvoxime forming *carbanilido-isocarvoxime,* $C_{10}H_{14}NO \cdot CO \cdot NHC_6H_5$, which melts at 150°.[2]

When boiled with dilute sulphuric acid it does not yield the corresponding ketone, but is converted into carvacrol, together with hydroxylamine and inactive carvoxime. It may be changed into carvacrylamine by heating with potassium hydroxide at 230° to 240° (Wallach and Neumann[3]).

Benzoylcarvoxime, $C_{10}H_{14}NOCOC_6H_5$, is prepared by treating an ethereal solution of carvoxime with the calculated quantity of benzoyl chloride; the crystalline mass obtained on evaporation of the ether is pressed on a porous plate, and purified by recrystallization first from petroleum ether and then from ethyl acetate. The active modifications melt at 96°, and the inactive derivative,[4] prepared from the active compounds, melts at 105° to 106°. Carvoxime is regenerated by treating benzoyl carvoxime with sodium alcoholate (Goldschmidt[5]).

Carbanilidocarvoxime, $C_6H_5NH\text{-}CO\cdot ONC_{10}H_{14}$, is the addition-product of dextro-carvoxime and phenylisocyanate; when recrystallized from benzene it forms splendid, brilliant prisms, which melt at 130° (Goldschmidt[2]).

Hydrochlorocarvoxime, $C_{10}H_{15}ClNOH$, is obtained when a solution of carvoxime in methyl alcohol is saturated with hydrogen chloride (Goldschmidt[5]). It may also be prepared by treating hydrochlorocarvone with hydroxylamine (Goldschmidt and Kisser[6]), or by passing hydrochloric acid gas through an alcoholic solution of α- or β-limonene nitrosochloride (Wallach[7]); compare Baeyer.[1] The optically active modifications crystallize from petroleum ether in transparent, lustrous prisms or tablets, which melt at 135°;[7] Baeyer[1] found the decomposition point (171°) to be characteristic for this compound.

[1] Baeyer, Ber., *29*, 3.
[2] Goldschmidt, Ber., *22*, 3104.
[3] Wallach and Neumann, Ber., *28*, 1160.
[4] Wallach, Ann. Chem., *252*, 149.
[5] Goldschmidt, Ber., *18*, 1732.
[6] Goldschmidt and Kisser, Ber., *20*, 488.
[7] Wallach, Ann. Chem., *270*, 178.

Racemic hydrochlorocarvoxime, obtained by crystallizing a mixture of the dextro- and levo-modifications, dissolves readily in petroleum ether and crystallizes from it in leaflets, which have a mother-of-pearl luster and melt at 125.5°. According to investigations of Baeyer,[3] inactive hydrochlorocarvoxime is also formed when isocarvoxime, hydrochlorodipentene nitrosochloride, terpineol nitrosochloride, pinene nitrosochloride or nitrosopinene is allowed to stand for a long time in an ethereal or alcoholic solution of hydrochloric acid.

Benzoyl hydrochlorocarvoxime, $C_{10}H_{15}Cl \cdot NOCOC_6H_5$, results by warming a solution of hydrochlorocarvoxime in dry ether with the calculated amount of benzoyl chloride. When recrystallized several times from ethyl acetate, the optically active substance melts at 114° to 115°, while the inactive compound melts at 111° (Goldschmidt[1]).

Benzoyl hydrochlorocarvoxime is isomeric with benzoyl limonene nitrosochloride; in the former the elements of hydrochloric acid are quite firmly fixed, while in the latter they are not so closely united.

Hydrobromocarvoxime, $C_{10}H_{15}BrNOH$, is produced by saturating a methyl alcoholic solution of carvoxime with hydrobromic acid, or by allowing hydrobromocarvone to react with the theoretical quantity of hydroxylamine (Goldschmidt and Kisser[2]). According to Baeyer,[3] hydrobromocarvoxime may be formed in a manner analogous to that suggested under hydrochlorocarvoxime, by treating α-limonene nitrosochloride, pinene nitrosochloride or terpineol nitrosochloride with an ethereal solution of hydrobromic acid. The optically active modifications melt and decompose at 133° to 134°; the inactive derivative melts with decomposition at 128° to 129°; the melting points are not sharp. Hydrobromocarvoxime is soluble in alkalis, and may be reprecipitated from alkaline solutions by acids; it is very unstable.

Hydroxylaminocarvoxime,[4] $C_{10}H_{15}(NH\,OH)(NOH)$, is prepared by the action of two molecules of hydroxylamine dissolved in methyl alcohol on carvone, at the ordinary temperature It melts at about 60° to 65°, occasionally as high as 83° to 84°; it boils at 190° at 6 to 7 mm. pressure with considerable decomposition. The *picrate* melts at 150° to 151° The *dibenzoyl*

[1] Goldschmidt, Ber, *18*, 2222, compare Wallach and Macheleidt, Ann. Chem, *270*, 179

[2] Goldschmidt and Kisser, Ber, *20*, 2071.

[3] Baeyer, Ber, *29*, 3.

[4] C Harries, Ber, *31*, 1810; Harries and Mayrhofer, Ber, *32*, 1345, see Wallach and Schrader, Ann. Chem., *279*, 366

derivative crystallizes from absolute alcohol, and melts at 171° to 172°; the *diphenylcarbimide* and *diphenylthiocarbimide* melt at 96° to 97°, and 142° to 143°, respectively.

The *dioxime*, $C_{10}H_{14}(NOH)_2$, is formed by oxidizing the preceding compound with mercuric oxide; it crystallizes from absolute alcohol, melts with decomposition at 193° to 194° when heated rapidly, and at 188° when the temperature is raised more slowly. It has the property of reducing Fehling's solution. An isomeric *compound*, $C_{10}H_{16}N_2O_2$, melting at 153° to 155°, is obtained from the mother-liquors of the dioxime.

The *diketone*, $C_{10}H_{14}O_2$, results by boiling the dioxime with dilute sulphuric acid; it crystallizes in large prisms, and melts at 194°. This compound[1] (1-methyl-4-propenyl-dihydroresorcinol) is also formed when carvone, barium hydroxide, and methyl alcohol are shaken for some time in contact with oxygen (auto-oxidation of carvone).

Semicarbazones of dextro- and levo-carvone,

$$C_{10}H_{14} = N \cdot NHCO \cdot NH_2,$$

crystallize in hexagonal tablets and melt at 162° to 163°. The semicarbazone of inactive carvone is more sparingly soluble than the other modifications, and melts at 154° to 156° (Baeyer[2]).

Carvone semioxamazone,[3] $C_{10}H_{14} = N - C_2O_2N_2H_3$, crystallizes in aggregates of white needles, and melts at 187° to 188°.

Benzylidene carvone,[4] $C_{10}H_{12}O = CH \cdot C_6H_5$.—Benzaldehyde condenses with carvone in the presence of sodium methylate, forming a solid product, which does not cystallize well.

Sodium carvonedihydrodisulphonate,[5] $C_{10}H_{14}O \cdot Na_2H_2S_2O_6$, is formed by boiling carvone with a solution of acid sodium sulphite and sodium carbonate for about an hour, in a reflux apparatus. It is a deliquescent, yellowish-white powder, is not decomposed by alkalis, and yields a *semicarbazone*, which indicates that the union of the carvone with the acid sulphite is accomplished by the ethylene linkages of carvone, while the carbonyl group remains unchanged. It has been suggested to use this compound in the estimation of carvone in essential oils.

Carvone does not yield a normal compound with acid sodium sulphite.

[1] Harries, Ber., *34*, 2105.
[2] Baeyer, Ber., *27*, 811 and 1923; *28*, 640.
[3] Kerp and Unger, Ber., *30*, 585.
[4] Wallach, Ber., *29*, 1595; Ann. Chem., *305*, 274.
[5] H. Labbé, Bull. Soc. Chim., *23*, 1900 (III.), 280.

Carvone combines with aceto-acetic ester and hydrochloric acid, forming a *compound*,[1] $C_{16}H_{25}ClO_4$, melting at 146°.

Oxymethylene carvone, $C_{10}H_{12}O = CH(OH)$, is formed when d-carvone is dissolved in ether and treated with amyl formate and sodium, according to Claisen's method. It is an oil, soluble in alkalis, is readily decomposed, boils at 132° under a pressure of 12 mm., and gives a deep purple colored solution on the addition of ferric chloride (Wallach[2]).

Reduction Products of Carvone.

When carvone is reduced by means of zinc dust and acetic acid, zinc and sodium hydroxide, or alcohol and metallic sodium, dihydrocarvone, $C_{10}H_{16}O$, is formed, together with a crystalline compound, $C_{20}H_{30}O_2$, which was at first regarded as a pinacone,[3]

$$C_{10}H_{14}(OH)-(HO)C_{10}H_{14}.$$

Closer investigation, however, proves that this dimolecular reduction-product of carvone is not a pinacone, but is a *diketone*, and is called *dicarvelone*.[4] It exists in nine different modifications, a dextro-, levo-, and inactive α-dicarvelone, three β-modifications, and three γ-modifications; only the α-modifications result by the direct reduction of carvone.

α-Dicarvelones, $C_{20}H_{30}O_2$.—These compounds may be prepared from either dextro- or levo-carvone. Thirty cc. of carvone are dissolved in 250 cc. of alcohol, and treated with a solution of twenty-five to thirty grams of potassium hydroxide in 150 cc. of water, and fifty grams of zinc; after a thorough agitation, the mixture is warmed on the water-bath for five to six hours. The excess of zinc is removed by filtration, and the filtrate is distilled with steam, which removes the alcohol and dihydrocarvone. The residue in the distilling flask is separated from the water, extracted with chloroform, and after the addition of some alcohol, the solution is allowed to evaporate slowly. α-Dicarvelone separates in crystals, is washed with a little cold alcohol, and purified by recrystallization from hot alcohol. The yield is about twenty to twenty-five per cent. of the carvone employed.

[1] Goldschmidt and Kisser, Ber., *20*, 489

[2] Wallach, Ber., *28*, 32

[3] Wallach and Schrader, Ann Chem, *279*, 379.

[4] Wallach, Ann. Chem, *305*, 223; compare Harries and Kaiser, Ber, *31*, 1807.

α-Dicarvelone crystallizes in splendid, rhombic crystals, and the *two active* modifications melt at 148° to 149°. D-α-l-Dicarvelone, prepared from dextro-carvone, is levorotatory, $[\alpha]_D = -73.92°$, and L-α-d-dicarvelone from levo-carvone is dextrorotatory, $[\alpha]_D = +73.28°$. A racemic, *inactive* α-dicarvelone is obtained by crystallizing together molecular quantities of D-α-l- and L-α-d-dicarvelone; it separates from alcohol in rhombic crystals, and melts at 120° to 121°.

That α-dicarvelone is a diketone, is proved by the formation of the *phenylhydrazone*, $C_{20}H_{30}(N_2HC_6H_5)_2$, the hydrazones of the active modifications melt and decompose at 215°, and the inactive hydrazone decomposes at about 200°.

α-Dicarvelonoxime, $C_{20}H_{30}(NOH)_2$, is prepared according to the method of preparation of carvoxime. The active modifications melt at 223°, and the inactive derivative melts and decomposes at 287°. The active *acetyl* derivatives of the oxime melt at 187°, and the inactive modification melts at 166°.

α-Dicarvelone dihydrobromide, $C_{20}H_{30}O_2 \cdot 2HBr$.—α-Dicarvelone contains two ethylene linkages, and unites with two molecules of hydrogen bromide. The D-α-l-dicarvelone dihydrobromide separates from alcohol in white crystals, and melts at 165°.

β-Dicarvelones, $C_{20}H_{30}O_2$.—When α-dicarvelone dihydrobromide is heated with an equivalent amount of alcoholic potash, hydrobromic acid is eliminated, and a compound isomeric with α-dicarvelone is obtained; this substance is termed *β-dicarvelone*. D-α-l-Dicarvelone dihydrobromide yields a *dextrorotatory* β-modification, $[\alpha]_D = +79.18°$, and L-α-d-dicarvelone gives rise to L-β-l-dicarvelone, $[\alpha]_D = -82.66°$; both active modifications crystallize well, and melt at 207°. By the union of D-β-d- and L-β-l-dicarvelone, an *inactive* derivative is produced, which melts at 168°. The β-dicarvelones form *phenylhydrazones*, and also combine with two molecules of hydrogen bromide, forming *dihydrobromides*, which are *identical* with the bromides prepared from the α-dicarvelones.

γ-Dicarvelones, $C_{20}H_{30}O_2$.—These compounds are prepared by adding the α- or β-dicarvelones, in small portions at a time, to well cooled, concentrated sulphuric acid; after standing for a short time, the product is poured onto ice, the resulting precipitate is filtered, dried, and crystallized from alcohol. D-γ-l-Dicarvelone, prepared from D-α-l- or D-β-d-dicarvelone, is levorotatory, $[\alpha]_D = -213.4°$ and 201.8°, respectively; L-γ-d-dicarvelone is dextrorotatory, $[\alpha]_D = +236.8°$. Both active modifications melt at 126°, and the *inactive* γ-derivative melts at 112°

The γ-dicarvelones differ from the corresponding α- and β-compounds in that they do not form phenylhydrazones.

Dieucarvelone, $C_{20}H_{30}O_2$.—When hydrochloro- or hydrobromocarvone is treated with zinc and potassium hydroxide in a manner similar to that described in the reduction of carvone, a number of crystalline products result, among which the compound, $C_{20}H_{30}O_2$, dieucarvelone, melting at 172°, has been isolated and studied; the same compound is likewise produced in the reduction of eucarvone, $C_{10}H_{14}O$, with sodium hydroxide and zinc.

Dieucarvelone melts at 172°, yields a *phenylhydrazone* and an *oxime*, but does not form a solid addition-product with hydrobromic acid.

A *compound*, $C_{20}H_{30}O_2$, isomeric with dieucarvelone, is also formed in the reduction of eucarvone; it melts at 128°. A *compound*, melting at 110° to 112°, is likewise produced in the same reaction; it may possibly prove to be identical with inactive γ-dicarvelone, melting at 112°.

The behavior of carvone towards potassium permanganate has been studied by Best,[1] and by Wallach,[2] but only the most important results of these investigations will be briefly mentioned here.

When carvone is treated with aqueous potassium permanganate, it yields *oxyterpenylic acid*, $C_8H_{12}O_5$, melting at 192.5°; when this acid is distilled under diminished pressure, it loses water and yields a neutral compound, $C_8H_{10}O_4$ (*dilactone*), melting at 129°. According to Best, oxyterpenylic acid is reduced by hydriodic acid to *terpenylic acid*, melting at 55° to 56°. According to Schryver,[3] terpenylic acid has the constitution of a lactone of *diaterpenylic acid:*

```
           (CH3)2C———————O                       (CH3)2COH
                 |       |                            |
HOCO—CH2—CH—CH2—CO              HOCO—CH2—CH—CH2—COOH
        Terpenylic acid.                 Diaterpenylic acid.
```

According to Wallach, another acid isomeric with oxyterpenylic acid is formed, together with the latter, by the action of permanganate on carvone; this acid melts at 94° to 95°. (Compare with Tiemann and Semmler.[4])

[1] O. Best, Ber., 27, 1218 and 3333.

[2] Wallach, Ann. Chem., 275, 155; Ber., 27, 1496.

[3] Schryver, Journ. Chem. Soc., 63, 1327; Mahla and Tiemann, Ber., 29, 928.

[4] Tiemann and Semmler, Ber., 28, 2141.

The values for the specific rotatory powers of dextro- and levo-carvone and their derivatives are given in the following table.

Compounds of the Carvone Series.	Prepared from		Observer.
	Dextro-carvone or levo-limonene $[\alpha]_D$.	Levo-carvone or dextro-limonene $[\alpha]_D$.	
Carvone,	+62.00°	—62.00°	A. Beyer, Arch. Pharm., *221*, 283.
Carvone hydrogen sulphide,	+ 5.53°	— 5.55°	A. Beyer, Arch. Pharm., *221*, 283.
Carvoxime,	+39.71°	—39.34°	Wallach and Conrady, Ann. Chem., *252*, 148.
Benzoyl carvoxime,	+26.47°	—26.97°	Wallach and Conrady, Ann. Chem., *252*, 148.
Benzoyl hydrochlorocarvoxime,	—10.58°	+ 9.92°	Macheleidt, Ann. Chem., *270*, 179.

2. CARVEOL METHYL ETHER, $C_{10}H_{15}OCH_3$.

When carvone, $C_{10}H_{14}O$, is reduced in an alcoholic solution with sodium, dihydrocarveol, $C_{10}H_{17}OH$, is formed. An alcohol, $C_{10}H_{15}OH$, corresponding to carvone is not at present known, although the methyl ether of carveol, $C_{10}H_{15}OCH_3$, has been obtained.

When one hundred grams of limonene tetrabromide are warmed on the water-bath with a solution of fifteen grams of sodium in two hundred cc. of methyl alcohol for eight hours, a compound is produced which has the constitution, $C_{10}H_{14}BrOCH_3$; it is volatile with steam, boils at 137° to 140° under 14 mm. pressure, has the specific gravity of 1.251 and the coefficient of refraction, $n_D = 1.51963$, at 18° (Wallach[1]).

If a solution of forty-two grams of this compound, $C_{10}H_{14}BrOCH_3$, in two hundred cc. of ethyl alcohol be treated with thirty-six grams of sodium, the bromine atom is replaced by hydrogen and carveol methyl ether results. The reaction-product is distilled in a current of steam, and the ether, being volatile, is separated from the distillate by the addition of water; it is dried with potassium hydroxide and rectified.

Carveol methyl ether boils at 208° to 209°, and has a specific gravity of 0.9065 at 18°; the refractive index is $n_D = 1.47586$ at 18°, from which a molecular refraction is calculated that indicates the presence of two double linkages in the molecule. The ether

[1] Wallach, Ann. Chem., *281*, 129.

is optically active, and unites with halogens and halogen hydrides forming additive products. It yields inactive carvone by oxidation with chromic anhydride in glacial acetic acid solution.

Optically inactive carveol methyl ether may be obtained from crystalline terpineol (Wallach [1]). If terpineol dibromide be treated with hydrogen bromide, it yields a tribromide, which was formerly designated as 1, 2, 4-, more recently as 1, 2, 8-tribromoterpane. When this tribromide is submitted to the action of sodium methylate, the bromine atom, 2, is replaced by a methoxyl-group, while the bromine atoms, 1 and 8, are eliminated as hydrogen bromide:

Terpineol (solid). → Terpineol dibromide. → 1, 2, 8-Tribromoterpane.

→ Carveol methyl ether. → Carvone.

3. EUCARVONE, $C_{10}H_{14}O$.

According to Baeyer,[2] a ketone isomeric with carvone is obtained, when hydrobromocarvone, prepared by the action of hydrogen bromide on carvone, is treated with alcoholic potash; the purification of the hydrobromocarvone is not necessary. After saturating carvone dissolved in glacial acetic acid with hydrobromic acid, the solution is poured into water; the oil which

[1] Wallach, Ann. Chem., *281*, 140.

[2] Baeyer, Ber., *27*, 812; compare also Wallach, Ann. Chem., *305*, 237.

separates is washed with water, extracted with ether, and, after agitating the ethereal solution with sodium bicarbonate, it is carefully dried with anhydrous sodium sulphate. This solution is then well cooled with ice and treated with methyl alcoholic potash (one part of potassium hydroxide in two parts of methyl alcohol) until a separation of potassium bromide is no longer noticeable. The mixture is then poured without delay into cold, dilute sulphuric acid; the ethereal solution is separated, washed with bicarbonate of sodium, the ether allowed to evaporate, and the resulting oil distilled with steam. Eucarvone prepared in this manner boils at 210° to 215° under ordinary pressure; it is better, however, to distill in vacuum, since the ketone is partially decomposed into carvacrol by distillation under atmospheric pressure.

It has an odor differing from that of carvone, but similar to that of peppermint and of menthone; it is optically inactive, boils at 104° to 105° (25 mm.) without decomposition, and has a specific gravity of 0.948 at 20°. Its boiling point and specific gravity are, therefore, lower than those of carvone. It is quantitatively converted into carvacrol by heating at its boiling point for an hour.

Eucarvone derives its name from the production of a pure, deep blue color on boiling a small quantity of the substance in a test-tube with about two cc. of concentrated methyl alcoholic potash; the color is very unstable and disappears at once on the addition of water.

It does not combine with acid sodium sulphite; it differs from carvone in that it reacts very slowly with phenylhydrazine, forming an oily *phenylhydrazone* (Baeyer).

Eucarvoxime, $C_{10}H_{14}NOH$, results by treating an alcoholic solution of eucarvone with the theoretical quantities of hydroxylamine hydrochloride and sodium bicarbonate. After standing for one week, the reaction-product is poured onto ice, and eucarvoxime separates at once in very small crystals. It is obtained in the form of leaflets by dissolving in alcohol and diluting the solution with water. It melts at 106°.

According to Wallach,[1] the oxime is more readily prepared as follows. Fifty grams of eucarvone are dissolved in 750 cc. of ninety per cent. alcohol and to this is added a solution of fifty grams of hydroxylamine hydrochloride in fifty cc. of hot water. A concentrated solution of fifty grams of *sodium* hydroxide is then slowly added, and the liquid is warmed in a flask with reflux condenser on the water-bath, for about one hour. After cool-

[1] Wallach, Ann. Chem., *305*, 239.

ing, the reaction-product is poured into ice water and acidified with some acetic acid. The oxime separates at once; it is pressed on a porous plate, and recrystallized from four times its quantity of methyl alcohol. It melts at 106°.

It is very stable towards dilute sulphuric acid, and when it is boiled with this acid for half an hour, only traces of regenerated eucarvone can be detected by means of methyl alcoholic potash. It is more readily decomposed into eucarvone by dilute sulphuric acid if substances are present which combine easily with hydroxylamine, for example methyl isonitrosoacetone. It dissolves in concentrated sulphuric acid without development of heat and without change. Beckmann's chromic acid mixture colors crystals of carvoxime black; crystals of eucarvoxime are not affected.

Eucarvone semicarbazone,[1] $C_{10}H_{14} = N \cdot NH \cdot CO \cdot NH_2$, crystallizes in concentric aggregates of prisms, and melts at 183° to 185°.

Condensation-products of eucarvone and benzaldehyde.[2]—**Benzylidene eucarvone,** $C_6H_5CH = C_{10}H_{12}O$, is the chief product obtained in the condensation of eucarvone and benzaldehyde in alcoholic solution by means of sodium ethylate. It crystallizes from alcohol in well defined, slightly yellowish prisms, melting at 112° to 113°; it is the normal condensation-product of these two compounds. A second *product* is also formed; it has the composition, $C_{24}H_{24}O_2$, and seems to be formed by the elimination of one molecule of water from one molecule of eucarvone and two molecules of benzaldehyde. It crystallizes from a mixture of chloroform and alcohol in white leaflets, and melts at 193° to 194°.

Dieucarvelone,[3] $C_{20}H_{30}O_2$, is formed in the reduction of eucarvone with sodium hydroxide and zinc; it melts at 172°. (See under carvone.)

Eucarvone yields dihydroeucarveol, $C_{10}H_{17}OH$, when it is reduced in alcoholic solution with sodium.[1]

Unsymmetrical or *gem*[4]-dimethyl succinic acid is formed, together with a considerable quantity of acetic acid, by the oxidation of eucarvone with a permanganate solution (Baeyer[5]).

An alcohol, $C_{10}H_{15}OH$, corresponding to eucarvone is not known.

[1] Baeyer, Ber., *27*, 1922.
[2] Wallach, Ber., *29*, 1600; Ann. Chem., *305*, 242.
[3] Wallach, Ann. Chem., *305*, 242.
[4] Baeyer, Ber., *31*, 2067.
[5] Baeyer, Ber., *29*, 3.

4. PINOCARVONE, $C_{10}H_{14}O$.

This ketone was formerly called "*isocarvone*" owing to its supposed similarity to carvone. More recent investigations, however, have shown that it possesses no similarity with the compounds of the carvone series, and, accordingly, Wallach[1] has changed its name to pinocarvone. The corresponding alcohol, $C_{10}H_{15}OH$, was called "*isocarveol*," but is now designated as *pinocarveol*.

When pinylamine nitrate is heated with a solution of sodium nitrite, an alcohol, $C_{10}H_{15}OH$ (pinocarveol), is produced; the latter yields pinocarvone by oxidation with chromic acid (Wallach[2]).

A solution of ten grams of pinocarveol in forty grams of glacial acetic acid is very gradually treated with a solution of ten grams of chromic anhydride in a mixture of five cc. of water and ten cc. of glacial acetic acid. A very vigorous reaction takes place at once, and, on its completion, the product is distilled with steam; the resultant crude ketone is converted into the oxime, and the latter is purified by steam distillation. Pure pinocarvone is obtained by boiling the oxime with dilute sulphuric acid.

Pinocarvone is a liquid having a characteristic odor, which differs from that of carvone, but when warm resembles that of peppermint. It boils at 222° to 224°, and at 19° has the specific gravity 0.989; its refractive index at 19° is 1.506, corresponding to a molecular refraction of 45.42, which indicates the presence of two double linkages in the molecule. Since this supposition respecting the constitution of pinocarvone has not yet been proved by chemical methods, and more especially since a transformation of pinocarvone into carvacrol has not been accomplished, it is possible that pinocarvone and pinocarveol are not to be regarded as derivatives of dihydrocymene.

It combines with acid sodium sulphite forming a crystalline compound, which is decomposed by water. It produces a deep red color when treated with acids.

When pinocarvone is dissolved in alcoholic ammonia and saturated with hydrogen sulphide, *pinocarvone hydrogen sulphide* is precipitated as a white, amorphous substance; it is readily soluble in chloroform, sparingly in alcohol, and is slowly decomposed by boiling with caustic soda.

Pinocarvoxime, $C_{10}H_{14}NOH$, is prepared by the action of hydroxylamine on crude pinocarvone and is purified by distillation with steam. It separates from alcohol or ether in well defined crystals, and melts at 98°.

[1] Wallach, Ann. Chem., *300*, 286.
[2] Wallach, Ann. Chem., *277*, 150; *279*, 387.

Pinocarvone semicarbazone,[1] $C_{10}H_{14}=N\cdot NH\cdot CO\cdot NH_2$, is sparingly soluble, and does not crystallize well. It separates from aqueous methyl alcohol in slightly yellowish crystals, and melts at 204°.

5. PINOCARVEOL, $C_{10}H_{15}OH$.

Pinylamine, $C_{10}H_{15}NH_2$, obtained by the reduction of nitrosopinene, may be converted into a secondary alcohol, $C_{10}H_{15}OH$, which is called pinocarveol because of its relation to pinocarvone.

Pinocarveol is prepared according to the following method (Wallach[2]).

Twenty grams of pinylamine nitrate are heated with a solution of ten grams of sodium nitrite in 100 cc. of water for some time. A yellow oil separates, and is distilled in a current of steam; the distillate is shaken with an oxalic acid solution in order to remove basic compounds, and is again distilled with steam. The alcohol so obtained is dried over potassium hydroxide, and boils at 215° to 218°.

It has a turpentine-like odor, and a specific gravity of 0.978 at 22°; its refractive power is 1.49787 at 22°, corresponding to the molecular refraction of 45.55.

6. PINENOL, $C_{10}H_{15}OH$.

According to Genvresse,[3] a terpene alcohol, $C_{10}H_{15}OH$, is formed by passing nitrous acid fumes into well cooled pinene; the product is distilled with steam, and the resulting oil is fractionally distilled under reduced pressure.

Pinenol is a slightly yellow colored liquid, and possesses an agreeable odor; it is insoluble in water, but readily soluble in the usual organic solvents. It boils at 143° under 38 mm. pressure, and at 225° under 740 mm.; it is partially decomposed by distillation at atmospheric pressure. It has the specific gravity 0.9952 at 0°, and the refractive index, $n_D = 1.497$, from which the molecular refraction 44.563 is calculated; the theoretical molecular refraction is 44.85, if the presence of one double linkage in the molecule be assumed. Its specific rotatory power is $[\alpha]_D = -14.66°$.

It unites with one molecule of bromine, forming an additive compound. It is converted into cymene on treatment with phosphoric oxide.

Pinenol acetate, $C_{10}H_{15}O\cdot COCH_3$, has an odor recalling that of lavender, and boils at 150° under 40 mm. pressure.

[1] Wallach, Ann. Chem., *300*, 286.
[2] Wallach, Ann. Chem., *277*, 149; *300*, 286.
[3] P. Genvresse, Compt. rend., *130*, 918.

7. PINENONE, $C_{10}H_{14}O$.

Pinenone [1] is the ketone corresponding to pinenol, $C_{10}H_{15}OH$, and results from the oxidation of the latter with a chromic acid mixture.

It is a yellow liquid, has an agreeable odor, and boils at 132° (42 mm.); it has a specific gravity 0.9953 at 0°, and is levorotatory, $[\alpha]_D = -21.12°$. Its refractive index is $n_D = 1.5002$, giving the molecular refraction 44.33; the calculated value for the molecular refraction is M = 43.84, if it be assumed that the molecule contains one double linkage. The ketone is unsaturated, and adds one molecule of bromine.

Pinenonoxime, $C_{10}H_{14}$:NOH, is produced by heating pinenone with an alcoholic solution of hydroxylamine. It is also formed in small quantity during the preparation of pinenol from pinene.

It crystallizes in rhombic crystals, melting at 89°; it boils with partial decomposition at 170° under a pressure of 40 mm. It is levorotatory, $[\alpha]_D = -22.3°$.

The *dibromide*, $C_{10}H_{14}(NOH)\cdot Br_2$, melts at 152°. The *phenyl carbimide*, $C_{10}H_{14}\cdot NO\cdot CO\cdot NHC_6H_5$, crystallizes in needles, and melts at 135°. The *benzoyl* and *butyryl* derivatives melt at 105° and 74°, respectively.

Pinenone semicarbazone, $C_{10}H_{14}{=}N{-}NH\cdot CO\cdot NH_2$, melts at 82°.

8. LIMONENOL, $C_{10}H_{15}OH$.

This alcohol [2] is produced by the action of nitrous fumes on dextro-limonene cooled by a freezing mixture of ice and salt; the reaction-product is neutralized with sodium carbonate, distilled with steam, and the alcohol is then separated from unaltered limonene by extraction with a concentrated solution of sodium salicylate, this solvent having the property of dissolving terpene alcohols, but not terpenes.

Limonenol is a colorless liquid having an agreeable odor, differing from that of pinenol or limonene. It boils at 135° under a pressure of 15 mm., has a sp. gr. 0.9669 at 18°, a refractive index, $n_D{=}1.497$, and a rotatory power, $[\alpha]_D{=}+19°21'$ at 17°. Its molecular refraction is 45.99, which corresponds with the calculated value of a compound containing two double linkings. It absorbs two molecules of bromine without evolution of hydrogen bromide. On oxidation with chromic acid it yields the ketone, limonenone, $C_{10}H_{14}O$.

[1] P. Genvresse, Compt. rend., *130*, 918.
[2] P. Genvresse, Compt. rend., *132*, 414.

9. LIMONENONE, $C_{10}H_{14}O$.

Limonenone[1] is the ketone corresponding to the alcohol, limonenol, and is prepared by oxidizing this alcohol with a chromic acid mixture.

It is a colorless liquid, having an agreeable odor. At 20° it has the sp. gr. 0.9606, the refractive index, $n_D = 1.487$, and the specific rotatory power $[\alpha]_D = +16° 4'$. Its molecule contains two double linkings.

Limonenonoxime, $C_{10}H_{14}NOH$, is formed by treating the ketone with alcoholic solutions of hydroxylamine hydrochloride and potassium hydroxide; it is purified by steam distillation. It melts at 85.5°; but after the fused material has solidified, it then melts at 72°. It is formed in small quantity by the action of nitrous fumes on limonene.

This compound is perhaps identical with levo-carvoxime, since the melting point of the latter corresponds with the lower melting point (72°) of limonenonoxime; the two compounds have the same specific rotatory power, $[\alpha]_D = -39° 42'$, and their benzoyl derivatives (m. p. 95°), and phenylcarbimides (m. p. 133°) agree in properties.

10. SABINOL, $C_{10}H_{15}OH$.

The chemists of Schimmel & Co.[2] observed that the principal constituent of the oil of savin is an alcohol, *sabinol*, which occurs partly free and partly combined as an acetic acid ester. It is obtained by the fractional distillation of the saponified oil of savin, and boils at 210° to 213°, or at 105° to 107° under 20 mm. pressure.

It was at first assumed that sabinol had the composition, $C_{10}H_{17}OH$, but more recent investigations of Fromm[3] and Semmler[4] indicate that its formula is $C_{10}H_{15}OH$.

The fraction of oil of savin boiling at 195° to 235°, when further fractionated, yields an oil boiling at 222° to 224°, and consisting largely of the acetate of sabinol. When this acetate is hydrolyzed with alcoholic potash, sabinol is obtained. The alcohol is more readily obtained by boiling the crude oil of savin with alcoholic potash for half an hour, and distilling the product with steam; the oil which passes over is purified by repeated fractionation. The yield is about fifty per cent. of the crude oil.

[1] P. Genvresse, Compt. rend., *132*, 414.
[2] Schimmel & Co., Semi-Annual Report, Oct., *1895*, 44.
[3] E. Fromm, Ber., *31*, 2025.
[4] F. Semmler, Ber., *33*, 1455.

Properties.—Pure sabinol is a colorless oil, with a faint odor resembling that of thujone; it boils at 208° to 209°, has a specific gravity 0.9432 at 20°, a refractive index, $\mu_D = 1.488$, and a molecular refraction, $M = 46.5$.

Sabinol absorbs bromine, iodine, and hydrogen chloride forming oily addition-products.

Semmler[1] regards it as a *pseudo*-terpene alcohol. It does not lose oxygen when heated with zinc dust, nor does it react with phthalic anhydride. It is probably a secondary alcohol, although it does not yield the corresponding ketone, $C_{10}H_{14}O$, on oxidation.

It is converted into thujone (tanacetone) by distillation with zinc dust, and, when boiled with absolute alcohol and a few drops of sulphuric acid, it gives rise to cymene.

Sabinol acetate, $C_{10}H_{15}O \cdot COCH_3$, boils at 222° to 224°.

Sabinyl glycerol, $C_{10}H_{15}(OH)_3$, results on the oxidation of sabinol with aqueous potassium permanganate at 0°; it crystallizes from water, and melts at 152° to 153°. Upon warming with water containing a trace of acid, it is converted into *cuminyl alcohol*, $C_{10}H_{13}OH$.

When further oxidized with permanganate, sabinol forms *tanacetogendicarboxylic acid*, $C_9H_{14}O_4$.

On reduction with sodium and amyl alcohol, sabinol yields *thujyl alcohol*, $C_{10}H_{17}OH$, which is readily oxidized to *thujone*.

[1] Semmler, Ber., *34*, 708.

B. SUBSTANCES CONTAINING ONE ETHYLENE LINKAGE. KETONES, $C_{10}H_{16}O$, ALCOHOLS, $C_{10}H_{17}OH$, AND OXIDES, $C_{10}H_{16}O$.

1. DIHYDROCARVONE, $C_{10}H_{16}O$.

Dihydrocarvone is a ketone which has not yet been observed in nature. It was obtained almost simultaneously by Wallach and Kerkhoff,[1] and by Baeyer[2] through the oxidation of dihydrocarveol, $C_{10}H_{17}OH$, with chromic anhydride. Wallach and Schrader[3] then showed that it is not necessary to employ the indirect method through dihydrocarveol in order to secure dihydrocarvone, but that it may be prepared by the direct reduction of carvone by means of zinc dust and sodium hydroxide, or zinc dust and acetic acid.

Dihydrocarvone is prepared from dihydrocarveol[1] by dissolving ten grams of the latter in twenty cc. of glacial acetic acid and treating the solution with a concentrated, aqueous solution of four to six grams of chromic anhydride; the mixture is heated in a flask, fitted with reflux condenser, on a water-bath for about twenty minutes. The resulting dihydrocarvone is distilled in a current of steam and purified by the method given below.

For the preparation of dihydrocarvone from carvone, introduce into a medium sized flask in the order named, one hundred cc. of water, fifty grams of zinc dust, twenty-five grams of potassium hydroxide dissolved in fifty cc. of water, twenty cc. of carvone, and two hundred and fifty cc. of alcohol. Shake vigorously the contents of the flask, and then boil for four or five hours, with reflux condenser, on the water-bath. When the smell of carvone can no longer be recognized, distill off the alcohol, the last portions of which may carry over some dihydrocarvone. Distill the residue with steam, and separate the dihydrocarvone from the distillate.

Crude dihydrocarvone, obtained by these methods, always contains some dihydrocarveol as an impurity. It is purified by agitating with a solution of acid sodium sulphite, and, after standing for twenty-four hours, the resulting crystals are filtered, washed with a mixture of alcohol and ether, pressed on a porous plate and decomposed with sodium hydroxide.

[1] Wallach and Kerkhoff, Ann. Chem., *275*, 114.

[2] Baeyer, Ber., *26*, 823.

[3] Wallach and Schrader, Ann. Chem., *279*, 377.

Twenty-six to thirty grams of pure dihydrocarvone may be obtained from forty grams of carvone, if the last described method be employed.

Dihydrocarvone is also obtained by the reduction of hydrobromocarvone.[1]

PROPERTIES.[2]—Dihydrocarvone boils at 221° to 222°, and its vapor has an odor recalling that of menthone, or of carvone; its specific gravity at 19° is 0.928 and its refractive index, $n_D =$ 1.47174, corresponding to the molecular refraction 45.84. It is optically active; the product obtained from dextro-carvone or dextro-dihydrocarveol is levorotatory, while that prepared from levo-carvone or levo-dihydrocarveol is dextrorotatory (Wallach).

An intramolecular change of dihydrocarvone into an isomeric ketone, which is identical with the carvenone discovered by Wallach, is effected when dihydrocarvone is treated with concentrated sulphuric acid at 0° (Baeyer[3]). The same transformation results by boiling dihydrocarvone with dilute sulphuric acid (Wallach[4]), or with formic acid.[5] Carvenone is also formed when a solution of dihydrocarvone in petroleum ether is saturated with hydrogen bromide;[6] a small quantity of a bromine derivative is formed during this reaction, and it may be completely converted into carvenone on treatment with zinc dust.

Carvacrol is formed by boiling this ketone with ferric chloride (Wallach).

Dihydrocarvone combines with one molecule of hydrogen bromide, forming the oily *dihydrocarvone hydrobromide*, which, on treatment with sodium acetate and glacial acetic acid, yields a mixture of dihydrocarvone and carvenone. If, however, a glacial acetic solution of dihydrocarvone hydrobromide be treated with silver acetate, the acetyl ester of a ketone-alcohol is produced; this acetate boils at 153° to 160° under a pressure of 25 mm., and is converted into a *glycol*, $C_{10}H_{18}(OH)_2$, by hydrolysis and subsequent reduction with sodium and alcohol. This glycol crystallizes in slender, white needles, melts at 112°, and is likewise formed when dihydrocarveol hydrobromide is treated with silver acetate (Baeyer[7]).

Bromine reacts with dihydrocarvone hydrobromide, forming dihydrocarvone dibromide (Baeyer).

[1] Harries, Ber., *34*, 1924.

[2] Kondakoff and Lutschinin, Journ. pr. Chem., *60* (II), 257.

[3] Baeyer, Ber., *27*, 1921.

[4] Wallach, Ann. Chem., *279*, 388.

[5] Klages, Ber., *32*, 1516; compare Kondakoff and Lutschinin, Journ. pr. Chem., *60* (II), 257.

[6] Kondakoff and Gorbunoff, Journ. pr. Chem., *56*, 248.

[7] Baeyer, Ber., *28*, 1589.

Dihydrocarvone hydrochloride,[1] $C_{10}H_{16}O \cdot HCl$, is produced by treating an acetic acid solution of dihydrocarvone with hydrogen chloride. It boils at 155.5° to 157° under 15 mm. pressure, has the sp. gr. 1.0266 and refractive index, $n_D = 1.47877$, at 20°. It is converted into carone by boiling with alcoholic soda.

The action of phosphorus pentachloride converts dihydrocarvone into a *chloride*,[2] $C_{10}H_{15}Cl$, which boils at 208° under ordinary pressure and at 105° to 106° under 16 mm. pressure; it has the sp. gr. 1.025 and the refractive index, $n_D = 1.51622$, at 18°. It is possibly identical with the chloride obtained by a similar treatment of carvenone.

Dihydrocarvone dibromide, $C_{10}H_{15}BrO \cdot HBr$, is obtained, when two atoms of bromine are added to a cold solution of dihydrocarvone in glacial acetic acid containing hydrobromic acid.

The reaction-product is poured into ice-water, and the dibromide, which separates, is crystallized from ether or methyl alcohol; it forms brilliant crystals. The active modifications melt at 69° to 70°. The racemic derivative, obtained by recrystallizing a mixture of equal weights of the dextro- and levo-compounds, melts at 96° to 97° (Wallach[3]).

Inactive dihydrocarvone dibromide is also formed by bromination of the trioxyhexahydrocymene (m. p. 121° to 122°), which is obtained by oxidation of terpineol. Ten grams of trioxyhexahydrocymene are suspended in glacial acetic acid, allowed to stand with fifty cc. of a saturated solution of hydrogen bromide in glacial acetic acid for three or four hours, and then treated with nine cc. of bromine; the dibromide is precipitated by pouring the reaction-mixture into ice-water, and recrystallized from ether; it separates in triclinic crystals, melting at 96° to 97°.

Baeyer[4] has further observed the formation of dihydrocarvone dibromide in the following reactions.

1. Bisnitroso-4-bromotetrahydrocarvone is obtained, when dihydrocarvone hydrobromide (two grams) is treated at a low temperature with a mixture of ethyl nitrite (1.3 grams) and a few drops of acetyl chloride; its active modifications melt at 131°, and its inactive derivative melts at 142°. Inactive dihydrocarvone dibromide (m. p. 96° to 97°) is formed, together with another product, by the action of a saturated glacial acetic acid solution of hydrobromic acid on the inactive modification of the bisnitroso-compound.

[1] Kondakoff and Gorbunoff, Journ. pr. Chem., *56*, 248.
[2] Klages and Kraith, Ber., *32*, 2550.
[3] Wallach, Ann. Chem., *286*, 127.
[4] Baeyer, Ber., *28*, 1589.

2. Inactive bisnitrosocarone yields caronbisnitrosylic acid and inactive dihydrocarvone dibromide on treatment with a glacial acetic acid or alcoholic solution of hydrobromic acid. This experiment was also performed by Baeyer with the optically active modifications.

1 : 8-Oxybromotetrahydrocarvone,[1] $C_{10}H_{16}Br(OH)O$, is produced in the form of its sodium derivative when dihydrocarvone dibromide (1 : 8-dibromotetrahydrocarvone) is diluted with ether and treated with a solution of sodium hydroxide (sp. gr. 1.23); the sodium salt is decomposed with dilute sulphuric acid. It crystallizes from dry ether in large prisms, melts at 69° to 72°, is optically active, and is rather unstable, being decomposed both by acids and alkalis. Methyl alcoholic potash converts it into *oxycarone*, $C_{10}H_{16}O_2$. When it is recrystallized from methyl alcohol, a small quantity of an isomeric compound, melting at 136° to 138°, is obtained. If oxybromotetrahydrocarvone be allowed to remain in contact with water or dilute acids, it is converted into an optically active *keto-terpine*, $C_{10}H_{16}(OH)_2O$, melting at 78° to 80°.

Dihydrocarvone tribromide, $C_{10}H_{15}OBr_3$, is produced by the action of one molecular proportion of bromine on a glacial acetic acid solution of dextro- or levo-dihydrocarvone dibromide; its active modifications form hemihedral orthorhombic crystals, and melt at 88° to 89°, while the racemic derivative melts at 65° (Wallach [2]).

Dihydrocarvone dichloride, $C_{10}H_{15}ClO \cdot HCl$, is prepared like the dibromide by treating bisnitrosocarone, or the bisnitroso-compound obtained from dihydrocarvone hydrochloride, with alcoholic hydrochloric acid. The optically active derivatives melt at 42°, and the inactive modification melts at 66° to 68° (Baeyer [3]).

Dihydrocarvoxime, $C_{10}H_{16}NOH$, was prepared by Wallach and Kerkhoff.[4] A warm solution of six grams of hydroxylamine hydrochloride in six cc. of water is added to the warm solution of six cc. of dihydrocarvone in twenty-five cc. of alcohol; six grams of potassium hydroxide dissolved in five cc. of water are then added, with constant agitation, and the cold reaction-product is poured into a large quantity of cold water. The oxime so formed crystallizes on the slow evaporation of an alcoholic solution in thick prisms, and melts at 88° to 89°. A physical isomeric modification,[5] which separates in more difficultly soluble needles, is always formed, together with the oxime crystallizing in prisms.

[1] Baeyer and Baumgärtel, Ber., *31*, 3208.
[2] Wallach, Ann. Chem., *286*, 127.
[3] Baeyer, Ber., *28*, 1589.
[4] Wallach and Kerkhoff, Ann. Chem., *275*, 116.
[5] Wallach, Ann. Chem., *279*, 381.

Dihydrocarvoxime is dextro- or levorotatory according as it originates from dextro- or levo-dihydrocarvone. The inactive oxime is prepared by recrystallizing a mixture of the two active modifications, and melts at 115° to 116°; thus, inactive dihydrocarvoxime, like inactive carvoxime, has a higher melting point than the active derivatives :—

	ACTIVE	INACTIVE.
Carvoxime,	72°	93°
Dihydrocarvoxime,	88° to 89°	115° to 116°

Dihydrocarvoxime hydrobromide, $C_{10}H_{17}BrNOH$, is formed by the treatment of dextro- or levo-dihydrocarvoxime with a glacial acetic acid solution of hydrobromic acid; it crystallizes from ether or ethyl acetate in flat prisms or tablets, and melts and decomposes at 109° (Wallach[1]), according to Baeyer,[2] it melts at 118° to 120°.

According to Wallach,[1] when this hydrobromide melts, it loses water, becomes yellow, and again solidifies. This process is accompanied by a conversion of the substance into carvacrylamine hydrobromide; this change may also be effected by boiling a solution of dihydrocarvoxime hydrobromide in xylene :—

$$C_{10}H_{17}Br\ NOH = H_2O + C_{10}H_{13}NH_2\ HBr$$

An oxime, which Baeyer[2] at first called "*carveoloxime*," and which was not isolated in a condition of purity, is obtained when dihydrocarvoxime hydrobromide is subjected to the action of methyl alcoholic potash in the cold. This oxime, however, is identical with the oxime of carvenone; when it is boiled with sulphuric acid, carvenone is obtained, and may be identified by conversion into carvenone semicarbazone, which melts at 202° to 205°. This transformation of dihydrocarvoxime into carvenonoxime is analogous to the conversion of dihydrocarvone into carvenone, which was observed by Baeyer.

In consideration of Baeyer's experiments, it would be anticipated that an isomeric oxime,[1] which Wallach obtained by the action of concentrated sulphuric acid on dihydrocarvoxime, would be identical with the oxime of carvenone. This does not seem to be the case, for this isomeric oxime melts at 87° to 88° (carvenonoxime melts at 91°), and Wallach mentions nothing regarding the identity of this compound with the oxime of carvenone,[3] which he had previously prepared.

[1] Wallach, Ann Chem, *279*, 381.
[2] Baeyer, Ber, *27*, 1921.
[3] Wallach, Ann Chem, *277*, 126

Semicarbazone of dihydrocarvone, $C_{10}H_{16} = N \cdot NH \cdot CONH_2$, melts at 189° to 191°. The melting point is not sharp (Wallach[1]).

Benzylidene dihydrocarvone,[2] $C_{10}H_{14}O = CH \cdot C_6H_5$, is the condensation-product obtained from benzaldehyde and dihydrocarvone; it is an oil, boiling at 187° to 190° under 10 mm. pressure. It yields an *oxime*, which crystallizes from methyl alcohol in colorless needles, and melts at 145° to 146°.

Benzyldihydrocarveol,[2] $C_{10}H_{16}(OH) \cdot CH_2C_6H_5$, is formed by the reduction of the preceding compound with alcohol and sodium; it boils at 182° to 183° at 10 mm. The action of phosphoric anhydride converts it into the *hydrocarbon*, $C_{17}H_{22}$, which boils at 166° to 169° under 10 mm. pressure.

Oxydihydrocarvone,[3] $C_{10}H_{15}(OH)O$, is produced by the oxidation of pinole hydrate with chromic acid in glacial acetic acid solution. Its *semicarbazone* melts at 174°, and its *oxime* crystallizes from alcohol and melts at 133° to 134°. Oxydihydrocarvoxime is likewise obtained by the elimination of hydrochloric acid from terpineol nitrosochloride; it yields a *diacetyl derivative*, melting at 107°. Dilute sulphuric acid converts the oxime into inactive carvone, while concentrated acid gives rise to amidothymol.

Dihydrocarveolacetic acid,[4] $C_{10}H_{16}(OH) \cdot CH_2 \cdot COOH$, boils at 196° to 208° under 14 mm. pressure; when distilled under ordinary pressure, it yields an unsaturated hydrocarbon which is possibly to be regarded as *homolimonene*. The *ethyl* ester, prepared from dihydrocarvone and ethyl bromoacetate, boils at 150° to 170° (14 mm.) and at 282° to 288° under atmospheric pressure; it has a sp. gr. 0.997 and $n_D = 1.47664$ at 20°.

The *oxymethylene derivative of dihydrocarvone*, $C_{10}H_{14}O = CHOH$, is an oil, boiling at about 115° at 15 mm. pressure (Wallach[5]).

Dihydrocarvone is converted into a *diketone*, $C_9H_{14}O_2$, on oxidation with chromic anhydride; it boils at 152° to 160° under a pressure of 22 mm. Its *dioxime* crystallizes in two modifications, one of which is sparingly soluble and melts at 197° to 198°, and the other is readily soluble and melts at 175° to 176° (Tiemann and Semmler[6]). This diketone corresponds to the ketone-alcohol, $C_9H_{16}O_2$, which is obtained by oxidation of dihydrocarveol.

[1] Wallach, Ber., *28*, 1955.
[2] Wallach, Ann. Chem., *305*, 268.
[3] Wallach, Ann. Chem., *291*, 342.
[4] Wallach, Ann. Chem., *314*, 147.
[5] Wallach, Ber., *28*, 33.
[6] Tiemann and Semmler, Ber., *28*, 2141.

Wallach and Scharpenack[1] oxidized dihydrocarvone with dilute permanganate solution, and obtained the following products.

1. A *ketone-glycol*, $C_{10}H_{16}O(OH)_2$, which melts at 115° to 120°, and boils at 130° under 10 mm. pressure; it forms a *semicarbazone*, melting at 202°. Dilute sulphuric acid converts this compound into a ketone ($C_{10}H_{14}O$?), boiling at 220°.

2. A *diketone*, $C_9H_{14}O_2$, which is probably identical with the diketone described by Tiemann and Semmler (see above), but it solidifies when placed in a freezing mixture. Its *dioxime* melts at 195°, and its *semicarbazone* at 203° to 204°.

3. *Oxalic acid*, and an *acid* melting at 203° to 204°.

The reduction of carvone with zinc dust and sodium hydroxide yields as a by-product, *dicarvelone*, $C_{20}H_{30}O_2$ (see under carvone).

It should also be recalled that the *ketone*,[2] $C_{10}H_{16}O$, obtained in the reduction of nitrosopinene dibromide with zinc and acetic acid, is identical with inactive dihydrocarvone, it gives an oxime, melting at 113° to 114°.

2 DIHYDROCARVEOL, $C_{10}H_{17}OH$.

Leuckart[3] determined that an alcohol is formed by the reduction of carvone in an alcoholic solution with sodium. A more detailed investigation of this compound by Lampe[4] led to the result that it is not *carveol*, $C_{10}H_{15}OH$, as Leuckart had believed, but that it has the constitution, $C_{10}H_{17}OH$, and must therefore be regarded as *dihydrocarveol*. Lampe's observations have since been confirmed by the researches of Wallach, Kruse, and Kerkhoff.[5]

Dihydrocarveol is prepared by the reduction of either dextro- or levo-carvone with sodium and alcohol, according to Wallach's method of preparing borneol from camphor.

Twenty grams of carvone are dissolved in 200 cc. of absolute alcohol, and twenty-four grams of sodium are added rather rapidly. Towards the end of the reaction it is generally essential to add more alcohol or water in order to effect the complete solution of the sodium, and the product is then distilled with steam. As soon as the distillate appears cloudy the receiver is changed; dihydrocarveol distills over rather slowly, and is then separated, dried with potassium hydroxide, and rectified. The dihydrocarveol, which remains dissolved in the aqueous-alcoholic distillate, may be recovered by adding common salt and extracting with ether.

[1] Wallach and Scharpenack, Ber, *28*, 2704.
[2] Wallach, Ann Chem, *300*, 291; *313*, 345.
[3] Leuckart, Ber, *20*, 114
[4] Lampe, Inaug Diss Göttingen, *1889*.
[5] Wallach, Kruse and Kerkhoff, Ann Chem, *275*, 110

The formation of dihydrocarveol from dihydrocarvylamine is mentioned below.

PROPERTIES.—Dihydrocarveol has an agreeable odor, recalling that of terpineol. It boils at 224° to 225° at ordinary pressure, and at 112° under a pressure of 14 mm. At 20° it has a specific gravity of 0.927 and a refractive index, $n_D = 1.48168$, corresponding to the molecular refraction of 47.33; it rotates the plane of polarized light in the same direction as the carvone from which it is derived.

It behaves as an unsaturated compound towards bromine and the halogen hydrides. In its reaction it exhibits a great similarity to terpineol, with the one exception that the latter is a tertiary alcohol, which, in contrast to dihydrocarveol, does not yield a ketone on oxidation with chromic anhydride. Like terpineol, it is converted into terpenes by treatment with dehydrating agents; terpinene is formed when dihydrocarveol is boiled with dilute sulphuric acid. It has not been ascertained with certainty whether, under other conditions, different terpenes are formed, but it is highly probable that they are.

Dihydrocarveol is produced, together with dipentene,[1] when an aqueous solution of equal molecular proportions of dihydrocarvylamine hydrochloride and sodium nitrite is heated.

Dihydrocarvyl phenylurethane,

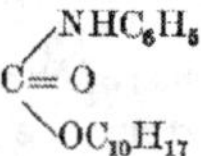

is obtained when theoretical quantities of carbanile and dihydrocarveol are brought together. After a few days the mixture becomes very thick, and eventually solidifies; it is washed with ligroine, and recrystallized from dilute alcohol. The urethanes obtained from the active modifications of dihydrocarveol melt at 87°; the racemic compound, formed by the combination of the active derivatives, is more readily soluble in alcohol than its components, and melts at 93°.

Methyl dihydrocarvylxanthate,[2] $C_{10}H_{17}O \cdot CS_2 \cdot CH_3$, is produced by successively treating dihydrocarveol, dissolved in dry toluene, with sodium, carbon bisulphide, and methyl iodide; it is a thick, yellow oil. On distillation, it yields a mixture of limonene and another hydrocarbon.

[1] Wallach, Ann. Chem., *275*, 128.

[2] L. Tschügaeff, Ber., *33*, 735.

Dihydrocarvyl acetate, $C_{10}H_{17}OCOCH_3$, results on boiling dihydrocarveol with acetic anhydride; it is a liquid, boiling at 232° to 234°, is readily oxidized by permanganate, and is converted into a hydriodide by the action of hydriodic acid in a glacial acetic acid solution. This hydriodide yields tetrahydrocarvyl acetate by reduction with zinc dust and glacial acetic acid; the latter is converted into tetrahydrocarveol, $C_{10}H_{19}OH$, by hydrolysis (Baeyer[1]).

Dihydrocarveol hydrobromide, $C_{10}H_{17}OH \cdot HBr$, is formed by the action of a glacial acetic acid solution of hydrogen bromide on dihydrocarveol; it is a heavy oil, and, when treated with silver acetate, it yields an acetate, boiling at 150° to 155° under a pressure of 15 mm.; this acetate may be converted by hydrolysis into a *glycol*, $C_{10}H_{18}(OH)_2$, which is soluble in water and alcohol, and melts at 110.5° to 112°. When oxidized with chromic acid, this glycol is converted into a liquid oxytetrahydrocarvone, whose semicarbazone melts at 139° (compare under dihydrocarvone and carone).

Wallach[2] has published a preliminary notice concerning the oxidation of dihydrocarveol with potassium permanganate. He found that dihydrocarveol is oxidized into a trioxyhexahydrocymene; the product is a viscous liquid, and may be distilled without decomposition in vacuum. When trioxyhexahydrocymene is warmed with dilute sulphuric acid, it yields a *ketone*, $C_{10}H_{16}O$, boiling at 196° to 199°; its specific gravity at 20° is 0.962, and its refractive index, $n_D = 1.484$. This ketone unites with nitrosyl chloride, forming a deep blue oil, and combines with hydrobromic acid, giving a solid addition-product.

This compound, $C_{10}H_{16}O$, was at first regarded as an unsaturated oxide; but, in the light of further investigation, it appears to be a ketone allied to pulegone, since it reacts with hydroxylamine yielding a mixture of two hydrated oximes, $C_{10}H_{16}NOH + H_2O$, one of which melts at 111° to 112°, and the other at 164° to 165°.

Tiemann and Semmler[3] have investigated in another direction respecting the constitution of the trioxyhexahydrocymene obtained by Wallach. By treating this substance with very dilute chromic acid, they obtained a ketone-alcohol, $C_9H_{16}O_2$, which melted at 58° to 59°; on oxidizing this ketone-alcohol with a solution of bromine in sodium hydroxide, it was converted into an acid, $C_7H_{13}O \cdot COOH$, which melted at 153°. When heated with bromine

[1] Baeyer, Ber., *26*, 821.
[2] Wallach, Ann. Chem., *275*, 155; *277*, 151; *279*, 386.
[3] Tiemann and Semmler, Ber., *28*, 2141.

(six atoms) at 190°, the acid was changed into meta-oxy-para-toluic acid, together with a small quantity of para-toluic acid, thus corresponding to the observations of Einhorn and Willstätter respecting the behavior of hydro-aromatic acids. From these facts, Tiemann and Semmler have proposed the following constitutional formulas of trioxyhexahydrocymene and its oxidation products:

```
      CH3                              CH3
      CH                               CH
  H2C    CHOH                      H2C    CHOH
  H2C    CH2          →            H2C    CH2
      CH                               CH
      COH                              CO
  H3C    CH2OH                         CH3
Trioxyhexahydrocymene            Methyl-1-ethyl-on-4-
from dihydrocarveol.               cyclohexanol-6
                                 (m. p. 58° to 59°).
                     ↙
      CH3                              CH3
      CH                               C
  H2C    CHOH                      HC    COH
  H2C    CH2          →            HC    CH
      CH                               C
      COOH                             COOH
Methyl-1-cyclohexanol-6-         m-Oxy-p-toluic acid.
methyl-acid-4 (m. p.
153°).
```

Tiemann and Semmler believe that they have thus explained the constitution of dihydrocarveol and of carvone, and consequently that of limonene; they ascribe the following formulas to these compounds:

```
      CH3              CH3              CH3
      CH               C                C
  H2C    CHOH      HC     CO        HC     CH2
  H2C    CH2       H2C    CH2       H2C    CH2
      CH               CH               CH
      C                C                C
  H3C    CH2       H3C    CH2       H3C    CH2
 Dihydrocarveol.     Carvone.         Limonene.
```

These formulas, which are the natural consequence of the formula of terpineol founded on the researches carried on by Wallach,[1] and, directly following him, by Tiemann and Semmler,[2] had been presented by G. Wagner[3] one year previous to their publication by Tiemann and Semmler.

3. CARVENONE, $C_{10}H_{16}O$.

Crystallized terpineol (melting point 35°) yields a trivalent alcohol, $C_{10}H_{17}(OH)_3$, on oxidation with potassium permanganate. This substance melts at 121° to 122° and, when heated with dilute sulphuric acid, is converted into cymene and a compound, $C_{10}H_{16}O$ (Wallach[4]):

$$C_{10}H_{17}(OH)_3 - 3H_2O = C_{10}H_{14},$$
$$C_{10}H_{17}(OH)_3 - 2H_2O = C_{10}H_{16}O.$$

Wallach supposed that a monovalent, unsaturated alcohol, $C_{10}H_{15}OH$, belonging to the carvone series, might be formed, together with cymene, from this trivalent alcohol, and that it should be designated as carveol. Nevertheless, he at once determined that the substance which he had obtained was not an alcohol, but reacted like a ketone ; a name was not immediately given to this ketone.

The same ketone, $C_{10}H_{16}O$, was subsequently obtained by Baeyer,[5] who gave to it the provisional name "*carveol.*" After further examination Wallach[6] called it *carvenone*.

Carvenone also results when dihydrocarvone is treated with cold, concentrated sulphuric acid, and the resulting solution is precipitated with ice (Baeyer[5]) ; or, when dihydrocarvone is boiled with dilute sulphuric acid (Wallach[6]). It may likewise be produced from carone, since dihydrocarvone unites with hydrobromic acid forming an additive compound from which hydrogen bromide may be withdrawn, yielding carone ; when the latter is heated for some time in a flask with reflux condenser, carvenone is formed (Baeyer[5]).

According to Klages,[7] carvenone is produced when dihydrocarvone is heated with formic acid in a reflux apparatus.

Carvenone is the intermediate product formed in the conversion of camphor into cymene and into carvacrol. Carvenone is also

[1] Wallach, Ber., *28*, 1773.

[2] Tiemann and Semmler, Ber., *28*, 1778.

[3] G. Wagner, Ber., *27*, 1653 and 2270.

[4] Wallach, Ann. Chem., *277*, 110 and 122.

[5] Baeyer, Ber., *27*, 1917.

[6] Wallach, Ann. Chem., *286*, 129.

[7] A. Klages, Ber., *32*, 1516; compare Kondakoff and Gorbunoff, Journ. pr. Chem., *56*, 248; Kondakoff and Lutschinin, Journ. pr. Chem., *60* [II.], 257.

produced by the action of concentrated sulphuric acid on camphor at 105° to 110° (Bredt[1]).

According to Bredt,[1] carvenone may be separated from the more volatile constituent of "*camphrene*"[2] (a mixture obtained by the action of hot, concentrated sulphuric acid on camphor).

Carvenone, prepared according to Wallach from the oxidation product of terpineol and separated by fractional distillation from cymene and other by-products, has the following properties: it boils at 231° to 233°, has a specific gravity at 20° equal to 0.929, and a specific refractive power, $n_D = 1.48197$.

Wallach[3] found that carvenone, regenerated from its semicarbazone, boils at 232° to 233°, and has the specific gravity 0.927 at 20°; its refractive index is $n_D = 1.48217$ at 20°, from which the molecular refraction of 46.76 is calculated, indicating that the molecule of carvenone contains two ethylene linkages.

It has a slight odor of carvone, but when it is rubbed on the skin, a peppermint-like odor is noticeable. It does not combine with acid sodium sulphite. It is converted into carvacrol by boiling with ferric chloride (Wallach).

Carvenonoxime, $C_{10}H_{16}NOH$, is produced when carvenone is treated with hydroxylamine hydrochloride; it is purified by distillation in a current of steam, and crystallized from methyl alcohol. It forms transparent, thick prisms, and melts at 91°. Carvenone is regenerated by warming the oxime with dilute sulphuric acid.

A *compound*, $C_{10}H_{20}N_2O_2$, melting at 162° to 163°, is formed, together with carvenonoxime, if an excess of hydroxylamine hydrochloride be allowed to react with carvenone.

Carvenone unites with four atoms of hydrogen when it is reduced with sodium and alcohol, and forms tetrahydrocarveol, $C_{10}H_{19}OH$ (Wallach). This secondary alcohol is identical with Baeyer's carvomenthol, and is an isomeride of position of menthol.

Carvenone semicarbazone, $C_{10}H_{16} = N \cdot NH \cdot CO \cdot NH_2$, crystallizes in spindles or six-sided leaflets, melting at 202° to 205° (Baeyer[4]). According to Wallach, carvenone yields two isomeric semicarbazones, one of which is a sparingly soluble α-semicarbazone, melting at 200° to 201°, and the other a readily soluble β-semicarbazone, melting at 153° to 154°.

Nitrosocarvenone, $C_{10}H_{15}O \cdot NO$, is prepared by adding ten drops of strong hydrochloric acid to a mixture of seven grams of carvenone and five grams of amyl nitrite, well cooled by a freezing

[1] Bredt, Rochussen and Monheim, Ann. Chem., *314*, 369.
[2] Armstrong and Kipping, Journ. Chem. Soc., *63*, 77.
[3] Wallach, Ber., *28*, 1955.
[4] Baeyer, Ber., *27*, 1915.

mixture; the addition of the acid should require about three hours. A colorless, crystalline powder separates, which is difficultly soluble in alcohol; it is purified by precipitating its solution in chloroform with methyl alcohol. It melts with decomposition at 133°, and is to be regarded as a bisnitroso-compound (Baeyer[1]).

Condensation-product of carvenone and benzaldehyde.[2]—When dry hydrogen chloride is passed into a well cooled mixture of two molecular proportions of benzaldehyde and one of carvenone, the *compound*, $C_{24}H_{26}O_2 \cdot HCl$, is obtained; it separates from acetic ether in colorless crystals, and melts with decomposition at 197°. When this substance is heated in vacuum for a short time and is then distilled, hydrogen chloride is eliminated and the *compound*, $C_{24}H_{26}O_2$, results; it crystallizes from hot methyl alcohol, and melts at 170° to 171°.

Oxidation Products of Carvenone.[3]

When carvenone is oxidized with a two per cent. alkaline solution of potassium permanganate (three atoms of oxygen to one molecule of carvenone) some lower fatty acids are formed, together with the following chief products.

1. **α-Oxy-α^1-methyl-α-isopropyl adipic acid**, $C_{10}H_{18}O_5$, is the chief oxidation product; it crystallizes from water, and melts at 136° to 137°. When heated above its melting point, it loses water and yields a *lactonic acid*, $C_{10}H_{16}O_4$, melting at about 100°.

2. **2:6-Dimethyl-heptan-5-onoic acid**, $C_9H_{16}O_3$, is a very feeble acid; it is an oil, boiling at 166° to 168° under 14 mm. pressure. It is also formed by the gentle oxidation of the acid $C_{10}H_{18}O_5$. It is a ketonic acid and yields an *oxime*, $C_9H_{16}O_2(NOH)$, which is sparingly soluble in water and melts at 67° to 68°.

3. **α-Methyl glutaric acid.**—This is also formed, together with acetone, by the oxidation of the preceding acid, $C_9H_{16}O_3$.

In consideration of these oxidation products, Tiemann and Semmler suggest the following formula for carvenone:

```
        CH3
        |
        CH
      /    \
    OC      CH2
    |       |
    HC      CH2
      \\   /
        C
        |
        CH
       /  \
    H3C    CH3
```

[1] Baeyer, Ber., 28, 646.
[2] Wallach, Ann. Chem., 305, 270.
[3] Tiemann and Semmler, Ber., 31, 2889.

It should further be mentioned that Marsh and Hartridge[1] have described a compound, $C_{10}H_{16}O$, under the name "*carvenol*";[1] they prepared it by the action of concentrated sulphuric acid on chlorocamphene, $C_{10}H_{16}Cl_2$ (obtained by the action of phosphorus pentachloride on camphor). It seems quite probable that this "carvenol" is identical with carvenone. On reduction, "carvenol" yields a saturated alcohol, $C_{10}H_{19}OH$, "*carvanol*," which is converted into the ketone, $C_{10}H_{18}O$, "*carvanone*," by oxidation. The properties of these compounds agree so completely with those of tetrahydrocarveol and tetrahydrocarvone, that it is probable that they are identical.

4. CARONE, $C_{10}H_{16}O$.

Carone, like its isomeride carvenone, was obtained by Baeyer[2] by the intramolecular change of dihydrocarvone.

In order to prepare it, dihydrocarvone is allowed to stand with an excess of a glacial acetic acid solution of hydrogen bromide for fifteen minutes; the resulting dihydrocarvone hydrobromide is precipitated with ice, and extracted with ether. The ethereal solution is washed with bicarbonate of sodium, dried over anhydrous sodium sulphate, and carefully treated with alcoholic potash, the mixture being well cooled with ice. When all of the bromine is removed, the reaction-product is poured onto ice and sulphuric acid, the ethereal solution is separated, and treated with a solution of permanganate until the violet color remains permanent, in order to remove small quantities of unsaturated by-products; the ether is then allowed to evaporate.

Carone is a colorless oil having an odor resembling that of camphor and of peppermint, and similar to that of eucarvone only not as pronounced. It boils at about 210°, but an accurate determination of its boiling point can not be made owing to its transformation into carvenone. Carone prepared from caraway oil is dextrorotatory, having the specific rotatory power, $a_D = +173.8°$; levo-carvone yields levo-carone, $a_D = -169.5°$ (Brühl[3]).

It does not combine with acid sodium sulphite; it is converted into carvenone and certain condensation-products by continued

[1] March and Hartridge, Journ. Chem. Soc., *73*, 852; March and Gardner, Journ. Chem. Soc., *71*, 290, refer to this compound as "camphenol"; see Bredt, Ann. Chem., *314*, 369.

[2] Baeyer, Ber., *27*, 1915.

[3] Brühl, Ber., *28*, 639.

boiling. The latter reaction resembles that observed by Semmler in the transposition of tanacetone into carvotanacetone.

Carone is very stable towards potassium permanganate, and its chloroform solution is only very slowly attacked by bromine. A liquid *dibromide* results by the action of bromine (two atoms) on a solution of carone in chloroform; the bromine is slowly absorbed without evolution of hydrogen bromide, hence the product is probably an additive compound.

Carone dissolved in acetic acid unites with hydrobromic acid, forming an oil which reacts with hydroxylamine and yields dihydrocarvoxime hydrobromide (m. p. 118° to 120°); this reaction indicates that the oil is dihydrocarvone hydrobromide (Baeyer).

Oxytetrahydrocarvone is formed by the addition of the elements of water to carone, when the latter is allowed to stand with dilute sulphuric acid and alcohol for several hours; when this oxytetrahydrocarvone is reduced with sodium and alcohol, it is converted into the same glycol, melting at 112°, which is obtained by heating dihydrocarveol hydrobromide with silver acetate (Baeyer[1]).

Caronoxime, $C_{10}H_{16}NOH$.—The oximes of the optically active modifications of carone are liquids. An inactive caronoxime is obtained by mixing the solutions of equal quantities of the oximes having opposite rotatory powers; it separates in crystals, melting at 77° to 79°. When the inactive oxime is reduced in an alcoholic solution with sodium, carylamine is formed (Baeyer[2]).

The *semicarbazones* of dextro- and levo-carone are readily soluble in alcohol, and crystallize in long needles, which melt at 167° to 169°; the inactive semicarbazone forms very insoluble, small, acute prisms, and melts at 178°. The semicarbazones decompose at once into semicarbazide and carone on boiling with dilute sulphuric acid.

Bisnitrosocarone, $(C_{10}H_{15}O)_2N_2O_2$, is obtained by a method similar to that employed by Baeyer and Manasse in the preparation of nitrosomenthone.

Forty drops of acetyl chloride are cautiously added to a well cooled mixture of twenty grams of carone and fifteen grams of amyl nitrite. Crystals separate, and are washed with methyl alcohol; the yield is forty-five per cent. of the theoretical.

Bisnitrosocarone is readily soluble in chloroform, sparingly in alcohol and ether. The active modifications melt and decompose at 112° to 118°; the inactive derivative is more difficultly sol-

[1] Baeyer, Ber., 29, 3.
[2] Baeyer, Ber., 27, 3485; 28, 640.

uble in chloroform, and melts with decomposition at 145° (Baeyer[1]).

Baeyer's original publication must be referred to for a description of other derivatives of bisnitrosocarone. The treatment of bisnitrosocarone with alcoholic hydrobromic or hydrochloric acid has already been mentioned; by means of this reaction Baeyer[2] obtained *caronbisnitrosylic acid*, $C_{10}H_{15}O \cdot N_2O_2 \cdot H$, together with dihydrocarvone dibromide or dichloride.

The *oxymethylene compound of tetrahydrocarvone*[2] is formed instead of the oxymethylene derivative of carone, when carone is treated with amyl formate in an ethereal solution.

Oxycarone,[3] $C_{10}H_{16}O_2$, is produced when one molecule of 1 : 8-oxybromotetrahydrocarvone, $C_{10}H_{16}Br(OH)O$ (prepared from dihydrocarvone dibromide), is treated with a methyl alcoholic solution of potassium hydroxide (1.5 molecules); it is a viscous oil, boils at 134° to 135° under 19 mm. pressure, and dissolves readily in water, the solution having a feebly acid reaction. Its *oxime* crystallizes in prisms, and melts at 138°; its *semicarbazone* forms needles, melting at 197°, and its *phenylurethane* crystallizes in prisms, melting and decomposing at 190°.

Oxycarone is optically active. Hydrobromic acid converts it into dibromotetrahydrocarvone, and hydrochloric acid yields the corresponding dichloro-derivative, melting at 41° to 42°.

The *keto-terpine*, $C_{10}H_{16}(OH)_2O$, is readily formed by treating oxycarone with ice-cold, dilute sulphuric acid, neutralizing the solution with sodium carbonate, and extracting with ether and alcohol. It crystallizes from ether in prisms, melts at 78° to 80°, boils at 163° to 165° (16 mm.), and dissolves readily in water, alcohol and chloroform; it is levorotatory. It is completely converted into carvacrol by boiling with dilute sulphuric acid. Its *oxime* melts at 163°, its *semicarbazone* at 184° to 185°, and its *phenylhydrazone* at 150° to 160°.

On reduction with alcohol and sodium, the keto-terpine gives rise to a *1 : 2 : 8-trioxyterpane*, $C_{10}H_{20}O_3$, which, when distilled under diminished pressure and recrystallized from ether, forms plates, melting at 97° to 98°; it is soluble in water and alcohol, and is levorotatory. When this trioxyterpane is oxidized with chromic anhydride and sulphuric acid, it yields an optically active *methyl ketone of homoterpenylic acid* (a *keto-lactone*), $C_{10}H_{16}O_3$, melting at 48° to 49°. (Compare with the keto-lactone obtained from terpineol.)

[1] Baeyer, Ber., *28*, 641.
[2] Baeyer, Ber., *28*, 1589.
[3] Baeyer and Baumgärtel, Ber., *31*, 3208.

Oxidation of Carone.[1]

When carone is oxidized with an alkaline solution of potassium permanganate, it yields oxalic acid and another acid which is capable of existing in *cis*- and *trans*-modifications; the latter acid is termed *caronic acid* or *gem*-dimethyltrimethylene-1 : 2-dicarboxylic acid. (The prefix *gem* is employed by Baeyer for compounds containing two alkyl groups attached to the same carbon atom.)

The *caronic acids*,

$$\begin{matrix} CH_3 \\ CH_3 \end{matrix}\!\!>\!C\!\!<\!\begin{matrix} CH{-}COOH \\ |\quad\quad \\ CH{-}COOH \end{matrix}$$

are formed by heating carone with potassium permanganate in a reflux apparatus on the water-bath, for thirty-six hours; after the removal of the oxalic acid, the neutral liquid is extracted with ether, rendered acid, and again extracted with ether, the acid syrup thus obtained depositing the *cis*-acid in crystals, while the *trans*-acid is separated by conversion into its ammonium salt.

Cis-caronic acid, $C_7H_{10}O_4$, crystallizes from water in plates, and melts at 174° to 175°; it is soluble in chloroform, but dissolves sparingly in ether and petroleum. It forms a crystalline *ammonium* salt. Its *anhydride* is produced by melting the acid, and separates from ether in crystals, melting at 54° to 56°. When the acid is heated with a solution of hydrobromic acid, it is converted into the isomeric terebic acid.

Trans-caronic acid, $C_7H_{10}O_4$, crystallizes from water in prisms, and melts at 212°. It does not yield an anhydride, but may be converted into terebic acid in the same manner as the *cis*-modification.

Caronic acid has also been synthetically prepared by Perkin and Thorpe in such a manner as to confirm the above constitutional formula which Baeyer assigned to it.

According to Baeyer, carone has the constitution represented by the formula,

$$\begin{matrix} CH_3 \\ CH_3 \end{matrix}\!\!>\!C\!\!<\!\begin{matrix} CH{-}CO{-}CH{-}CH_3 \\ |\quad\quad\quad\quad\quad | \\ CH{-}CH_2{-}CH_2 \end{matrix}$$

Baeyer regards it as probable that carone differs from eucarvone merely by the presence of a double linkage in the latter compound.

[1] Baeyer and Ipatieff, Ber., *29*, 2796; Baeyer and Villiger, Ber., *31*, 1401; Perkin and Thorpe, Proc. Chem. Soc., *1898*, 107; Baeyer and Villiger, Ber., *31*, 2067.

5. DIHYDROEUCARVONE, $C_{10}H_{16}O$.

Dihydroeucarvone is formed when dihydroeucarveol is oxidized with Beckmann's chromic acid mixture. It boils at 86° to 88° under 14 mm. pressure, and, like eucarvone, has a faint odor of peppermint and of camphor (Baeyer[1]). It is unstable towards permanganate, and yields an oily oxime, which forms a very characteristic, crystalline hydriodide.

Dihydroeucarvoxime hydriodide, $C_{10}H_{17}I \cdot NOH$, is prepared when dihydroeucarvoxime is allowed to remain in a glacial acetic acid solution of hydriodic acid for twelve hours. It is obtained in splendid, colorless prisms, melts at 161°, and is only slightly soluble in the ordinary solvents. When it is reduced with alcohol and sodium, it yields *dihydroeucarvylamine,* $C_{10}H_{17}NH_2$; but on reduction with zinc dust and alcoholic hydrochloric acid, it is converted into *tetrahydroeucarvone,*[2] $C_{10}H_{18}O$.

Dihydroeucarvone semicarbazone, $C_{10}H_{16}{=}N \cdot NH \cdot CO \cdot NH_2$, crystallizes in thin plates; it is readily soluble in alcohol, and melts at 189° to 191°.

Nitrosodihydroeucarvone, $C_{10}H_{15}ONO$, is prepared by adding ten drops of hydrochloric acid to a mixture of seven grams of dihydroeucarvone and five grams of amyl nitrite, which is well cooled by a freezing mixture; three hours should be required for the addition of the hydrochloric acid.[3] It forms large, colorless prisms, melts and decomposes at 121° to 124°, and is very characteristic of dihydroeucarvone. Baeyer regards it as a bisnitroso-derivative, $(C_{10}H_{15}O)_2N_2O_2$.

According to Baeyer,[2] dihydroeucarvone is a methyl-*gem*-dimethylcycloheptenone, and, when oxidized with a saturated solution of potassium permanganate, it gives rise to unsymmetrical or *gem*-dimethylsuccinic acid. Baeyer regards this as evidence of the presence of the *gem*-dimethyl group in the molecule of dihydroeucarvone, as well as in that of eucarvone.

Dihydroeucarvone yields dihydroeucarveol when it is reduced with alcohol and sodium.

On treating dihydroeucarvone with phosphorus pentachloride, a *chloride,* $C_{10}H_{15}Cl$, is formed, which boils at 92° to 93° under 18 mm. pressure, and has a sp. gr. 1.02 and refractive index, $n_D = 1.51250$, at 18°.

[1] Baeyer, Ber., 27, 1922.
[2] Baeyer and Villiger, Ber., *31*, 2067.
[3] Baeyer, Ber., 27, 1923; 28 646.

6. DIHYDROEUCARVEOL, $C_{10}H_{17}OH$.

Dihydroeucarveol is formed when eucarvone, $C_{10}H_{14}O$, or dihydroeucarvone, $C_{10}H_{16}O$, is reduced in an alcoholic solution with sodium; during the reaction the solution changes in color from a deep bluish-violet to red, and eventually becomes colorless. It was discovered by Baeyer.[1]

It is a colorless, thick oil, which has a camphor-like odor, and boils at 109° to 110° under a pressure of 21 mm. It is an unsaturated alcohol, and, when oxidized with chromic anhydride, yields dihydroeucarvone.

Dihydroeucarvyl acetate,[2] $C_{10}H_{17}O \cdot COCH_3$, boils at 223° to 224°, and has a sp. gr. 0.951 and a refractive index, $n_D = 1.46315$, at 20°.

Dihydroeucarvyl chloride,[2] $C_{10}H_{17}Cl$, boils at 85° under 20 mm. pressure. It does not form 2-chlorocymene, but may be converted into Baeyer's euterpene.

When 100 grams of dihydroeucarveol are treated with 200 grams of phosphorus pentachloride, and the resulting chloride is boiled with quinoline during half an hour, a hydrocarbon, *euterpene*,[3] $C_{10}H_{16}$, is produced; this terpene boils at 161° to 165°, and yields acetic, oxalic and *gem*-dimethylsuccinic acids on oxidation with permanganate.

7. THUJONE (TANACETONE), $C_{10}H_{16}O$.

The investigations of Schweizer[4] and of Jahns[5] determined that thuja oil contains a ketone, $C_{10}H_{16}O$. Wallach[6] has more recently examined thuja oil and found, as has already been indicated, that it consists principally of levorotatory fenchone and another ketone, $C_{10}H_{16}O$, for which he proposed the name thujone. The same name had been used by Jahns to designate the ketone which he obtained from thuja oil.

Simultaneous with Wallach's investigations, Semmler[7] was engaged in researches on the oil of tansy (*Tanacetum vulgare*), and he showed that it contains a compound which he identified as a ketone; the same substance had previously been discovered by

[1] Baeyer, Ber., *27*, 1922.
[2] Klages and Kraith, Ber., *32*, 2550.
[3] Baeyer and Villiger, Ber., *31*, 2067.
[4] Schweizer, Ann. Chem., *52*, 398.
[5] Jahns, Arch. Pharm. (1883), *221*, 748.
[6] Wallach, Ann. Chem., *272*, 109.
[7] Semmler, Ber., *25*, 3343.

Bruylants,[1] and described as an aldehyde under the name of tanacetone. Semmler found tanacetone to be identical with *absinthol*, which is the name given by Beilstein and Kupfer[2] to a constituent of the oil of absinth; he also regarded it as identical with *salviol*, a compound found by Muir and Sigiura[3] in the oil of sage. In his first publication, Semmler considered the thujone obtained by Jahus and Wallach as identical with tanacetone.

This view has been strengthened by Wallach's[4] subsequent investigations of thujone, and seems to be proved by the preparation of many derivatives of both compounds. Nevertheless, the behavior of tanacetone and thujone does not perfectly agree in all respects, and, therefore, Semmler[5] has denied the identity of tanacetone and thujone. However, there can be no doubt as to the chemical identity of these compounds, for Wallach[6] has proved that the same ketone may be separated from all of the above-mentioned oils by means of its acid sodium sulphite compound, and that the differences, which have been observed in the behavior of thujone and tanacetone, may be attributed to admixtures of foreign substances with the crude ketone.

It is also worthy of notice that experiments conducted in the laboratories of Schimmel & Co. have indicated that thujone occurs in specially large quantities in the ethereal oil of *Artemisia barrelieri*.

Preparation.—Thujone is contained in a comparatively pure condition in artemisia oil, and also in the more accessible oil of tansy. Two hundred grams of the latter oil are shaken with a mixture of two hundred cc. of a saturated solution of acid sodium sulphite, seventy-five cc. of water and three hundred cc. of alcohol; no further separation of crystals takes place after standing for about two weeks. The mixture is then well cooled, the crystals are filtered with the pump, washed with alcohol and ether, and decomposed with soda; pure thujone is obtained in a quantity equal to forty-seven per cent. of the crude oil. This product contains, as impurities, small quantities of substances having an aldehydic character; the latter are removed by heating with an ammoniacal silver solution (Semmler).

The other above-mentioned oils contain thujone in such small amounts that the acid sodium sulphite compound is obtained as a solid product only with difficulty; thujone is contained in the

[1]Bruylants, Ber., *11*, 450.
[2]Beilstein and Kupfer, Ann. Chem., *170*, 290.
[3]Muir and Sigiura, Jahresb. Chem., *1879*, 980.
[4]Wallach, Ann. Chem., *275*, 179; *279*, 383.
[5]Semmler, Ber., *27*, 897.
[6]Wallach, Ann. Chem., *286*, 90.

fractions of these oils boiling at 80° to 90° under a pressure of 14 mm, or at 195° to 200° under ordinary pressure.

PROPERTIES.—Pure thujone is an optically active oil, which boils at 84.5° under 13 mm. pressure, or at 203° under the ordinary pressure; it has a specific gravity of 0.9126 and refractive power, $n_D = 1.4495$, at 20° (Semmler[1]). Wallach[2] found similar constants. According to Semmler,[3] pure thujone has a specific rotatory power of about 68°; the rotatory power is diminished, and the capacity of the ketone to unite with acid sodium sulphite is lessened, by the continued boiling of thujone.

It is converted into the isomeride, carvotanacetone, by heating to high temperatures (Semmler). Isothujone is produced when thujone is boiled with dilute sulphuric acid. When thujone is heated with ferric chloride, it readily yields carvacrol; this is also formed as a by-product in the preparation of carvotanacetone from thujone (Wallach[4]).

Different opinions are held as to whether thujone should be regarded as an unsaturated compound. The molecular refraction indicates the presence of a diagonal linkage, whilst its extreme sensitiveness towards permanganate points against this assumption. Thujone behaves as a saturated compound towards bromine; it combines slowly with this element forming a substitution product, which Wallach regards as very characteristic.

Thujone tribromide, $C_{10}H_{13}OBr_3$, is prepared when five cc. of bromine are added in one portion to a solution of five grams of thujone in thirty cc. of petroleum ether, contained in a rather large beaker. An energetic reaction takes place, accompanied by a violent evolution of hydrogen bromide. When the petroleum ether is allowed to evaporate slowly, a crystalline mass is generally obtained; in case the reaction-product does not solidify at once, a little more petroleum ether and bromine are added. The product is pressed on a porous plate, and crystallized from ethyl acetate. It forms large, well defined, monoclinic prisms, is very sparingly soluble in cold alcohol, melts and decomposes at 121° to 122° (Wallach[5]).

When thujone tribromide is treated with a solution of sodium in methyl alcohol, one molecule of hydrogen bromide is eliminated, and one atom of bromine is replaced by a methoxyl-group, forming a compound which is phenolic in character (Wallach[5]):

$$C_{10}H_{13}OBr_3 + 2NaOCH_3 = 2NaBr + CH_3OH + C_{10}H_{11}Br(OH)(OCH_3)$$

[1] Semmler, Ber., *25*, 3343.
[2] Wallach, Ber., *28*, 1955.
[3] Semmler, Ber., *27*, 897.
[4] Wallach, Ann. Chem., *275*, 197, *286*, 109, see Semmler, Ber., *33*, 2454.
[5] Wallach, Ann. Chem., *275*, 197; *286*, 129.

This intramolecular change is analogous to the transposition of carvone into carvacrol, and may be graphically represented by the following formulas:

```
      CH3                              CH3
      |                                |
      CH                               C
    /    \                           //  \
 BrC      CO          →          BrC      COH
  ||      |                        |      ||
 BrC      CH2                 CH3OC      CH
    \    /                           \\  /
     CBr                               C
      |                                |
     C3H7                             C3H7
Thujone tribromide.            Methoxy-bromocarvacrol.
```

This phenol separates from methyl alcohol in colorless crystals, and melts at 156° to 157°; it forms an acetyl compound, melting at 63° to 64°, and a methyl ether, melting at 42° to 43° (Wallach [1]).

The action of sodium and ethyl alcohol converts thujone tribromide into an *ethoxyl-compound*, $C_{10}H_{11}Br(OH)(OC_2H_5)$, melting at 144° to 145°. When thujone tribromide is boiled with sodium acetate and glacial acetic acid, an acetyl compound is obtained, which yields a quinone by hydrolysis with ferric chloride. A more detailed examination of this quinone has not been made, but its formation indicates that the methoxyl-group of the phenol stands in the para-position to the hydroxyl-group.

Thujyl alcohol, $C_{10}H_{17}OH$, is formed when thujone is reduced with sodium and alcohol.

An amine, $C_{10}H_{17}NH_2$, results by the treatment of thujone with ammonium formate; the same base is also obtained by the reduction of thujonoxime with sodium and alcohol, and has been described by Semmler as tanacetylamine, and by Wallach as thujylamine.

Thujolacetic acid,[2] $C_{10}H_{16}(OH)\cdot CH_2\cdot COOH$, is produced by the action of zinc on a mixture of thujone and bromoacetic acid; it crystallizes from a mixture of benzene and petroleum in leaflets, and melts at 90° to 91°. The *ethyl ester*, prepared from thujone and ethyl bromoacetate, boils at 154° to 164° (14 mm.).

Thujonoxime, $C_{10}H_{16}NOH$, boils at 135° to 136° under a pressure of 20 mm., and solidifies in long prisms, which melt at 51.5° (Semmler). The oxime prepared from impure thujone is represented by Wallach as an oil, and the fact that Semmler was never able to obtain this oxime as a solid compound formed an important argument for his assumption that thujone and tanacetone are

[1] Wallach, Ann. Chem, *275*, 197; *286*, 109.
[2] Wallach, Ann. Chem., *314*, 147.

not identical Wallach,[1] however, has found that thujonoxime may always be obtained as a solid, if the thujone be previously purified by means of its acid sodium sulphite compound.

Thujonoxime melts at 54° to 55°, and may be converted into an isomeric oxime by treatment of its chloroform solution with phosphorus pentachloride. This isomeride is sparingly soluble, crystallizes in monoclinic prisms, and melts at 90°; it is not volatile with steam, and its alcoholic solution is feebly dextrorotatory (Wallach[1]).

When thujonoxime is dissolved in concentrated sulphuric acid and the temperature maintained below 50° to 60°, it is converted into optically inactive isothujonoxime, which is volatile with steam, and melts at 119° to 120° (Wallach[1]).

Phosphorus pentoxide converts thujonoxime into a nitrile, together with carvacrylamine; the properties of the nitrile are not described by Wallach.

Thujonoxime yields *carvacrylamine* on heating with alcoholic sulphuric acid (Semmler[2]); the same amine is also obtained in a similar manner from carvoxime (see page 190).

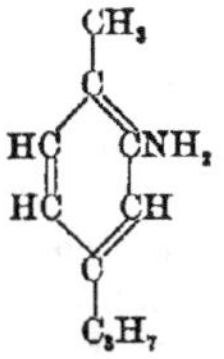

$$
\begin{array}{ccc}
 & CH_3 & \\
 & | & \\
 & C & \\
HC & & CNH_2 \\
\| & & | \\
HC & & CH \\
 & C & \\
 & | & \\
 & C_3H_7 &
\end{array}
$$

Carvacrylamine

Thujone semicarbazone, $C_{10}H_{16}{=}N\ NH{\cdot}CO\ NH_2$, forms acute prisms, and melts at 171° to 172° (Baeyer[3]).

According to Rimini,[4] thujonoxime, on treatment with amyl nitrite, yields crystals of *thujylimine nitrate*. By the action of nitrous acid, it gives rise to a *pernitroso-derivative*, which decomposes on heating, and, when distilled with steam in presence of potash, yields thujone and nitrous oxide; with hydroxylamine, thujonoxime is regenerated. When the pernitroso-compound is treated with an alcoholic solution of the calculated quantities of semicarbazide hydrochloride and sodium acetate, *thujone semicar-*

[1] Wallach, Ann Chem., 277, 159; 286, 94

[2] Semmler, Ber, 25, 3352

[3] Baeyer, Ber., 27, 1923

[4] E. Rimini, Gazz Chim, 30 [I], 600.

bazone is formed; it separates in needles, melting at 178°. Rimini gives the same melting point, 178°, for the semicarbazone which is prepared directly from thujone.

Oxymethylene thujone, $C_{10}H_{14}O = CHOH$, is obtained when an ethereal solution of pure thujone is treated with sodium and amyl formate. It is purified by distillation with steam, melts at 40°, and boils at 115° to 118° under a pressure of 16 mm. It gives an intensive reaction with ferric chloride, and decomposes easily when allowed to stand in the air (Wallach[1]).

The behavior of thujone and tanacetone towards potassium permanganate and towards bromine and sodium hydroxide has been carefully studied by Wallach[2] and by Semmler[3]; the fact that the same very characteristic acids were obtained during the investigations of both compounds supports the view that thujone and tanacetone are identical.

α- and *β*-**Thujaketonic acids (tanacetoketocarboxylic acids),**

$$C_7H_{12}\begin{matrix}\diagup COCH_3 \\ \diagdown COOH\end{matrix}$$

are produced when pure thujone or the fraction of thuja oil boiling between 190° and 200° (compare with the preparation of levorotatory fenchone, see page 157) is agitated with permanganate solution at a medium temperature; the quantity of potassium permanganate employed is so regulated that two atoms of oxygen may act on one molecule of thujone. When the oxidation is complete, the unchanged oil is distilled off with steam, the residue is filtered, and the resultant acids are separated from the filtrate by the usual method. According to the conditions under which the oxidation is performed, more or less of one of the two isomeric acids is obtained.

α-**Thujaketonic acid,**[4] $C_{10}H_{16}O_3$, crystallizes from water in well defined, transparent, brittle plates, and melts at 75° to 76°; it is soluble in about forty parts of boiling water, and does not crystallize at once on cooling, but only after long standing. Alkaline hypobromite converts it into *α-tanacetogendicarboxylic acid*, $C_9H_{14}O_4$, which melts at 141° to 142°.

β-**Thujaketonic acid**[4] **(3-metho-ethyl-2-heptene-6-onoic acid),** $C_{10}H_{16}O_3$, is produced generally in larger quantities than the *α*-acid;

[1] Wallach, Ber., *28*, 33.
[2] Wallach, Ann. Chem., *272*, 111; *275*, 164.
[3] Semmler, Ber., *25*, 3346 and 3513.
[4] Wallach, Ber., *30*, 423; Tiemann and Semmler, Ber., *30*, 429.

it is also formed by heating an aqueous solution of the α-acid for some time, and is rapidly formed when the α-acid is heated at 150° under reduced pressure. It is soluble in seventy parts of boiling water, and crystallizes at once on cooling; it forms small, fine needles, melting at 78° to 79°.

Both thujaketonic acids form *silver salts*, $C_{10}H_{15}O_3Ag$, which are sparingly soluble in water.

The liberation of iodoform or bromoform by the treatment of both acids with iodine or bromine and sodium hydroxide, and the formation of a ketone, $C_9H_{16}O$, by the dry distillation of these acids, indicate that they are to be regarded as ketonic acids, and that they contain the group, $CO{\cdot}CH_3$. Wallach regards the β-acid as unsaturated, but the α-acid is saturated, and is so constructed as to form an ethylene linkage under the influence of acids and high temperature.

β-Tanacetogendicarboxylic acid (3-metho-ethyl-2-hexene-dioic acid), $C_9H_{14}O_4$, results by the action of alkaline hypobromite on β-thujaketonic (β-tanacetoketonic) acid; it crystallizes from water, and melts at 116° to 118° (Tiemann and Semmler), or at 113° to 114° (Wallach).

α-Tanacetogendicarboxylic acid, $C_9H_{14}O_4$, is formed by the action of sodium hydroxide and bromine on α-thujaketonic (α-tanacetoketonic) acid, bromoform being eliminated. It is a dibasic acid, melts at 141° to 142°, and may be readily converted into an *anhydride*, $C_9H_{12}O_3$, when it is heated with acetic anhydride; the anhydride crystallizes in white needles, melts at 55°, and boils at 171.5° under 16 mm. pressure.

When α-tanacetogendicarboxylic acid is fused with potash, it readily yields *pimelic acid*,

$$\begin{array}{lll} CH_2 & —CH & —CH(CH_3)_2 \\ | & | & \\ COOH & COOH & \end{array}$$

whilst by the distillation with soda-lime it is changed into *tanacetophorone*, $C_8H_{12}O$. The latter compound is an oil, having an odor similar to that of camphorone; it boils at 89° to 90° under a pressure of 13 mm., has a specific gravity 0.9378 and a refractive power, $n_D = 1.4817$, at 20°. By the oxidation of tanacetophorone with potassium permanganate, a solid lactone, $C_7H_{12}O_3$, is produced, which boils at 145° under 11 mm. (Semmler).

ω-Dimethyl laevulinic methyl (isobutyryl ethyl methyl) ketone, or 2-methylheptone-3 : 6-dione, $C_8H_{14}O_2$, is formed by the oxidation of β-thujaketonic acid in an alkaline solution with a two per cent. solution of potassium permanganate; it boils at 102° to 106° at

23 mm., has the specific gravity 0.9402 at 20°, and the refractive index, $n_D = 1.4321$; the molecular refraction is $M = 39.47$. Its *oxime* separates from water in prisms, and melts at 132°.

ω-Dimethyl laevulinic (3-methyl hexan-3-onoic) acid, $C_7H_{12}O_3$, is formed by treating the preceding diketone with alkaline hypobromite, bromoform being eliminated; it melts at 32°, and boils at 145° to 146° under a pressure of 20 mm. This acid also results on the oxidation of β-tanacetogendicarboxylic acid with potassium permanganate. It yields a sparingly soluble *silver salt*, and an *oxime*,[1] melting at 88° to 89°. This acid is identical with δ-dimethyl laevulinic acid prepared by Fittig and Silberstein.[2]

2-Methyl-5-isopropylpyrroline, $C_8H_{12}NH$, is produced by heating the diketone, $C_8H_{14}O_2$, with alcoholic ammonia in sealed tubes at 180°, for two hours; it has the specific gravity 0.9051 at 20°, the refractive index, $n_D = 1.4988$, and the molecular refraction, $M = 39.86$.

α- and β-Thujaketoximic acids (tanacetoketoximic acids),

$$C_7H_{12}\begin{cases} C(NOH)-CH_3 \\ COOH \end{cases}$$

are prepared by the action of a warm, concentrated solution of one part of hydroxylamine hydrochloride on one part of the ketonic acid dissolved in one part of potassium hydroxide. The α-ketoximic acid melts and decomposes at 168°, the β-acid melts at 104° to 106°. The formation of these acids indicates that the α- and β-thujaketonic acids contain a ketone group. The α-ketoximic acid yields a *hydrochloride*, $C_{10}H_{16}O_2 \cdot NOH \cdot HCl$, melting at 128° to 129°, and a *hydrobromide*, $C_{10}H_{16}O_2 \cdot NOH \cdot HBr$, which melts at 176° to 177°.

Methyl heptylene ketone, $C_7H_{13} \cdot CO \cdot CH_3$, is obtained when β-thujaketonic acid is submitted to dry distillation. It is also formed by a similar process from the α-ketonic acid, which is at first converted into the β-acid during the distillation.

It boils at 184° to 186°, has the specific gravity 0.854 at 20°, and the refractive index, $n_D = 1.44104$; it combines directly with bromine, forming additive products. It is converted into *dihydropseudocumene*, C_9H_{14}, when heated with zinc chloride (Wallach). It forms a *semicarbazone*,[3] which melts at 143°. Its *benzylidene derivative*,[3] $C_9H_{14}O = CH \cdot C_6H_5$, crystallizes in white needles, and melts at 170°.

[1] Tiemann and Semmler, Ber., *31*, 2311.

[2] Fittig and Silberstein, Ann. Chem., *283*, 269; Fittig and Wolff, Ann. Chem., *288*, 176.

[3] Wallach, Ber., *30*, 423.

Tiemann and Semmler[1] describe a compound, $C_9H_{16}O$, under the name *tanacetoketone* (*thujaketone*, or *2-methyl-3-metheneheptane-6-one*); they obtain it by the elimination of carbon dioxide from β-tanacetoketonic (thujaketonic) acid, and represent its constitution by the formula,

$$CH_2=C(C_3H_{7\beta})-CH_2-CH_2-CO-CH_3.$$

It is probably identical with Wallach's methyl heptylene ketone.

Thujaketoxime (methyl heptylene ketoxime),[2] $C_9H_{16}NOH$, is derived from methyl heptylene ketone, and boils at 118° to 120° under 15 mm. On reduction, it yields a *base*, $C_9H_{17}NH_2$, which boils at 78° to 79° (26 mm.), and forms a *carbamide*, melting at 104° to 105°. Phosphoric oxide acts vigorously on the oxime, giving rise to the *base*, $C_9H_{13}NH_2$, which boils at 180° to 183°, and has a specific gravity 0.892 at 25°; its *picrate* decomposes above 170° without melting, and its *platinochloride* melts and decomposes at 179°.

When methyl heptylene ketone is reduced with sodium and alcohol, it yields an unsaturated *alcohol*, $C_7H_{13}\cdot CH(OH)\cdot CH_3$, boiling at 185° to 187°; it has an odor recalling that of linalool; its specific gravity is 0.848 and specific refractive power, $n_D =$ 1.4458, at 21°. If this alcohol be heated with zinc chloride, or better with dilute sulphuric acid (one part of sulphuric acid and three parts of water), it yields an isomeric, saturated *oxide*, $C_9H_{18}O$, which boils at 149° to 151°, hence considerably lower than the alcohol from which it is derived. This oxide has the specific gravity 0.847 and the index of refraction, $n_D = 1.42693$, at 20°.

Thus, methyl heptylene ketone reacts like a homologue of methyl hexylene ketone, which is formed by the dry distillation of cineolic anhydride. The constitutional formulas of methyl heptylene ketone and its above-mentioned derivatives are (Wallach):

$$\begin{matrix}CH_3\\CH_3\end{matrix}\!\!>CH.C(CH_3)=CH-CH_2-CO-CH_3$$

Methyl heptylene ketone.

$$\begin{matrix}CH_3\\CH_3\end{matrix}\!\!>CH.C(CH_3)=CH-CH_2-CH(OH)-CH_3$$

Methyl heptylene carbinol.

$$\begin{matrix}CH_3\\CH_3\end{matrix}\!\!>CH.C(CH_3)-CH_2-CH_2-CH-CH_3 \quad (\text{C and CH joined through } O)$$

Dimethyl isopropyl butylene oxide.

[1] Tiemann and Semmler, Ber., *30*, 429.

[2] Wallach, Ann. Chem., *309*, 1.

Tiemann and Semmler[1] regard them as having a somewhat different constitution.

According to Wallach,[2] when the alcohol, $C_9H_{17}OH$, obtained by the reduction of methyl heptylene ketone, is oxidized with potassium permanganate, a *glycerol*, $C_9H_{17}(OH)_3$, is produced; it is a syrupy liquid, and boils at 160° to 165° under 10 mm. pressure. Hot, dilute sulphuric acid converts the glycerol into an *oxide*, $C_9H_{16}O$, which has an odor recalling that of pinole, and boils at 160° to 165°; its *bromine derivative*, $C_9H_{15}BrO$, crystallizes from alcohol in white needles, and melts at 124.5°.

According to Tiemann and Semmler,[3] when tanacetoketone (thujaketone or methyl heptylene ketone) is oxidized with potassium permanganate, it yields a small quantity of δ-(ω)-dimethyl laevulinic methyl ketone; the chief product, however, is the ketoglycol, *2-methyl-3-methyl-ol-heptan-6-one-3-ol*, $C_9H_{16}O(OH)_2$.

Tanacetogen dioxide, $C_9H_{16}O_2$, results on distilling the ketoglycol under reduced pressure, water being eliminated. It boils at 72° to 75° (19 mm.), has the specific gravity 0.9775 at 20°, the refractive index, $n_D = 1.4450$, and the molecular refraction, $M = 42.50$; it has an odor resembling that of menthol (Tiemann and Semmler).

Oxidation of Thujone with Alkaline Hypobromite.

Varying results are obtained according to the different conditions under which the oxidation may take place. Wallach first observed, and was later confirmed by Semmler, that an acid, $C_{10}H_{16}O_4$, isomeric with camphoric acid, is obtained when the following method is employed.

Thirty grams of thujone are allowed to stand for two weeks with a solution of seventy grams of bromine in 1250 cc. of a four per cent. solution of sodium hydroxide. Any unchanged oil is then removed by shaking with ether, the aqueous solution is concentrated and acidified with dilute sulphuric acid; the acid, $C_{10}H_{16}O_4$, is thus precipitated in brilliant, crystalline leaflets. It is recrystallized from water or dilute alcohol, and is obtained in orthorhombic crystals, melting at 146° to 147°; it is saturated, and is apparently a dibasic acid.

According to Semmler, if sixty parts of thujone (tanacetone) are treated with a solution of 186 parts of bromine in 2,500 parts of a four per cent. solution of sodium hydroxide, bromoform is

[1] Tiemann and Semmler, Ber., *28*, 2136.
[2] Wallach, Ber., *30*, 423.
[3] Tiemann and Semmler, Ber., *30*, 429.

liberated and *tanacetogenic* acid, $C_9H_{13}COOH$, is formed. This acid is an oil, which boils at 113.5° under a pressure of 15 mm., and solidifies when placed in a freezing mixture; it behaves as a saturated compound.

The investigations respecting thujone are by no means complete. While Wallach is inclined to regard it as an unsaturated ketone related to dihydrocarvone, Semmler[1] considers it as having a diagonal linkage, and proposes the following formula:

CH_3
CH
HC CO
H_2C CH
CH
C_3H_7

Thujone.

Wallach[2] gives numerous reasons for not accepting this constitutional formula.

Semmler[3] has more recently proposed the following formula for thujone:

CH_3
CH
HC CO
H_2C CH_2
C
$C_3H_7\beta$

8. **THUJYL ALCOHOL (TANACETYL ALCOHOL), $C_{10}H_{17}OH$.**

Thujone is quantitatively changed into thujyl alcohol, when twenty-four parts of thujone are dissolved in 100 parts of alcohol and reduced by the gradual addition of eighteen parts of sodium; sufficient alcohol is subsequently added to dissolve all of the sodium. Thujyl alcohol boils at 92.5° under 13 mm. pressure, has a sp. gr. 0.9249 and index of refraction, $n_D = 1.4635$, at 20°. It behaves as a saturated compound (Semmler[4]).

[1] Semmler, Ber, *27*, 898

[2] Wallach, Ann. Chem, *286*, 116.

[3] Semmler, Ber., *33*, 275 and 2454

[4] Semmler, Ber, *25*, 3344; compare Wallach, Ann. Chem, *272*, 109.

An impure alcohol, obtained from thujone by Wallach, boiled at 210° to 212°, and had the sp. gr. of 0.9265 at 20°.

Thujyl chloride (tanacetyl chloride), $C_{10}H_{17}Cl$, results by treating thujyl alcohol with phosphorus pentachloride, petroleum ether being used as a diluent. It is an oil, boiling at 72° under 10 mm. pressure. It is very stable, and can not be converted into a terpene, $C_{10}H_{16}$, by boiling with aniline and alcohol. It will be recalled, however, that such a terpene, *thujene*, may be prepared indirectly from thujone by the dry distillation of thujylamine hydrochloride.

9. ISOTHUJONE, $C_{10}H_{16}O$.

Isothujone is obtained by boiling twenty-five grams of thujone with seventy-five cc. of a mixture of one volume of concentrated sulphuric acid and two volumes of water for eight to ten hours, in a reflux apparatus, the product being then distilled in a current of steam (Wallach[1]).

Isothujone differs from thujone in its higher specific gravity and higher boiling point. It boils at 231° to 232°, has the sp. gr. 0.927 and the refractive index, $n_D = 1.48217$ at 20°; it immediately reduces a cold solution of potassium permanganate, thus indicating that it is an unsaturated compound.

Isothujolacetic acid,[2] $C_{10}H_{16}(OH) \cdot CH_2 \cdot COOH$, melts at 168° to 170°.

Isothujonoxime, $C_{10}H_{16}NOH$, may be obtained by treating thujonoxime (m. p. 54° to 55°) with concentrated sulphuric acid according to the method given on page 228; it is, however, more conveniently prepared from isothujone.

Twenty grams of hydroxylamine hydrochloride are covered with fifty cc. of methyl alcohol, and the well cooled mixture is treated with a solution of twenty grams of potassium hydroxide in fifteen grams of water; the filtered solution is then boiled with ten grams of isothujone for ten minutes. The oxime is precipitated with water, and on recrystallization forms long needles, melting at 119°; it is sparingly soluble in petroleum ether (Wallach[1]).

Isothujone yields two isomeric semicarbazones, which melt at 208° to 209°, and at 184° to 185°, respectively; if they are warmed with dilute sulphuric acid, isothujone is regenerated (Wallach[3]).

[1] Wallach, Ann. Chem., *286*, 101.
[2] Wallach, Ann. Chem., *314*, 147.
[3] Wallach, Ber., *28*, 1955.

Dihydroisothujol or thujamenthol, $C_{10}H_{19}OH$, is formed by reducing isothujone with sodium and alcohol. It boils at 211° to 212°, has a sp. gr. of 0.9015 and index of refraction, $n_D = 1.46306$, at 20°; it is not identical with menthol or tetrahydrocarveol (carvomenthol) (Wallach[1])

Thujamenthone, $C_{10}H_{18}O$, is obtained when dihydroisothujol is oxidized in glacial acetic acid solution with chromic anhydride; it is isomeric, but not identical, with carvomenthone.

Isothujaketonic acid, $C_{10}H_{16}O_3$, is produced by the oxidation of isothujone with potassium permanganate; it is a saturated acid, and boils at 271° to 273° at ordinary pressure, and at 142° to 143° under a pressure of 12 mm Its *semicarbazone* melts at 193°, and its *oxime* at 153°.

Sodium hypobromite converts isothujaketonic acid into isopropyl succinic acid and bromoform (Wallach[2]).

When isothujaketonic acid is distilled under atmospheric pressure, it is converted into the *keto-lactone*, $C_{10}H_{16}O_3$, which melts at 43°; its *oxime* melts at 155°. The same keto-lactone is also formed on oxidizing thujamenthone with chromic acid. On further oxidation, this keto-lactone yields β-isopropyl laevulinic acid (Semmler[3]).

10. CARVOTANACETONE, $C_{10}H_{16}O$.

Pure thujone, when heated alone in a sealed tube at 280° for twenty-four hours, is converted into an isomeric compound, carvotanacetone, which has an intensive odor resembling that of caraway, and a higher boiling point than that of thujone (Semmler[4]). Wallach's[5] experiments show that it is highly probable that carvotanacetone is also contained in the high boiling fractions of thuja oil. It may be surmised, therefore, that even during the fractional distillation of thuja oil under ordinary pressure a portion of the thujone is transformed into carvotanacetone; a definite conclusion, however, has not yet been reached.

In order to prepare pure carvotanacetone, heat thujone in a sealed tube, as above suggested, and submit the product to a fractional distillation, collecting the largest fraction at 220° to 225°. Convert this fraction into the oxime, and regenerate pure carvotanacetone by heating the oxime with dilute sulphuric acid (Semmler[6]).

[1] Wallach, Ann. Chem, *286*, 101
[2] Wallach, Ber., *30*, 423
[3] Semmler, Ber, *33*, 275
[4] Semmler, Ber., *27*, 895
[5] Wallach, Ann Chem, *275*, 183; *279*, 385.
[6] Semmler, Ber, *27*, 895, *33*, 2454

PROPERTIES.—Carvotanacetone is a liquid boiling at 228°, has a specific gravity of 0.9373 and refractive power, $n_D = 1.4835$, at 17° (Semmler[2]). Wallach[1] found similar constants. The specific gravity, refractive index and boiling point are, therefore, considerably higher than those of thujone. Its odor is very like that of carvone.

It is an unsaturated ketone, and combines with four atoms of hydrogen forming an alcohol, $C_{10}H_{19}OH$, when it is reduced in an alcoholic solution with sodium. Semmler regards this alcohol as identical with oxy-2-hexahydro-p-cymene (tetrahydrocarveol), which was prepared by Baeyer in the reduction of dihydrocarveol, and by Wallach by the reduction of carvenone. The results of Wallach's[1] researches fully establish Semmler's view.

Carvotanacetone unites with hydrogen sulphide in ammoniacal solution;[2] the product melts at about 95°.

Carvotanacetoxime, $C_{10}H_{16}NOH$, is obtained from crude carvotanacetone, as already indicated; it crystallizes from methyl alcohol, and melts at 92° to 93°. It is optically inactive (Wallach[1]).

Wallach obtained an oxime having the same melting point (93° to 94°) from the fraction of thuja oil, which boils at 220° to 230°.

Carvotanacetone semicarbazone forms orthorhombic tablets or acute prisms, and melts at 177° (Baeyer[3]).

According to Harries, the *oxaminoxime* of carvotanacetone sinters at 155° and melts at 162°; it was not obtained quite pure, hence Harries[4] regards it as probable that carvotanacetone is a mixture of the racemic form of dihydrocarvone with other compounds.

When carvotanacetone is oxidized with a dilute solution of potassium permanganate, it yields pyruvic and isopropylsuccinic acids. From this fact Semmler[2] concludes that carvotanacetone is an *ortho*-terpene ketone, and that the *pseudo*-ketone corresponding to it is found in *terpenone*,[5] $C_{10}H_{16}O$ (obtained from tetrahydrocarvone).

11. PULEGONE, $C_{10}H_{16}O$.

The ethereal oils of *Mentha pulegium* and *Hedeoma pulegioides* Persoon, which are sold under the name of pennyroyal oil, contain a

[1] Wallach, Ber., *28*, 1955.

[2] Semmler, Ber., *27*, 895; *33*, 2454.

[3] Baeyer, Ber., *27*, 1923; see Harries, Ber., *34*, 1924.

[4] Harries, Ber., *34*, 1924.

[5] Baeyer and Oehler, Ber., *29*, 35.

ketone, $C_{10}H_{16}O$, as their chief constituent; this ketone was subjected to a detailed investigation by Beckmann and Pleissner.[1] The most valuable result of this research is the establishment of the fact that pulegone may be converted into *menthone* by the addition of hydrogen; all of the other ketones, which have been mentioned up to this point, may be derived from *carvomenthone.*

Beckmann and Pleissner isolated pulegone from Spanish oil of pennyroyal by the fractional distillation of this oil under diminished pressure. They found that on fractionating the oil under atmospheric pressure some decomposition always takes place with formation of a dark yellow oil; the specific rotatory power of the original oil is also diminished. Nearly all of the oil of pennyroyal distills at 130° to 131° under a pressure of 60 mm.; this fraction consists of pure pulegone.

Pulegone[1] is dextrorotatory, $[\alpha]_D = +22.89°$; its specific gravity is 0.9323 and refractive index, $n_D = 1.47018$, at 20°. It quickly turns yellow, even when kept in closed vessels; it is a rather thick liquid, does not solidify when cooled to −20°, and has an odor recalling that of peppermint.

Wallach[2] gives the following properties of pulegone regenerated from its acid sodium sulphite compound.

Boiling point, 221° to 222°; specific gravity, 0.936; refractive index, $n_D = 1.4868$.

Pulegone does not combine with hydrogen sulphide; it imparts an intense violet color to a fuchsine-sulphurous acid solution, and reduces an ammoniacal silver nitrate solution after continued boiling

Although Beckmann and Pleissner did not obtain a compound of pulegone with acid sodium sulphite, Baeyer and Henrich[3] prepared such a derivative by allowing 100 cc. of pulegone to stand for a long time with 210 cc. of acid sodium sulphite solution and fifty cc. to sixty cc. of alcohol. The properties of pulegone regenerated from its bisulphite compound by means of potash agree completely with those of the product obtained by the vacuum distillation of oil of pennyroyal.

Pulegone hydrochloride, $C_{10}H_{16}O \cdot HCl$, is produced by the treatment of pure pulegone with a solution of hydrochloric acid in glacial acetic acid. It is crystallized from ligroine, forming large

[1] Beckmann and Pleissner, Ann Chem, *262*, 1; compare Kane, Ann Chem, *32*, 286 (1839), Butlerow, Jahresb Chem, *1854*, 595; Kremer's Analysis of the volatile oil of *Hedeoma pulegoides*, Cincinnati, *1887*.

[2] Wallach, Ber, *28*, 1955

[3] Baeyer and Henrich, Ber, *28*, 652

crystals, which are often one centimeter in length and melt at 24° to 25°. Pulegone is regenerated when the hydrochloride is warmed with methyl alcoholic potash (Baeyer and Henrich [1]).

Pulegone hydrobromide, $C_{10}H_{16}O \cdot HBr$, is prepared when dry hydrobromic acid is passed into a well cooled solution of pulegone in petroleum ether. On evaporation of the solvent, it is deposited in small, brilliant, colorless crystals, which are filtered and washed with fifty per cent. alcohol. For further purification, its ethereal solution is shaken with cold, dilute sodium hydroxide, the ether is evaporated, and the residue crystallized from dilute alcohol. It separates in hard, colorless crystals, melting at 40.5°. It is optically levorotatory, $[\alpha]_D = -33.88°$; it gradually decomposes on keeping, forming a dark colored, viscous oil. When dissolved in ether, it is converted into pulegone by freshly precipitated silver oxide. Pulegone and another compound (inactive pulegone?) are formed by boiling an ethereal solution of the hydrobromide with lead hydroxide (Beckmann and Pleissner). When pulegone hydrobromide is boiled with alcohol and lead hydroxide, the chief product is methyl cyclohexanone, $C_7H_{12}O$ (Harries [2]).

Hydrobromopulegonoxime, $C_{10}H_{17}Br \cdot NOH$, melts at 38°, and readily loses hydrogen bromide; in the presence of water hydrobromic acid is eliminated, and the compound is converted into the "hydrated pulegonoxime" described below.

When pulegone hydrobromide is reduced with zinc dust in an alcoholic solution, it yields a ketone, $C_{10}H_{18}O$, which possesses all the properties of levorotatory menthone, except that it yields an oxime, melting at 84° to 85°, while levorotatory menthonoxime melts at 59°. The close relation of this ketone to levo-menthone is shown by the fact that when it is reduced with sodium in an ethereal solution, according to Beckmann's [3] method, it yields levo-menthol, whose benzoyl derivative may be isolated and characterized by its melting point and specific rotatory power.

The close relation of pulegone to menthone was proved by the observations of Beckmann and Pleissner in a much simpler manner than by the above-suggested transformation. When pulegone is reduced in an ethereal solution with sodium, levo-menthol is formed. If the treatment of pulegone with sodium be repeated three times, solid menthol is obtained, which can be identified

[1] Baeyer and Henrich, Ber., *28*, 652.
[2] Harries and Roeder, Ber., *32*, 3357.
[3] Beckmann, German patent, No. 42458; Ber., *22*, 912.

not only by its melting point and the preparation of its benzoyl ester, but also by its transformation into levorotatory menthone and the oxime of the latter.

Pulegonoxime, $C_{10}H_{16}NOH$.—Although Beckmann and Pleissner obtained only the "hydrated oxime" from pulegone, Barbier[1] has described a normal pulegonoxime, $C_{10}H_{16}NOH$, as an oil, which boils at 170° under 48 mm. pressure. Wallach[2] found that normal pulegonoxime can be obtained as a solid, if it be prepared according to the method described in the preparation of carvoxime, and the product be distilled in a current of steam. The volatile, solid oxime is pressed on a plate, and crystallized from ether or petroleum ether; it crystallizes in transparent prisms, and melts at 118° to 119°.

The pulegone regenerated by treatment of this oxime with dilute sulphuric acid seems to be impure, since it boils at 220° to 225°; nevertheless, it yields the oxime, melting at 118° to 119°, by the action of hydroxylamine.

Pulegylamine, $C_{10}H_{17}NH_2$, results by reducing an alcoholic solution of pulegonoxime with sodium (Wallach[3]).

BECKMANN AND PLEISSNER'S "HYDRATED PULEGONOXIME," $C_{10}H_{19}NO_2$, AND ITS DERIVATIVES.

An oxime of pulegone, differing from the normal pulegonoxime by containing one molecule of water, was obtained by Beckmann and Pleissner as follows. Twenty parts of pulegone, ten parts of ninety per cent. alcohol, thirty parts of ether and twelve parts of hydroxylamine hydrochloride are heated in a reflux apparatus for two hours. The alcoholic ethereal solution is then filtered, most of the alcohol and ether distilled off, and the residue allowed to evaporate; the crystals resulting are recrystallized from ether.

"Hydrated pulegonoxime" crystallizes in long needles, and melts at 157°; when pure, it is sparingly soluble in ether, cold alcohol, benzene and petroleum ether; it is readily soluble in dilute acids, but it is not decomposed by cold acids. It is levorotatory, having a specific rotatory power, $[\alpha]_D = -83.44°$. Molecular weight determinations indicate that it has the simple molecular formula, $C_{10}H_{19}NO_2$.

[1] Barbier, Compt. rend., *114*, 126; Ber., *25*, 110, Ref.
[2] Wallach, Ann. Chem., *277*, 160.
[3] Wallach, Ann. Chem., *289*, 337.

The *hydrochloride*, $C_{10}H_{19}NO_2 \cdot HCl$, is produced by passing hydrogen chloride into a solution of "Pleissner's oxime" in glacial acetic acid, and is precipitated from this solution by the addition of ether. It separates from alcoholic ether in beautiful, orthorhombic[1] crystals, melts at 117° to 118°, and is levorotatory, $[\alpha]_D = -32.43°$. Soda precipitates the "hydrated oxime" (m. p. 157°) from aqueous solutions of this hydrochloric acid salt.

The following derivatives indicate that the molecule of water in "hydrated pulegonoxime" is chemically combined.

Benzoyl ester, $C_{10}H_{18}O \cdot NO \cdot COC_6H_5$, is prepared by treating the ethereal solution of the "oxime" with benzoyl chloride; it crystallizes from dilute alcohol or a mixture of benzene and ligroine, and melts at 137° to 138° with decomposition.

Acetyl ester, $C_{10}H_{18}O \cdot NO \cdot COCH_3$, melts at 149°.

According to more recent researches of Harries,[2] Beckmann and Pleissner's "hydrated pulegonoxime" should be called *pulegone hydroxylamine;* its constitution is expressed by the following formula:

CH_3
CH
H_2C CH_2
H_2C CO
CH
$NH \cdot OH$
C
H_3C CH_3

Oxidation converts it into *nitrosomenthone* (m. p. 35°) and *nitromenthone* (m. p. 80°).

Pulegone hydroxylamine forms an *oxalate*,[3] $(C_{10}H_{19}O_2N)C_2O_4H_2$, which crystallizes in needles, and melts with decomposition at 151° to 152°.

With nitrous acid, the hydroxylamine derivative yields a white, crystalline mass, which is probably a *nitroso-amine*,[3] but is exceedingly unstable.

Pulegone hydroxylamine also reacts with hydriodic acid, giving rise to *8-amidomenthone.*

Pulegonamine, $C_{10}H_{19}ON$, is formed when "Pleissner's oxime" is warmed with hydriodic acid and red phosphorus.

[1] Fock, Ann. Chem., *262*, 9.
[2] Harries and Roeder, Ber., *31*, 1809.
[3] Harries and Roeder, Ber., *32*, 3357.

Pulegone semicarbazone,[1] $C_{10}H_{16} = N - NH \cdot CO \cdot NH_2$, dissolves in cold alcohol, and melts at 172°; it yields pulegone on treatment with boiling acids, even acetic acid being sufficient to decompose it.

Bisnitrosopulegone, $(C_{10}H_{15}O)_2N_2O_2$.—According to Baeyer and Henrich,[1] this compound is so characteristic that it may be employed for the identification of pulegone. In order to prepare it, two cc. of pulegone are mixed with two cc. of ligroine and one cc. of amyl nitrite; the mixture is cooled with ice, and treated with a drop of concentrated hydrochloric acid, the acid being introduced by a glass rod. In twenty to twenty-five seconds the liquid becomes cloudy, and solidifies to a crystalline mass; it is allowed to stand for twenty minutes, is filtered, washed with ligroine, pressed on a porous plate, and again washed with ether. It decomposes on recrystallization. Baeyer[2] regards this compound as a bisnitroso-derivative, but it differs from members of this class in that it yields an *oxime* in addition to a *bisnitrosylic acid;* this feature is explained by the fact that the bisnitroso-group $- NO_2N -$ is joined to the methylene carbon atom, in juxtaposition to the ketone group in the pulegone molecule.

Bisnitrosopulegone dissolves in ammonia, yielding an *oxime.*

Isonitrosopulegone,[2] $C_{10}H_{15}NO_2$, is prepared by the action of caustic soda on bisnitrosopulegone; it crystallizes in yellow needles, and decomposes at 122° to 127°.

Pulegondioxime hydrate,[2] $C_{10}H_{18}N_2O_3$, is formed by the action of hydroxylamine on isonitrosopulegone.

Pulegonbisnitrosylic acid,[2] $C_{10}H_{16}N_2O_3$, results by the action of hydrogen chloride upon an ethereal solution of bisnitrosopulegone. It separates from petroleum ether in slender, colorless needles, and melts at 115° to 116°.

2-Chloropulegone,[2] $C_{10}H_{15}ClO$, which crystallizes in long needles and melts at 124° to 125°, and *diisonitroso-methyl-cyclohexanone,* $C_7H_{10}N_2O_3$, are obtained in the same reaction with bisnitrosopulegone. The diisonitroso-derivative decomposes at 190°; its formation depends on the elimination of the C_3H_6-group from the pulegone molecule. Its *diacetate* melts at 125° to 130°. The diisonitroso-derivative yields the *anhydride of triisonitroso-methyl-cyclohexanone,* $C_7H_9N_3O_2$, by the action of hydroxylamine; it melts at 128° to 129°, and yields an *acetate,* melting at 139° to 140°.

Benzylidene pulegone,[3] $C_{10}H_{14}O = CH \cdot C_6H_5$, is formed by the condensation of pulegone and benzaldehyde with sodium ethylate;

[1] Baeyer and Henrich, Ber., *28*, 652.
[2] Baeyer and Prentice, Ber., *29*, 1078.
[3] Wallach, Ber., *29*, 1595; Ann. Chem., *305*, 267.

it boils at 202° to 203° under a pressure of 12 mm. On reduction with sodium and alcohol, it yields *benzylpulegol*, $C_{10}H_{16}(OH)$-$CH_2 \cdot C_6H_5$.

Pulegenacetone,[1] $C_{13}H_{20}O$, is formed by warming a mixture of pulegone, ethyl acetoacetate, and glacial acetic acid with fused zinc chloride, for ten hours, on the water-bath. It boils at 148° to 153° under a pressure of 8 mm., solidifies in the receiver, and crystallizes from light petroleum in prisms, which melt at 72° to 73°. Its *oxime* is crystalline, melts at 134° to 135°, and yields a *benzoyl* derivative, which crystallizes in yellow needles, and melts at 178° to 179°.

3-Chloro-$\Delta^{2(4:8)}$-terpadiëne,[2] $C_{10}H_{15}Cl$, is produced by the action of phosphorus pentachloride on pulegone; it is a colorless oil, boils at 101° (25 mm.), has a sp. gr. 0.983 at 19°, and $n_D = 1.49928$. With an excess of bromine, it yields a *tetrabromide*, $C_{10}H_{11}ClBr_4$. Formic acid converts the chloroterpadiëne into methyl cyclohexanone.

Bispulegone,[3] $C_{20}H_{34}O_2$, results by the action of aluminium amalgam on pulegone; it crystallizes in needles, melts at 118° to 119°, and is readily soluble in benzene, ether and acetic acid. When pulegone is reduced with sodium amalgam in an acetic acid solution, menthone and menthol are also formed.

Oxidation of pulegone.—Pulegone yields acetone and optically dextrorotatory *β-methyl adipic acid*, $C_7H_{12}O_4$ (m. p. 84.5°), on oxidation with potassium permanganate.

β-Methyl adipic acid is converted into a *lactonic acid*, $C_7H_{10}O_4$, by oxidation; when the calcium salt of β-methyl adipic acid is distilled with soda-lime, it yields a ketone, $C_6H_{10}O$, *β-methyl ketopentamethylene*. According to Semmler,[4] these reactions indicate that β-methyl adipic acid has the following constitution:

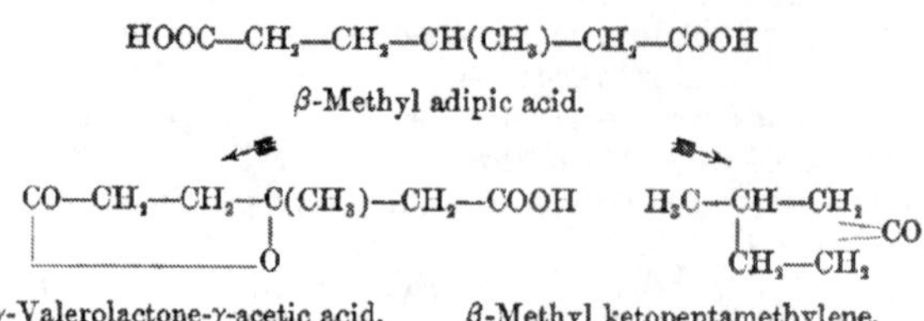

[1] Barbier, Compt. rend., *127*, 870.
[2] Klages, Ber., *32*, 2564.
[3] Harries and Roeder, Ber., *32*, 3357.
[4] Semmler, Ber., *25*, 3515; *26*, 774.

Semmler derives the following constitutional formula of pulegone from these transformations:

```
      CH3
      |
      CH
    /    \
H2C      CH2
 |        |
H2C      CO
    \    /
      C
      ||
      C
    /   \
H3C      CH3
```

Pulegone.

This formula has further been proved by Wallach.[1] He showed that when pulegone is boiled with anhydrous formic acid, or is heated with water in an autoclave at 250°, a hydrolytic decomposition takes place with the production of acetone and methyl cyclohexanone (boiling point 169°).

```
      CH3                           CH3
      |                             |
      CH                            CH
    /    \                        /    \
H2C      CH2  + H—O—H =      H2C      CH2  + CH3 CO CH3
 |        |                   |        |
H2C      CO                  H2C      CO
    \    /                        \    /
      C                             CH2
      ||
      C
    /   \
H3C      CH3
```

Pulegone Methyl cyclohexanone. Acetone

The formyl derivative of cycloheptylenamine (hexahydro-meta-toluidine), $C_7H_{13}NH_2$, is formed in an analogous manner, when pulegone is boiled with ammonium formate.

Methyl cyclohexanone,[1] $C_7H_{12}O$, is obtained from pulegone as above mentioned. It is also formed during the action of concentrated sulphuric acid on pulegone,[2] by boiling pulegone hydrobromide with alcohol and lead hydroxide, by boiling pulegone with alcohol and basic lead acetate, or when it is distilled with quinoline.[3]

It boils at 169°, has the specific gravity 0.915 at 21°, and the refractive index, $n_D = 1.4456$, at the same temperature, $M =$

[1] Wallach, Ann Chem., *289*, 337.

[2] Harries and Roeder, Ber., *32*, 3357.

[3] Zelinsky, Ber, *30*, 1532.

32.59. Its *oxime* melts at 43° to 44°, and the *semicarbazone* at 180°.

When methyl hexanone is reduced with sodium and alcohol, *methyl cyclohexanol* (*meta-oxyhexahydrotoluene*), $C_7H_{13}OH$, is formed; it boils at 175° to 176°.

For the numerous derivatives of methyl cyclohexanone, reference must be made to the original publications.[1]

PULEGENIC ACID, $C_{10}H_{16}O_2$.

Pulegone forms a liquid *dibromide*, which yields pulegenic acid when it is heated with a solution of sodium methylate:

$$C_{10}H_{16}OBr_2 + H_2O = 2HBr + C_{10}H_{16}O_2.$$

This acid boils without decomposition at 150° to 155° under a pressure of 13 mm.; when distilled at atmospheric pressure, it decomposes into carbonic anhydride and a *hydrocarbon*, C_9H_{16}. This hydrocarbon boils at 138° to 140°, has the sp. gr. 0.790 and refractive index, $n_D = 1.44$, at 20°; it yields a *nitrosochloride*, melting at 74° to 75° (Wallach[2]).

The *amide* of pulegenic acid crystallizes in woolly needles, and melts at 121° to 122°. When it is treated with phosphoric anhydride, it is converted into the *nitrile*, which boils at 218° to 220°, has the sp. gr. 0.8935 and index of refraction, $n_D = 1.47047$, at 22°.

The preparation of pulegenic acid from pulegone is accomplished by a break in the ring structure; its formation resembles, in certain respects, that of campholenic acid from camphor and of fencholenic acid from fenchone.

Pulegenic acid is an unsaturated compound; when its solution in methyl alcohol is saturated with hydrochloric acid gas, the *hydrochloride of pulegenic methyl ester* is formed. It boils at 113° to 116° (13 mm.), and solidifies at a low temperature.

Methyl pulegenate,[3] $C_{10}H_{15}O_2CH_3$, boils at 89° to 90° (10 mm.), and is formed by the action of a methyl alcoholic solution of sodium methylate upon the hydrochloride. On acidifying the alkaline solution which remains after the removal of the methyl

[1] Wallach, Ann. Chem., *289*, 337; *309*, 1; *312*, 171; *314*, 147; Ber., *29*, 1595; *29*, 2955; Klages, Ber., *32*, 2564; Harries and Roeder, Ber., *32*, 3357; methyl hexanone prepared from β-methyl pimelinic acid, see Einhorn and Ehret, Ann. Chem., *295*, 181; Kondakoff and Schindehneiser, Journ. pr. Chem., 1900 [II], *61*, 477; J. von Braun, Ann. Chem., *314*, 168; Harries, Ber., *34*, 300; Bouveault and Tetry, Bull. Soc. Chim., 1901 [III], *25*, 441.

[2] Wallach, Ann. Chem., *289*, 337.

[3] Wallach, Ann. Chem., *300*, 259.

alcohol and ethereal salt by distillation with steam, the *lactone*, $C_{10}H_{16}O_2$, is precipitated; it boils at 125° to 127° (15 mm.). The *acid*, $C_{10}H_{16}O_2$, produced together with the lactone, boils at 145° to 147° (15 mm.) and at 256° to 260° at 760 mm.; sp. gr. = 0.9955, n_D = 1.47547, at 21°. It closely resembles, but is not identical with, pulegenic acid; its *amide* crystallizes from methyl alcohol in needles, and melts at 152°.

A *brominated lactone* is formed by treating pulegenic acid with potassium hypobromite; by the action of alcoholic sodium methylate, it yields *pulegenolide*, $C_{10}H_{14}O_2$, which melts at 44° to 45°, and boils at 265° to 268°. An *oxy-acid*, $C_{10}H_{16}O_3$, is produced on hydrolyzing the lactone with aqueous alkali; it melts at 95°, and forms a *silver salt*.

An *oxy-lactone*, $C_{10}H_{16}O_3$, is formed by oxidizing pulegenic acid with a cold solution of potassium permanganate; it melts at 129° to 130°. This compound is also obtained by the action of moist silver oxide on the brominated lactone above mentioned. The oxy-lactone is converted into pulegenolide by the action of phosphorus pentachloride, and subsequent treatment of the product with sodium methylate.

The *ketone*, $C_9H_{16}O$, is produced when the oxy-lactone, $C_{10}H_{16}O_3$, is treated with moderately dilute sulphuric acid, carbon dioxide being eliminated; it is a saturated compound, boils at 183°, has the specific gravity 0.8925 and refractive power, n_D = 1.44506, at 21°. Its *oxime* melts at 94°.

When pulegone dibromide is heated, it loses hydrogen bromide and yields methyl cyclohexanone and *m-cresol*.

Synthetical (Ortho-iso- (?)) Pulegone, $C_{10}H_{16}O$.

When methyl cyclohexanone, $C_7H_{12}O$, and acetone are condensed by means of alcoholic sodium methylate, a ketone,[1] $C_{10}H_{16}O$, is obtained, which closely resembles natural pulegone, and is isomeric, but not identical, with it. If natural pulegone be termed *para*-pulegone, then the structure of this synthetical ketone will be either that of *pseudo*- or *ortho*-iso-pulegone. Wallach is inclined to regard it as an ortho-iso-pulegone, but the investigations are not yet complete.

Synthetical pulegone is purified by conversion into the semicarbazone; when regenerated from this compound, it boils at 94° to 95° under 14 mm. pressure, or at 214° to 215° at atmospheric pressure. It has the specific gravity 0.918 and the refractive

[1] Wallach, Ber., *29*, 1595 and 2955; Ann. Chem., *300*, 268.

index, $n_D = 1.46732$, at 20°. Its odor is scarcely distinguishable from that of natural pulegone, but its chemical properties are widely different. It is strongly dextrorotatory.

It yields a *semicarbazone*, which exists in two modifications, the one melting at 70° to 85°, and the second at 144°; both modifications yield the same synthetical pulegone on treatment with dilute acids.

Synthetical pulegone is *not* converted into methyl hexanone and acetone by the action of formic or dilute sulphuric acid.

The **benzylidene** derivative of synthetical pulegone, $C_{10}H_{14}O = CH{\cdot}C_6H_5$, melts at 83° to 84°.

A **compound**, $C_{13}H_{20}O$, is also formed during the condensation of methyl hexanone and benzaldehyde; it boils at 179° to 183° under reduced pressure.

Synthetical pulegol, $C_{10}H_{17}OH$, is produced by reducing synthetical pulegone in ethereal or alcoholic solution with sodium. It is a viscous liquid, has an odor of terpineol, and boils at 103° to 104° (15 mm.), and at 215° under atmospheric pressure. Its specific gravity at 20° is 0.912 and refractive power, $n_D = 1.4792$. When treated with phosphoric anhydride, it yields a *terpene*, $C_{10}H_{16}$, boiling at 173° to 175°.

Wallach[1] suggests the following formula for synthetical pulegone:

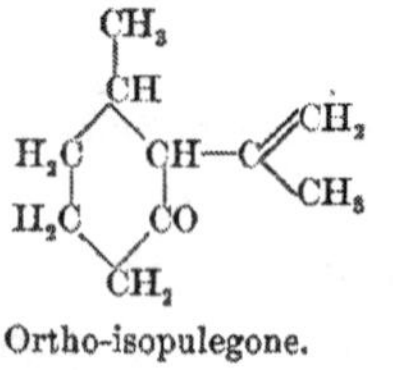

CH_3
CH
H_2C CH—C($=CH_2$)(CH_3)
H_2C CO
CH_2

Ortho-isopulegone.

12. ISOPULEGOL, $C_{10}H_{17}OH$, and ISOPULEGONE, $C_{10}H_{16}O$.

An alcohol, $C_{10}H_{17}OH$, corresponding with natural pulegone, has not yet been obtained free from menthol by the reduction of pulegone. An alcohol, $C_{10}H_{17}OH$, *isopulegol*, is, however, produced from citronellal, $C_{10}H_{16}O$, an aliphatic terpene aldehyde.

It results in the form of its *acetate* by heating citronellal with an equal weight of acetic anhydride in an autoclave at 180° to

[1] Wallach, Ann. Chem., *300*, 275.

200°, for ten or twelve hours; or by heating citronellal with anhydrous sodium acetate for fifteen to twenty hours at 150° to 160° (Tiemann and Schmidt[1]).

According to Barbier,[2] when citronellal is agitated with ten parts of five per cent. sulphuric acid for twelve hours, isopulegol is formed, together with *menthoglycol*, $C_{10}H_{18}(OH)_2$; the latter compound is also obtained from isopulegol.

According to Tiemann,[3] commercial citronellal contains some isopulegol, together with other compounds; its presence in the mixture may be recognized by its conversion into isopulegone upon oxidation.

PROPERTIES.—Isopulegol has an odor like menthol, boils at 91° under a pressure of 13 mm., and has the rotatory power, $[\alpha]_D = -2.65°$. Its specific gravity is 0.9154 at 17.5°, the refractive index, $n_D = 1.47292$, and the molecular refraction, $M =$ 47.20.

Menthoglycol[2] **(menthandiol-3, 8)**, $C_{10}H_{18}(OH)_2$, is a compound closely related to isopulegol. It is formed, together with some isopulegol and a *compound*, $C_{20}H_{34}O$ (b. p. 185° at 10 mm.), by agitating citronellal with ten parts of five per cent. sulphuric acid for twelve hours. It crystallizes from petroleum ether in white plates, melting at 81° to 81.5°. Acetic anhydride at 100° converts it into a *monoacetate* (b. p. 137° to 138° at 10 mm.), while at 150°, in the presence of fused sodium acetate, the acetyl derivative of isopulegol results. Hydrogen chloride in presence of glacial acetic acid changes the glycol into a mixture of two isomerides, $C_{10}H_{18}Cl \cdot O \cdot COCH_3$, boiling at 124° to 125° (10 mm.). This glycol may also be obtained directly from isopulegol.

Isopulegone, $C_{10}H_{16}O$, is formed by the oxidation of isopulegol with an acetic acid solution of chromic anhydride;[4] the product seems to consist of a mixture of two stereo-isomeric modifications, which are designated as α- and β-isopulegone.[5]

According to Tiemann, the mixture of α- and β-isopulegone, obtained by the oxidation of isopulegol, boils at 90° (12 mm.), has the specific gravity 0.9213, the index of refraction, $n_D = 1.4690$, the molecular refraction, M = 45.98, and the specific rotatory power, $[\alpha]_D = +10° 15'$, in a one decimeter tube. On treating with boiling dilute sulphuric acid and alcohol or with

[1] Tiemann and Schmidt, Ber., *29*, 903.
[2] Barbier and Leser, Compt. rend., *124*, 1308.
[3] Tiemann, Ber., *32*, 825.
[4] Tiemann and Schmidt, Ber., *29*, 903; *30*, 22; Tiemann, Ber., *32*, 825.
[5] Harries and Roeder, Ber., *32*, 3357.

formic acid, methyl cyclohexanone is obtained which is identical in every respect with the compound produced from natural pulegone. Isopulegone differs widely from natural and synthetical pulegones in its chemical behavior. It does not combine with acid sodium sulphite. When reduced with sodium and alcohol, it yields isopulegol, no menthol being produced; menthol is *not* formed by the action of sodium and alcohol on isopulegol.

α-Isopulegone[2] is also obtained in a yield of seventy per cent. by heating natural pulegone with methyl alcohol and basic lead nitrate on the water-bath for half an hour; it is separated from unchanged pulegone by treating its ethereal solution with aluminium amalgam, distilling with steam and converting into its oxime (m. p. 120° to 121°). When regenerated from the latter compound, α-isopulegone is obtained as a colorless oil, which boils at 98° to 100° (13 mm.), has a specific gravity 0.9192 at 19.5°, and a specific rotatory power, $[\alpha]_D = -7° 8'$; when allowed to stand in contact with dilute sulphuric acid for some time it is rendered inactive. It is converted into dextrorotatory, natural pulegone when its alcoholic solution is left in contact with baryta water for twenty-four hours (Harries and Roeder).

α-Isopulegonoxime, $C_{10}H_{16}NOH$, is formed, together with the β-derivative, by the action of hydroxylamine on isopulegone. It melts at 120° to 121°, and is volatile with steam.

β-Isopulegonoxime, $C_{10}H_{16}NOH$, is prepared with the α-modification; it melts at 143° (Harries and Roeder).

According to Tiemann, isopulegone yields two oximes, one melting at 120° to 121° (α-isopulegonoxime), the other melting at 134°; the latter is non-volatile with steam and may possibly be a mixture of the α- and β-oximes.

α-Isopulegone semicarbazone, $C_{10}H_{16} = N \cdot NH \cdot CO \cdot NH_2$, crystallizes from dilute alcohol in needles, and melts and decomposes at 173° to 174° (Harries). According to Tiemann, it melts at 171° to 172°, and is readily soluble in ether.

β-Isopulegone semicarbazone, $C_{10}H_{16} = N \cdot NH \cdot CO \cdot NH_2$, melts at 183° (Harries). According to Tiemann, it melts at 180°, and is sparingly soluble in ether.

A mixture of the α- and β-semicarbazones melts at 173° to 174°. It is obtained by treating the isopulegone, resulting from the oxidation of isopulegol, with semicarbazide solution; it is separable into the α- and β-derivatives, having the above-described properties (Tiemann).

When α-isopulegonoxime (m. p. 121°) or the α-semicarbazone (m. p. 173° to 174°) is acted upon by boiling dilute sulphuric acid and alcohol, it yields methyl cyclohexanone.

According to Tiemann and Harries, isopulegone is represented by the formula

$$
\begin{array}{c}
CH_3 \\
| \\
CH \\
H_2C \quad CH_2 \\
OC \quad CH_2 \\
CH \\
| \\
C \\
H_2C \quad CH_3
\end{array}
$$

The following table may serve to illustrate some of the points of difference between natural pulegone, isopulegone and synthetical or ortho-isopulegone.

	Natural Pulegone.	Isopulegone.	Synthetical Pulegone.
Boiling point,	99° to 101° (12 mm.)	90° (12 mm.).	94° to 95° (14 mm.).
Acid sodium sulphite,	forms a crystalline derivative.	does not yield a derivative.	
Heated with formic acid,	yields methyl cyclohexanone.	yields methyl cyclohexanone.	does not yield methyl cyclohex anone.
Reduction with alcohol and sodium,	yields pulegol (?) containing menthol; b. p. 108° to 110° (14 mm.).	yields isopulegol, b. p. 91° (13 mm.)	yields synthetical pulegol, b. p. 103° to 104° (15 mm.),
Oximes,	normal oxime, $C_{10}H_{16}NOH$, m. p. 118° to 119°. pulegone hydroxylamine, $C_{10}H_{19}NO_2$, m. p. 157°.	α-derivative, $C_{10}H_{16}NOH$, m. p. 121°. β-derivative, $C_{10}H_{16}NOH$, m. p. 143°. mixture (?), m. p. 134°.	liquid, b. p. 145° (15 mm.).
Semicarbazones,	m. p. 172°.	α-derivative, m. p. 171° to 172°. β-derivative, m. p. 180°. mixture (α- and β-), m. p. 173° to 174°.	exists in two modifications; m. p. 70° to 85°, and 144°.

13. MENTHENONE, $C_{10}H_{16}O$.

A ketone, $C_{10}H_{16}O$, was obtained by Urban and Kremers[1] by boiling nitrosomenthene (m. p. 65° to 67°) with dilute hydrochloric acid (1 : 1), and in the year 1899 Wallach[2] gave it the name *menthenone*.

[1] Urban and Kremers, Amer. Chem. Journ., *16*, 401.
[2] Wallach, Ann. Chem., *305*, 272.

Menthenone boils at 205° to 208°, and has the specific gravity of 0.916 at 20°; the ketone prepared from the optically active and inactive nitrosomenthenes is optically active. It has a decided odor of peppermint (Richtmann and Kremers[1]).

According to Wallach, menthenone boils at 95° to 97° under 12 mm. pressure, has the refractive index, $n_D = 1.4733$, at 20°, the molecular refraction, M = 46.42, and the specific gravity 0.919 at 20°.

Menthenone hydrogen sulphide,[1] $C_{10}H_{16}O \cdot 2H_2S$, is readily formed by passing hydrogen sulphide into a solution of the ketone in alcohol, and subsequently adding concentrated ammonia. It forms crystals, melting at 212° to 215°, and is soluble in chloroform and hot methyl alcohol.

Nitrosomenthenone, $C_{10}H_{15}O \cdot NO$, is prepared according to Baeyer's method for the preparation of bisnitrosopulegone; it melts at 115° to 115.5°.

Menthenone phenylhydrazone, $C_{10}H_{16} = N \cdot NHC_6H_5$, crystallizes with considerable decomposition from warm alcohol, and melts at 73.5° to 74° (Richtmann and Kremers).

Menthenone is reverted into nitrosomenthene by the action of hydroxylamine (Urban and Kremers).

When menthenone is reduced with sodium and ether, according to Beckmann's method, it yields an oil (possibly a new alcohol, $C_{10}H_{17}OH$, or unchanged menthenone), and a solid compound (a pinacone (?)); the latter substance crystallizes from hot methyl alcohol, and melts at 160° to 162° (Richtmann and Kremers).

Dibenzylidene menthenone, $C_{10}H_{12}O(=CH \cdot C_6H_5)_2$, results by the condensation of menthenone and benzaldehyde; it crystallizes from hot alcohol in light yellow needles, and melts at 129° to 130°. When reduced with zinc dust and glacial acetic acid it gives rise to the corresponding *alcohol*, $C_{24}H_{26}O$, which forms colorless crystals, and melts at 72° to 75° (Wallach).

14. ISOCAMPHOR, $C_{10}H_{16}O$.

When camphoroxime, in glacial acetic acid solution, is treated with nitrous acid (sodium nitrite), it yields a compound, $C_{10}H_{16}N_2O_2$, which Angeli and Rimini[2] call *pernitrosocamphor* and which Tiemann[3] terms *camphenylnitramine*; it melts at 43°. Pernitrosocamphor is attacked by cold concentrated sulphuric acid with evolution of nitric oxide and formation of a ketone,

[1]Richtmann and Kremers, Amer. Chem. Journ., *18*, 771.

[2]Angeli and Rimini, Ber., *28*, 1077 and 1127; Gazz. Chim., *26* [II], 29, 34, 45, 228, 502 and 517; 28 [I], 11.

[3]Tiemann, Ber., *28*, 1079; *29*, 2807.

$C_{10}H_{16}O$, *isocamphor*. This ketone should possibly be classified with the ketodihydrocymenes.

Isocamphor is also formed by treating *isopernitrosofenchone*, $C_{10}H_{16}N_2O_2$, with concentrated sulphuric acid.

Isocamphor [1] is an oil having a pleasant odor, boils with slight resinification at 214° to 216° under ordinary pressure, and slowly changes in the air; it immediately reduces permanganate solution, and behaves as an unsaturated compound. It combines with bromine and hydrogen bromide forming additive products, and seems to differ from dihydrocarvone and dihydroeucarvone. It is resinified by alkalis; it does not condense with benzaldehyde or ethyl formate. The pure ketone is obtained by treating its oxime with dilute sulphuric acid.

Isocamphoroxime,[1] $C_{10}H_{16}NOH$, melts at 106°. It is dissolved unaltered by concentrated sulphuric acid, but is converted into isocamphor by boiling with dilute sulphuric acid.

Isocamphor semicarbazone, $C_{10}H_{16} = N \cdot NH \cdot CO \cdot NH_2$, melts at 215°.

Isocamphor bisnitrosochloride, $(C_{10}H_{16}O)_2(NOCl)_2$, is produced by the action of acetyl chloride on a mixture of isocamphor and amyl nitrite, cooled with ice; it forms small, white crystals, and melts with decomposition at 120° to 121°.

Tetrahydroisocamphor,[1] $C_{10}H_{19}OH$, is formed by the reduction of isocamphor with sodium and alcohol; it is a heavy, colorless oil, having a lavender-like odor. It is an alcohol and yields a *phenylurethane*, which forms colorless crystals and melts at 155°.

Dihydroisocamphor, $C_{10}H_{18}O$, is formed by oxidizing the preceding compound with chromic acid; it is a colorless oil, boiling at 203°. Its *semicarbazone* crystallizes in thin, white needles, melting at 162°; dilute sulphuric acid reconverts it into dihydroisocamphor.

Dihydroisocamphor is stable towards permanganate, and yields a crystalline *acid sodium sulphite* derivative.

On mixing dihydroisocamphor with one molecule of benzaldehyde and gradually adding an alcoholic solution of sodium ethylate (one molecule), *benzylidene dihydroisocamphor*,[2] $C_{10}H_{14}O = CH \cdot C_6H_5$, is formed; it crystallizes from alcohol in small, white needles, melting at 217°. The formation of this compound indicates that dihydroisocamphor contains the group —CO—CH_2—.

When isocamphor is oxidized with an alkaline solution of potassium permanganate, it yields *α-isopropyl glutaric acid*, $C_8H_{14}O_4$, which crystallizes in white needles and melts at 96°; it has been synthetically prepared by W. H. Perkin.[3] It forms an

[1] Compare M. Spica, Gaz. Chim. Ital., *31* [II], 286.

[2] Rimini, Gazzetta (1900), *30*, 596.

[3] W. H. Perkin, jun., Journ. Chem. Soc., *69*, 1495.

anhydride, $C_8H_{12}O_3$, which crystallizes in long needles, and melts at 60°. It is converted into *succinic acid* by oxidation with chromic acid, and also gives rise to an *anilide*, melting at 160°.

It may further be mentioned that a *ketone*,[1] $C_{10}H_{16}O$, isomeric with camphor, is formed by the dry distillation of 3-*methyl*-6-*iso-propyl*-Δ^2-*cyclohexenone carboxylic acid*, $C_{10}H_{15}O \cdot COOH$; it is an oil, having a camphor-like odor, and boils at 217° to 219°. Its *oxime* forms beautiful, monoclinic crystals.

β-Isocamphor, $C_{10}H_{15}OH$, is an unsaturated alcohol which Duden[2] obtained by the action of nitrous acid on *camphenamine*, $C_{10}H_{15}NH_2$; it sublimes in long needles having the odor and appearance of camphor, and melts at 102°. It has the specific rotatory power, $[\alpha] = + 17.65°$, in methyl alcohol. Its *phenyl-urethane* crystallizes from petroleum in long needles and melts at 112°.

15. PINOLONE, $C_{10}H_{16}O$, and PINOLOL, $C_{10}H_{17}OH$.

Wallach[3] obtained the ketone, pinolone, by treating *isopinole dibromide*, $C_{10}H_{16}OBr_2$, with zinc dust and glacial acetic acid, and also by the reduction of pinole tribromide. It has an odor recalling that of amyl acetate; it boils at 214° to 217°, has a specific gravity 0.916 and refractive index, $n_D = 1.46603$, at 20°.

Pinolonoxime, $C_{10}H_{16}NOH$, boils at 150° under a pressure of 15 mm.; on reduction it yields a *base*, the *carbamide* of which crystallizes from methyl alcohol and melts at 186°.

Pinolone semicarbazone, $C_{10}H_{16}{=}N \cdot NH \cdot CO \cdot NH_2$, melts at 158°.

Pinolol, $C_{10}H_{17}OH$, is the alcohol obtained by reducing pinolone with sodium and alcohol. It possesses a linalool-like odor, boils at 108° under 15 mm., has a specific gravity 0.913 and an index of refraction, $n_D = 1.47292$, at 20°.

16. Δ^6-MENTHENE-2-ONE, $C_{10}H_{16}O$.

According to Harries,[4] when hydrobromocarvone is reduced in methyl alcoholic solution with zinc dust, about one-quarter of the product consists of carvone and the remainder is a ketone, $C_{10}H_{16}O$, called Δ^6-menthene-2-one.

It is a yellow colored oil, boils at 227° to 228°, or at 96° to 97° under 9 mm. pressure; it has a sp. gr. 0.9411 at 10° and 0.9351 at 19°, and a specific rotatory power, $[\alpha]_D = + 49.5°$, in a 10 cm. tube.

[1] J. A. Callenbach, Ber., *30*, 639.
[2] Duden and Macintyre, Ann. Chem., *313*, 59.
[3] Wallach, Ann. Chem., *306*, 275; *281*, 154; Ber., *28*, 2710.
[4] Harries, Ber., *34*, 1924.

Its *semicarbazone* crystallizes in plates and melts at 173° to 174°; its *oxime* crystallizes in large prisms and melts at 75° to 77°. The *hydrogen sulphide derivative*, $2C_{10}H_{16}O \cdot H_2S$, crystallizes in lustrous needles and melts at 222° to 225°.

The *oxaminoxime*, $C_{10}H_{16}(NOH)(NH_2OH)$, crystallizes with one-half molecule of water in needles, and melts at 95° to 97°; it forms an *oxalate*, melting at 130° to 135°. When it is oxidized by a current of air, it gives rise to a *dioxime*, $C_{10}H_{16}(NOH)_2$, which crystallizes in colorless prisms and melts with decomposition at 194° to 196°.

When Δ^6-menthene-2-one is reduced with zinc dust and alcoholic sodium hydroxide, it yields dextro-carvomenthone. When reduced with aluminium amalgam, it gives a dimolecular compound, $C_{20}H_{34}O_2$; the latter yields a phenylhydrazone, melting at 260°.

The ketone unites slowly with hydrobromic acid, forming a yellow oil.

17. TERPINEOL, $C_{10}H_{17}OH$.

The name terpineol was formerly used to designate a substance which to-day is recognized as a mixture of isomeric alcohols, $C_{10}H_{17}OH$. It will be well first to consider the preparation and properties of this mixture, which was termed "terpineol," before entering into a discussion of the individual alcohols contained in it. These alcohols occupy an intermediate position between dipentene and terpine:

$$\underset{\text{Dipentene.}}{C_{10}H_{16}} \rightleftarrows \underset{\text{Terpineol.}}{C_{10}H_{17}OH} \rightleftarrows \underset{\text{Terpine.}}{C_{10}H_{18}(OH)_2}$$

Therefore, those terpenes which can be converted into terpine may also be transformed into "terpineol" by the addition of one molecule of water, while "terpineol" may also be obtained by the elimination of water from terpine hydrate.

Deville [1] probably obtained "terpineol" as a by-product in the preparation of terpine hydrate from turpentine oil. According to Flawitzky,[2] "terpineol" is prepared when one part of levorotatory turpentine oil is mixed with one-half part of sulphuric acid and one and one-half parts of ninety per cent. alcohol, the mixture being allowed to stand for twelve hours.

Tilden [3] first obtained "terpineol" from terpine hydrate, and Wallach [4] more closely defined the conditions under which "terpineol" could be most conveniently prepared from this compound. He found that dilute phosphoric acid gave relatively

[1] Deville, Ann. Chem., *71*, 351.

[2] Flawitzky, Ber., *12*, 2354.

[3] Tilden, Journ. Chem. Soc., *1878*, 247; *1879*, 287; Ber., *12*, 848; Jahresb. Chem., *1878*, 1132.

[4] Wallach, Ann. Chem., *230*, 247 and 264.

small quantities of terpenes, and a large yield of "terpineol." In order to prepare it, twenty-five grams of terpine hydrate are boiled with fifty cc. of a twenty per cent. solution of phosphoric acid in a reflux apparatus, for fifteen minutes; the product is distilled in a current of steam, and the resultant oil submitted to a fractional distillation, the "terpineol" being contained in the fraction boiling at 215° to 218° (Wallach).

The French chemists Bouchardat and Voiry[1] prepared "terpineol" by the action of very dilute sulphuric acid (1 to 1000) on terpine hydrate; they showed that five-sixths of the resulting "terpineol" solidified at — 50° to crystals, melting at 30° to 32°. This product is designated as "*solid terpineol.*"

It is certain that solid terpineol is also contained in Wallach's "terpineol,"[2] although for some time it was impossible to isolate the solid compound from the liquid product.

If terpine be given the formula:

```
        CH3
        |
        COH
       /   \
    H2C     CH2
     |       |
    H2C     CH2
       \   /
        COH
        |
        CH
       /  \
    H3C    CH3,
```

Terpine.

it will be seen that three isomeric, unsaturated alcohols, $C_{10}H_{17}OH$, may be derived from it, thus:

```
       Ia.                   IIa.                  III.
       CH3                   CH3                   CH3
       |                     |                     |
       C                     COH                   COH
     //  \                  /   \                 /   \
  H2C     CH             H2C     CH2           H2C     CH2
   |       |              |       |             |       |
  H2C     CH2            H2C     CH            H2C     CH2
     \   /                  \   //                \   /
      COH                    C                     C
      |                      |                     ||
      CH                     CH                    C
     /  \                   /  \                  /  \
  H3C    CH3             H3C    CH3            H3C    CH3
```

Δ[1]-Terpen-4-ol. Δ[3]-Terpen-1-ol. Δ[4(8)]-Terpen-1-ol.

[1] Bouchardat and Voiry, Compt. rend., *104*, 996; Ber., *20*, 286.

[2] Tiemann and R. Schmidt, Ber., 28, 1781; Semi-Annual Report of Schimmel & Co., April and May, 1901, 75.

By totally different methods, Wallach and Baeyer came to the same conclusion, that solid terpineol (m. p. 35°) should be considered as a Δ^1-terpen-4-ol, expressed by formula Ia. This formula, however, is hardly conformable to the results of experiments which have more recently been published by Wallach,[1] and by Tiemann and Semmler;[2] according to their researches it appears possible, and even probable, that terpine should be represented by the formula:

```
      CH3
      |
      COH
     /   \
  H2C     CH2
   |       |
  H2C     CH2
     \   /
      CH
      |
      COH
     /   \
  H3C     CH3
```

Terpine.

Of the three terpenols which may be derived from this terpine, one has the constitution represented in formula III; the other two have the formulas:

```
        Ib.                    IIb.
        CH3                    CH3
        |                      |
        C                      COH
       / \\                   /   \
    H2C    CH              H2C     CH2
     |     |                |       |
    H2C    CH2             H2C     CH2
       \  /                   \   /
        CH                     CH
        |                      |
        COH                    C
       /  \                   /  \\
    H3C    CH3             H3C    CH2
```

Δ^1-Terpen-8-ol. $\Delta^{8(9)}$-Terpen-1-ol.

Formula Ib is to be regarded as expressing the constitution of solid terpineol (m. p. 35°), since it represents the facts at present known better than formula Ia. This formula was first proposed by G. Wagner.[3]

[1] Wallach, Ber., 28, 1773.
[2] Tiemann and Semmler, Ber., 28, 1778.
[3] G. Wagner, Ber., 27, 1652.

It now remains to consider the nature of the oily constituent which occurs, together with solid terpineol (m. p. 35°), in Wallach's "terpineol." Baeyer has synthetically prepared a solid alcohol, melting at 69° to 70°, which he calls $\Delta^{4(8)}$-terpen-1-ol, corresponding to formula III; this alcohol and its acetate yield blue nitrosochlorides, hence, according to Baeyer, the alcohol and its acetate must contain a tertiary-tertiary double linkage, since only those compounds possessing such a double linkage are capable of producing blue nitrosochlorides. Baeyer recognized this terpinol in the liquid "terpineol" prepared from terpine hydrate by means of oxalic or phosphoric acid.

It is quite certain that liquid "terpineol" contains a mixture of isomeric terpinols. The chemists of Schimmel & Co.[1] have carefully investigated this liquid product, and, by submitting it to continued cold, have isolated the solid terpineol, m. p. 35°, and an isomeric terpineol, melting at 32° to 33°; the two compounds are readily distinguished by their chemical and physical properties.

Liquid terpineols have been isolated from camphor, cardamom,[2] erigeron, kesso,[3] kuromoji,[4] and marjoram[5] oils; but since it has been determined that the terpineol from cardamom oil may be obtained in a crystalline form (m. p. 35°), it is possible that the terpineols from the other oils may be procured in a crystalline condition.[6]

Wallach's "terpineol" is an optically inactive liquid and contains terpineol of the melting point 35° and terpineol of the melting point 32° as its chief constituents.

Liquid "terpineol" is readily converted into dipentene dihydrochloride, dihydrobromide, etc., when the halogen hydrides are passed into its ethereal solution. Terpine hydrate is easily formed when it is acted upon by dilute acids.

"Terpineol" is an unsaturated compound; when bromine is added to its solution in petroleum ether, a bromide is produced, which crystallizes on cooling with solid carbon dioxide and ether, but it becomes liquid again at higher temperatures. When it is treated with an excess of bromine, dipentene tetrabromide results (Wallach).

[1] Schimmel & Co., Semi-Annual Report, April and May, *1901*, 75.
[2] Weber, Ann. Chem., *238*, 98.
[3] Bertram and Gildemeister, Arch. Pharm., *228*, 483.
[4] Kwasnick, Ber., *24*, 81.
[5] Biltz, Ber., *32*, 995.
[6] Schimmel & Co., Semi-Annual Report, Oct., *1897*, 11.

TERPINEOL MELTING AT 35°.

It has been mentioned that Bouchardat and Voiry isolated a solid terpineol from the liquid reaction-product obtained by heating terpine hydrate with very dilute sulphuric acid. This solid alcohol was called "*terpilenol*" or "*caoutchin hydrate*"; it melted at 30° to 32°, and boiled at 218°. It was also obtained in the form of its acetyl ester by the continued heating of dipentene with glacial acetic acid at 100° (Bouchardat and Lafont [1]).

It is worthy of notice that inactive, solid terpineol occurs in the form of its acetate in cajuput oil (Voiry [2]). The chemists of Schimmel & Co.[3] have made a careful investigation of the chemical and physical constants of pure, inactive terpineol from cajuput oil and also of its derivatives; they found that these properties agreed completely with those of solid terpineol melting at 35°.

Kremers [4] has found terpineol (m. p. 35°) in the oil of *Erigeron canadensis*.

Terpineol (m. p. 35°) is also obtained by the action of formic acid on *geraniol* at a temperature of 15° to 20°; *terpinyl formate* is the primary product of this reaction, and yields the inactive terpineol on hydrolysis. A similar conversion of geraniol into terpineol is accomplished by the action of acetic acid containing one or two per cent. of sulphuric acid; this reaction takes place slowly at the ordinary temperature, rapidly on warming. By shaking with five per cent. sulphuric acid for ten days, and boiling the terpine hydrate thus formed with dilute sulphuric acid, geraniol may be converted into a *liquid "terpineol"* identical with that formed from pinene (Stephan [5]).

The solid terpineol, sold by Schimmel & Co., served as the material which was used by Wallach and by Baeyer in the following described experiments. It melts at 35° to 36°, boils at 98° to 99° (10 mm.) or 218.8° to 219.4° (752 mm.), has the specific gravity 0.9391 at 15° or 0.9345 at 20°, and the index of refraction, $n_D = 1.48132$ at 20° (Schimmel & Co.[3]).

According to Tiemann and Schmidt,[6] terpine hydrate is quantitatively formed, when terpineol is agitated with benzene and a five per cent. solution of sulphuric acid for five days.

The behavior of terpineol towards dehydrating agents was the subject of a systematic investigation by Wallach and Kerkhoff[7];

[1] Bouchardat and Lafont, Compt. rend., *102*, 1555.
[2] Voiry, Compt. rend., *106*, 1538.
[3] Schimmel & Co., Semi-Annual Report, April and May, *1901*, 76.
[4] Kremers, Pharm. Rundschau, *13*, 137.
[5] K. Stephan, Journ. pr. Chem., *60* [II], 244.
[6] Tiemann and Schmidt, Ber., *28*, 1781.
[7] Wallach and Kerkhoff, Ann. Chem., *275*, 103.

their researches were carried out in the same direction as previous investigations of Wallach[1] regarding the liquid "terpineol."

Dipentene is produced when solid terpineol is heated with acid potassium sulphate at 180° to 190°. Terpinene, cineole, terpinolene and traces of dipentene are formed when it is boiled with dilute sulphuric acid; almost the same result is obtained by boiling terpineol with twenty per cent. phosphoric acid, but in this case no dipentene results. On boiling terpineol with a solution of oxalic acid or with anhydrous formic acid[2] for a *short time*, the product consists chiefly of terpinolene; when the boiling is of longer duration considerable quantities of terpinene and small amounts of cineole are obtained, together with terpinolene.

The primary reaction-product obtained by the removal of water from terpineol consists of the very unstable terpinolene; at higher temperatures this hydrocarbon is transformed into dipentene, while by the action of acids it is converted into terpinene.

Terpinyl formate is formed, as above mentioned, by the action of formic acid on geraniol at 15° to 20°.

Terpinyl acetate,[3] $C_{10}H_{17}O \cdot COCH_3$, is obtained when terpineol is heated with sodium acetate and acetic anhydride for forty-five minutes; the yield is about eighty-four per cent.

Terpinyl phenylurethane,

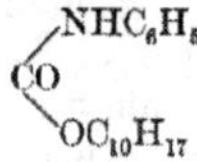

is obtained when equal parts by weight of terpineol and phenyl carbimide are allowed to remain in a closed vessel for several days; the solid reaction-product is washed with petroleum ether, and crystallized from warm alcohol. It dissolves readily in ether, and melts at 113° (Wallach and Kerkhoff[4]).

Wallach[1] had previously obtained this urethane from liquid "terpineol."

Terpinyl methyl ether, $C_{10}H_{17}OCH_3$, is produced when crystallized terpineol is dissolved in three times its amount of toluene, and boiled with an excess of the liquid alloy of potassium and sodium in a flask, fitted with a reflux condenser, for eight hours; the liquid is then cooled, decanted from unchanged alloy, and treated with methyl iodide. The reaction commences at a moderate

[1] Wallach, Ann. Chem., *230*, 268; *239*, 20.
[2] Wallach, Ann. Chem., *291*, 342.
[3] Schimmel & Co., Semi-Annual Report, Oct., 1897, 64.
[4] Wallach and Kerkhoff, Ann. Chem., *275*, 103.

temperature, and is complete after warming on a water-bath for one hour. The potassium and sodium iodides are filtered off, and the filtrate is submitted to a fractional distillation. The resultant terpinyl methyl ether is a mobile liquid, which boils at 212°, smells like cymene, and is vigorously attacked by permanganate (Baeyer[1]). It combines with hydriodic acid in a glacial acetic acid solution to form a hydriodide, which yields the methyl ether of tertiary menthol by reduction with acetic acid and zinc dust.

$$\begin{array}{ccc} & CH_3 & \\ & | & \\ & CH & \\ H_2C & & CH \\ H_2C & & \overset{2}{CH_2} \\ & COCH_3 & \\ & | & \\ & C_3H_7 & \end{array}$$

Tertiary menthyl methyl ether.

Terpineol dibromide, $C_{10}H_{17}OH \cdot Br_2$, results by the gradual addition of two atoms of bromine to a well cooled solution of solid terpineol in glacial acetic acid; it is precipitated from this solution by water, forming a heavy oil.

When this bromide is digested with an excess of moist silver oxide or lead hydroxide on the water-bath, *pinole hydrate*, $C_{10}H_{17}O \cdot OH$, is formed, together with a small quantity of *pinole;* large quantities of pinole, $C_{10}H_{16}O$, are obtained, together with a small amount of cymene, when terpineol dibromide is heated with sodium alcoholate (Wallach[2]).

Baeyer[3] states that when the dibromide of Wallach's liquid "terpineol" is treated with a solution of two molecules of hydrogen bromide in glacial acetic acid, *1, 2, 4 (or 1, 2, 8 (?))-tribromoterpane*, $C_{10}H_{17}Br_3$, is produced; this is a liquid, which, on bromination in an acetic acid solution, is converted into dipentene tetrabromide.

According to Wallach,[4] when 1, 2, 4 (or 1, 2, 8 (?))-tribromoterpane is heated with sodium methylate, the bromine atom 2 is replaced by a methoxyl-group, whilst the remaining two atoms of bromine are eliminated as hydrogen bromide, and optically inactive carveol methyl ether results. Optically active carveol methyl ether is formed, as already mentioned, by reducing the bromide,

[1] Baeyer, Ber., *26*, 2560; *26*, 826.
[2] Wallach, Ann. Chem., *277*, 113.
[3] Baeyer, Ber., *27*, 440.
[4] Wallach, Ann. Chem., *281*, 140.

$C_{10}H_{14}BrOCH_3$, which is obtained by treating limonene tetrabromide with sodium methylate. Carveol methyl ether yields inactive carvone by oxidation with chromic anhydride.

The following formulas illustrate the transformation of solid terpineol into carvone :

```
      CH3                              CH3
      |                                |
      C                                CBr
    /   \\                            /   \
H2C      CH          →           H2C      CHBr
 |        |                       |        |
H2C      CH2                     H2C      CH2
    \   /                            \   /
     COH                              COH
      |                                |
     C3H7                             C3H7
Terpineol (Δ1-terpen-4-ol).      Terpineol dibromide.

      CH3                              CH3
      |                                |
      CBr                              C
    /   \                            //  \
H2C      CHBr        →           HC       CH(OCH3)
 |        |                       |        |
H2C      CH2                     HC       CH2
    \   /                            \\  /
     CBr                               C
      |                                |
     C3H7                             C3H7
1, 2, 4-Tribromoterpane.         Carveol methyl ether.

                  CH3
                  |
                  C
                //  \
              HC      CO
              |        |
              HC      CH2
                \\  /
                  C
                  |
                 C3H7
               Carvone.
```

The development of those formulas which indicate that terpineol should be regarded as a Δ^1-terpen-8-ol is given on page 198.

Terpineol nitrosochloride, $C_{10}H_{17}(OH) \cdot NOCl$, is obtained by adding eleven cc. of ethyl nitrite to a solution of fifteen grams of crystallized terpineol in fifteen cc. of glacial acetic acid, well cooled by a freezing mixture, and subsequently adding very slowly a mixture of six cc. of concentrated hydrochloric acid and six cc. of glacial acetic acid. When the reaction is complete, water is added and the nitrosochloride separates as an oil which soon solidifies. The yield is quantitative (Wallach[1]).

It is a comparatively stable compound and may be recrystallized from methyl alcohol or ethyl acetate, melting at 102° to 103°.

[1] Wallach, Ann. Chem., 277, 121.

When hydrogen chloride is eliminated from terpineol nitrosochloride, *oxydihydrocarvoxime*,[1] $C_{10}H_{15}(OH)NOH$, melting at 133° to 134°, is obtained; this compound, when boiled with dilute acids, loses water and hydroxylamine, yielding a mixture of carvacrol and inactive carvone. It may, therefore, be concluded that in terpineol the ethylene linkage is, without doubt, in the Δ^1-position (Wallach[2]).

Terpineol nitrosate, $C_{10}H_{17}(OH)\cdot N_2O_4$, was prepared by Wallach,[3] but has not been carefully studied.

Terpineol nitrolpiperidide,[4] $C_{10}H_{17}(OH)\cdot NO\cdot NC_5H_{10}$, is prepared by the interaction of the nitrosochloride with piperidine. It crystallizes from methyl alcohol in needles and dissolves sparingly in ether from which it separates in prisms, melting at 159° to 160°.

Terpineol nitrolanilide, $C_{10}H_{17}(OH)\cdot NO\cdot NHC_6H_5$, is obtained by warming ten grams of terpineol nitrosochloride with ten cc. of aniline and twenty or twenty-five cc. of alcohol. The reaction-mixture is diluted with a little water and yields splendid, yellow crystals on cooling. These are washed with a little ether and, when recrystallized from alcohol, form colorless prisms, which melt at 155° to 156°.

Terpineol yields various products on oxidation with potassium permanganate; the first of these is a compound, $C_{10}H_{20}O_3$, which must be regarded as methyl isopropyl trioxyhexahydrobenzene, or, according to Baeyer, *trioxyterpane.* By further action of permanganate, trioxyterpane loses four atoms of hydrogen, and forms the *keto-lactone*, $C_{10}H_{16}O_3$, a compound which is likewise derived from a number of other terpene derivatives; hence, in order to prepare pure trioxyterpane, an excess of permanganate must be carefully avoided (Wallach[5]).

Trioxyhexahydrocymene [1, 2, 8-trioxyterpane or 1, 2, 8-trioxymenthane], $C_{10}H_{20}O_3$.—For the preparation of this compound, dissolve one hundred and fifty grams of permanganate in six liters of water contained in a metallic, double-walled vessel; add one hundred and five grams of melted terpineol, and agitate for several minutes on a shaking-machine, keeping the liquid well cooled by passing water through the space between the walls of the vessel. The reaction is complete in a very short time. Filter off the manganese oxides, evaporate the filtrate to dryness while passing a current of carbonic anhydride through the liquid, and extract

[1] Wallach, Ann. Chem., *291*, 342.
[2] Wallach, Ber., *28*, 1773.
[3] Wallach, Ann. Chem., *277*, 121.
[4] Wallach, Ann. Chem., *281*, 140.
[5] Wallach, Ann. Chem., *275*, 150.

the dry residue with alcohol. On evaporation of the alcohol, the product soon solidifies to a light colored, crystalline mass. This is best distilled in vacuum, and boils at 170° to 180° under 11 mm. pressure; the distillate solidifies, and is rubbed up with ether, which readily dissolves the impurities. When purified in this manner, trioxyhexahydrocymene is almost insoluble in ether, somewhat sparingly soluble in chloroform, and separates from a mixture of alcohol and ether in transparent crystals. It melts at 121° to 122°, and boils above 300° with slight decomposition.

It is very readily soluble in water, and is precipitated from its concentrated aqueous solution by alkalis; it yields iodoform when treated with iodine and alkalis, and forms carbon tetrabromide by the action of bromine and alkalis. Phosphoric chloride converts it into a chloride.

Trioxyhexahydrocymene loses three molecules of water and forms cymene, when it is heated with dilute sulphuric acid (Wallach[1]),

$$C_{10}H_{20}O_3 - 3H_2O = C_{10}H_{14}.$$

Under suitable conditions it may part with but two molecules of water, yielding carvenone, $C_{10}H_{16}O$:

$$C_{10}H_{20}O_3 - 2H_2O = C_{10}H_{16}O.$$

According to Ginzberg,[1] trioxymenthane is converted into cymene, and the *diacetate* of a glycol, when it is heated with three molecules of acetic anhydride for six hours at 150°. On hydrolysis, the diacetate yields the *glycol*, $C_{10}H_{16}(OH)_2$, isomeric with pinole hydrate; it crystallizes from petroleum ether in triclinic prisms, melts at 63° to 64°, and boils at 259° to 260° under 754 mm. pressure. Oxidation with dilute permanganate converts the glycol into an inactive *tetrahydric alcohol*, $C_{10}H_{20}O_4$, which is isomeric with limonetriol, and melts at 168.5° to 169.5°. The glycol is regarded as a *$\Delta^{8(9)}$-menthene-1:2-diol.*

When trioxyterpane is heated with acetic anhydride at 200°, more cymene than glycol is produced; when heated with acetyl chloride, pinole hydrate (m. p. 130.5° to 131°) and a little cymene are formed (Ginzberg[2]).

Keto-lactone,[3] $C_{10}H_{16}O_3$, is quantitatively formed by oxidizing trioxyterpane, $C_{10}H_{20}O_3$, which is also almost quantitatively obtained by the oxidation of terpineol as described above. The following method is well adapted for the preparation of this compound.

[1] Wallach, Ann. Chem., *277*, 110 and 122.
[2] A. Ginzberg, Ber., *29*, 1198.
[3] Wallach, Ann. Chem., *275*, 153.

Eleven grams of trioxyterpane are dissolved in seven cc. of warm water; the solution is then well cooled, and treated very carefully with a solution of eight grams of chromic anhydride in twenty cc. of sulphuric acid, sp. gr. 1.25. The reaction is accompanied by a rapid rise in the temperature; the chromic acid is reduced to a sulphate, and an oil separates, which solidifies in large crystals on cooling. Additional quantities of this substance may be obtained by extracting the aqueous chromium sulphate solution with chloroform. It is washed with a small quantity of water and ether, and crystallized from hot water.

This keto-lactone is characterized by its exceptional power of crystallization; it separates in monoclinic pyramids, and forms quite as well defined crystals as any member of the terpene series. It boils at about 330° without decomposition, and melts at 62° to 63°.

This compound, $C_{10}H_{16}O_3$, yields an *oxime*, melting at 77°, as well as a *semicarbazone*, melting at 200°, and, on the other hand, is converted into the potassium salt of an acid, $C_{10}H_{18}O_4$, by the action of potassium hydroxide; therefore, Wallach[1] assumes that it is a keto-lactone. Wallach[2] further determined that it is readily converted into acetic acid and terpenylic acid by oxidation with permanganate.

Tiemann and Semmler[3] also obtained this keto-lactone as a by-product in the oxidation of commercial pinene with permanganate. They determined its constitution in much the same manner as Wallach, and arrived at the same constitutional formula, according to which it is represented as *methyl-3¹-ethyl-3-heptanon-6-olide-1-3¹*. Tiemann and Schmidt[4] confirmed these results; they also showed that the keto-lactone, $C_{10}H_{16}O_3$, is formed, together with terpenylic acid, by the oxidation of terpineol and of trioxyhexahydrocymene with a mixture of chromic and glacial acetic acids.

According to Mahla and Tiemann,[5] oxidation with chromic and sulphuric acids converts methoethylheptanonolide (keto-lactone) into terpenylic acid,[6] $C_8H_{12}O_4$, while oxidation with nitric acid gives rise to terebic acid, $C_7H_{10}O_4$.

According to Tiemann,[7] the keto-lactone melts at 64°, and its *oxime*, $C_{10}H_{16}O_2(NOH)$ (see above), crystallizes in rhombs, and

1 Wallach, Ber., 28, 1773.
2 Wallach, Ann. Chem., 277, 118.
3 Tiemann and Semmler, Ber., 28, 1778.
4 Tiemann and R. Schmidt, Ber., 28, 1781.
5 Mahla and Tiemann, Ber., 29, 2621.
6 Mahla and Tiemann, Ber., 29, 928.
7 Tiemann, Ber., 29, 2616.

melts at 79° to 80°; when heated with concentrated sulphuric acid at 100°, the oxime is converted into acetic acid and a base, *methyl-2-aminoethyl-3-pentolide*, $C_8H_{13}O_2NH_2$.

The keto-lactone is also formed by treating the pinonic acids with dilute sulphuric acid (see under pinene).

According to Bredt, terpenylic acid is readily obtained, when solid terpineol is treated with a chromic acid mixture.

If we accept the constitution of terpenylic acid as represented by the formula proposed by Wallach[1] and supported by Schryver,[2] we may formulate the oxidation of terpineol in the following manner:

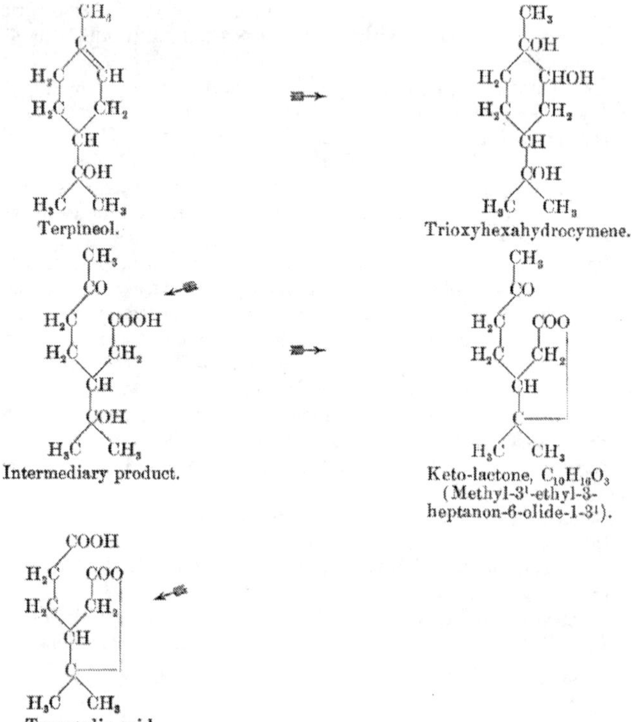

CH_3
C
H_2C CH
H_2C CH_2
CH
COH
H_3C CH_3
Terpineol.

→

CH_3
COH
H_2C CHOH
H_2C CH_2
CH
COH
H_3C CH_3
Trioxyhexahydrocymene.

CH_3
CO
H_2C COOH
H_2C CH_2
CH
COH
H_3C CH_3
Intermediary product.

→

CH_3
CO
H_2C COO
H_2C CH_2
CH
C
H_3C CH_3
Keto-lactone, $C_{10}H_{16}O_3$
(Methyl-3[1]-ethyl-3-heptanon-6-olide-1-3[1]).

COOH
H_2C COO
H_2C CH_2
CH
C
H_3C CH_3
Terpenylic acid.

[1] Wallach, Ann. Chem., *259*, 322.
[2] Schryver, Journ. Chem. Soc., *1893*, 1327.

The above-described terpineol (m. p. 35°) is optically inactive, but a number of optically active terpineols have been obtained and will be briefly mentioned here.[1]

Semmler[2] obtained an active terpineol, $C_{10}H_{17}OH$, by the substitution of the hydroxyl-group for an atom of chloride in limonene hydrochloride; it boils at 215°, has the odor of hawthorn blossom and lilac, and its optical rotation is of the same sign as that of the limonene derivate from which it is produced.

Bouchardat and Tardy[3] obtained a strongly dextrorotatory terpene (pinene) from the eucalyptus oil of *Eucalyptus globulus*; by treating this terpene with anhydrous formic acid at a low temperature *terpinyl formate* is produced, which yields a solid, dextrorotatory terpineol on hydrolysis. This terpineol melts at 33° to 34°, boils at 218° and has the specific rotatory power, $[\alpha]_D = + 88°$.

The fraction boiling at 150° to 164° at 14 mm. pressure of Ceylon cardamom oil contains a terpineol,[4] melting at 35° to 37°; it is dextrorotatory, $[\alpha]_D = 83°31'$, at 21°. It yields a *terpinyl phenylurethane*, melting at 112° to 113°, which is optically active, $[\alpha]_D = + 33°58'$, at 20°. It also forms a *nitrosochloride*, and *nitrolpiperidide*, melting at 151° to 152°, while the nitrolpiperidide obtained from inactive terpineol melts at 159° to 160°.

An active terpineol is also obtained from the oil of lovage[5]; it boils at 217° to 218°, melts at 35°, and is dextrorotatory, $[\alpha]_D = + 79°18'$, at 22°. It yields a terpinyl phenylurethane (m. p. 112°), and a nitrolpiperidide (m. p. 151°).

Godlewsky[6] obtains a levorotatory terpineol by treating French turpentine oil with alcoholic sulphuric acid, according to Flawitzky's method, the mixture being shaken and the product poured onto ice. The reaction is allowed to proceed for ten hours. The resulting terpineol melts at 34°, has the specific rotatory power, $[\alpha]_D = - 95°28'$, in an alcoholic solution. Oxidation with a one per cent. solution of permanganate converts it into *trioxymenthane* (*menthanetriol* or *trioxyhexahydrocymene*), $C_{10}H_{20}O_3$; when this compound is oxidized with chromic acid, the *keto-lactone* (*methoethylheptanonolide*), $C_{10}H_{16}O_3$, is formed, which differs by its optical activity, $[\alpha]_D = + 55.3°$, in alcoholic solution, and a considerably lower melting point (45° to 46°), from the keto-lactone,

[1]For optically active terpineol prepared by action of alcohol and nitrous acid on dextro- or levo-pinene, see P. Genvresse, Compt. rend., *132*, 637.

[2]Semmler, Ber., *28*, 2189.

[3]Bouchardat and Tardy, Compt. rend., *121*, 1417.

[4]Schimmel & Co., Semi-Annual Report, Oct., *1897*, 11.

[5]Schimmel & Co., Semi-Annual Report, April, *1897*, 27.

[6]J. Godlewsky, J. Russ. Chem. Soc., *31*, 203; Chem. Centr., *1899* [I], 1241.

$C_{10}H_{16}O_3$, derived from inactive terpineol, which melts at 63° to 64°. This keto-lactone is perhaps identical with the optically active *keto-lactone* (*active methyl ketone of homoterpenylic acid*), $C_{10}H_{16}O_3$, melting at 48° to 49°, which Baeyer[1] obtained from levorotatory trioxyterpane (m. p. 97° to 98°), prepared indirectly from optically active *1:8-oxybromotetrahydrocarvone*, $C_{10}H_{16}BrO(OH)$.

In the oxidation of the above-mentioned levo-terpineol, optically active terpenylic acid is also produced.

According to Stephan,[2] when levo-linalool is heated with acetic anhydride during five to eight hours at 150° to 160°, a product is obtained which consists of about eighty-five parts of geraniol and fifteen parts of *dextro-terpineol;* the latter separates out in a crystalline condition after repeated fractionation and cooling in a freezing mixture.

Dextro-terpineol is also produced in larger quantities by treating linalool with acetic acid containing a little sulphuric acid. Formic acid also converts l-linalool into d-terpineol, and d-linalool into l-terpineol, if the reaction proceeds below 20°; a crystalline terpineol is formed in each case.

The crystalline active modifications of terpineol are readily obtained in the form of their acetates by the action of glacial acetic and sulphuric acids on the limonenes, or of glacial acetic acid and zinc chloride on the pinenes.[3]

According to Biltz,[4] the essential oil of *Origanum majorana* (marjoram oil) contains a dextrorotatory, *liquid* "terpineol," the presence of which is shown by its oxidation products, trioxyhexahydrocymene, $C_{10}H_{20}O_3$, and the keto-lactone, $C_{10}H_{16}O_3$.

A solid, levorotatory terpineol is also said to be contained in niaouli oil.

The active and inactive modifications of terpineol are alike in their chemical behavior; a few derivatives, however, differ slightly in their melting points.

Since terpineol (m. p. 35°) shows such a close relation to so many compounds of the terpene series, and is of importance for the determination of the constitution of these compounds, the following table is introduced in order to render more apparent the close relationship of terpineol with other terpene derivatives.

[1]Baeyer and Baumgaertel, Ber., *31*, 3208.

[2]K. Stephan, Journ. pr. Chem., *58* [II], 109.

[3]Ertschikowsky, Journ. d. russ. phys.-chem. Ges., *28*, 132; Abs. Bull. Soc. Chim., *16* [III], 1584.

[4]W. Biltz, Ber., *32*, 995.

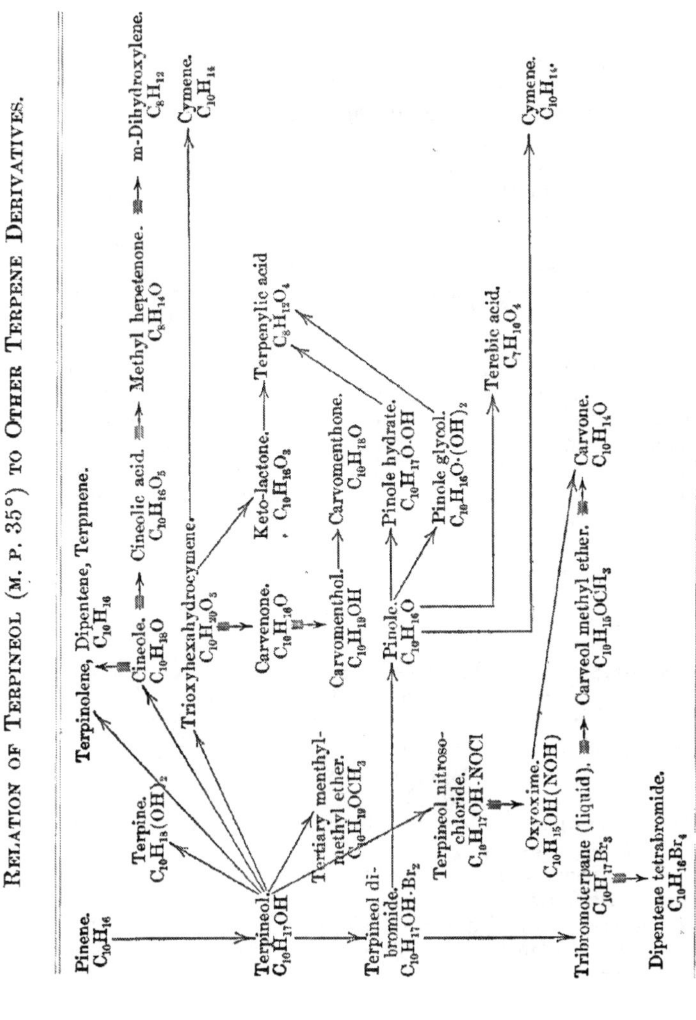

Relation of Terpineol (m. p. 35°) to Other Terpene Derivatives.

18. ISOMERIC TERPINEOL, $C_{10}H_{17}OH$, MELTING AT 69° TO 70°. ($\Delta^{4(8)}$-TERPEN-1-OL.)

When the tribromoterpane (m. p. 110°), which Wallach obtained by brominating dipentene dihydrobromide, is reduced with zinc dust and acetic acid, it yields the acetate of an isomeric terpenol (terpineol); this is converted, on hydrolysis, into a crystalline alcohol, melting at 69° to 70°, which is to be regarded as a $\Delta^{4(8)}$-terpen-1-ol (Baeyer[1]).

In order to prepare the acetate of this alcohol, a solution of thirty grams of the tribromide (m. p. 110°) in 200 grams of glacial acetic acid is cooled to 0° (a portion of the acetic acid solidifies at this temperature) and is treated carefully and with constant shaking with thirty grams of zinc dust. After standing for half an hour the product is filtered and the filtrate is diluted with water, neutralized with soda and extracted with ether. The ethereal solution is then washed with soda, the ether distilled off and the resultant terpenol acetate purified by distillation in vacuum; it boils at 110° to 120° under a pressure of 17 mm. The yield amounts to eighty per cent. of the theoretical.

$\Delta^{4(8)}$-Terpen-1-ol separates in the form of long needles when the acetate is heated with an excess of alcoholic potash and the solution is subsequently diluted with water. It crystallizes from ether in thick prisms which melt at 69° to 70° and, like terpineol (m. p. 35°), it has an agreeable odor of lilac. It is rather volatile, distills undecomposed and reacts with dilute acids like the isomeric terpenols.

According to Baeyer,[2] $\Delta^{4(8)}$-terpen-1-ol is also contained in the liquid "terpineol," which is obtained when terpine hydrate is heated with oxalic or phosphoric acids. When this liquid "terpineol" is boiled with acetic anhydride, an acetate is produced from which the blue, crystalline nitrosochloride of $\Delta^{4(8)}$-terpen-1-ol acetate may be readily obtained.

Liquid "terpineol" prepared by Schimmel & Co. does not contain $\Delta^{4(8)}$-terpen-1-ol.

When terpenol acetate is dropped into boiling quinoline, terpinolene distills over.[2]

$\Delta^{4(8)}$-Terpen-1-ol and its acetate readily give dipentene dihydrobromide when treated with a glacial acetic acid solution of hydrogen bromide.

[1] Baeyer, Ber., 27, 443.
[2] Baeyer, Ber., 27, 815.

Terpenol dibromide,[1] $C_{10}H_{17}OH\ Br_2$ (4, 8-dibromoterpen-1-ol), results by the addition of the theoretical quantity of bromine to the alcoholic ethereal solution of terpenol; it crystallizes in long needles and melts at 114° to 115°.

Terpenol acetate dibromide,[1] $C_{10}H_{17}(OCOCH_3)\cdot Br_2$, is prepared like the preceding compound, and forms brilliant leaflets, melting at 103°.

If the dibromide of terpenol or its acetate be treated with hydrobromic acid in glacial acetic acid solution, Wallach's tribromoterpane (m. p. 110°) is produced.

Nitrosochloride of $\Delta^{4(8)}$-terpen-1-ol acetate, $C_{10}H_{17}(OCOCH_3)\cdot NOCl$.—This very characteristic compound is prepared according to the directions given by Thiele[2] for the preparation of tetramethyl ethylene nitrosochloride.

Terpenol acetate is dissolved in an alcoholic solution of hydrochloric acid, and, when well cooled, is treated slowly with slight excess of a concentrated solution of sodium nitrite. The liquid immediately assumes a pure blue color, and only becomes green when an excess of sodium nitrite is added. On the addition of ice a heavy, blue oil separates, which solidifies to microscopic, blue prisms. By dissolving in alcohol and precipitating with water, brilliant blue leaflets result, which melt at 82°. It decomposes into its components when warmed with alcohol (Baeyer[1]).

$\Delta^{4(8)}$-Terpen-1-ol also gives a blue nitrosochloride, but it has not been thoroughly examined.

Nitrosobromide of $\Delta^{4(8)}$-terpenol acetate, $C_{10}H_{17}(OCOCH_3)\ NOBr$, crystallizes in blue needles, and melts at 81° to 82°. According to Baeyer and Blau,[3] this substance undergoes a remarkable transformation when it is treated with red phosphorus and a solution of hydrogen bromide in glacial acetic acid; the acetyl group is replaced by a bromine atom, and the hydrobromic acid salt of a base results, which contains a hydroxylamine group. The constitution of this salt is expressed by the empirical formula, $C_{10}H_{17}Br_2NHOH\ HBr$. It crystallizes in thin, quadratic plates, and melts at 182° to 184°.

When this salt is dissolved in water and treated with potash or ammonia, two molecules of hydrogen bromide are eliminated, and a base, $C_{10}H_{16}Br\ NHOH$, is formed. It melts at 100° to 102°. Nitrous acid changes it into a nitroso-compound, melting at 138° to 139°.

[1] Baeyer, Ber, 27, 443.
[2] Thiele, Ber, 27, 455.
[3] Baeyer and Blau, Ber, 28, 2289

It is mentioned on page 93 that when 1-bromo-$\Delta^{4(8)}$-terpene is treated with sodium nitrite and hydrobromic acid, a nitrosobromide is obtained, which crystallizes in blue crystals and melts at 44°. When this nitrosobromide is treated with a solution of hydrogen bromide in acetic acid, it yields the hydrobromic acid salt described above. Thus, the nitrosobromide of 1-bromo-$\Delta^{4(8)}$-terpene and of $\Delta^{4(8)}$-terpenol acetate yield the same product, $C_{10}H_{17}Br_2NHOH \cdot HBr$.

According to Baeyer, only those substances which contain a tertiary-tertiary double linkage are capable of forming blue nitrosochlorides, for example, tetramethylethylene. Consequently, there is but one terpenol which conforms to this condition, and at the same time contains the hydroxyl-group in such a position that renders possible a transformation of the terpenol into dipentene dihydrobromide. Accordingly, Baeyer assumes that terpenol (m. p. 69° to 70°) has the following constitution:

CH_3
COH
H_2C CH_2
H_2C CH_2
C
‖
C
H_3C CH_3

$\Delta^{4(8)}$-Terpen-1-ol.

Since this alcohol is readily converted into terpinolene, the above formula supports Baeyer's formula of terpinolene and also agrees with the constitution which Wallach ascribes to tribromoterpane (m. p. 110°). The following formulas illustrate these relations:

```
      CH3                        CH3
      COH                        C
  H2C     CH2      →         H2C     CH
  H2C     CH2                H2C     CH2
      C                          C
      ‖                          ‖
      C                          C
  H3C   CH3                  H3C   CH3
```

$\Delta^{4(8)}$-Terpen-1-ol. Terpinolene.

```
      CH3
      CBr
  H2C     CH2
  H2C     CH2            ⇅              ↓
      CBr
      CH
  H3C   CH3
```

Dipentene dihydrobromide

```
           CH3                        CH3
           CBr                        C
  →    H2C     CH2       ←        H2C     CH
       H2C     CH2                H2C     CH2
           CBr                        CBr
           CBr                        CBr
       H3C   CH3                  H3C   CH3
```

1, 4, 8-Tribromoterpane. (m. p. 110°). Terpinolene dibromide.

These formulas would be quite as probable if the constitution of dipentene dihydrobromide were represented by the formula:

```
      CH3
      CBr
  H2C     CH2
  H2C     CH2
      CH
      CBr
  H3C   CH3
```

Trioxyhexahydrocymene, according to Baeyer's nomenclature,[1] *1, 4, 8-trioxyterpane*, $C_{10}H_{20}O_3$, is obtained, when $\Delta^{4(8)}$-terpenol (m. p. 69° to 70°) is dissolved in ether and oxidized with a dilute potassium permanganate solution. It forms crystals containing one molecule of water, and melts at 95° to 96°. It loses the water of crystallization when heated to 50° or 60° in a vacuum; the anhydrous substance melts at 110° to 112°. Hydrobromic acid converts it into Wallach's tribromoterpane, melting at 110° to 111° (Baeyer and Blau[1]).

19. ISOMERIC TERPINEOL, $C_{10}H_{17}OH$, MELTING AT 32° TO 33°.

In an investigation of liquid "terpineol," which is largely employed in perfumes, the chemists of Schimmel & Co. succeeded in preparing two phenylurethane derivatives; the one melted at 112° to 113° and was found to be identical with the terpinyl phenylurethane from terpineol, melting at 35°; the second proved to be a new isomeric phenylurethane and melted at 85°. By hydrolysis of the latter, a new terpineol, melting at 32° to 33°, was obtained.

According to more recent investigations,[2] the new terpineol is prepared as follows. A large quantity of liquid "terpineol" is repeatedly fractionated under reduced pressure, two chief fractions being obtained. Fraction 1 is optically inactive, boils at 213° to 215°, and has the sp. gr. 0.930 at 15°; fraction 2 is also optically inactive, boils at 218° to 220° and has the sp. gr. 0.940 at 15°. Both fractions congeal when exposed to continued winter cold. The solid compounds are separated and purified by repeated crystallization from alcohol. Fraction 1 gives the new terpineol, m. p. 32° to 33°, while fraction 2 yields the solid terpineol, m. p. 35°. The two substances have a slightly different odor.

The new terpineol crystallizes in long needles, melts at 32° to 33°, and boils at 90° (10 mm.) or at 209° to 210° (752 mm.); it has the sp. gr. 0.923 at 15° and 0.919 at 20°, and the refractive index, $n_D = 1.47470$, at 20°. About seventy per cent. of ester is formed by acetylization. When agitated with concentrated hydriodic acid (sp. gr. 1.96), it yields the same dipentene dihydriodide (m. p. 77°) as is formed by similar treatment of terpineol melting at 35°.

[1]Baeyer and Blau, Ber., *28*, 2289.

[2]Schimmel & Co., Semi-Annual Report, April-May, *1901*, 75.

The *phenylurethane*, $C_{17}H_{23}O_2N$, is formed by treating the terpineol with phenyl isocyanate; it melts at 85°. On hydrolysis it is reconverted into terpineol melting at 32°.

The *nitrosochloride*, $C_{10}H_{17}OH \cdot NOCl$, is produced by the action of amyl nitrite and hydrochloric acid on the alcohol; it melts at 102° to 103°.

Nitrolamines are formed only with difficulty from the nitrosochloride; by the action of piperidine only a small quantity of nitrolpiperidide is obtained.

Oxy-ketone, $C_9H_{16}O_2$.—When the terpineol, m. p. 32° to 33°, is oxidized, first with potassium permanganate and then with a chromic acid mixture, an oxy-ketone, $C_9H_{16}O_2$, is formed; under similar conditions terpineol, m. p. 35°, gives rise to the keto-lactone, $C_{10}H_{16}O_3$. This oxy-ketone boils at 140° to 145° under 19 mm. pressure, has the sp. gr. 1.023 at 20° and the refractive index, $n_D = 1.47548$, at 20°. Its *semicarbazone* crystallizes from alcohol and melts at 195° to 196°.

When this oxy-ketone is treated with a sodium hypobromite solution, it yields bromoform and an *oxy-acid*, $C_8H_{14}O_3$; the latter crystallizes from ethyl acetate, melts at about 130° and probably consists of a number of isomeric compounds. On heating this oxy-acid with concentrated sulphuric acid, it is converted into paratoluic acid, melting at 176°.

The following formula is suggested by the chemists of Schimmel & Co. as the best representation of the constitution of this terpineol:

```
          CH3
          |
          COH
        /     \
    H2C         CH2
    H2C         CH2
        \     /
          CH
          |
          C
        /   \\
    H3C       CH2
```

$\Delta^{8(9)}$-Terpen-1-ol.

20. PINOLE, $C_{10}H_{16}O$.

Pinole is an unsaturated oxide, and may be obtained from pinene or terpineol by the greatest variety of reactions. It was discovered in the oily by-products formed in the preparation of pinene nitrosochloride by Wallach and Otto,[1] and named pinole.

[1] Wallach and Otto, Ann. Chem., *253*, 249.

When the oily by-products, which are formed in considerable quantity in preparing pinene nitrosochloride, are distilled with steam, the distillate contains a mixture of cymene, pinole, and other substances. This crude product distills between 160° and 190°, the principal portion boiling at 180° to 186° and consisting for the most part of pinole.

Soon after Wallach and Otto's investigations, Armstrong[1] showed that pinole is produced when the crystalline compound, $C_{10}H_{18}O_2$, obtained by Sobrero[2] by exposing oil of turpentine to the action of moist oxygen in the sunlight, is distilled with dilute sulphuric acid. In the meantime, Wallach[3] prepared pinole hydrate,

$$C_{10}H_{16}O\langle{}^{H}_{OH}$$

by the addition of the elements of water to pinole, and proved the identity of this hydrate with the crystalline substance, $C_{10}H_{18}O_2$, which was first observed by Sobrero.

Pinole may also be regenerated from pinole dibromide, $C_{10}H_{16}O{\cdot}Br_2$, by boiling with alcoholic potash,[4] or by heating a benzene solution of the dibromide with sodium wire.[3] According to Wallach,[5] pinole may be very conveniently obtained from the dibromide of terpineol (m. p. 35°); the resulting pinole is very pure, hence this method is to be highly recommended for its preparation. The details of this process are as follows.

One molecular proportion of terpineol dibromide is added to a solution of one molecule of sodium in an excess of alcohol, and is heated; sodium bromide is thrown out, and, on completion of the reaction, the product is distilled with steam. Alcohol distills over at first, and contains considerable pinole, which is best isolated in the form of its dibromide by treating the alcoholic solution with bromine until a yellow color is produced, and then allowing the alcohol to evaporate. The receiver is changed when all of the alcohol is removed, and the distillation with steam is continued as long as the resultant oil is lighter than water. The oil is separated, dried over potassium hydroxide, and fractionally distilled (Wallach[5]).

[1] Armstrong, Chem. Ztg., *1890*, 838; Journ. Chem. Soc., *1891*, I., 311; Ber., *24*, 763, Ref.; Armstrong and Pope, Journ. Chem. Soc., *1891*, I., 315; Ber., *24*, 764c.

[2] Sobrero, Ann. Chem., *80*, 108.

[3] Wallach, Ann. Chem., *259*, 309.

[4] Wallach and Otto, Ann. Chem., *253*, 249.

[5] Wallach, Ann. Chem., *277*, 113.

PROPERTIES.—Pinole is a liquid, boiling at 183° to 184°, and has a characteristic odor resembling that of cineole and of camphor. It has a specific gravity 0.942 and refractive power, $n_D = 1.47145$, at 20°.[1] It is optically inactive; even the product obtained from the active pinole hydrate does not rotate the plane of polarized light.

It is readily converted into cymene on treatment with mineral acids, hence this hydrocarbon generally results as a by-product during the preparation of pinole.—

$$C_{10}H_{16}O - H_2O = C_{10}H_{14}$$

It does not react with hydrogen sulphide, hydroxylamine, phenylhydrazine, or benzoyl chloride.

Pinole behavès as an unsaturated compound; when dissolved in a dry or moist solvent, it readily unites with hydrobromic acid, forming an additive product, this has not been obtained in a pure condition, but it may be converted into pinole hydrate by shaking with alkalis.

Pinole hydrate,

$$C_{10}H_{16}O\langle^{H}_{OH}$$

It has been mentioned that this compound was obtained by Sobrero[2] in 1851 by the action of oxygen and water on turpentine oil. Armstrong found that pinole hydrate obtained in this manner is optically active, but that it yields inactive pinole on warming with dilute acids; he suggested the names "*sobrerol*" for pinole hydrate and "*sobrerone*" for pinole.

In order to convert pinole into the hydrate, it is mixed with an equal volume of glacial acetic acid, and the cooled solution is saturated with hydrobromic acid; the resultant, dark-colored liquid is poured into an excess of cold sodium hydroxide solution, and well shaken to decompose the pinole hydrobromide. Steam is now passed through the liquid in order to remove cymene, which is usually found in crude pinole; the hydrate is extracted from the alkaline solution by agitating with ether. Pinole hydrate remains as a crystalline product after evaporation of the ether, and may be recrystallized from water or alcohol. It is soluble in water (one part in thirty parts of water at 15°), and melts at 131° (Wallach[3]).

According to Wagner,[4] pinole hydrate is to be regarded as a *cis*-compound.

[1] Wallach, Ann Chem, *281*, 148
[2] Sobrero, Ann Chem, *80*, 108
[3] Wallach, Ann Chem, *259*, 313
[4] Wagner and Slawinski, Ber, *32*, 2068

The active modifications of pinole hydrate separate from alcoholic solutions in long, tabular crystals, which possess enantiomorphous, hemihedral forms of the monoclinic system, and, according to Armstrong and Pope, melt at 150°; Wallach[1] found the melting point 131°.

Inactive pinole hydrate is obtained by mixing the solutions of equal weights of the two active modifications; the crystals separate in flat, colorless, transparent tables belonging to the orthorhombic system, and melt at 131° (Armstrong and Pope).

Pinole hydrate readily loses water and is converted into pinole when warmed with dilute sulphuric acid. According to Wallach, it may be recrystallized unchanged from boiling acetic anhydride; on the other hand, Ginzberg[3] finds that when it is treated with boiling acetic anhydride, it yields a *diacetate*, which is a viscous liquid of agreeable odor, and has the specific gravity 1.0385 at 18°.

According to Wagner,[2] pinole hydrate is to be classified as an unsaturated γ-glycol; this view is in harmony with the fact that, when oxidized with potassium permanganate, it yields a tetrahydric alcohol, *cis-trans-sobrerytrite* (*menthane-1, 2, 6, 8-tetrol*),[3] $C_{10}H_{20}O_4$. Accordingly, pinole hydrate (sobrerol) is termed *Δ^6-menthene-2, 8-diol*, or *Δ^1-menthene-6, 8-diol.*[3]

Cis-trans-sobrerytrite, $C_{10}H_{20}O_4$, is very hygroscopic, and readily forms the *hydrate*, $C_{10}H_{20}O_4 + 2H_2O$, which separates from water in monoclinic crystals, melts at 100° to 105°, and loses water at 120°, after which it melts at 155.5° to 160°. Oxidation with potassium permanganate converts sobrerytrite into terpenylic acid as the chief product, together with acetic and terebic acids.

Wallach[4] obtained *oxydihydrocarvone*, $C_{10}H_{15}O(OH)$, whose oxime melts at 134°, by the oxidation of pinole hydrate with chromic acid. This result is in harmony with the view which regards pinole hydrate as an unsaturated glycol containing one hydroxyl-group united with a secondary and the other with a tertiary carbon atom.

By a more vigorous oxidation of pinole hydrate with permanganate, Wallach[1] obtained terpenylic acid, oxalic acid and carbon dioxide.

Cis-pinole hydrate dibromide[4] (1, 6, 2, 8 **dibromodioxyhexahydrocymene**), $C_{10}H_{16}Br_2(OH)_2$, is formed by the addition of a solution of bromine in chloroform to a solution of pinole hydrate in

[1] Wallach, Ann. Chem., *259*, 313.
[2] Wagner, Ber., *27*, 1648; Ber., *32*, 2069.
[3] Ginzberg, Ber., *29*, 1195.
[4] Wallach, Ann. Chem., *291*, 342.

the same solvent; it melts at 131° to 132°. Sodium methylate converts this dibromide into the *anhydride of cis-pinole glycol*, $C_{10}H_{16}O_2$.

Cis-pinole dibromide,[1] $C_{10}H_{16}O \cdot Br_2$, is one of the most characteristic and beautiful compounds of the terpene series. It is prepared by diluting pinole with twice its volume of glacial acetic acid, and adding bromine, drop by drop, until a permanent yellow coloration is produced. On evaporation of the solvent, pinole dibromide separates in splendid, well defined, orthorhombic crystals, which are recrystallized from ethyl acetate or a mixture of alcohol and ether. It melts at 94°, and boils undecomposed at 143° to 144° under 11 mm. pressure. It is moderately volatile with steam, and readily soluble in ether, alcohol, chloroform and ethyl acetate

Pure pinole is easily prepared by removing the bromine from pinole dibromide by treatment with alcoholic potash or metallic sodium.

When pinole dibromide is heated at 100° with an excess of pure formic acid[2] and a small quantity of ammonium formate, it is converted into cymene; the same hydrocarbon is produced, together with pinole glycol diacetate, if the dibromide be boiled with glacial acetic acid and zinc dust.[3] A far more important result was obtained by Wallach[3] by the reduction of the dibromide with zinc dust and glacial acetic acid in the cold; under these conditions, crystalline terpineol (m. p. 35°) is formed.

Hydrobromopinole dibromide, $C_{10}H_{17}OBr_3$.—According to Wallach,[2] pinole dibromide combines quantitatively with one molecule of hydrobromic acid, forming a tribromide.

A solution of fifty grams of pinole dibromide in fifty cc. of glacial acetic acid is warmed very gently, and treated, with shaking, with 100 cc. of a forty to fifty per cent. solution of hydrogen bromide in glacial acetic acid. A portion of the dibromide separates at once in the form of leaflets. If the mixture is now allowed to stand in a closed vessel for two days, the crystals gradually undergo a complete change The new compound is purified by diluting the reaction-product with water, filtering with the pump, washing with water and recrystallizing from ethyl acetate; the tribromide is thus obtained in brittle needles or prisms, melting at 160°. It is also formed as a by-product in the bromination of crude pinole.

[1] Wallach and Otto, Ann Chem, *253*, 253
[2] Wallach, Ann Chem, *268*, 224
[3] Wallach, Ann Chem, *281*, 148

On reduction, the tribromide yields an unsaturated ketone, *pinolone*, $C_{10}H_{16}O$, which has an odor resembling that of amyl acetate (Wallach [1]). When a solution of this tribromide in glacial acetic acid is digested with silver acetate, a *compound*, $C_{12}H_{20}Br_2O_3$, is obtained; it crystallizes from methyl alcohol, and melts at 118° to 120° (Wallach [1]).

Isopinole dibromide,[2] $C_{10}H_{16}O{\cdot}Br_2$, is formed by the elimination of hydrogen bromide from hydrobromopinole dibromide by means of quinoline in benzene, or of silver acetate in ethyl acetate; it separates from ether in transparent, well defined crystals, and melts at 94°. It is an unsaturated compound, and unites with hydrogen bromide, forming the pinole tribromide from which it is derived. It combines with two atoms of bromine, yielding *pinole tetrabromide*, $C_{10}H_{16}O{\cdot}Br_4$, which melts at 132°.

On reducing isopinole dibromide with zinc and glacial acetic acid, the ketone, *pinolone*, $C_{10}H_{16}O$ (b. p. 214° to 217°), is produced.

Isopinole dibromide and pinole tribromide are converted into *inactive carvone* by means of a hot, ten per cent. solution of potassium hydroxide; sodium methylate, however, gives rise to the methyl ether of carveol or carvacrol.

Cis-pinole glycol, $C_{10}H_{16}O(OH)_2$, may be prepared directly from pinole dibromide by the replacement of the bromine atoms with hydroxyl-groups. This can be effected by boiling seven grams of the dibromide with five grams of freshly precipitated lead hydroxide and 100 cc. of water, in a reflux apparatus, for several hours. The reaction-product is cooled, the lead bromide is filtered off, and the filtrate extracted with chloroform, or the aqueous solution may be evaporated at a relatively low temperature until crystallization commences (Wallach and Früstück[3]).

It may also be obtained by the hydrolysis of *cis*-pinole glycol diacetate.

It separates from its solutions in chloroform by the addition of petroleum ether, and crystallizes from water in hard crystals, which melt at 125°. It is changed into *cis*-pinole glycol diacetate by boiling with acetic anhydride. Terpenylic acid is formed by oxidizing pinole glycol with potassium permanganate (Wallach).

Cis-trans-pinole glycol, $C_{10}H_{16}O(OH)_2$.—According to Wagner,[4] pinole is oxidized by a very dilute solution of potassium permanganate to a glycol, isomeric with that obtained from pinole dibro-

[1] Wallach, Ber., *28*, 2708.
[2] Wallach, Ann. Chem., *306*, 267.
[3] Wallach and Früstück, Ann. Chem., *268*, 223.
[4] Wagner, Ber., *27*, 1644; Wagner and Slawinski, Ber., *32*, 2067.

mide. It appears to be a dimorphous compound, crystallizing from ether and ethyl acetate in orthorhombic pyramids, which melt at 126° to 127°, and from water in monoclinic tablets, which melt at 128° to 129°. Acetic anhydride converts this glycol into a diacetate, which boils at 154° to 155° (10.5 mm.), or at 166° to 167° (17 mm), after standing during a long time (Wagner reports two years), it solidifies, and melts at 37° to 38°. (Compare with Wallach.[1])

According to Wagner, the glycol obtained from pinole dibromide is to be regarded as the *cis*-modification, and that derived by the oxidation of pinole as the *cis-trans*-derivative.

d-Cis-trans-pinole glycol is the dextrorotatory modification of the above described glycol. It melts at 73° to 74 5° (See under cis-pinole glycol-2-chlorhydrin, page 282.)

Cis-pinole glycol diacetate, $C_{10}H_{16}O(OCOCH_3)_2$, is produced by the treatment of pinole dibromide with silver or lead acetate (Wallach[2]).

Twenty-five grams of pulverized pinole dibromide are heated with thirty grams of lead acetate in glacial acetic acid solution in an oil-bath at 150°; the reaction commences at a moderate temperature, and is complete in a short time. The resultant lead bromide is filtered off, acetic acid is removed from the filtrate by distillation, and the residue is submitted to distillation in vacuum. The diacetate passes over as an oil, which boils at 155° under 20 mm. pressure, or at 127° under 13 mm., and soon solidifies. It may be recrystallized from water, although when its aqueous solution is boiled it is changed into pinole glycol It melts at 97° to 98°.

The diacetate is also formed, together with cymene, when pinole dibromide is boiled with zinc dust and glacial acetic acid.[3]

Cis-pinole glycol dipropionate,[2] $C_{10}H_{16}O(OCOC_2H_5)_2$, results on heating pinole dibromide with propionic acid and silver propionate, or by warming the glycol with propionic anhydride. It is insoluble in water, soluble in alcohol, and melts at 106°.

Cis-pinole glycol diethyl ether,[4] $C_{10}H_{16}O\,(OC_2H_5)_2$, results, together with pinole, by the action of alcoholic potash on pinole dibromide It forms hard needles when recrystallized from ether, and melts at 52° to 53°.

Anhydride of cis-pinole glycol[5] **(cis-pinole oxide),** $C_{10}H_{16}O_2$, is produced by the action of sodium methylate on the dibromide of

[1] Wallach, Ber, *28*, 2708

[2] Wallach, Ann Chem, *259*, 311, *268*, 222

[3] Wallach, Ann Chem, *281*, 149

[4] Wallach and Otto, Ann. Chem, *253*, 260

[5] Wallach and Guericke, Ann Chem, *291*, 342

cis-pinole hydrate. It is an oil, which boils at 206° to 207°, and at 82° under a pressure of 12 mm.; it has the specific gravity 1.0335 and the refractive index, $n_D = 1.4588$, at 20°. It is a saturated compound, and hydrolysis converts it into *cis*-pinole glycol (m. p. 124°); it is, therefore, a true anhydride of the latter compound.

Cis-pinole glycol anhydride is also described by Wagner[1] under the name *cis-pinole oxide;* he obtained it as one of the products formed during the action of hypochlorous acid on levo-pinene and subsequent treatment with potassium hydroxide. It boils at 206° to 208°, is optically inactive, or in some cases feebly levorotatory, and is immediately converted into the corresponding inactive *cis*-pinole glycol (m. p. 124°) by agitation with two per cent. sulphuric acid; the latter yields the diacetate (m. p. 97°), and on oxidation is converted into terpenylic acid.

The anhydride is also produced by the action of potassium hydroxide at the ordinary temperature on *cis*-pinole glycol-1-chlorhydrin.[2]

Cis-pinole glycol-1-chlorhydrin,[2] $C_{10}H_{16}OCl(OH)$, is formed by the action of hypochlorous acid on pinole; it crystallizes from petroleum ether in long needles, melts at 52° to 54° and is readily soluble in the usual organic solvents and water. Its aqueous solution soon gives an acid reaction. Potassium hydroxide converts it into the anhydride of cis-pinole glycol. Oxidation with chromic acid at 0° converts this chlorhydrin into a *chloroketone*, $C_{10}H_{15}$-ClO_2, which crystallizes in long needles, melts at 74° to 75.5°, and yields a *hydrazone*, melting at 107° to 108°.

Cis-pinole glycol-2-chlorhydrin, $C_{10}H_{16}OCl(OH)$, is another compound, which Wagner obtained by treating turpentine oil with hypochlorous acid and subsequent treatment of the product with potash. It separates from acetic ether in large, transparent, rhombic crystals. The chlorhydrin prepared from French turpentine oil (levo-pinene) melts at 131° to 132°, and is dextrorotatory, $[\alpha]_D = + 88° 23'$; that obtained from dextro-pinene melts at the same temperature, but is levorotatory, $[\alpha]_D = - 87° 39'$. When equal weights of the two active derivatives are crystallized from petroleum ether, the *inactive* modification results, which melts at 104° to 105°.

It is not readily acted upon by aqueous alkali, but after long-continued boiling it is converted into *cis*-pinole glycol (m. p. 123° to 124°).

[1] Wagner and Slawinski, Ber., *32*, 2065.

[2] A. Ginzberg, Journ. Russ. Chem. Soc., *30*, 681; Wagner and Slawinski, Ber., *32*, 2073.

When this chlorhydrin is heated with zinc dust and alcohol on the water-bath for three weeks, it yields pinole as the only product; when this pinole is oxidized in the cold with dilute permanganate, it yields a dextrorotatory glycol which Wagner terms *d-cis-trans-pinole glycol*, $C_{10}H_{18}O_3$. This compound melts at 73° to 74.5°, is dextrorotatory, $[\alpha]_D = +8° 20'$ (one decimeter tube, alcoholic solution), and is readily soluble in ether and ethyl acetate; on oxidation with permanganate, it yields acetic, terpenylic, and terebic acids. The pinole from which it is derived is probably the optically active modification of ordinary pinole, although it combines with two atoms of bromine, yielding the inactive pinole dibromide (m. p. 94°).

Cis-menthane-1, 2-dichlor-6, 8-diol, $C_{10}H_{18}O_2Cl_2$, is also formed during the reaction of hypochlorous acid upon pinene; it crystallizes from boiling ether in small crystals, and melts at 136° to 137°. In contrast to the monochlorhydrin (m. p. 131° to 132°), this dichlorhydrin readily loses its chlorine atoms when warmed with aqueous potash, and is converted into the anhydride of *cis*-pinole glycol. It is also acted upon by cold, aqueous potash solution, yielding the anhydride of *cis*-pinole glycol and a new crystalline, saturated *chlorhydrin*, which, however, has not yet been carefully investigated; the latter compound is further formed in small quantity by the action of hypochlorous acid on pinene.

When the dichlorhydrin is treated with zinc dust and alcohol, it yields limonene (?) and pinole hydrate (m. p. 129° to 129.5°).

Cis-sobrerytrite (menthane-1, 2, 6, 8-tetrol), $C_{10}H_{20}O_4$, is formed during the action of hypochlorous acid upon pinene. It is sparingly soluble in ether, but dissolves readily in alcohol or water; it has a sweet taste, is optically inactive, and melts at 193° to 194°. Potassium permanganate oxidizes it, yielding terpenylic and acetic acids.

This compound is also produced when *cis*-pinole glycol is treated with a glacial acetic acid solution of hydrogen bromide, and the resulting bromine derivative is treated with aqueous sodium hydroxide. It is isomeric with the *cis-trans*-sobrerytrite obtained in the oxidation of inactive pinole hydrate; both isomerides are optically inactive, but are characterized by different melting points, and by the fact that the *cis-trans*-derivative easily forms a *hydrate*, $C_{10}H_{20}O_4 + 2H_2O$, while the *cis*-modification does not.

Nopinole glycol, $C_{10}H_{18}O_3$, a product of the action of hypochlorous acid on pinene, melts at 126° to 127° and is a derivative of an isomeride of pinene, while the preceding compounds may be regarded as derivatives of ordinary pinene. Its *diacetate* is an oil. Oxidation converts it into formic acid and a non-volatile, syrupy acid, no acetic or terpenylic acid being produced.

Pinole bisnitrosochloride,[1] $(C_{10}H_{16}O)_2N_2O_2Cl_2$, is formed when six cc. of fuming hydrochloric acid are very gradually added to a well cooled mixture of five cc. of pinole, seven cc. of amyl nitrite, and ten cc. of glacial acetic acid; the liquid assumes a deep blue color, and the bisnitroso-compound separates slowly as a white, crystalline precipitate. It is filtered and purified by washing with methyl alcohol and ether. It melts at 103° when heated slowly, but on rapid heating the melting point of 116° to 120° is found.

It is almost insoluble in methyl alcohol, but dissolves in chloroform or benzene, the solution having a blue color at the ordinary temperature, becoming darker on heating. A dry solution of this chloride in chloroform is colorless at —12°, becoming blue as the temperature rises, and is again colorless on strong cooling. The pure bisnitrosochloride forms a colorless solution at low temperatures, but on dissociation with rise in temperature, yields the mono-molecular derivative, $C_{10}H_{16}NOCl$, which dissolves in chloroform forming a blue colored solution. The same assumption may be made with many other colorless nitrosochlorides which dissolve, forming blue colored solutions.

When pinole bisnitrosochloride is allowed to stand for a long time, it is partially converted into an isomeride, pinole isonitrosochloride, which is soluble in methyl alcohol.

Pinole isonitrosochloride,[2] $C_{10}H_{16}O \cdot NOCl$, is produced, as above mentioned, by the slow spontaneous change of the dimolecular compound. Thus, if an old specimen of the bisnitrosochloride is treated with methyl alcohol, the iso-compound is dissolved, and is obtained in splendid crystals.

It is more readily prepared by saturating a solution of the bisnitrosochloride in ethyl acetate with hydrogen chloride; on evaporation of the solvent, the isonitrosochloride separates in well defined crystals, which dissolve in acetic ether forming a colorless solution, and crystallize in colorless, transparent prisms. It melts at 131°, becoming brown and decomposing at 150°; it is a monomolecular compound. It reacts with bases (aniline, piperidine, β-naphthylamine, etc.), forming nitrolamines which are identical with those obtained from pinole bisnitrosochloride (see below).

[1]Wallach and Otto, Ann. Chem., *253*, 260; Wallach and Sieverts, Ann. Chem., *306*, 278.

[2]Wallach and Sieverts, Ann. Chem., *306*, 279.

When the bisnitrosochloride or the isonitrosochloride is heated with alcohols, the chlorine atom is replaced by the oxy-alkyl group, yielding the following compounds.

Methoxyl-derivative,

$$C_{10}H_{15}\begin{cases}NOH\\OCH_3\end{cases}$$

forms well defined crystals, and melts at 138°.

Ethoxyl-derivative,

$$C_{10}H_{15}\begin{cases}NOH\\OC_2H_5\end{cases}$$

crystallizes in prisms, and melts at 100°.

Benzoyl chloride reacts with the pinole nitrosochlorides forming *benzoyl*-derivatives.

When the nitrosochlorides are treated with sodium ethylate, a white, amorphous *compound* is formed.

Ammonia or organic bases readily convert pinole bisnitrosochloride into the following nitrolamines, all of which were prepared by Wallach and Otto.[1] Since the same compounds are also derived from pinole isonitrosochloride, it is probable that, in contact with bases, the bisnitrosochloride is at first changed into the monomolecular isonitrosochloride, which then gives rise to the nitrolamines. It is also probable that a similar change takes place in all cases in which *bis*-nitrosochlorides are converted into nitrolamines, since, according to the observations so far reported, the nitrolamines are always monomolecular compounds (Wallach[2]).

Pinole nitrolamine, $C_{10}H_{16}O \cdot NO \cdot NH_2$, is produced when pinole nitrosochloride is treated with excess of alcoholic ammonia; the mixture becomes warm, ammonium chloride is thrown out and filtered off, and pinole nitrolamine hydrochloride separates from the cold filtrate, while the free base remains dissolved in the alcohol. Wallach and Otto did not isolate the free amine, but analyzed its hydrochloric acid salt, $C_{10}H_{18}N_2O_2 \cdot HCl$, which crystallizes well from water or dilute alcohol.

Pinole nitrolpiperidide, $C_{10}H_{16}O \cdot NO \cdot NC_5H_{10}$, is formed by gently warming one molecule by weight of the nitrosochloride with a solution of two molecules of piperidine in alcohol; after diluting the reaction-product with water the base separates as an oil, which quickly solidifies, and, on recrystallization from alcohol, melts at 154°.

[1] Wallach and Otto, Ann. Chem., *253*, 260.
[2] Wallach and Sieverts, Ann. Chem., *306*, 281.

The hydrochloride is precipitated from an ethereal solution of the base, and is very readily soluble in water.

Pinole nitrolbenzylamine, $C_{10}H_{16}O \cdot NO \cdot NHCH_2C_6H_5$, crystallizes from ether in well defined, transparent prisms, which become opaque on standing in the air; it melts at 135° to 136°. It separates from alcoholic solutions with one molecule of alcohol of crystallization.

Pinole nitrolanilide, $C_{10}H_{16}O \cdot NO \cdot NHC_6H_5$, is easily soluble in alcohol and ether, and forms brilliant plates, melting at 174° to 175°. When the base is dissolved in warm hydrochloric acid, the hydrochloride results and crystallizes from the cold solution; this salt loses a part of its hydrogen chloride on continued exposure to the air.

Pinole nitrol- β**-naphthylamide,** $C_{10}H_{16}O \cdot NO \cdot NHC_{10}H_7$.—This base is only sparingly soluble in warm alcohol, but is readily purified by recrystallization from alcoholic ether, and melts at 194° to 195°; solutions of the free amine and its salts are highly fluorescent. This compound is isomeric with quinine.

Oxidation of Pinole.

According to Wagner,[1] the first product of the oxidation of pinole with a one per cent. solution of potassium permanganate at about 0° is *cis-trans*-pinole glycol; if a more concentrated solution be used, there are formed, in addition to pinole glycol, terpenylic acid and a trace of terebic acid.

Wallach[2] showed that pinole is oxidized by warm, relatively concentrated potassium permanganate solution, as well as by dilute nitric acid, yielding terebic acid (m. p. 175° to 176°), together with oxalic acid and carbonic acid. On the other hand, pinole hydrate and pinole glycol give terpenylic acid, when oxidized with permanganate.

21. EUDESMOLE, $C_{10}H_{16}O$.

A compound, $C_{10}H_{16}O$, which apparently contains neither a hydroxyl- nor a ketone group, was discovered by Smith[3] in the oil of *Eucalyptus piperita*. Although a very complete investigation of this compound has not yet been made, it seems probable

[1] Wagner, Ber., *27*, 1645.

[2] Wallach and Otto, Ann. Chem., *253*, 256; Wallach, Ann. Chem., *259*, 317; Ber., *28*, 2708.

[3] Baker and Smith, Journ. and Proc. of the Royal Soc. of N. S. Wales; *32*, 104; *33*, 86; Semi-Annual Report of Schimmel & Co., April, *1900*, 27.

that the substance is an unsaturated oxide, and is called eudesmole.

Its presence has been determined in the oils of *Eucalyptus piperita, goniocalyx, camphora, smithii, macrorrhyncha, stricta* and *elæophora.*

Eudesmole is best obtained by the fractional distillation of the oil of *Eucalyptus macrorrhyncha;* the fractions boiling up to 190°, which contain a trace of phellandrene and cineole, are removed, and, on cooling, the crude eudesmole separates from the residue as a butter-like, crystalline mass. It is purified by pressing on porous plates and repeatedly crystallizing from dilute alcohol.

PROPERTIES.—Eudesmole crystallizes from dilute alcohol in white, very fine needles, which melt at 79° to 80°; it boils at 270° to 272°. It is insoluble in water and aqueous alkali solutions, but dissolves readily in the usual organic solvents; it sublimes easily, and is optically inactive. It fails to give the characteristic reactions of alcohols and ketones, and for this reason alone it is classified in this book as an oxide. It is an unsaturated compound.

Eudesmole dibromide, $C_{10}H_{16}O \cdot Br_2$, is formed on adding one molecular proportion of bromine to a cold solution of eudesmole in glacial acetic acid; the dibromide separates in a hard, plastic mass, which can not be obtained in a crystalline condition. It melts at 55° to 56°.

Dinitroeudesmole, $C_{10}H_{14}(NO_2)_2O$, is produced by the action of cold, concentrated nitric acid on eudesmole. It melts at 90°, is soluble in alcohol, ether and acetone, but is not crystalline.

When eudesmole is oxidized with dilute nitric acid, an acid, melting at 165° to 168°, is formed; it is possibly inactive camphoronic acid.

C. SUBSTANCES WITHOUT AN ETHYLENE LINKAGE.

(KETONES, $C_{10}H_{18}O$, ALCOHOLS, $C_{10}H_{19}OH$, AND $C_{10}H_{18}(OH)_2$, OXIDES, $C_{10}H_{18}O$, etc.).

1. TETRAHYDROCARVONE (CARVOMENTHONE), $C_{10}H_{18}O$.

Tetrahydrocarvone has the constitutional formula:

CH_3
CH
H_2C CO
H_2C CH_2
CH
CH
H_3C CH_3

It is known in two optically active modifications which are obtained, together with optically active tetrahydrocarveol and tetrahydrocarvylamine, when phellandrene nitrosite is reduced with sodium and alcohol.[1] Inactive tetrahydrocarvone is formed when equal portions of dextro- and levo-tetrahydrocarvone are united. The inactive modification is also obtained as a product of the oxidation of tetrahydrocarveol (carvomenthol), $C_{10}H_{19}OH$. It should be mentioned here that tetrahydrocarveol may be obtained by three different methods: from solid terpineol (m. p. 35°) (Wallach), from carvotanacetone (Semmler, Wallach), and from carvone (Baeyer).

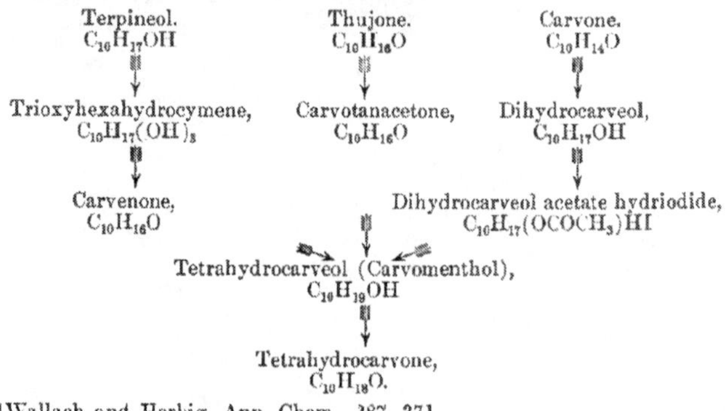

[1] Wallach and Herbig, Ann. Chem., *287*, 371.

Only inactive tetrahydrocarvone can be prepared from terpineol and carvotanacetone, but the method proposed by Baeyer by means of carvone renders possible the formation of optically active modifications.[1]

In order to prepare it, Baeyer[2] oxidizes tetrahydrocarveol with Beckmann's chromic acid mixture, whilst Wallach[3] recommends a solution of chromic anhydride in glacial acetic acid as the oxidizing agent. The resultant tetrahydrocarvone is distilled in a current of steam, and is purified by conversion into its acid sodium sulphite compound (Baeyer), or into its oxime or semicarbazone[4] which may be reconverted quantitatively into pure tetrahydrocarvone by warming with dilute sulphuric acid.

PROPERTIES.—Tetrahydrocarvone is an oil, which smells more like carvone than menthone. According to Baeyer, it boils at 222° to 223° (corr.). According to Wallach, it boils at 220° to 221°, has a specific gravity of 0.904 at 20°, and a specific refractive power, $n_D = 1.45539$.

It is relatively stable towards permanganate. Its acid sulphite compound is decomposed into its components by cold water. In a moist ethereal solution carvomenthone is reduced by sodium to the corresponding alcohol, tetrahydrocarveol.

According to Baeyer and Oehler,[5] when tetrahydrocarvone is gently oxidized at 40° with potassium permanganate, 5-isopropylheptan 2-onic acid (m. p. 40°) is formed :—

$$\begin{array}{l} CH_3CO \cdot CH_2 \cdot CH_2 \cdot \underset{\displaystyle CH(CH_3)_2}{\underset{|}{C}H}—CH_2—COOH. \end{array}$$

By more vigorous action with hot permanganate solution, this acid is converted into isopropyl succinic acid, which melts at 114° to 115°. The oxime of isopropyl heptanonic acid melts at 75° to 78°, and is formed, together with *bisnitrosotetrahydrocarvone*,[6] $C_{20}H_{34}N_2O_4$, melting at 119° with decomposition, by the action of amyl nitrite and hydrochloric acid on tetrahydrocarvone.

When bisnitrosotetrahydrocarvone is treated with ethereal hydrogen chloride, it yields *tetrahydrocarvone bisnitrosylic acid*, $C_{10}H_{18}N_2O_3$, and a *chlorinated ketone*, $C_{10}H_{17}ClO$; the bisnitrosylic acid crystallizes in leaflets and melts at 82° ; its *oxime* is also formed in the same reaction and melts at 75° to 77°.

[1] Baeyer, Ber., *28*, 1586.
[2] Baeyer, Ber., *26*, 822.
[3] Wallach, Ann. Chem., *277*, 133.
[4] Wallach, Ber., *28*, 1955.
[5] Baeyer and Oehler, Ber., *29*, 27.
[6] Baeyer, Ber., *28*, 1588; *29*, 33.

When the chlorinated ketone, $C_{10}H_{17}ClO$, above mentioned, is treated with sodium acetate and acetic acid for the elimination of hydrochloric acid, a ketone, $C_{10}H_{16}O$, is produced, which is called terpenone.

Terpenone,[1] $C_{10}H_{16}O$, is purified by steam distillation; it boils at 233° to 235° and has an odor somewhat similar to that of carvone. It forms a *semicarbazone*, which crystallizes from dilute alcohol in prisms or needles containing water of crystallization, and melts at 222° to 223°.

According to Semmler,[2] when terpenone, $C_{10}H_{16}O$, is oxidized with potassium permanganate, it yields a liquid acid, $C_9H_{16}O_4$, which on further oxidation forms isopropyl succinic acid (m. p. 112°). From its behavior towards oxidizing agents, Semmler regards terpenone as the *pseudo*-ketone corresponding to carvotanacetone; the latter is regarded as an *ortho*-ketone.

Tetrahydrocarvoxime, $C_{10}H_{18}NOH$, is prepared from tetrahydrocarvone in the same manner as carvoxime from carvone. The crude ketone obtained by the oxidation of tetrahydrocarveol is employed, and in order to insure a successful result it is important that this oxidation product should not contain any considerable quantities of tetrahydrocarveol; if, however, a large amount of the latter compound is present, the crude product must be again treated with chromic acid.

Tetrahydrocarvoxime may be recrystallized from dilute alcohol or better from petroleum ether. The inactive modification melts at 105° (Wallach). Optically active tetrahydrocarvoxime crystallizes from dilute alcohol in prisms resembling those of calcite, melts at 97° to 99°, and possesses the opposite rotatory power to that of the phellandrene from which it is prepared (Wallach and Herbig).

When tetrahydrocarvoxime is gently heated with sulphuric acid containing some water, it yields an *aminodecoic acid*, $C_{10}H_{21}O_2N$, which separates from water in small crystals, melting at 201° to 202°; nitrous acid converts it into *decenoic acid*, $C_{10}H_{18}O_2$, which boils at 257° to 260°, has a sp. gr. 0.936, the refractive index, $n_D =$ 1.4554, at 20°, and a molecular refraction, $M = 49.21$ (Wallach[3]).

α-Isotetrahydrocarvoxime, $C_{10}H_{19}NO$, is obtained by treating a chloroform solution of tetrahydrocarvoxime with one molecule by weight of phosphorus pentachloride; when the resultant, energetic reaction is complete, the solution is repeatedly shaken with water, and on evaporation of the chloroform a syrup remains,

[1] Baeyer and Oehler, Ber., *29*, 35.
[2] Semmler, Ber., *33*, 2459.
[3] Wallach, Ann. Chem., *312*, 171.

which solidifies to a crystalline mass. This is dissolved, without regeneration of tetrahydrocarvone, by warming for a short time with dilute sulphuric acid, the oily impurities are separated by filtering through a wet filter paper, and the α-isoxime is precipitated by neutralizing the filtrate with ammonia. Additional amounts may be obtained by extracting the aqueous solution with ether (Wallach). It is very soluble in all solvents, is recrystallized from petroleum ether, and melts at 51° to 52°. It is converted into the β-isoxime by heating above its melting point (to about 100° to 110°).

β-Isotetrahydrocarvoxime, $C_{10}H_{19}NO$, like the α-isoxime, is stable towards warm, dilute sulphuric acid, but is distinguished from the α-compound by being less soluble in all solvents, and by its great power of crystallization. It melts at 104°.

i-Amido-2-hexahydrocymene (tetrahydrocarvylamine), $C_{10}H_{19}NH_2$, is formed when tetrahydrocarvoxime is reduced with sodium and alcohol.

α-Semicarbazone[1] **and β-semicarbazone**[2] **of inactive tetrahydrocarvone** are formed simultaneously; the former melts at 174°, and the latter at 135° to 140°. The *semicarbazone of optically active tetrahydrocarvone* forms hard needles, which melt at 185° to 187° (Wallach and Herbig[3]); according to Baeyer,[4] it melts at 194° to 195°.

Oxymethylene tetrahydrocarvone, $C_{10}H_{16}O = CH(OH)$, is produced by the action of amyl formate and sodium on an ethereal solution of carone. It is optically active (Baeyer[4]).

Condensation-product of tetrahydrocarvone and benzaldehyde,[5] $C_{24}H_{28}O_2$.—A mixture of twenty grams of tetrahydrocarvone and fourteen grams of benzaldehyde are well cooled, and saturated with *dry* hydrochloric acid; the product is allowed to stand for a day, is then washed with soda and ligroine, and the resultant solid compound is dissolved in chloroform. It is further purified by distilling off the chloroform, recrystallizing the residue from ethyl acetate, and then digesting the product for a short time with a solution of sodium ethylate in order to remove the last traces of hydrochloric acid. The pure compound separates from acetic ether in colorless crystals, and melts at 175°. It is almost insoluble in alcohol and ligroine, sparingly soluble in ethyl acetate, and readily soluble in chloroform.

[1] Wallach, Ann. Chem., *286*, 107.
[2] Wallach, Ber., *28*, 1955.
[3] Wallach and Herbig, Ann. Chem., *287*, 371.
[4] Baeyer, Ber., *28*, 1586.
[5] Wallach, Ann. Chem., *305*, 266.

It is formed according to the equation:

$$C_{10}H_{18}O + 2C_6H_5CHO = H_2O + C_{24}H_{28}O_2.$$

It does not unite with the elements of hydrogen chloride; on reduction, it seems to combine with two atoms of hydrogen.

1, 8-Oxybromotetrahydrocarvone,[1] $C_{10}H_{16}Br(OH)O$, is produced in the form of its sodium salt when Wallach's dihydrocarvone dibromide (1, 8-dibromotetrahydrocarvone), $C_{10}H_{15}BrO \cdot HBr$, is diluted with ether and is agitated with sodium hydroxide solution (sp. gr. 1.23) for about one hour; the sodium derivative is decomposed with dilute sulphuric acid, and the oxybromotetrahydrocarvone is rapidly filtered. It is recrystallized from dry ether or a mixture of amylene and petroleum ether, and is obtained in large prisms, melting at 69° to 72°. It is optically active, is readily soluble in most solvents, and is somewhat unstable, being decomposed both by acids and alkalis.

When recrystallized from methyl alcohol, a small quantity of an isomeric substance, melting at 136° to 138°, is obtained.

An optically active *oxycarone*, $C_{10}H_{16}O_2$ is formed by treating oxybromotetrahydrocarvone with methyl alcoholic potash.

The ketone, $C_{10}H_{18}O$, described by Marsh and Hartridge[2] under the name *carvanone*, is probably identical with tetrahydrocarvone.

For the action of Caro's reagent upon tetrahydrocarvone, reference must be made to the original publication.[3]

2. TETRAHYDROCARVEOL (CARVOMENTHOL), $C_{10}H_{19}OH$.

Tetrahydrocarveol was first described by Baeyer,[4] and shortly afterward by Wallach.[5] Baeyer obtained it from dihydrocarveol, the alcohol formed by the reduction of carvone. Dihydrocarveol acetate combines with hydriodic acid in a glacial acetic acid solution; when the resultant hydriodide is washed with water, extracted with ether, and reduced with zinc duct and acetic acid at a temperature not exceeding 25°, tetrahydrocarveol acetate is formed, which, on careful saponification with alcoholic potash, yields tetrahydrocarveol. This is purified by digesting with permanganate, which is added until its color remains permanent for a short time; nevertheless, a product purified in such a manner contains impurities, which decompose by distillation.[6]

[1] Baeyer and Baumgärtel, Ber., *31*, 3208.
[2] Marsh and Hartridge, Journ. Chem. Soc., *73*, 857.
[3] Baeyer and Villiger, Ber., *32*, 3625.
[4] Baeyer, Ber., *26*, 822.
[5] Wallach, Ann. Chem., *277*, 130.
[6] Baeyer, Ber., *26*, 2558.

Wallach's method of preparation of tetrahydrocarveol is more convenient. He employs carvenone, $C_{10}H_{16}O$, which is obtained, together with cymene, when trioxyhexahydrocymene (formed by oxidation of terpineol, melting at 35°) is heated with dilute sulphuric acid. Twenty grams of carvenone are dissolved in 100 grams of absolute alcohol, and gradually treated with twenty grams of metallic sodium. The reaction-product is distilled with steam, the oil is separated, dried with potash, and purified by repeated fractional distillations. It boils at 218° to 220°.

The product obtained by Semmler[1] in the reduction of carvotanacetone, $C_{10}H_{16}O$, with alcohol and sodium is identical with tetrahydrocarveol. This compound, designated by Semmler as *tetrahydrocarvotanacetone*, boils at 219° to 220°, has the sp. gr. 0.9014, and refractive index, $n_D = 1.4685$. (Compare with Wallach.[2])

Optically active tetrahydrocarveol is also formed in the reduction of phellandrene nitrosite with sodium and alcohol[3] (see tetrahydrocarvone).

Wallach[4] prepares pure tetrahydrocarveol by reduction of pure tetrahydrocarvone with sodium and alcohol; it boils at 220°, has the specific gravity of 0.900 and refractive power, $n_D = 1.46246$, at 23°.

The odor of tetrahydrocarveol is very similar to that of terpineol and of dihydrocarveol. It is a very thick liquid at ordinary temperature, and becomes hard, brittle and vitreous, but not crystalline, on cooling with a mixture of solid carbonic anhydride and ether. It is perceptibly soluble in water, and is capable of uniting with it. Chromic anhydride converts it into tetrahydrocarvone.

Carvomenthene, $C_{10}H_{18}$, is prepared by warming tetrahydrocarveol with acid potassium sulphate; it boils at 175° to 176° (Wallach). It is also formed when the bromide, $C_{10}H_{19}Br$, obtained by the action of warm, concentrated hydrobromic acid on tetrahydrocarveol, is heated with quinoline (Baeyer, and Kondakoff and Lutschinin).

Tetrahydrocarvyl phenylurethane, $C_{10}H_{19}O{\cdot}CO{\cdot}NHC_6H_5$, is produced when pure tetrahydrocarveol is allowed to stand for one day with one molecular proportion of carbanile; the reaction-product is washed with petroleum ether, and crystallized from a mixture of ether and petroleum ether; it separates in needles, and

[1] Semmler, Ber., 27, 895.
[2] Wallach, Ber., 28, 1955.
[3] Wallach and Herbig, Ann. Chem., 287, 371.
[4] Wallach, Ann. Chem., 277, 130; Kondakoff and Lutschinin, Journ. pr. Chem., 60 [II.], 257.

melts at 74° to 75°. It dissolves very readily in alcohol and ether (Wallach[1]).

Tetrahydrocarvyl acetate (carvomenthyl acetate[2]), $C_{10}H_{19}O \cdot CO$-CH_3, boils at 235° to 238° under a pressure of 761 mm., and at 105° to 107° at 11 mm. It is a colorless, fairly mobile liquid having a faint odor of cherries; it has the specific gravity 0.9280 at 22°/4°, a refractive index, $n_D = 1.45079$, a molecular refraction, $M = 57.42$, and a specific rotatory power, $[\alpha]_D = + 4° 7'$.

Tetrahydrocarvyl chloride,[2] $C_{10}H_{19}Cl$, is a colorless liquid having the odor of menthyl chloride; it boils at 90° to 95° (15 mm.), and at 82° to 85° (11 mm.). It is optically inactive, has a specific gravity 0.9450 at 21°/4°, a refractive index, $n_D = 1.46534$, at 21°, and a molecular refraction, $M = 50.48$.

Tetrahydrocarvyl bromide,[2] $C_{10}H_{19}Br$, is colorless, boils at 95° to 99° (10 mm.), has a specific gravity 1.1870 at 21°, a refractive index, $n_D = 1.49060$, at 21°/21°, and a molecular refraction, $M = 53.39$.

The properties of carvomenthyl chloride and bromide are almost identical with those of carvomenthene hydrochloride and hydrobromide.

When carvomenthyl chloride or bromide is treated with moist silver oxide, tertiary carvomenthol is formed, together with a small quantity of a *compound*, $C_{10}H_{22}O_3$, which crystallizes in slender needles, and melts at 101° to 102°.

"**Carvanol,**"[3] $C_{10}H_{20}O$, a compound obtained by the reduction of "*carvenol*," $C_{10}H_{16}O$, is probably identical with tetrahydrocarveol; on oxidation "carvanol" is converted into "*carvanone*" (tetrahydrocarvone), $C_{10}H_{18}O$.

3. TETRAHYDROEUCARVONE, $C_{10}H_{18}O$.

When dihydroeucarvoxime hydriodide, $C_{10}H_{16}NOH \cdot HI$, is reduced with zinc dust and an alcoholic solution of hydrogen chloride at 0°, it is converted into the ketone, tetrahydroeucarvone.[4] It is freed from unsaturated compounds by treatment with potassium permanganate. The pure ketone boils at 108° to 115° under a pressure of 20 mm.

It yields a liquid *oxime*, $C_{10}H_{18}NOH$.

Its *semicarbazone*, $C_{10}H_{18} = N \cdot NH \cdot CO \cdot NH_2$, crystallizes from ethyl acetate in fine needles, melts at 191°, and is sparingly soluble in ether and ethyl acetate.

[1] Wallach, Ann. Chem., *277*, 130.
[2] Kondakoff and Lutschinin, Journ. pr. Chem., 60 [II.], 257.
[3] Marsh and Hartridge, Journ. Chem. Soc., *73*, 857.
[4] Baeyer and Villiger, Ber., *31*, 2067.

Tetrahydroeucarvone is not acted upon by amyl nitrite and hydrochloric acid.

When it is oxidized with the theoretical quantity of a cold, four per cent. potassium permanganate solution, it is partially converted into the *ketonic acid*, $C_{10}H_{18}O_3$; this acid is purified by regeneration from its semicarbazone. It is a liquid acid, and is probably a methyl ketone. Its *semicarbazone*, $C_{10}H_{18}O_2 = N \cdot NH \cdot CO \cdot NH_2$, is sparingly soluble, but crystallizes from warm ethyl acetate in long needles, melting at 191°. Its *oxime*, $C_{10}H_{18}O_2 = NOH$, crystallizes in transparent prisms, which melt at 101° to 102°.

Gem-dimethyl adipic acid, $C_8H_{14}O_4$, is the chief product of the oxidation of tetrahydroeucarvone with cold permanganate; it crystallizes from petroleum ether in prisms, and melts at 87° to 88°.

When tetrahydroeucarvone is oxidized with a warm, fairly concentrated solution of permanganate, it gives rise to a mixture of acetic, oxalic, dimethyl malonic, and *gem*-dimethyl succinic acids.

4. THUJAMENTHONE, $C_{10}H_{18}O$.

On heating thujone at 280°, it is converted into carvotanacetone; this differs from isothujone, and yields carvomenthol (tetrahydrocarveol) by reduction. When thujone is treated with dilute sulphuric acid, it is converted into isothujone; on reduction, this compound forms an alcohol, $C_{10}H_{19}OH$, thujamenthol (dihydroisothujol), which can be very readily distinguished from tetrahydrocarveol (Wallach[1]).

Thujamenthone is obtained by oxidizing thujamenthol in glacial acetic acid solution with chromic anhydride. It is a ketone, and is purified by means of its semicarbazone. It boils at 208° to 209°, has a specific gravity of 0.891 and index of refraction, $n_D = 1.44708$, at 20°. It is optically inactive, and is stable towards a cold solution of potassium permanganate (Wallach).

Thujamenthonoxime, $C_{10}H_{18}NOH$, crystallizes from dilute methyl alcohol in transparent prisms, and melts at 95° to 96°.

Isothujamenthonoxime, $C_{10}H_{19}NO$, is obtained by treating thujamenthonoxime with phosphorus pentachloride; it crystallizes from hot water in long, thin needles, melting at 113° to 114°, and is more readily soluble than the oxime, melting at 95° to 96°. Unlike isomenthonoxime, isothujamenthonoxime is very unstable, and is even reconverted into thujamenthonoxime, melting at 95° to 96°, by standing for some time with water.

Thujamenthone semicarbazone, $C_{10}H_{18} = N \cdot NH \cdot CO \cdot NH_2$, melts at 179°. It is slowly reconverted into thujamenthone by boiling with dilute sulphuric acid.

[1] Wallach, Ber., 28, 1955; Ann. Chem., *286*, 104.

Oxidation of thujamenthone.[1]—When thujamenthone is carefully oxidized with potassium permanganate, it yields the *ketonic acid*, $C_{10}H_{18}O_3$, which boils at 273°, being converted into the keto-lactone, $C_{10}H_{16}O_3$. The *semicarbazone* of the ketonic acid melts at 174.5°. A solution of sodium hypobromite changes the ketonic acid into a *dibasic acid*, $C_9H_{16}O_4$, melting at 134.5°.

The *keto-lactone*, $C_{10}H_{16}O_3$, is produced on oxidizing thujamenthone with chromic acid; it melts at 41°, and yields an *oxime*, melting at 156° (Wallach).

According to Semmler, the above-mentioned ketonic acid boils at 273°, being converted into the preceding keto-lactone, $C_{10}H_{16}O_3$, melting at 43°; the oxime melts at 155°. On oxidation, the keto-lactone gives rise to *β-isopropyl laevulinic acid.*

5. THUJAMENTHOL, $C_{10}H_{19}OH$.

Thujamenthol or dihydroisothujol is obtained by reducing isothujone with sodium and alcohol.[2] It is a viscous liquid, having an odor resembling that of terpineol. It boils at 211° to 213°, has a sp. gr. of 0.895 and a refractive index, $n_D = 1.46345$, at 22°. It yields thujamenthone by oxidation with chromic acid (Wallach[2]).

6. MENTHONE, $C_{10}H_{18}O$.

Menthone has the constitutional formula :—

```
        CH3
        |
        CH
       /  \
   H2C    CH2
   H2C    CO
       \  /
        CH
        |
        CH
       /  \
   H3C    CH3
```

It occurs, together with menthol, esters of menthol, menthene and limonene, in peppermint oil.[3] According to Power and Kleber,[3] the amount of menthone in American oil of peppermint reaches 12.3 per cent. Andres and Andrejew[4] found it in Russian peppermint oil.

The separation of pure menthone from peppermint oil by fractional distillation is impossible, since menthone boils but a few

[1] Wallach, Ber., *30*, 423; Semmler, Ber., *33*, 275.

[2] Wallach, Ber., *28*, 1955.

[3] Schimmel & Co., Semi-Annual Report, April, *1895*, 56.

[4] Andres and Andrejew, Ber., *24*, 560, Ref.; Ber., *25*, 609.

degrees lower than menthol, and cannot, therefore, be separated from the latter compound. It is prepared, however, by oxidation of menthol. In this manner optically inactive menthone was first prepared by Moriya,[1] who heated menthol with potassium chromate and sulphuric acid in a sealed tube at 120° for ten hours. Later, Atkinson and Yoshida[2] succeeded in the preparation of strongly dextrorotatory menthone by repeated treatments of menthol with a chromic acid mixture at 135°; they assumed, therefore, that the product obtained by Moriya contained levo-menthone as an impurity, and that for this reason alone it appeared optically inactive.

The comprehensive experiments of Beckmann[3] have led to a very simple method for the preparation of menthone, and have further shown that its optical behavior is quite unusual. Menthone is very readily inverted by acids, as will be shown later more in detail.

Levo-menthone results by the oxidation of levo-menthol if the action of an excess of acid be avoided as much as possible. Beckmann has suggested the following method. To a solution of sixty grams (one molecule) of potassium dichromate and fifty grams (two and one-half molecules) of concentrated sulphuric acid in 300 grams of water, which is warmed to about 30°, forty-five grams of crystallized menthol are added in one portion; the surface of the mixture immediately assumes a deep black color, due to the formation of a chromium compound. If the mixture be now vigorously shaken, the liquid takes on a dark color, and becomes warm; the menthol at first softens, and is then completely converted into a black, crystalline chromium compound. The oily menthone is not formed until the temperature rises above 53°, which is generally accomplished, without heating, in about thirty minutes; at this point the chromium compound is suddenly decomposed into a brown mass with separation of liquid menthone. If large quantities of menthol are employed, care must be taken to cool the mixture so that the temperature does not rise above 55°.

The menthone forms a dark, oily layer on the cold reaction-product; it is taken up in ether, and agitated successively with water and dilute sodium hydroxide in order to remove the chromium compounds. For further purification, portions of ten to twenty grams of menthone are *rapidly* distilled with steam, the oil is separated, dried over anhydrous sodium sulphate, and rectified.

[1] Moriya, Journ. Chem. Soc., *1881*, 77; Jahresb. Chem., *1881*, 629.

[2] Atkinson and Yoshida, Journ. Chem. Soc., *1882*, 50; Jahresb. Chem., *1882*, 775.

[3] Beckmann, Ann. Chem., *250*, 322; *289*, 362.

Levorotatory menthone, prepared in this way, is a mobile liquid; it does not solidify when placed in a freezing mixture, has a soft, peppermint-like odor, and differs from menthol in its bitter and sharp taste. It boils at 207°, and has the specific gravity 0.896 at 20°. Menthone, regenerated from its semicarbazone, boils at 208°, has a sp. gr. 0.894 and refractive index, $n_D = 1.4496$ (Wallach[1]).

The following specific rotatory powers were obtained for five quantities of menthone prepared at different times, and in each case the menthone contained no menthol:

$$[\alpha]_D = -24.78°, -25.51°, -26.98°, -27.12°, -28.18°.$$

The menthone was prepared by oxidizing menthol according to the above-described method; the menthol melted at 43°, and had a specific rotatory power, $[\alpha]_D = -50.59°$, in a ten per cent. alcoholic solution, and $-49.35°$ in a twenty per cent. solution.

Dextrorotatory menthone is produced by the action of acids on levo-menthone. A mixture of ten parts of concentrated sulphuric acid and one part of water is allowed to stand for some time in a freezing mixture; two parts of levo-menthone are then added and the mixture is gently shaken until the menthone dissolves in the slowly melting acid, forming a yellow liquid. When solution is complete, the temperature is gradually raised to 30° and the reaction-product poured onto ice. The resulting dextro-menthone is immediately extracted with ether and the ethereal solution washed with soda; the menthone is distilled *rapidly* with steam and dried with fused sodium sulphate (Beckmann).

If pure levo-menthone, free from menthol, be employed, the resultant dextro-menthone does not differ from the levo-modification in odor, boiling point, etc. Various preparations showed the specific rotatory powers: $[\alpha]_D = +26.33°, +26.67°$, etc., to $+28.14°$.

An *inactive* product is produced by mixing equal quantities of dextro- and levo-menthone, having rotatory powers of the same degree but of opposite direction; this product, however, must be regarded as a mixture, since, if it be converted into the oxime, pure levo menthonoxime may be isolated.

When levorotatory menthone is treated with dilute sulphuric acid, its levorotatory power diminishes until it reaches zero, and then becomes dextrorotatory to about $+8°$; this change in the rotatory power is dependent on the temperature, time of action and concentration of the acid. If dextrorotatory menthone be treated in the same manner, its dextrorotatory power also di-

[1] Wallach, Ber., 28, 1955.

minishes, and finally reaches a value of about + 8°, which seems to correspond to a condition of equilibrium. The two modifications of menthone suffer similar transformations by the action of dry hydrogen chloride, acetic acid, hot sodium hydroxide solution, cold sodium alcoholate or boiling water. The rotatory powers of the menthones slowly change on standing at the ordinary temperature. Respecting the large number of similar observations of Beckmann, reference must be made to his original publications.

Menthone does not combine with acid sodium sulphite. It is converted into menthol by reduction in a moist ethereal solution with sodium.[1] When levo-menthone is heated with ammonium formate at 190° to 200°, according to Leuckart's method, the product consists chiefly of dextrorotatory menthylamine, $C_{10}H_{19}$-NH_2, together with some of the levorotatory isomeride.[2] Levomenthylamine is also formed by reducing levo-menthonoxime.

When menthone is added in small portions to a cold mixture of phosphorus pentachloride and ligroine, hydrochloric acid is given off, and a *monochloride*, $C_{10}H_{17}Cl$, and a *dichloride*, $C_{10}H_{18}Cl_2$, are obtained. The monochloride boils at 205° to 208°, has the specific gravity at 0° of 0.9833, and is dextrorotatory; it does not lose hydrogen chloride even when boiled with quinoline. The dichloride boils at 150° to 155° under 60 mm. pressure, and has the specific gravity of 1.0824 at 0° (Berkenheim[3]).

According to Jünger and Klages,[4] *chlorotetrahydrocymene*, $C_{10}H_{17}Cl$, is obtained by the action of phosphoric chloride on menthone; by successive treatment with bromine and quinoline it is converted into *chlorodihydrocymene*, $C_{10}H_{15}Cl$, which boils at 210° to 212° under atmospheric pressure. When chlorodihydrocymene is further treated with bromine, and the product is distilled with quinoline, *3-chlorocymene* is produced:

```
          CH₃
          |
          C
        //  \
      HC     CH
       |     ||
      HC     CCl
        \\  /
          C
          |
         C₃H₇
```

3-Chlorocymene.

[1] Beckmann, German patent, No. 42,458; Ber., *21*, 321, Ref.; Ber., *22*, 912.
[2] Wallach, Ber., *24*, 3992; *25*, 3313; Wallach and Kuthe, Ann. Chem., *276*, 296.
[3] Berkenheim, Ber., *25*, 693.
[4] Jünger and Klages, Ber., *29*, 314.

Dibromomenthone,[1] $C_{10}H_{16}Br_2O$, is produced by adding two molecular proportions of bromine to *l*- or *d*-menthone dissolved in chloroform. It separates from alcohol in colorless crystals, melts at 79° to 80°, and is dextrorotatory. It is reconverted into menthone by the action of glacial acetic acid and zinc dust. With hydroxylamine, it yields the *oxime*, $C_{10}H_{16}Br(OH) = NOH$, which melts at 136° to 137°. When the dibromo-compound is heated with boiling quinoline, thymol is formed.

By the action of an excess of bromine on menthone, a crystalline tetrabromo-m-cresol is obtained, together with a *compound*,[2] $C_{10}H_8OBr_6$; the latter melts and decomposes at 148° to 149°.

β-Methyl adipic acid, $C_7H_{12}O_4$, is formed by the oxidation of menthone with potassium permanganate (Manasse and Rupe[3]); it is also obtained, together with the so-called *oxymenthylic acid*, $C_{10}H_{18}O_3$, by oxidation of menthol with potassium permanganate or chromic acid, and, according to Semmler, it is one of the products formed in the oxidation of pulegone. The acid is optically active.

Manasse and Rupe explain the formation of β-methyl adipic acid from menthone by means of the following formulas:

CH₃ | CH | H₂C CH₂ | H₂C CO | CH | CH | H₃C CH₃

Menthone.

→

CH₃ | CH | H₂C CH₂ | H₂C COOH | CO | CH | H₃C CH₃

Oxymenthylic acid, the intermediate ketonic acid.

←

CH₃ | CH | H₂C CH₂ | H₂C COOH | COOH

β-Methyl adipic acid.

[1] Beckmann and Eichelberg, Ber., *29*, 418.

[2] Baeyer and Seuffert, Ber., *34*, 40.

[3] Manasse and Rupe, Ber., *27*, 1820.

Oxymenthylic acid is also formed by oxidizing menthone with chromic acid.[1]

When menthone is oxidized with Caro's reagent (potassium persulphate and concentrated sulphuric acid), it forms the corresponding *ε-lactone*,[2] $C_{10}H_{18}O_2$; it crystallizes from methyl alcohol, and melts at 46° to 48°. It yields an oxy-acid (m. p. 65° to 66°), and a ketonic acid, whose oxime melts at 100° to 102°.

Levo-menthonoxime, $C_{10}H_{18}NOH$, is prepared by the following method (Beckmann[3]). Twenty parts (one molecule) of menthone are dissolved in two and one-half times its amount of ninety per cent. alcohol, and treated with twelve parts (1.3 molecules) of hydroxylamine hydrochloride and a little more than the theoretical quantity of acid sodium carbonate. The reaction takes place in the cold in less than one day, but if the mixture be warmed it is complete in a few minutes. On the addition of water, the oxime separates as an oil which soon solidifies; it is pressed on a plate, recrystallized from dilute alcohol, and melts at 59°. According to Wallach,[4] it boils at 250° to 251°.

If the levo-menthone used in the preparation of the oxime contains menthol, or is partially inverted, liquid products are formed which prevent the immediate separation of the solid oxime; when these oily compounds are cooled, levo-menthonoxime separates in crystals.

Beckmann found the specific rotatory powers of levo-menthonoxime obtained at different times, as:

$$[\alpha]_D = -40.75°, -41.97°, -42.51°.$$

Levo-menthonoxime dissolves in dilute acids and alkalis and may be recovered from these solutions by means of ether. Menthone is formed by allowing the oxime to remain in contact with dilute sulphuric acid for some time, or by boiling its sulphuric acid solution; the rotatory power of this regenerated menthone is, of course, less than that of the ketone from which the oxime was prepared, since a portion of the menthone is inverted by the action of the acid. Concentrated sulphuric acid at 100° converts it into an isomeric compound, melting at 68° to 83°.

The *hydrochloric acid salt of levo-menthonoxime* is precipitated by passing dry hydrogen chloride into an ethereal solution of the oxime; it crystallizes from alcohol in small tablets, which melt at 118° to 119°, and have the specific rotatory power, $[\alpha]_D = -61.16°$. This salt is converted into the levo-oxime by the action of sodium hydroxide.

[1] Beckmann and Mehrländer, Ann. Chem., *289*, 367.

[2] Baeyer and Villiger, Ber., *32*, 3625.

[3] Beckmann, Ann. Chem., *250*, 329.

[4] Wallach, Ann. Chem., *277*, 157.

Dextro-menthonoxime, $C_{10}H_{18}NOH$, is prepared in the same manner as the levo-oxime; it is an oil having a slight levorotatory power: $[\alpha]_D = -4.85°$ to $-6.67°$. Thus, the replacement of the oxygen atom in dextrorotatory menthone by the isonitroso-group (NOH), causes a change in direction of its optical rotation.

Dextro-menthonoxime hydrochloride is prepared like the levo-compound; it melts at 95° to 100°, and is deliquescent. Its specific rotatory power is $[\alpha]_D = -24.83°$.

Levo-menthylamine, $C_{10}H_{19}NH_2$, results by the reduction of levo-menthonoxime with alcohol and sodium.

Several substances derived from levo-menthonoxime have been prepared by Wallach;[1] they are of special interest since they manifestly stand in a close relation to the olefinic members of the terpene series.

Iso-levo-menthonoxime,[1] $C_{10}H_{18}NOH$, is formed when levo-menthonoxime is dissolved in chloroform, and the molecular proportion of phosphorus pentachloride is added to the solution; the product is shaken with water when the reaction is complete. It is also obtained by heating a solution of levo-menthonoxime in acetic anhydride with phosphoric anhydride for a short time. It is, however, more conveniently prepared, when twenty grams of levo-menthonoxime are added slowly at first and then more rapidly, with constant agitation, to forty cc. of cold, concentrated sulphuric acid; the liquid is then warmed very cautiously until all of the oxime is dissolved. The color of the solution changes from yellow to red and brown, and traces of sulphur dioxide are given off; as soon as the brown color appears, the liquid is poured into a limited amount of ice-water. Most of the isoxime separates in small needles, and the residue may be precipitated by neutralization with sodium hydroxide. (Compare with Beckmann and Mehrländer.[2])

It is very readily soluble in methyl and ethyl alcohols, and may be recrystallized from hot water; it melts at 119° to 120°, and boils at 295°. Its specific rotatory power is $[\alpha]_D = -52.25°$. It behaves as a saturated compound, and does not yield menthone when boiled with acids; dehydrating agents convert it into menthonitrile.

It has been mentioned above that when levo-menthonoxime is dissolved in chloroform and treated with phosphorus pentachloride, and the product is then mixed with water, iso-l-menthonox-

[1] Wallach, Ann. Chem., *278*, 302; *277*, 154.

[2] Mehrländer, Inaug. Diss. Breslau, 1887; Beckmann and Mehrländer, Ann. Chem., *289*, 367.

ime is produced; however, if the reaction-product be distilled in vacuum to remove the chloroform and phosphorus oxychloride, and then heated for some time at 100°, a strong base, $C_{20}H_{35}ClN_2$, is obtained. This amine crystallizes in well defined prisms, and melts at 59° to 60°; it is levorotatory, $[\alpha]_D = -186.35°$, and yields stable salts as $C_{20}H_{35}ClN_2 \cdot 2HCl$.

Phosphoric chloride converts dextro-menthonoxime into an *isomeric compound*, melting at 88°; an oily product results, together with the solid substance (Beckmann and Mehrländer [1]).

Menthonitrile, $C_9H_{17}CN$, may be prepared directly from levomenthonoxime by the action of phosphoric anhydride; however, since this reaction takes place very violently, it is better to employ iso-l-menthonoxime. Thirty grams of the latter are dissolved in eighty cc. of chloroform and treated with forty-five grams of phosphorus pentachloride; when the evolution of hydrochloric acid is complete, the chloroform and phosphorus oxychloride are removed by distillation in vacuum. If the residue be heated with the free flame under diminished pressure, hydrogen chloride is split off, and menthonitrile distills over. The reaction takes place in two phases: first, the chlorinated base (m. p. 59° to 60°) is formed from the chloride of iso-l-menthonoxime, and then, at a higher temperature, it is decomposed into menthonitrile and hydrochoric acid:—

$$\text{I. } 2C_{10}H_{18}NCl = HCl + C_{20}H_{35}ClN_2;$$
$$\text{II. } C_{20}H_{35}ClN_2 = HCl + 2C_9H_{17}CN.$$

It can, therefore, be prepared from the pure base, $C_{20}H_{35}ClN_2$. The crude nitrile is washed with sodium hydroxide and purified by distillation with steam. It is an oil, which rotates the plane of polarized light to the left, and boils at 225° to 226°; it has a specific gravity 0.8355 and index of refraction, $n_D = 1.44406$, at 20°.

Menthonitrile differs from iso-l-menthonoxime in behaving as an unsaturated compound; it immediately decolorizes bromine and permanganate. The formation of this nitrile is, therefore, accompanied by a break in the hexamethylene ring; hence, *menthonitrile and its derivatives belong to the fatty series.*

Menthonenic amide,[2] $C_9H_{17}CONH_2$, is produced by boiling menthonitrile with sodium alcoholate for half an hour; it crystallizes from hot water in brilliant leaflets, melts at 105° to 106°, and decolorizes bromine.

Menthonenic (decenoic) acid,[2] $C_9H_{17}COOH$, results by the prolonged action of alcoholic potash on the nitrile or acid amide; it

[1] Beckmann and Mehrländer, Ann. Chem., *289*, 367.
[2] Wallach, Ann. Chem., *296*, 120.

is conveniently prepared on hydrolyzing the nitrile with sodium ethylate in sealed tubes at 120°. It boils at 257° to 261°, has the sp. gr. 0.918 and $n_D = 1.45109$ at 20°; it forms a sparingly soluble *silver salt.* Oxidation with permanganate yields β-methyl adipic acid.

Aminodecoic acid,[1] $C_{10}H_{21}O_2N$, is prepared from menthone isoxime; it separates from water in well formed crystals, melting at 194° to 195°. Nitrous acid converts it into decenoic acid, $C_{10}H_{18}O_2$, which boils at 257° to 259° and is identical with menthonenic acid.

When menthonitrile is reduced in an alcoholic solution with sodium, it yields *menthonylamine,* $C_{10}H_{19}NH_2$, and *oxyhydromenthonylamine,* $C_{10}H_{20}(OH)NH_2$; the former is an aliphatic isomeride of menthylamine. If menthonylamine be treated with nitrous acid, an alcohol, *menthocitronellol,* $C_{10}H_{19}OH$, is formed; when this alcohol is oxidized with chromic acid, an aldehyde, *menthocitronellal,* $C_{10}H_{18}O$, is obtained. *Dimethyl octylene glycol,* $C_{10}H_{20}(OH)_2$, is formed by the action of nitrous acid upon oxyhydromenthonylamine. These substances possess the properties of aliphatic compounds, and bear a close relation to the naturally occurring aliphatic members of the terpene series. They will be described with the aliphatic alcohols and aldehydes.

A *decoic acid,* $C_{10}H_{20}O_2$, an open-chain acid, is formed by heating menthonoxime with an aqueous solution of caustic potash for one hour, at 220° to 230°; it boils at 249° to 251°, has the sp. gr. 0.905, and the refractive index, $n_D = 1.4373$. Its *amide* crystallizes from water and melts at 108° to 109° (Wallach).

Menthone semicarbazones, $C_{10}H_{18} = N{\cdot}NH{\cdot}CO{\cdot}NH_2$.—The derivative obtained from dextro-menthone melts at 172°, and has the specific rotatory power, $[\alpha]_D = -3°$ (ten per cent. glacial acetic acid solution at 20°); the semicarbazone derived from levomenthone crystallizes from alcohol in small needles, melts at 178°, and has $[\alpha]_D = -3.67°$, under same condition as above. A mixture of the two modifications melts at 175° (Beckmann[2]). According to Wallach,[3] menthone yields a semicarbazone, melting at 184°. Rimini[3] has also obtained a semicarbazone from pernitrosomenthone, which melts at 192° to 193°.

Menthone semioxamazone,[4] $C_{10}H_{18} = N{\cdot}C_2O_2N_2H_3$, crystallizes from alcohol in white needles, and melts at 177°.

[1] Wallach, Ann. Chem., *312*, 171.

[2] Beckmann, Ann. Chem., *289*, 362.

[3] Wallach, Ber., *28*, 1955; compare Rimini, Gazz. Chim., *30* [I.], 600; Beckmann, Ann. Chem., *289*, 366.

[4] Kerp and Unger, Ber., *30*, 585.

Pernitrosomenthone,[1] $C_{10}H_{18}N_2O_2$, is formed by the action of sodium nitrite on an acetic acid solution of menthonoxime; it is an oil, which decomposes at 140° when distilled under diminished pressure. Sulphuric acid and alkalis convert it into menthone. When treated in an alcoholic solution with semicarbazide hydrochloride and sodium acetate, it is converted into a menthone semicarbazone, melting at 192° to 193°.

Bisnitrosomenthone, $[C_{10}H_{17}O(NO)]_2$, results, together with menthoximic acid, when amyl nitrite is added very slowly and with constant agitation to a well cooled mixture of one hundred grams of menthone and twenty-five grams of concentrated hydrochloric acid; after two hours standing the mixture is again treated with twenty-five grams of hydrochloric acid, and, in the course of another two hours, amyl nitrite is continuously added until the total amount of nitrite employed equals seventy-six grams. The thick reaction-product, containing some crystals, is shaken with ice and treated with a dilute solution of sodium hydroxide, which dissolves the menthoximic acid. The nitrosomenthone remains undissolved, and is obtained in a yield of about eight per cent. It is filtered and crystallized from ether; it separates in lustrous needles, and melts at 112.5° (Baeyer and Manasse[2]).

It may also be prepared in a yield of forty per cent. if acetyl chloride be used in place of hydrochloric acid (Baeyer[2]).

Bisnitrosomenthone reacts with alcoholic hydrochloric acid forming *menthobisnitrosylic acid*, which is a crystalline solid, and *monochloromenthone*, which is an oil. When monochloromenthone is distilled with sodium acetate and glacial acetic acid, it gives a ketone, $C_{10}H_{16}O$, which is apparently identical with *menthenone*, obtained by Kremers from nitrosomenthene (Baeyer[3]).

Menthoximic acid, $C_{10}H_{18}O_2 = NOH$, is formed together with bisnitrosomenthone, and is identical with the oxime of oxymenthylic acid, prepared by Beckmann and Mehrländer[4] by the action of hydroxylamine on oxymenthylic acid; the latter acid is a product of the oxidation of menthol. By treatment with dilute acids, menthoximic acid is readily converted into oxymenthylic acid.

According to Baeyer and Manasse, menthoximic acid is produced in a yield of sixty per cent. by the action of amyl nitrite and hydrochloric acid on menthone; they assume that tertiary nitrosomenthone is first formed, which then combines with the

[1]Rimini, Gazz. Chim., *26* [II.], 502; *30* [I.], 600.

[2]Baeyer and Manasse, Ber., *27*, 1912.

[3]Baeyer, Ber., *28*, 1586.

[4]Beckmann and Mehrländer, Ann. Chem., *289*, 367.

elements of water and is converted into menthoximic acid (dimethyl-(2, 6)-oximido-3-octanic acid):

```
     CH3                                   CH3
     |                                     |
     CH                                    CH
    /  \                                  /  \
 H2C    CH2                            H2C    CH2
  |      |        +H2O   ──>            |      |
 H2C    CO                             H2C    COOH
    \  /                                  \
     CNO                                   CNOH
     |                                     |
     CH                                    CH
    /  \                                  /  \
 H3C    CH3                            H3C    CH3
Nitrosomenthone.                      Menthoximic acid.

                     CH3
                     |
                     CH        <──
                    /  \
                 H2C    CH2
                  |      |
                 H2C    COOH
                    \
                     CO
                     |
                     CH
                    /  \
                 H3C    CH3
              Oxymenthylic acid.
```

According to Oehler,[1] menthoximic acid melts at 103°; according to Baeyer and Manasse, it melts at 98.5°.

Oxymethylene menthone,

$$C_8H_{16}\left<\begin{matrix}C{=}CH(OH)\\ |\\ CO\end{matrix}\right.$$

is prepared by the action of sodium and amyl formate on an ethereal solution of menthone; it is a colorless oil, boils at 121° under a pressure of 12 mm. to 13 mm., and has a specific gravity of 1.002 at 15°. It dissolves in alkalis, and decomposes into menthone and the alkali salts of formic acid on boiling its alkaline solutions. It forms a liquid acetyl derivative, boiling at 160° to 162° under 12 mm. to 13 mm. pressure, and a solid benzoyl compound, melting at 75° to 76° (Claisen [2]).

Nitromenthone, $C_{10}H_{17}O(NO_2)$, is formed by heating menthone with nitric acid (sp. gr. 1.075) in a sealed tube. It is a light yellow liquid, boils with slight decomposition at 135° to 140° (15 mm.), and has the sp. gr. 1.059 at 20°/0°. When reduced with tin and hydrochloric acid, it yields *amidomenthone*, $C_{10}H_{17}$-$O{\cdot}NH_2$, which boils at 235° to 237°; it forms *amidomenthonoxime*

[1] Baeyer and Oehler, Ber., *29*, 27.

[2] Claisen, Ann. Chem., *281*, 394.

hydrochloride (m. p. 110°) by the action of an excess of hydroxylamine hydrochloride. Amidomenthonoxime is converted by reduction into a *diamine* (b. p. 240° to 243°), whose *hydrochloride* reacts with potassium nitrite, forming an unsaturated ketone (?), which is possibly isomeric or identical with pulegone.

When amidomenthone is reduced, it yields *amidomenthol*, boiling at 254°.

An *acid*, $C_{10}H_{19}NO_4$, is formed by the action of sodium ethylate on nitromenthone; it boils at 190° to 195° under 13 mm. pressure (Konowaloff[1]).

Benzylidene menthone,[3] $C_{10}H_{16}O = CH{\cdot}C_6H_5$, is readily obtained in the form of its hydrochloride by saturating a mixture of molecular proportions of menthone and benzaldehyde with *dry* hydrochloric acid gas; after standing for about twelve hours in a cold place, the solid hydrochloride is washed with a soda solution to remove excess of hydrogen chloride, is dried, and crystallized from hot alcohol or petroleum ether. On treating the hydrochloride with a solution of sodium ethylate for twenty minutes on the water-bath, benzylidene menthone is obtained; it is a yellow oil, and boils at 188° to 189° under 12 mm. pressure. Its *hydrochloride* $(C_{10}H_{16}O = C_7H_6){\cdot}HCl$, crystallizes from alcohol in white needles, and melts at 140°. The *hydrobromide* is produced by passing hydrogen bromide into a glacial acetic acid solution of benzylidene menthone; it crystallizes well, and melts with decomposition at 115° to 116°.

According to Martine,[2] benzylidene menthone is formed by the action of benzaldehyde on sodium menthylate; it boils at 195° to 196° (15 mm.), has the rotatory power, $[\alpha]_D = +22.8°$ to $+24.3°$, and forms the hydrobromide, melting at 115°.

Benzylidene menthonoxime, $C_{10}H_{16}(NOH) = CH{\cdot}C_6H_5$, crystallizes from alcohol or ether in needles and melts at 161°. On reduction with alcohol and sodium, it gives rise to a base, *benzylidene menthylamine*, $C_{17}H_{23}NH_2$, which boils at 200° to 205° under 10 mm. pressure.

Benzyl menthol,[3] $C_{10}H_{18}(OH){\cdot}CH_2{\cdot}C_6H_5$, is produced by the reduction of benzylidene menthone or its hydrochloride with sodium and alcohol; it separates as a thick oil, boiling at 181° to 183° (10 mm.). After standing during several months, a small portion of this oil solidifies, and, after recrystallization from ether, forms colorless crystals, melting at 111° to 112°. Both oil and crystals

[1]Konowaloff, Compt. rend., *121*, 652; Ber., *31*, 1478.

[2]Martine, Compt. rend., *133*, 41.

[3]Wallach, Ann. Chem., *305*, 261; Ber., *29*, 1595; compare Martine, Compt. rend., *133*, 41.

have the same composition, $C_{17}H_{25}OH$, and are probably two physical-isomeric modifications of the same compound. When treated with phosphorus pentoxide, benzyl menthol yields a hydrocarbon, *methyl isopropyl hexahydrofluorene*, $C_{17}H_{24}$, boiling at 153° to 155° (10 mm.).

Benzyl menthone, $C_{17}H_{24}O$, results on the oxidation of benzyl menthol in glacial acetic acid solution with chromic acid; it is a viscous oil, boils at 177° to 179° (10 mm.), and yields an oily *oxime;* on reduction, this oxime gives rise to *benzyl menthylamine.*

Menthone pinacone,[1] $C_{20}H_{38}O_2$, is formed on reducing menthone in ethereal solution with sodium; it melts at 94°.

When menthone in an absolute ethereal solution is treated with sodium wire, and is then saturated with carbon dioxide, a mixture of products is obtained, which contains, besides unchanged menthone and menthol, menthone pinacone, menthone carboxylic and dicarboxylic acids.[2]

Menthone carboxylic acid, $C_{10}H_{17}O{\cdot}COOH$, is a heavy, colorless oil, is sparingly soluble in water, and its solution gives a violet coloration with ferric chloride; when heated with dilute sulphuric acid, it is reconverted into menthone. Its *silver salt* is a white solid.

On treating the acid with nitrous acid at ordinary temperature, *isonitrosomenthone*, $C_{10}H_{16}O(NOH)$, and an *ortho-diketone*, $C_{10}H_{16}O_2$, are formed; the former is an oil, is soluble in alkalis, and yields *menthone amine*, $C_{10}H_{17}O{\cdot}NH_2$, on reduction with zinc dust and acetic acid; the ortho-diketone is a reddish oil, insoluble in alkalis.

Menthone dicarboxylic acid, $C_{10}H_{16}O(COOH)_2$, melts and decomposes at 140° to 141°.

It should be mentioned that Flatau and Labbé[3] separated a ketone, boiling at 204° to 206°, from Bourbon geranium oil; they called this ketone "*a-menthone.*" It yields a semicarbazone, melting at 180°. It will probably be safe to regard "*a*-menthone" as identical with ordinary levo-menthone, until a more complete investigation shall prove to the contrary.

A ketone, $C_{10}H_{18}O$, was obtained by Kondakoff[4] from the ethereal oil of buchu leaves; this ketone is called *ketomenthone.* It is a colorless liquid with a peppermint-like odor; it boils at 208.5° to 209.5° under 760 mm. pressure, has the sp. gr. 0.9004 at 19°/19°,

[1] Beckmann, Journ. pr. Chem., *55* [II.], 14.

[2] Oddo, Gazz. Chim., *27* [II.], 97.

[3] Flatau and Labbé, Bull. Soc. Chim., *19* [III.], 788; compare Schimmel & Co., Semi-Annual Report, Oct., *1898*, 52.

[4] Kondakoff, Journ. pr. Chem., *54* [II.], 433; Kondakoff and Bachtschéeff, Journ. pr. Chem., *63* [II.], 49.

the optical rotation, $[\alpha]_D = -16°6'$, the index of refraction, $n_D = 1.45359$, and molecular refraction, 46.28. Its *oxime* is liquid and optically active.

When ketomenthone is reduced in methyl alcoholic solution with sodium, it yields a solid and a liquid *menthol*, $C_{10}H_{19}OH$. The solid menthol crystallizes in needles, melts at 38.5° to 39°, has the sp. gr. 0.9006 at 32°/32°, and the index of refraction, $n_D = 1.45869$, at 32°; its *benzoate* melts at 82°. When this menthol is treated with phosphoric oxide, it is converted into a *menthene*, $C_{10}H_{18}$, which boils at 166.5° to 168.5° (785 mm.), has the sp. gr. 0.8112 at 19°, $n_D = 1.45109$, and $[\alpha]_D = -13°46'$.

The isomeric, liquid menthol boils at 106.5° to 109° (18 mm.), has the sp. gr. 0.9041 at 21.6°, $n_D = 1.461793$, and $[\alpha]_D = +26°30'$; it yields a levorotatory menthene.

Neither of these isomeric menthols appears to be identical with the natural menthol.

Sym-menthone[1] **(1,3-methylisopropyl cyclohexanone-5)**, $C_{10}H_{18}O$, is formed by oxidizing *sym*-menthol with chromic acid; it is a colorless oil of peppermint-like odor, and readily forms a crystalline derivative with acid sodium sulphite. It boils at 222° (749 mm.), has the sp. gr. 0.9040 at 18°/4°, the refractive index, $n_D = 1.45359$, at 18°, and the molecular refraction, $R = 45.98$. Its *semicarbazone* crystallizes from benzene and melts at 176° to 177°.

7. MENTHOL, $C_{10}H_{19}OH$.

Menthol,[2] formerly designated as "*mentha camphor*," or "*peppermint camphor*," occurs, together with menthone, menthene and terpenes, in peppermint oil. It is deposited in crystals when the essential oil is cooled; for its preparation, however, it is better to first distill off the terpenes and menthene, and then cool the remaining oil.

When menthone, $C_{10}H_{18}O$, is reduced in the presence of an excess of nascent hydrogen, as with sodium and alcohol or water, menthol is the only product; but with sodium and solvents which do not themselves liberate hydrogen, as absolute ether, some *menthone pinacone*, $C_{20}H_{38}O_2$, is formed, together with menthol.[3] Levo- and dextro-menthone yield by both methods a strongly levorotatory mixture of menthols. From this mixture the natural

[1] Knoevenaugel and Wiedermann, Ann. Chem., *297*, 169.

[2] Oppenheim, Ann. Chem., *120*, 350; *130*, 176; Journ. pr. Chem., *91*, 502; Gorup-Besanez, Ann. Chem., *119*, 245; Beckett and Wright, Journ. Chem. Soc., *1* [2], 1; Ber., *1875*, 1466; Charabot, Compt. rend., *130*, 518.

[3] Beckmann, Journ. pr. Chem., *55* [II.], 14.

levo-menthol (m. p. 43°), and a dextrorotatory *isomenthol* (m. p. 78° to 81°, $[\alpha]_D = +2°$) may be separated.

Menthol and menthone may be separated by converting the latter into its oxime, extracting with ether, evaporating the extract, and again extracting with dilute sulphuric acid. This removes the menthone in the form of its oxime, and leaves the menthol; it does not give rise to a transformation into optical isomerides (Beckmann).

Menthol is readily prepared when an ethereal solution of menthone is treated successively with sodium and water, these operations being repeated several times. By this method it is possible to convert the menthone, occurring together with menthol in peppermint oil, into menthol, thus considerably increasing the yield of the latter compound (Beckmann[1]).

Menthol is also formed in the reduction of pulegone,[2] $C_{10}H_{16}O$.

It crystallizes in colorless, brilliant prisms, which have a strong smell of peppermint, and a burning taste; it melts at 43°, boils at 212°, and possesses a specific gravity of 0.890 at 15°. Its molecular refractive power[3] is 47.52, and its heat of combustion[4] equals 1509.1 calorimetric units (for one molecule expressed in grams). Menthol obtained from peppermint oil is optically levorotatory, $[\alpha]_D = -59° 6'$.

Chromic acid converts menthol into menthone. Phosphoric anhydride, zinc chloride, potassium bisulphate, etc., dehydrate it, forming menthene, $C_{10}H_{18}$; this hydrocarbon is more readily prepared by distilling menthyl chloride with quinoline. According to Beckmann,[5] menthene also results by the action of concentrated sulphuric acid on menthol, whilst Wagner[6] finds that this reaction gives rise to a polymeric product, $C_{20}H_{36}$, together with cymene sulphonic acid and hexahydrocymene (menthane), $C_{10}H_{20}$. The transformation of menthol into cymene may be effected by heating with anhydrous copper sulphate at 250° to 280° (Brühl[7]). Hexahydrocymene ("*menthonaphthene*"), $C_{10}H_{20}$, is produced by heating menthol with hydriodic acid and red phosphorus at 200°; it boils at 169° to 170.5° (Berkenheim[8]).

Potassium permanganate oxidizes menthol, forming oxymenthylic (ketomenthylic) acid, $C_{10}H_{18}O_3$, carbonic, formic, propionic

[1] Beckmann, German Patent, No. 42,458; Ber., *22*, 912.

[2] Beckmann and Pleissner, Ann. Chem., *262*, 1.

[3] Brühl, Ber., *21*, 457.

[4] Luginin, Ann. Chim. Phys. [5], *23*, 387.

[5] Beckmann, Ann. Chem., *250*, 358.

[6] G. Wagner, Ber., *27*, 1637; St. Tolloczko, Chem. Centr., *1895* [I.], 543; *1898* [I.], 105.

[7] Brühl, Ber., *24*, 3374.

[8] Berkenheim, Ber., *25*, 686.

and butyric acids, together with the dibasic β-methyl adipic acid (Arth's[1] β-pimelic acid), $C_7H_{12}O_4$.

Oxymenthylic acid (2, 6-dimethyl octan-3-onoic acid), $C_{10}H_{18}O_3$, is a thick liquid, sparingly soluble in water, and boils at 280° at ordinary pressure, or at 173° to 175° (15 mm.); with alkalis it forms crystalline salts which are readily soluble, whilst its silver salt is sparingly soluble. Its *semicarbazone*[2] crystallizes in prisms and melts at 152°. Its *methyl* ester boils at 136° to 137° (17 mm.), and the *ethyl* ester at 145° (15 mm.). When the ethyl ester is heated with sodium and xylene, it yields a *1, 3-diketone*[2] (*isobutyryl methyl ketopentamethylene*), $C_{10}H_{16}O_2$; it boils at 115° to 116° (25 mm.), forms a *dioxime* (m. p. 144°), and is reconverted into oxymenthylic acid on heating with aqueous potash.

Oxymenthylic acid is most conveniently prepared by the oxidation of menthol in an acetic acid solution with chromic anhydride. It is a ketonic acid and is converted into *menthoximic acid*[3] (m. p. 96.5°), by treating with hydroxylamine.

β-Methyl adipic acid[4] (Arth's *β-pimelic acid*), $C_7H_{12}O_4$, melts at 88.5° to 89°. Mehrländer described it as normal propyl succinic acid, but Arth[5] proved the error of this statement. According to Semmler,[6] this acid is likewise formed, together with acetone, during the oxidation of pulegone with permanganate.

The constitution of the oxidation products of menthol are, therefore, expressed by the same formulas as given under menthone.

The *sodium salt*[7] of l-menthol is formed by heating the latter compound with sodium in an atmosphere of hydrogen. When it is heated with acid anhydrides for several hours at 160° to 170°, it yields the corresponding esters of menthol; the *stearate*, prepared in this manner, melts at 39°.

Methylenic acetal of menthol[8] **(dimentholic formal or dimenthylmethylal),** $CH_2(O \cdot C_{10}H_{19})_2$, is produced by the condensation of menthol and formaldehyde in the presence of mineral acids; it separates from alcohol in colorless needles, melts at 56.5°, and boils with slight decomposition at 337°; $[\alpha]_D = -77.94°$ at 24°. It is indifferent to boiling acids and alkalis.

[1] Arth, Ann. Chim. Phys., 7 [6], 440.
[2] Baeyer and Oehler, Ber., *29*, 27.
[3] Beckmann and Mehrländer, Ann. Chem., *289*, 367.
[4] Manasse and Rupe, Ber., 27, 1818.
[5] Arth, Ber., *21*, 645, Ref.
[6] Semmler, Ber., *25*, 3515; *26*, 774.
[7] Beckmann, Journ. pr. Chem., *55* [II.], 14.
[8] Brochet, Compt. rend., *128*, 612; Wedekind, Ber., *34*, 813.

Chloromethyl menthyl oxide,[1] $C_{10}H_{19}O \cdot CH_2Cl$, is obtained by saturating a mixture of menthol and formalin solution with hydrogen chloride at the temperature of the water-bath. It is a colorless oil, boils at 160° to 163° under 13 mm. to 16 mm. pressure, has the sp. gr. 0.9821 at 4° and the rotatory power, $[\alpha]_D = -172°.57$, at 27°. The action of water converts it into menthol, formaldehyde and hydrogen chloride; when distilled under reduced pressure it suffers partial decomposition and yields methylenic acetal of menthol, $C_{21}H_{40}O_2$.

Menthyl acetoacetate,[2] $C_{14}H_{25}O_2$, is obtained by heating menthol and ethyl acetoacetate at 140° to 150° during four hours; it crystallizes in needles, melts at 30° to 32°, boils at 145° under 11 mm. pressure, and has the specific rotatory power, $[\alpha]_D = -56.6°$. Its *phenylhydrazone* melts at 81° to 83°.

Menthyl ethyl ether, $C_{10}H_{19}OC_2H_5$, is produced by the action of ethyl iodide on sodium menthylate. It is a liquid, boiling at 211.5° to 212° under 750 mm., and has a slight odor of menthol; it has a specific gravity of 0.8513 at 20° or 0.8535 at 17.1°, and the refractive power, $n_D = 1.44347$, at 17.1° (Brühl[3]).

Menschutkin[4] investigated the speed of the ester formation of menthol and from his results determined that it is a secondary alcohol.

Menthyl acetate, $C_{10}H_{19}O \cdot COCH_3$, is a thick, strongly refractive liquid, which boils at 224° and is levorotatory, $[\alpha]_D = -114°$. (Compare with Power and Kleber[6]).

Menthyl butyrate, $C_{10}H_{19}O \cdot COC_3H_7$, boils at 230° to 240° and has the rotatory power, $[\alpha]_D = -88°8'$.

The following esters were prepared by Arth.[5]

Menthyl succinoxyl ester, $C_{10}H_{19}O \cdot CO \cdot CH_2 \cdot CH_2 \cdot COOH$, melts at 62°, and has the specific rotatory power, $[\alpha]_D = -59.63°$.

Menthyl succinyl ester, $C_2H_4(COOC_{10}H_{19})_2$, forms triclinic crystals, and melts at 62°; it decomposes into succinic acid and menthene when heated in a sealed tube at 220°. Its specific rotatory power is $[\alpha]_D = -81.52°$.

Menthyl benzoyl ester,[7] $C_6H_5COOC_{10}H_{19}$, crystallizes in triclinic crystals, melts at 54°, and has the rotatory power, $[\alpha]_D = -90.92°$.

[1] Wedekind, German Patent, No. 119,008; Ber., *34*, 813.
[2] Cohn, Monatsh., *21*, 200.
[3] Brühl, Ber., *24*, 3375 and 3703.
[4] Menschutkin, Journ. Russ. Chem. Soc., *13*, 569.
[5] Arth, Ann. Chim. Phys. [6], 7, 433 to 499; Ber., *19*, 436, Ref.
[6] Power and Kleber, Pharm. Rund., *12*, 162; Archiv. d. Pharm., *232*, 653.
[7] Compare with Beckmann, Ann. Chem., *262*, 31; Journ. pr. Chem., 55 [II.], 16.

Menthyl phthaloxyl ester, $HOOC \cdot C_6H_4 \cdot CO \cdot OC_{10}H_{19}$, melts at 110°, and has the specific rotatory power, $[\alpha]_D = -105.55°$. Its magnesium salt is almost insoluble in water.

Menthyl phthalyl ester, $C_6H_4(COOC_{10}H_{19})_2$, separates from ether in triclinic crystals, and melts at 133°. $[\alpha]_D = -94.72°$.

Menthyl carbonate, $CO(OC_{10}H_{19})_2$, is obtained, together with menthyl carbamate, when cyanogen is allowed to act on sodium menthylate suspended in toluene; the toluene is removed by steam distillation when the reaction is complete. The carbamate crystallizes from the cold residue, and is filtered off; the carbonate is obtained by evaporation of the filtrate. It is recrystallized from alcohol or toluene, and melts at 105°.

It is also formed when a well cooled mixture of a solution of menthol in chloroform and pyridine is treated very slowly with a solution of carbonyl chloride in chloroform; after standing for a day in a cold place, the product is distilled with steam, the solid residue is washed with hot water, and crystallized from alcohol (Erdmann [1]).

Menthyl carbamate, $C_{10}H_{19}O \cdot CO \cdot NH_2$, is purified by recrystallizing the crystals, obtained as suggested under the preceding compound, from alcohol. It crystallizes in orthorhombic prisms, melts at 165°, and has the specific rotatory power, $[\alpha]_D = -85.11°$. It combines with benzaldehyde, forming benzylidene menthyl carbamate; this compound melts at 143°.

Menthyl phenylcarbamate, $C_{10}H_{19}O \cdot CO \cdot NHC_6H_5$, is formed by the combination of phenylcarbimide with menthol; it separates from alcohol in silky needles, melting at 111° (Leuckart [2]).

When this compound, prepared from natural menthol, is saponified with alcoholic sodium ethylate at 150°, it yields some *inactive menthol*,[3] melting at 49° to 51°.

Sodium menthylxanthate,[4] $C_{10}H_{19}O \cdot CS \cdot SNa$, results when carbon bisulphide is allowed to act on sodium menthylate suspended in ether. The free acid is an oil, which decomposes very readily. The dark, amorphous cupric salt, which is precipitated from aqueous solutions of the sodium salt by copper sulphate, is converted into the yellow, crystalline cuprous salt, $C_{10}H_{19}O \cdot CS \cdot SCu$, by heating.

Methyl menthylxanthate,[4] $C_{10}H_{19}O \cdot CS \cdot SCH_3$, is formed when a solution of menthol in dry toluene is successively treated with sodium, carbon bisulphide, and methyl iodide; it melts at 39°.

[1] Erdmann, Journ. pr. Chem., *56* [II.], 1.
[2] Leuckart, Ber., *20*, 115.
[3] Beckmann, Journ. pr. Chem., *55* [II.], 14.
[4] Bamberger and Lodter, Ber., *23*, 213.

When submitted to distillation, it yields methyl mercaptan and a menthene, $C_{10}H_{18}$, of a high specific rotatory power, $[\alpha]_D = 114.77°$ to $116.06°$.

Menthyl dixanthate,[1] $(C_{10}H_{19}O)_2C_2S_4$, is formed by the condensation of sodium menthylxanthate with iodine; it forms yellow crystals. When distilled it gives a menthene, having the rotatory power, $[\alpha]_D = 111.56°$.

A number of the fatty acid esters of menthol have been prepared, and investigated by Tschúgaeff.[2]

Menthyl chloride, $C_{10}H_{19}Cl$, **bromide** and **iodide**, prepared by the action of the phosphorus pentahalogen derivatives on menthol, are identical with menthene hydrochloride, hydrobromide and hydriodide, which are produced by the addition of the halogen hydride to menthene. They react like derivatives of tertiary menthol, but are doubtless to be regarded as mixtures of at least two isomerides.

Menthyl chloride (menthene hydrochloride[3]**)**, $C_{10}H_{19}Cl$, is formed, together with menthene, by treating menthol with phosphorus pentachloride, by heating menthol with concentrated hydrochloric acid, or by heating menthone with concentrated hydrochloric acid at 205° for six hours. It boils at 209.5° to 210.5°, and has the specific gravity 0.947 at 15°. It yields menthene when treated with zinc dust and acetic acid or with sodium mentholate; on reduction with sodium and alcohol, it gives rise to hexahydrocymene (menthane), $C_{10}H_{20}$.

According to Kursanoff,[4] when menthyl chloride is dissolved in ether and the solution is boiled with sodium, it yields a mixture of menthene, menthane, and two dimenthyls, $C_{20}H_{38}$, one of which is a liquid. The crystalline *dimenthyl*, $C_{20}H_{38}$, is readily soluble in ether and benzene, and crystallizes from cold alcohol or benzene in well developed crystals, which melt at 105.5° to 106°, and boil at 185° to 186° (21 mm.); it has the specific rotatory power, $[\alpha]_D = -51° 18'$, in a 19.4 per cent. benzene solution. The liquid *dimenthyl* is probably a stereoisomeride of the crystalline derivative.

The formation of the crystalline dimenthyl from crude menthyl chloride, as well as by the action of sodium on an ethereal solution of menthyl iodide, indicates that the crude halogen esters of

[1] Tschúgaeff, Ber., *32*, 3332.

[2] Tschúgaeff, Ber., *31*, 364.

[3] Waller, Ann. Chem., *32*, 292; Oppenheim, Ann. Chem., *130*, 177; Berkenheim, Ber., *29*, 686; Kondakoff, Ber., *28*, 1619; Jünger and Klages, Ber., *29*, 317; Kursanoff, Journ. Russ. Phys. Chem. Soc., *33*, 289.

[4] Kursanoff, Journ. Russ. Phys. Chem. Soc., *33*, 289.

menthol contain some secondary compounds, together with derivatives of tertiary menthol (Kursanoff).

When l-menthyl chloride is treated with zinc ethyl, it gives rise to *ethyl menthane*, $C_{10}H_{19}.C_2H_5$; the latter boils at 209° to 210° at 730 mm. pressure, has the sp. gr. 0.8275 at 0°/0°, and the specific rotation, $[\alpha]_D = -12° 15'$.

Menthyl bromide (menthene hydrobromide[1]**)**, $C_{10}H_{19}Br$, is produced by the action of phosphorus pentabromide or hydrobromic acid on menthol; it also results by treating menthene with a saturated solution of hydrobromic acid. It boils at 100° to 103° at 13 mm., and has the specific gravity 1.155 to 1.166 at 23°.

Menthyl iodide (menthene hydriodide[2]**)**, $C_{10}H_{19}I$, is obtained by the action of hydriodic acid on menthol or menthene; it boils at 124° to 126° (18 mm.), and has the specific gravity 1.3155 at 16.5°. Moist silver oxide converts it into tertiary menthol, thus giving rise to a transformation of secondary into tertiary menthol.

Menthol is a saturated secondary alcohol, and its constitution is represented by the accompanying formula:

CH_3
|
CH
H_2C CH_2
H_2C $CHOH$
CH
|
CH
H_3C CH_3

Menthol.

It has already been mentioned that when d- or l-menthone is reduced with sodium, the corresponding d- and l-menthols are not obtained, but rather a strongly levorotatory mixture of menthols is formed, from which the ordinary l-menthol (m. p. 43,° $[\alpha]_D = -49.3°$), and a dextrorotatory isomenthol may be separated.

Isomenthol[3] is separated from the mixture by converting the menthols into their benzoyl esters; menthyl benzoate is a solid (m. p. 54°), while *isomenthyl benzoate* is a liquid. On saponification of the liquid ester, isomenthol is obtained and crystallizes after standing some time. It melts at 78° to 81° and is slightly dextrorotatory, $[\alpha]_D = +2.03°$. On oxidation with chromic

[1] Kondakoff, Ber., 28, 1618.

[2] Kondakoff and Lutschinin, Journ. pr. Chem., 60 [II.], 257; Berkenheim, Ber., 25, 696.

[3] Beckmann, Journ. pr. Chem., 55, 14.

acid, isomenthol yields a *dextro*-menthone, which has a stronger dextrorotatory power than the d-menthone prepared by the inversion of l-menthone.

Dextro-menthol, corresponding to the natural levo-menthol, has not yet been obtained.

In an investigation of the ethereal oil of buchu leaves, Kondakoff[1] found that the best samples of oil from *Barosma betulina* and *B. serratifolia* contain about ten per cent. of hydrocarbons, $C_{10}H_{16}$ (d-limonene and dipentene), sixty per cent. of ketomenthone, $C_{10}H_{18}O$ (see under menthone), and five per cent. of diosphenol.

Diosphenol, $C_{10}H_{18}O_2$ or $C_{10}H_{16}O_2$, is an inactive, phenolic aldehyde, and melts at 82°. On reduction with hydriodic acid and phosphorus at 210°, it yields a hydrocarbon, $C_{10}H_{20}$, of the hexahydrocymene series; it boils at 165° to 168° (762 mm.). When reduced with sodium and alcohol, diosphenol gives an inactive menthol, a crystalline glycol, $C_{10}H_{20}O_2$, and a stereomeric, liquid glycol, $C_{10}H_{20}O_2$.

The inactive *menthol*, $C_{10}H_{19}OH$, is volatile with steam, boils at 215° to 216° (763 mm.), has a sp. gr. 0.9052 at 20°, and the index of refraction, $n_D = 1.464456$. It yields an inactive *iodide*, $C_{10}H_{19}I$, which boils at 126.5° (17 mm.). When this iodide is treated with alcoholic potash, an active *menthene*, $C_{10}H_{18}$, results, which boils at 168° to 169°, has the sp. gr. 0.8158 at 19.8°, $n_D = 1.45909$, and $[a]_D = -37'$.

The crystalline *glycol*, $C_{10}H_{20}O_2$, is optically active and odorless; it crystallizes in colorless needles, melts at 92°, has a sharp, cooling taste, and is not volatile with steam. When heated with hydriodic acid it gives a liquid *menthyl iodide*, $C_{10}H_{19}I$, which boils at 112° to 114° (9 mm.), has the sp. gr. 1.359 at 20.6°, and $n_D = 1.520771$.

The liquid *glycol*, $C_{10}H_{20}O_2$, is stereomeric with the crystalline glycol; it boils at 141.5° to 145° (13 mm.), has the sp. gr. 0.995 at 21.6°, and $n_D = 1.47877$.

In conclusion, two alcohols, $C_{10}H_{19}OH$, isomeric with menthol, but synthetically prepared, should be mentioned.

Cis-symmetrical menthol (cis-1, 3-methyl isopropyl cyclohexanol-5), $C_{10}H_{19}OH$, is an alcohol, isomeric with natural menthol, which Knoevenagel[2] prepared synthetically by the action of hydriodic acid, zinc dust and glacial acetic acid on *trans*-hexahydro-1, 3, 5-carvacrol, $C_{10}H_{17}OH$. It boils at 226° to 227° (760 mm.), has a specific gravity 0.9020 and refractive index, $n_D = 1.46454$, at

[1] Kondakoff and Bachtschéeff, Journ. pr. Chem., 63 [II.], 49.

[2] Knoevenagel and Weidermann, Ann. Chem., 297, 169.

13.6°, and a molecular refraction, $M = 47.67$. It has an odor suggesting that of natural menthol, is not acted upon by bromine or potassium permanganate, but is converted into symmetrical menthone on oxidation with chromic acid. Its *acetate* boils at 235° to 236° (752 mm.), and the *phenylurethane* crystallizes from a mixture of alcohol and petroleum ether, and melts at 88°. The *chloride*, *bromide* and *iodide* are liquids.

An *alcohol*,[1] $C_{10}H_{19}OH$, isomeric with, and having the same structure as, natural l-menthol, is formed by the reduction of *3-methyl-6-isopropyl-Δ^2-keto-R-hexene*. It boils at 202° to 204°, has the sp. gr. 0.910 at 20°, and possesses an odor recalling that of peppermint; it does not yield a phenylurethane. When treated with phosphoric anhydride, it gives rise to an inactive menthene, $C_{10}H_{18}$, boiling at 165° to 167°.

8. TERTIARY CARVOMENTHOL, $C_{10}H_{19}OH$.

Tertiary carvomenthyl iodide, $C_{10}H_{19}I$, is formed, when carvomenthene is dissolved in acetic acid and treated with hydriodic acid; the iodine atom in this compound is attached to that atom of carbon which carries the methyl group. This follows the common rule that when a halogen hydride combines with an unsaturated compound, the halogen atom attaches itself to the least hydrogenized carbon atom. If this iodide, $C_{10}H_{19}I$, be dissolved in acetic acid, and decomposed with silver acetate, it is partially reverted into carvomenthene, while the remaining portion is converted into the acetate of tertiary carvomenthol (Baeyer[2]).

```
       CH3                    CH3                   CH3
       |                      |                     |
       C                      CI                    COCOCH3
     /   \\                  /    \                 /     \
 H2C      CH     ⇄     H2C       CH2     →    H2C        CH2
  |        |             |        |             |         |
 H2C      CH2          H2C       CH2          H2C        CH2
     \   /                  \    /                 \     /
      CH                     CH                     CH
      |                      |                      |
      C3H7                   C3H7                   C3H7
Carvomenthene.      Tertiary carvomenthyl   Tertiary carvomenthyl
                          iodide.                 acetate.
```

Tertiary carvomenthol is obtained by the hydrolysis of its acetate. It[3] is also produced by treating carvomenthyl chloride or bromide with moist silver oxide; a small quantity of the compound, $C_{10}H_{22}O_3$ (m. p. 101° to 102°), is formed at the same time.

[1] S. H. Baer, Inaug. Diss., Leipzig, 1898; Schimmel & Co., Semi-Annual Report, Oct., *1898*, 49.

[2] Baeyer, Ber., *26*, 2270.

[3] Kondakoff and Lutschinin, Journ. pr. Chem., *60* [II.], 257.

Tertiary carvomenthol has a slight odor, and boils at 96° to 100° under a pressure of 17 mm. It reacts as a tertiary alcohol towards chromic acid. Hydrobromic acid in a glacial acetic acid solution converts it at once into tertiary carvomenthyl bromide;[1] this is a heavy oil, which yields carvomenthene, boiling at 174.5°, when distilled with quinoline.

9. TERTIARY MENTHOL, $C_{10}H_{19}OH$.

Tertiary menthyl iodide is produced by treating menthene with an acetic acid solution of hydrogen iodide; if this halogen derivative be decomposed with silver acetate and acetic acid, it gives menthene and the acetate of tertiary menthol (Baeyer[2]).

Menthene		Tertiary menthyl iodide		Tertiary menthyl acetate
CH_3		CH_3		CH_3
CH		CH		CH
H_2C CH_2	⇄	H_2C CH_2	→	H_2C CH_2
H_2C CH		H_2C CH_2		H_2C CH_2
C		CI		$COCOCH_3$
C_3H_7		C_3H_7		C_3H_7
Menthene.		Tertiary menthyl iodide.		Tertiary menthyl acetate.

Tertiary menthol is obtained by the saponification of its acetate. It is also formed by the action of moist silver oxide on menthyl iodide.[1]

Tertiary menthol is produced by heating menthene with trichloracetic acid at 70° to 90° for half an hour, and agitating the product with potash for 12 hours.[3]

It has a faint odor of peppermint, is decomposed on distillation at ordinary pressure, but boils undecomposed at 97° to 101° under a pressure of 20 mm. It solidifies to a vitreous mass when cooled with solid carbonic anhydride. It behaves as a tertiary alcohol towards chromic acid.

Tertiary menthyl bromide, $C_{10}H_{19}Br$, is readily prepared by treating a glacial acetic acid solution of tertiary menthol with hydrogen bromide. It yields menthene, boiling at 167.5°, when heated with quinoline.

Tertiary menthyl methyl ether, $C_{10}H_{19}OCH_3$, is obtained, together with a monomethyl terpine, by the following method.

[1] Kondakoff and Lutschinin, Journ. pr. Chem., *60* [II.], 257.

[2] Baeyer, Ber., *26*, 2270.

[3] Masson and Reychler, Ber., *29*, 1843.

The methyl ether of crystallized terpineol (m. p. 35°) is shaken with hydriodic acid (sp. gr. 1.7) for fifteen minutes, thus forming the hydriodide. This is washed with sodium sulphite and bicarbonate, extracted with ether, and the ethereal solution dried and treated directly with glacial acetic acid and zinc dust, care being taken not to allow the temperature to rise above 25°. When the reaction is complete, an excess of sodium hydroxide is added, and the product distilled with steam. Some terpinyl methyl ether is regenerated during the reaction, and is eliminated by treating the crude product with potassium permanganate. The acetate of a methyl terpine, $C_{10}H_{18}(OCH_3)OCOCH_3$, is also formed by the replacement of the iodine atom in the above-mentioned hydriodide with the acetyl group. This acetate yields monomethyl terpine by boiling with sodium hydroxide. The terpine is separated from menthyl methyl ether by distillation over the alloy of sodium and potassium, the terpine being quantitatively retained in the residue, while the pure methyl ether of tertiary menthol is found in the distillate (Baeyer[1]).

It has a faint odor of cymene, boils at about 210°, and is not attacked by permanganate. It combines with hydrobromic acid, forming tertiary menthyl bromide, which is converted into menthene on distillation with quinoline; the resultant menthene boils at 167.5°, and forms a nitrosochloride, melting at 146°.

Baeyer's conclusions as to the orientation of these compounds are opposed to the views regarding the constitution of terpineol (m. p. 35°), which have been expressed by both Wallach and Tiemann. (Compare also with the publications of Kondakoff.[2])

10. TERPINE, $C_{10}H_{18}(OH)_2$.

Terpine is the alcohol corresponding to dipentene dihydrochloride. It was believed until quite recently that the constitutions of these two compounds were represented by the formulas:—

```
        CH3                          CH3
        |                            |
        CCl                          COH
       /   \                        /   \
   H2C       CH2                H2C       CH2
    |         |       and        |         |
   H2C       CH2                H2C       CH2
       \   /                        \   /
        CCl                          COH
        |                            |
        CH                           CH
       /  \                         /  \
    H3C    CH3                   H3C    CH3
```

Dipentene dihydrochloride. Terpine.

1 Baeyer, Ber., *26*, 2560.

2 Kondakoff, Ber., *28*, 1618; Journ. pr. Chem., *60* [II.], 257.

This terpine formula, however, does not readily conform with the formation of terebic acid by the oxidation of terpine, since terebic acid possesses the constitution :—

```
HOOC—CH—CH2—CO
      |      |
      C——————O
     / \
  H3C   CH3
```

Moreover, the oxidation of terpine[1] with chromic anhydride yields the keto-lactone, $C_{10}H_{16}O_3$, which is obtained by the oxidation of terpineol (m. p. 35°). Hence, it is possible that a chlorine atom in dipentene dihydrochloride and a hydroxyl-group in terpine are not attached to carbon atom 4, but rather to carbon atom 8; the two compounds would then be represented by the formulas :—

```
      CH3                        CH3
      |                          |
      CCl                        COH
     /  \                       /  \
  H2C    CH2                 H2C    CH2
   |      |         and       |      |
  H2C    CH2                 H2C    CH2
     \  /                       \  /
      CH                         CH
      |                          |
      CCl                        COH
     /  \                       /  \
  H3C    CH3                 H3C    CH3
```

Dipentene dihydrochloride. Terpine.

The determination of the exact constitution of terpine is, naturally, of fundamental importance for the orientation in the terpene series. Perhaps two terpines exist which correspond to the above formulas, since Baeyer[2] has found that the dihydrochloride and dihydrobromide of dipentene, and terpine itself exist in two forms designated as the *trans-* and *cis-*modification.

Trans-terpine corresponds to the well known dipentene dihydrobromide, melting at 64°, and is prepared by dissolving this compound in ten times its amount of glacial acetic acid and gradually treating the ice-cold solution with an excess of silver acetate. The product is filtered after standing for some time, and the filtrate is neutralized with soda and extracted with ether. The ethereal solution is treated with alcoholic potash to saponify the acetyl compound, and the reaction-product is then distilled with steam; hydrocarbons and terpineol are so removed, while trans-terpine is obtained from the cold residue (Baeyer[2]).

[1] Tiemann and Schmidt, Ber., *28*, 1781.

[2] Baeyer, Ber., *26*, 2865.

Trans-terpine crystallizes without water of crystallization, melts at 156° to 158° and boils at 263° to 265°. It is readily soluble in alcohol, more sparingly in water, ether and ethyl acetate, and separates from the latter solvent in beautiful, short prisms or six-sided tablets, having a strong, vitreous luster. When it is treated with hydrogen bromide in a glacial acetic acid solution, it yields almost exclusively trans-dipentene dihydrobromide, melting at 64°. Dilute sulphuric acid converts trans- and cis-terpine into terpineol.

Cis-terpine corresponds to cis-dipentene dihydrobromide (m. p. 39°), and may be obtained from this dihydrobromide according to the method described under trans-terpine (Baeyer[1]).

While many terpenes yield trans-dipentene dihydrochloride and dihydrobromide exclusively or in preponderant quantities, on the other hand the transformation of the same terpenes into terpine always gives cis-terpine, which has the peculiarity of crystallizing with one molecule of water; in such cases, therefore, terpine hydrate, $C_{10}H_{18}(OH)_2 + H_2O$, is always produced and may be converted into cis-terpine by the elimination of the water of crystallization.

It further merits notice that Tiemann and Schmidt[2] do not regard terpine hydrate as a terpine containing water of crystallization, but rather as an aliphatic alcohol.

Terpine hydrate, $C_{10}H_{18}(OH)_2 + H_2O$, results when pinene or limonene (dipentene) is allowed to stand in contact with dilute mineral acids for a long time at ordinary temperature. Of the following methods which have been proposed for its preparation, the one suggested by Hempel is to be preferred.

According to Wiggers[3] and Deville,[4] a mixture of three liters of eighty-five per cent. alcohol, one liter of ordinary nitric acid, and four liters of turpentine oil is allowed to stand for one or one and one-half months.

According to Tilden,[5] two and one-half volumes of turpentine are mixed with one volume of methyl alcohol and one volume of nitric acid of sp. gr. 1.4; the mixture is allowed to stand for two days, and is then poured into a flat basin, small quantities of methyl alcohol being added every two days.

According to Hempel,[6] whose method was employed by Wallach,[7] a mixture of eight parts of turpentine oil, two parts of alco-

[1] Baeyer, Ber., *26*, 2865.
[2] Tiemann and Schmidt, Ber., *28*, 1781.
[3] Wiggers, Ann. Chem., *57*, 247.
[4] Deville, Ann. Chem., *71*, 348.
[5] Tilden, Jahresb. Chem., *1878*, 638.
[6] Hempel, Ann. Chem., *180*, 73.
[7] Wallach, Ann. Chem., *227*, 284.

hol, and two parts of nitric acid of sp. gr. 1.255 is placed in flat basins. After standing for a few days the mother-liquor is poured off from the crystals of terpine hydrate, and is neutralized with an alkali, after which treatment a second crop of crystals separates. The preparation of this compound is most successful during the cool seasons of the year.[1]

Terpine hydrate is also formed when dipentene dihydrochloride is treated with aqueous alcohol,[2] or when limonene hydrochloride is mixed with water and allowed to stand for some time.[3] It results if terpineol be shaken with dilute acid for a considerable time.

It crystallizes from alcohol in transparent, well defined, monoclinic[4] prisms, and dissolves in 200 parts of cold, and twenty-two parts of boiling water;[5] 14.49 parts of terpine hydrate dissolve in 100 parts of eighty-five per cent. alcohol[4]; it is insoluble in ligroine. Contrary to the earlier publications, Wallach[6] found that when it is heated in a capillary tube it commences to coagulate and soften above 100°, and melts at 116° to 117°, the fusion being accompanied by frothing and sublimation of some of the substance due to the removal of water of crystallization. It does not melt when boiled with a quantity of water insufficient for its solution. On distillation the water of crystallization is first given off and carries over some terpine hydrate; the anhydrous terpine, $C_{10}H_{18}(OH)_2$, then boils at 258° (corr.). Terpine is likewise formed when the hydrate is dried over sulphuric acid.

Anhydrous terpine (cis-terpine) melts at 102° or at 104° to 105°, according to its purity. It is very hygroscopic. It behaves as a saturated compound, being readily converted into dipentene dihydrochloride or dihydrobromide on treatment with phosphorus trichloride or tribromide; the halogen hydrides also react with terpine, forming the corresponding dipentene addition-products. It has already been noted under the derivatives of dipentene that the above suggested reactions yield a mixture of the cis- and trans-isomerides (Baeyer).

The behavior of terpine hydrate towards dehydrating agents has frequently been a subject of investigation. It was formerly believed that a homogeneous substance resulted by heating terpine hydrate with dilute acids; Tilden[7] recognized, however, that an oxidized compound, $C_{10}H_{18}O$, was formed, together with terpenes,

[1] Wallach, Ann. Chem., *227*, 284.
[2] Flawitzky, Ber., *12*, 2358.
[3] Wallach and Kremers, Ann. Chem., *270*, 188.
[4] Deville, Ann. Chem., *71*, 348.
[5] Blanchet and Sell, Ann. Chem., *6*, 268.
[6] Wallach, Ann. Chem., *230*, 247.
[7] Tilden, Jahresb. Chem., *1878*, 639.

$C_{10}H_{16}$. Detailed researches regarding this reaction have been made by Wallach.

When terpine hydrate is boiled with dilute sulphuric acid (one part of acid to two parts of water), terpinene, terpinolene and terpineol are formed; when a very dilute acid (one volume of sulphuric acid to seven volumes of water) is used, it yields a product consisting largely of terpinene, with almost no terpineol.

If the hydrate be heated with twenty per cent. phosphoric acid, it is changed chiefly into terpineol, while a small quantity of terpinolene and dipentene, but no terpinene, results. Boiling glacial acetic acid slowly converts terpine hydrate into terpineol; but when heated with glacial acetic acid in a sealed tube at 190° to 200°, terpinene is the principal product. It is converted into dipentene and terpineol by heating with acid potassium sulphate at 190° to 200°. In all these reactions small quantities of cineole are produced.

The elimination of water from terpine hydrate, under all conditions, at first yields "terpineol" and a little cineole. It was explained under terpineol that this "terpineol" obtained by Wallach by dehydrating terpine hydrate was later found to be a mixture. (See page 254.)

If ten grams of terpine hydrate are dissolved in twenty grams of cold, colorless, concentrated nitric acid, and the resultant clear, rose-colored liquid be very gently warmed, an oil separates which, according to Wallach,[1] is to be regarded as the nitric acid ester of terpine (or terpineol?); when this oil is treated with sodium hydroxide and distilled with steam, it yields some terpine hydrate and products similar to those obtained by the action of other acids on terpine hydrate.

A *mono-acetyl ester of terpine*, $C_{10}H_{19}O(C_2H_3O_2)$, was obtained by Oppenheim[2] by heating terpine hydrate with acetic anhydride. It has an odor like that of orange, and boils at 140° to 150° under a pressure of 20 mm.

Hexahydrocymene, $C_{10}H_{20}$, is formed by the action of concentrated hydriodic acid on terpine hydrate at 210°. It boils at 168° to 170°, and has the specific gravity of 0.797 at 15° (A. Schtschukarew[3]).

The oxidation of terpine hydrate with nitric acid yields terebic, para-toluic, and terephthalic acids, whilst chromic anhydride converts it into acetic and terpenylic acids (Hempel[4]).

[1] Wallach, Ann. Chem., *230*, 253; *239*, 17; compare Bouchardat and Voiry, Compt. rend., *104*, 996; *106*, 663; Ann. Chim. Phys. [6], *16*, 251; Wallach, Ann. Chem., *246*, 265; *252*, 133.

[2] Oppenheim, Ann. Chem., *129*, 157.

[3] Schtschukarew, Ber., *23*, 433, Ref.

[4] Hempel, Ann. Chem., *189*, 71.

An aqueous solution of terpine hydrate is not acted on by potassium permanganate at the ordinary temperature, but, on warming, it is resolved into acetic acid, oxalic acid, etc.; terpenylic acid is not formed in this reaction (Tiemann and Schmidt[1]).

Cis-terpine in a hot, glacial acetic acid solution is converted by chromic anhydride into an orange-colored chromium compound, which, on heating with glacial acetic acid, yields terpine hydrate and the keto-lactone, $C_{10}H_{16}O_3$, described by Tiemann and Schmidt as methoethylheptanonolide; the same keto-lactone was obtained by Wallach in the oxidation of terpineol (m. p. 35°) with potassium permanganate.

11. MENTHENE GLYCOL, $C_{10}H_{18}(OH)_2$.

Menthene glycol was obtained, together with other substances, by Wagner by the action of potassium permanganate on menthene; it has been described under menthene.

12. CINEOLE, $C_{10}H_{18}O$.

Cineole is a widely distributed constituent of many ethereal oils. It was first characterized as a chemical individual and called cineole by Wallach and Brass,[2] who separated it in a condition of purity from oil of levant wormseed, by means of its hydrochloric acid derivative. A compound having the formula, $C_{10}H_{18}O$, had already been detected in wormseed oil by earlier investigators, but had never been isolated in a pure condition.

Simultaneous with the recognition of cineole in wormseed oil, Wallach[3] showed that it is identical with the oxidized constituent of oil of cajeput, which was formerly called "*cajeputol.*" Cineole was then found in various ethereal oils, among which may be mentioned oil of rosemary, in which cineole was discovered by Weber,[4] in eucalyptus oil by Jahns[5] and by Wallach and Gildemeister,[6] in oil of sage, laurel leaf oil and laurel berry oil by Wallach.[7] It also occurs in the oil of cheken-leaves, galangal

[1] Tiemann and Schmidt, Ber., *28*, 1781.

[2] Wallach and Brass, Ann. Chem., *225*, 291.

[3] Wallach, Ann. Chem., *225*, 315.

[4] Weber, Ann. Chem., *238*, 90.

[5] Jahns, Ber., *17*, 2941.

[6] Wallach and Gildemeister, Ann. Chem., *246*, 278; compare Arch. Pharm., *1885*, 52.

[7] Wallach, Ann. Chem., *252*, 94.

oil, lavender oil, spike oil, cinnamon oils, zedoary oil, myrtle oil, canella oil, iva oil, basilicum oil, peppermint oil, Russian spearmint oil, camphor oil, different eucalyptus and cardamom oils, etc.

Cineole is formed, together with terpenes and terpineol, when terpine hydrate is boiled with dilute acids. Crystallized terpineol (m. p. 35°) and liquid "terpineol," which is known to be a mixture of various compounds, may be partially converted into cineole by boiling with dilute phosphoric acid or oxalic acid (Wallach [1]). Similar observations were subsequently made by Bouchardat and Voiry,[2] who called it "*terpane.*" Cineole has also been termed "*eucalyptol.*"

In order to prepare it, rectified oil of levant wormseed is cooled by a freezing mixture and saturated with dry hydrochloric acid gas; the resultant crystalline cineole hydrochloride is pressed on a porous plate in the cold, decomposed by water, and the separated oil distilled in a current of steam. Chemically pure cineole is obtained by a repetition of this operation (Wallach and Brass [3]). A similar method is used by Schimmel and Co. for the preparation of large quantities of pure cineole, but in this case it is obtained from the oil of *Eucalyptus globulus*, and not from the oil of wormseed.

PROPERTIES.—Cineole is a liquid which has a characteristic odor resembling that of camphor, and is optically inactive. The purest commercial product[4] boils at 176°, has a sp. gr. 0.930 at 15°, and a refractive index, $n_D = 1.45961$, at 17°. When cooled to a low temperature, it solidifies to crystals, melting at $-1°$; this property may be used for the purification of cineole. According to Wallach, it has a refractive index, $n_C = 1.45590$.[5]

It combines with concentrated phosphoric acid, forming the compound, $C_{10}H_{18}O \cdot H_3PO_4$, which may also be employed for the preparation of pure cineole from eucalyptus oil.[6] It also forms addition-products with α- and β-naphthol and iodol.

It is not attacked by sodium, phosphoric chloride or benzoyl chloride. It does not unite with hydroxylamine or phenylhydrazine. The oxygen atom in cineole is, therefore, combined in a position similar to that in which it occurs in ethylene oxide.

[1] Wallach, Ann. Chem., *239*, 20; *275*, 106.
[2] Bouchardat and Voiry, Compt. rend., *106*, 663.
[3] Wallach and Brass, Ann. Chem., *225*, 291.
[4] Schimmel & Co., Semi-Annual Report, April, *1895*, 34.
[5] Wallach and Pulfrich, Ann. Chem., *245*, 195.
[5] Scammel, German patent, No. 80,118.

Cineole is generally regarded as an anhydride of terpine:

```
       CH3                                CH3
       |                                  |
       COH                                C
      /   \                              /|\
  H2C       CH2                      H2C  |  CH2
  |         |              -->        |   O   |
  H2C       CH2                      H2C  |  CH2
      \   /                              \|/
       COH                                C
       |                                  |
       CH                                 CH
      /  \                               /  \
   H3C    CH3                         H3C    CH3
     Terpine.                           Cineole.
```

If we assume the correctness of the terpine formula, then the above formula would represent the constitution of cineole; this view is supported by the formation of cineole from terpine, and by the general behavior of cineole. The dihydrochloride or dihydrobromide of dipentene is obtained when a glacial acetic acid solution of cineole is saturated with hydrochloric or hydrobromic acid. Dipentene dihydriodide is even formed when dry hydriodic acid is passed through cold cineole, whilst under the same conditions hydrochloric and hydrobromic acids combine with cineole, forming addition-products (Wallach and Brass).

It is manifest, therefore, that cineole may be changed by the action of acids in a manner similar to terpine and terpineol; thus, it is converted into terpinene and terpinolene by the action of alcoholic sulphuric acid (Wallach[1]).

Cineole hydrochloride, $(C_{10}H_{18}O)_2 \cdot HCl$ (?), was first obtained by Völkel.[2] It is prepared by treating a well cooled mixture of light petroleum and cineole with dry hydrochloric acid gas (Wallach and Brass).

It is readily soluble in terpenes, hence it is not suitable for the detection of cineole in ethereal oils. Its behavior towards water has already been mentioned. It decomposes into water, hydrogen chloride and dipentene when dry distilled (Wallach and Brass).

Simultaneous with the researches of Wallach and Brass, a detailed investigation of cineole was carried on by Hell and Ritter;[3] according to these chemists, the hydrochloride has the formula, $C_{10}H_{18}O \cdot HCl$.

Cineole hydrobromide, $C_{10}H_{18}(OH)Br$, was obtained in an impure condition by Hell and Ritter;[4] it was also prepared by Wallach and Brass.

In order to prepare it, cineole is dissolved in petroleum ether,

[1] Wallach, Ann. Chem., *239*, 22.
[2] Völkel, Ann. Chem., 87, 315.
[3] Hell and Ritter, Ber., *17*, 1977.
[4] Hell and Ritter, Ber., *17*, 2610.

and the solution, well cooled by a freezing mixture, is treated with dry hydrogen bromide, which at once produces a white precipitate; this is filtered, washed with petroleum ether and dried. It is rather more stable than the hydrochloride, and melts at 56° to 57°. Since it is very sparingly soluble, the presence of cineole in mixtures of terpenes may be recognized by the formation of the hydrobromide; this reaction is so sensitive that one per cent. of cineole in limonene may be readily detected (Wallach and Gildemeister).

Cineole hydrobromide is decomposed by water into pure cineole and hydrobromic acid.

Cineole combines with the halogens, yielding unstable, additive products.

Cineole dibromide, $C_{10}H_{18}O \cdot Br_2$, is obtained in red needles if bromine be added to a cold solution of cineole in petroleum ether (Wallach and Brass). It easily decomposes on keeping. If crystals of the dibromide are placed in closed vessels and kept in a cool place for some time, they decompose with elimination of water and formation of an oil, which partially solidifies to a crystalline mass and yields dipentene tetrabromide on recrystallization; the same tetrabromide may also be produced in considerable quantities by treating the admixed oil with alcohol and bromine.

Cineole diiodide, $C_{10}H_{18}O \cdot I_2$, is likewise prepared by the action of iodine on a solution of cineole in petroleum ether; it crystallizes in long, dark needles, which are more stable than those of cineole dibromide (Wallach and Brass).

Addition-product of cineole and iodol,[1] $C_{10}H_{18}O \cdot C_4I_4NH$, is well adapted for the rapid detection and isolation of cineole in volatile oils. A small quantity of iodol, C_4I_4NH, is dissolved in a few drops of the oil under investigation, using a moderate heat; if cineole be present, the addition-product soon separates in the form of yellowish-green crystals. It may be recrystallized from alcohol or benzene, and melts at 112°. It is very sparingly soluble in petroleum ether. It is decomposed by sodium hydroxide, with regeneration of cineole.

CINEOLIC ACID, $C_{10}H_{16}O_5$.

Cineole is oxidized by potassium permanganate, yielding cineolic acid, oxalic acid, acetic acid and carbonic acid (Wallach and Gildemeister[2]). The preparation of small quantities of racemic cineolic acid is best accomplished by the method described by the above-mentioned chemists. Large quantities are obtained by the following process.

[1] Hirschsohn, Pharm. Zeitschr. f. Russl., *32*, 49 and 67; Bertram and Walbaum, Archiv. d. Pharm., *235*, 178.

[2] Wallach and Gildemeister, Ann. Chem., *246*, 265.

One hundred cc. of cineole are mixed with a solution of 420 grams of potassium permanganate in 6.3 liters of water, and the mixture is placed in a double-walled, metallic vessel, which is connected with an upright condenser. The vessel is so constructed that steam may be passed, during the entire operation, between the outer and inner walls. It is then vigorously agitated on a shaking-machine for about three and one-half hours, or until the color of the permanganate solution is removed. The manganese oxides, which separate, are filtered off, and the filtrate is evaporated to dryness; the residue, consisting of the potassium salt of cineolic acid, is extracted with alcohol in which it is readily soluble, and the free acid is precipitated from the alcoholic solution by the addition of dilute sulphuric acid. The crude acid is freed from admixed potassium sulphate by dissolving in ether, and, on evaporation of this solvent, is recrystallized from twenty times its amount of boiling water. The yield is forty-five per cent. of the weight of cineole employed.

Pure cineolic acid separates from water in colorless, well defined crystals, which often appear as twins; it is optically inactive, and melts[1] and decomposes at 196° to 197°. It is soluble in seventy parts of water at 15°, and in about fifteen parts of boiling water. It is readily soluble in alcohol and ether, more sparingly in chloroform. By means of its strychnine salt it is resolved into the optically active cineolic acids.[1]

The following compounds are derivatives of racemic cineolic acid.

Calcium cineolate, $C_{10}H_{14}O_5Ca + 4H_2O$, is characteristic. If a cold aqueous solution of the acid be saturated with calcium carbonate and then filtered, calcium cineolate separates from the filtrate on boiling. It is insoluble in boiling water.

Silver cineolate is rather easily soluble in alcohol and water.

Methyl cineolic ester,[2] $C_8H_{14}O(COOCH_3)_2$, is obtained by saturating a methyl alcoholic solution of cineolic acid with hydrochloric acid gas. It melts at 31°.

Ethyl cineolic ester, $C_8H_{14}O(COOC_2H_5)_2$, is prepared in an analogous manner to the preceding compound. It is a colorless liquid, boiling at 155° under a pressure of 11 mm. to 12 mm.

Ethyl hydrogen cineolate,[3]

$$C_8H_{14}O\left\langle\begin{matrix}COOH\\ COOC_2H_5\end{matrix}\right.$$

[1] According to Rupe and Ronus (Ber., *33*, 3544), pure, inactive cineolic acid melts at 204° to 206°.

[2] Wallach, Ann. Chem., *258*, 319.

[3] Rupe, Ber., *33*, 1133.

crystallizes from dilute alcohol in slender needles, and melts at 99° to 100°.

Cineolic anhydride,[1] $C_{10}H_{14}O_4$, is produced when cineolic acid is heated with several times its weight of acetic anhydride until all of the acid is dissolved. The excess of acetic anhydride and acetic acid is then distilled off under diminished pressure, and on continuing the distillation cineolic anhydride is obtained; it boils at 157° under 12 mm. to 13 mm. pressure, and when pure melts at 77° to 78°. It is readily soluble in chloroform or benzene, and crystallizes from a mixture of petroleum ether and benzene in long needles; it is reconverted into cineolic acid by boiling water.

Cineolic acid amides are produced by the action of one molecular proportion of anhydrous organic bases on one molecule of cineolic anhydride (Wallach and Elkeles[1]).

Cineolic piperidide,

$$C_8H_{14}O\begin{cases}CONC_5H_{10}\\COOH\end{cases}$$

results when an ethereal solution of the anhydride is treated with piperidine; it crystallizes in colorless needles by the slow evaporation of the solvent, and melts at 151° to 152°. It forms a sparingly soluble *silver salt* of the composition $AgOOC\cdot C_8H_{14}O\cdot$-$CONC_5H_{10}$.

Cineolic allylamide,

$$C_8H_{14}O\begin{cases}CONHC_3H_5\\COOH\end{cases}$$

is sparingly soluble in ether, crystallizes from a mixture of methyl alcohol and ether, and melts at 126°.

Cineolic diethylamide,

$$C_8H_{14}O\begin{cases}CON(C_2H_5)_2\\COOH\end{cases}$$

melts at 162° to 163°.

Cineolic anilide,

$$C_8H_{14}O\begin{cases}CONHC_6H_5\\COOH\end{cases}$$

is obtained as a syrup, which may be converted into a silver salt; this reacts with methyl iodide, yielding a *methyl ester* which melts at 78° to 79°.

[1] Wallach and Elkeles, Ann. Chem., *271*, 21.

Cineolic para-toluidide,

$$C_8H_{14}O\begin{cases}CONHC_6H_4CH_3\\COOH\end{cases}$$

separates from a mixture of ether and methyl alcohol in well defined crystals, melting at 125° to 126°.

Cineolic phenylhydrazide,

$$C_8H_{14}O\begin{cases}CONH\cdot NHC_6H_5\\COOH\end{cases}$$

crystallizes in needles, and melts at 110°.

When cineolic anhydride is subjected to dry distillation, it is quantitatively decomposed into carbonic oxide, carbonic anhydride, and methyl hexylene ketone :—

$$C_{10}H_{14}O_4 = CO + CO_2 + C_8H_{14}O.$$

Wallach regards as the probable explanation of this reaction, that a saturated, but unstable, oxide is at first formed, which then suffers an intramolecular change and is converted into an unsaturated ketone. Such a transformation would be analogous to that which is known to take place in the formation of pinacoline. The following formulas[1] illustrate this change :

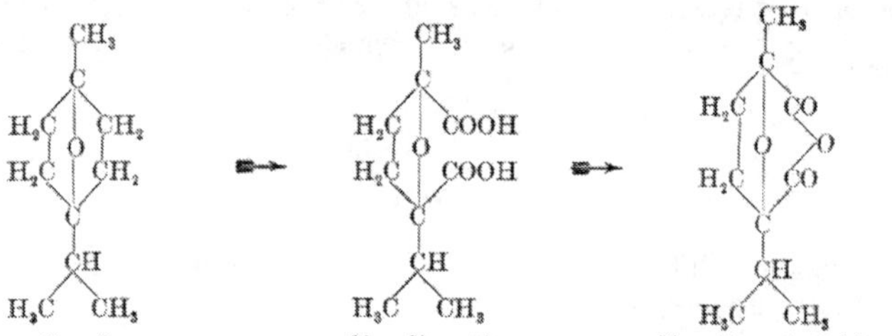

CH_3 — C — (H_2C, CH_2 / O / H_2C, CH_2) — C — CH — H_3C CH_3 → CH_3 — C — (H_2C, COOH / O / H_2C, COOH) — C — CH — H_3C CH_3 → CH_3 — C — (H_2C, CO / O / O / H_2C, CO) — C — CH — H_3C CH_3

Cineole. Cineolic acid. Cineolic anhydride.

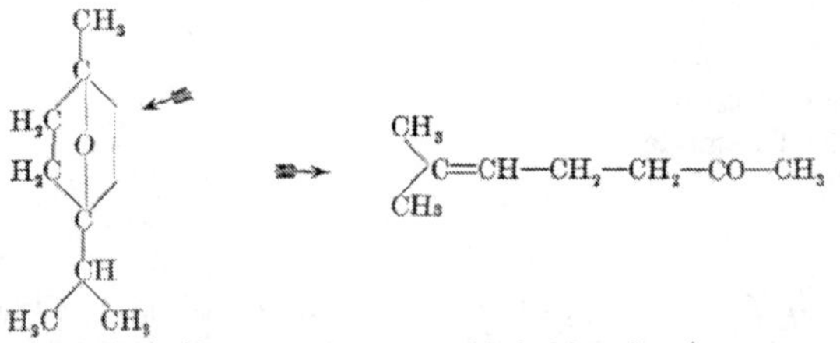

CH_3 — C — (H_2C / O / H_2C) — C — CH — H_3C CH_3 → $(CH_3)_2C{=}CH{-}CH_2{-}CH_2{-}CO{-}CH_3$

Oxide (hypothetical). Methyl hexylene ketone.

[1] For more recent formulas of cineole and cineolic acid, see Wallach, Ann. Chem., *291*, 350.

Methyl hexylene ketone (methyl heptenone), $C_8H_{14}O$, is a liquid, having an agreeable odor like that of amyl acetate; it boils at 173° to 174°, has a refractive power, $n_C = 1.44003$, and specific gravity of 0.8530 at 20°. According to Schimmel & Co., it boils at 170° to 171° (758 mm.), has the sp. gr. 0.858 and refractive index, $n_D = 1.44388$, at 15°. It unites readily with bromine, and is decomposed by permanganate. It does not decolorize a sulphurous acid solution of fuchsine, but forms an unstable additive compound with acid sodium sulphite, and combines with phenylhydrazine and hydroxylamine, yielding an oily hydrazone and oxime. Its *semicarbazone*[1] melts at 136° to 138°.

Meta-dihydroxylene, C_8H_{12}, is formed, together with a polymeride of this hydrocarbon, when methyl hexylene ketone is heated with zinc chloride at 90° to 95°. This transformation is probably expressed by the following equation:

```
          CH                                   CH
        //  \                                //  \
CH3—C       CH2          = H2O +      CH3—C       CH2
      |       |                             |       |
    H3C     CH2                            HC     CH2
              |                              \\   /
             CO                                C
              |                                |
             CH3                              CH3
```

Methyl hexylene ketone. Meta-dihydroxylene.

When meta-dihydroxylene is carefully treated with nitric acid, it yields nitro-m-xylene.

Methyl hexylene ketone has recently become quite important in consequence of its discovery in many ethereal oils, and because of its relation to the aliphatic members of the terpene series. Its constitution is completely explained by the researches of Tiemann and Semmler, who made the important observation that methyl heptenone is converted into acetone and laevulinic acid by oxidation.

For the various syntheses and methods of preparation of methyl heptenone, and an enumeration of its derivatives, the original publications[2] must be consulted.

An unsaturated alcohol,[3] *methyl heptenol* (*methyl hexylene carbinol*), $C_8H_{15}OH$, is formed, when methyl hexylene ketone is re-

[1] Tiemann and Krüger, Ber., *28*, 2124.

[2] Léser, Bull. Soc. Chim., *17* [III.], 108; Compt. rend., *127*, 763; *128*, 108; Barbier and Bouveault, Compt. rend., *121*, 168; *122*, 393 and 1422; Barbier and Léser, Bull. Soc. Chim., *17* [III.], 748; Barbier, Compt. rend., *128*, 110; Verley, Bull. Soc. Chim., *17* [III.], 175; Tiemann, Ber., *31*, 2989; *32*, 812 and 830; Tiemann and Semmler, Ber., *26*, 2719 and 2721; *28*, 2128; Wallach, Ann. Chem., *319*, 77.

[3] Wallach, Ann. Chem., *275*, 171.

duced with sodium and alcohol. This alcohol is also obtained as a decomposition product of geraniol, and further by the hydrolysis of geranic nitrile. It boils at 174° to 176°, has a sp. gr. of 0.850 and a refractive index, $n_D = 1.44889$. When this alcohol is boiled with dilute sulphuric acid, it is converted into an isomeric, saturated *oxide*, $C_8H_{16}O$. This reaction is quite analogous to that by which the homologous alcohol, $C_9H_{17}OH$, obtained from methyl heptylene ketone, is converted into an isomeric oxide, $C_9H_{18}O$ (see thujone).

Methyl hexylene oxide, $C_8H_{16}O$, boils at 127° to 129°, has a specific gravity of 0.850 and index of refraction, $n_D = 1.4249$. It has an odor resembling that of peppermint and of cineole, and is probably a homologue of the oxide, boiling at 78° to 83°, which Perkin and Freer[1] obtained from γ-pentylene glycol.

$$CH_3{\cdot}CH(OH){\cdot}CH_2{\cdot}CH_2{\cdot}CH_2(OH) = H_2O + O\begin{matrix} CH_2-CH-CH_2 \\ CH_2-CH_2 \end{matrix}$$

γ-Pentylene glycol. γ-Pentylene oxide.

$$\begin{matrix} CH_3 \\ CH_3 \end{matrix}{>}C{=}CH-CH_2-CH_2-CH(OH)-CH_3 = \begin{matrix} CH_3 \\ CH_3 \end{matrix}{>}CH-CH-CH_2 \quad O\!<\!\begin{matrix} \\ CH_2-CH-CH_2 \end{matrix}$$

Methyl hexylene carbinol. Methyl hexylene oxide.

Wallach and Elkeles also prepared methyl hexylene ketone by the distillation of cineolic amides :—

$$C_8H_{14}O\begin{matrix} \diagup CONHR \\ \diagdown COOH \end{matrix} = RNH_2 + CO + CO_2 + C_8H_{14}O.$$

When cineolic acid is submitted to dry distillation, it is partially converted into its anhydride, and partially into a liquid *monobasic acid*, $C_9H_{16}O_3$ (b. p. 135° under 11 mm.), together with some methyl hexylene ketone :[2]—$C_{10}H_{16}O_5 = CO_2 + C_9H_{16}O_3$.

Wallach and Elkeles have described the *methyl ester* of this monobasic acid, $C_9H_{16}O_3$; it is a liquid, boiling at 125° under a pressure of 13 mm.

Wallach and Gildemeister obtained only oxalic acid and carbon dioxide by the oxidation of cineolic acid with permanganate or dilute nitric acid. These two products are also formed when cineole is oxidized with dilute nitric acid; therefore, a relationship between cineolic acid and terebic acid or terpenylic acid does not appear to exist.

[1] Perkin and Freer, Ber., *19*, 2568; compare Lipp, Ber., *18*, 3285; *19*, 2843.
[2] Wallach, Ann. Chem., *246*, 274; *258*, 321; *271*, 26; Rupe, Ber., *33*, 1129.

According to Rupe,[1] when cineolic acid is heated with water at 160° for three hours, it yields a mixture of two isomeric acids, $C_9H_{16}O_3$; one of these acids is termed *α*-cinenic acid, and the other is called methoethylol-5-hexene-2-acid-6.

***α*-Cinenic acid**, $C_9H_{16}O_3$, is stable towards potassium permanganate, is not acted upon by bromine, does not react with phenylhydrazine, hydroxylamine, or semicarbazide, and probably contains a cyclic arrangement of the carbon atoms. It is a monobasic acid, crystallizes from petroleum ether in transparent crystals, melts at 83° to 84°, and boils at 127.5° to 129.5° (14 mm.) or at 245° to 247° under atmospheric pressure. It is soluble in most organic solvents, readily soluble in hot, sparingly in cold, water; it is volatile with steam. It forms *silver* and *calcium* salts, and *methyl* and *ethyl* esters. When *α*-cinenic acid is heated with water in a closed tube at 160°, it is partially converted into methoethylol-5-hexene-2-acid-6. When hydrochloric acid gas is allowed to act upon the alcoholic solution of *α*-cinenic acid, without cooling, *ethyl-δ-chloro-α-methoethylol-5-hexoate*, $C_8H_{15}Cl(OH)·COOC_2H_5$, is formed; this ester boils at 131° to 136° (17 mm.), and is an open-chain compound.

When *α*-cinenic acid is treated with a glacial acetic acid solution of hydrogen bromide, it yields *δ-bromo-α-oxyisopropyl hexenoic acid*, $C_8H_{15}Br(OH)·COOH$, which crystallizes in needles and melts at 97° to 98°; when the latter acid is treated with alcoholic potash, it gives rise to methoethylol-5-hexene-2-acid-6, and when treated with water, it forms *cinogenic acid*, $C_8H_{15}(OH)_2·COOH$. Cinogenic acid (*δ*-oxy-*α*-oxyisopropyl hexenoic acid) is also one of the products of the action of water under pressure on cineolic acid; it is insoluble in ether, crystallizes from chloroform in tablets and melts at 104.5° to 105°; when distilled under diminished pressure, or heated under pressure with water, it yields *α*-cinenic acid.

***β*-Cinenic acid**, $C_9H_{16}O_3$, is formed by the action of sulphuric acid on cineolic acid, and also by heating *α*-cinenic acid with dilute sulphuric acid under pressure; it is stereoisomeric with *α*-cinenic acid, and is possibly an example of *cis*- and *trans*-isomerism. It is a liquid acid, boiling at 122° to 123° (10 mm.), has the refractive index, $n_D = 1.4486$, and forms a characteristic *calcium salt*, which crystallizes from water in needles; the corresponding salt of *α*-cinenic acid is amorphous. *β*-Cinenic acid may be converted into cinogenic acid in the same manner as the *α*-acid.

Methoethylol-5-hexene-2-acid-6 (*α*-**oxyisopropyl-**Δ^{γ}**-hexenoic acid**), $C_9H_{16}O_3$, is isomeric with the cinenic acids and is formed together with *α*-cinenic acid by the action of water on cineolic acid.

[1] Rupe, Chem. Centr., *1898* [II.], 1055; Ber., *33*, 1129; *34*, 2191.

It crystallizes from water in small leaflets and from petroleum in silky needles; it melts at 59° to 60°, and boils at 152° to 153° (10 mm.). It decolorizes aqueous permanganate solutions, combines directly with one molecule of bromine, and contains an open-chain of carbon atoms. It is much more soluble in water than α-cinenic acid, and forms *silver* and *magnesium* salts. This acid is a β-oxy-acid, and when distilled under atmospheric pressure, it loses one molecule of water, yielding *α-iso-propylidene-Δ^{γ}-hexenoic acid (methoethene-5-hexene-2-acid-6)*, $C_9H_{14}O_2$; this is a colorless, liquid acid, which boils at 136° to 138° (11 mm.), has the sp. gr. 0.9816 at 17°, and gradually resinifies in the air.

By means of the strychnine salt, Rupe and Ronus[1] have resolved cineolic acid into its optically active components. When cineolic acid is dissolved in hot water and is treated with one molecular weight of finely pulverized strychnine, the salts of the two optically active and the inactive acids are obtained; they are separated by fractional crystallization. The *strychnine salt of dextro-cineolic acid*, $C_{31}H_{36}O_6N_2$, separates first and may be recrystallized from hot water; it forms large prisms, which melt at 195° to 197°. On further evaporation, the mother-liquors of the dextro-salt yield successively the salts of the *inactive* and *levo*-cineolic acids.

The strychnine salts of the active cineolic acids are converted into the free acids by treatment with dilute hydrochloric acid at a temperature not exceeding 40°. The resulting *dextro-* and *levo-cineolic acids* are repeatedly crystallized from water in order to free them (especially the levo-acid) from admixed racemic cineolic acid. The optically active acids, $C_{10}H_{16}O_5 + H_2O$, separate from water in large, transparent crystals which contain one molecule of water of crystallization, and melt at 79°; the racemic acid never crystallizes with water of crystallization, and is formed by crystallizing a mixture of equal quantities of the two optically active acids.

When the hydrated crystals of the active acids are exposed to dry air, they lose their water, yielding anhydrous acids which melt at 138° to 139°, and have the specific rotatory powers, $[\alpha]_D = +18.56°$ and $-19.10°$. The racemic acid melts[2] at 204° to 206°.

The active acids are much more soluble in water and in chloroform than the racemic acid. On dry distillation they yield the anhydride, methyl heptenone and other decomposition products.

[1] Rupe and Ronus, Ber., *33*, 3541.

[2] According to Wallach and Gildemeister, the inactive acid melts at 196° to 197°.

d-Cineolic anhydride, $C_{10}H_{14}O_4$, is formed by the action of acetic anhydride on d-cineolic acid; it boils at 165° to 167° (15 mm.), dissolves sparingly in petroleum ether, and crystallizes from benzene in large tablets, melting at 108°. It has the specific rotatory power, $[\alpha]_D = +45.37°$, at 20° in a benzene solution.

13. TERPAN-1, 4, 8-TRIOL, $C_{10}H_{17}(OH)_3$.

This compound has already been mentioned as an oxidation product of Baeyer's $\Delta^{4(8)}$terpen-1-ol (see page 273). Its constitution may be regarded as proved by its transformation into tribromoterpane, melting at 110°.

14. TRIOXYHEXAHYDROCYMENE, $C_{10}H_{17}(OH)_3$.

This substance melts at 121° to 122°. (Compare under terpineol, page 262.)

15. PINOLE HYDRATE, $C_{10}H_{17}O{\cdot}OH$.

This compound is described under pinole; see page 276.

16. LIMONETROL, $C_{10}H_{16}(OH)_4$.

Limonetrol is prepared by the following method suggested by G. Wagner.[1]

Five liters of a one per cent. solution of permanganate are added drop by drop to a mixture of one liter of water and sixty-five grams of limonene, the mixture being continually shaken. When the reaction is complete, the product is filtered and the precipitate, consisting of manganese oxides, is carefully washed with water. The volatile compounds are removed from the filtrate by distillation with steam, and the residue is concentrated by evaporation and extracted with ether. On evaporation of this solvent, the resultant limonetrol is washed with a small quantity of ether, and crystallized from alcohol; it separates in small, lustrous needles. The yield is very good.

This tetrahydric alcohol is readily soluble in water, has a sweet taste, and melts at 191.5° to 192°.

17. PINOLE GLYCOLS, $C_{10}H_{16}O(OH)_2$.

These compounds are mentioned under pinole (see page 279).

The most important transformations of the various keto- and oxy-hydrocymenes, in so far as they are not represented in the tables given under terpineol, are shown in the accompanying table.

[1] G. Wagner, Ber., 23, 2315.

TRANSFORMATIONS OF THE KETO- AND OXY-HYDROCYMENES.

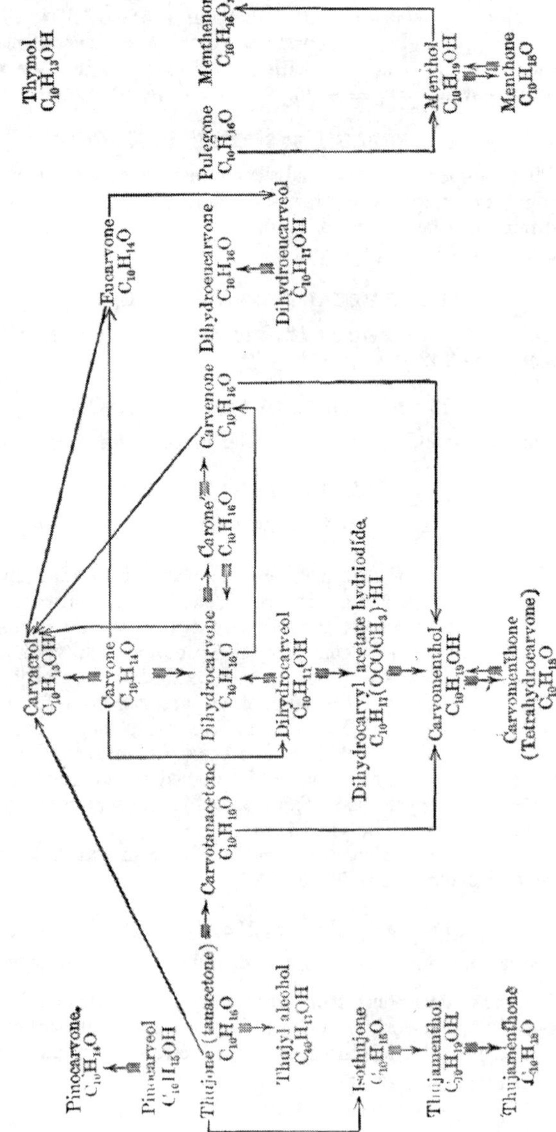

AMIDO-DERIVATIVES OF THE TERPENES.

I. BASES WHICH CAN NOT BE REGARDED AS DERIVATIVES OF THE HYDROCYMENES.

(Analogues of Pinene, Camphene, Fenchene, and of Campholenic Acid and Fencholenic Acid.[1])

1. PINYLAMINE, $C_{10}H_{15}NH_2$.

Pinylamine is formed by the reduction of nitrosopinene, the compound obtained by the action of alcoholic potash on pinene nitrosochloride :—

$$C_{10}H_{15}NO + 4H = H_2O + C_{10}H_{15}NH_2.$$

In order to prepare it, thirty grams of nitrosopinene are dissolved in about 200 cc. of warm glacial acetic acid; the solution is diluted with water until it commences to appear cloudy, and is then treated with zinc dust, which is added in small portions at a time. After the first violent evolution of hydrogen has abated, the reaction is accelerated by adding water and heating the mixture on the water-bath for several hours. The liquid is then poured off from the zinc, which must always be present in excess, and is diluted with a large amount of water; the zinc is precipitated from the hot solution by hydrogen sulphide, is filtered off, and the filtrate concentrated on the water-bath until a dark coloration appears. It is again filtered, and the sparingly soluble pinylamine nitrate is precipitated by the addition of a hot, saturated solution of sodium nitrate. It is crystallized from hot water. The yield of pinylamine is approximately fifty per cent. of the theoretical (Wallach and Lorentz[2]).

The free base is produced by treating pinylamine nitrate with sodium hydroxide; it is dried over potash, and distilled in vacuum.

[1] A series of papers has been published by P. Duden on "Synthetical bases of the series of terpenes and camphors"; the following references are mentioned: Ber., *33*, 481; Ann. Chem., *313*, 25 and 59.

[2] Wallach and Lorentz, Ann. Chem., *268*, 197; compare Ann. Chem., *258*, 346, and Ber., *24*, 1549.

When freshly distilled, it is a thick, colorless oil, which boils at 207° to 208° under ordinary pressure, and at 98° to 99° under 22 mm. to 23 mm. It may be kept unchanged in a sealed vessel, but in the air it soon decomposes with liberation of ammonia; it also takes up carbonic anhydride from the air. It is almost insoluble in water, but dissolves freely in alcohol, ether and chloroform. It has a strong basic smell, resembling that of borneol. Its specific gravity at 17° is 0.943. Pinylamine is an unsaturated compound.

Pinylamine hydrochloride, $C_{10}H_{15}NH_2{\cdot}HCl$, is precipitated from an ethereal solution of the amine by hydrochloric acid gas, and crystallizes from water in thin needles, melting at 229° to 230°. If this salt be heated above its melting point, it is very readily decomposed into ammonium chloride, cymene, and a small quantity of a compound which appears to unite with oxygen in the air, and has the composition, $C_{10}H_{16}O$; this oxygenated compound yields an oxime when treated with hydroxylamine. The decomposition of pinylamine hydrochloride is represented by the equation:—$C_{10}H_{15}NH_2{\cdot}HCl = NH_4Cl + C_{10}H_{14}$.

Pinylamine platinochloride, $(C_{10}H_{17}N{\cdot}HCl)_2PtCl_4$, is sparingly soluble in water, but freely in alcohol; it decomposes without melting when heated above 200°.

Pinylamine nitrate, $C_{10}H_{15}NH_2{\cdot}HNO_3$, is difficultly soluble in water. It crystallizes from dilute alcohol in long, colorless needles.

Pinylamine sulphate, $(C_{10}H_{15}NH_2)_2{\cdot}H_2SO_4$, forms small needles, and decomposes above 200° without melting.

Pinylamine thiocyanate, $C_{10}H_{15}NH_2{\cdot}HCNS$, is obtained, when the aqueous solutions of equal molecular proportions of pinylamine hydrochloride and potassium thiocyanate are mixed, allowed to evaporate, and the residue is extracted with alcohol. It crystallizes from water in well defined prisms, and melts at 135° to 136°.

Pinylamine oxalate, $(C_{10}H_{15}NH_2)_2H_2C_2O_4$, separates at once in the form of brilliant crystals, if a concentrated aqueous solution of one molecular proportion of oxalic acid be added to a dilute alcoholic solution of two molecules of pinylamine. It melts without decomposition at 247° to 248°, and dissolves sparingly in all ordinary solvents.

Pinylamine picrate forms yellow needles, and is slightly soluble in cold water.

Acetyl pinylamine, $C_{10}H_{15}NH{\cdot}COCH_3$, is prepared by heating pinylamine with acetic anhydride. It crystallizes from petroleum ether or alcohol, and melts at 108° to 109°.

Benzoyl pinylamine, $C_{10}H_{15}NH{\cdot}COC_6H_5$, is best obtained by the action of one molecule of benzoyl chloride on an ethereal solution of two molecular proportions of pinylamine; some pinylamine hydrochloride separates during the reaction, and is filtered off. The ethereal solution is evaporated, and the resulting benzoyl compound is washed with ammonia, and crystallized from glacial acetic acid or petroleum ether; it separates in small needles, melting at 125°.

Pinyl carbamide, $C_{10}H_{15}NH{\cdot}CO{\cdot}NH_2$, is produced by treating pinylamine hydrochloride with potassium cyanate; it crystallizes in long, colorless needles, and melts at 156°.

Benzylidene pinylamine, $C_{10}H_{15}N = CH{\cdot}C_6H_5$, results on mixing equal molecular weights of pinylamine and benzaldehyde; the mixture becomes warm, and the reaction takes place with elimination of water. It crystallizes from alcohol in splendid crystals, melts at 52° to 53°, and decomposes on keeping.

Furfuro-pinylamine, $C_{10}H_{15}N = CH{\cdot}C_4H_3O$, is the condensation-product of pinylamine and furfural; it separates from alcohol in well formed crystals, and melts at 80° to 81°.

***o*-Oxybenzylidene pinylamine**, $C_{10}H_{15}N = CH{\cdot}C_6H_4OH$, forms lustrous, yellow crystals, and melts at 108° to 109°.

The halogen alkyls react vigorously with pinylamine.

Pinocarveol,[1] $C_{10}H_{15}OH$, is formed when pinylamine is heated with a solution of sodium nitrite. Since this is a secondary alcohol, the following formula of pinylamine, originally proposed by Wallach, does *not* represent the facts:

```
        CH3
        |
        CNH2
       /    \
     HC      CH
      | \  / |
      |  \/  |
      |  /\  |
     HC      CH
       \    /
        CH
        |
        CH
       /  \
    H3C    CH3
```

2. AMIDOTEREBENTENE, $C_{10}H_{15}NH_2$.

Pesci and Betelli[2] also converted pinene into an amine, $C_{10}H_{15}NH_2$, which is isomeric with pinylamine. It is obtained from nitroterebentene.

[1] Wallach, Ann. Chem., *277*, 149; Wallach and Smythe, Ann. Chem., *390*, 286.

[2] Pesci and Betelli, Gazz. Chim., *16*, 337; Jahresb. Chem., 1886, 613.

Nitroterebentene, $C_{10}H_{15}NO_2$, is obtained by treating French or American [1] oil of turpentine (levo- or dextro-pinene) with nitrous acid. A seventy-five per cent. aqueous solution of 135 parts of potassium nitrite is gradually added to a cold mixture of 100 parts of the terpene and 545 parts of dilute sulphuric acid (145 parts of concentrated acid to 400 parts of water), the mixture being well shaken; a green oil is formed, and is separated by the addition of an excess of water. This product is shaken with ammonia, and purified by fractional distillation with steam (Pesci and Betelli [2]).

It is a yellow liquid, having an odor of peppermint, and is readily decomposed on heating.

Amidoterebentene is prepared by reducing nitroterebentene with zinc dust and glacial acetic acid. It is an oil, having an agreeable odor, and boils at 197° to 200°, undergoing slight decomposition; it boils without decomposition at 94° to 97° under a pressure of 9 mm. (Pesci and Betelli).

Amidoterebentene hydrochloride, $C_{10}H_{15}NH_2 \cdot HCl$, obtained from either levo- or dextro-pinene, is optically levorotatory,[1] $[\alpha]_D = -48.5°$. It crystallizes in rectangular tablets, having a mother-of-pearl luster. The *platinum* salt forms hexagonal plates, is insoluble in cold water, and is decomposed by boiling water. The *sulphate* separates in a gelatinous, hygroscopic mass. The *oxalate* is obtained in sparingly soluble leaflets.

Pinene phthalimide,

$$C_6H_4\left\langle\begin{matrix}CO\\CO\end{matrix}\right\rangle NC_{10}H_{15}$$

prepared by Pesci [3] by the action of phthalic anhydride on amidoterebentene, melts at 99° to 100°. It is insoluble in water, readily soluble in alcohol, ether, and chloroform, and has the specific rotatory power, $[\alpha]_D = -35.38°$. The potassium salt of pinene phthalamic acid is formed by dissolving pinene phthalimide in a hot solution of potash; it crystallizes in thin needles.

Pinene phthalamic acid,

$$C_6H_4\left\langle\begin{matrix}COOH\\CONHC_{10}H_{15}\end{matrix}\right.$$

results by decomposing its potassium salt with hydrochloric acid.

[1] Pesci, Gazz. Chim., *18*, 219; Jahresb. Chem., *1888*, 899.
[2] Pesci and Betelli, Gazz. Chim., *16*, 337; Jahresb. Chem., *1886*, 613.
[3] Pesci, Gazz. Chim., *21* (I.), 1; Chem. Centr., *1891* (I.), 542.

It is recrystallized from chloroform, melts at 109° to 111°, and is very unstable.

Trimethyl terebenthyl ammonium iodide, $C_{10}H_{15}N(CH_3)_3I$, is produced by the interaction of methyl iodide and amidoterebentene, and crystallizes in rectangular leaflets. The *chloride*, prepared from the iodide, is deliquescent, but yields a platinum salt which is nearly insoluble (Pesci and Betelli).

3. BORNYLAMINES, $C_{10}H_{17}NH_2$.

Bornylamine was discovered by Leuckart and Bach,[1] who obtained it by the treatment of camphor with ammonium formate, and also by the reduction of camphoroxime with sodium and alcohol. It was later made the subject of a detailed investigation by Wallach and Griepenkerl.[2]

It is best prepared by the method proposed by Leuckart and Bach and subsequently modified by Wallach and Griepenkerl. An intimate mixture of not more than four grams of camphor and the same weight of ammonium formate is heated at 220° to 230° for five hours. The reaction-product forms a syrupy mass consisting chiefly of formyl bornylamine, together with some free bornylamine, unchanged camphor, and ammonium salts, and solidifies when shaken with cold water. It is boiled with alcoholic potash for five or six hours, and the resulting bornylamine and camphor are distilled over with steam. The distillate is acidified with hydrochloric acid, filtered, concentrated and shaken with ether to remove impurities which may be present in the solution. The base is then set free by potash, extracted with ether, and the ethereal solution dried with potassium hydroxide; the ether is distilled off, and the bornylamine rectified, being careful to keep the receiver well cooled on account of the extreme volatility of the base. The yield is about eighty to eighty-two per cent.

Bornylamine melts at 159° to 160°, boils at 199° to 200°, and dissolves very easily in alcohol and ether. It has an intensive basic odor resembling that of camphor and piperidine; it sublimes at the ordinary temperature, and unites readily with carbonic anhydride in the air. It is optically active, a 12.5 per cent. solution having a specific rotatory power of $[\alpha]_D = -18° 35' 41''$ (Leuckart and Bach).

Bornylamine hydrochloride, $C_{10}H_{17}NH_2 \cdot HCl$, is precipitated in the form of small, white needles when hydrogen chloride is passed into an ethereal solution of bornylamine. When the hydrochloride

[1] Leuckart and Bach, Ber., *20*, 104.

[2] Wallach and Griepenkerl, Ann. Chem., *269*, 347.

is dissolved in water or alcohol, it suffers partial decomposition. It sublimes undecomposed in splendid needles without the formation of ammonium chloride and camphor.

The **platinochloride**, $(C_{10}H_{17}NH_2 HCl)_2PtCl_4$, dissolves readily in hot water and alcohol, and forms golden-yellow scales.

Bornylamine hydrobromide,[1] $C_{10}H_{17}NH_2 \cdot HBr$, separates as a colorless, crystalline precipitate on the addition of bromine to an ethereal bornylamine solution. It combines with bromine, forming an unstable, red product.

Bornylamine acid sulphate,[2] $C_{10}H_{17}NH_2 \cdot H_2SO_4$, is prepared from the theoretical quantities of dilute sulphuric acid and bornylamine; it separates in orthorhombic tablets on evaporation of the solution. Like the hydrochloride, its aqueous solution is decomposed by boiling.

Bornylamine tartrate, $C_{10}H_{17}NH_2 \cdot C_4H_6O_4 + H_2O$, is easily soluble in water, almost insoluble in cold alcohol, and crystallizes from hot alcohol in needles

Bornylamine picrate,[1] $C_{10}H_{17}NH_2 \cdot C_6H_2(NO_2)_3OH$, forms golden-yellow needles, which are almost insoluble in ether.

Bornylamine is very readily converted into the carbylamine derivative.[2]

When bornylamine or its formyl compound is heated at 200° to 210° with acetic anhydride, it is decomposed into camphene, $C_{10}H_{16}$, and ammonia:[1]

$$C_{10}H_{17}NH_2 = C_{10}H_{16} + NH_3$$

Formyl bornylamine,[2] $C_{10}H_{17}NH \cdot CHO$.—It has already been mentioned that this compound forms the chief constituent of the reaction-product produced by the action of ammonium formate on camphor; it may also be prepared by the action of formic acid on the free base When recrystallized from hot water, it forms white, glistening scales, melting at 61°.

Acetyl bornylamine,[2] $C_{10}H_{17}NH \cdot COCH_3$, is formed by the action of acetyl chloride on an ethereal solution of bornylamine; the bornylamine hydrochloride, which at first separates, is filtered off, the ethereal filtrate evaporated, and the resultant acetyl compound crystallized from dilute alcohol. It forms leaflets, melting at 141°, and is nearly insoluble in ligroine.

Benzoyl bornylamine, $C_{10}H_{17}NH \cdot COC_6H_5$, is prepared like the preceding compound, and is similar to it in appearance and solubility. It melts at 131°.

[1] Wallach and Griepenkerl, Ann Chem, *269*, 347.
[2] Leuckart and Bach, Ber, *20*, 104.

Bornylcarbamide,[1] $C_{10}H_{17}NH·CO·NH_2$, is formed from bornylamine hydrochloride and potassium isocyanate. It crystallizes in needles, which melt at 164°, and is readily soluble in hot water and alcohol.

Methyl bornylcarbamide,[1] $C_{10}H_{17}NH·CO·NHCH_3$, results by mixing the ethereal solutions of methyl isocyanate and bornylamine. It melts at 200°.

Phenyl bornylcarbamide,[1] $C_{10}H_{17}NH·CONHC_6H_5$, separates in the form of silvery leaflets when phenyl isocyanate is added to an ethereal solution of bornylamine. It melts and decomposes at 248°.

Bornyl phenylthiocarbamide,[1] $C_{10}H_{17}NH·CS·NHC_6H_5$, is produced from phenylthiocarbimide and the free base in an ethereal solution; it forms colorless needles, which melt at 170° and are almost insoluble in petroleum ether.

Dibornylthiocarbamide,[2] $CS(NHC_{10}H_{17})_2$, is formed when the dithiocarbamic acid salt, obtained by the interaction of carbon bisulphide and bornylamine, is boiled for some time with ten to fifteen times its weight of ninety-six per cent. alcohol. It separates from alcohol in compact, transparent crystals, which melt at 223° to 224°.

According to Wallach and Griepenkerl,[2] the alkyl chlorides act vigorously on bornylamine. When equal molecular quantities of benzyl chloride and the free amine are heated at 140° to 150° and the resulting product is treated with alkalis, a mixture of bases is obtained which is fractionally distilled in vacuum; the following compound is thus isolated.

Benzyl bornylamine, $C_{10}H_{17}NH·CH_2C_6H_5$, is a thick oil, boiling at 184° under 14 mm. pressure. The *hydrochloric acid salt* separates from water or alcohol in colorless crystals; its *platinochloride* crystallizes in red, transparent prisms.

Benzyl bornylamine unites with methyl iodide, forming a *methiodide*, which crystallizes from hot alcohol in thin needles, and is very difficultly soluble in hot water.

Benzylidene bornylamine,[2] $C_{10}H_{17}N = CHC_6H_5$, is an oil; its *hydrochloride*, which crystallizes in small needles, and its *platinochloride* have been analyzed.

The other condensation-products of bornylamine with aldehydes are liquids.

Bornylamine is very stable towards fuming nitric acid (Wallach and Griepenkerl[2]).

[1] Leuckart and Bach, Ber., *20*, 104.
[2] Wallach and Griepenkerl, Ann. Chem., *269*, 347.

When formyl bornylamine is oxidized with an acetic acid solution of chromic anhydride, it yields bornylamine and small quantities of a very volatile compound, which melts at 159°, and contains oxygen but no nitrogen, it appears to have the empirical formula, $C_{10}H_{16}O$ or $C_{10}H_{18}O$ A compound having the same melting point has also been observed by Lampe[1] in the decomposition of bornylamine nitrite.

Dibornylamine, $(C_{10}H_{17})_2NH$, is obtained in a yield of about nine per cent. from the product of the action between camphor and ammonium formate (Wallach and Griepenkerl[2]). It remains in the residue from the distillation of bornylamine with steam, and is obtained as an oil which slowly solidifies; it may be purified by distillation in vacuum.

Dibornylamine boils at 180° to 181° under a pressure of 12 mm, and crystallizes from alcohol in lustrous plates, melting at 43° to 44°.

Dibornylamine hydrochloride, $C_{20}H_{35}N\ HCl$, is precipitated by passing hydrochloric acid gas into an ethereal solution of the base It crystallizes in needles or plates, dissolves sparingly in cold, readily in hot, water and melts at 260° with partial decomposition. Its *platinochloride* crystallizes in red needles.

Dibornylamine nitrate, $C_{20}H_{35}N \cdot HNO_3$, is sparingly soluble in water; it is well adapted for the separation of dibornylamine from bornylamine.

A *compound,* $C_{20}H_{35}N \cdot HBr \cdot Br_2$, is formed when bromine is added to a solution of dibornylamine in petroleum ether. It is almost insoluble in ether and ethyl acetate, but crystallizes from alcohol in stable, golden-yellow plates, which melt at 184°.

Dibornylamine nitrite, $C_{20}H_{35}N\ HNO_2$, is rather sparingly soluble in water, but may be recrystallized unchanged from boiling alcohol.

On boiling with acetic anhydride, dibornylamine forms a compound, which crystallizes from alcohol in lustrous plates, melts at 59°, and seems to be isomeric with dibornylamine.

According to more recent investigations by Forster,[3] the bornylamine prepared by heating camphor with ammonium formate at 220° to 240° or by reducing camphoroxime with sodium and amyl alcohol is not an individual compound, but contains two isomeric bases, $C_{10}H_{17}NH_2$. One of these melts at 163°, is dextrorotatory, $[\alpha]_D = +45\ 5°$, and is termed *bornylamine,* whilst the other melts at 180°, is levorotatory, $[\alpha]_D = -31\ 3°$, and is

[1] Lampe, Inaug. Diss, Göttingen, *1889*, 41.

[2] Wallach and Griepenkerl, Ann. Chem, *269*, 347

[3] Martin O Forster, Journ Chem Soc, *73*, 386, *75*, 934 and 1149

called *neobornylamine*. (Leuckart and Bach's "bornylamine" melts at 159° to 160°, and is levorotatory, $[\alpha]_D = -18.6°$.)

Although bornylamine melts lower than neobornylamine, all its derivatives possess a higher melting point than those of the isomeride. The derivatives of bornylamine are also less readily soluble than those of the levorotatory base, and this property is employed in effecting the separation of the two isomerides.

The preparation of the two isomerides is accomplished as follows. Seventy-five grams of camphoroxime, dissolved in 750 cc. of amyl alcohol, are treated in a reflux apparatus with seventy-five grams of sodium; the process requires about four hours, after which 100 cc. of amyl alcohol are added. The reaction-mixture is then treated with 450 cc. of water, and the same volume of concentrated hydrochloric acid; the amyl alcohol is finally removed by distillation with steam, and on allowing the aqueous residue to cool, the hydrochlorides of the two amines crystallize rapidly in lustrous needles. The yield is practically quantitative.

The separation of the two isomeric bases is based on the greater solubility in water of the hydrochloride of neobornylamine. The free bases are obtained by decomposing the hydrochlorides with caustic soda. About sixty per cent. of the product obtained on reducing camphoroxime as above described consists of the dextrorotatory bornylamine, and forty per cent. is the levo-neobornylamine.

Bornylamine, $C_{10}H_{17}NH_2$, is a white volatile solid, melting at 163°; it somewhat resembles camphor, having a faint, pungent odor like that of piperidine. It dissolves very readily in cold organic solvents, but is insoluble in water (Forster).

Neobornylamine, $C_{10}H_{17}NH_2$, closely resembles its isomeride, but remains as a powder after being kept in a desiccator, which treatment causes bornylamine to become more camphor-like in consistence; it melts at 180°. It is insoluble in water, but more freely soluble in organic solvents than bornylamine.

Many derivatives of the two bases have been prepared and carefully studied by Forster. The most important of these are given in the accompanying table, which shows the differences in melting points of the derivatives of Forster's bornylamine and neobornylamine, and Leuckart and Bach's bornylamine; the latter may be regarded as a mixture of neobornylamine with about twenty per cent. of the dextro-bornylamine.

For the "influence of substitution on specific rotation in the bornylamine series," and the "influence of an unsaturated linking on the optical activity of certain derivatives of bornylamine," the original publications[1] must be consulted.

	Bornylamine (Forster)	Neobornylamine (Forster)	Bornylamine (Leuckart, Wallach)
Base	m p 163°, $[\alpha]_D = + 45.5°$	m p 180°, $[\alpha]_D = - 31.3°$	m p 159°–160°, $[\alpha]_D = -$ 18°35′41
Hydrochloride	infusible below 320°, $[\alpha]_D = + 22.7°$	infusible below 320°, $[\alpha]_D = - 39.0°$	——
Formyl derivative	m p 93°, $[\alpha]_D = - 42.1°$	m p 72°–73°, $[\alpha]_D = - 19.4°$	m p. 61°
Acetyl derivative	m p 145°, $[\alpha]_D = - 42.9°$	m p 143°, $[\alpha]_D = - 19.5°$	m p 141°
Benzoyl derivative	m p 139°, $[\alpha]_D = - 21.8°$	m p 130°, $[\alpha]_D = - 44.7°$	m p 131°
Platinochloride	m p 321°	m. p. 303°	——
Carbamide	m p 175°	m p. 169°	m p 164°
Phenylcarbamide	m p 270°	m p. 254°	m p 248°
Picrate	m p 256°	m p 248°	——
Methyl derivative	b p 205° (759 mm)	——	——
Ethyl derivative	b p 215°–216° (758 mm)	——	——
Benzyl derivative	b p 313°–315° (740 mm)	——	184° (14 mm) liquid
Benzylidene derivative	m p 58°–59°	——	

[1] Martin O Forster, Journ Chem. Soc, 75, 934 and 1149.

4. CAMPHYLAMINES, $C_9H_{15}CH_2NH_2$.

α-Camphylamine is produced by the reduction of the nitrile of α-campholenic acid (camphoroxime anhydride):—

$$C_9H_{15}CN + 4H = C_9H_{15}CH_2NH_2.$$

The reduction may be accomplished by zinc and alcoholic hydrochloric acid (Goldschmidt and Koreff[1]), or by sodium and alcohol (Goldschmidt[2]). Goldschmidt and Schulhof,[3] who made a special study of camphylamine, employed the last-mentioned method for its preparation.

α-Camphylamine[4] is a colorless liquid, boiling at 194° to 196°, and has a strong basic odor; when exposed to the air, it combines with carbon dioxide and solidifies to a waxy mass. In a one decimeter tube, $[\alpha]_D = +6°$.

α-Camphylamine hydrochloride,[1] $C_{10}H_{19}N{\cdot}HCl$, forms colorless, thin, orthorhombic plates; it is readily soluble.

α-Camphylamine platinochloride,[3] $(C_{10}H_{19}N)_2H_2PtCl_6$, crystallizes in brilliant, yellow leaflets, which decompose without melting when heated above 200°. The *mercuriochloride*[2] forms lustrous, orthorhombic plates.

Acid α-camphylamine oxalate, $C_{10}H_{19}N{\cdot}C_2O_4H_2 + \frac{1}{2}H_2O$, is precipitated when a solution of camphylamine hydrochloride is treated with a solution of oxalic acid; it separates in colorless, lustrous, orthorhombic crystals, and melts with decomposition at 194°.

α-Camphylamine sulphate, $(C_{10}H_{19}N)_2H_2SO_4 + H_2O$, crystallizes in orthorhombic prisms, which are readily soluble. It cannot be recrystallized from hot water without decomposition.

α-Camphylamine dichromate, $(C_{10}H_{19}N)_2H_2Cr_2O_7$, is precipitated from a solution of camphylamine hydrochloride by potassium dichromate.

α-Camphylamine picrate forms slender, yellow needles, and melts with decomposition at 194°.

Benzoyl α-camphylamine, $C_{10}H_{17}NH{\cdot}COC_6H_5$, is obtained when an ethereal solution of camphylamine is treated with benzoyl chloride. Some camphylamine hydrochloride separates and is filtered off; the ethereal filtrate is evaporated, and the residue consisting of the benzoyl compound is washed with a soda solution,

[1] Goldschmidt and Koreff, Ber., *18*, 1632.
[2] Goldschmidt, Ber., *18*, 3297.
[3] Goldschmidt and Schulhof, Ber., *19*, 708.
[4] Tiemann, Ber., *29*, 3006.

and crystallized from ligroine. It separates in colorless prisms, melting at 75° to 77°.

a-**Camphyl phenylthiocarbamide,** $C_{10}H_{17}NH \cdot CS \cdot NHC_6H_5$, is prepared by the action of phenylthiocarbimide on an ethereal solution of the base, it is crystallized from ligroine, and recrystallized from ether. It separates in compact, colorless, lustrous prisms, melts at 118°, and is readily soluble in alcohol and benzene, more sparingly in ether, and very difficultly in ligroine.

a-**Camphylamine dithiocamphylcarbamate,**[1] $C_{10}H_{17}NH \cdot CS\,SNH_3 \cdot C_{10}H_{17}$, is obtained by the action of carbon bisulphide on camphylamine.

a-**Camphyl thiocarbimide**[2] is formed in small quantity when the preceding compound is boiled with a solution of mercuric chloride.

a-Camphylamine reacts with ethyl iodide even in the cold, and, like bornylamine, it gives the isonitrile reaction.

β-**Camphylamine,**[2] $C_{10}H_{17}NH_2$, is produced by the reduction of *β*-campholenonitrile, $C_9H_{15}CN$, in alcoholic solution with sodium. It is optically inactive, and boils at 196° to 198°.

5. FENCHYLAMINE, $C_{10}H_{17}NH_2$.

Wallach[3] obtained this compound by treating fenchone with ammonium formate, and also by reducing fenchonoxime with sodium and alcohol.[4] Like fenchone, fenchylamine is known in two optically active modifications having opposite rotatory powers, as well as in an inactive form ; the derivatives of the racemic modification differ from those of its active components in melting point and in solubility. A detailed investigation of dextrorotatory fenchylamine and its derivatives was carried out by Wallach, Griepenkerl and Luhrig.[5]

In order to prepare fenchylamine by the ammonium formate method, five grams of pure fenchone are heated with an *equal* weight of ammonium formate at 220° to 230° for six hours. The resultant solid product contains unchanged fenchone, fenchylamine, formyl fenchylamine (the chief product) and ammonium salts. The fenchone is removed by distilling the acidulated reaction-product with steam. The formyl derivative remaining in the residue is saponified by boiling with concentrated hydrochloric

[1] Goldschmidt and Schulhof, Ber, *19*, 708.
[2] Tiemann, Ber, *30*, 242.
[3] Wallach, Ann. Chem., *263*, 140.
[4] Wallach, Ann Chem, *272*, 105.
[5] Wallach, Griepenkerl and Lührig, Ann. Chem, *269*, 358

acid, and fenchylamine hydrochloride is obtained on the evaporation of the hydrochloric acid solution; the free base results by decomposing the hydrochloride with potash. The yield of fenchylamine is about ninety per cent. of the theoretical.

For the preparation of fenchylamine from fenchonoxime,[1] twenty-five grams of sodium are added rather rapidly to a solution of twenty-one grams of the oxime in 100 cc. of absolute alcohol. Any undissolved metal is brought into solution by a further addition of alcohol, and the product is then distilled in a current of steam. The resulting amine is dried over potash, and rectified at ordinary pressure.

Fenchylamine boils at 195°, and has the specific gravity of 0.9095 at 22°; it has an odor resembling that of piperidine and of bornylamine. It absorbs carbonic anhydride from the air, forming solid fenchylamine fenchyl carbamate.[2]

Fenchylamine hydrochloride, $C_{10}H_{17}NH_2 \cdot HCl$, dissolves in water and alcohol, and by slow crystallization is obtained in transparent prisms. It is readily soluble in ether.

The *platinochloride*, $(C_{10}H_{17}NH_2)_2H_2PtCl_6$, crystallizes from water in long, thin, hydrated prisms, which effloresce when kept over sulphuric acid.

The *hydriodide* is also rather soluble in water and dilute alcohol, and separates in well defined crystals. The *nitrate* is distinguished by its great power of crystallization. *Fenchylamine sulphate* forms needles or plates, which are only moderately easily soluble. The *picrate* differs from bornylamine picrate in that it is readily soluble in ether. The *tartrate* may be precipitated from an aqueous solution by alcohol. The *neutral oxalate* is sparingly soluble.

Fenchylamine nitrite, $C_{10}H_{17}NH_2 \cdot HNO_2$, is moderately stable, readily soluble in water, and sparingly in a concentrated sodium nitrite solution; hence, small lustrous needles of fenchylamine nitrite are precipitated on the addition of a sodium nitrite solution to a concentrated, neutral solution of a fenchylamine salt.

Formyl fenchylamine,[3] $C_{10}H_{17}NH \cdot CHO$, is obtained by the action of ammonium formate on fenchone; it is also formed by the treatment of fenchylamine with chloral. It crystallizes from dilute alcohol in lustrous leaflets, and melts, for the most part, at 87°, although some portions remain solid until the temperature rises to 112°.

[1] Wallach, Ann. Chem., 272, 105.
[2] Wallach Griepenkerl and Lührig, Ann. Chem., *269*, 358.
[3] Wallach, Ann. Chem., *263*, 140.

Acetyl fenchylamine,[1] $C_{10}H_{17}NH\ COCH_3$, is prepared by heating the free amine with acetic anhydride, it crystallizes from ether, and melts at 98° It is not very characteristic.

Propionyl fenchylamine,[2] $C_{10}H_{17}NH{\cdot}COC_2H_5$, melts at 123°.

Butyryl fenchylamine,[2] $C_{10}H_{17}NH{\cdot}COC_3H_7$, melts at 77.5°.

Benzoyl fenchylamine,[1] $C_{10}H_{17}NH{\cdot}COC_6H_5$, is produced by the action of benzoyl chloride on an ethereal solution of the amine. After evaporation of the ether, the syrupy residue is washed with water which dissolves the fenchylamine hydrochloride formed in the reaction. The resultant solid product is then dissolved in alcohol, and the benzoyl compound is precipitated with dilute sodium hydroxide, free benzoic acid being thus removed. It melts at 133° to 135°.

Difenchyloxamide,[1] $(CONHC_{10}H_{17})_2$, results on mixing oxalic ester (one molecule) and fenchylamine (two molecules); it solidifies after standing for some time. It crystallizes from alcohol in long prisms or quadratic, thin plates, melting at 188°.

Fenchylcarbamide,[1] $C_{10}H_{17}NH{\cdot}CONH_2$, is prepared by boiling the solution of equal molecular proportions of fenchylamine hydrochloride and potassium isocyanate; it separates from the cold solution in small needles, melting at 170° to 171°.

Fenchyl phenylthiocarbamide,[1] $C_{10}H_{17}NH{\cdot}CS{\cdot}NHC_6H_5$, is formed when the dilute ethereal solutions of equal molecules of fenchylamine and phenylthiocarbimide are mixed; the reaction is rather violent This compound is especially well adapted for the characterization of fenchylamine; it is sparingly soluble in cold alcohol and separates from this solvent in brittle, acute crystals, while it is deposited from dilute solutions in colorless, brilliant, well defined crystals, melting at 153° to 154°. Optically inactive fenchyl phenylthiocarbamide melts at 169° to 170°.[3]

Difenchylthiocarbamide,[1] $CS(NHC_{10}H_{17})_2$, is obtained when carbon bisulphide is added to an ethereal solution of fenchylamine, and the resultant dithiocarbamic acid salt is boiled with alcohol for a short time. It separates from the cold solution in the form of white leaflets, melting at 210°.

Methyl fenchylamine, $C_{10}H_{17}NHCH_3$.—When an ethereal solution of fenchylamine is treated with methyl iodide, a mixture of mono- and di-methyl fenchylamine hydriodides is produced and gradually crystallizes from the ethereal solution. The two salts may be readily separated by crystallizing from water in which the

[1] Wallach, Griepenkerl and Luhrig, Ann Chem, *269*, 358

[2] Wallach and Binz, Ann Chem, *276*, 317, compare Zeitschr für physik Chem, *12*, 723

[3] Wallach, Ann Chem, *272*, 105

salt of the mono-methyl base is more sparingly soluble than that of the di-methyl derivative.

Mono-methyl fenchylamine, derived from its hydriodide, is an oil of specific gravity 0.8950 at 20°; it boils at 201° to 202°, has a refractive index, $n_D = 1.46988$, at 20°, and is a weaker base than fenchylamine. Its *hydrochloride* forms prismatic crystals, and is stable when exposed to the air; it is insoluble in ether, whilst fenchylamine hydrochloride is easily soluble (method of separation of fenchylamine and methyl fenchylamine).

Nitroso-methyl fenchylamine,

$$C_{10}H_{17}N\begin{cases}CH_3\\NO\end{cases}$$

is precipitated when a solution of methyl fenchylamine hydrochloride is treated with a solution of sodium nitrite; it first forms an oil which solidifies in the cold. It may be purified by dissolving in alcohol and precipitating with ice, and melts at 52° to 53°.

Benzyl fenchylamine,[1] $C_{10}H_{17}NH{\cdot}CH_2C_6H_5$, is prepared by boiling the molecular proportions of fenchylamine and benzyl chloride in a reflux apparatus for about one hour; benzyl fenchylamine hydrochloride separates on cooling, is washed with ether to remove fenchylamine hydrochloride, and saponified with alkali. It is a thick oil, boils at 190° to 191° at 16 mm. pressure, has a feeble basic odor, and a sp. gr. of 0.9735 at 20°.

Its *hydrochloride* and *platinochloride* form well defined crystals.

Nitroso-benzyl fenchylamine,

$$C_{10}H_{17}N\begin{cases}CH_2C_6H_5\\NO\end{cases}$$

crystallizes from alcohol or ether in prisms, and melts at 93°.

Benzylidene fenchylamine,[1] $C_{10}H_{17}N = CHC_6H_5$, is formed with development of heat and separation of water when the theoretical quantities of fenchylamine and benzaldehyde are allowed to react. On cooling, the reaction-product solidifies to a hard mass which crystallizes from methyl alcohol in splendid needles, melting at 42°. Inactive benzylidene fenchylamine is obtained as an oil by combining equal amounts of the levo- and dextro-rotatory modifications.[2]

The *hydrochloride* of the benzylidene derivative is hygroscopic, and readily decomposes with formation of benzaldehyde.

[1] Wallach, Griepenkerl and Lührig, Ann. Chem., *269*, 358.
[2] Wallach, Ann. Chem., *272*, 105.

Ortho-oxybenzylidene fenchylamine,[1] $C_{10}H_{17}N = CHC_6H_4OH$, results by gently warming salicylic aldehyde with fenchylamine; it crystallizes from alcohol in yellow needles, and melts at 95°. Acids readily resolve this compound into its components The optically inactive derivative melts at 64° to 65°.

Para-oxybenzylidene fenchylamine,[2] $C_{10}H_{17}N = CHC_6H_4OH$, is prepared in an analogous manner to the preceding compound by condensing p-oxybenzaldehyde with fenchylamine; it melts at 175°.

Ortho-methoxybenzylidene fenchylamine,[2] $C_{10}H_{17}N = CHC_6H_4O\text{-}CH_3$, is produced by the condensation of fenchylamine and o-methoxybenzaldehyde; it melts at 56°.

Para-methoxybenzylidene fenchylamine melts at 54° to 55°.

Fenchylamine forms a solid condensation-product, $C_{16}H_{27}NO_2$, with aceto-acetic ester; it has not been further investigated

The following table contains the mean values obtained for the specific and molecular rotatory powers of fenchylamine, prepared from dextro-fenchone, and of its derivatives in chloroform solutions (Wallach and Binz [2])

	Melting Point	$[\alpha]_D$	$[M]_D$
Fenchonoxime	165°	+52 44°	+ 87 40°
Fenchylamine	——	—24 89°	— 38 00°
Formyl fenchylamine	(114°)	—36 56°	— 66.04°
Acetyl fenchylamine	99°	—46 62°	— 90.73°
Propionyl fenchylamine	123°	—53 16°	—110 88°
Butyryl fenchylamine	77 5°	—53.11°	—118 19°
Benzylidene fenchylamine	42°	+73.14°	+175.90°
o-Oxybenzylidene fenchylamine	94°	+66 59°	+170 77°
p-Oxybenzylidene fenchylamine	175°	+72.00°	+184 65°
o-methoxybenzylidene fenchylamine	56°	+59 20°	+160 09°
p-methoxybenzylidene fenchylamine.	55°	+78 05°	+211 07°

6. FENCHOLENAMINE, $C_9H_{15}CH_2NH_2$.

A base of the composition, $C_{10}H_{17}NH_2$, which bears the same relation to camphylamine as fenchylamine to bornylamine, was obtained by Wallach[3] by the reduction of fenchonoxime anhydride (α-fencholenonitrile), $C_9H_{15}CN$. This amine was carefully studied by Wallach and Jenkel,[4] and designated as fencholenamine.

It is prepared by adding fifteen grams of sodium to a solution of twenty-five grams of α-fencholenonitrile in one hundred and

[1] Wallach, Griepenkerl and Luhrig, Ann Chem, *269*, 358

[2] Wallach and Binz, Ann Chem, *276*, 317, compare Zeitschr für physik. Chem, *12*, 723.

[3] Wallach, Ann Chem, *263*, 138

[4] Wallach and Jenkel, Ann Chem, *269*, 360

twenty-five grams of absolute alcohol. Toward the end of the reaction a small quantity of water is added, the liquid is heated until all sodium is dissolved, and the product is then poured into water. After acidulating with sulphuric acid, the undecomposed nitrile is distilled off in a current of steam, the free base is liberated from the residue by means of sodium hydroxide, is separated and fractionated in vacuum. The fencholenamine distills over at 110° to 115° under 21 mm. to 24 mm., while on continued distillation a small fraction is obtained at 115° to 147°, and then, at 147° to 148°, a base, $C_{10}H_{21}NO$, is obtained (see below).

Fencholenamine boils at 205° under atmospheric pressure; it readily absorbs carbonic anhydride, and is an unsaturated compound.

Fencholenamine nitrate, $C_{10}H_{17}NH_2 \cdot HNO_3$, is formed by dissolving five grams of the base in eleven grams of nitric acid of sp. gr. 1.105. It may be obtained in splendid crystals by recrystallization from twice its weight of water.

Fencholenamine sulphate, $(C_{10}H_{19}N)_2 \cdot H_2SO_4$, crystallizes in plates, and is sparingly soluble in water, readily in dilute sulphuric acid. Its aqueous solution is not decomposed by boiling.

Like an unsaturated amine, fencholenamine combines with two molecules of hydrochloric acid. When hydrogen chloride is passed into a methyl alcoholic solution of the base and the alcohol is then allowed to evaporate, *hydrochlorofencholenamine hydrochloride*, $C_{10}H_{18}ClNH_2 \cdot HCl$, is obtained in well defined crystals. This salt yields a fencholenamine containing only a small amount of chlorine when it is treated with a solution of sodium hydroxide in the cold.

Fencholenamine oxalate is sparingly soluble in water.

Acetyl fencholenamine, $C_{10}H_{17}NH \cdot COCH_3$, is prepared by the addition of acetic anhydride to an ethereal solution of the base. It is a thick oil, and boils at 180° under a pressure of 21 mm.

Benzoyl fencholenamine, $C_{10}H_{17}NHCOC_6H_5$, is easily obtained by the Schotten-Baumann method; it melts at 88° to 89°.

The condensation-products of fencholenamine with aldehydes are oils; the compound obtained from furfural boils at 167° under a pressure of 16 mm.

When fencholenamine is treated with nitrous acid, it is converted into fencholenyl alcohol.

The above-mentioned base, $C_{10}H_{21}NO$, formed together with fencholenamine by the reduction of α-fencholenonitrile, may be easily separated from fencholenamine by means of its very soluble oxalate. It boils at 147° to 148° under 21 mm. to 24 mm. By boiling with dilute sulphuric acid, this amine loses water and appears to be converted into fencholenamine.

7. CAMPHOLAMINE, $C_9H_{17}CH_2NH_2$.

Campholamine is prepared by reducing campholonitrile,[1] $C_9H_{17}CN$, with sodium in alcoholic solution. (Campholic acid, $C_9H_{17}COOH$, is obtained by heating a solution of camphor in benzene with sodium.)

This base is a colorless oil, lighter than water, and is only slightly soluble in water. It boils at 210°, and quickly absorbs carbonic anhydride from the air forming a crystalline salt (Errera[2]).

Campholamine hydrochloride, $C_{10}H_{21}N \cdot HCl$, is insoluble in ether, and crystallizes from water in silvery laminæ The *platino-chloride* separates from alcohol in yellow plates.

Campholamine nitrate, $C_{10}H_{21}N \cdot HNO_3$, is sparingly soluble in water, and may be recrystallized from boiling water. When heated rapidly, the salt melts and decomposes at 220°.

Benzoyl campholamine, $C_{10}H_{19}NH \cdot COC_6H_5$, is prepared by the action of benzoyl chloride on an ethereal solution of the base; it is insoluble in water, readily soluble in the other ordinary solvents, and melts at 98°.

Campholyl phenylthiocarbamide, $C_{10}H_{19}NH\ CS\ NHC_6H_5$, is produced by the action of phenylthiocarbimide on an ethereal solution of the base, the reaction being energetic. When recrystallized from dilute alcohol, it separates in colorless needles, melting at 117° to 118°; it is sparingly soluble in petroleum ether.

When a solution of campholamine hydrochloride is warmed with silver nitrite, campholyl alcohol, $C_{10}H_{19}OH$, and a hydrocarbon, $C_{10}H_{18}$, are formed. Errera[2] terms this hydrocarbon, *campholene.*

[1] Errera, Gazz Chim, **22**, I, 205; Ber., *25*, 466, Ref

[2] Errera, Gazz. Chim, **22**, II, 109, Ber., *26*, 21, Ref

II. BASES WHICH MAY BE REGARDED AS DERIVATIVES OF THE HYDROCYMENES.

A. AMINES, $C_{10}H_{15}NH_2$, CONTAINING TWO ETHYLENE LINKAGES.

1. CARVYLAMINES, $C_{10}H_{15}NH_2$.

By the reduction of carvoxime, $C_{10}H_{14}NOH$, with sodium amalgam and acetic acid, Goldschmidt[1] obtained a base which he called carvylamine, $C_{10}H_{15}NH_2$. The existence of this compound was subsequently questioned by Wallach,[2] since he obtained dihydrocarvylamine, $C_{10}H_{17}NH_2$, by reducing carvoxime with sodium and alcohol; Wallach also found dihydrocarvylamine, $C_{10}H_{17}NH_2$, to be identical with the base, prepared by Leuckart and Bach[3] and by Lampe[4] on the treatment of carvone with ammonium formate, which had previously been called "carvylamine," $C_{10}H_{15}NH_2$.

Although in the German edition of this book, Dr. Heusler considers Goldschmidt's and Leuckart's carvylamine as identical with Wallach's dihydrocarvylamine, it appears to the translator that Goldschmidt[5] has sufficiently proved the existence of his carvylamine, $C_{10}H_{15}NH_2$, and has shown it to be quite different from dihydrocarvylamine.

According to Goldschmidt,[5] when an alcoholic solution of dextrocarvoxime is reduced with sodium amalgam, or zinc dust, and acetic acid, two optically active, isomeric bases are formed, which are designated as *α-d-* and *β-d-*carvylamine, $C_{10}H_{15}NH_2$. Levo-carvoxime likewise gives rise to two bases *α*-l- and *β*-l-carvylamine, whose derivatives have the same melting point, solubility, etc., as those of the corresponding bases obtained from d-carvoxime, while their optical rotation is the opposite. Two racemic compounds, corresponding to the *α*- and *β*-carvylamines, have been separated in the form of their benzoyl derivatives, so that altogether six isomeric benzoyl carvylamines have been isolated.

[1] H. Goldschmidt, Ber., *19*, 3232; *20*, 486; *26*, 2084.
[2] Wallach, Ann. Chem., *275*, 120.
[3] Leuckart and Bach, Ber., *20*, 105.
[4] Lampe, Inaug. Diss., Göttingen, 1889.
[5] Goldschmidt and Fischer, Ber., *30*, 2069.

The reduction of carvoxime is accomplished as follows. An alcoholic solution of d-carvoxime is heated with zinc dust and acetic acid on the water-bath until no further precipitation of the oxime takes place on pouring a little of the reaction-mixture into water. The excess of zinc is filtered off, the filtrate is diluted with water, rendered acid with hydrochloric acid, and considerable regenerated carvone is extracted with ether. The acid liquid is then rendered alkaline with sodium hydroxide, and again extracted with ether, after drying over potash and distilling off the ether, the basic residue is rectified in vacuum, the product boiling at 94° under 10 mm. pressure.

The liquid distillate has a basic odor, is sparingly soluble in water, and consists of two bases, whose separation is accomplished by means of their nitrates; the nitrate of β-d-carvylamine is more difficultly soluble in water than its isomeride. The basic mixture is neutralized with dilute nitric acid, and the resultant salts are crystallized from a small quantity of warm water; the β-salt separates at first, and the filtrate may be used for the preparation of the α-derivatives.

The free bases may be obtained from their hydrochlorides or nitrates by the action of alkalis; they have a decided basic odor, and rapidly absorb carbon dioxide from the air, forming solid carbonates.

α-d-Carvylamine hydrochloride, $C_{10}H_{15}NH_2 HCl$, crytallizes from absolute alcohol in fine needles, melts with decomposition at 180°, and is readily soluble in water.

α-d-Carvyl phenylcarbamide, $C_{10}H_{15}NH \cdot CONHC_6H_5$, can not be obtained entirely free of the β-derivative; it is crystalline, and melts at 187° to 191°.

Benzoyl-α-d-carvylamine, $C_{10}H_{15}NH \cdot COC_6H_5$, is produced by treating an aqueous solution of the α-d-nitrate with alkali and benzoyl chloride; it usually contains some of the β-derivative as an impurity, but after repeated crystallization from methyl alcohol, it is freed from most of the β-compound. It crystallizes from methyl alcohol in long, white needles, and melts at 169°; it is levorotatory, $[\alpha]_D = -91.9°$.

α-d-Carvyl carbamide, $C_{10}H_{15}NH CONH_2$, is formed by warming a solution of the hydrochloride with potassium cyanate; it crystallizes from hot water in white, miscroscopic needles, and melts at 187°.

The β-d-carvylamine may be readily obtained in a pure condition, since its nitrate is much more sparingly soluble in water than the α-compound

β-d-Carvyl phenylcarbamide, $C_{10}H_{15}NH CONHC_6H_5$, crystallizes in small, white needles, and melts at 138°.

Benzoyl-β-d-carvylamine, $C_{10}H_{15}NH \cdot COC_6H_5$, is prepared from the β-d-nitrate by treating with alkali and benzoyl chloride; it crystallizes from methyl alcohol in colorless needles, melts at 103°, and is more readily soluble in all solvents than the α-compound. It is dextrorotatory, $[\alpha]_D = +176.6°$.

When l-carvoxime is reduced in alcoholic solution with zinc dust and acetic acid in a manner similar to that described above, a mixture of two isomeric bases is obtained, which boils at 94° to 95° under 10 mm. pressure. These bases are also separated by means of their nitrates, and the benzoyl derivatives are formed like the corresponding d-compounds.

Benzoyl-α-l-carvylamine, $C_{10}H_{15}NH \cdot COC_6H_5$, crystallizes from methyl alcohol in long, white needles, melts at 169°, and is dextrorotatory, $[\alpha]_D = +92.6°$.

Benzoyl-β-l-carvylamine, $C_{10}H_{15}NH \cdot COC_6H_5$, crystallizes from methyl alcohol, melts at 103°, and is levorotatory, $[\alpha]_D = -175.4°$.

Racemic benzoyl-α-carvylamine, $(C_{10}H_{15}NH \cdot COC_6H_5)_2$, is obtained by crystallizing together equal weights of the α-d- and α-l-derivatives from methyl alcohol; it forms fine, white needles, and melts at 141°.

Racemic benzoyl-β-carvylamine, $(C_{10}H_{15}NH \cdot COC_6H_5)_2$, is produced from the two β-compounds; it crystallizes from methyl alcohol in small prisms, and melts at 140°. It is more readily soluble in all solvents than the preceding compound.

When the two isomeric racemic derivatives are rubbed together, a mixture results, which melts at about 132°.

B. AMINES, $C_{10}H_{17}NH_2$, CONTAINING ONE ETHYLENE LINKAGE.

1. DIHYDROCARVYLAMINE, $C_{10}H_{17}NH_2$.

By the treatment of carvone with ammonium formate, Leuckart and Bach,[1] and Lampe [2] obtained a base which they called "carvylamine," $C_{10}H_{15}NH_2$. Wallach [3] subsequently showed that this compound could be more conveniently prepared by reducing carvoxime with sodium and alcohol, and further that its composition was not expressed by the formula, $C_{10}H_{15}NH_2$, but that it had the constitution, $C_{10}H_{17}NH_2$, *dihydrocarvylamine*. Wallach has

[1] Leuckart and Bach, Ber., *20*, 105.

[2] Lampe, Inaug. Diss., Göttingen, *1889*.

[3] Wallach, Ann. Chem., *275*, 120; Ber., *24*, 3984.

also regarded dihydrocarvylamine as chemically identical with Goldschmidt's carvylamine, $C_{10}H_{15}NH_2$, but more recent publications[1] by Goldschmidt indicate that this view can no longer be maintained.

For the preparation of dihydrocarvylamine according to Leuckart's method, ten grams of carvone are heated with eleven grams of ammonium formate in sealed tubes at 180° to 200°, for five or six hours. On cooling, the tubes contain the formyl derivative of the base as a dark, viscous mass, together with some unchanged ammonium formate. The formyl compound is treated with water and extracted with ether; the ethereal solution is separated, the ether distilled off, and the resultant product saponified with alcoholic potash. After the alcohol is removed by distillation, the base is distilled with steam, and rectified in vacuum. The yield is seventy to eighty per cent. of the theoretical (Wallach[2]).

In order to prepare the base by the reduction of carvoxime,[2] twenty grams of the oxime are dissolved in one hundred and seventy-five cc. of absolute alcohol and treated gradually with twenty-five grams of sodium, the operation requiring one-half hour; the last particles of sodium are dissolved by the addition of more alcohol. The product is distilled with steam, and the base purified by distillation in vacuum.

Dihydrocarvylamine boils without appreciable decomposition at 218° to 220°; under 15 mm. pressure it boils at 93° to 95°. It has a specific gravity of 0.889 and refractive power, $n_D = 1.48294$, at 20°. It is optically active; on mixing the solutions of equal quantities of the dextro- and levo-modifications, a racemic compound is obtained, whose derivatives differ materially from those of the active bases in melting point and solubility. It readily absorbs carbonic anhydride from the air.

Dihydrocarvylamine hydrochloride, $C_{10}H_{17}NH_2 \cdot HCl$, is precipitated by passing hydrochloric acid gas into a dry ethereal solution of the base; by the long-continued action of hydrogen chloride, this salt is dissolved owing to the formation of a dihydrochloride, which is soluble in ether. The monohydrochloride melts at about 200°, and *decomposes readily into ammonium chloride and terpinene;* at a higher temperature this terpene is partially converted into cymene by the elimination of hydrogen:—

$$C_{10}H_{17}NH_2 \cdot HCl = NH_4Cl + C_{10}H_{16};$$
$$C_{10}H_{16} = H_2 + C_{10}H_{14}.$$

[1] Goldschmidt and Fischer, Ber., *30*, 2069.
[2] Wallach, Ann. Chem., *275*, 120; Ber., *24*, 3984.

Dihydrocarvylamine sulphate crystallizes in characteristic, lustrous leaflets, and is sparingly soluble. The *oxalate* is also difficultly soluble.

When a solution of dihydrocarvylamine hydrochloride is warmed with a solution of sodium nitrite, dihydrocarveol is formed, together with dipentene (inactive limonene); the formation of this hydrocarbon is of interest since it indicates a transformation of carvone into limonene.

Acetyl dihydrocarvylamine, $C_{10}H_{17}NHCOCH_3$, is obtained by warming the free base with acetic anhydride; it separates at first as an oil which solidifies after some time, and may be crystallized from hot water. It melts at 132°.

Benzoyl dihydrocarvylamine, $C_{10}H_{17}NH{\cdot}COC_6H_5$, crystallizes from methyl alcohol in needles, and melts at 181° to 182°.

Dihydrocarvyl phenylcarbamide, $C_{10}H_{17}NH{\cdot}CO{\cdot}NHC_6H_5$, melts at 191°.

Dihydrocarvyl phenylthiocarbamide, $C_{10}H_{17}NH{\cdot}CS{\cdot}NHC_6H_5$, is prepared by mixing the methyl alcoholic solutions of the molecular proportions of the base and phenylcarbimide; it forms small, transparent prisms, which melt at 125° to 126°. When equal quantities of the dextro- and levo-modifications are crystallized together from methyl alcohol, the inactive thiocarbamide is obtained; it is more readily soluble, and does not form as well defined crystals as the active modifications, and melts at 119°.

Dihydrocarvyldiamine,[1] $C_{10}H_{16}(NH_2)_2$, is produced on the reduction of hydroxylaminocarvoxime with alcohol and sodium. It is a colorless liquid, having a basic odor, boils at 258° to 260° under atmospheric pressure, and at 122° to 123° (10 mm.); it absorbs carbon dioxide from the atmosphere. Its *hydrochloride* is hygroscopic, and the *aurichloride* crystallizes in long needles. The *oxalate* melts at 135° to 140°, the *dibenzoyl* derivative at 275° to 276°, the *diphenylcarbamide* at 214° to 216°, and the *diphenylthiocarbamide* at 179° to 180°.

On the dry distillation of dihydrocarvyldiamine, a hydrocarbon, $C_{10}H_{14}$, isomeric with cymene, is formed; it is an unsaturated compound, and boils at 170° to 175°.

2. CARYLAMINE, $C_{10}H_{17}NH_2$.

Carylamine is formed when one part of the oily caronoxime, $C_{10}H_{16}NOH$, is dissolved in twenty-one parts of alcohol and reduced with three parts of sodium (Baeyer[2]).

[1] Harries and Mayrhofer, Ber., 32, 1345.
[2] Bayer, Ber., 27, 3486.

It has no characteristic odor. Its alcoholic solution is stable towards potassium permanganate, hence Baeyer assumes that the hexamethylene ring in carylamine contains either a para-linking or a trimethylene ring.

Carylamine hydrochloride, $C_{10}H_{17}NH_2$ HCl, is obtained by saturating an ethereal solution of the base with hydrochloric acid gas. On evaporation of the ether, the salt remains as a crystalline mass, which is readily soluble in water, alcohol and ether. When its aqueous solution is evaporated, it is converted into the isomeric vestrylamine hydrochloride. The aqueous solution of carylamine hydrochloride gives no precipitate with platinic chloride.

Benzoyl carylamine, $C_{10}H_{17}NH \cdot COC_6H_5$, is prepared by Schotten-Baumann's method, and crystallizes from ethyl acetate in large, flat prisms, which melt at 123°.

Caryl phenylthiocarbamide, $C_{10}H_{17}NH \cdot CS \cdot NHC_6H_5$, melts at 145° to 146°.

3 VESTRYLAMINE, $C_{10}H_{17}NH_2$.

Carylamine is readily transformed into the isomeric, unsaturated vestrylamine[1] by saturating an alcoholic solution of carylamine with hydrogen chloride, and heating the reaction-product on the water-bath for one and one-half days; the hydrochloride of vestrylamine is so obtained as a syrup, which gradually solidifies to a crystalline mass.

Vestrylamine resembles carylamine in odor, but is immediately attacked by permanganate. When treated with benzoyl chloride and sodium hydroxide, it yields a resinous product from which crystals of benzoyl carylamine may be separated, hence the conversion of carylamine into vestrylamine is not quantitative.

When vestrylamine hydrochloride is subjected to dry distillation, it is decomposed into carvestrene and ammonium chloride:

$$C_{10}H_{17}NH_2\ HCl = C_{10}H_{16} + NH_4Cl$$

Carylamine hydrochloride likewise forms carvestrene by distillation, but in this case the change is probably preceded by an intramolecular transformation of carylamine hydrochloride into vestrylamine hydrochloride.

4. DIHYDROEUCARVYLAMINE, $C_{10}H_{17}NH_2$.

Dihydroeucarvylamine was obtained by Baeyer[2] in the reduction of eucarvoxime and of dihydroeucarvoxime hydriodide with

[1] Bayer, Ber, 27, 3486.

[2] Bayer, Ber, 27, 3487, Baeyer and Villiger, Ber, 31, 2067

sodium and alcohol. It has no characteristic odor, and its alcoholic solution immediately reduces potassium permanganate. It boils at 116° to 117° under a pressure of 40 mm.[1]

Dihydroeucarvylamine hydrochloride is crystalline and rather sparingly soluble. The *platinochloride* is also crystalline and difficultly soluble.

Benzoyl dihydroeucarvylamine, $C_{10}H_{17}NH \cdot COC_6H_5$, obtained by Schotten-Baumann's method, is sparingly soluble in ether, and crystallizes from ethyl acetate in long needles, melting at 155° to 156°. It is unstable towards permanganate.

Dihydroeucarvyl phenylcarbamide,[1] $C_{10}H_{17}NH \cdot CO \cdot NHC_6H_5$, melts at 142°, and the *phenylthiocarbamide*, $C_{10}H_{17}NH \cdot CS \cdot NH$-$C_6H_5$, crystallizes from methyl alcohol in transparent plates, and melts at 120° to 121°.

5. THUJYLAMINE (TANACETYLAMINE), $C_{10}H_{17}NH_2$.

Tanacetylamine, $C_{10}H_{17}NH_2$, is formed when ten parts of tanacetoxime (m. p. 51.5°) are reduced with twenty-five parts of sodium and fifty parts of alcohol (Semmler[2]). The same base, designated by Wallach as thujylamine, is obtained by reducing thujonoxime (m. p. 54°) with alcohol and sodium (Wallach[3]).

According to Semmler, this compound boils at 80.5° under a pressure of 14 mm., has the specific gravity 0.8743 and a refractive power, $n_D = 1.462$, at 0°.

According to Wallach, it boils at 195°, has a specific gravity of 0.8735 and refractive index, $n_D = 1.4608$, at 20°.

Thujylamine absorbs carbonic anhydride with great readiness, forming the *carbamate*, which melts at 106° to 107°.

The *nitrate* is rather difficultly soluble in water, and melts at 167° to 168°.

The *hydrochloride* is precipitated from the ethereal solution of the base as a gelatinous mass, which melts at 260° to 261°. When dry distilled, it yields ammonium chloride and a terpene, $C_{10}H_{16}$, which Wallach calls thujene and Semmler designates as tanacetene. This hydrocarbon boils at 60° to 63° under a pressure of 14 mm., has the specific gravity 0.8508 and refractive power, $n_D = 1.476$, at 20° (Semmler). According to Tschugaeff,[4] the dry distillation of thujylamine hydrochloride gives *isothujene* and not thujene. It contains two ethylene linkages.

[1] Wallach, Ann. Chem., *305*, 223.
[2] Semmler, Ber., *25*, 3345.
[3] Wallach, Ann. Chem., *286*, 96.
[4] Tschugaeff, Ber., *34*, 2276.

Thujyl phenylcarbamide, $C_{10}H_{17}NH \cdot CO \cdot NHC_6H_5$, results by the interaction of thujylamine and phenylcarbimide; it crystallizes in prisms, and melts at 120° (Wallach).

Dimethylthujylamine,[1] $C_{10}H_{17}N(CH_3)_2$, is formed as a by-product during the preparation of thujyl trimethyl ammonium iodide; it boils at 213.5° to 214°, has a sp. gr. 0.8606 at 20°/4°, and $[\alpha]_D = +141.76°$. Its *hydrochloride* is very easily soluble in water and alcohol, the *platinochloride* separates from hot alcohol as an orange red, crystalline powder, and the *nitrate* crystallizes readily and is only sparingly soluble in water and alcohol.

Thujyl trimethyl ammonium iodide,[1] $C_{10}H_{17}N(CH_3)_3I$, is formed by the action of methyl iodide and potassium hydroxide on thujylamine; it crystallizes from a mixture of chloroform and methyl alcohol in long, prismatic crystals, has the specific rotatory power in chloroform solution, $[\alpha]_D = +42.61°$, and is only sparingly soluble in cold water.

Thujyl trimethyl ammonium hydroxide,[1] $C_{10}H_{17}N(CH_3)_3OH$, is obtained as a crystalline mass by treating the preceding compound with moist silver oxide; on dry distillation it is decomposed with the formation of thujene, $C_{10}H_{16}$ (b. p. 151° to 153°, sp. gr. 0.8263 at 20°/4°, $n_D = 1.45022$ at 20°, and $[\alpha]_D = -8.23°$).

It has already been mentioned that three isomeric thujonoximes are known (see page 228). These oximes yield three different amines on reduction. Thujonoxime, melting at 54°, gives the above described thujylamine; the isomeric thujonoxime, melting at 90°, forms the isomeric thujylamine, boiling at 193°; and isothujonoxime, melting at 119°, yields isothujylamine, boiling at 200° to 201°.

ISOMERIC THUJYLAMINE, $C_{10}H_{17}NH_2$, PREPARED FROM THE ISOMERIC THUJONOXIME, MELTING AT 90°.

When the isomeric thujonoxime, melting at 90°, is reduced with sodium and alcohol, it yields a base, $C_{10}H_{17}NH_2$, which boils at 193°, and at 20° has the specific gravity 0.875 and refractive index, $n_D = 1.46256$ (Wallach[2]). It absorbs carbonic anhydride slowly. Its *nitrate* crystallizes in needles, is readily soluble, and melts at 124°; the *hydrochloride* separates in tablets, and melts at 216°; the *phenylcarbamide* forms transparent tablets, which melt at 110°.

[1] Tschugaeff, Ber., *34*, 2276.
[2] Wallach, Ann. Chem., *286*, 96.

Wallach[1] had previously obtained a thujylamine, boiling at 198° to 199°, by heating crude thujone with ammonium formate. When the hydrochloride of this base is submitted to dry distillation, it is decomposed into ammonium chloride and thujene, $C_{10}H_{16}$; this hydrocarbon boils at 172° to 175°, has the specific gravity 0.840 and refractive index, $n_D = 1.4761$, at 20°. Whether this amine is identical with the thujylamine prepared from thujonoxime (m. p. 54°), or is to be regarded as a derivative of carvotanacetone—the latter view is suggested by the high temperature at which the compound is formed—can only be determined by a renewed investigation.

6. ISOTHUJYLAMINE, $C_{10}H_{17}NH_2$.

Isothujylamine is produced when isothujonoxime (m. p. 119° to 120°) is reduced with sodium and alcohol (Wallach[2]).

It boils at 200° to 201°, has a specific gravity of 0.865 and a refractive index, $n_D = 1.468$, at 20°; it absorbs carbonic anhydride very feebly.

The *nitrate* is sparingly soluble, and melts at 163°.

The *hydrochloride* is precipitated from a solution of the base in dry ether by hydrochloric acid gas; it may be crystallized from a mixture of chloroform and petroleum ether, and melts at 180° to 181°. When this salt is submitted to dry distillation, it is decomposed into ammonium chloride and a terpene, which seems to be identical with the above-mentioned thujene; the terpene boils at 170° to 172°, its sp. gr. is 0.836 and refractive power, $n_D = 1.47145$, at 22°.

Isothujylcarbamide, $C_{10}H_{17}NH{\cdot}CO{\cdot}NH_2$, is prepared by the interaction of isothujylamine hydrochloride and potassium isocyanate; it melts at 158° to 159°.

Isothujyl phenylcarbamide, $C_{10}H_{17}NH{\cdot}CO{\cdot}NHC_6H_5$, forms small needles, which are readily soluble in alcohol, and melt at 178°.

Isothujyl phenylthiocarbamide, $C_{10}H_{17}NH{\cdot}CS{\cdot}NHC_6H_5$, crystallizes in needles, dissolves sparingly in methyl alcohol, and melts at 152° to 153°.

7. PULEGYLAMINE, $C_{10}H_{17}NH_2$.

Pulegylamine is obtained by reducing the normal pulegonoxime, $C_{10}H_{16}NOH$, in an alcoholic solution with sodium. It is a crystalline compound, and is purified by means of its readily soluble oxalate; it melts at about 50°, boils at 205° to 210°, and combines with great readiness with carbonic anhydride.

[1] Wallach, Ann. Chem., *272*, 109.
[2] Wallach, Ann. Chem., *286*, 97.

Pulegylamine hydrochloride is insoluble in ether, and yields a *carbamide*, melting at 104° to 105°, when treated with potassium isocyanate.

Pulegyl phenylcarbamide, obtained from the free amine and carbanile, melts at 154° to 155° (Wallach[1]).

Beckmann and Pleissner[2] obtained a base, $C_{10}H_{19}ON$, which they termed pulegonamine, by the action of hydriodic acid on the "hydrated pulegonoxime," $C_{10}H_{19}NO_2$. According to these chemists, this amine is prepared when ten parts of "hydrated pulegonoxime" are treated with twenty parts of strong hydriodic acid and a little red phosphorus; the mixture is warmed until the reaction commences, and is then allowed to stand for some time. Two layers are formed, a light colored aqueous solution and a dark oil. The product is diluted with water, and decolorized with thiosulphate, the oil being dissolved. The sulphur and phosphorus are filtered off, the solution is shaken with ether, and then rendered alkaline; the resulting pulegonamine is extracted with ether. On evaporation of the ether, the base remains as a yellowish oil, having a basic odor and bitter taste; it decomposes when distilled.

This amine does not reduce Fehling's solution, and does not give the isonitrile reaction. If hydrochloric acid gas be passed through its ethereal solution an oil is precipitated, which solidifies after repeated washing with ether, and crystallizes from absolute alcohol in long needles, melting at 117°. This salt is not homogeneous, but contains more chlorine than the formula, $C_{10}H_{19}NO \cdot HCl$, demands.

Pulegonamine phenylthiocarbamide,

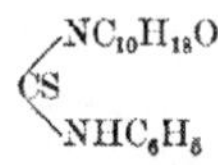

is obtained by the action of phenylthiocarbimide on a solution of pulegonamine in benzene; it crystallizes from benzene in white plates, and melts at 198°.

Benzoyl pulegonamine, $C_{10}H_{18}ON \cdot COC_6H_5$, is formed by treating an ethereal solution of the base with benzoyl chloride; it separates from dilute alcohol in lustrous, feathery crystals, which melt at 100.5° to 101°.

Methyl pulegonamine, $C_{10}H_{18}ON \cdot CH_3$, is produced by boiling pulegonamine with methyl iodide and decomposing the reaction-product with potash; it is a light yellow oil, having a penetrating,

[1] Wallach, Ann. Chem., *289*, 347.
[2] Beckmann and Pleissner, Ann. Chem., *262*, 13.

fish-like smell. Its *platinochloride*, $(C_{11}H_{22}NOCl)_2PtCl_4$, crystallizes in well defined needles.

When pulegonamine is boiled with potash, it is converted into pulegone and ammonia; under the same conditions, methyl pulegonamine yields pulegone and methylamine; in both cases, however, the resultant pulegone apparently contains a nitrogenous substance as an impurity.

The constitution of pulegonamine, therefore, differs entirely from that of the other terpene bases. Beckmann and Pleissner assume that the isonitroso-group (NOH) in pulegonoxime is changed into the NH-group by treatment with hydriodic acid.

C. AMINES, $C_{10}H_{19}NH_2$, WITHOUT AN ETHYLENE LINKAGE.

1. CARVOMENTHYLAMINE (TETRAHYDROCARVYLAMINE), $C_{19}H_{19}NH_2$.

(Amido-2-hexahydrocymene.)

When the oxime of tetrahydrocarvone (carvomenthone), $C_{10}H_{18}NOH$, melting at 105°, is reduced with sodium and alcohol by the same method which serves for the preparation of menthylamine from menthonoxime (see page 368), an amine isomeric with menthylamine is obtained. Wallach[1] regards this compound as having the constitution of an amido-2-hexahydrocymene; it may be designated as carvomenthylamine or tetrahydrocarvylamine:

```
          CH3
          |
          CH
        /    \
    H2C       CHNH2
     |          |
    H2C       CH2
        \    /
          CH
          |
          CH
        /    \
     H3C      CH3.
```

The optically active modifications of this base are obtained, together with optically active tetrahydrocarveol and tetrahydrocarvone, when phellandrene nitrosite is reduced with sodium and alcohol (Wallach and Herbig[2]).

[1] Wallach, Ann. Chem., 277, 137.
[2] Wallach and Herbig, Ann. Chem., 287, 371.

Carvomenthylamine is a liquid, and boils at 211° to 212°, considerably higher than menthylamine; the other properties of both amines are very similar. It unites with carbon dioxide with great readiness, forming a solid salt.

Carvomenthylamine hydrochloride, $C_{10}H_{19}NH_2$ HCl, is insoluble in ether and sparingly soluble in cold water, its optically active modifications melt at 199° to 204°, while the inactive derivative melts at 221° to 222°. It resembles menthylamine hydrochloride in that it may be distilled at a high temperature with only slight decomposition. The *platinochloride* is very easily soluble in alcohol, more sparingly in water.

Formyl carvomenthylamine, $C_{10}H_{19}NHCOH$, is obtained as an oil by the distillation of the formate. It solidifies gradually, but on recrystallization it separates at first from all solvents as an oil. The inactive modification melts at 61° to 62°.

Acetyl carvomenthylamine, $C_{10}H_{19}NHCOCH_3$, is formed by warming the base with acetic anhydride; it crystallizes from dilute alcohol in small needles The active derivatives melt at 158° to 159°, whilst the inactive modification melts at 124° to 125°.

Carvomenthyl phenylthiocarbamide, $C_{10}H_{19}NH{\cdot}CS{\cdot}NHC_6H_5$, is prepared by the action of phenylthiocarbimide on carvomenthylamine; it forms a viscous mass, which solidifies slowly. The pure, inactive derivative crystallizes from methyl alcohol in small, white needles, which melt at 117°.

Carvomenthyl carbamide, $C_{10}H_{19}NH{\cdot}CO\,NH_2$, is best adapted for the characterization of carvomenthylamine. It is precipitated by heating carvomenthylamine hydrochloride with a solution of potassium isocyanate; it is insoluble in water, and is not readily soluble in hot alcohol The racemic compound crystallizes from methyl alcohol in brilliant leaflets or needles, and melts at 193° to 194°, the active modifications melt at 201° to 203°.

Carvomenthyl phenylcarbamide,[1] $C_{10}H_{19}NH{\cdot}CO\,NHC_6H_5$.—The inactive modification melts at 145° to 150°, and the active derivatives at 185° to 186°.

Optically active carvomenthol[1] is formed when the salts of optically active carvomenthylamine are treated with a solution of sodium nitrite.

2. MENTHYLAMINE, $C_{10}H_{19}NH_2$.

Menthylamine was first prepared by Moriya[2] by the reduction of a nitro-compound, obtained by the action of strong nitric acid

[1] Wallach and Herbig, Ann Chem, *287*, 371

[2] Moriya, Journ Chem. Soc, *1881*, 77

on menthol, with tin and sulphuric acid; the properties of this amine were very incompletely described. Andres and Andreef[1] subsequently showed that a base having a strong levorotatory power was formed by reducing levo-menthonoxime with sodium and alcohol. Wallach and Kuthe[2] then obtained the same results, although Wallach[3] had previously shown that a base, $C_{10}H_{19}NH_2$, could be produced by the treatment of menthone with ammonium formate.

According to Wallach and Kuthe, levo-menthylamine prepared from levo-menthonoxime is strongly levorotatory, and is chemically different from the feebly dextrorotatory menthylamine, which may be obtained, together with some of the levorotatory isomeride, by the action of ammonium formate on levo-menthone. Wallach explains the simultaneous formation of both bases by the following considerations.

Levorotatory menthone contains two asymmetric carbon atoms. When menthone is converted into menthylamine, the carbonyl group is changed into the group, $CH{\cdot}NH_2$, and a third asymmetric carbon atom is introduced, as shown by the formulas in which the asymmetric atoms are represented by heavy type:

```
      CH3                         CH3
      |                           |
      CH                          CH
     /  \                        /  \
 H2C    CH2                  H2C    CH2
  |      |        →           |      |
 H2C    CO                   H2C    CHNH2
     \  /                        \  /
      CH                          CH
      |                           |
      C3H7                        C3H7
 Menthone.                    Menthylamine.
```

If it be assumed that the two asymmetric carbon atoms in levo-menthone and levo-menthonoxime influence the levorotatory power of these compounds in the same direction although to an unequal extent, the two substances can be represented:

$$(-, -)C_{10}H_{18}O \text{ and } (-, -)C_{10}H_{18}{:}NOH.$$

By the transformation into menthylamine, the third asymmetric carbon atom may increase this levorotation and a levorotatory menthylamine may be formed which would be expressed by the symbol:

$$(-, -, -)C_{10}H_{19}NH_2;$$

or, the third asymmetric atom may act in the opposite direction

[1] Andres and Andreef, Ber., *25*, 618; *24*, 560, Ref.
[2] Wallach and Kuthe, Ann. Chem., *276*, 296; compare Ber., 25, 3313.
[3] Wallach, Ber., *24*, 3992.

to those already present, and a compound be obtained which has a weaker power of rotation, or, as in the case under consideration, it may rotate the plane of polarized light slightly to the right; the symbol of the resultant dextrorotatory menthylamine would be:

$$(-, -, +)C_{10}H_{19}NH_2.$$

This hypothesis, proposed by Wallach, explains the facts that levo- and dextro-menthylamines are not related to each other in the same manner that an object is to its reflection, and, moreover, that they are chemically different.

It would be expected that compounds having rotatory powers exactly opposite to those of the above-mentioned menthylamines would result if dextro-menthone were employed instead of levo-menthone. Experiments in this direction were made by Wallach and Kuthe, and by Negoworoff,[1] but the preparation of such bases in a condition of purity has not succeeded.

The behavior of the two menthylamines towards nitrous acid is quite characteristic. Under the influence of this reagent, l-menthylamine is readily converted into the ordinary, solid l-menthol, while under the same conditions, d-menthylamine yields large quantities of menthene. Consequently d-menthol, corresponding to d-menthylamine, possesses a much greater tendency to lose the elements of water than the common l-menthol; therefore, the hydroxyl-group in d-menthol probably stands in a closer structural relation to the tertiary hydrogen atom attached to the adjoining carbon atom than is the case in the molecule of l-menthol. From this Wallach concludes that the isomerism in the menthylamine series is to be explained as a *cis-* and *trans-*isomerism; l-menthylamine and l-menthol are to be regarded as *trans-*compounds, and the dextro-isomers as *cis-*derivatives. The following formulas will illustrate this.

```
      CH3                          CH3
      |                            |
      CH                           CH
     /  \                         /  \
  H2C    CH2                   H2C    CH2
   |      |                     |      |
  H2C    CH·NH2                H2C    CH·NH2
     \  /                         \  /
      C                            C
     / \                          / \
    H   C3H7                  H7C3   H
```

Trans-(*l*)-Menthylamine. *Cis-*(*d*)-Menthylamine.

If, in the above formulas, the NH_2 group be replaced by the (OH) group, the corresponding menthols result, and it will be

[1] Negoworoff, Ber., 25, 162c.; compare Ber., 25, 620.

observed that menthene can be formed more readily by the elimination of water from *cis*-menthol than from *trans*-menthol.

(a) l-(TRANS-) MENTHYLAMINE.

l-Menthylamine was first obtained pure by Andres and Andreef. It may be prepared by the following method.

Ten grams of pure levo-menthonoxime are dissolved in seventy-five grams of absolute alcohol, and fifteen grams of sodium are added in small portions at a time to the boiling solution. The crystallization of sodium alcoholate is prevented by the occasional addition of absolute alcohol, the total amount added being about sixty cc. When the sodium is dissolved, the product is distilled with steam, and the receiving vessel is changed as soon as the distillate appears cloudy. The yield is nearly quantitative. After drying over potash, the amine boils at 209° to 210°; it has a disagreeable, strongly basic odor, and rapidly absorbs carbonic anhydride from the air. It has the sp. gr. 0.86 and refractive index, $n_D = 1.46058$, at 20°; $[\alpha]_D = -38.07°$.

l-Menthylamine hydrochloride, $C_{10}H_{19}NH_2 \cdot HCl$, is precipitated from ethereal solutions of the base as a white powder; it dissolves readily in alcohol and warm water. It does not melt at 280°, and at higher temperatures it may be distilled without decomposition.

l-Menthylamine hydrobromide, $C_{10}H_{19}NH_2 \cdot HBr$, is more sparingly soluble in water than the hydrochloride, and crystallizes from water in needles. The *hydriodide* is more difficultly soluble than the hydrobromide.

l-Menthylamine nitrite, $C_{10}H_{19}NH_2 \cdot HNO_2$, is prepared from molecular proportions of the hydrochloride of the base and sodium nitrite; on heating, it is converted into menthol,

$$C_{10}H_{19}NH_2 \cdot HNO_2 = C_{10}H_{19}OH + H_2O + N_2.$$

l-Formyl menthylamine, $C_{10}H_{19}NH \cdot COH$, is best prepared by the distillation of the molecular quantities of the base and anhydrous formic acid. It is washed with water, and separates from methyl alcohol in splendid crystals, which melt at 102° to 103°.

l-Acetyl menthylamine, $C_{10}H_{19}NH \cdot COCH_3$, is obtained by the addition of the theoretical quantity of acetic anhydride to a solution of the base in three times its volume of ethyl acetate; a vigorous reaction takes place, and the acetyl derivative crystallizes from the cold solution. It is readily soluble in alcohol, ether and chloroform, but almost insoluble in petroleum ether; it crystallizes from ethyl acetate, and melts at 145°.

l-Propionyl menthylamine, $C_{10}H_{19}NH{\cdot}COC_2H_5$, is more readily soluble than the formyl and acetyl derivatives ; it crystallizes from ethyl acetate or acetone, and melts at 89°.

l-Butyryl menthylamine, $C_{10}H_{19}NH{\cdot}COC_3H_7$, tends to separate from most solvents as an oil, but by recrystallization from acetone it is obtained in prisms, which melt at 80°.

l-Menthyl carbamide, $C_{10}H_{19}{\cdot}NH{\cdot}CONH_2$, is obtained as an oil by the action of potassium isocyanate on l-methylamine hydrochloride ; it solidifies after standing some time, and melts at 134° to 136°.

l-Menthyl phenylcarbamide, $C_{10}H_{19}NH{\cdot}CONHC_6H_5$, results by the action of carbanile on the free base ; it crystallizes from alcohol, and melts at 140° to 141°.

l-Menthyl phenylthiocarbamide, $C_{10}H_{19}NH{\cdot}CS{\cdot}NHC_6H_5$, results when an ethereal solution of menthylamine is treated with the molecular amount of phenylthiocarbimide ; the reaction is energetic. It separates from ethyl acetate in lustrous crystals, and melts at 135°.

l-Benzylidene menthylamine, $C_{10}H_{19}N{=}CHC_6H_5$, is obtained by the action of benzaldehyde on menthylamine in a methyl alcoholic solution ; it is crystallized from methyl alcohol, and melts at 69° to 70°.

l-Ortho-oxybenzylidene menthylamine, $C_{10}H_{19}N = CH{\cdot}C_6H_4OH$, is produced in an analogous manner to the preceding compound ; it separates at first as an oil, which solidifies after washing with soda and cooling in a freezing mixture. It crystallizes in yellow needles, and melts at 56° to 57°.

The nitroso-derivatives of the monoalkyl menthylamines are formed by treating one molecular proportion of menthylamine with one molecule of an alkyl iodide, liberating the free base from the resulting mixture, dissolving in hydrochloric acid, and treating with sodium nitrite. The resultant nitroso-derivatives of the secondary amines are distilled with steam, dried and rectified in vacuum.

l-Menthyl methylnitrosamine, $C_{10}H_{19}N(NO){\cdot}CH_3$, is a yellow oil, boiling at 145° to 146° under 18 to 20 mm. pressure.

l-Menthyl ethylnitrosamine, $C_{10}H_{19}N(NO){\cdot}C_2H_5$, crystallizes from dilute methyl alcohol in colorless needles, melts at 52° to 53°, and boils at 155° to 156° (22 mm.).

l-Menthyl propylnitrosamine, $C_{10}H_{19}N(NO)C_3H_7$, boils at 159° to 161° (20 mm.).

l-Menthyl isobutylnitrosamine, $C_{10}H_{19}N(NO)C_4H_9$, crystallizes in white needles, melts at 52° to 53°, and boils at 160° to 161°.

l-Menthyl trimethyl ammonium iodide, $C_{10}H_{19}N(CH_3)_3I$, crystallizes from water in large, colorless crystals, and melts at 190°.

Its alcoholic solution absorbs one molecule of iodine, forming a *triiodide*, $C_{10}H_{19}N(CH_3)_3I_3$, melting at 117° to 118°.

l-Menthyl trimethyl ammonium hydroxide, $C_{10}H_{19}N(CH_3)_3OH$, is produced by digesting the preceding compound with moist silver oxide; it is a colorless, crystalline, hygroscopic mass. On distillation under atmospheric pressure, it is decomposed into water, trimethylamine, and menthene, $C_{10}H_{18}$; the latter boils at 170° to 171°, has the specific rotatory power, $[\alpha]_D = + 89.307°$, and does not yield a nitrosochloride.

(*b*) d-(CIS-)MENTHYLAMINE.

When five grams of levorotatory menthone are heated with six grams of ammonium formate in sealed tubes at 190° to 200° for several hours, a mixture of the formyl derivatives of l- and d-menthylamines is obtained. *d*-Formyl menthylamine is characterized by its great power of crystallization, and is more sparingly soluble than the isomeric l-compound. Therefore, the contents of the tubes are washed out with ether and water, the ethereal solution is separated and allowed to evaporate slowly; most of the d-formyl derivative separates in well defined crystals. On further evaporation of the mother-liquors, an oil is obtained, which is distilled in vacuum; the fraction boiling at 180° to 183° at a pressure of 18 mm. to 20 mm. yields, on cooling, additional quantities of the d-formyl derivative, which may be completely freed from the mother-liquor by washing with petroleum ether. d-Formyl menthylamine is recrystallized from acetic ether. The yield amounts to fifty or sixty per cent. of the theoretical.

Together with d-formyl menthylamine, of which considerable quantities remain in the oily mother-liquors, l-formyl menthylamine and menthol are formed by the action of ammonium formate on levo-menthone; the presence of the l-base may be proved by its transformation into l-menthylamine hydrochloride, which is insoluble in ether.

Larger quantities of the d-base may be conveniently prepared by the following method.[1] In a 250 cc. round-bottom flask having a glass tube, one meter in length, sealed to it, ten grams of menthone and twelve grams of dry ammonium formate are heated over a direct flame for two days. The reaction-product separates into two layers, the lower, aqueous layer being light colored, the upper, a thick, brown oil. The latter is separated from the aqueous liquid, and is freed from unaltered menthone by steam distillation; the residual oil is then distilled under reduced

[1] Wallach and Werner, Ann. Chem., *300*, 283.

pressure, the largest portion of which boils at 165° to 175° (20 mm.), and forms a colorless syrup; on cooling, or after standing for several days, the oil begins to solidify. The crystallization of the oil may be accelerated by rubbing up the syrupy mass with ether; the crystals are filtered, recrystallized from ether, and consist of d-formyl menthylamine, melting at 117° to 118°. The l-derivative is more soluble in ether, and only crystallizes after allowing the ethereal filtrate to stand during a considerable time.

The formyl derivative of d-menthylamine, obtained by either of the above-mentioned methods, is saponified by heating with alcoholic potash, or better by boiling for two hours with concentrated hydrochloric acid; the resulting acid solution is concentrated until crystallization commences, and the free base is separated by means of alkali.

d-Menthylamine boils at 207° to 208°, has the specific gravity 0.857, the refractive index, $n_D = 1.45940$, and the specific rotatory power, $[\alpha]_D = + 14.71°$; in other properties the two menthylamines are similar, but their derivatives differ very decidedly in melting point, solubility, etc.

d-Menthylamine hydrochloride, $C_{10}H_{19}NH_2 \cdot HCl$, can not be precipitated from the ethereal solution of the base; one hundred parts of ether at 15° dissolve twenty-two grams of this salt. It crystallizes from ether in splendid, transparent prisms, which, however, soon become opaque, and decompose. It is rather easily soluble in water and crystallizes from it in anhydrous plates, melting at 189°.

d-Menthylamine hydrobromide, $C_{10}H_{19}NH_2 \cdot HBr$, is sparingly soluble in ether, and crystallizes from water in fine, small needles, which melt at 225°.

d-Menthylamine hydriodide, $C_{10}H_{19}NH_2 \cdot HI$, is slightly soluble in water and ether, and melts at 270° with decomposition.

d-Formyl menthylamine, $C_{10}H_{19}NH \cdot COH$, is prepared according to the above-described method; it is also formed by heating the free base with formic acid at 200°. It separates from methyl alcohol in very beautiful crystals, which melt at 117.5°; it is sparingly soluble in ether and ethyl acetate, more difficultly in ligroine.

d-Acetyl menthylamine, $C_{10}H_{19}NH \cdot COCH_3$, is obtained in the same manner as the corresponding l-derivative; it crystallizes from ethyl acetate in lustrous prisms, melts at 168° to 169°, and is readily soluble in ether and methyl alcohol.

d-Propionyl menthylamine, $C_{10}H_{19}NH \cdot COC_2H_5$, melts at 151°.

d-Butyryl menthylamine, $C_{10}H_{19}NH \cdot COC_3H_7$, melts at 105° to 106°, dissolves readily in methyl alcohol, sparingly in ethyl acetate, and very difficultly in ether and ligroine.

d-Menthyl carbamide, $C_{10}H_{19} \cdot NH \cdot CONH_2$, crystallizes from dilute alcohol, and melts 155° to 156°.

d-Menthyl phenylcarbamide, $C_{10}H_{19}NH \cdot CONHC_6H_5$, crystallizes from alcohol in fine needles, and melts at 177° to 178°.

d-Menthyl phenylthiocarbamide, $C_{10}H_{19}NH \cdot CS\ NHC_6H_5$, is prepared like the l-derivative; it separates from methyl alcohol in small crystals, having a diamond-like luster, and melts at 178° to 179°.

d-Menthyl allylthiocarbamide, $C_{10}H_{19}NH \cdot CS \cdot NHC_3H_5$, is formed by the action of allylthiocarbimide on an ethereal solution of d-menthylamine; it is very soluble in methyl alcohol, and crystallizes from a mixture of ether and ligroine in brilliant prisms, which melt at 110°. The analogous compound of the levo-series is an oil.

d-Menthyl trimethyl ammonium iodide, $C_{10}H_{19}N(CH_3)_3I$, crystallizes from hot water, and melts at 160° to 161°.

d-Menthyl trimethyl ammonium hydroxide, $C_{10}H_{19}N(CH_3)_3OH$, is prepared from the iodide by means of moist silver oxide. On heating, it is resolved into water, trimethylamine, and *menthene;* the latter boils at 167°, and readily yields a nitrosochloride.

d-Benzylidene menthylamine, $C_{10}H_{19}N = CHC_6H_5$, is obtained by the condensation of the base with benzaldehyde in an ethereal solution. It crystallizes in lustrous needles, which melt at 42° to 43°.

d-Ortho-oxybenzylidene menthylamine, $C_{10}H_{19}N = CHC_6H_4OH$, crystallizes from methyl alcohol in yellow needles, melting at 96° to 97°.

When an aqueous solution of d-menthylamine hydrochloride is boiled with sodium nitrite, and the reaction-product is distilled with steam, a liquid results, which boils at 55° to 95° under a pressure of 20 mm.; on repeated fractionation, this oil is separated chiefly into low boiling portions from which *menthene* is obtained. It boils at 164° to 165°, has the sp. gr. 0.8175, and $[\alpha]_D = + 55.44°$. It forms a nitrosochloride, from which menthene nitrolbenzylamine (m. p. 107° to 108°) is obtained.

The higher boiling fractions contain a small quantity of menthol, and possibly a little menthone; on oxidation with chromic acid, a product is formed which gives a semicarbazone (m. p. 184°), probably identical with l-menthone semicarbazone.

l-Menthylamine is not converted into d-menthylamine at high temperatures, and the derivatives of the levo-base can not be transformed into those of the dextrorotatory amine.

An investigation regarding the optical behavior of l- and d-menthylamines, and of their salts and derivatives has been carried out by Wallach and Binz.[1] The following table presents the most important values obtained for the specific and molecular rotatory powers of these compounds.

	Solvent.	$[\alpha]_D$.	$[M]_D$.
l-Menthylamine	——	—38.07°	—58.90°
" hydrochloride	Water	—35.66	—68.15
" hydrobromide	"	—29.32	—69.04
" hydriodide	"	—24.72	—69.77
d-Menthylamine	——	+14.71	+22.76
" hydrochloride	Water	+17.24	+32.94
" hydrobromide	"	+13.83	+32.56
" hydriodide	"	+11.79	+33.28
" hydrochloride	Ether	+ 8.34	+15.94
" hydrobromide	"	+ 5.26	+12.38
l-Formyl menthylamine	Chloroform	—83.37	—152.27
l-Acetyl "	Chloroform	—81.81	—160.84
l-Propionyl "	Chloroform	—76.53	—161.15
l-Butyryl "	Chloroform	—72.10	—161.90
d-Formyl "	Chloroform	+54.03	+98.68
d-Acetyl "	Chloroform	+50.57	+99.42
d-Propionyl "	Chloroform	+45.14	+95.05
d-Butyryl "	Chloroform	+40.59	+91.14

Wallach and Binz have also obtained values for the rotatory powers of these compounds in other solvents.

3. TERTIARY CARVOMENTHYLAMINE, $C_{10}H_{19}NH_2$.

According to Baeyer,[2] tertiary carvomenthylamine results, together with regenerated carvomenthene, when tertiary carvomenthyl iodide or bromide, formed by the addition of hydriodic acid or hydrobromic acid to carvomenthene, is treated in an ethereal solution with silver cyanide, and the resultant oil is saponified with potash.

$$
\begin{array}{ccc}
 & CH_3 & \\
 & | & \\
 & CNH_2 & \\
 / & & \backslash \\
H_2C & & CH_2 \\
| & & | \\
H_2C & & CH_2 \\
 \backslash & & / \\
 & CH & \\
 & | & \\
 & C_3H_7 &
\end{array}
$$

Tertiary carvomenthylamine.

[1] Wallach and Binz, Ann. Chem., *276*, 317; compare Zeitschr. für physik. Chem., *12*, 723.

[2] Baeyer, Ber., *26*, 2271.

Tertiary carvomenthylamine hydrochloride is soluble in ether, and on evaporation of the solvent it remains as a syrup, which solidifies gradually.

The *platinochloride* is a solid; the *gold double salt* is precipitated as an oil, which soon solidifies, forming large, lustrous plates.

The *benzoyl* derivative crystallizes in large needles, melting at 110°; the *phenylthiocarbamide* forms prisms, which melt at 128°.

4. TERTIARY MENTHYLAMINE, $C_{10}H_{19}NH_2$.

Tertiary menthyl iodide or bromide, obtained by direct addition of hydriodic acid or hydrobromic acid to menthene, forms tertiary menthylamine when treated according to the method given under the preceding compound; the yield is about ten per cent. of the theoretical. According to Baeyer,[1] this amine has the constitution:

```
        CH3
        |
        CH
       /  \
   H2C     CH2
    |       |
   H2C     CH2
       \  /
        CNH2
        |
        C3H7.
```

Tertiary menthylamine hydrochloride, $C_{10}H_{19}NH_2 \cdot HCl$, is soluble in, and crystallizes from, ether; it melts at about 205°. The *platinochloride* crystallizes from alcohol in lustrous leaflets, and melts at 235°. The *gold double salt* forms an oil, which partially solidifies in needles.

The *phenylthiocarbamide* crystallizes in leaflets, and melts at 118° to 119°. The *benzoyl* derivative separates in needles, which melt at 154.5°.

AMIDO-DERIVATIVES OF PHELLANDRENE.

1. AMIDOPHELLANDRENE, $C_{10}H_{15}NH_2$.

The so-called nitrophellandrene, $C_{10}H_{15}NO_2$, obtained by Pesci by the action of ammonia on phellandrene nitrosite, may be converted into amidophellandrene by the following method (Pesci[2]).

Twenty grams of nitrophellandrene are dissolved in a mixture of sixty grams of glacial acetic acid and an equal volume of alcohol; the solution is gradually treated with thirty grams

[1]Baeyer, Ber., *26*, 2270 and 2562.

[2]Pesci, Gazz. Chim., *16*, I., 228; Jahresb. Chem., *1884*, 547.

of zinc dust, and is heated on the water-bath at 70° after the first violent reaction has taken place. The reaction-product is diluted with water, neutralized with sodium hydroxide, and shaken with ether. The base is removed from the ethereal solution by dilute hydrochloric acid, the acid solution is rendered alkaline, and the amidophellandrene is again extracted with ether and purified by distillation with steam.

It is an oily liquid, having a penetrating odor like that of conine; it is moderately soluble in water, and absorbs carbonic anhydride with great readiness

Amidophellandrene sulphate, $(C_{10}H_{15}NH_2)_2 H_2SO_4$, is rather sparingly soluble in cold water. The *hydrochloride* is crystalline, and easily soluble in alcohol and water. The *platinochloride*, $(C_{10}H_{15}NH_2 \cdot HCl)_2PtCl_4$, forms yellow, hexagonal, microscopic plates which are insoluble in water, but readily soluble in warm alcohol. The *mercuric double salt* is crystalline, and sparingly soluble.

It has been mentioned that phellandrene nitrosite, and the compound, $C_{10}H_{15}NO_2$, obtained by Wallach in the treatment of phellandrene nitrosite with sodium alcoholate, are both converted into optically active tetrahydrocarvylamine on reduction with sodium and alcohol.

2. DIAMIDOPHELLANDRENE, $C_{10}H_{16}(NH_2)_2$.

A diamine, $C_{10}H_{16}(NH_2)_2$, was obtained by Pesci[1] by the reduction of phellandrene nitrosite.

For the preparation of this base, phellandrene nitrosite is mixed with alcohol to form a thick paste, and is reduced by the addition of about ten per cent. of glacial acetic acid and zinc dust; the zinc dust is added to the well cooled mixture in small portions at a time until the reaction is complete. The reaction-product is warmed at 40° to 50° for some time, then for one hour at 90,° and is diluted with water The zinc is precipitated with hydrogen sulphide, filtered off, and the filtrate acidified with hydrochloric acid; this solution is evaporated to a small volume, made alkaline, and distilled with steam The distillate is acidified with hydrochloric acid and evaporated, the residue is treated with potash, and the free base extracted with ether, after drying the ethereal solution with solid potassium hydroxide, the ether is distilled off, and the amine is rectified.

Phellandrene diamine is a colorless, odorless liquid, having a strong refractive power; it boils at 209° to 214° with slight de-

[1] Pesci, Gazz Chim, *16*, I., 229, Jahresb. Chem, *1885*, 698

composition. It is readily soluble in water and alcohol, more sparingly in ether, chloroform and ligroine.

The *hydrochloride* is crystalline but hygroscopic; it yields a *platinochloride*, $C_{10}H_{16}(NH_2)_2 \cdot 2HCl \cdot PtCl_4$, which crystallizes in monoclinic prisms.

The sulphate, acetate, nitrate and tartrate of phellandrene diamine are hygroscopic.

OLEFINIC MEMBERS OF THE TERPENE SERIES.

A. HYDROCARBONS.

1. MYRCENE, $C_{10}H_{16}$.

Bay oil contains eugenol, methyl eugenol, chavicol, methyl chavicol, geranial and two hydrocarbons, $C_{10}H_{16}$. Mittmann [1] regarded these hydrocarbons as pinene and another terpene, probably dipentene; Power and Kleber,[2] however, proved that bay oil contains levorotatory phellandrene and a hydrocarbon, $C_{10}H_{16}$, which they called myrcene. This hydrocarbon has an open chain and may be designated as an aliphatic terpene. Myrcene is also found in the oil of sassafras leaves [3]

According to Power and Kleber, myrcene is obtained from the oil of bay by the following process. The oil is first shaken with a five per cent. solution of sodium hydroxide to remove phenols, and is then subjected to a fractional distillation in vacuum. (Myrcene is very readily polymerized by distillation under ordinary pressure.) About eighty per cent. of the oil from which the phenols are removed distills between 67° and 80° under a pressure of 20 mm. By repeated fractionation of this distillate in vacuo, a colorless liquid results, which boils at 67° to 68° under 20 mm. pressure; this liquid has a characteristic odor unlike that of the other terpenes. It has a specific gravity 0.8023 at 15°, considerably lower than that of the common terpenes. The coefficient of refraction, $n_D = 1.4673$, is also remarkably small, and indicates that myrcene contains three double linkages.

When a mixture of one part of myrcene, three parts of glacial acetic acid, and a small amount of dilute sulphuric acid is digested for three hours at 40°, according to Bertram's [4] method, the product contains an oil, having a lavender-like odor; if this oil be saponified with potash, and subsequently fractionated in a vacuum, a product is obtained which consists of unchanged myrcene, dipentene and *linalool*, $C_{10}H_{17}OH$. The presence of linalool is proved

[1] Mittmann, Arch Pharm, *1889*, 529

[2] Pharm Rund, New York, *1895*, No. 13; Semi-Annual Report, Schimmel & Co, April, *1895*, 11

[3] Power and Kleber, Pharm Review, *1896*

[4] German Patent, No 80,711

by its conversion into the aldehyde geranial (citral), $C_{10}H_{16}O$, by careful oxidation, and by the characterization of the latter compound in the formation of the crystalline geranial-β-naphthocinchonic acid (see geranial, page 399). Since myrcene may be converted into linalool, $C_{10}H_{17}OH$, it bears the same relation to this alcohol as does camphene to isoborneol, and pinene or dipentene to terpineol (Power and Kleber).

According to Barbier,[1] however, the alcohol, $C_{10}H_{17}OH$, obtained by Power and Kleber on hydrating myrcene as above mentioned, is *not identical* with linalool (Barbier's "licareol"), but is *isomeric* with it; Barbier designates it by the name *myrcenol*, $C_{10}H_{17}OH$. He describes it as a colorless, oily liquid boiling at 99° to 101° (10 mm.), and slowly undergoing polymerization; it has the sp. gr. 0.9012 and the refractive index, $n_D = 1.47787$, at 14.5°. *Myrcenyl acetate*, $C_{10}H_{17}OOCCH_3$, is a colorless liquid boiling at 111° to 112° (10 mm.). When myrcenol is oxidized with a sulphuric acid solution of chromic acid, it yields acetone, laevulinic acid, and an *aldehyde*, $C_{10}H_{16}O$ (not geranial), boiling at 110° (10 mm.). This aldehyde forms an *oxime*, $C_{10}H_{16}{\cdot}NOH$, which boils at 148° to 150° (10 mm.), and is converted into the aldehyde by boiling with a solution of oxalic acid. The *semicarbazone* is a crystalline powder, melting at 195° to 196°. When myrcenol is oxidized with a one per cent. permanganate solution and then with a chromic acid mixture, it yields laevulinic and succinic acids.

According to Barbier, myrcene and myrcenol are to be represented by the formulas,

$$\begin{matrix}CH_3\\CH_3\end{matrix}\!\!>C{=}CH{-}CH_2{-}CH{=}\underset{\displaystyle CH_3}{\underset{|}{C}}{-}CH{=}CH_2.$$

Myrcene.

$$\begin{matrix}CH_3\\CH_3\end{matrix}\!\!>C{=}CH{-}CH_2{-}CH_2{-}\underset{\displaystyle CH_3}{\underset{|}{C}}(OH){-}CH{=}CH_2.$$

Myrcenol.

Characteristic additive products of myrcene can not be prepared because most reagents seem to polymerize it. Bromine is absorbed in a somewhat smaller quantity than corresponds to the addition of six atoms, but this is attributed to the polymerization of the hydrocarbon. Myrcene is easily oxidized by permanganate with the formation of succinic acid (Power and Kleber).

[1] P. Barbier, Compt. rend., *132*, 1048.

Dihydromyrcene,[1] $C_{10}H_{18}$, is formed by reducing myrcene with alcohol and sodium; it boils at 171.5° to 173.5°, has the specific gravity 0.7802, and the refractive index, $n_D = 1.4501$. On oxidation with permanganate, it yields laevulinic acid and a *keto-glycol*, $C_8H_{16}O_3$, which, on oxidation with chromic acid, gives rise to a *diketone*, $C_7H_{12}O_2$

Cyclodihydromyrcene,[1] $C_{10}H_{18}$, is produced by treating dihydromyrcene with a mixture of acetic and sulphuric acids; it boils at 169° to 172°, has a sp. gr. 0 828, and a refractive index, $n_D = 1.462$ It unites with bromine, forming a *dibromide* (sp. gr. 1.524), and when oxidized it yields a *ketonic acid*, $C_{10}H_{18}O_3$.

It should also be mentioned that the chemists of Schimmel & Co.[2] have isolated a hydrocarbon, $C_{10}H_{16}$, from basil oil, which boils at 73° to 74° (22 mm.), has the sp gr. 0.794 at 22° and 0.801 at 15°, and the index of refraction, $n_D = 1.4861$. It is optically inactive, has an agreeable odor, and is termed *ocimene.* The properties of ocimene resemble those of myrcene, but it differs from the latter in its behavior towards oxygen, it readily absorbs oxygen and becomes resinified. The examination of ocimene is not complete.

2 ANHYDROGERANIOL, $C_{10}H_{16}$.

Anhydrogeraniol was the first known representative of the class of *olefinic terpenes.* It is formed by heating geraniol, $C_{10}H_{17}OH$, in small portions at a time with twice its weight of acid potassium sulphate at 170°. When the reaction-product is distilled in a current of steam, an oil results, which, after purification by repeated distillation over sodium, boils at 172° to 176° (uncorr.). This oil consists of anhydrogeraniol, $C_{10}H_{16}$; it has a peculiar smell, a specific gravity 0.8232 and refractive power, $n_D = 1.4835$, at 20°. It yields a hydrocarbon, $C_{10}H_{22}$, by reduction, and unites with bromine, forming the compound, $C_{10}H_{16}Br_6$ (Semmler[3]).

No additional observations seem to have been made by Semmler regarding the behavior of this terpene However, his assumption that it contains three double linkages, as indicated by its molecular refraction, is in harmony with the fact that it combines with six bromine atoms or six atoms of hydrogen, forming addition-products.

In the same preliminary publication,[3] Semmler mentions that similar olefinic terpenes are obtained from linalool and coriandrol by treatment with acid potassium sulphate as above described.

[1]Semmler, Ber., *34*, 3122.
[2]Schimmel & Co, Semi-Annual Report, April–May, *1901*, 12
[3]Semmler, Ber, *24*, 682

3. OLEFINIC TERPENES IN OIL OF HOPS AND OIL OF ORIGANUM.

Investigations of Chapman[1] on the oil of hops, and of Gildemeister[2] on the oil of origanum from Smyrna indicate that these oils also contain olefinic terpenes. On fractional distillation both oils yield small quantities of a fraction which has the same boiling point as pinene, but is distinguished from the ordinary terpenes by its remarkably low specific gravity. Nothing further is known at present regarding these hydrocarbons.

4. LINALOLENE, $C_{10}H_{18}$.

Linalolene is obtained by reducing linalool with sodium and alcohol, or better by heating equal weights of linalool and zinc dust in sealed tubes at 220° to 230°; the resultant hydrocarbon is purified by distillation with steam, and by subsequent distillation over sodium. It boils at 165° to 168°, has a specific gravity 0.7882 and a refractive power, $n_D = 1.455$, at 20° (Semmler[3]).

The values obtained for the specific and molecular refractive powers show that linalolene contains two ethylene linkages, and therefore belongs to the aliphatic series. When gently warmed with concentrated sulphuric acid, linalolene undergoes a transformation into an isomeric hydrocarbon, which boils at 165° to 167°, has the sp. gr. 0.8112 and the index of refraction, $n_D = 1.4602$, at 17°. Semmler considers this isomeride as a hydrobenzene derivative, and calls it *cyclolinalolene.*

5. HYDROCARBON, $C_{10}H_{18}$, OBTAINED FROM MENTHONYLAMINE.

When menthonylamine is treated with nitrous acid in the preparation of menthocitronellol, $C_{10}H_{19}OH$, a by-product is formed which contains a hydrocarbon, $C_{10}H_{18}$. It boils at 153° to 156°, has the specific gravity of 0.7545 at 15°, and a refractive power, $n_D = 1.4345$ (Wallach[4]).

[1] Chapman, Jour. Chem. Soc., *1894*, 1, 54; Ber., *28*, 303, Ref.
[2] Gildemeister, Arch. Pharm., *233*, 182.
[3] Semmler, Ber., *27*, 2520.
[4] Wallach, Ann. Chem., *278*, 317.

B. OXYGENATED COMPOUNDS.

(*a*) ALCOHOLS.

1. LINALOOL, $C_{10}H_{17}OH$.

Morin[1] showed that the oil of linaloe contains an alcohol, $C_{10}H_{17}OH$, which Semmler[2] in the year 1891 identified as an aliphatic terpene alcohol; he called it linalool. In the following year Barbier[3] submitted linalool, prepared from oil of linaloe, to a detailed investigation, and designated this alcohol as "*licareol.*" Barbier at first doubted the identity of his "licareol" and linalool, but subsequently recognized that they were identical.[4]

Linalool is very widely distributed in nature. Simultaneous with Semmler and Tiemann,[5] Bertram and Walbaum[6] found linalool and linaloyl acetate in the oil of bergamot. The alcohols, $C_{10}H_{17}OH$, which Semmler and Tiemann[5] called "*aurantiol*" and "*lavendol,*" and which occur partially in a free condition and partially in the form of fatty acid esters in the oil of petitgrain and in lavender oil, are to be regarded as linalool (Bertram and Walbaum[6]). In a subsequent publication, Tiemann and Semmler[7] assented to the views expressed by Bertram and Walbaum and added that the alcoholic constituent of the oil of neroli, the so-called "*nerolol,*" is in all probability to be regarded as linalool. According to Reychler, linalool is also found in oil of ylang-ylang[8] and in oil of cananga[9]; according to Gildemeister,[10] it occurs together with levorotatory linaloyl acetate in oil of limes (*Citrus limetta* Risso), and likewise in Smyrnan oil of origanum. Linaloyl acetate is found in sage oil (*Salvia sclarea* L.).

l-Linalool, partly free, partly as ester, forms a constituent of Palermo lemon oil, spike oil, thyme oil,[11] Russian spearmint oil, German[12] and French[13] basilicum oil, and sassafras leaf oil.

[1] Morin, Ann Chim Phys [5], *25*, 427

[2] Semmler, Ber, *24*, 207

[3] Barbier, Compt. rend, *114*, 674, Ber, *25*, 463, Ref

[4] Barbier and Bouveault, Compt rend, *121*, 168

[5] Semmler and Tiemann, Ber., *25*, 1180

[6] Bertram and Walbaum, Journ pr Chem. [2], 45, 590

[7] Tiemann and Semmler, Ber, *26*, 2708.

[8] Reychler, Bull Soc Chim [3], 11, 407 and 576, Ber, *27*, 751, Ref; *28*, 151, Ref

[9] Reychler, Bull Soc Chim. [3], *11*, 1045.

[10] Gildemeister, Arch Pharm, *233*, 174

[11] Labbé, Bull Soc Chim, *19* [III], 1009, Schimmel & Co, Semi Annual Report, Oct, *1894*, 57

[12] Bertram and Walbaum, Arch Pharm, *235*, 176

[13] Dupont and Guerlain, Compt rend, *124*, 300

According to our present knowledge, linalool yields no crystalline derivative which may be employed for the preparation of a chemically pure product from the above-mentioned ethereal oils. Therefore, linalool is separated by the fractional distillation of these oils; but oils which contain esters of linalool, together with the free alcohol, must first be treated with alcoholic potash, and then rectified. The properties of linalool so prepared vary in certain respects according to its origin. These variations are rendered apparent by the following table.

LINALOOL OBTAINED FROM,

	Lavender Oil (Bertram and Walbaum).[1]	Bergamot Oil (Bertram and Walbaum).[1]	Linaloe Oil (Bertram and Walbaum).[1]	Linaloe Oil (Semmler).[2]	Oil of Limes (Gildemeister).[3]	Oil of Origanum (Gildemeister).[3]
Boiling point.	197° to 199°	197° to 199°	197° to 200°	195° to 199°	198° to 199° under 760 mm.	197.8° to 199° under 752 mm.
Specific gravity.	0.8725 at 15°	0.8720 at 15°	0.8770 at 15°	0.8702 at 20°	0.870 at 15°	0.8704 at 15°
Refractive index, n_D.	1.4640 at 20°	1.4629 at 18°	1.4630 at 20°	1.4695 at 20°	1.4668 at 20°	1.4633 at 20°
Angle of rotation (100 mm.).	—10°35′	—16°	—2°	——	—17°37′ at 15°	—15°56′ at 15°

The difference in the properties of these various samples of linalool was at times explained by the supposition that they contained different, although closely allied, alcohols. Recently, however, all these alcohols have been regarded as identical, and the anomalies in their properties as being dependent on the presence of impurities; this view is rendered more probable by the fact that they exhibit exactly the same chemical behavior. If linalool, obtained from any of the above-mentioned oils, be oxidized with chromic acid, it is converted into an optically inactive aldehyde, geranial (citral), $C_{10}H_{16}O$, which is characterized by its transformation into cymene, and by the formation of the crystalline geranial (citral)-β-naphthocinchonic acid, melting at 198° to 199°.

All alcohols of the formula, $C_{10}H_{17}OH$, having the properties given in the above table, are termed linalool if they are optically

[1] Bertram and Walbaum, Journ. pr. Chem. [2], *45*, 590.
[2] Semmler, Ber., *24*, 207.
[3] Gildemeister, Arch. Pharm., *233*, 174.

levorotatory, and yield geranial on oxidation. If this definition of linalool be accepted, then an optically dextrorotatory alcohol, which Semmler[1] called "*coriandrol*," must be designated as *dextro-linalool*. This compound occurs in oil of coriander, and has the properties of linalool; it boils at 194° to 198°, has the specific gravity 0.8679 and refractive index, $n_D = 1.4652$, at 20°, and is converted into geranial by oxidation; its optical rotation is reported as $[\alpha]_D = +13° 19'$ and $+15° 1'$.

It is of course possible with the increase of knowledge respecting this group of compounds, that the various alcohols, which we designate at present as linalool, will be distinguished from one another, and characterized as chemical individuals. Theoretically, numerous isomerides of geranial may be predicted. As Tiemann and Semmler have indicated, a transposition of the ethylene linkages may take place in such substances by treatment with certain reagents, and this has been especially observed by Fittig; hence, the formation of the same geranial from isomeric alcohols could be explained by the acceptance of a similar hypothesis. One observation seems to point to the fact that an intramolecular change of this nature takes place in linalool. When linalool is heated with acetic anhydride, it is rendered inactive, and is converted into the acetyl derivative of the isomeric, inactive alcohol, geraniol. Geraniol boils 30° higher than linalool, and, therefore, can not have the same connection with the latter compound as dipentene with limonene. In consideration of the results obtained by the oxidation of these alcohols, Tiemann and Semmler[2] represent the transformation of linalool into geraniol by the following formulas:

$$\underset{\substack{|\\CH_3}}{CH_3{-}C}{=}CH{-}CH_2{-}CH_2{-}\underset{\substack{|\\CH_3}}{C}(OH){-}CH{=}CH_2$$

Linalool (dimethyl-2-6-octadiene-2-7-ol-6)

$$\underset{\substack{|\\CH_3}}{CH_3{-}C}{=}CH{-}CH_2{-}CH_2{-}\underset{\substack{|\\CH_3}}{C}{=}CH{-}CH_2OH$$

Geraniol (dimethyl-2-6-octadiene-2-6-ol-8)

According to more recent investigations by Barbier,[3] this formula for linalool represents the constitution of myrcenol, and

[1]Semmler, Ber., *24*, 206, compare Kawalier, Jahresb. Chem., *1852*, 624, and Grosser, Ber., *14*, 2485

[2]Tiemann and Semmler, Ber., *28*, 2126

[3]Barbier, Bull Soc. Chim., *25* [III], 828

Barbier therefore suggests that linalool is stereoisomeric with geraniol ("lemonol"), and is to be represented by the formula:

$$CH_3-\underset{\displaystyle CH_3}{\underset{|}{C}}=CH-CH_2-CH_2-\underset{\displaystyle CH_3}{\underset{|}{C}}=CH-CH_2OH.$$

Linalool.

According to Barbier, the compound previously regarded as pure linalool is a mixture of levo-terpineol, active myrcenol and unsaturated ethers of the formula, $C_{10}H_{18}O$; and since linalool has not been obtained free from these substances, the optical rotation of the *pure* alcohol is not at present known. Barbier regards *pure* linalool as inactive, and since the oxidation products of linalool are identical with those of geraniol, he considers that all the reactions of linalool are more readily explained by his formula.

According to Tiemann,[1] a fairly pure linalool, free from terpenes, may be obtained from the essential oils by the following process. Sodium is added to the crude linalool contained in a retort, and the liquid is heated under reduced pressure as long as the sodium continues to be dissolved; after cooling, the unchanged metallic sodium is removed, the sodium salt of linalool is suspended in dry ether, and treated with succinic, or, better, phthalic anhydride. After standing for several days, the liquid is agitated with water, which dissolves the *linaloyl sodium phthalate,* while any unchanged linalool or linalolene remains in the ether; the aqueous solution is repeatedly washed with ether, the solution is acidified, and again extracted with ether. The resulting linaloyl acid phthalate is hydrolyzed with alcoholic potash, and the purified linalool is extracted with ether.

An inactive linalool may be artificially prepared by heating geraniol with water in an autoclave for some time at 200°; it boils at 198° to 200° (753 mm.), and has the sp. gr. 0.877 at 15°.[2] Another method of preparing inactive linalool consists in treating geraniol with hydrochloric acid, and saponifying the resultant, isomeric chlorides, $C_{10}H_{17}Cl$, with alcoholic potash; some geraniol is regenerated, and about fifty per cent. of inactive linalool is obtained (Tiemann[3]). According to Stephan,[4] a third method of converting geraniol into inactive linalool consists in

[1]Tiemann and Krüger, Ber., *29*, 901; Tiemann, Ber., *31*, 837.
[2]Schimmel & Co., Semi-Annual Report, April, *1898*, 27.
[3]Tiemann, Ber., *31*, 832.
[4]Stephan, Journ. pr. Chem., *60* [II.], 252.

passing steam into an aqueous solution of sodium geranyl phthalate; some geraniol is also regenerated.

It is reported that levo-linalool may be converted into dextro-linalool by the influence of acid reagents[1]; thus, this transformation is said to take place on heating a solution of linaloyl acid phthalate, and during the preparation of linaloyl acetate by the action of acetic and dilute sulphuric acids on linalool.

Linalool absorbs four atoms of bromine. When reduced with sodium and alcohol, or when heated with zinc dust at 220° or 230°, it is converted into linalolene, $C_{10}H_{18}$ (Semmler). By the action of hydrochloric acid on linalool, water is eliminated, and a mixture of liquid chlorides, $C_{10}H_{18}Cl_2$, results; they decompose when distilled in vacuum (Bertram and Walbaum).

According to Barbier,[2] when this mixture of chlorides is heated with potassium acetate and glacial acetic acid, terpenes, geranyl acetate and geraniol are formed.

The action of dehydrating agents on linalool has been studied by Bertram and Walbaum. Water may be removed by acid potassium sulphate or by dilute sulphuric acid. When linalool is heated gently with formic acid of sp. gr. 1.22, a somewhat violent reaction takes place, and water is very readily separated with the formation of terpinene and dipentene; this reaction is worthy of special notice, since by means of it the first transformation of an aliphatic compound into a true terpene, $C_{10}H_{16}$, was effected. According to Semmler, aliphatic terpenes may also be obtained from linalool, but nothing definite has been published regarding such compounds. (See anhydrogeraniol.)

When formic acid is allowed to act on levo-linalool at a temperature below 20°, fifty per cent. of the linalool is converted into *dextro-terpineol*; in the same manner, formic acid converts dextro-linalool (coriandrol) into *levo-terpineol* (Stephan[3]).

When l-linalool is warmed with acetic acid, some d-terpineol is produced. Cold acetic acid does not act upon it, but if a solution of linalool in three times its weight of acetic acid be treated with one half a per cent. of sulphuric acid at a temperature below 20°, about forty-five per cent. is changed into *d*-terpineol, and ten per cent. into geraniol (Stephan[3]).

Hydrogen peroxide converts linalool into a crystalline compound, melting at 110° to 111°; this substance has been shown to

[1] Schimmel & Co., Semi-Annual Report, Oct., *1896*, 85; compare with Charabot, Bull. Soc. Chim., *21*, 549.

[2] Barbier and Bouveault, Bull. Soc. Chim., *15* [III.], 594.

[3] Stephan, Journ. pr. Chem., *58* [II.], 109.

be identical with terpine hydrate, the formation of which is probably due to the presence of a mineral acid impurity in the reagent (Bertram and Walbaum).

Terpine hydrate is almost quantitatively formed, when linalool is agitated with five per cent. sulphuric acid for several days.[1]

Chromic acid oxidizes linalool into the aldehyde geranial (citral). The oxidation sometimes proceeds further, yielding oxidation products of geranial, as methyl heptenone, laevulinic acid, etc.

Tiemann and Semmler[2] obtained rather remarkable results in the oxidation of linalool. By successive treatment with potassium permanganate and chromic acid, they accomplished quite readily a decomposition of this alcohol into acetone, laevulinic acid and oxalic acid. They concluded, therefore, that linalool contains the grouping,

$$C(CH_3)_2 = CH - CH_2 - CH_2 - C(CH_3) = ;$$

and considering that it must also contain an asymmetric carbon atom, they derived the formula of linalool which has already been presented.

The alcohol obtained from coriander oil, which must be designated as dextro-linalool, yields compounds, $C_{10}H_{17}Cl$ and $C_{10}H_{17}I$, when treated with hydrochloric and hydriodic acids; these substances are oils which can not be distilled. When dextro-linalool is oxidized with permanganate, it is converted into a ketone, $C_{10}H_{16}O$, carbonic anhydride, acetic acid and a gelatinous acid, having the constitution $C_6H_{10}O_4$ (Grosser[3]).

Linaloyl acetate, $C_{10}H_{17}OCOCH_3$, is found in many ethereal oils, especially in the oil of orange blossoms and in the oil of bergamot, whose odor is dependent on it. It is formed when myrcene is treated with a mixture of glacial acetic and sulphuric acids (Power and Kleber[4]).

In order to prepare it, linalool is boiled with acetic anhydride for several hours, the product is washed with water and soda solution, and the ester distilled with steam. The terpenes which result during its preparation are separated by fractional distillation in vacuum (Bertram and Walbaum).

Linaloyl acetate has a strong odor of bergamot, and boils and decomposes at 220° when distilled under ordinary pressure. It boils at 105° to 108° under a pressure of 11 mm., and has the

[1] Tiemann and Semmler, Ber., *28*, 2137.
[2] Tiemann and Semmler, Ber., *28*, 2126.
[3] Grosser, Ber., *14*, 2494 and 2497.
[4] Power and Kleber, Pharm. Rundsch, *1895*, No. 13; A. Hesse, Journ. pr. Chem., *64* [II.], 245.

specific gravity 0.912 at 15°; $[\alpha]_D = -6° 25'$. Alcoholic potash changes it into linalool.

Pure linaloyl acetate may be prepared from sodium linaloolate and acetic anhydride; it boils at 96.5° to 97° under 10 mm. pressure (Hesse).

If the acetate be prepared from levo-linalool by means of a mixture of glacial acetic and sulphuric acids, dextro-linaloyl acetate is obtained; this yields dextro-linalool when saponified (Gildemeister[1]).

Linaloyl propionate, $C_{10}H_{17}OCOC_2H_5$, is a fragrant oil, which boils at 115° under 10 mm. pressure. It occurs naturally in lavender oil.

Linaloyl butyrate occurs in lavender oil, and the *valerianate* is contained in lavender oil and sassafras oil.

It is to be noted that the esters of linalool, which are prepared synthetically by heating linalool with acid anhydrides, are not chemically pure compounds; they consist largely of the esters of linalool, together with some esters of geraniol and terpineol, and are usually optically inactive or slightly dextrorotatory. The naturally occurring esters are levorotatory.

2. GERANIOL, $C_{10}H_{17}OH$.

Geraniol is an alcohol closely related to linalool, but is distinguished from it by its optical inactivity and by its higher boiling point (linalool boils at 197° to 200°, geraniol at 229° to 230°).

The conversion of linalool into geraniol was first observed by Barbier.[2] This chemist found that the boiling point of linalool increases and its optical rotatory power decreases when it is heated with acetic anhydride at 120° for a long time; the resultant alcohol, having a rose-like odor, was thought to be different from geraniol, and was called "*licarhodol.*" Bouchardat[3] at once expressed the opinion that this licarhodol was identical with geraniol. The correctness of Bouchardat's statement was conclusively proved by Bertram and Gildemeister[4] by the isolation of the calcium chloride compound of geraniol from Barbier's licarhodol.

[1] Gildemeister, Arch Pharm, *233*, 174; German Patent, No 80,711, compare with Tiemann and Semmler, Ber, *25*, 1184 and 1187, Bertram and Walbaum, Journ pr Chem, *45* [II], 598

[2] Barbier, Compt rend, *116*, 1200, Ber, *16*, 490, Ref

[3] Bouchardat, Compt rend, *116*, 1253, compare Barbier, Compt rend, *117*, 122

[4] Bertram and Gildemeister, Journ. pr Chem. [2], *49*, 185, compare Stephan, Journ pr Chem [2], *58*, 109, Schimmel & Co, Semi-Annual Report, April, *1898*, 33

Tiemann and Semmler[1] also confirmed Bouchardat's view, and Barbier and Bouveault[2] have admitted its accuracy.

Geraniol is widely distributed in nature. Indian oil of geranium and palmarosa oil contain ninety-two per cent. of geraniol as shown by the experiments of Jacobsen[3] and, more recently, by those of Semmler.[4] It has also been found in pelargonium oil (African geranium oil) by Gintl,[5] and in the oil of citronella by Schimmel & Co.[6] It occurs in the oil of *Eucalyptus maculata*, var. *citriodora*, and occurs, together with linalool, in lavender oil, lemon grass oil and ylang-ylang oil. It is also found in small quantities in neroli and petitgrain oils, oil of spike, lignaloe oil, and sassafras oil. According to Smith,[7] the oil from the fresh leaves and branchlets of *Eucalyptus macarthuri* contain sixty per cent. of geranyl acetate, 10.64 per cent. of free geraniol, as well as some eudesmol.

Of especial interest, however, is the fact that the greatest part of the alcoholic constituents of Turkish and German oil of rose consists of geraniol (Bertram and Gildemeister[8]).

In an investigation of the oil of rose, Eckart[9] discovered an alcohol, $C_{10}H_{18}O$, to which he gave the name "*rhodinol*." Markownikoff and Reformatzky[10] examined rose oil and came to the conclusion that it contained an alcohol, $C_{10}H_{20}O$, which they called "*roseol*"; Barbier[11] rejected this conclusion, and confirmed Eckart's observations. Tiemann and Semmler[1] further determined that "*rhodinal*," $C_{10}H_{16}O$, which is obtained by the oxidation of Eckart's "rhodinol," $C_{10}H_{18}O$, is identical with garanial, $C_{10}H_{16}O$. The conclusive proof that rose oil contains geraniol was given by Bertram and Gildemeister by the isolation of the calcium chloride compound of geraniol from rose oil. More recent investigations have proved that rose oil[12] and the ethereal

[1] Tiemann and Semmler, Ber., *26*, 2708.

[2] Barbier and Bouveault, Compt. rend., *121*, 168.

[3] Jacobsen, Ann. Chem., *157*, 232.

[4] Semmler, Ber., *23*, 1098.

[5] Gintl, Jahresb. Chem., *1879*, 941.

[6] Semi-Annual Report of Schimmel & Co., Oct., *1893*, and German Patent, No. *76,435;* Ber., 27, 953, Ref.; compare Journ. pr. Chem. [2], *49*, 191, and Dodge, Amer. Chem. Journ., *1889*, 456; Ber., *23*, 175, Ref.

[7] H. G. Smith, Chem. News, *83*, 5.

[8] Bertram and Gildemeister, Journ. pr. Chem. [2], *49*, 185; Gildemeister and Stephan, Arch. Pharm., *234*, 321.

[9] Eckart, Arch. Pharm., *229*, 355.

[10] Markownikoff and Reformatzky, Journ. pr. Chem. [2], *48*, 293; Ber., *27*, 625, Ref.

[11] Barbier, Compt. rend., *117*, 177 and 1092.

[12] Dupont and Guerbain, Compt. rend., *123*, 700.

oils of the genus *Pelargonium* contain geraniol, $C_{10}H_{18}O$, together with considerable quantities of another alcohol, *citronellol*, $C_{10}H_{20}O$.

The terpene alcohol "*réuniol*," prepared by A. Hesse[1] from Réunion geranium oil by means of its camphoric acid ester, has been shown to be a mixture[2] of geraniol, $C_{10}H_{18}O$, and citronellol, $C_{10}H_{20}O$.

Erdmann and Huth[3] suggested that the name "*rhodinol*" be substituted for that of geraniol; this suggestion, however, can not be accepted.

Barbier and Bouveault[4] obtained an alcohol from the volatile oil of *Andropogon schœnanthus;* they considered it an individual chemical compound, and called it "*lemonol*." Bertram and Gildemeister[5] have proved that this "lemonol" is a mixture, containing considerable quantities of geraniol.

Very different opinions have been expressed from time to time by different chemists regarding the constituents of the above-mentioned essential oils, and the nature of the alcohols obtained from them. The use of different names for geraniol and citronellol, or for mixtures of these two alcohols has led to considerable confusion in the study of these compounds and their derivatives. It must suffice here merely to note that the recent investigations, especially those of Bertram and Gildemeister,[6] chemists of Schimmel & Co., Leipzig, have practically proved that geraniol, $C_{10}H_{18}O$, is *identical* with "lemonol" (Barbier and Bouveault), and with "rhodinol" (Erdmann and Huth, and Poleck); citronellol, $C_{10}H_{20}O$ (Tiemann and Schmidt) is identical with "rhodinol" of Barbier and Bouveault and with "réuniol" (Hesse, Naschold); Eckart's "rhodinol" is a mixture of geraniol and citronellol, and the same may be said of "roseol" (Markownikow); "licarhodol" (Barbier) is a mixture of about eighty-five parts of geraniol and fifteen parts of dextro-terpineol.

[1] A. Hesse, Journ. pr. Chem., *50* [II.], 474; *53* [II.], 23; Wallach and Naschold, Naschold's Inaug. Diss., Göttingen, *1896*.

[2] Schimmel & Co., Semi-Annual Report, April, *1895*, 37 and 63; Tiemann and Schmidt, Ber., *29*, 903.

[3] Erdmann and Huth, Journ. pr. Chem., *53* [II], 42; *56* [II], 1; Poleck, Ber., *31*, 29; Journ. pr. Chem., *56* [II.], 515; Bertram and Gildemeister, Journ. pr. Chem., *56* [II.], 506.

[4] Barbier and Bouveault, Compt. rend., *118*, 1154 and 1208; *119*, 281 and 334; *122*, 393; Bull. Soc. Chim., *15* [III.], 594; Barbier, Compt. rend., *126*, 1423; Tiemann, Ber., *31*, 2989; Barbier, Bull. Soc. Chim., *21* [II.], 635.

[5] Bertram and Gildemeister, Journ. pr. Chem., *53* [II.], 225; Schimmel & Co., Semi-Annual Report, April, *1898*, 33.

[6] Schimmel & Co., Semi-Annual Report, April, *1896*, 37; Oct., *1896*, 85, 87 and 90; April, *1897*, 32; Oct., *1897*, 67; Oct., *1898*, 55.

In order to prepare geraniol, the oils which contain large quantities of this alcohol are treated with alcoholic potash to remove esters, and are then fractionated in vacuo. The resulting geraniol, however, generally contains impurities. The method for the purification of this product depends on the property observed by Jacobsen [1] that geraniol combines with calcium chloride. According to Bertram and Gildemeister,[2] the crude geraniol is carefully dried and intimately mixed with an equal amount of freshly dried and finely pulverized calcium chloride; the mixture is allowed to stand in a desiccator at a temperature of $-4°$ to $-5°$ for twelve to sixteen hours. The resultant, more or less tough, mass is rubbed up with anhydrous benzene or petroleum ether, and filtered with the pump. The substance remaining on the filter is again mixed with benzene and filtered, the same process being repeated for a third time; the product is then decomposed with water. The oil which separates is washed with water and distilled, the geraniol boiling at 228° to 230°. As a rule the separation of geraniol by this method is only applicable when the ethereal oil contains at least twenty-five per cent. of geraniol. Chloride of magnesium, and calcium or magnesium nitrate also form crystalline additive compounds with geraniol, and may be used in place of calcium chloride.

Several other methods [3] have been proposed for the separation of geraniol from mixtures with terpenes, etc., depending on the production of an acid geranyl ester by the action of succinic, or, preferably, phthalic anhydride on the sodium salt of crude geraniol, or by heating geraniol with phthalic anhydride on the water-bath. This acid ester or its sodium salt (prepared from the pure silver salt) is saponified with alcoholic potash, and a very pure geraniol is obtained. These methods have no great superiority over the calcium chloride process.

Properties.—Geraniol is an optically inactive alcohol, which has a very pleasant odor of roses, and boils at 229° to 230° under atmospheric pressure and at 120.5° to 122.5° under a pressure of 17 mm. Its specific gravity at 15° is 0.8801 to 0.8834, according to its origin; the refractive power is $n_D = 1.4766$ to 1.4786. The specific gravity of geraniol increases rapidly when it is allowed to stand in the air (Tiemann and Semmler [4]).

[1] Jacobsen, Ann. Chem., *157*, 232.

[2] Semi-Annual Report of Schimmel & Co., *1895*, 38.

[3] Tiemann and Krüger, Ber., *29*, 901; Haller, Compt. rend., *122*, 865; Erdmann, Journ. pr. Chem., *56* [II.], 17; Flatau and Labbé, Compt. rend., *126*, 1725; Bull. Soc. Chim., *19* [III.], 635.

[4] Tiemann and Semmler, Ber., *26*, 2711.

Jacobsen recognized geraniol as an alcohol, and prepared geranyl chloride, $C_{10}H_{17}Cl$, geranyl bromide and iodide by the action of the halogen hydrides on geraniol; he described these compounds as oils which could not be distilled, and further stated that their halogen atoms could be replaced by sulphur, oxygen and acid radicals.

According to Reychler,[1] when geraniol is saturated with hydrogen chloride, the compound, $C_{10}H_{18}Cl_2$, is formed, when this substance is boiled with water, it yields a product intermediate between $C_{10}H_{18}Cl_2$ and $C_{10}H_{18}O$.

Isomeric chlorides, $C_{10}H_{17}Cl$, are probably produced by the action of hydrogen chloride on geraniol; they are converted into geraniol and linalool by the action of alcoholic potash.[2]

Geranyl bromide dihydrobromide,[3] $C_{10}H_{17}Br\ 2HBr$, is formed by the action of hydrobromic acid on geraniol in glacial acetic acid solution; it decomposes on distillation. Silver acetate converts it into geranyl acetate and a *diacetate of a glycol*, $C_{10}H_{18}(OH)_2$.

According to Semmler, geraniol absorbs four atoms of bromine or iodine.

The conversion of geraniol into the isomeric linalool was mentioned under linalool. On the other hand, linalool may be converted into a mixture of geraniol and dextro-terpineol or its acetate (Barbier's "licarhodol") by heating with acetic anhydride.[4]

On heating geraniol with water in an autoclave at 240° to 250°, it is decomposed into hydrocarbons (dipentene).[3]

Geraniol is more stable towards acids than linalool. Boiling acetic anhydride converts it quantitatively into geranyl acetate; no terpineol is formed during this reaction. Acetic acid containing one to two per cent. of sulphuric acid converts it into terpineol.[5]

Formic acid acts on geraniol at 0° to 5° yielding geranyl formate; on warming, terpinene is produced; at 15° to 20°, however, the product consists chiefly of terpinyl formate, which yields terpineol (m p. 35°) on hydrolysis (Stephan).

When geraniol is shaken with a five per cent. sulphuric acid for several days, terpine hydrate is formed.[6]

[1] Reychler, Bull Soc. Chem, *15* [III], 364; Barbier and Bouveault, Bull Soc Chim, *15* [III], 594.

[2] Tiemann, Ber, *31*, 808

[3] Naschold, Inaug Diss, Göttingen, *1896*

[4] Bouchardat, Compt rend, *116*, 1253, Stephan, Journ. pr Chem, *58* [II], 111.

[5] Stephan, Journ pr Chem, *60* [II], 244

[6] Tiemann and Semmler, Ber, 28, 2137

Semmler found that geraniol is converted into *anhydrogeraniol*, an aliphatic terpene, by the action of potassium bisulphate; dilute sulphuric acid converts geraniol into terpinene, and concentrated formic acid gives rise to terpinene and dipentene.[1] The action of phosphoric anhydride on geraniol also causes the formation of terpenes and polyterpenes having a cyclic structure of the carbon atoms.

Cold solutions of alkalis are without action on geraniol. According to Barbier,[2] when "lemonol" (geraniol) is heated with a concentrated, alcoholic solution of potash at 150° for eight hours, it yields a tertiary alcohol, $C_9H_{18}O$, *dimethyl heptenol*. According to Tiemann,[3] however, this reaction gives rise to *methyl heptenol* (methyl hexylene carbinol), $C_8H_{16}O$. On similar treatment, linalool is hardly altered.

On oxidation of geraniol with chromic acid, geranial, $C_{10}H_{16}O$, is produced; the reaction frequently proceeds further giving oxidation products of geranial. Since the latter compound is an aldehyde, geraniol must be a primary alcohol. The oxidation of geraniol with potassium permanganate converts it into isovaleric acid, see under linalool (Semmler, Jacobsen).

Geraniol, like linalool, is readily decomposed into acetone, laevulinic acid and oxalic acid by gentle oxidation. If geraniol (fifty grams) be oxidized in the cold with a very dilute solution of potassium permanganate (seventy grams), a product results which is probably a polyvalent alcohol, although it has never been isolated. This compound is contained in the filtrate from the manganese oxides, and is in its turn oxidized by heating the aqueous solution with chromic anhydride (one hundred and fifty grams) and sulphuric acid (two hundred and fifty grams). The products of this oxidation are, as above stated, acetone, laevulinic and oxalic acids. From this reaction, Tiemann and Semmler[4] derive the formula for geraniol:

$$\underset{\displaystyle CH_3}{CH_3-\overset{|}{C}}=CH-CH_2-CH_2-\underset{\displaystyle CH_3}{\overset{|}{C}}=CH-CH_2OH.$$

Dimethyl-2, 6-octadiëne-2, 6-ol-8.

Geranyl acetate, $C_{10}H_{17}OCOCH_3$, is found, together with geraniol, in certain ethereal oils, and may be prepared by boiling gera-

[1] Bertram and Walbaum (Gildemeister), Journ. pr. Chem., *49* [II.], 185; *53*, 236.

[2] Barbier, Compt. rend., *126*, 1423.

[3] Tiemann, Ber., *31*, 2991; Schimmel & Co., Semi-Annual Report, Oct., *1898*, 61.

[4] Tiemann and Semmler, Ber., *28*, 2126.

niol with acetic anhydride (Bertram and Gildemeister). It is decomposed into the alcohol and acetic acid when distilled under atmospheric pressure, but boils without decomposition at 127.8° to 129.2° under a pressure of 16 mm. It has a specific gravity of 0.9174 and refractive power, $n_D = 1.4628$, at 15°. Since terpenes are not formed by boiling geraniol with acetic anhydride, the determination of the saponification figure may be employed for the quantitative estimation of geraniol in mixtures of this alcohol with terpenes.

Other fatty acid esters of geraniol are prepared by the action of the acid anhydrides on geraniol, or from the acid chlorides and geraniol in the presence of pyridine. These esters are all liquids.

Geranyl diphenylurethane,[1] $(C_6H_5)_2N \cdot CO \cdot OC_{10}H_{17}$, is a compound well adapted for the characterization of geraniol; it crystallizes from eighty per cent. alcohol in long, silky needles, melting at 82.2°. It forms a *tetrabromide*, which melts at 129° to 132°.

Geranyl hydrogen phthalate, $C_{10}H_{17}O \cdot CO \cdot C_6H_4 \cdot COOH$, may be used for the isolation and preparation of pure geraniol. It was obtained by Erdmann[2] as a colorless oil by heating "rhodinol" with finely powdered phthalic anhydride on the water-bath. According to Flatau and Labbé,[3] geraniol may be separated from citronellol by boiling a mixture of the two alcohols, in a reflux apparatus, with an equal weight of phthalic anhydride dissolved in benzene; the resultant ethereal salts are purified, and dissolved in petroleum ether. On cooling the solution to − 5°, geranyl phthalate separates in the crystalline form, while on evaporation of the remaining liquid citronellol phthalate is obtained as a yellow oil.

Geranyl phthalate crystallizes in rhombic tablets, melting at 47°, and is readily soluble in most organic solvents in the cold, with the exception of petroleum ether. When dissolved in ether and treated with bromine, it yields *tetrabromogeranyl phthalate*, $C_{10}H_{17}Br_4O \cdot CO \cdot C_6H_4 \cdot COOH$; it crystallizes from petroleum ether, and melts at 114° to 115°.

The *silver salt* of geranyl phthalate melts at 133°; it is purified by dissolving in benzene and precipitating with warm methyl alcohol.

3. MENTHOCITRONELLOL, $C_{10}H_{19}OH$.

As has already been mentioned under menthone, menthonitrile, on reduction, yields two bases, menthonylamine, $C_{10}H_{19}NH_2$, and oxyhydromenthonylamine, $C_{10}H_{20}(OH)NH_2$.

[1] Erdmann, Journ. pr. Chem., *53* [II.], 42; *56* [II.], 28.

[2] H. Erdmann and Huth, Journ. pr. Chem., *56* [II.], 17; see Erdmann, Ber., *31*, 356.

[3] Flatau and Labbé, Compt. rend., *126*, 1725.

When menthonylamine oxalate (twenty grams) is warmed with a concentrated solution of sodium nitrite (twelve grams in eighty grams of water), an oil separates immediately; it has a rose-like odor, and may be distilled in a current of steam. This oil contains menthocitronellol (menthonyl alcohol), $C_{10}H_{19}OH$, together with its nitrous acid ester, and small quantities of a hydrocarbon, $C_{10}H_{18}$ (b. p. 153° to 156°). The ester is removed by treating with sodium methylate; the reaction-product is distilled with steam, and the resulting oil is dried over potash, and fractionated under diminished pressure. The hydrocarbon distills over first, and is followed by menthocitronellol at 95° to 105° under a pressure of 7 mm.

This alcohol is an isomeride of menthol, has a specific gravity 0.8315 and refractive index, $n_D = 1.44809$, at 20°; it is feebly dextrorotatory, $[\alpha]_D = +2.008°$. In some respects it is similar to linalool, and, like the latter, it yields an acetate having a bergamot-like odor. When oxidized with chromic anhydride it yields an aldehyde, menthocitronellal, $C_{10}H_{18}O$; it is, therefore, a primary alcohol (Wallach[1]).

Menthocitronellol shows considerable similarity to citronellol, and future investigations may show them to be identical; but for the present they are to be regarded as individual compounds.

Dimethyl octylene glycol (2, 6-dimethyl octane-2, 8-ol), $C_{10}H_{20}(OH)_2$, is formed by the action of nitrous acid on oxyhydromenthonylamine, $C_{10}H_{20}(OH)NH_2$; it boils at 153° to 156° (19 mm.), and is converted into menthocitronellol by the action of dilute sulphuric acid (Wallach[2]).

4. CITRONELLOL, $C_{10}H_{19}OH$.

It has already been mentioned that mixtures of geraniol and an alcohol, $C_{10}H_{20}O$, have been described under the names of "rhodinol,"[3] "réuniol,"[4] and "roseol."[5] These mixtures were obtained from geranium oil and the oil of rose, and were at first regarded as definite chemical compounds. After it had been proved that these substances contained geraniol and an alcohol, $C_{10}H_{20}O$, the terms "rhodinol" and "réuniol" were applied to the latter compound. Owing to the close relation which this alcohol bears to citronellal, being prepared from the latter com-

[1] Wallach, Ann. Chem., *278*, 315; *296*, 120.

[2] Wallach, Ann. Chem., *296*, 120.

[3] Eckart, Archiv. d. Pharm., *229*, 355; Barbier and Bouveault, Compt. rend., *119*, 281 and 334; *122*, 529.

[4] A. Hesse, Journ. pr. Chem., *50* [II.], 472.

[5] Markownikow, Journ. pr. Chem., *48* [II.], 293.

pound by reduction, Tiemann and Schmidt[1] proposed the name citronellol.

Citronellol occurs in the geranium oils in two optically active modifications, while rose oil appears to contain only levo-citronellol; esters of citronellol are also found in nature.

It was not until quite recently that a pure citronellol was obtained, and characterized as a chemical compound. The chief difficulty was to separate it from geraniol, since the two alcohols can not be separated by fractional distillation. Wallach and Naschold[2] obtained pure l-citronellol by heating a mixture of this alcohol and geraniol with water in an autoclave at 250°; by this treatment geraniol is entirely decomposed into hydrocarbons, while citronellol remains unaltered. According to Tiemann and Schmidt, citronellol may be separated from geraniol by heating the mixture with phthalic anhydride at 200° for two hours; geraniol is thus converted into hydrocarbons, and the resulting liquid phthalic acid salt of citronellol is separated, washed and saponified. When phosphorus trichloride is allowed to act on a mixture of the two alcohols in ethereal solution, it converts geraniol into hydrocarbons and geranyl chloride; citronellol, however, gives rise to a chlorinated acid phosphoric acid ester, which dissolves in alkalis, and may thus be separated (Tiemann and Schmidt) Flatau and Labbé convert the mixture of the two alcohols into the acid phthalic esters; the geraniol derivative is crystalline (m. p. 47°), while the citronellol compound is an oil (see under geraniol).

Dextro-citronellol may be prepared by reducing the corresponding aldehyde, citronellal, with sodium amalgam and glacial acetic acid.[3] When obtained by this method, it boils at 117° to 118° under 17 mm. pressure, has the specific rotatory power, $[\alpha]_D = +4°$, the sp. gr 0.8565 and the refactive index, $n_D = 1.45659$ (Tiemann and Semmler).

According to Wallach, citronellol ("réuniol") boils at 114° to 115° (12 to 13 mm.), has the sp. gr. 0.856 at 22°, $n_D = 1.45609$ at 22°, and $[\alpha]_D = -1°40'$.

Citronellol is a colorless liquid, has a pleasant, rose-like odor, and boils at 225° to 226° under a pressure of 764.5 mm.

It is not acted upon by heating with alkalis, but when agitated with a ten per cent. sulphuric acid, it unites with one molecule of water, yielding a diatomic alcohol; the latter is a colorless oil,

[1] Tiemann and Schmidt, Ber, *29*, 921

[2] Naschold, Inaug Diss, Gottingen, *1896*

[3] Dodge, Amer. Chem Journ, *11*, 463; Tiemann and Schmidt, Ber., *29*, 906

boils at 144° to 146° (10 mm.), and is reverted into citronellol on treatment with dehydrating agents (Tiemann and Schmidt).

Although citronellol occurs in the ethereal oils with geraniol, and appears to bear a close relation to the latter alcohol, the reduction of geraniol, $C_{10}H_{18}O$, to citronellol, $C_{10}H_{20}O$, has not yet been accomplished.

Oxidation with chromic acid converts citronellol into the aldehyde, citronellal; the former is, therefore, a primary alcohol. This oxidation frequently proceeds further, yielding oxidation products of the aldehyde, as citronellic acid, etc.

When oxidized with a dilute solution of potassium permanganate, citronellol yields a polyatomic alcohol; if the latter be oxidized in turn with chomic anhydride, acetone and β-methyl adipic acid (m. p. 84° to 85°) are obtained. Dextro- and levo-β-methyl adipic acid result on the oxidation of the corresponding active modifications of citronellol; the inactive β-methyl adipic acid crystallizes in needles and melts at 93° to 94°.

According to Tiemann and Schmidt, citronellol is to be regarded as dimethyl-2, 6-octene-2-ol-8, and its constitution is represented by the formula,

$$\begin{matrix} CH_3 \\ CH_3 \end{matrix}\!\!>C{=}CH{-}CH_2{-}CH_2{-}\underset{\displaystyle CH_3}{\underset{|}{C}H}{-}CH_2{-}CH_2OH.$$

The fatty acid esters of citronellol may be readily formed by treating the alcohol with the corresponding acid anhydrides.

Citronellol acetate, $C_{10}H_{19}OCOCH_3$, is a colorless liquid, having a pleasant odor somewhat similar to that of bergamot oil; it boils at 119° to 121° (15 mm.), has the rotatory power, $[\alpha]_D = +2° 37'$, the sp. gr. 0.8928, and refractive index, $n_D = 1.4456$, at 17.5°.

Citronellol formate boils at 97° to 100° (10 mm.).

Citronellol hydrogen phthalate,[1] $C_{10}H_{19}O{\cdot}CO{\cdot}C_6H_4COOH$, is formed by heating the free alcohol with phthalic anhydride; it is a yellow oil. It forms a crystalline *silver salt*, melting at 120° to 124°, from which pure citronellol may be regenerated.

Citronellol diphenylurethane[1] is a liquid.

(*b*) ALDEHYDES.

1. GERANIAL (CITRAL), $C_{10}H_{16}O$.

In the year 1888, the chemists of Schimmel & Co., Leipzig, determined that lemon oil contains about six to eight per cent. of

[1] H. Erdmann, Journ. pr. Chem., *56* [II.], 1; Flatau and Labbé, Compt. rend., *126*, 1725.

an aldehyde, $C_{10}H_{16}O$, and that the characteristic odor of oil of lemon is due to this aldehyde, which was termed *citral.*[1]

Semmler[2] had also obtained an aldehyde, $C_{10}H_{16}O$, in the oxidation of geraniol; he then made a careful investigation of citral and showed that his aldehyde, called *geranial*, was identical with citral, hence the two names, citral and geranial, have been employed to designate this compound. Although the name citral is historically correct, nevertheless geranial is to be preferred in most instances since it indicates that this compound is the aldehyde corresponding to geraniol.

Geranial has been found in bay oil (Power and Kleber[3]), in citronella fruit oil, in cedro oil, in eucalyptus oils of *Backhousia citriodora* and *Eucalyptus staigeriana*, in lemongrass oil, Japanese pepper oil of *Xanthoxylum piperitum* DC. (Schimmel & Co.), and in the oil of orange peel (Semmler). It also occurs in mandarin oil, West Indian limette oil, verbena oil, balm oil, pimenta oil, and the oil of sassafras leaves.

Geranial may be isolated from the ethereal oils by means of its crystalline acid sodium sulphite compound It is prepared from geraniol by the following method (Semmler[4]).

Fifteen grams of geraniol are added, all at once, to a solution of ten grams of potassium dichromate in 12 5 grams of concentrated sulphuric acid and one hundred cc. of water; the mixture is at first well cooled, and afterwards allowed to become warm, and vigorously shaken for half an hour. The reaction-product is then made slightly alkaline and distilled in a current of steam; the resulting oil is mixed with a solution of acid sodium sulphite, and allowed to remain for twenty-four hours. The crystals are then collected, pressed between filter-paper, and decomposed with soda.

PROPERTIES.—Geranial has a specific gravity of 0.8972 at 15° or 0 8844 at 22°; at the same temperatures its refractive index is $n_D = 1.934$, and $n_D = 1.486116$. It boils at 110° to 112° at 12 mm. pressure, 117° to 119° at 20 mm., and 120° to 122° at 23 mm. Under atmospheric pressure it boils with slight decomposition at 228° to 229°.

Geranial is a mobile, slightly yellowish oil, having a penetrating lemon-like odor; it is optically inactive (Tiemann and Semmler[5]). It has the characteristic properties of an aldehyde, reducing a silver solution, and coloring a fuchsine-sulphurous acid solution.

[1] For the history of citral, compare Tiemann, Ber, *31*, 3278

[2] Semmler, Ber, *23*, 2965, *24*, 201.

[3] Power and Kleber, Pharm Rundsch, *1895*, No 13

[4] See also Tiemann, Ber, *31*, 3311

[5] Tiemann and Semmler, Ber, *26*, 2708

It has been mentioned that, on oxidation with chromic acid, linalool suffers an intramolecular transformation into geraniol, and then yields geranial. The latter compound has also been synthetically prepared by Tiemann[1] by the distillation of a mixture of the calcium salts of formic and geranic acids.

Geranial forms a liquid, additive compound with four atoms of bromine. It is very sensitive towards acids. According to Semmler,[2] geranial is characterized by the great readiness with which it loses water and is converted into cymene, when heated with twice its weight of potassium bisulphate for twenty minutes at 170° ; dilute sulphuric acid also changes it into cymene. Alkalis[3] also decompose geranial; when treated with caustic soda, it suffers a partial decomposition into methyl heptenone, $C_8H_{14}O$, acetaldehyde, and resinous substances. Geranial is converted into the corresponding primary alcohol, geraniol, on reduction.[4]

The behavior of geranial towards sodium bisulphite has been studied by Tiemann and Semmler.[5] The *normal* additive compound of geranial and sodium bisulphite, $C_9H_{15}\cdot CH(OH)\cdot SO_3Na$, is formed when geranial (100 parts), sodium thiosulphate (100 parts), water (200 parts), and acetic acid (25 parts) are shaken at a low temperature; it is decomposed by dissolving in water, but may be recrystallized from methyl alcohol containing some acetic acid ; a *quantitative* yield of geranial is never obtained from this compound on treatment with sodium carbonate or caustic soda. A *stable dihydrosulphonic acid* derivative of geranial is produced when the normal compound is submitted to steam distillation, or is boiled with chloroform, one-half of the geranial being regenerated. A *labile dihydrosulphonic acid* derivative, $C_9H_{17}(SO_3Na)_2\cdot CHO$, results when geranial is agitated with sodium sulphite, and the sodium hydroxide, which is liberated, is neutralized. It is also formed when the normal crystallized compound is allowed to stand for some time with an excess of an acid sulphite solution. It is readily soluble in water, and does not yield geranial on treatment with alkali carbonates, but is converted into the aldehyde by an excess of caustic alkalis. It reacts with semicarbazide, forming *sodium geranial semicarbazone dihydrodisulphonate.* In the purification of geranial, it is sufficient to form the *labile* disulphonic derivative in solution, and then to decompose it with alkali. *Sodium geranial hydrosulphonate* results on shaking the labile di-

[1] Tiemann, Ber., *31*, 827.
[2] Semmler, Ber., *23*, 2965; *24*, 201; Tiemann, Ber., *32*, 107.
[3] Verley, Bull. Soc. Chim., *17* [III.], 175; Tiemann, Ber., *32*, 107.
[4] Tiemann, Ber., *31*, 828.
[5] Tiemann and Semmler, Ber., *26*, 2708; Tiemann, Ber., *31*, 3297.

hydrosulphonate with geranial, it is soluble in methyl alcohol, and is readily decomposed by sodium hydroxide.

This peculiar behavior of geranial towards sodium bisulphite solution is obviously similar to the reactions which have been observed with various unsaturated aldehydes and ketones, and which have been studied in detail by Muller[1] in the case of acrolein, and by Heusler[2] and by Tiemann[3] regarding cinnamic aldehyde.

Geranial- (citral-) β-naphthocinchonic acid, $C_{23}H_{23}NO_2$.—This derivative of geranial, first prepared by Doebner,[4] is very characteristic, and especially well adapted for the detection of small amounts of geranial in ethereal oils According to this chemist, aldehydes may be condensed with pyroracemic acid and β-naphthylamine, yielding alkyl-β-naphthocinchonic acids; the geranial derivative is obtained according to the equation:

$$C_9H_{15}CHO + CH_3COCOOH + C_{10}H_7\overset{\beta}{N}H_2 = 2H_2O + H_2 +$$

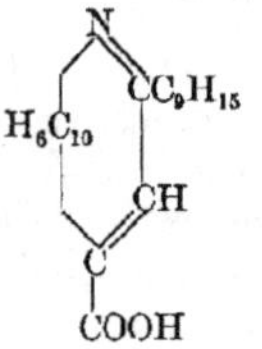

$$H_6C_{10}\left\langle\begin{array}{l} N = CC_9H_{15} \\ \qquad | \\ C = CH \\ | \\ COOH \end{array}\right.$$

It is prepared by boiling an alcoholic solution of twenty grams of geranial, twelve grams of pyroracemic acid and twenty grams of β-naphthylamine for three hours; fourteen grams of the compound are produced. It crystallizes from dilute alcohol in lemon-yellow leaflets, which contain one-half molecule of water of crystallization, and melt at 197°.[5] The *hydrochloride* of geranial-β-naphthocinchonic acid crystallizes from alcohol in orange-yellow needles.

Geranyl phenylhydrazone, $C_{10}H_{16}N_2HC_6H_5$, is an oil, which decomposes when distilled in a vacuum (Tiemann and Semmler).

The *anilide*, $C_{10}H_{16}=NC_6H_5$, is formed by heating geranial and aniline at 150°, it is a yellow liquid, boiling at 200° under a pressure of 20 mm.

[1] Muller, Ber, *6*, 1441

[2] Heusler, Ber, *24*, 1805

[3] Tiemann, Ber, *31*, 3297.

[4] Doebner, Ber, *27*, 352 and 2020, *31*, 1888 and 3195, compare also Ber, *31*, 3331; *32*, 115

[5] The melting point is frequently reported at 200° or slightly above this point

Dry ammonia also reacts with geranial, yielding an oil which can not be distilled without decomposition in a vacuum.

Geranialoxime, $C_{10}H_{16}NOH$, is formed by the action of the molecular amounts of hydroxylamine hydrochloride and soda on an alcoholic solution of geranial. It is a yellow oil, boils at 143° to 145° under 12 mm. pressure, has a specific gravity of 0.9386 at 20° and an index of refraction, $n_D = 1.51433$. When the oxime is distilled at atmospheric pressure, water is removed and the nitrile of geranic acid is produced, together with an amine which has not been carefully investigated (Tiemann and Semmler).

Geranial semicarbazones, $C_{10}H_{16} = N \cdot NHCONH_2$.—A number of isomeric semicarbazones appear to have been obtained from geranial by different investigators. Wallach [1] mentions two such derivatives, melting at 150° and 160°; Tiemann and Semmler [2] describe a semicarbazone, melting at 130° to 135°. Barbier and Bouveault [3] state that the fraction of the oil of lemongrass (b. p. 107° to 110° at 10 mm.) yields a semicarbazone, melting at 171°; it forms white crystals and is very sparingly soluble in boiling alcohol. The fraction of the same oil, boiling at 110° to 112° (10 mm.), gives three isomeric derivatives, melting at 171°, 160° and 135°, respectively.

According to more recent investigations by Tiemann,[4] ordinary geranial yields two isomeric semicarbazones; one is produced in large amount and melts at 164°, and the other is formed in small quantity and melts at 171°. A mixture of the low melting derivative with six to ten per cent. of the other melts at 135°.

Geranial- (citral-) a.—According to Tiemann,[5] ordinary geranial consists of two geometrical isomerides termed geranial *a* and geranial *b*. These compounds are separated by converting geranial into the sodium bisulphite compound, decomposing it with sodium carbonate, and repeatedly agitating with ether; a portion of the geranial is changed into the hydrosulphonic acid compound, while the remainder, about one-half of the total quantity, is dissolved by the ether. The fraction dissolved in the ether yields exclusively the semicarbazone, melting at 164°. It is called geranial *a*. It boils at 118° to 119° (20 mm.), has the sp. gr. 0.8898, and a

[1] Wallach, Ber., *28*, 1957.
[2] Tiemann and Semmler, Ber., *28*, 2133.
[3] Barbier and Bouveault, Compt. rend., *121*, 1159.
[4] Tiemann, Ber., *32*, 115; *31*, 3324.
[5] Tiemann, Ber., *32*, 115; *33*, 877.

refractive index, $n_D = 1.4891$. Its chemical properties are precisely like those of ordinary geranial.

Geranial- (citral-) b.—The geranial produced on decomposing the hydrosulphonic acid derivative referred to under geranial *a* yields large amounts of the semicarbazone, melting at 171°, together with small quantities of the lower melting compound; it consists, therefore, chiefly of geranial *b*, and some geranial *a*. Geranial *b* is separated from the mixture by means of its compound with cyanoacetic acid (*b-geranialidene cyanoacetic acid*, see below); the latter is formed less rapidly than the corresponding *a*-derivative.

Geranial *b* has the same chemical properties as geranial *a*; it boils at 102° to 104° (12 mm.), sp. gr. = 0.888 and $n_D = 1.49001$, at 19°. Its *oxime* boils at 136° to 138° (11 mm.), its *semicarbazone* melts at 171°, and its *β-naphthocinchonic acid* melts at 200°.

Geranionitrile, $C_9H_{15}CN$, is obtained almost quantitatively by boiling one part of geranialoxime with two and one-half parts of acetic anhydride for half an hour; the nitrile is separated by fractionally distilling the reaction-product in vacuum. It boils at 110° under 10 mm. pressure, has the specific gravity 0.8709 and the refractive index, $n_D = 1.4759$, at 20° (Tiemann and Semmler).

Geranic acid, $C_9H_{15}COOH$, is prepared by warming geranial with moist silver oxide (Semmler[1]). It may be more conveniently obtained by boiling geranionitrile with alcoholic potash until ammonia is no longer eliminated (Tiemann and Semmler[2]).

It is a colorless liquid, and is readily soluble in alcohol, ether, benzene, and chloroform; its odor resembles that of the higher fatty acids. It boils at 153° (13 mm.), has the specific gravity 0.964 and index of refraction, $n_D = 1.4797$, at 20°.

A partial synthesis[3] of this acid consists in the condensation of methyl heptenone with ethyl iodoacetate in the presence of zinc; the product is decomposed with water, yielding a colorless oil, $C_{10}H_{17}O_2 \cdot OC_2H_5$. When this compound is boiled with acetic acid and some zinc chloride, the ethyl ester of geranic acid is formed; or, if the acid, $C_{10}H_{17}O_2 \cdot OH$, corresponding to the compound, $C_{10}H_{17}O_2 \cdot OC_2H_5$, is boiled with acetic anhydride, it is converted into geranic acid.

Geranic acid is converted into citronellic acid, $C_{10}H_{18}O_2$, when it is reduced with sodium and amyl alcohol.

[1] Semmler, Ber., *23*, 2965, *24*, 201.

[2] Tiemann and Semmler, Ber., *26*, 2708; *28*, 2137.

[3] Barbier and Bouveault, Compt. rend., *122*, 393; compare Tiemann, Ber., *33*, 559.

Geraniolene, C_9H_{16}.—When geranic acid is distilled at the ordinary pressure, it decomposes into carbonic anhydride and geraniolene; this hydrocarbon is a liquid, boiling at 142° to 143°, has the sp. gr. 0.757 and the refractive power, $n_D = 1.4368$, at 20°. It forms a liquid tetrabromide, $C_9H_{16}Br_4$.

Geranic acid, geraniolene, and other compounds of the geranial series may be very readily converted into a mixture of two isomeric *cyclic* compounds by the action of dilute acids. The isomerism of these two classes of compounds is explained by the difference in position of the double linkage in the ring. They are designated as α- and β-cyclo-compounds; the α-cyclo-geranial derivatives may be regarded as derived from isogeronic acid or β, β-dimethyl adipic acid, while those of the β-series may be referred back to geronic acid and α, α-dimethyl adipic acid.[1]

α- and β-Cyclo-geranic acids,[1] $C_9H_{15}COOH$.—When geranic acid is shaken with sixty-five to seventy per cent. sulphuric acid at 0° for several days, a mixture of the two cyclo-acids, together with some other products, is formed. After two or three days, α-cyclo-geranic acid separates from the reaction-product in crystals, which are filtered, pressed on a plate, and recrystallized from petroleum ether; the pure acid melts at 106°. When the liquid filtrate from the crystalline α-acid is extracted with ether, the ether evaporated, and the resulting oil repeatedly distilled under atmospheric pressure, a mixture of α- and β-cyclo-geranic acids is obtained; the β-acid can not be separated from this liquid mixture in a crystalline condition, but its presence may be proved by its characteristic oxidation products.

A larger yield of β-cyclo-geranic acid is obtained if geranic acid is introduced into four parts of concentrated sulphuric acid at 0°, and the mixture is then gradually warmed to 50° and poured into water. This method, however, does not give a crystalline β-acid, but that it is formed in considerable quantity is shown by its oxidation products.

α-Cyclo-geranic acid crystallizes from water or ligroine in needles, melts at 106°, and boils at 138° (11 mm.); it may also be distilled without decomposition under atmospheric pressure. It unites directly with bromine, producing a dibromide which melts at 121°. Oxidation with potassium permanganate converts the α-acid into *dioxydihydrocyclogeranic acid*, $C_9H_{15}(OH)_2$.-COOH, melting at 198° to 200°, and *keto-oxydihydrocyclogeranic*

[1]Tiemann and Krüger, Ber., *26*, 2693; Tiemann and Semmler, Ber., *26*, 2725; Tiemann, Ber., *33*, 3703, 3710, 3713, 3719 and 3726; Tiemann and Schmidt, Ber., *31*, 881.

acid, $C_{10}H_{16}O_4$, melting at 145°, the latter acid yields a *semicarbazone*, melting at 216°. On oxidizing either the dioxy-acid or the keto-oxy-acid with one molecular proportion of chromic acid, *isogeronic acid*, $C_8H_{15}O \cdot COOH$, is formed; this is an open-chain, ketonic acid, which forms a *semicarbazone*, melting at 226°. When the ethyl ester of dioxydihydrocyclogeranic acid is oxidized with chromic acid, it yields the *hydrogen ethyl ester of α-acetyl-β, β,-dimethyl adipic acid*,

$$C_8H_{14}O\begin{cases} COOH \\ COOC_2H_5 \end{cases},$$

this is an oil, which gives a *semicarbazone* melting at 157°. When this ester is heated with an aqueous solution of potassium hydroxide, it undergoes a ketone hydrolysis and forms isogeronic acid.

These oxidation products of α-cyclo-geranic acid indicate that it is a β, γ-unsaturated acid, and that it may be termed methyl-1-dimethyl-5-cyclohexene-1-methyl-acid-6.

β-Cyclo-geranic acid is formed, as above mentioned, during the inversion of the aliphatic geranic acid by means of sixty-five to one hundred per cent. sulphuric acid; this method, however, does not give a pure product. The pure acid may be readily formed by the careful oxidation of *β-cyclo-geranial* with air or with the calculated quantity of permanganate in the cold. It crystallizes from ligroine in large, transparent prisms or plates, and melts at 93° to 94°; it distills undecomposed at atmospheric pressure. It decolorizes bromine very slowly, yielding hydrogen bromide. Its behavior towards oxidizing agents is quite different from that of the α-cyclo-acid. Oxidation with alkaline potassium permanganate converts β-cyclo-geranic acid into an *oxy-acid*, $C_{10}H_{16}O_3$, which melts with decomposition at 186°, a *ketonic acid*, $C_9H_{12}O_3$, which melts at 189° and yields a *semicarbazone* melting at 240°, and, as chief product, α, α-dimethyl glutaric acid.

α- and β-Cyclo-geranionitriles,[1] $C_9H_{15}CN$.—A mixture of the two nitriles is produced by shaking geranionitrile with seventy per cent. sulphuric acid; a separation of the two nitriles has not yet been accomplished, but their presence in the reaction-product is proved by their conversion into the α- and β-cyclo-acids and their derivatives. The mixture of the two nitriles boils at 87° to

[1] Tiemann and Semmler, Ber, *26*, 2725, Tiemann and Schmidt, Ber., *31*, 881, Tiemann, Ber, *33*, 3705, compare Barbier and Bouveault, Bull. Soc Chim, *15* [III.], 1002.

88° (11 mm.), has the sp. gr. 0.9208 and the refractive index, n_D = 1.4734, at 20°. It forms an *amidoxime*, melting at 165°, whilst the corresponding compound of the aliphatic geranionitrile is a liquid.

α- **and** *β*-**Cyclo-geraniolenes,** C_9H_{16}, cannot be obtained by the distillation of the corresponding cyclo-geranic acids, but a mixture of the two hydrocarbons may be prepared by shaking geraniolene with ten parts of sixty-five per cent. sulphuric acid for three days; the yield is sixty to seventy per cent. It boils at 138° to 140°, has the sp. gr. 0.7978 and refractive index, n_D = 1.4434, at 22°.

Oxidation with permanganate converts this mixture of *α*- and *β*-cyclo-geraniolenes into *isogeronic acid*, $C_8H_{15}O.COOH$, which gives a *semicarbazone* melting at 198° and insoluble in ethyl acetate, and *geronic acid*, $C_8H_{15}O.COOH$, which yields a *semicarbazone* melting at 164° and readily soluble in ethyl acetate; geronic acid[1] is an open-chain compound and is also a product of the oxidation of ionone with permanganate.

α- **and** *β*-**Cyclo-geranials,**[2] $C_{10}H_{16}O$.—While the compounds of the geranial series in general yield cyclo-derivatives on the action of acids, by the union of the carbon atoms in positions 1 and 6 geranial itself is converted into cymene. If, however, the sensitive aldehyde group in geranial be protected, as in geranialidene cyanoacetic acid, the normal cyclo-derivatives may be obtained. Thus, when either a- or b-geranialidene cyanoacetic acid is boiled for twenty hours with dilute sulphuric acid (1 part of acid to 8 parts of water), it is converted into the solid cyclo-geranialidene cyanoacetic acid (a mixture of the *α*- and *β*-cyclo-derivatives); when the latter is hydrolyzed with potash, a mixture of *α*- and *β*-cyclogeranial is formed, of which only the *β*-compound has so far been obtained in a pure condition.

β-**Cyclo-geranial** is a colorless oil, having the odor of carvone; it boils at 88° to 91° (10 mm.) or 95° to 100° (15 mm.), has the sp. gr. 0.959 at 15° and 0.957 at 20°, and the refractive index, n_D = 1.49715, at 15°. Its *semicarbazone* crystallizes from methyl alcohol in large prisms containing methyl alcohol and melting at 165° to 166°; it separates from ethyl acetate in thin leaflets melting at 166° to 167°. By the action of acids, it is quantitatively converted into *β*-cyclo-geranial.

β-Cyclo-geranial forms an *additive compound*, $C_{11}H_{21}O_2N_3$, with semicarbazide, which crystallizes from a mixture of ethyl acetate and benzene in needles, and melts with decomposition at 250°.

[1] Tiemann, Ber., *31*, 808.
[2] Tiemann, Ber., *33*, 3719; Schmidt, Ber., *34*, 2451.

When β-cyclo-geranial is condensed with acetone, β-*ionone* is formed.

β-Cyclo-geranial is readily oxidized into β-cyclo-geranic acid on exposure to the air. On oxidation with potassium permanganate, β-cyclo-geranial yields β-cyclo-geranic acid and oxidation products of this acid, together with *geronic acid*, $C_9H_{16}O_3$, the methyl ketonic acid corresponding to α, α-dimethyl adipic acid.

Geranialidene cyanoacetic acid,[1] $C_9H_{15} \cdot CH = C(CN) \cdot COOH$, is formed when cyanoacetic acid is shaken with geranial in the presence of aqueous sodium hydroxide; on acidifying the reaction-mixture, the product separates as an oil which soon solidifies. The crude product melts at 85° to 90°, but after repeated crystallizations from benzene, it melts at 122°.

It is probable that this compound consists of a mixture of the cyanoacetic acid derivatives of geranial *a* and geranial *b*. By the action of dilute sulphuric acid it is converted into the *cyclo*-derivative.

b-Geranialidene cyanoacetic acid crystallizes from petroleum ether in yellowish needles, and melts at 94° to 95°

Geranialidene bisacetylacetone[2] is formed by the condensation of geranial and acetyl acetone in the presence of a few drops of piperidine; it crystallizes from a mixture of alcohol, ether and ligroine, and melts at 46° to 48°.

Labbé[3] mentions a *polymeride* of geranial, $(C_{10}H_{16}O)_x$, which results by the action of alcoholic potash on geranial. It melts at 81° to 82°.

It should be mentioned that, according to Stiehl,[4] lemongrass oil contains three isomeric aldehydes which he terms "*citriodoraldehyde*," "*allolemonal*" ("l-licarhodol"), and "*geranial*." Subsequent investigations by other chemists seem to have indicated that Stiehl's three aldehydes are all identical with geranial (citral).

When geranial is carefully oxidized with a chromic acid mixture or with a glacial acetic acid solution of chromic anhydride at a very low temperature, methyl hexylene ketone (methyl heptenone), $C_8H_{14}O$, is formed (Tiemann and Semmler[5]). This ketone is identical with the compound previously prepared by Wallach by the distillation of cineolic anhydride. The identity of these two

[1] Tiemann, Ber, *31*, 3324, *33*, 877 and 3720; Verley, Bull. Soc Chim., *21* [III.], 413 and 414

[2] K Wedemeyer, Inaug Diss., Heidelberg, *1897*

[3] Labbé, Bull Soc Chim, *21*, 407

[4] W Stiehl, Journ pr Chem, *58*, 51

[5] Tiemann and Semmler, Ber, *26*, 2708.

ketones, $C_8H_{14}O$, has been determined by Tiemann and Semmler by the formation of tribromo-methyl hexylene carbinol (tribromo-heptanonol), $C_8H_{12}Br_3O{\cdot}OH$; this substance is produced by the action of bromine and sodium hydroxide on methyl hexylene ketone, and melts at 98° to 99°.

The ketone, $C_8H_{14}O$, is likewise obtained by the oxidation of geraniol, and is also formed as a by-product during the preparation of geranic acid from geranionitrile by the action of alcoholic potash. Methyl hexylene carbinol, $C_8H_{15}OH$, results, together with geranic acid and methyl hexylene ketone, in the hydrolysis of geranionitrile.

It should be especially noted that methyl heptenone, $C_8H_{14}O$, occurs, together with geraniol and geranial, in many ethereal oils. Its constitution has been explained by Tiemann and Semmler's[1] investigations, according to which the ketone is almost quantitatively converted into acetone and laevulinic acid by successive oxidation with potassium permanganate and chromic acid.

When geranial is carefully oxidized with chromic anhydride, an uncrystallizable acid, $C_9H_{15}(OH)_2COOH$, is obtained which gives methyl hexylene ketone on distillation (Tiemann and Semmler). According to Barbier and Bouveault,[2] when geranial is oxidized with sodium dichromate and sulphuric acid at a low temperature, it yields formic acid, acetic acid, and a methyl heptenoncarboxylic acid; this acid is probably identical with the acid, $C_9H_{15}(OH)_2COOH$, obtained by Tiemann and Semmler. By more vigorous oxidation with boiling chromic acid mixture, geranial is converted into carbon dioxide, formic acid, acetic acid and terebic acid (Barbier and Bouveault).

In this connection it should be mentioned that some of the derivatives of geranial described in the preceding were prepared by different chemists before Tiemann and Semmler obtained them, but such compounds were generally designated by different names. Thus, Barbier[3] first prepared geranialoxime, and converted it into geranionitrile and then into geranic acid. Geranic acid was previously described by Eckart[4] under the name "*rhodinolic acid.*"

From the results of their experiments, Tiemann and Semmler[1]

[1] Tiemann and Semmler, Ber., *28*, 2126.
[2] Barbier and Bouveault, Compt. rend., *118*, 1050; *122*, 393.
[3] Barbier, Compt. rend., *116*, 883.
[4] Eckart, Arch. Pharm., *229*, 355.

regard the following formulas as expressing the true constitution of geranial and its derivatives:

$$CH_3-\underset{\displaystyle CH_3}{\underset{|}{C}}=CH-CH_2-CH_2-\underset{\displaystyle CH_3}{\underset{|}{C}}=CH-CHO,$$

Geranial (citral) (dimethyl-2, 6-octadiene-2, 6-al-8)

$$CH_3-\underset{\displaystyle CH_3}{\underset{|}{C}}=CH-CH_2-CH_2-\underset{\displaystyle CH_3}{\underset{|}{C}}=CH-COOH$$

Geranic acid (dimethyl-2, 6-octadiene-2, 6-acid-8)

$$CH_3-\underset{\displaystyle CH_3}{\underset{|}{C}}=CH-CH_2-CH_2-CO-CH_3$$

Methyl hexylene ketone (methyl-2-heptene-2-on-6).

It should further be mentioned that geranial undergoes condensation with acetone, yielding a ketone, *pseudoionone*,[1] $C_{13}H_{20}O$; its constitution is represented by the formula,

$$CH_3-\underset{\displaystyle CH_3}{\underset{|}{C}}=CH-CH_2-CH_2-\underset{\displaystyle CH_3}{\underset{|}{C}}=CH-CH=CH-CO-CH_3$$

Pseudoionone, $C_{13}H_{20}O$, boils at 143° to 145° under a pressure of 12 mm., has the specific gravity 0.9044, and the refractive power, $n_D = 1.5275$.

When it is boiled with dilute sulphuric acid and a little glycerol, it is converted into a mixture of two isomeric, cyclic ketones, *a- and β-ionone.* This mixture was at first thought to be an individual chemical compound and was called *ionone*,[1] $C_{13}H_{20}O$. It boils at 126° to 128° (12 mm.), has the sp. gr. 0.9351 and the refractive index, $n_D = 1.507$, at 20°.

a-Ionone,[2] $C_{13}H_{20}O$, is prepared from a mixture of the *a*- and *β*-ionones ("commercial ionone") by conversion into its oxime, crystallizing this compound from petroleum, and regenerating the ketone with dilute sulphuric acid. It boils at 123° to 124° (11 mm.) or 134° to 136° (17 mm.), has the sp. gr. 0.932 and the refractive index, $n_D = 1.4980$. Its *oxime* crystallizes from petroleum and melts at 89° to 90°, while the oxime of *β*-ionone is a liquid, hence a separation of the two ketones is rendered possible. The *semicarbazone* dissolves more readily than the *β*-derivative in petroleum, and melts at 107° to 108°. Other characteristic derivatives have been prepared.

[1] Tiemann and Krüger, Ber., *26*, 3691.

[2] Tiemann, Ber., *31*, 808 and 867, *33*, 3704 and 3726; compare Lemme, Chem. Centrl., *1900* [I], 576

β-Ionone, $C_{13}H_{20}O$, is obtained from the mixture of the isomeric ketones by means of its semicarbazone, which crystallizes more readily than the corresponding α-derivative. The ketone boils at 127° to 128.5° (10 mm.) or 140° (18 mm.), has the sp. gr. 0.946 and the refractive index, $n_D = 1.521$. Its *oxime* is an oil, and its *semicarbazone* melts at 148° to 149°.

Oxidation with permanganate converts α-ionone into *isogeronic acid*, $C_9H_{16}O_3$, and oxidation products of the latter, while β-ionone gives rise to *geronic acid* and its oxidation products. The constitutional formulas of the two ketones are:

```
    CH3 CH3
       C      H
  H2C     C
   |      |  CH = CH—CO—CH3
  H2C     C—CH3
      C
        H
```

α-Ionone.

```
    CH3 CH3
       C
  H2C     C—CH = CH—CO—CH3
   |      ||
  H2C     C—CH3
      CH2
```

β-Ionone.

Commercial ionone has the characteristic odor of violets, and for this reason it is of considerable practical importance.[1]

Irone,[1] $C_{13}H_{20}O$, is a structural isomeride of ionone, and is the fragrant constituent of violets. It is an oil which is readily soluble in alcohol, boils at 144° (16 mm.), has the sp. gr. 0.939 and refractive index, $n_D = 1.50113$, at 20°; it is dextrorotatory.

Since it is impracticable to introduce into this book the results of many investigations on geranial, reference may be made to the following publications:

Bouveault, Bull. Soc. Chim., *21* [III.], 419 and 423.
Barbier, Bull. Soc. Chim., *21* [III.], 635.
Corie, C. and D., *54*, 650.
Doebner, Ber., *31*, 3195.
Flatau, Bull. Soc. Chim., *21* [III.], 158.
Flatau and Labbé, Bull. Soc. Chim., *19* [III.], 1012.
Ipatieff, Ber., *34*, 594.
Labbé, Bull. Soc. Chim., *21* [III.], 77, 407 and 1026.
Semmler, Ber., *31*, 3001.
Stiehl, Journ. pr. Chem., *58*, 51.

[1] Tiemann and Krüger, Ber., *26*, 2675; *28*, 1754; Barbier and Bouveault, Bull. Soc. Chim., *15* [III.], 1002; Tiemann, Ber., *31*, 808, 867, 1736, 2313, and 3324; *32*, 115; *33*, 877, 3704 and 3726; Ziegler, Journ. pr. Chem., *57* [II.], 493.

Tiemann, Ber., *31*, 2313, 3278, 3297 and 3324, *32*, 107, 250, 812, 827 and 830.

Verley, Bull. Soc Chim., *21* [III.], 408, 413 and 414.

Ziegler, Journ. pr. Chem, *57* [II.], 493.

2 MENTHOCITRONELLAL, $C_{10}H_{18}O$.

This aldehyde,[1] previously termed menthonyl aldehyde, results on the oxidation of menthocitronellol (menthonyl alcohol) with chromic acid. It has an odor like that of sweet orange, boils at 86° to 88° (16 mm.), and at about 200° under atmospheric pressure; it has the specific gravity 0.8455 and the refractive index, n_D = 1.43903, at 20°.

Menthocitronellal-β-naphthocinchonic acid is formed by the condensation of the aldehyde with β-naphthylamine and pyroracemic acid; it melts at 214° to 215° (the corresponding derivative of natural citronellal melts at 225°).

Menthocitronellal semicarbazone melts at 89°, and is optically inactive.

3 CITRONELLAL, $C_{10}H_{18}O$.

This compound was formerly called "*citronellone*"; it has, however, been characterized as an aldehyde, and, in order to indicate the aldehydic nature, is now termed citronellal. It derives its name from its occurrence in oil of citronella (from *Andropogon nardus*); this oil has been carefully studied by Gladstone,[2] Wright,[3] Kremers,[4] and Dodge.[5] It has been found by Schimmel & Co. in the oils of *Eucalyptus maculata* and *Eucalyptus maculata* var. *citriodora*, and, according to Dóbner, it also accompanies geranial in the oil of lemon.

In order to prepare citronellal from citronella oil or eucalyptus oil, the ethereal oil is shaken with a solution of acid sodium sulphite, and the resulting crystalline, additive compound is decomposed with sodium carbonate, pure citronellic aldehyde is then obtained by distilling the reaction-product in a current of steam. The citronellal so obtained from the ethereal oils is dextrorotatory; it is possible, however, that the specimens of citronellal having low rotatory powers will prove to be mixtures of the two optically active modifications.

[1] Wallach, Ann Chem, *278*, 313; *296*, 120.

[2] Gladstone, Journ Chem Soc, *1872*, 7

[3] Wright, Journ Chem Soc, *1875*, 1

[4] Kremers, Proc Amer. Pharm Assoc, *1887;* Amer. Chem. Journ, *14*, 203; Ber, *25*, 644, Ref

[5] Dodge, Amer. Chem. Journ., *11*, 456; *12*, 553; Ber., *23*, 175, Ref; *24*, 90, Ref

Citronellal may also be prepared by the oxidation of citronellol with chromic acid; the yield, however, is small. By means of this method a levo-citronellal may be obtained from the l-citronellol of rose oil.

Citronellal is a colorless liquid, boils at 205° to 208° at ordinary pressure, and at 103° to 105° under a pressure of 15 mm.; the specific gravity is 0.8538 at 17.5°, and the refractive index, $n_D = 1.4481$. Its optical rotation was found by Kremers to be $[\alpha]_D = + 8.18°$, and by Tiemann and Schmidt,[1] $[\alpha]_D = + 12°30'$.

Pure citronellal is very unstable; when allowed to stand for several months, it is almost entirely converted into isopulegol;[2] the same isomeric change is effected much more rapidly by the action of acids.[3] When citronellal is treated with alkalis, it is completely resinified.

When it is reduced in alcoholic solution with glacial acetic acid and sodium amalgam, it yields citronellol, $C_{10}H_{19}OH$ (Dodge, Tiemann and Schmidt).

On oxidizing citronellal with silver oxide, citronellic acid, $C_{10}H_{18}O_2$, is obtained (Semmler). Oxidation with potassium permanganate, followed by chromic and sulphuric acids, converts citronellal, like citronellol and citronellic acid, into acetone and β-methyl adipic acid. The aldehyde is, therefore, to be regarded as dimethyl-2, 6-octene-2-al-8 (Tiemann and Schmidt):

$$\begin{array}{l} CH_3-\underset{|\atop CH_3}{C}=CH-CH_2-CH_2-\underset{|\atop CH_3}{CH}-CH_2-CHO. \end{array}$$

It unites with two atoms of bromine, forming a liquid additive product (Dodge, Semmler).

According to Barbier,[4] menthoglycol, $C_{10}H_{18}(OH)_2$, is formed by agitating citronellal with dilute sulphuric acid.

The *normal* addition-product of citronellal and sodium bisulphite,[5] $C_{10}H_{18}O \cdot NaHSO_3$, is a crystalline compound, and is formed by shaking a cold solution of sodium bisulphite (free from sulphurous anhydride) with citronellal; it is soluble in water, but may be precipitated by the addition of a saturated salt solution. Sodium carbonate or hydroxide converts it into citronellal. A *mono-* and *dihydrosulphonic acid* are also described.[5]

[1] Tiemann and Schmidt, Ber., *29*, 905.

[2] Labbé, Bull. Soc. Chim., *21* [III.], 1023; compare Tiemann, Ber., *32*, 825.

[3] Tiemann and Schmidt, Ber., *29*, 913; *30*, 22.

[4] Barbier and Leser, Compt. rend., *124*, 1308.

[5] Tiemann, Ber., *31*, 3297.

Citronellylidene cyanoacetic acid,[1] $C_{11}H_{18}(CN)\cdot COOH$, is formed by shaking citronellal with an aqueous solution of cyanoacetic acid and sodium hydroxide; it crystallizes from benzene or alcohol, and melts at 137° to 138°. Its *sodium* salt is sparingly soluble, and is especially characteristic.

Citronellal dimethylacetal,[2] $C_{10}H_{18}(OCH_3)_2$, is obtained by treating citronellal with a one per cent. solution of hydrogen chloride in methyl alcohol. It boils at 110° to 112° (12 to 13 mm.), and has the specific gravity 0.885 at 11.5°.

Phosphoric anhydride converts citronellal into a mixture of a terpene (b. p. 175° to 178°), and *citronellal phosphoric acid;* the latter crystallizes from water in prisms, melting at 203°. It is a monobasic acid, forms crystalline salts, and has the formula (Dodge):

$$C_9H_{17}CH\begin{matrix}\diagup O \diagdown \\ -O- \\ H-O\diagup\end{matrix}P=O.$$

Citronellal-β-naphthocinchonic acid,

$$C_{10}H_6\begin{matrix}\diagup N=C-C_9H_{17} \\ \quad\quad | \\ \diagdown C=CH \\ | \\ COOH\end{matrix}$$

was discovered by Dobner.

It is especially valuable for the characterization of this aldehyde, and is prepared by heating an alcoholic solution of an excess of citronellal with the molecular proportions of pyroracemic acid and β-naphthylamine, for three hours. On cooling, citronellal-β-naphthocinchonic acid separates in crystals; these are washed with ether, and recrystallized from alcohol containing hydrochloric acid. The resultant hydrochloride is dissolved in ammonium hydroxide, and the pure acid is precipitated from the ammoniacal liquid by acetic acid; it is again crystallized from dilute alcohol, and forms colorless needles, melting at 225°.

When heated above its melting point, this compound loses carbonic anhydride and yields citronellal-β-naphthyl quinoline; this amine crystallizes from dilute alcohol or petroleum ether in bright needles, which melt at 53°.

[1] Tiemann, Ber., *32*, 824

[2] Harries, Ber., *33*, 857, *34*, 1498 and 2981

Citronellaloxime,[1] $C_{10}H_{18}NOH$, was obtained by Kremers, and subsequently by Semmler,[1] by the action of hydroxylamine on an alcoholic solution of citronellal. It is an oil, which boils at 135° to 136° (14 mm.), has a specific gravity of 0.9055 and refractive index, $n_D = 1.4763$, at 20°.

Citronellonitrile,[1] $C_9H_{17}CN$, results on boiling the oxime with acetic anhydride. It boils at 94° under 14 mm. pressure, has the specific gravity 0.8645 and the index of refraction, $n_D = 1.4545$, at 20°; the molecular refraction is 47.43.

Citronellic acid, $C_9H_{17}COOH$, was prepared by Dodge,[2] Semmler,[3] and Kremers[4] by the oxidation of citronellal with moist silver oxide. It is more readily formed by the saponification of the corresponding nitrile with alcoholic potash (Semmler[5]). It boils at 143.5° (10 mm.) and at 257° under atmospheric pressure; its specific gravity is 0.9308 and the refractive power, $n_D = 1.4545$, at 20°. The molecule of citronellic acid appears to contain one double linkage.

Citronellic acid is further obtained from geranic acid, $C_9H_{15}COOH$, by reduction with sodium and amyl alcohol.[6]

A small amount of citronellal is formed by strongly heating a mixture of calcium citronellate and formate.[6]

Citronellamide,[6] $C_9H_{17}CONH_2$, is produced by boiling citronellonitrile with a fifteen per cent. alcoholic potash solution during five or six hours. It crystallizes from petroleum ether in colorless needles, melts at 81.5° to 82.5°, is sparingly soluble in water, but dissolves readily in most organic solvents.

Dioxycitronellic acid, $C_9H_{17}(OH)_2COOH$, is formed by oxidizing citronellic acid with a very dilute solution of permanganate at 0°. It is a viscous liquid, and appears not to yield a lactone. On further oxidation with a chromic acid mixture, it yields β-methyl adipic acid, $C_7H_{12}O_4$ (Semmler's citronellapimelic acid).

Citronellal semicarbazone,[7] $C_{10}H_{18} = N \cdot NHCONH_2$, is obtained by shaking an alcoholic solution of citronellal with a solution of semicarbazide hydrochloride and sodium acetate; it crystallizes from chloroform and ligroine in white leaflets, and melts at 84°.

[1] Semmler, Ber., *26*, 2254; compare Tiemann and Krüger, Ber., *29*, 926; Tiemann and Schmidt, Ber., *30*, 33.

[2] Dodge, Amer. Chem. Journ., *11*, 456; *12*, 553.

[3] Semmler, Ber., *24*, 208.

[4] Kremers, Amer. Chem. Journ., *14*, 203.

[5] Semmler, Ber., *26*, 2254; compare Tiemann and Schmidt, Ber., *30*, 33; Barbier and Bouveault, Compt. rend., *122*, 673, 737, 795 and 842.

[6] Tiemann, Ber., *31*, 2899.

[7] Tiemann and Schmidt, Ber., *30*, 34; *31*, 3307; compare Barbier and Bouveault, Compt. rend., *122*, 737.

C. AMINES.

1. MENTHONYLAMINE, $C_{10}H_{19}NH_2$.

According to Wallach,[1] menthonylamine, $C_{10}H_{19}NH_2$, is formed, together with oxyhydromenthonylamine, $C_{10}H_{20}(OH)NH_2$, by the reduction of menthonitrile with sodium and alcohol. Thirty grams of sodium are gradually added to the solution of fifty grams of the nitrile in two hundred and fifty grams of absolute alcohol; when the reaction is complete, the product is distilled in a current of steam, the distillate is treated with a solution of thirty-five grams of oxalic acid, and the non-basic impurities are removed from the oxalic acid solution by redistillation with steam. On cooling, the sparingly soluble menthonylamine oxalate crystallizes in leaflets, whilst the oxalate of the base, $C_{10}H_{23}NO$, remains in solution.

Menthonylamine, obtained from its oxalate, boils without decomposition at 207° to 208°; it resembles the isomeric menthylamine in readily absorbing carbonic anhydride from the air. It has the specific gravity 0.8075 at 20° (the sp. gr. of menthylamine is 0.8600), and the index of refraction, $n_D = 1.4500$. It is feebly dextrorotatory.

Menthonylamine hydrochloride, $C_{10}H_{19}NH_2 \cdot HCl$, is a crystalline salt, stable in the air, and forms a sparingly soluble *platinochloride.*

The *acid oxalate* is slightly soluble in water, and separates from it with one-half molecule of water of crystallization.

Acetyl menthonylamine is a liquid.

The *oxamide*,

$$\begin{array}{l} CONHC_{10}H_{19} \\ | \\ CONHC_{10}H_{19} \end{array}$$

is very soluble in alcohol, and melts at 82° to 83°.

Menthocitronellol (menthonyl alcohol) and a hydrocarbon, $C_{10}H_{18}$, are produced on treating menthonylamine oxalate with sodium nitrite.

Oxyhydromenthonylamine, $C_{10}H_{20}(OH)NH_2$, boils at 252° to 255°, and forms very soluble salts. On treatment with nitrous acid, this amine yields *dimethyloctylene glycol* (2, 6-dimethyloctane-2, 8-diol), $C_{10}H_{20}(OH)_2$; it is non-volatile with steam, and boils at 153° to 156° under 19 mm. pressure.

[1] Wallach, Ann. Chem., *278*, 313; *296*, 120.

SESQUITERPENES AND POLYTERPENES.

SESQUITERPENES, $C_{15}H_{24}$, AND SESQUITERPENE ALCOHOLS, $C_{15}H_{25}OH$.

1. CADINENE, $C_{15}H_{24}$.

Cadinene resembles limonene in its behavior and in its distribution in ethereal oils. Like limonene it yields solid additive products with two molecules of halogen hydrides, but these compounds are optically active, and, by elimination of the hydrogen chloride, etc., may be reverted into optically active cadinene.

Although cadinene has been recognized in many ethereal oils, it is, nevertheless, doubtful whether this hydrocarbon is actually the most widely distributed of the sesquiterpenes, since reactions by which cadinene can be definitely identified are, as a rule, unknown for the other sesquiterpenes.

The name cadinene was introduced by Wallach[1] owing to the occurrence of this sesquiterpene in large quantities in the oil of cade (*Oleum cadinum*). This oil is the most convenient and cheapest source for its preparation. The investigations of Wallach,[2] Schmidt,[3] Oglialoro,[4] Soubeiran and Capitaine[5] have shown that cadinene occurs in the oil of cubeb. Wallach[2] also proved that it occurs in patchouly oil, galbanum oil and oil of savin; Wallach and Rheindorf[6] subsequently discovered it in the oil of paracoto bark, and Wallach and Walker[7] detected it as a constituent of oil of olibanum. Bertram and Gildemeister[8] found cadinene in the oil of betel leaves and in camphor oil; Bertram and Walbaum[9] recognized it in pine needle oil from *Picea excelsa* and *Pinus montana*, and in the German oil of *Pinus silvestris*. Schimmel &

[1] Wallach, Ann. Chem., *271*, 297; compare Troeger and Feldmann, Arch. Pharm., *236*, 692.

[2] Wallach, Ann. Chem., *238*, 78.

[3] Schmidt, Arch. Pharm. [2], *141*, 1.

[4] Oglialoro, Gazz. Chim., *5*, 467.

[5] Soubeiran and Capitaine, Journ. Pharm., *26*, 75; Pharm. Centr., *1840*, 177.

[6] Wallach and Rheindorf, Ann. Chem., *271*, 303.

[7] Wallach and Walker, Ann. Chem., *271*, 295.

[8] Bertram and Gildemeister, Journ. pr. Chem., N.F., *39*, 349.

[9] Bertram and Walbaum, Arch. Pharm., *231*, 290.

Co. obtained it from oil of cedar wood, Florida oil of pepper, and oil of juniper. The same sesquiterpene is also found, according to Semmler,[1] in oil of asafetida, and, according to Reychler,[2] in oil of ylang-ylang. It also occurs in the oils of elderberry, wormwood, goldenrod, peppermint and angostura bark.

Preparation.—Pure cadinene is prepared from pure cadinene dihydrochloride, obtained from the fractions boiling at 260° to 280° of the above-mentioned oils; the fraction obtained from *Oleum cadinum* is best. The hydrogen chloride is removed from the dihydrochloride by boiling with twice its weight of aniline, or by heating with sodium acetate. In the latter method, the following process is employed.

Twenty grams of cadinene dihydrochloride and twenty grams of anhydrous sodium acetate are covered with eighty cc. of glacial acetic acid, and heated in a flask fitted with a reflux condenser. At first the solids are dissolved, but very soon sodium chloride is thrown out and the reaction is complete in about half an hour. The product is diluted with water, the resultant hydrocarbon is washed with sodium hydroxide, distilled in a current of steam and rectified (Wallach[3]).

Properties.[4]—Cadinene boils at 274° to 275°, has the specific gravity 0.9180 at 20° and 0.9210 at 16°; the refractive power is 1.50647. Wallach and Conrady found the specific rotatory power, $[\alpha]_D = -98.56°$. It shows a very great tendency to decompose into resinous substances on exposure to the air. It is sparingly soluble in alcohol and glacial acetic acid, readily in ether.

When cadinene is dissolved in chloroform and then shaken with a few drops of concentrated sulphuric acid, the liquid assumes an intensive green color, which passes into blue and is converted into red by warming. The beautiful indigo-blue color is rendered more apparent if the hydrocarbon be dissolved in an excess of glacial acetic acid instead of chloroform, and then treated very slowly with a little sulphuric acid. These color-reactions are facilitated by allowing the cadinene to stand for some time in the air.

On oxidation with chromic acid, this sesquiterpene yields the lower fatty acids. If the hydrocarbon be added drop by drop to fuming nitric acid, a violent reaction takes place and a yellow

[1] Semmler, Arch. Pharm., *229*, 17.

[2] Reychler, Bull. Soc. Chim. [3], *11*, 576; Ber., *28*, 151, Ref.

[3] Wallach, Ann. Chem., *238*, 80 and 84.

[4] Wallach, Ann. Chem., *238*, 80 and 84; compare Wallach and Conrady, Ann. Chem., *252*, 150; Wallach, Ann. Chem., *271*, 297.

compound is formed; this substance is quite insoluble in water, soluble in sodium hydroxide, and appears to be amorphous.

Cadinene seems to be changed by continued heating with dilute sulphuric acid (Wallach).

Cadinene dihydrochloride, $C_{15}H_{24} \cdot 2HCl$, was first obtained by Soubeiran and Capitaine, subsequently by Schmidt, and Oglialoro, from the oil of cubeb. According to Wallach,[1] it is most conveniently prepared from *Oleum cadinum.* The fraction of the latter oil boiling between 260° and 280° is diluted with twice its volume of ether and saturated with hydrochloric acid gas; after standing for a few days, a portion of the ether is distilled off, and on further evaporation of the liquid the dihydrochloride crystallizes. The crystals are filtered by the pump, washed with a little alcohol, and recrystallized from ethyl acetate; the compound is readily soluble in warm acetic ether, but difficultly in the cold solvent. When crystallized slowly from ether, it separates in hemihedral rhombic prisms, which show a close resemblance to those of limonene tetrabromide (Hintze[2]).

Cadinene dihydrochloride melts at 117° to 118°, and has the specific rotatory power, $[\alpha]_D = -36.82°$ (Wallach and Conrady).

When it is heated with aniline or sodium acetate, it is decomposed into cadinene; the resultant hydrocarbon may be readily reconverted into pure cadinene dihydrochloride, having the same rotatory power as the original dihydrochloride, by treatment with a glacial acetic acid solution of hydrogen chloride.

A saturated *hydrocarbon,* $C_{15}H_{28}$, is formed when cadinene dihydrochloride is heated with hydriodic acid at 180° to 200°; it boils at 257° to 260°, has the specific gravity 0.872 at 18°, and the refractive power, $n_D = 1.47439$ (Wallach and Walker[3]).

Cadinene dihydrobromide, $C_{15}H_{24} \cdot 2HBr$, is obtained by shaking an acetic acid solution of pure cadinene with fuming hydrobromic acid; it forms white needles resembling those of the dihydrochloride. It melts at 124° to 125°, is difficultly soluble in alcohol, but dissolves readily in ethyl acetate. The rotatory power is $[\alpha]_D = -36.13°$ (Wallach).

Cadinene dihydriodide, $C_{15}H_{24} \cdot 2HI$, is prepared like the dihydrobromide. It crystallizes from petroleum ether in white, woolly needles, and melts with decomposition at 105° to 106°. The rotatory power is $[\alpha]_D = -48.00°$.

Cadinene nitrosochloride,[4] $C_{15}H_{24} \cdot NOCl$, is obtained when a so-

[1] Wallach, Ann. Chem., *238*, 82; compare Cathelineau and Hauser, Bull. Soc. Chim., *25* [III.], 247 and 931.

[2] Hintze, Ann. Chem., *238*, 82.

[3] Wallach and Walker, Ann. Chem., *271*, 295.

[4] Schreiner and Kremers, Pharm. Arch., *2*, 273.

lution of cadinene in glacial acetic acid is well cooled with a freezing mixture, ethyl nitrite is added, and the mixture is carefully treated with a saturated solution of hydrogen chloride in glacial acetic acid. It melts with decomposition at 93° to 94°.

Cadinene nitrosate,[1] $C_{15}H_{24} \cdot N_2O_4$, is produced on treating a well cooled mixture of a solution of the sesquiterpene in glacial acetic acid, and ethyl nitrite, with strong nitric and glacial acetic acids; the reaction-mixture is diluted with alcohol, the nitrosate being precipitated. The yield is over forty per cent. It melts and decomposes at 105° to 110°.

2. CARYOPHYLLENE, $C_{15}H_{24}$.

Caryophyllene, which occurs in the oil of cloves and clove stems, in copaiba balsam oil, and in the oil of *Canella alba*, was characterized as a definite sesquiterpene by Wallach and Walker[2] by means of its conversion into caryophyllene alcohol; it has not, however, been prepared absolutely pure. When the elements of water are eliminated from caryophyllene alcohol, it is not converted into caryophyllene, but is changed into the isomeric sesquiterpene, *clovene.*

Impure caryophyllene, obtained by the fractional distillation of the oil of cloves, boils at 258° to 260°, has a specific gravity 0.9085 at 15°, and the refractive power, $n_D = 1.50094$. It is optically active (Wallach).

According to Schreiner and Kremers,[3] a comparatively pure specimen of caryophyllene boils at 136° to 137° under a pressure of 20 mm., has the specific gravity 0.90301 and refractive index, $n_D = 1.49976$, at 20°, and the specific rotatory power, $[\alpha]_D = -8.959°$ at 20°. The physical constants have also been determined by Erdmann,[4] and by Kremers.[5]

According to Wallach, caryophyllene combines with the halogen hydrides, yielding liquid addition-products, while caryophyllene alcohol (see below) forms solid derivatives when it is treated with the phosphorus halides. These reactions, and the fact that it is impossible to reconvert caryophyllene alcohol into caryophyllene, indicate that the formation of this alcohol is preceded by a molecular rearrangement.

Caryophyllene dihydrochloride, $C_{15}H_{24} \cdot 2HCl$.—According to Kremers,[3] it appears that this compound may be obtained in a crys-

[1] Schreiner and Kremers, Pharm. Arch., *2*, 273.
[2] Wallach and Walker, Ann. Chem., *271*, 285.
[3] Schreiner and Kremers, Pharm. Arch., *2*, 282.
[4] Erdmann, Journ. pr. Chem., *56* [II.], 146.
[5] Kremers, Pharm. Arch., *1*, 211.

talline form by saturating an ethereal solution of the sesquiterpene with hydrogen chloride, and exposing the solution to intense cold. It melts at 69° to 70°.

When it is treated with glacial acetic acid and anhydrous sodium acetate, it yields a sesquiterpene which is not regenerated caryophyllene; it has a sp. gr. 0.9191 at 20°, $n_D = 1.49901$, and $[a]_D = -35.39°$; it is perhaps identical with *clovene*.

Caryophyllene bisnitrosochloride, $(C_{15}H_{24})_2 \cdot N_2O_2Cl_2$, forms a white powder, which is sparingly soluble and melts with decomposition at 161° to 163°. The yield is small (Wallach).

According to more recent investigations, the bisnitrosochloride may be obtained in a crystalline form, when a mixture of the sesquiterpene, alcohol, ethyl acetate and ethyl nitrite is well cooled with a freezing mixture, and treated with a saturated, alcoholic solution of hydrogen chloride; the reaction-mixture is allowed to stand for one hour in the cold, and is then exposed to the sunlight. It melts and decomposes at 158°, and has the bimolecular formula. It reacts with benzylamine forming two derivatives, *a- and β-benzylnitrolamine;* the *a*-compound melts at 167° and is sparingly soluble in alcohol, while the *β*-modification melts at 128° and is readily soluble (Schreiner and Kremers[1]).

Caryophyllene nitrosite,[1] $C_{15}H_{24} \cdot N_2O_3$, is formed by treating a mixture of equal volumes of the sesquiterpene and petroleum ether with a concentrated solution of sodium nitrite and glacial acetic acid. It crystallizes in blue needles, melts at 107°, and dissolves in alcohol forming a blue solution; the blue color of the crystals may be removed by recrystallization. It has a specific rotatory power, $[a]_D = +103°$, in a 1.6 per cent. benzene solution. Cryoscopic determinations in benzene solution indicate that this compound has the simple molecular formula above indicated. When this nitrosite is exposed to the sunlight in an absolute alcoholic solution, it is converted into a colorless *a-isomeride*, having the same molecular weight; it melts at 113° to 114°, is optically inactive, and is soluble in alcohol and benzene. When the nitrosite is dissolved in benzene and is exposed to the sunlight, it is transformed into a colorless *β-isomeride;* this compound melts at 146° to 148°, and is insoluble in benzene and alcohol.

The nitrosite reacts with benzylamine, forming a *benzylnitrolamine* (m. p. 167°).

Caryophyllene isonitrosite (bisnitrosite), $(C_{15}H_{24})_2 \cdot (N_2O_3)_2$, results on heating the alcoholic solution of the nitrosite; it forms colorless crystals, and melts at 53° to 56°.

Caryophyllene nitrosate, $C_{15}H_{24} \cdot N_2O_4$, is readily prepared by

[1] Schreiner and Kremers, Pharm. Arch., *1*, 209; *2*, 273.

adding a mixture of glacial acetic acid and concentrated nitric acid to a well cooled mixture of ten cc. of the fraction of oil of cloves containing caryophyllene, nine cc. of amyl nitrite and sixteen cc. of glacial acetic acid; the separation of the crystalline nitrosate is hastened by the addition of alcohol. It is insoluble in alcohol and ether, sparingly soluble in glacial acetic acid, and rather soluble in benzene and chloroform; it crystallizes from benzene in slender needles, and melts at 148° to 149° (Wallach and Tuttle).

According to Kremers, this nitrosate is to be regarded as having a *bimolecular* structure and should be termed caryophyllene *bis*nitrosate, $(C_{15}H_{24} \cdot N_2O_4)_2$. It yields a benzylnitrolamine, melting at 128°.

When the nitrosate is boiled with alcoholic potash for a short time, it yields a compound which crystallizes in white needles, melting at 220° to 223°; it is possibly an *oxime* derivative of caryophyllene.

Caryophyllene nitrolbenzylamines,

$$C_{15}H_{24}\Big\langle{}^{NO}_{NH \cdot CH_2C_6H_5}.$$

The α- and β-modifications are obtained from the bisnitrosochloride and benzylamine; the α- melts at 167°, and the β-nitrolamine at 128°. The nitrolamine prepared from the nitrosate and benzylamine is identical with the β-derivative and melts at 128°. The compound produced from the nitrosite and benzylamine appears to be identical with the α-nitrolamine and melts at 167°. The α-compound is less soluble in alcohol than the β-modification.

Caryophyllene nitrolpiperidide,[1]

$$C_{15}H_{24}\Big\langle{}^{NO}_{NC_5H_{10}}$$

results by treatment of the nitrosate with piperidine; it separates from alcohol in transparent crystals, melting at 141° to 143°.

Caryophyllene alcohol, $C_{15}H_{25}OH$, is obtained according to the method of preparation of terpene alcohols proposed by Bertram,[2] and modified for this substance by Wallach and Walker.

Twenty-five grams of the fraction of oil of cloves boiling at 250° to 260° are introduced into a mixture of one kilogram of

[1] Wallach and Tuttle, Ann. Chem., *279*, 391; compare Kremers, Schreiner and James, Pharm. Arch., *1*, 209.

[2] Bertram, German Patent, No. 80,711.

glacial acetic acid, twenty grams of concentrated sulphuric acid and forty grams of water; the solution is heated for twelve hours on the water-bath. As large a quantity of oil of cloves can be subsequently added as the warm acid mixture is capable of dissolving. The dark colored reaction-product is distilled in a current of steam. At first, acetic acid and a mobile oil pass over, but towards the end of the operation caryophyllene alcohol collects in the receiver, and gradually solidifies; it is dried, and then distilled from a retort.

Caryophyllene alcohol boils without decomposition at 287° to 289°, sublimes in lustrous needles, and may be recrystallized from alcohol, the melting point changing from 94° or 95° to 96°. It is almost insoluble in cold, and only sparingly soluble in hot, water, but dissolves freely in most of the ordinary organic solvents. The crystalline alcohol is almost without odor, but its vapors have a characteristic smell resembling that of pine needles. It is optically inactive.

Caryophyllene phenylurethane, $C_{15}H_{25}O \cdot CO \cdot NHC_6H_5$, is produced by the action of carbanile on the alcohol. It crystallizes from a mixture of alcohol and ether in needles, and melts at 136° to 137° (Wallach and Tuttle[1]).

Caryophyllene acetate, $C_{15}H_{25}OCOCH_3$, may be prepared by heating the iodide, $C_{15}H_{25}I$, with sodium acetate and glacial acetic acid. The product partially solidifies and is recrystallized from methyl alcohol (Wallach and Tuttle[1]).

Caryophyllene chloride,[2] $C_{15}H_{25}Cl$, is readily formed by treating the theoretical quantity of phosphorus pentachloride with caryophyllene alcohol, care being taken to exclude all moisture. After removal of the phosphorus oxychloride formed during the reaction, the product is washed with soda solution, and crystallized from alcohol, ethyl acetate or ligroine. It separates in well defined crystals, melts at 63°, and boils without decomposition at 293° to 294°.

Caryophyllene bromide,[2] $C_{15}H_{25}Br$, results when the alcohol is treated with phosphorus tribromide; it separates from alcohol in rhombic crystals, which melt at 61° to 62°.

Caryophyllene iodide, $C_{15}H_{25}I$, is prepared by adding a quantity of iodine, sufficient for the formation of phosphorus triiodide, to a solution of yellow phosphorus in carbon bisulphide, and treating this solution with the theoretical amount of caryophyllene alcohol. It crystallizes in long, colorless needles or rhombic prisms, and melts at 61°.

[1] Wallach and Tuttle, Ann. Chem., *279*, 391.
[2] Wallach and Walker, Ann. Chem., *271*, 285.

A *hydrocarbon*, $C_{30}H_{50}$, is obtained when the above-mentioned iodide is dissolved in ether and treated at the ordinary temperature with sodium in the form of wire. After repeated crystallization, first from ethyl acetate and then from alcohol, it forms well defined, transparent prisms, and melts at 144° to 145°. It is a saturated hydrocarbon, and is as stable towards oxidizing agents as paraffin (Wallach and Tuttle).

Caryophyllene nitrate, $C_{15}H_{25}ONO_2$, is produced by dissolving caryophyllene alcohol in a very small quantity of ethyl alcohol, and gradually adding a large excess of fuming nitric acid to the well cooled solution; on keeping this mixture for several hours at the ordinary temperature, the nitric acid ester is deposited in splendid, colorless needles, which are filtered on glass wool. A further quantity of this substance is precipitated, but in an impure condition, by adding water to the acid mother-liquor; it is then purified by distillation with steam.

It crystallizes in rhombic prisms, melts at 96°, and is more sparingly soluble in alcohol, ether and benzene than caryophyllene alcohol. It is saponified only with great difficulty.

Caryophyllene alcohol, its halogen derivatives, and the nitrate are saturated compounds, and are extremely stable.

3. CLOVENE, $C_{15}H_{24}$.

When caryophyllene alcohol is treated with dehydrating agents, it is converted into the hydrocarbon clovene, isomeric with caryophyllene.

Ten grams of caryophyllene alcohol are heated for fifteen minutes almost to its boiling point with excess of phosphoric anhydride, and, after cooling, the resultant hydrocarbon is distilled over in a current of steam. The oil is again treated with phosphoric anhydride as before, the product distilled with steam and rectified (Wallach and Walker[1]).

Clovene boils at 261° to 263°, has a specific gravity of 0.930 and refractive power, $n_D = 1.50066$, at 18°. It cannot be converted into caryophyllene alcohol from which it is derived, hence it must be different from caryophyllene. It does not yield a nitrosochloride, and apparently has only one ethylene linkage.

4. HUMULENE, $C_{15}H_{24}$.

The ethereal oil of hops contains a terpene, $C_{10}H_{16}$, which possibly belongs to the series of olefinic terpenes, a hydrocarbon, $C_{10}H_{18}$, an oxidized compound which resembles geraniol, and, as

[1] Wallach and Walker, Ann. Chem., *271*, 294 and 298.

the chief constituent, a sesquiterpene which boils at 166° to 171° under a pressure of 60 mm.; this sesquiterpene is called humulene (Chapman[1]).

Humulene boils at 263° to 266° at ordinary pressure, and at 166° to 171° under 60 mm. pressure; it has a specific gravity of 0.9001 at 20°. It forms a liquid tetrabromide and a liquid dihydrochloride, and does not yield an alcohol when boiled in glacial acetic acid solution with dilute sulphuric acid.

Humulene nitrosochloride, $C_{15}H_{24} \cdot NOCl$, is a white, crystalline substance, which melts and decomposes at 164° to 165°.

Humulene nitrosate, $C_{15}H_{24} \cdot N_2O_4$, melts at 162° to 163°.

Humulene nitrolpiperidide,

$$C_{15}H_{24}\begin{cases} NO \\ NC_5H_{10} \end{cases}$$

crystallizes from alcohol in small, white, glistening plates, and melts at 153°. Its *hydrochloride* crystallizes from boiling water in hard, nodular masses; the *platinochloride* separates from alcohol in reddish needles, and melts with decomposition at 187° to 189°.

Humulene nitrolbenzylamine,

$$C_{15}H_{24}\begin{cases} NO \\ NH \cdot CH_2C_6H_5 \end{cases}$$

crystallizes from boiling alcohol and melts at 136°. Its *hydrochloride* is formed by passing hydrogen chloride into the dry ethereal solution of the base, and melts with some decomposition at 187° to 189°.

Humulene nitrosite, $C_{15}H_{24} \cdot N_2O_3$.—Nitrous acid reacts with humulene forming two compounds, one of which is probably a true *nitroso-*, the other an *isonitroso-* or *bisnitroso-*derivative. The nitroso-compound crystallizes from alcohol in magnificent, blue needles, and melts at 120°. The isonitroso-compound is formed in small quantity together with the nitroso-derivative; it separates from alcoholic solutions in colorless crystals, and melts at 165° to 168°. When the blue nitroso-derivative is crystallized several times from alcohol, it is completely converted into the colorless isonitroso-derivative.

It should also be noted that humulene occurs in the oil of poplar buds. According to Fichter and Katz,[2] the principal fraction

[1] Chapman, Journ. Chem. Soc., *1895* (1), 54 and 780; Ber., *28*, 303 and 920, Ref.; compare Kremers, Pharm. Arch., *1*, 209.

[2] Fichter and Katz, Ber., *32*, 3183.

obtained from this oil boils at 132° to 137° (13 mm.), and at 263° to 269° at ordinary pressure. It has the sp. gr. 0.8926 at 15°/4°, and a specific rotatory power, $[\alpha]_D = 10°48'$ at 22°; its vapor density corresponds with that of a compound, $C_{15}H_{24}$. It yields a *nitrosochloride*, $C_{15}H_{24}\cdot NOCl$, melting at 164° to 170°, from which a *nitrolpiperidide* (m. p. 151° to 152°) and a *nitrolbenzylamine* (m. p. 132° to 133°) are obtained. The *nitrosite* forms blue needles (m. p. 127°), but on recrystallization from alcohol, it becomes colorless and melts at 172°. The *nitrosate* melts at 162° to 163°. It will be observed that the properties of this sesquiterpene from the oil of poplar buds and of its derivatives resemble those of humulene from oil of hops in all respects except the optical rotation; the humulene in oil of hops is optically inactive, while that in the oil of poplar buds is active.

5. CEDRENE, $C_{15}H_{24}$, AND CEDROL ("CEDAR CAMPHOR"), $C_{15}H_{25}OH$.

The ethereal oil of cedar wood consists almost entirely of a liquid sesquiterpene, $C_{15}H_{24}$, and a solid compound, $C_{15}H_{25}OH$, having the properties of a tertiary alcohol; the sesquiterpene has not been identified with any of the other known members of this class, and is called cedrene (Wallach[1]).

When rectified by distillation over sodium, cedrene is obtained as a viscous, colorless liquid, boiling at 131° to 132° (10 mm.), and at 262° to 263° under atmospheric pressure. It is levorotatory, $[\alpha]_D = -47° 54'$ (Rousset[2]).

Cedrene unites with bromine and the halogen hydrides, forming very unstable, liquid addition-products.

On oxidation with an excess of chromic acid in a sulphuric acid solution, cedrene yields an *acid*, $C_{12}H_{18}O_3$, which boils at 220° to 230° (9 mm.).

Cedrene is not converted into an alcohol, $C_{15}H_{25}OH$, on treatment with glacial acetic and sulphuric acids.

The solid compound, $C_{15}H_{25}OH$, occurring with cedrene in cedar wood oil, is termed cedrol or "cedar camphor." It forms a lustrous, crystalline mass, melts at 74° and boils at 282° (Walter[3]). It crystallizes from dilute methyl alcohol in colorless needles, and, after repeated crystallizations, it softens at about 78°, and melts at 85° to 86°.[4] It is optically active.

[1] Wallach, Ann. Chem., *271*, 299.

[2] Rousset, Bull. Soc. Chim., *17* [III.], 485.

[3] Walter, Ann. Chem., *39*, 247; 48, 35.

[4] Schimmel & Co., Semi-Annual Report, Oct., *1897*, 14; compare Rousset, Bull. Soc. Chim., *17* [III.], 485; Chapman and Burgess, Chem. News, *74*, 95.

Walter observed that, when "cedar camphor" is heated with phosphoric anhydride, it is decomposed into water and a sesquiterpene, $C_{15}H_{24}$, which he called cedrene. Rousset reports that cedrol is dehydrated with formation of a sesquiterpene by the action of benzoyl chloride, and by chromic acid, and partially by acetic anhydride; however, on heating with the latter reagent at 100°, a part of the cedrol is converted into an *acetate*, $C_{15}H_{25}O\cdot COCH_3$, which boils at 157° to 160° (8 mm.).

According to Schimmel & Co., water is very readily eliminated from cedrol by the action of concentrated formic acid at the ordinary temperature; the hydrocarbon, $C_{15}H_{24}$, thus obtained boils at 262° to 263°, and is levorotatory, $[a]_D = -80°$. It appears to be identical with the cedrene occurring in cedar wood oil.

Cedrol reacts like a tertiary alcohol since it does not give rise to an aldehyde or ketone on oxidation.

Cedrone, $C_{15}H_{24}O$, is a ketone which is formed on the oxidation of natural cedrene with an acetic acid solution of chromic anhydride; it boils at 147° to 151° (7.5 mm.), does not form a crystalline derivative with sodium bisulphite, but yields iodoform on treatment with sodium hypobromite and potassium iodide. Its *oxime* boils at 175° to 180° (8 mm.), and is converted into an *acetate* (b. p. 185° to 190° at 9 mm.) by acetic anhydride.

Isocedrol, $C_{15}H_{25}OH$, results on reducing cedrone in an ethereal solution with sodium. This alcohol, isomeric with "cedar camphor," boils at 148° to 151° (7 mm.), and yields a *benzoate*, boiling at 221° to 223° under 6 mm. pressure.

6. CUBEB CAMPHOR, $C_{15}H_{25}OH$.

The oil of cubeb, prepared from old cubebs, contains the sesquiterpene cadinene, and a sesquiterpene alcohol, $C_{15}H_{25}OH$; this alcohol has been the subject of investigations by Blanchet and Sell,[1] Winkler,[2] Schaer and Wyss,[3] and Schmidt.[4] Cubeb camphor separates from a mixture of ether and alcohol in large, odorless, rhombic crystals, melts at 65°, and boils at 248° with the elimination of a small quantity of water. It is optically levorotatory. It loses water when it is heated at 200° to 250° or allowed to remain in a desiccator over sulphuric acid; the nature of the resultant sesquiterpene, *cubebene* has not been explained.

[1] Blanchet and Sell, Ann. Chem., *6*, 294.
[2] Winkler, Ann. Chem., *8*, 203.
[3] Schaer and Wyss, Jahresb. Chem., *1875*, 497.
[4] Schmidt, Zeitschr. für Chem., *1870*, 190; Ber., *10*, 189.

7. LEDUM CAMPHOR, $C_{15}H_{25}OH$, AND LEDENE, $C_{15}H_{24}$.

Ledum camphor[1] occurs in the oil of Labrador tea, obtained from the leaves of *Ledum palustre.* When purified by recrystallization from alcohol, it melts at 104° to 105°, and boils at 282° to 283°. It sublimes in long, white needles, and its solution in alcohol is feebly dextrorotatory, $[\alpha]_j = +7.98°$. It is a powerful poison, affecting the central nervous system.

Ledum camphor readily loses water by warming with acetic anhydride or dilute sulphuric acid and yields *ledene*, $C_{15}H_{24}$, which is an oil boiling at 255°.

The *chloride*, $C_{15}H_{25}Cl$, is obtained as a yellowish oil by the careful action of phosphorus pentachloride on a solution of the camphor in petroleum ether.

Ledum camphor must be considered as a tertiary sesquiterpene alcohol, since it is not attacked by potassium permanganate (Hjelt[2]).

8. PATCHOULY ALCOHOL, $C_{15}H_{25}OH$, AND PATCHOULENE, $C_{15}H_{24}$.

The oil of patchouly contains liquid substances, together with a solid compound which was investigated by Gal,[3] and Montgolfier,[4] and named *"patchouly camphor."* More recently, Wallach and Tuttle[5] recognized the alcoholic nature of this compound and called it patchouly alcohol. It forms hexagonal prisms, melting at 56°, boils at 206°, and is optically levorotatory.

It has long been known that patchouly alcohol can be decomposed by the action of acetic anhydride into water and a sesquiterpene, $C_{15}H_{24}$. According to Wallach and Tuttle, the same hydrocarbon, *patchoulene*, is obtained by the action of feeble dehydrating agents on the alcohol. The best method for preparing this sesquiterpene is by heating patchouly alcohol with acid potassium sulphate at 180°, for one and one-half hours.

Patchoulene boils at 254° to 256°, has the specific gravity of 0.939 at 23°, and the index of refraction, $n_D = 1.50094$. It has an odor recalling that of cedrene, and apparently contains one ethylene linkage.

[1] Rizza, Journ. Russ. Chem. Soc., *19*, 319; Iwanow, Jahresb. Chem., *1879*, 909; Trapp, Ber., *8*, 542; Hjelt and Collan, Ber., *15*, 2501; Hjelt, Ber., *28*, 3087.

[2] Hjelt, Ber., *28*, 3087.

[3] Gal, Zeitschr. für Chem., *1869*, 220.

[4] Montgolfier, Bull. Soc. Chim., *28*, 414.

[5] Wallach and Tuttle, Ann. Chem., *279*, 394.

9. GUAIOL, $C_{15}H_{25}OH$.

The sesquiterpene alcohol obtained by Schimmel & Co.[1] from the oil of guaiac wood is identical with a product subsequently obtained from the so-called Champaca wood oil by distillation with steam. This compound, which is called guaiol or champacol according to its source, has been investigated by Wallach and Tuttle.[2]

Guaiol is purified by distillation in vacuum, and then washing with ether. It boils at 155° to 165° under a pressure of 13 mm. When recrystallized several times from alcohol, it forms lustrous, transparent prisms, which melt at 91°, boil at 288°, and are levorotatory.

The brilliant colors which are formed by the action of dehydrating agents on guaiol are especially characteristic. When heated with zinc chloride at 180° and then distilled with steam, a blue oil is obtained. This is a sesquiterpene, and boils at 124° to 132° under 13 mm. pressure; its specific gravity at 20° is 0.910 and the refractive index, $n_D = 1.50114$. The blue color of this hydrocarbon is due to impurities consisting of oxidation products of the sesquiterpene (Wallach and Tuttle).

According to Schimmel & Co., acetic anhydride reacts with guaiol forming a liquid acetate, which boils at 155° under a pressure of 10 mm.

10. SANTALOL, $C_{15}H_{25}OH$, AND SANTALENE, $C_{15}H_{24}$.

East Indian sandalwood oil consists chiefly of a mixture of two sesquiterpene alcohols, $C_{15}H_{25}OH$, which are called α- and β-santalol; the two isomeric santalenes also occur in the oil, together with other compounds. A mixture of the two alcohols is frequently called "*santalol*," and is known commercially as "*gonorol*."

α-Santalol,[3] $C_{15}H_{25}OH$, is a colorless, oily liquid, having a faint odor; it boils at 300° to 301°, has the sp. gr. 0.9854 at 0°, and the specific rotatory power, $[\alpha]_D = -1.2°$. Its acetate boils at 308° to 310°.

β-Santalol, $C_{15}H_{25}OH$, resembles its isomeride, boils at 309° to 310°, has the sp. gr. 0.9868 at 0°, and $[\alpha]_D = -56°$. Its acetate boils at 316° to 317°.

These alcohols are probably primary alcohols, and, when treated

[1] Schimmel & Co., Semi-Annual Report, April, *1892*, 42; April, *1893*, 33.

[2] Wallach and Tuttle, Ann. Chem., *279*, 394.

[3] Guerbet, Compt. rend., *130*, 417 and 1324; Soden and Müller, Pharm. Zeit., *44*, 258; compare Parry, C. and D., *53*, 708; *55*, 1023; Schimmel & Co., Semi-Annual Report, April, *1899*, 38 and 40; April, *1900*, 42 and 43.

with dehydrating agents, are converted into two isomeric sesquiterpenes, α- and *β-isosantalene*, $C_{15}H_{24}$. These compounds are colorless liquids, having an odor of turpentine; the α-isosantalene boils at 255° to 256°, and has $[\alpha]_D = +0.2°$, while the β-derivative boils at 259° to 260°, and has $[\alpha]_D = +6.1°$.

α-Santalene, $C_{15}H_{24}$, boils at 252° to 252.5°, has the sp. gr. 0.9134 at 0°, and $[\alpha]_D = -13.98°$. When heated in a closed tube with glacial acetic acid at 180° to 190°, it forms an *acetate*, $C_{15}H_{24} \cdot C_2H_4O_2$, boiling at 164° to 165° (14 mm.). When dissolved in ether and treated with dry hydrogen chloride, it forms a *dihydrochloride*, $C_{15}H_{24} \cdot 2HCl$, which decomposes on distillation in vacuum; its specific rotatory power is $[\alpha]_D = +6°$.

α-Santalene forms a *nitrosochloride*, $C_{15}H_{24} \cdot NOCl$, which crystallizes from benzene in prisms, and melts and decomposes at 122°; the *nitrolpiperidide* crystallizes from alcohol in needles, and melts at 108° to 109°.

β-Santalene, $C_{15}H_{24}$, boils at 261° to 262°, has the sp. gr. 0.9139 at 0°, and the rotatory power, $[\alpha]_D = -28.55°$. Its *acetate*, $C_{15}H_{24} \cdot C_2H_4O_2$, boils at 167° to 168° (14 mm.); its *dihydrochloride*, $C_{15}H_{24} \cdot 2HCl$, is decomposed on distillation, and has the rotatory power $[\alpha]_D = +8°$.

β-Santalene yields a mixture of two *nitrosochlorides*, $C_{15}H_{24} \cdot NOCl$, on heating its solution in petroleum ether with nitrosyl chloride; they are separated by fractional crystallization from alcohol. The less soluble derivative melts at 152°, and the other, which is formed in larger quantities, melts at 106°; the corresponding *nitrolpiperidides* melt at 101°, and 104° to 105°, respectively.

According to Soden and Müller, when santalene (β-santalene) is treated with glacial acetic and sulphuric acids by Bertram's method, it yields a sesquiterpene *alcohol*, $C_{15}H_{25}OH$, which has a strong odor of cedar; it boils at 160° to 165° (6 mm.), and has the sp. gr. 0.9780 at 15°.

In addition to the santalols and santalenes, East Indian sandalwood oil contains the following compounds (Guerbet[1]).

Santalal, $C_{15}H_{24}O$.—This substance has the properties of an aldehyde, and boils at 180° (14 mm.); it is a colorless, oily liquid, having a strong odor of peppermint. It yields a *semicarbazone*, which crystallizes in small needles, and melts at 212°.

Santalic acid, $C_{15}H_{24}O_2$, is a liquid, boiling at 210° to 212° under 20 mm. pressure.

[1]Guerbet, Compt. rend., *130*, 417; compare Chapoteant, Bull. Soc. Chim., *37* [II.], 303; Chapman and Burgess, Proc. Chem. Soc., *1896*, 140; Chapman, Journ. Chem. Soc., *79*, 134.

Teresantalic acid, $C_{10}H_{14}O_2$, crystallizes from alcohol in prisms, melting at 157°.

When West Indian sandalwood oil is saponified with alcoholic potash, and fractionally distilled in a vacuum, a sesquiterpene alcohol, *amyrol*, $C_{15}H_{25}OH$, is obtained. It is a colorless, viscous liquid, having a faint odor and bitter taste; it boils at 299° to 301° (748 mm.) and at 151° to 152° (11 mm.). Its sp. gr. is 0.981 at 15°, and $[\alpha]_D = +27°$. When heated with phthalic anhydride at 110°, it loses water and yields a sesquiterpene.[1] It is possible that amyrol, like santalol, may consist of two similar alcohols, having different rotatory powers.

In a more recent publication, Soden[2] states that α-santalol is probably a sesquiterpene alcohol having the formula, $C_{15}H_{23}OH$, and not $C_{15}H_{25}OH$; it forms the chief constituent of "santalol" and East Indian sandalwood oil. β-Santalol may also have the formula $C_{15}H_{23}OH$.

11. GALIPOL, $C_{15}H_{25}OH$, AND GALIPENE, $C_{15}H_{24}$.

According to investigations by Beckurts and Troeger,[3] the oil of angostura bark contains about fourteen per cent. of a sesquiterpene alcohol, $C_{15}H_{25}OH$, called galipol. It boils at 264° to 265°, has the specific gravity 0.9270 at 20°, and is optically inactive; its refractive index is $n_D = 1.50624$.

The sesquiterpene, $C_{15}H_{24}$, galipene, is also contained in angostura bark oil; it is further obtained by treating galipol with phosphoric anhydride. It boils at 255° to 260°, has the specific gravity 0.912 at 19°, and is optically inactive. It yields a liquid, unstable additive product with hydrogen bromide.

12. CAPARRAPIOL, $C_{15}H_{25}OH$, AND CAPARRAPENE, $C_{15}H_{24}$.

The acid-free oil obtained from the essential oil of caparrapi contains a sesquiterpene alcohol, caparrapiol,[4] which boils at 260° (757 mm.); it has the specific gravity 0.9146, the refractive index, $n_D = 1.4843$, and the rotatory power, $[\alpha]_D = -18.58°$. When distilled with phosphoric or acetic anhydride, it is converted into the sesquiterpene, caparrapene. This sesquiterpene is a colorless liquid, which boils at 240° to 250°, has the sp. gr. 0.9019 at 16°,

[1] Soden, Pharm. Zeit., *45*, 229 and 878; compare Parry, C. and D., *53*, 708.

[2] Soden, Arch. Pharm., *238*, 353; compare Müller, Arch. Pharm., *238*, 366; Schimmel & Co., Semi-Annual Report, April, *1900*, 43.

[3] Beckurts and Troeger, Arch. Pharm., *235*, 518 and 634; *236*, 392; compare Beckurts and Nehring, Arch. Pharm., *229*, 612; Herzog, Arch. Pharm., *143*, 146.

[4] Tapia, Bull. Soc. Chim., *19* [III.], 638.

the refractive index, $n_D = 1.4953$, and a rotatory power, $[\alpha]_D = -2.21°$. Its glacial acetic acid solution gives a rose coloration, changing to deep violet, on the addition of a few drops of sulphuric acid.

The commercial "white oil" of caparrapi oil also contains a monobasic *acid*, $C_{15}H_{26}O_3$, which crystallizes in white needles, melts at 84.5°, and has the specific rotatory power, $[\alpha]_D = +3°$. It is sparingly soluble in cold water, soluble in hot water, and readily soluble in alcohol. Its *calcium salt*, $Ca(C_{15}H_{25}O_3)_2 + 5H_2O$, crystallizes in needles, melting at 250°; the silver, sodium, and ammonium salts are crystalline.

13. ZINGIBERENE, $C_{15}H_{24}$.

The sesquiterpene, $C_{15}H_{24}$, which is the chief constituent of the oil of ginger, has been studied by Soden[1] and by Schreiner and Kremers.[2]

It is obtained by the repeated fractional distillation of ginger oil under reduced pressure, and is a colorless and almost odorless oil; it boils at 134° (14 mm.), 160° to 161° (32 mm.) and at 269° to 270° under atmospheric pressure. It has the sp. gr. 0.872 at 15° or 0.8731 at 20°, the refractive index, $n_D = 1.49399$, at 20°, and the specific rotatory power, $[\alpha]_D = -69°$ to $-73.38°$ (100 mm. tube).

Zingiberene dihydrochloride,[2] $C_{15}H_{24}\cdot 2HCl$, is obtained by saturating a solution of zingiberene in an equal volume of glacial acetic acid, cooled to 0°, with *dry* hydrochloric acid gas, and allowing to stand during one or two days; it crystallizes from hot alcohol in fine, white needles, which melt at 168° to 169°.

Zingiberene nitrosochloride,[3] $C_{15}H_{24}\cdot NOCl$, is formed when a mixture of zingiberene, glacial acetic acid and ethyl nitrite is cooled in a freezing mixture and is treated gradually with a saturated solution of hydrogen chloride in glacial acetic acid; the nitrosochloride is precipitated by shaking the reaction-product with alcohol and is purified by dissolving in ethyl acetate and reprecipitating with alcohol. It forms a white powder and melts with decomposition at 96° to 97°.

Zingiberene nitrosite,[3] $C_{15}H_{24}\cdot N_2O_3$, results when the sesquiterpene is dissolved in ten times its volume of petroleum ether, the solution well cooled and treated with a solution of sodium nitrite and glacial acetic acid. It crystallizes from hot methyl alcohol in fine needles and melts at 97° to 98°.

[1] H. von Soden and Rojahn, Pharm. Zeit., *45*, 414.
[2] Schreiner and Kremers, Pharm. Arch., *4*, 141 and 161.
[3] Schreiner and Kremers, Pharm. Arch., *4*, 161.

Zingiberene nitrosate, $C_{15}H_{24}\cdot N_2O_4$, is prepared by dissolving zingiberene in an equal volume of glacial acetic acid and ethyl nitrite, cooling in a freezing mixture, and carefully treating with a mixture of nitric and glacial acetic acids; the product is precipitated by shaking with cold alcohol. The nitrosate is purified by dissolving in acetic ether and precipitating with alcohol; it forms a yellow powder, which melts and decomposes at 86° to 88°.

Zingiberene unites with bromine, forming a liquid tetrabromide (Soden).

14. OLEFINIC SESQUITERPENE, $C_{15}H_{24}$, FROM THE OIL OF CITRONELLA.

According to Schimmel & Co.,[1] citronella oil contains a "light sesquiterpene" which appears to bear the same relation to the sesquiterpenes proper, as do the olefinic terpenes to the cyclic terpenes.

This sesquiterpene boils at 157° (15 mm.), has the sp. gr. 0.8643 and index of refraction, $n_D = 1.51849$, at 15°; it is dextrorotatory, $[\alpha]_D = +1° 28'$. Under ordinary pressure, it boils with decomposition at 270° to 280°.

It is readily decomposed by the action of the halogens or halogen hydrides. It has an odor similar to that of cedar wood, and is oxidized by dilute permanganate solutions, yielding carbon dioxide, oxalic acid and a glycol. It is acted upon by a mixture of glacial acetic and sulphuric acids, forming a product having a saponification-number of 43.6.

During the year 1901, Kremers[2] suggested a classification of the sesquiterpenes according to which these hydrocarbons, $C_{15}H_{24}$, may be separated into five groups as follows.

Group I. Sesquiterpenes having an open-chain of carbon atoms and containing four double linkages. An example of this class is possibly to be found in the "light sesquiterpene" obtained by Schimmel & Co. from citronella oil.

Group II. Monocyclic sesquiterpenes having three double linkages. This group probably includes zingiberene and the sesquiterpene obtained by Semmler from the oil of *Carlina acaulis*.

Group III. Dicyclic sesquiterpenes having two double linkages. This class embraces most of the sesquiterpenes, including cadinene, caryophyllene and probably humulene.

[1] Schimmel & Co., Semi-Annual Report, Oct., *1899*, 23.
[2] Schreiner and Kremers, Pharm. Arch., *4*, 141.

Group IV. Tricyclic sesquiterpenes having one double linkage. Clovene belongs to this group.

Group V. Tetracyclic sesquiterpenes without a double linkage. Representatives of this class are not at present known.

A further division of Group II. may be made according to whether the ring contains three, four, five or six carbon atoms. Groups III., IV. and V. may likewise be subdivided according to the number of carbon atoms contained in the ring.

Many sesquiterpenes are known which have not been mentioned in the preceding pages; but they probably consist, in part at least, of mixtures of the above described hydrocarbons, although they may also contain chemical individuals which have not yet been characterized as such. Such sesquiterpenes are found in the products of the distillation of caoutchouc,[1] and in the polymerization-products of valerylene,[2] C_5H_8. Many ethereal oils also contain sesquiterpenes of an unknown nature.

DITERPENES, $C_{20}H_{32}$.

Very many diterpenes are known, but they have never been thoroughly characterized. Hence, only a brief enumeration of a few of these compounds which have been investigated will be given in the following.

Colophene is formed by the action of concentrated sulphuric acid[3] or phosphoric anhydride[4] on oil of turpentine, and also by heating turpentine oil with benzoic acid,[5] and by the distillation of colophonium.[6] It is an oily, viscid liquid,[4] boils at 318° to 320°, and unites with hydrogen chloride, producing a very unstable compound.

Metaterebentene[7] is produced by heating turpentine oil at 300°. It is an oily, viscous liquid, is optically levorotatory, and boils above 360°; it has a specific gravity of 0.913 at 20°, and absorbs hydrogen chloride. *Meta-australene* is prepared from dextro-pinene in the same manner that metaterebentene is obtained from levo-pinene.

[1] Bouchardat, Bull. Soc. Chim., *24*, 108; compare Himly, Ann. Chem., *27*, 40; Williams, Jahresb. Chem., *1860*, 495.

[2] Bouchardat, Bull. Soc. Chim., *33*, 24; Reboul, Ann. Chem., *143*, 373.

[3] Deville, Ann. Chem., *37*, 192.

[4] Deville, Ann. Chem., *71*, 350.

[5] Bouchardat and Lafont, Compt. rend., *113*, 551; Ber., *1891*, 904, Ref.

[6] Riban, Ann. Chim. Phys. [5], *6*, 40; Armstrong and Tilden, Ber., *1879*, 1755.

[7] Berthelot, Ann. Chim. Phys. [3], *39*, 119.

Dicinene[1] is obtained by the action of phosphoric anhydride on wormseed oil; it boils at 328° to 333°.

Diterpilene[2] is formed when oil of turpentine is heated with crystalline formic acid for twelve hours, or when limonene is allowed to remain in contact with formic acid at the ordinary temperature for some time. It is a thick oil, is optically inactive, and has an odor like that of balsam of copaiba; it boils at 212° to 215° under 40 mm. pressure, and has the sp. gr. 0.9404 at 0°. It readily changes into a resinous mass on exposure to the air; it combines with hydrogen chloride, forming a semi-solid of the composition $C_{20}H_{32}\cdot HCl$.

Paracajeputene[3] is produced by the action of phosphoric anhydride on the oil of cajeput; it boils at 310° to 316°, dissolves in ether, but is insoluble in alcohol and turpentine oil.

Diterpene[4] is obtained by heating terpine hydrate with phosphoric anhydride or hydriodic acid; it is a thick, oily liquid, which boils at 320° to 325°, and has a specific gravity of 0.9535 at 0°. It unites with hydrogen bromide and chloride, forming additive compounds, and also yields a yellow, amorphous nitro-product.

TRITERPENES, $C_{30}H_{48}$.

Several well characterized compounds which occur in elemi-resin belong to the class of triterpenes. When elemi-resin is washed with alcohol, the resinous substances are dissolved, and a crystalline compound is obtained; this has been investigated by many chemists, and is called *amyrin*. Vesterberg's[5] detailed investigation showed that amyrin, purified by recrystallization from alcohol, consists of a mixture of two isomeric triterpene alcohols, $C_{30}H_{49}OH$. The separation of these alcohols is effected by boiling amyrin, which is obtained from elemi-resin in a yield of 16.5 per cent., with acetic anhydride, and crystallizing the resultant acetyl compounds from ligroine; the crude acetyl derivative melts at about 200°. By fractional crystallization of the crude acetyl compound, two substances of different crystalline form are obtained, the one, *β-amyrin acetate*, consisting of aggregates of prisms, the other, *α-amyrin acetate*, separating in single leaflets. Both acetates may be obtained in a condition of chemical purity by repeated recrystal-

[1] Hell and Stürcke, Ber., *1894*, 1973.

[2] Lafont, Compt. rend., *106*, 140; Ber., *1888*, 138; Bull. Soc. Chim., *49*, 17; Ber., *1888*, 605, Ref.; Bouchardat and Lafont, Compt. rend., *107*, 916; Ber., *1889*, 9, Ref.

[3] Schmidt, Jahresb. Chem., *1860*, 481.

[4] Berkenheim, Ber., *1892*, 686.

[5] Vesterberg, Ber., *20*, 1242; *23*, 3186; *24*, 3834 and 3836.

lization from petroleum ether or benzene. Pure α- and β-amyrin are secured by the saponification of the pure acetates.

The total amount of α-amyrin in the crude amyrin is about sixty-six to seventy-five per cent.

α-Amyrin, $C_{30}H_{49}OH$, crystallizes in long, lustrous, elastic needles, which are quite readily soluble in ethyl acetate, ether, benzene and hot alcohol, but are sparingly soluble in cold alcohol and ligroine. It melts at 181° to 181.5°, and is optically dextrorotatory, $[\alpha]_D = +91.59°$.

β-Amyrin, $C_{30}H_{49}OH$, shows a striking resemblance to the α-modification, but is more difficultly soluble in alcohol, and melts at 193° to 194°. It is dextrorotatory, $[\alpha]_D = +99.81°$.

The acetates of α- and β-amyrin have already been mentioned.

Both α- and β-amyrin are apparently secondary alcohols. When oxidized with chromic acid, they yield the corresponding ketones (or, possibly, aldehydes), *α- and β-amyrone*, which, on treatment with hydroxylamine, are readily converted into oximes, $C_{30}H_{48}:NOH$.

When α- or β-amyrin is dissolved in petroleum ether and treated with phosphorus pentachloride, *α- or β-amyrilene*, $C_{30}H_{48}$, is formed; both modifications are optically dextrorotatory. Levorotatory α-amyrilene is obtained by treating a solution of α-amyrin in benzene with phosphorus pentoxide.

By the action of bromine on α- or β-amyrin, or their acetates, substitution products are produced.

When α-amyrin acetate is subjected to the action of chromic anhydride in glacial acetic acid solution, it yields *oxy-α-amyrin acetate*, $C_{30}H_{47}O(OCOCH_3)$; this is converted into *oxy-α-amyrin*, $C_{30}H_{47}O(OH)$, by hydrolysis. The analogous compound of the β-series has not been isolated in a condition of purity (Vesterberg[1]).

The properties of α- and β-amyrin and their derivatives are given in the following table.

Almost all amyrin derivatives give characteristic colors with Liebermann's cholesterine reagent (acetic anhydride and concentrated sulphuric acid), the bromine compounds giving a blue, and the others a violet or purple-red coloration. These colors are best shown by dissolving about one milligram of the substance in a few drops of chloroform, adding five to ten drops of acetic anhydride and one or two drops of concentrated sulphuric acid, and then warming very gently.

[1] Vesterberg, Ber., 24, 3836.

According to O. Hesse,[1] β-amyrin occurs as the palmitic acid ester in the wax obtained from Trujillo coca and Java coca.

Palmityl-β-amyrin, $C_{46}H_{80}O_2$, melts at 75°, and has the specific rotatory power, $[a]_D = + 54.5°$.

	a-Series.	β-Series.
Amyrin, $C_{30}H_{49}OH$.	Melting point, 181° to 181.5°; slender needles; one part of a-amyrin dissolves in 21.36 parts of 98.3 per cent. alcohol at 19° to 19.5°. $[a]_D = +91.6°$.	Melting point, 193° to 194°; slender needles; one part of β-amyrin dissolves in 36.44 parts of 98.3 per cent. alcohol at 19° to 19.5°. $[a]_D = +99.8°$.
Amyrin acetate, $C_{30}H_{49}OCOCH_3$.	Melting point, 221°; large plates. $[a]_D = +77.0°$.	Melting point, 236°; long prisms. $[a]_D = +78.6°$.
Amyrin benzoate, $C_{30}H_{49}OCOC_6H_5$.	Melting point, 192°; needles or flat prisms.	Melting point, 230°; leaflets.
Bromoamyrin, $C_{30}H_{48}BrOH$.	Melting point, 177° to 178°; slender needles. $[a]_D = +72.8°$.	Melting point, 182° to 186° (?); gelatinous.
Bromoamyrin acetate, $C_{30}H_{48}BrOCOCH_3$.	Melting point, 268°; tablets or flat prisms.	Melting point, 238°; prisms.
Amyrilene, $C_{30}H_{48}$, prepared by means of phosphorus pentachloride.	Melting point, 135°; very sparingly soluble in alcohol; crystallizes from ether in splendid, thick, rhombic prisms, and sometimes separates in sphenoidal hemihedral crystals. Axial ratio, $a:b:c = 0.66733:1:0.40489$. $[a]_D = +109.5°$.	Melting point, 175° to 178°; crystallizes from benzene in long, slender, rhombic prisms. $a:b:c = 0.91655:1:0.54032$. $[a]_D = +111.3°$.
Levo-a-amyrilene, $C_{30}H_{48}$, prepared by means of phosphoric oxide.	Melting point, 193° to 194°; sparingly soluble in ether, more readily in hot ligroine, and quite easily in hot benzene; at 5°, however, only one part of the hydrocarbon is soluble in fifty-nine parts of benzene. It separates in rhombic crystals. $a:b:c = 0.789:1:0.505$. $[a]_D = -104.9°$.	

[1] Hesse, Ann. Chem., *271*, 216.

	α-Series.	β-Series.
Amyrone, $C_{30}H_{48}O$.	Melting point, 125° to 130°; it separates from a mixture of alcohol and glacial acetic acid in crystals containing one molecule of water of crystallization; dissolves readily in ether, hot benzene and glacial acetic acid, sparingly in cold benzene and glacial acetic acid and more difficultly in alcohol.	Melting point 178° to 180°; forms nodular aggregates of small prisms which do not contain water of crystallization, and are readily soluble in chloroform, ether, benzene and glacial acetic acid, sparingly in ligroine and alcohol.
Amyronoxime, $C_{30}H_{48}NOH$.	Melting point, 233° to 234°; needles, readily soluble in hot benzene, sparingly in alcohol and ether, insoluble in petroleum ether and potash.	Melting point, 262° to 263°; leaflets, insoluble in alcohol, sparingly soluble in ligroine and ether, quite readily in hot benzene.
Oxyamyrin, $C_{30}H_{47}O(OH)+2H_2O$.	Melting point, 207° to 208°; contains two molecules of water of crystallization which are slowly evolved at 100°; readily soluble in benzene, ether and alcohol, sparingly in petroleum ether. $[\alpha]_D = +108.6°$.	
Oxyamyrin acetate, $C_{30}H_{47}O(OCOCH_3)$.	Melting point, 278°; crystallizes from benzene in six-sided plates, which belong to the sphenoidal-hemihedral division of the orthorhombic system.	Melting point, 240° (?).

TETRATERPENES, $C_{40}H_{64}$.

Tetraterebentene is formed, together with colophene, when French oil of turpentine is shaken with twenty to twenty-five per cent. of antimony chloride at a temperature not exceeding 50° (Riban[1]). It is a transparent, amorphous mass, and has a specific gravity of 0.977; it is optically levorotatory, has a conchoidal fracture, and is soluble in ether, carbon bisulphide, ligroine, benzene and turpentine oil, insoluble in alcohol. It melts above 100°, is not volatile at 350°, and yields colophene and a terpene, $C_{10}H_{16}$, when it is distilled.

Tetraterebentene hydrochloride, $C_{40}H_{64}.HCl$, is formed when hydrochloric acid gas is led over pulverized tetraterebentene. The *dihydrochloride*, $C_{40}H_{64}\cdot 2HCl$, is obtained when hydrogen chloride is passed into a well cooled, ethereal solution of tetraterebentene. The latter compound and the corresponding *dihydrobromide* are amorphous (Riban[1]).

[1]Riban, Ann. Chim. Phys. [5], 6, 40.

INDEX.

D

E

F

G

P

CPSIA information can be obtained
at www.ICGtesting.com
Printed in the USA
BVHW042138300120
571069BV00007B/27